Strategic Management Theory

AN INTEGRATED APPROACH

Fourth Edition

Charles W. L. Hill
University of Washington

Gareth R. Jones
Texas A&M University

HOUGHTON MIFFLIN COMPANY
Boston   New York

For Jennifer, Nicholas, and Julia
G.R.J.

For Alexandra, Elizabeth, Charlotte, and Michelle
C.W.L.H.

Sponsoring Editor: *Jennifer B. Speer*
Senior Associate Editor: *Susan M. Kahn*
Senior Project Editor: *Fred Burns*
Production/Design Coordinator: *Jennifer Meyer*
Manufacturing Coordinator: *Marie Barnes*
Marketing Manager: *Michael B. Mercier*
Cover design: *Diana Coe*
Cover image: *David Weiss*

Printed in the U.S.A.

Library of Congress Catalog Card Number: 97-72484

ISBN: 0-395-85778-3

123456789-DW-01 00 99 98 97

Brief Contents

PART ONE   **INTRODUCTION TO STRATEGIC MANAGEMENT**   I

1. The Strategic Management Process   2
2. Stakeholders and the Corporate Mission   35

PART TWO   **THE NATURE OF COMPETITIVE ADVANTAGE**   69

3. External Analysis: The Identification of Industry Opportunities and Threats   70
4. Internal Analysis: Resources, Capabilities, and Competitive Advantage   107

PART THREE   **STRATEGIES**   141

5. Building Competitive Advantage Through Functional-Level Strategy   142
6. Business-Level Strategy   185
7. Competitive Strategy and the Industry Environment   213
8. Strategy in the Global Environment   243
9. Corporate Strategy—Vertical Integration, Diversification, and Strategic Alliances   279
10. Corporate Development—Building and Restructuring the Corporation   312

PART FOUR   **IMPLEMENTING STRATEGY**   345

11. Designing Organizational Structure   346
12. Designing Strategic Control Systems   380
13. Matching Structure and Control to Strategy   410
14. Implementing Strategic Change   442

APPENDIX   **ANALYZING AND WRITING A CASE STUDY**   A3

Contents

Preface XII

PART I   INTRODUCTION TO STRATEGIC MANAGEMENT   1

Chapter 1   The Strategic Management Process   2

Opening Case: Jill Barad's Strategy for Mattel   2
Overview   3
Strategic Planning   4
  A Basic Planning Model • Mission and Major Goals • External Analysis • Internal Analysis • SWOT and Strategic Choice • Strategy Implementation • The Feedback Loop
Strategic Managers   10
  Corporate-Level Managers • Business-Level Managers • **Strategy in Action 1.1: Larry Bossidy, CEO** • Functional-Level Managers
Strategic Leadership   14
  Vision, Eloquence, and Consistency • Commitment • Being Well Informed • Willingness to Delegate and Empower • Astute Use of Power
Strategy as an Emergent Process   16
  Strategy Making in an Unpredictable World • Strategy Making by Lower-Level Employees • **Strategy in Action 1.2: A Strategic Shift at Microsoft** • Intended and Emergent Strategies
Strategic Planning in Practice   22
  Planning Under Uncertainty • **Strategy in Action 1.3: Strategic Planning at Royal Dutch/Shell** • Ivory Tower Planning • Planning for the Present
Improving Strategic Decision Making   26
  Cognitive Biases and Strategic Decisions • Groupthink and Strategic Decisions • Techniques for Improving Decision Making • **Strategy in Action 1.4: Groupthink at Imperial Tobacco**
Summary of Chapter   30 • Discussion Questions   31
Practicing Strategic Management   32
  Small-Group Exercise: Designing a Planning System • Exploring the Web: Visiting Compaq. • Article File 1 • Strategic Management Project: Module 1 • Closing Case: Southwest Airlines

Chapter 2   Stakeholders and the Corporate Mission   35

Opening Case: Bill Agee and the Fall of Morrison Knudsen   35
Overview   36
Stakeholders   37
The Mission Statement   39
  Strategy in Action 2.1: Dick Ferris and United Airlines • Vision, or Mission • **Strategy in Action 2.2: Strategic Intent at 3M** • Values • Goals
Corporate Governance and Strategy   51
  Strategy in Action 2.3: Short-Term Emphasis, Long-Term Loss • The Corporate Governance Problem • Corporate Governance Mechanisms
Strategy and Ethics   59

The Purpose of Business Ethics • Shaping the Ethical Climate of an Organization • Thinking Through Ethical Problems • **Strategy in Action 2.4: The Jack-in-the-Box Poisonings— Questionable Ethics?** • Corporate Social Responsibility

Summary of Chapter 63 • Discussion Questions 64

Practicing Strategic Management 65
Small-Group Exercise: Constructing a Mission Statement • Exploring the Web: Visiting Merck • Article File 2 • Strategic Management Project: Module 2 • Closing Case: Body Shop International

PART II THE NATURE OF COMPETITIVE ADVANTAGE 69

Chapter 3 External Analysis: The Identification of Industry Opportunities and Threats 70

Opening Case: Boom and Bust in the Market for DRAMs 70
Overview 72
The Five Forces Model 72
Potential Competitors • Rivalry Among Established Companies • **Strategy in Action 3.1: Barriers to Entry in the Japanese Brewing Industry** • **Strategy in Action 3.2: The Great European Soap War** • The Bargaining Power of Buyers • The Bargaining Power of Suppliers • **Strategy in Action 3.3: Changing Buyer-Supplier Relationships in Health Care** • The Threat of Substitute Products • The Role of the Macroenvironment

Strategic Groups Within Industries 87
The Concept of Strategic Groups • Implications of Strategic Groups

Limitations of the Five Forces and Strategic Group Models 89
Innovation and an Industry's Structure • An Industry's Structure and Company Differences

Competitive Changes During an Industry's Evolution 92
Embryonic Industry Environment • Growth Industry Environment • Shakeout Industry Environment • Mature Industry Environment • Declining Industry Environment • Variations on the Theme

Globalization and Industry Structure 96
The National State and Competitive Advantage 97
Factor Endowments • Demand Conditions • Related and Supporting Industries • Strategy, Structure, and Rivalry • **Strategy in Action 3.4: The Rise of Finland's Nokia**

Summary of Chapter 102 • Discussion Questions 103
Practicing Strategic Management 104
Small-Group Exercise: Entering the Regional Airline Market • Exploring the Web: Visiting Boeing and Airbus • Article File 3 • Strategic Management Project: Module 3 • Closing Case: Wang Laboratories

Chapter 4 Internal Analysis: Resources, Capabilities, Competencies, and Competitive Advantage 107

Opening Case: The Rise of Intel 107
Overview 109
Competitive Advantage: Value Creation, Low Cost, and Differentiation 110
The Generic Building Blocks of Competitive Advantage 113
Strategy in Action 4.1: Productivity in the Automobile Industry • Efficiency • Quality • Innovation • Customer Responsiveness • **Strategy in Action 4.2: Time-Based Competition and Customer Responsiveness at Citicorp** • Summary

Business Functions, the Value Chain, and Value Creation   119
Primary Activities   •   Support Activities   •   **Strategy in Action 4.3: Value Creation at Pfizer**   •   Cross-Functional Goals

Distinctive Competencies, Resources, and Capabilities   123
Resources and Capabilities   •   Strategy and Competitive Advantage   •   The Role of Luck   •   **Strategy in Action 4.4: Lucky Microsoft**

The Durability of Competitive Advantage   127
Barriers to Imitation   •   Capability of Competitors   •   Industry Dynamism   •   Summary

Why Do Companies Fail?   131
Inertia   •   Prior Strategic Commitments   •   The Icarus Paradox   •   **Strategy in Action 4.5: The Road to Ruin at DEC**

Avoiding Failure and Sustaining Competitive Advantage   134
Focus on the Building Blocks of Competitive Advantage   •   Institute Continuous Improvement and Learning   •   Track Best Industrial Practice and Use Benchmarking   •   Overcome Inertia

Summary of Chapter   136   •   Discussion Questions   136

Practicing Strategic Management   137
Small-Group Exercise: Analyzing Competitive Advantage   •   Exploring the Web: Visiting Johnson & Johnson   •   Article File 4   •   Strategic Management Project: Module 4   •   Closing Case: Marks & Spencer

PART III   STRATEGIES   141

Chapter 5   Building Competitive Advantage Through Functional-Level Strategy   142

Opening Case: Reengineering Lloyds Bank   142

Overview   143

Achieving Superior Efficiency   144
Production and Efficiency: Economies of Scale   •   Production and Efficiency: Learning Effects   •   **Strategy in Action 5.1: Chemical and Chase Banks Merge to Realize Economies of Scale**   •   Production and Efficiency: The Experience Curve   •   **Strategy in Action 5.2: Too Much Experience at Texas Instruments**   •   Production and Efficiency: Flexible Manufacturing   •   **Strategy in Action 5.3: Toyota's Lean Production System**   •   Marketing and Efficiency   •   Materials Management, JIT, and Efficiency   •   R&D Strategy and Efficiency   •   Human Resource Strategy and Efficiency   •   Infrastructure and Efficiency   •   Summary: Achieving Superior Efficiency

Achieving Superior Quality   160
The TQM Concept   •   **Strategy in Action 5.4: The Impact of TQM Programs on Quality**   •   Implementing TQM   •   **Strategy in Action 5.5: Total Quality Management at Intermountain Health Care**

Achieving Superior Innovation   166
The High Failure Rate of Innovation   •   **Strategy in Action 5.6: Whatever Happened to the Digital Compact Cassette?**   •   Building Competencies in Innovation   •   **Strategy in Action 5.7: Slow Cycle Time at Apollo Computer**   •   Summary: Achieving Superior Innovation

Achieving Superior Customer Responsiveness   175
Focusing on the Customer   •   Satisfying Customers' Needs   •   **Strategy in Action 5.8: Materials Management and Information Systems Help Bose Improve Its Customer Responsiveness**   •   Summary: Achieving Superior Customer Responsiveness

Summary of Chapter   180   •   Discussion Questions   181

Practicing Strategic Management   182
Small-Group Exercise: Identifying Excellence   •   Exploring the Web: Visiting Applied Materials   •   Article File 5   •   Strategic Management Project: Module 5   •   Closing Case: Xerox Corp.

Chapter 6   Business-Level Strategy   **185**

Opening Case: Ford's Difficult Balancing Act   185

Overview   186

What Is Business-Level Strategy?   186
Customers' Needs and Product Differentiation   •   Customer Groups and Market Segmentation   •   Distinctive Competencies

Choosing a Generic Business-Level Strategy   188
Cost-Leadership Strategy   •   **Strategy in Action 6.1: Nissan's New Cost-Leadership Strategy**   •   Differentiation Strategy   •   Cost Leadership *and* Differentiation   •   **Strategy in Action 6.2: Who Wants an American Express Card?**   •   Focus Strategy   •   **Strategy in Action 6.3: Finding a Niche in the Outsourcing Market**   •   Stuck in the Middle   •   **Strategy in Action 6.4: Holiday Inns Makes a Comeback**

Strategic Groups and Business-Level Strategy   202

Choosing an Investment Strategy at the Business Level   203
Competitive Position   •   Life Cycle Effects   •   Choosing an Investment Strategy   •   **Strategy in Action 6.5: Campbell Soup Heats Up**

Summary of Chapter   209   •   Discussion Questions   210

Practicing Strategic Management   211
Small-Group Exercise: Finding a Strategy for a Restaurant   •   Exploring the Web: Visiting the Luxury-Car Market   •   Article File 6   •   Strategic Management Project: Module 6   •   Closing Case: Liz Claiborne, Inc.

Chapter 7   Competitive Strategy and the Industry Environment   **213**

Opening Case: The Burger Wars   213

Overview   214

Strategies in Fragmented Industries   215
Chaining   •   Franchising   •   Horizontal Merger

Strategies in Embryonic and Growth Industries   217
Complementary Assets   •   Height of Barriers to Imitation   •   Capable Competitors   •   Three Innovation Strategies   •   **Strategy in Action 7.1: The Body Shop Opens Too Late**

Strategy in Mature Industries   222

Strategies to Deter Entry in Mature Markets   223
Product Proliferation   •   Price Cutting   •   **Strategy in Action 7.2: Ups and Downs in the Airline Industry**   •   Maintaining Excess Capacity

Strategies to Manage Rivalry in Mature Industries   226
Price Signaling   •   Price Leadership   •   Nonprice Competition   •   **Strategy in Action 7.3 Warfare in Toyland**   •   Capacity Control

Supply-and-Distribution Strategy in Mature Industries   233
Strategy in Action 7.4: Compaq and Dell Go Head-to-Head in Distribution

Strategies in Declining Industries   235
The Severity of Decline   •   Choosing a Strategy   •   **Strategy in Action 7.5: How to Make Money in the Vacuum Tube Business**

Summary of Chapter   239   •   Discussion Questions   240

Practicing Strategic Management   241
Small-Group Exercise: How to Keep the Hot Sauce Hot   •   Exploring the Web: Visiting Wal-Mart   •   Article File 7   •   Strategic Management Project: Module 7   •   Closing Case: The Goodyear Tire & Rubber Company

| Chapter 8 | Strategy in the Global Environment | 243 |

Opening Case: IKEA   243

Overview   244

Profiting from Global Expansion   245
  Transferring Distinctive Competencies • **Strategy in Action 8.1: Its a McWorld** • Realizing Location Economies • Moving Down the Experience Curve • Global Expansion and Business-Level Strategy

Pressures for Cost Reductions and Local Responsiveness   249
  Pressures for Cost Reductions • Pressures for Local Responsiveness

Strategic Choice   253
  International Strategy • Multidomestic Strategy • Global Strategy • Transnational Strategy • **Strategy in Action 8.2: Proctor & Gamble** • Summary

The Choice of Entry Mode   260
  Exporting • Licensing • Franchising • Joint Ventures • **Strategy in Action 8.3: Fuji-Xerox** • Wholly Owned Subsidiaries • Choosing Among Entry Modes

Global Strategic Alliances   268
  Advantages of Strategic Alliances • Disadvantages of Strategic Alliances

Making Strategic Alliances Work   270
  Partner Selection • **Strategy in Action 8.4: General Motors and Daewoo** • Alliance Structure • Managing the Alliance

Summary of Chapter   275 • Discussion Questions   275

Practicing Strategic Management   276
  Small-Group Exercise: Developing a Global Strategy • Exploring the Web: Visiting IBM • Article File 8 • Strategic Management Project: Module 8 • Closing Case: The Ford-Mazda Alliance

| Chapter 9 | Corporate Strategy—Vertical Integration, Diversification, and Strategic Alliances | 279 |

Opening Case: Rockwell International   279

Overview   280

Concentration on a Single Business   281

Vertical Integration   282
  Creating Value Through Vertical Integration • **Strategy in Action 9.1: Specialized Assets and Vertical Integration in the Aluminum Industry** • Arguments Against Vertical Integration • Bureaucratic Costs and the Limits of Vertical Integration

Alternatives to Vertical Integration: Cooperative Relationships and Strategic Outsourcing   290
  Short-Term Contracts and Competitive Bidding • Strategic Alliances and Long-Term Contracting • Building Long-Term Cooperative Relationships • **Strategy in Action 9.2: Chrysler Builds an American Keiretsu** • Strategic Outsourcing and the Virtual Corporation • **Strategy in Action 9.3: Strategic Outsourcing at Boeing**

Diversification   297
  Creating Value Through Diversification • Bureaucratic Costs and the Limits of Diversification • Diversification That Dissipates Value • **Strategy in Action 9.4: Diversification and Divestments at ICI** • Related Versus Unrelated Diversification

Strategic Alliance as an Alternative to Diversification   306

Summary of Chapter   308 • Discussion Questions   308

Structure and Control at the Corporate Level   427
  Strategy in Action 13.3: Reengineering Nestlé's Global Structure   •   Unrelated
  Diversification   •   Vertical Integration   •   **Strategy in Action 13.4: Alco Standard Gets It
  Right**   •   Related Diversification
Special Issues in Strategy/Structure Choice   433
  Mergers, Acquisitions, and Structure   •   **Strategy in Action 13.5: No Problems for ABP**   •
  Internal New Ventures and Structure   •   Network Structure and the Virtual Organization   •
  Strategy in Action 13.6: NIKE's Network Structure
Summary of Chapter   438   •   Discussion Questions   438
Practicing Strategic Management   439
  Small-Group Exercise: Deciding on an Organizational Structure   •   Exploring the Web: Matching
  Strategy and Structure   •   Article File 13   •   Strategic Management Project: Module 13   •   Closing
  Case: Hughes Aircraft Reengineers Its Structure

Chapter 14	Implementing Strategic Change	**442**

Opening Case: Raising Quality at Eastman Chemicals   442
Overview   443
Strategic Change   444
  Reengineering   •   Restructuring   •   **Strategy in Action 14.1: A New Approach at IBM
  Credit**   •   Innovation   •   **Strategy in Action 14.2: Turnaround at Sunbeam-Oster**
Determining the Need for Change   449
Determining the Obstacles to Change   450
  Types of Obstacles to Change   •   **Strategy in Action 14.3: The Shakeout at Tenneco**   •
  Organizational Conflict: An Important Obstacle to Change   •   **Strategy in Action 14.4: Father and
  Son Go Head-to-Head**
Implementing Strategic Change and the Role of Organizational Politics   456
  Sources of Organizational Politics   •   Legitimate Power and Politics   •   **Strategy in Action 14.5:
  Who Has Power in a Merger?**   •   Informal Sources of Power and Politics   •   Summary   •   Effects
  of Power and Politics on Strategic Change
Managing and Evaluating Change   465
Summary of Chapter   467   •   Discussion Questions   468
Practicing Strategic Management   469
  Small-Group Excercise: Handling Change   •   Exploring the Web: Managing Change   •   Article File
  14   •   Strategic Management Project: Module 14   •   Closing Case: Which Way for Merck?

APPENDIX ANALYZING AND WRITING A CASE STUDY   **345**

Endnotes   E1
Index   I1

Preface

Increased support for and acceptance of our integrated approach to strategic management greeted the publication of the third edition of *Strategic Management Theory*. We have revised the fourth edition of our book in significant ways to build on this successful approach. Enthusiasm for our interactive approach to involving students in strategic management has also led us to develop more "hands-on" learning experiences for students. As discussed in detail later, we have a new section at the end of each chapter called Practicing Strategic Management, which includes both a new Internet exercise and a new experiential exercise.

We are grateful to the many instructors using our text and have continued to utilize feedback from them as well as from instructors not using our text to increase the value of *Strategic Management Theory*. We have continued to update our coverage of all the flourishing strategic management literature while keeping the text readable. We believe that together, the text and interactive teaching approach in our Practicing Strategic Management sections provides students with a learning experience that is second to none.

COMPREHENSIVE AND UP-TO-DATE COVERAGE

Significant Content Changes

Nearly every chapter in the fourth edition has been significantly revised either to include new material or to change the way the material is presented, in accordance with market feedback. We have continued our thrust toward exploring the *sources of competitive advantage*—efficiency, quality, innovation, and customer responsiveness—and have revised our explanation of how organizations build strengths in these areas through functional-, business-, and corporate-level strategy. We have totally changed Chapter 10, now called "Corporate Development," to provide students with a clear picture of the *major currents* that have been taking place in contemporary corporate strategy. Also, we have substantially reorganized the chapters on *strategy implementation* to show how organizational design can be used to build competitive advantage and to manage the process of *strategic change*. This new focus has enabled us to give a more comprehensive and integrated picture of the strategic management process.

We have also continued to emphasize the importance of the *global dimension* of strategy throughout the book. For example, beyond our chapter on global strategy (8), discussion of the global environment is found in the chapter on analyzing the environment (3), and discussion of the appropriate structure for managing global strategy is discussed in the chapter on matching strategy to structure (13). The global strategy chapter itself has been revised and updated to incorporate all recent research and thinking.

While each chapter has been thoroughly revised and updated, we have been careful to preserve the *balanced and integrated* nature of our account of the strategic management process. Moreover, as we added new material, we deleted less current or less important concepts and information to ensure that students would concentrate on the core concepts and issues in the field. We have paid close attention to retaining the book's readability.

Besides integrating recent research and global concerns into the fourth edition, we have striven to enhance the book's value for students in our use of *current examples*. The chapter-opening case is completely new in almost every chapter, and the Strategy in Action boxes, which provide graphic examples of the real-world implications of strategic management theory, are either new or have been updated. The opening cases from the third edition have been updated and are now the chapter closing cases—hence they will be familiar to previous users of the book.

Some examples of specific chapter changes or additions include:

- Strategy making by autonomous actions by lower-level managers. (Chapter 1)

- New and expanded material on the organizational mission, strategic intent, organizational values, and performance. (Chapter 2)

- Expanded coverage of Porter's theory of the relationship between national context and competitive advantage. (Chapter 3)

- New approach to value creation. (Chapter 4)

- Expanded coverage of the relationship between technology and innovation. (Chapter 5)

- Discussion of strategic outsourcing and the virtual corporation. (Chapter 9)

- Introduction of Hamel and Prahalad's Core Competence Approach. (Chapter 10)

- More on cross-functional and product team structures. (Chapter 11)

- Introduction of the Balanced Scorecard Model of Organizational Control. (Chapter 12)

- Expanded coverage of organizational culture. (Chapter 12)

- New discussion of network structures and virtual organizations. (Chapter 13)

- New focus on the process of managing strategic change and in-depth discussion of restructuring and reengineering. (Chapter 14)

PRACTICING STRATEGIC MANAGEMENT: AN INTERACTIVE APPROACH

We hope you will be excited by the new hands-on learning possibilities provided by the exercises/assignments in the end-of-chapter *Practicing Strategic Management* sections. Following the Chapter Summary and Discussion Questions, each chapter contains the following assignments/exercises:

- ***Small Group Exercise***.   This short (20 minute) experiential exercise asks students to divide into groups and discuss a scenario concerning some aspect of strategic management. For example, the scenario in Chapter 11 asks students to discuss how they would reengineer the structure of a greeting cards company to increase the speed of product innovation.

■ ***Exploring the Web***.   The Internet exercise requires students to explore a particular web site and answer chapter-related questions. For example, the Chapter 11 assignment is to go to the website of Bertelsmann, the giant German media company, and analyze the nature of and reasoning behind its organizational structure. This section also asks students to explore the web for relevant sites of their own choosing and answer questions.

■ ***Article File***.   As in the last edition, this exercise requires students to search business magazines to identify a company that is facing a particular strategic management problem. For instance, students are asked to locate and research a company pursuing a low-cost or a differentiation strategy, and to describe this company's strategy, its advantages and disadvantages, and the core competencies required to pursue it. Students' presentations of their findings lead to lively class discussions.

■ ***Strategic Management Project***.   Students, in small groups, choose a company to study for the whole semester and then analyze the company using the series of questions provided at the end of every chapter. For example, students might select Ford Motor Co. and, using the series of chapter questions, collect information on Ford's top managers, mission, ethical position, domestic and global strategy and structure, and so on. Eventually, students would write a case study of their company and present it to the class at the end of the semester. Normally, we also have students present one or more of the cases in the book early in the semester, but in our classes we now treat the students' own projects as the major class assignment and their case presentations as the climax of the semester's learning experience.

■ ***Closing case study***.   A new feature to this edition, a short closing case provides an opportunity for a short class discussion of a chapter-related theme.

In creating these exercises it is not our intention to suggest that they should *all* be used for *every* chapter. For example, over a semester an instructor might combine a group strategic management project with five to six article file assignments and five to six exploring the web exercises, while doing eight to ten small group experiential exercises in class.

Another tool we provide in *Strategic Management Theory* is a special section that helps students learn how to effectively analyze and write a case study. This thoroughly revised section includes a checklist and explanation of areas to consider, suggested research tools, tips on financial analysis, and guidelines for using the Strategic Management Project.

We have found that our new interactive approach to teaching strategic management appeals to students. It also greatly improves the quality of their learning experience. Our approach is more fully discussed in the *Instructor's Resource Manual*.

Teaching and Learning Aids

Taken together, the teaching and learning features of *Strategic Management Theory* provide a package that is unsurpassed in its coverage and that supports the integrated approach, which we have taken throughout the book. Further details for using the supplementary materials can also be found in the *Instructor's Resource Manual*.

For the Instructor

■ The **Instructor's Resource Manual**, which users liked so much in the first three editions of *Strategic Management,* has been refined and expanded. For each chapter we provide a *synopsis,* a list of *teaching objectives,* a *comprehensive lecture outline,* and *answers to discussion questions.* Each of the new chapter opening cases also has a corresponding *teaching note* to help guide class discussion. Furthermore, the lecture outlines include summaries of the material in the *Strategy in Action* boxes.

■ The **Test Bank** (in the *Instructor's Resource Manual*) has been revised and offers a set of comprehensive true/false and multiple-choice questions, and the answers to them, for each chapter in the book. The **Electronic Test Bank** version allows instructors to generate and change tests easily on the computer.

■ A package of **color transparencies** accompanies the book. These include nearly all the art found in the chapters.

■ Completely new to this edition is a set of **PowerPoint slides,** developed by Milton Pressley, University of New Orleans. This lecture tool includes over twenty-five slides per chapter combining clear, concise text and art to create a total presentation package. Instructors with PowerPoint can edit slides; a viewer is included for those without. Slides can also be printed for lecture notes and class distribution.

■ A **videotape** pertaining to several of the examples and concepts in the text is available to instructors. It helps highlight many issues of interest and can be used to spark class discussion.

For the Student

■ **Micromatic** is a computer-based simulation that introduces students to tools and concepts of today's business world, such as spreadsheet calculations, "what-if" scenarios, financial analysis, and competitive analysis.

■ **Policy Expert** includes four computer tools—business calculator, ratio analysis, portfolio models, and environmental scan—that assist students in analyzing actual businesses or cases in a strategic management text.

ACKNOWLEDGMENTS

This book is the product of far more than two authors. We are grateful to Jennifer Speer, our sponsoring editor, for her help in promoting and developing the book and for providing us with timely feedback and information from professors and reviewers that have allowed us to shape the book to meet the needs of its intended market. We are also grateful to Susan Kahn, senior associate editor, for ably coordinating the planning of our book and for managing the creation of the ancillary materials, to Fred Burns for his handling of production, and to Elisa Adams for her help in developing the manuscript. We are also grateful to the case authors for allowing us to use their materials. We also want to thank the departments of management at the University of Washington and Texas A&M University for providing the setting and atmosphere in which the book could be written, and the students of these universities who reacted to and provided input for many of our ideas. In addition, the following reviewers of this and earlier editions gave us valuable suggestions for improving the manuscript from its original version to its current form:

Ken Armstrong
Anderson University
Kunal Banerji
West Virginia University
Glenn Bassett
University of Bridgeport
Thomas H. Berliner
The University of Texas at Dallas
Richard G. Brandenburg
University of Vermont
Steven Braund
University of Hull
Philip Bromiley
University of Minnesota
Geoffrey Brooks
Western Oregon State College
Lowell Busenitz
University of Houston
Gene R. Conaster
Golden State University
Steven W. Congden
University of Hartford
Catherine M. Daily
Ohio State University
Helen Deresky
SUNY—Plattsburgh
John Fahy
Trinity College, Dublin
Patricia Feltes
Southwest Missouri State University
Mark Fiegener
Oregon State University
Isaac Fox
Washington State University
Craig Galbraith
University of North Carolina at Wilmington

Eliezer Geisler
Northeastern Illinois University
Gretchen Gemeinhardt
University of Houston
Lynn Godkin
Lamar University
Robert L. Goldberg
Northeastern University
Graham L. Hubbard
University of Minnesota
Tammy G. Hunt
University of North Carolina at Wilmington
James Gaius Ibe
Morris College
W. Grahm Irwin
Miami University
Marios Katsioloudes
University of South Carolina Coastal Carolina College
Robert Keating
University of North Carolina at Wilmington
Geoffrey King
California State University— Fullerton
Rico Lam
University of Oregon
Robert J. Litschert
Virginia Polytechnic Institute and State University
Franz T. Lohrke
Louisiana State University
Lance A. Masters
California State University—San Bernardino
Charles Mercer
Drury College

Van Miller
University of Dayton
Joanna Mulholland
West Chester University of Pennsylvania
Paul R. Reed
Sam Houston State University
Rhonda K. Reger
Arizona State University
Malika Richards
Indiana University
Ronald Sanchez
University of Illinois
Joseph A. Schenk
University of Dayton
Brian Shaffer
University of Kentucky
Pradip K. Shukla
Chapman University
Dennis L. Smart
University of Nebraska at Omaha
Barbara Spencer
Clemson University
Lawrence Steenberg
University of Evansville
Kim A. Stewart
University of Denver
Ted Takamura
Warner Pacific College
Bobby Vaught
Southwest Missouri State
Robert P. Vichas
Florida Atlantic University
Daniel L. White
Drexel University
Edgar L. Williams, Jr.
Norfolk State University

Finally, thanks are due to our families for their patience and support during the revision process. We especially thank our wives, Alexandra Hill and Jennifer George, for their ever increasing support and affection.

Charles W. L. Hill
Gareth R. Jones

PART ONE

Introduction to Strategic Management

1. The Strategic Management Process

2. Stakeholders and the Corporate Mission

CHAPTER I

The Strategic Management Process

Opening Case: Jill Barad's Strategy For Mattel

Overview

Strategic Planning

Strategic Managers

Strategic Leadership

Strategy as an Emergent Process

Strategic Planning in Practice

Improving Strategic Decision Making

Closing Case: Southwest Airlines

OPENING CASE

Jill Barad's Strategy for Mattel

On August 22, 1996, Jill Barad was named the new chief executive officer (CEO) of Mattel. At 45 years of age, she had become one of the youngest women to head a major U.S. corporation. For Barad, the announcement was the fulfillment of a fifteen-year career at Mattel during which she was best known for transforming Mattel's flagging line of Barbie dolls into the most profitable toy brand in the world. As product manager for Barbie, she had pioneered a brand extension strategy that had tripled Barbie sales to $1.4 billion between 1988 and 1995. In the process she had gained a reputation for being a hard-driving manager and skilled marketing visionary. As CEO, one of Barad's first tasks was to decide on a strategy that would enable Mattel to grow earnings per share in line with the company's stated goal of 15 percent per annum.

Mattel is the world's largest toymaker, with 1995 revenues of $3.64 billion. The company's strengths lie in its Barbie brand; its Fisher-Price line of toys for young children, which generated 1995 revenues of more than $1 billion; the Hot Wheels brand; and its Disney licenses. Negotiated in 1988, the Disney licenses give Mattel exclusive rights to make products based on Disney's movies for kids. In 1995 Mattel earned revenues of $450 million from its Disney connection alone. Between 1988 and 1995 these four core product areas helped power Mattel to a compound annual growth rate of 20 percent for sales and 38 percent for operating income. In total, Mattel commands about 16 percent of the market share for toys sold in the United States, although its share in Europe, the other great toy market, is less than 8 percent.

Despite Mattel's glittering past and Jill Barad's own starring role in it, many knowledgeable observers of the toy industry believe that the company's goal of 15 percent growth in earnings represents a difficult challenge for the new CEO. Barad takes over the top spot at a time when

Mattel's growth rate appears to be slowing. In June 1996 Mattel reported that sales for its most recent quarter would be "approximately the same as last year," marking the first time quarterly results had been flat in eight years. To be sure, part of the slowdown was due to lackluster sales of its toys based on Disney's latest film, *The Hunchback of Notre Dame*. Although this shortfall could easily be made up by a strong showing from toys linked to future Disney films, critics charge that the toy industry in general seems to be suffering from a chronic lack of creativity. Of the fifteen top-selling toys in 1996, only three were toy company inventions that originated within the last year. Mattel is very much a case in point. The Barbie brand has been around since 1959; Hot Wheels and Fisher-Price were acquired rather than developed internally; while the creative minds behind the Disney line of toys clearly lie with that company, not Mattel.

Of course, it can be argued that given the fickle nature of the toy business, in which last year's mega-hit can become this year's bust (remember Cabbage Patch Kids?), Mattel is right to focus on established and enduring brands. However, by emphasizing established brands over innovation, Mattel runs the risk of missing out on successful new blockbusters. That's what happened with video games. Having given up after some early forays into video

games, Mattel watched Nintendo and Sega take that business from zero to $6 billion in sales.

So what strategy will Barad pursue in order to attain the goal of 15 percent growth in earnings? The early signs are that her strategy for Mattel will have four main elements. First, she has made it clear that she intends to continue with the highly profitable practice of extending the company's existing brands. For example, she has plans to develop a line of collectable Barbies. Second, she intends to develop new product categories, particularly in boys' toys and board games, two areas in which Mattel has traditionally been weak. This could be accomplished either by developing the toys in house or by acquiring an existing company and then growing its business through further investments. Third, she intends to focus more effort on expanding sales in overseas markets, where Mattel's presence is more limited than in the United States. Her goal is to increase overseas sales to more than 50 percent of Mattel's total, up from 40 percent today. Finally, she will try to increase earnings by driving down costs. Cost reductions will be achieved by moving production to low-cost foreign factories in places such as China and Thailand. This will represent a major shift for Mattel, which currently manufactures two-thirds of its core product lines in its own plants.[1]

OVERVIEW

Why do some organizations succeed while others fail? In the toy industry, what distinguishes successes such as Mattel from failures such as Coleco Industries, which rode to fame with the Cabbage Patch Kids only to see sales slump as the brand lost its appeal among the young of America? In the retail industry, what distinguishes successes such as Wal-Mart from failures such as rival American discount retailer Kmart? Why has Wal-Mart consistently outperformed the industry, even in difficult years such as 1995, whereas Kmart found itself facing the possibility of going bankrupt in 1995? Similarly, in the computer industry, why have Apple Computer and Digital Equipment (DEC), once regarded as two of world's most successful computer companies, found it difficult to remain profitable for much of the 1990s, whereas rival companies such as Compaq Computer and Dell Computer are considered successes? In the microprocessor segment of the semiconductor industry, why has Intel been able to outperform its closest rivals, such as Advanced Micro Devices, so consistently?

This book argues that the strategies an organization pursues have a major impact upon its performance relative to that of competitors. A **strategy** is a specific pattern of decisions and actions that managers take to achieve an organization's goals. For most if not all organizations, an overriding goal is to achieve superior performance. Thus, a strategy can often be defined more precisely as the specific pattern of decisions and actions that managers take to achieve superior organizational performance. The overriding goal of Mattel, for example, is to achieve 15 percent annual growth in earnings, which is an ambitious goal for a company with revenues closing in on $4 billion. Mattel's strategies for attaining this goal include extending its established brands, developing new products, expanding into overseas markets, and cutting costs.

This book is devoted to identifying and describing the various strategies a company can pursue to achieve superior performance. Many of these strategies are generic—that is, they apply to all organizations, large or small, manufacturing or service, and profit seeking or not for profit. A central aim of this book is to give you a thorough understanding of the analytical techniques and skills necessary to identify and exploit strategies successfully. The first step toward achieving this objective is to give you an overview of the **strategic management process,** that is, the process by which managers choose a set of strategies for the enterprise. By the end of this chapter, you will understand the processes managers use to choose strategies for their company and you will have an appreciation for the strengths and weaknesses of these processes.

STRATEGIC PLANNING

Ask the average person in the street how an organization chooses its strategy, and they will probably answer that its strategy is the result of a *rational planning* process that is orchestrated by, if not dominated by, the *top management* of the organization. To a certain extent, this emphasis on a rational planning process dominated by top management reflects the military roots of strategy, with its imagery of generals clustered around a map table with their staff plotting out a strategy for defeating their enemy. This imagery has been propagated in the business literature by a number of writers who have emphasized that strategy is the outcome of a formal planning process and that top management plays the most important role in this process.[2] The story of Mattel, discussed in the Opening Case, provides us with an example of the role of top management in strategy formulation. Jill Barad, Mattel's CEO, seems to have played a major role in identifying the strategies that the company will pursue to attain its goal of earnings growth.

However, while the view of strategy as the product of a rational planning process driven by top management certainly has some basis in reality, it is not the whole story. As we shall learn later in the chapter, by no means all of an organization's strategies are the result of formal strategic planning exercises. Strategies often emerge from deep within the organization without prior planning. Nevertheless, a consideration of planning is a useful starting point for our journey into the world of strategy. Accordingly, this section considers what might be described as a stereotypical strategic planning model.

A Basic Planning Model

The strategic planning process can be broken down into the five main steps illustrated in Figure 1.1. You might want to think of Figure 1.1 as a plan of the book, for it also shows how the different chapters relate to the different steps of the strategic

FIGURE 1.1

The Main Components
of the Strategic
Planning Process

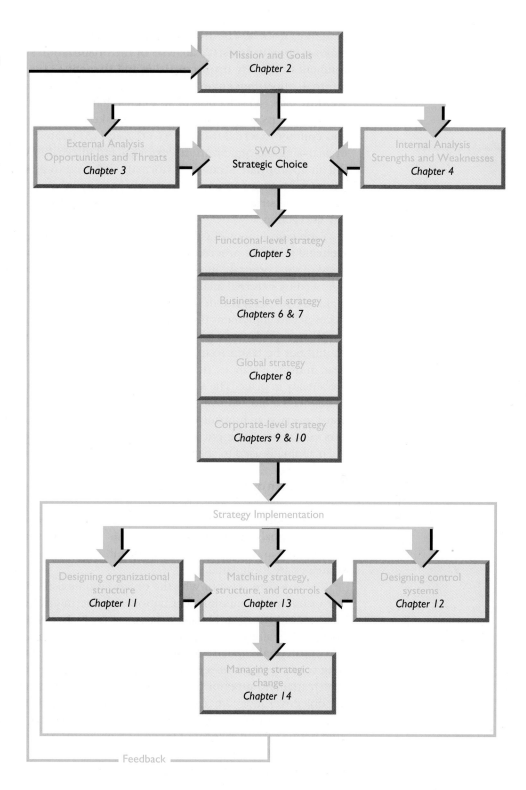

planning process. The five steps are (1) selection of the corporate mission and major corporate goals; (2) analysis of the organization's external competitive environment to identify **opportunities** and **threats**; (3) analysis of the organization's internal operating environment to identify the organization's **strengths** and **weaknesses**; (4) selection of strategies that build on the organization's strengths and correct its weaknesses in order to take advantage of external opportunities and counter external threats (SWOT); and (5) strategy implementation. The task of analyzing the organization's external and internal environment and then selecting an appropriate strategy is normally referred to as **strategy formulation**. In contrast, **strategy implementation** typically involves designing appropriate organizational structures and control systems to put the organization's chosen strategy into action.

Each component illustrated in Figure 1.1 constitutes a *sequential* step in the strategic planning process. Each *cycle* of the planning process begins with a statement of the corporate mission and major corporate goals. The mission statement is followed by external analysis, internal analysis, and strategic choice. The strategy making ends with the design of the organizational structure and control systems necessary to implement the organization's chosen strategy.

Many organizations go through this kind of process every year, although this should not be taken to imply that the organization chooses a new strategy each year. In many instances, the result is simply to reaffirm a strategy and structure that are already in place. The strategic plans generated by this kind of process generally encompass a one- to five-year period, with the plan being updated, or "rolled forward," every year. In many organizations, the results of the annual strategic planning process are used as input into the budget process for the coming year. Thus, strategic planning is used to shape resource allocation within the organization.

Mission and Major Goals

The first component of the strategic management process is defining the mission and major goals of the organization. This topic is covered in depth in Chapter 2. The mission and major goals of an organization provide the context within which strategies are formulated.

The **mission** sets out why the organization exists and what it should be doing. For example, the mission of a national airline might be defined as satisfying the needs of individual and business travelers for high-speed transportation at a reasonable price to all the major population centers of North America.

Major goals specify what the organization hopes to fulfill in the medium to long term. Most profit-seeking organizations operate with a hierarchy of goals, in which attaining superior performance is placed at or near the top. Secondary goals are objectives judged necessary by the company if it is to attain superior performance. For example, under the leadership of Jack Welch, General Electric has operated with a secondary goal of being first or second in every major market in which it competes. This secondary goal reflects Welch's belief that building market share is the best way to achieve superior performance. Similarly, a major goal of Coca-Cola has been to put a Coke within an arm's reach of every consumer in the world. If Coca-Cola achieves this goal, superior performance is likely to follow. Not-for-profit organizations typically have a more diverse set of goals.

External Analysis

The second component of the strategic management process is the analysis of the organization's external operating environment. This topic is covered in detail in Chapter 3. The objective of external analysis is to identify strategic *opportunities* and *threats* in the organization's operating environment. Three interrelated environments should be examined at this stage: the immediate, or industry, environment in which the organization operates; the national environment; and the wider macroenvironment.

Analyzing the industry environment requires an assessment of the competitive structure of the organization's industry, including the competitive position of the focal organization and its major rivals, as well as the stage of industry development. Since many markets are now global markets, analyzing the industry environment also means assessing the impact of globalization upon competition within an industry. Analyzing the national environment requires an assessment of whether the national context within which a company operates facilitates the attainment of a competitive advantage in the global marketplace. If it does not, then the company might have to consider shifting a significant part of its operations to countries where the national context does facilitate the attainment of a competitive advantage. Analyzing the macroenvironment consists of examining macroeconomic, social, governmental, legal, international, and technological factors that may affect the organization.

Internal Analysis

Internal analysis, the third component of the strategic management process, serves to pinpoint the *strengths* and *weaknesses* of the organization. Such issues as identifying the quantity and quality of resources available to the organization are considered in Chapter 4, in which we probe the sources of competitive advantage. We look at how companies attain a competitive advantage, and we discuss the role of distinctive competencies (unique company strengths), resources, and capabilities in building and sustaining a company's competitive advantage. One conclusion we reach in Chapter 4 is that building and maintaining a competitive advantage requires a company to achieve superior efficiency, quality, innovation, and customer responsiveness. A company's strengths lead to superiority in these areas, whereas a company's weaknesses translate into inferior performance.

SWOT and Strategic Choice

The next component requires generating a series of strategic alternatives, given the company's internal strengths and weaknesses and its external opportunities and threats. The comparison of **s**trengths, **w**eaknesses, **o**pportunities, and **t**hreats is normally referred to as a **SWOT** analysis.[3] The central purpose of the SWOT analysis is to identify strategies that *align, fit,* or *match* a company's resources and capabilities to the demands of the environment in which the company operates. To put it another way, the purpose of the strategic alternatives generated by a SWOT analysis should be to build on a company's strengths in order to exploit opportunities, counter threats, and correct weaknesses.

Strategic choice is a process of selecting among the alternatives generated by a SWOT analysis. The organization has to evaluate various alternatives against each other with respect to their ability to achieve major goals. The strategic alternatives generated can encompass functional-level, business-level, global, and corporate-level strategies. The process of strategic choice requires the organization to identify the set of functional-level, business-level, global, and corporate-level strategies that would best enable it to survive and prosper in the fast-changing and globally competitive environment that characterizes most modern industries.

Functional-Level Strategy   Competitive advantage stems from a company's ability to attain superior efficiency, quality, innovation, and customer responsiveness—a point made in Chapter 4. In Chapter 5 we examine the different functional-level (operations) strategies that can be employed to achieve these four crucial aims. By functional-level strategies, we mean strategies directed at improving the effectiveness of functional operations within a company, such as manufacturing, marketing, materials management, research and development, and human resources.

Business-Level Strategy   The business-level strategy of a company encompasses the overall competitive theme that a company chooses to stress, the way it positions itself in the marketplace to gain a competitive advantage, and the different positioning strategies that can be used in different industry settings. The various strategic options available are discussed in Chapter 6. We review the pros and cons of three generic business-level strategies: a strategy of **cost leadership**, a strategy of **differentiation**, and a strategy of **focusing** on a particular market niche. Mattel pursues a differentiation strategy, the overall competitive theme the company has chosen to stress differentiating its brands from those of competitors through marketing.

In Chapter 7 we build on Chapter 6 to consider the relationship between business-level strategy and industry structure. We concentrate on the different strategic options confronting companies in radically different industry settings, such as the benefits and drawbacks of establishing a first-mover advantage in a newly formed or embryonic industry. We also discuss the role of market signaling, price leadership, and product differentiation for sustaining a competitive advantage in mature industries, and we explore the different strategic options that a company can choose from in a declining industry.

Global Strategy   In today's world of global markets and global competition, achieving a competitive advantage and maximizing a company's performance increasingly require a company to expand its operations outside its home country. Accordingly, a company must consider various global strategies. In Chapter 8 we assess the benefits and costs of global expansion and examine four different strategies—multidomestic, international, global, and transnational—that a company can adopt to compete in the global marketplace. In addition, Chapter 8 explores the benefits and costs of strategic alliances between global competitors, the different entry modes that can be used to penetrate a foreign market, and the role of host-government policies in influencing a company's choice of global strategy.

Corporate-Level Strategy   We deal with the issue of corporate-level strategy in Chapters 9 and 10. An organization's corporate-level strategy must answer this question: What businesses should we be in to maximize the long-run profitability of the organization? For many organizations, competing successfully often means **vertical integration**—integrating its operations either backward into the production of inputs for the company's main operation or forward into the disposal of outputs from the operation. Beyond this, companies that succeed in establishing a sustainable competitive advantage may find that they are generating resources *in excess* of their investment requirements within their primary industry. For such organizations, maximizing long-run profitability may entail **diversification** into new business areas. Accordingly, in Chapter 9 we look closely at the costs and benefits of different diversification strategies. In addition, we examine the role of **strategic alliances** as alternatives to diversification and vertical integration. In Chapter 10 we review the different vehicles that companies use to achieve vertical integration and diversification, including **acquisitions** and **new ventures**. We also consider how diversified companies can **restructure** their portfolio of businesses in order to improve performance.

Strategy Implementation

Having chosen a strategy to achieve the goals of the company, that strategy then has to be put into action; it has to be implemented. In this book we break down the topic of strategy implementation into four main components: (1) designing appropriate organizational structures; (2) designing control systems; (3) matching strategy, structure, and controls; and (4) managing strategic change.

Designing Organizational Structure   Implementing a strategy requires the allocation of roles and responsibilities for different aspects of that strategy to different managers and subunits within the company. A company's organizational structure maps out roles and responsibilities, along with reporting relationships. In this sense, strategy is implemented through structure. At Mattel, for example, under the CEO, Jill Barad, there is a product group for each of Mattel's major brands: Barbie, Hot Wheels, Fisher-Price, and Disney license products. Each of these subunits is headed by a vice president, who reports directly to Barad. It is the responsibility of each vice president to make sure that his or her product group successfully implements the company's brand extension strategy for the brand they are responsible for.

If the existing structure of an organization is not appropriate given the company's strategy, it may have to design a new structure. Consider again the case of Mattel; another of Barad's strategies is to build new brands for boys' toys and board games. To achieve this, Barad will probably create two new subunits within Mattel, each headed by a vice president, one for boys' toys and one for board games. It will be the responsibility of these vice presidents to develop or acquire products that can become enduring brands. In other words, Barad will probably alter the structure of Mattel to reflect her strategic priorities. We discuss the different kinds of organization structures that managers can use to implement strategy in Chapter 11.

Designing Control Systems   Besides choosing a structure, an organization must also establish appropriate organizational control systems. It must decide how best to assess the performance and control the actions of subunits. The options range from market and output controls to bureaucratic controls and control through organizational culture, all of which we tackle in Chapter 12. An organization also needs to decide what kind of reward and incentive systems to set up for employees. Chapter 12 reviews those options as well.

Matching Strategy, Structure, and Controls   If it wants to succeed, a company must achieve a *fit* among its strategy, structure, and controls. Chapter 13 focuses on the various means employed toward this end. Since different strategies and environments place different demands on an organization, they call for different structural responses and control systems. For example, a strategy of cost leadership demands that an organization be kept simple (so as to reduce costs) and that controls stress productive efficiency. On the other hand, a strategy of differentiating a company's product by unique technological characteristics generates a need for integrating the company's activities around its technological core and for establishing control systems that reward technical creativity.

Managing Strategic Change   We live in a world in which the only constant is change. In the Opening Case we saw how Mattel is trying to cope with a change in its competitive environment. Because change is so pervasive, companies that succeed in the long run are those that are able to adapt their strategy and structure to a changing world. Accordingly, in Chapter 14 we take a close look at the process of managing strategic change and we discuss the different tactics that managers can utilize in order to implement strategic change successfully.

The Feedback Loop

The feedback loop in Figure 1.1 indicates that strategic planning is an ongoing process. Once a strategy has been implemented, its execution must be monitored to determine the extent to which strategic objectives are actually being achieved. This information passes back to the corporate level through feedback loops. At the corporate level, it is fed into the next round of strategy formulation and implementation. It serves either to reaffirm existing corporate goals and strategies or to suggest changes. For example, when put into practice, a strategic objective may prove to be too optimistic, and so the next time more conservative objectives are set. Alternatively, feedback may reveal that strategic objectives were attainable but implementation was poor. In that case, the next round in strategic management may concentrate more on implementation. Because feedback is an aspect of organizational control, it is considered in detail in Chapter 12.

STRATEGIC MANAGERS

We have already alluded to the fact that within the context of the traditional strategic planning model, a major responsibility for orchestrating the planning process is placed upon the shoulders of top managers. Who are these top managers, and what precisely is their strategic role? What about lower-level managers within the organization? What is their role in the strategic management process? In this section we look at the strategic role of managers at different levels in the organization *through the lens of traditional strategic management theory*. Later in the chapter we modify this view somewhat, but for now it constitutes a useful starting point.

In most modern organizations, there are two types of managers: **general managers** and **functional managers**. General managers are individuals who bear responsibility for the overall performance of the organization or for one of its major self-contained divisions. Their overriding concern is for the health of the *total* organization under their direction. Functional managers, on the other hand, bear responsibility for specific business functions, such as personnel, purchasing, production, sales, marketing, customer service, and accounts. Their sphere of authority is generally confined to one organizational activity, whereas general managers oversee the operation of the whole organization. This responsibility puts general managers in the unique position of directing the total organization in a strategic sense.

A typical multibusiness company has three main levels of management: the corporate level, the business level, and the functional level (see Figure 1.2). General managers are found at the first two of these levels, but their strategic roles differ, depending on their sphere of responsibility. Functional managers have a strategic role, too, though of a different kind. We now look at each of the three levels and the strategic roles assigned to managers within them.

Corporate-Level Managers

The corporate level of management consists of the CEO, other senior executives, the board of directors, and corporate staff. These individuals occupy the apex of decision making within the organization. The CEO is the main general manager at this level. His or her strategic role is *to oversee* the development of strategies for the total organization. This role includes defining the mission and goals of the organization, determining what businesses it should be in, allocating resources among the different businesses, formulating and implementing strategies that span individual businesses, and providing leadership for the organization.

FIGURE 1.2

Levels of Strategic Management

Consider General Electric. The company is active in a wide range of businesses, including lighting equipment, major appliances, motor and transportation equipment, turbine generators, construction and engineering services, industrial electronics, medical systems, aerospace, and aircraft engines. The main strategic responsibilities of its CEO, Jack Welch, include setting overall strategic objectives, allocating resources among the different business areas, deciding whether the firm should divest itself of any of its businesses, and determining whether it should acquire any new ones. In other words, it is up to Welch to develop strategies that span individual businesses. He is concerned with building and managing the corporate portfolio of businesses. It is not his specific responsibility, however, to develop strategies for competing in the individual business areas, such as aeroengines or financial services. The development of such strategies is the responsibility of business-level strategic managers.

Besides overseeing resource allocation and managing the divestment and acquisition processes, corporate-level general managers also provide a link between the people who oversee the strategic development of a firm and those who own it (stockholders). Corporate-level general managers, and particularly the CEO, can be viewed as the guardians of stockholder welfare. It is their responsibility to ensure that corporate strategies pursued by the company are consistent with maximizing stockholder wealth. If they are not, then ultimately the CEO is likely to be called to account by the stockholders.

For another look at the roles and responsibilities of a general manager, see Strategy in Action 1.1, which looks at Larry Bossidy, the hard-driving, hard-nosed CEO of AlliedSignal. Bossidy sets the overall goals and strategic direction for AlliedSignal. However, because AlliedSignal is a diversified company with more than twenty different business units, Bossidy leaves it up to individual business managers to decide upon the best strategy for their particular operation. Bossidy's involvement is limited to vigorously probing managers with questions to test the logic underlying their strategic decisions.

Business-Level Managers

In a multibusiness company, such as General Electric or AlliedSignal, the business level consists of the heads of individual business units within the organization and their support staff. In a single-industry company, the business and corporate levels are the same. A business unit is an organizational entity that operates in a distinct business area. Typically, it is self-contained and has its own functional departments (for example, its own finance, purchasing, production, and marketing departments). Within most companies, business units are referred to as **divisions**.

The main strategic managers at the business level are the heads of the divisions. Their strategic role is to translate general statements of direction and intent from the corporate level into concrete strategies for individual businesses. Thus, while corporate-level general managers are concerned with strategies that span individual businesses, business-level managers are concerned with strategies that are specific to a particular business. At General Electric, Jack Welch has committed the company to the objective of being first or second in every business in which the corporation competes. However, it is up to the general managers who head each division to work out for their business the details of a strategy that is consistent with this objective. Similarly, at AlliedSignal it is left to the heads of each division to work out

Larry Bossidy, CEO

Larry Bossidy, the CEO of the diversified engineering company, AlliedSignal, is reputed to be one of the most sought-after CEOs in corporate America. Since leaving the number two spot at General Electric in 1991 to join AlliedSignal, Bossidy has been approached by IBM, Merck, Kodak, and Westinghouse, all of whom were looking for a new CEO. The reasons for all of this attention are not hard to find. When Bossidy joined AlliedSignal, the company was widely perceived as a poorly performing enterprise based in a number of dull businesses in aerospace, auto parts, and engineered materials. At around $14 per share, the stock price was no higher than it had been in 1984, while the 1991 net profit of $342 million was well below the peak profit of $559 million earned in 1986. Under Bossidy's leadership, however, earnings surged to more than $600 million in 1995 and the stock price climbed to $50 per share by early 1996.

How has Bossidy done it? He has articulated a handful of challenging goals that he wants AlliedSignal to attain and then relentlessly pushed the managers of each of AlliedSignal's twenty-odd businesses, or divisions, to find ways of meeting those goals. The primary goal of AlliedSignal under Bossidy has been growth. Bossidy wants to increase earnings per share by 15 percent annually. To achieve that, he reckons that AlliedSignal must grow sales by 8 percent per annum and that it must increase productivity at a compound annual rate of 6 percent "forever." These are challenging "stretch" goals for a company such as AlliedSignal, which is

based in mature low-growth industries. To achieve these goals, Bossidy has been pushing his managers to do three things—enter foreign markets, particularly those in fast-growing Asia; make selected niche acquisitions that can help to round out a business's product line; and develop new products that can boost earnings growth, a particularly difficult challenge for a company that was once known for its aversion to new ideas.

Technically, Bossidy "negotiates" goals with the heads of each of AlliedSignal's twenty-odd businesses, but in reality he pushes them to accept goals that require a significant improvement in the performance of their businesses. He then tirelessly monitors his managers to make sure they follow through. Nearly every week Bossidy visits at least one of AlliedSignal's businesses. He is known for vigorously probing managers in all-day meetings to find out what strategies they are adopting to meet the goals he has set for them. If they fail? Well, they better not. Bossidy has an award that he bestows on business units that don't meet their cost of capital—it's called the "leaky bucket" award. More significantly, when people fail to meet his stretch targets, he fires them. In the automotive division, which makes brake parts and where profits are below par, Bossidy fired or transferred six of the top ten executives in the course of a year. Bossidy admits that he is demanding, relentless, and tough, but in his view such a management style offers the only way forward for companies such as AlliedSignal that have to compete with aggressive low-cost foreign competitors.[4]

how they are going to meet Bossidy's demanding goals of 15 percent earnings growth per year, 8 percent sales growth per year, and 6 percent productivity growth "forever" (see Strategy in Action 1.1).

Functional-Level Managers

Functional managers bear responsibility for specific business functions, such as human resources, manufacturing, materials management, marketing, and research and development (R&D). They are not in a position to look at the big picture. Nevertheless, they have a major strategic role, for their responsibility is to develop functional strategies in manufacturing, marketing, R&D, and so on, that help fulfill the strategic objectives set by business- and corporate-level general managers. In the case of General Electric's financial services business, for instance, manufacturing managers are responsible for developing manufacturing strategies consistent with the corporate objective of being first or second in that industry. Moreover, functional managers provide most of the information that makes it possible for business- and corporate-level general managers to formulate realistic and attainable strategies. Indeed, because they are closer to the customer than the typical general manager, functional managers may themselves generate important strategic ideas, which subsequently become major strategies for the company. Thus, it is important for general managers to listen closely to the ideas of their functional managers. An equally important responsibility for managers at the functional level is strategy implementation, the execution of corporate- and business-level decisions.

STRATEGIC LEADERSHIP

One of the key strategic roles of managers, whether they are general or functional managers, is to provide strategic leadership for their subordinates. **Strategic leadership** refers to the ability to articulate a strategic vision for the company, or a part of the company, and to motivate others to buy into that vision. An enormous amount has been written about leadership, and it is beyond the scope of this book to review this complex topic in detail. However, a few key characteristics of good leaders have been identified by several authors, and we discuss them here.[5] These characteristics are (1) vision, eloquence, and consistency; (2) commitment; (3) being well informed; (4) willingness to delegate and empower; and (5) astute use of power.

Vision, Eloquence, and Consistency

One of the key tasks of leadership is to give the organization a sense of direction. Strong leaders seem to have a vision of where the organization should go. Moreover, they are eloquent enough to communicate this vision to others within the organization in terms that can energize people, and they consistently articulate their vision until it becomes part of the culture of the organization.[6] John F. Kennedy, Martin Luther King, Jr., and Margaret Thatcher are often held up as examples of visionary leaders. All three had their own clear vision of the society they would like to see, and all were able to communicate it eloquently to people using evocative language that energized the audience. Think of the impact of Kennedy's challenge, "Ask not what your country can do for you; ask what you can do for your country," and of King's "I Have a Dream" speech. Kennedy and Thatcher were also able to use their political office to push for governmental actions that were consistent with their vision, while King was able to pressure the government from outside to make changes in society. Examples of strong business leaders include Jill Barad (profiled in the Opening Case); Jack Welch of General Electric; Lee Iacocca, formerly of Chrysler; Herb Kelleher of Southwest Airlines; and Larry Bossidy of AlliedSignal (profiled in Strategy in Action 1.1).

Commitment

A strong leader is someone who demonstrates commitment to his or her particular vision, often leading by example. Consider the case of Nucor's CEO, Ken Iverson. Nucor is a very efficient steelmaker with perhaps the lowest cost structure in the steel industry. The company has turned in twenty years of profitable performance in an industry in which most companies have lost money. It has done so by relentlessly focusing on cost minimization, which starts with Iverson himself. Iverson answers his own phone, employs only one secretary, drives an old car, flies coach class, and is proud of being one of the lowest-paid CEOs in the *Fortune* 500. This kind of commitment sends a powerful signal to employees within Nucor that Iverson is serious about doing everything possible to minimize costs. It earns him the respect of Nucor employees, which in turn makes them more willing to work hard.

Being Well Informed

Good leaders do not operate in a vacuum. Rather, they develop a network of formal and informal sources that keep them well informed about what is going on within their company. They develop back-channel ways of finding out what is going on within the organization so that they do not have to rely on formal information channels. Herb Kelleher at Southwest Airlines, for example, was able to find out a lot about the health of his company by dropping in unannounced on aircraft maintenance facilities and helping workers there to perform their tasks. Using informal and unconventional ways to gather information is wise, since formal channels can be captured by special interests within the organization or by gatekeepers, who may misrepresent the true state of affairs within the company to the leader. People such as Kelleher and Iverson, who are constantly interacting with their employees at all levels within the organization, are better able to build informal information networks than leaders who closet themselves away in a remote corporate headquarters and never interact with lower-level employees.

Willingness to Delegate and Empower

Good leaders are skilled delegators. They recognize that unless they delegate, they can quickly become overloaded with responsibilities. They also recognize that empowering subordinates to make decisions is a good motivation tool. Delegating also makes sense when it results in decisions being made by those who must implement them. At the same time, good leaders recognize that they need to maintain control over certain key decisions. Thus, although they will delegate many decisions to lower-level employees, they will not delegate those decisions that they judge to be critical to the future success of the organization under their leadership.

Astute Use of Power

Edward Wrapp has noted that good leaders tend to be very astute in their use of power.[7] By this he means three things. First, good leaders play the power game with skill, preferring to build consensus for their ideas rather than use their authority to force ideas through. They act as members or democratic leaders of a coalition, rather than as dictators. Second, good leaders often hesitate to commit themselves publicly to detailed strategic plans or precise objectives, since in all probability the emergence of unexpected contingencies will require adaptation. Thus, a successful leader might commit the organization to a particular vision, such as minimizing costs or boosting product quality, without stating precisely how or when this will be achieved. It is important to note that good leaders often have precise private objectives and strategies that they would like to see the organization pursue. However, they recognize the futility of public commitment, given the likelihood of change and the difficulties of implementation. Third, Wrapp claims that good leaders possess the ability to push through programs in a piecemeal fashion. They recognize the futility of trying to push total packages or strategic programs through the organization, since significant objections to at least part of such programs are likely to arise. Instead, the successful leader is willing to take less than total acceptance in order to achieve modest progress toward a goal. The successful leader tries to push through his or her ideas one piece at a time, so that they appear as incidental to other ideas, though in fact they are part of a larger program or hidden agenda that moves the organization in the direction of the manager's objectives.

Jeffery Pfeffer has articulated a similar vision of the politically astute manager who gets things done in organizations by the intelligent use of power.[8] In Pfeffer's view power comes from control over resources, which include budgets, positions, information, and knowledge that is important to the organization. Politically astute managers use these resources to acquire another critical resource—allies. Allies can then help managers to attain their strategic objectives. Pfeffer stresses that one does not need to be a CEO to assemble power in an organization. Sometimes quite junior functional managers can build a surprisingly effective power base and use it to influence organizational outcomes.

STRATEGY AS AN EMERGENT PROCESS

The planning model we reviewed earlier in the chapter suggests that an organization's strategies are the result of a plan; that the strategic planning process itself is rational and highly structured; and that the process is orchestrated by, and indeed dominated by, top management. In recent years several scholars have advocated an alternative view of strategy making that has called into question the traditional planning-centric view.[9] These scholars have two main criticisms of the planning model; one focuses upon the unpredictability of the real world, while the other looks at the role lower-level managers can play in the strategic management process.

Strategy Making in an Unpredictable World

Critics of formal planning systems argue that we live in a world in which uncertainty, complexity, and ambiguity dominate and in which small chance events can have a large and unpredictable impact upon outcomes.[10] In such an environment, they claim, even the most carefully thought out strategic plans are prone to being rendered useless by rapid and unforeseen changes in the environment. This is something that military historians and thinkers have long recognized. Carl von Clausewitz, the famous Prussian military strategist of the early 1800s, once noted that "the principles, rules, or even systems of strategy must always fall short, undermined by the world's endless complexities. . . . In strategy most things are uncertain and variable."[11] Although von Clausewitz was talking about military strategy, his observations are just as relevant to business strategy. Witness, for example, how Microsoft was caught off guard by the rapid rise of the Internet and the sudden emergence of companies such as Netscape and Sun Microsystems as potential competitors (see Strategy in Action 1.2 for details).

In an unpredictable world, there is a premium on being able to respond quickly to changing circumstances, altering the strategies of the organization accordingly (as Microsoft did in response to the threat posed by Netscape—see Strategy in Action 1.2). According to critics, such a flexible approach to strategy making is not possible within the framework of the traditional strategic planning process, with its implicit assumption that an organization's strategies need to be reviewed only during the annual strategic planning exercise.

Strategy Making by Lower-Level Employees

Another criticism leveled at the rational planning model of strategy is that too much importance is attached to the role of top management.[12] An alternative view now gaining wide acceptance is that individual managers deep within an organization can and often do exert a profound influence over the evolution of strategy.[13] Writing with Robert Burgelman of Stanford University, Andy Grove, the CEO of Intel, has recently described how many important strategic decisions at Intel were initiated not by top managers, but by the autonomous action of mid-level managers deep within Intel.[14] These strategic decisions included the decision to exit an important market (the DRAM memory chip market) and the decision to develop a certain class of microprocessors (RISC-based microprocessors) in direct contrast to the stated strategy of Intel's top managers.

Another famous example of autonomous action occurred at 3M corporation back in the 1920s. At that time 3M was primarily a manufacturer of sandpaper. Richard Drew, who was a young laboratory assistant at the time, came up with what he thought would be a great new product, a glue-covered paper. Drew saw applications for the product in the automobile industry, where it could be used to mask parts of a vehicle during painting. He presented the idea to the company's president, William McKnight. An unimpressed McKnight suggested that Drew drop the research. Drew didn't; instead he developed the paper and then went out and got endorsements from potential customers in the auto industry. Armed with this information he approached McKnight again. A chastened McKnight reversed his original position and gave Drew the go ahead to start developing what was to become one of 3M's main product lines—sticky tape—a business it dominates to this day.[15] The point of this story, of course, is that it illustrates how autonomous action by a lower-level employee can shape the strategic destiny of a company.

Intended and Emergent Strategies

Henry Mintzberg has incorporated the ideas discussed above into a model of strategy development that provides us with a more encompassing view of what strategy actually is. According to this model, which is illustrated in Figure 1.3, a company's **realized strategy** is the product of whatever planned, or **intended, strategies** are

1.2   STRATEGY *in* ACTION

A Strategic Shift at Microsoft

Over the last decade Microsoft has emerged as the dominant software company in the desktop computing market. By 1995 Microsoft's Windows operating system was to be found on 90 percent of all personal computers, while the company enjoyed a market share in excess of 50 percent for a large number of popular desktop computing applications, including word processing, presentation software, and spreadsheets. So complete was Microsoft's dominance that in the early 1990s several of its competitors filed complaints with the United States Department of Justice, alleging that Microsoft engaged in unfair trade practices, a charge that Microsoft vigorously denies. Meanwhile, the business press hailed the company's founder and CEO, Bill Gates, as one of the greatest strategic thinkers in the computer industry. The linchpin of Gate's strategy was to ensure the continued dominance of Microsoft's Windows operating system as the standard of choice in the personal computer environment.

In mid 1995, however, Microsoft suddenly began to look vulnerable when it was blind-sided by two related and unexpected developments. The first of these was the explosive growth of the global network of interlinked computers known as the Internet and the associated World Wide Web, or WWW, that sits on top of the Internet. In the late 1980s, Tim Bernes Lee, a physicist at the CERN research institute for particle physics in Switzerland, developed a method for encoding, displaying, and transmitting text and graphics over the Internet using HTML (hypertext markup language). In effect, Lee had invented the World Wide Web. In 1993 a young computer programmer, Mark Andreessen, at the University of Illinois masterminded the development of a "browser" that could be used to travel the Internet, read HTML documents, and display them on a personal computer screen. In 1994 he left Illinois to help found Netscape, a software company that produced an improved version of the HTML browser, Netscape Navigator, along with "Web server software," which could be placed upon the computer servers that were the nodes of the rapidly developing WWW to manage Web files and handle Web traffic. The growth of the WWW was nothing short of stunning. In 1990 less than 1 million users were connected to the Internet. By late 1995, largely as a result of the popularity of the WWW, the figure was approaching 80 million, and Netscape, not Microsoft, had supplied more than 70 percent of all Web browsers and Web server software.

The second development was the invention of the Java computer programming language at Sun Microsystems, one of the leading suppliers of computer workstations and servers. A program written in Java can be

actually put into action *and* of any unplanned, or **emergent, strategies.** In Mintzberg's view, emergent strategies are the unplanned responses to unforeseen circumstances, and they often arise from autonomous action by individual employees deep within the organization (such as Richard Drew at 3M). They are *not* the product of formal top-down planning mechanisms.

Mintzberg maintains that emergent strategies are often successful and may be more appropriate than intended strategies. Richard Pascale has described how this was the case for the entry of Honda Motor into the U.S. motorcycle market.[16] When a number of Honda executives arrived in Los Angeles from Japan in 1959 to establish a U.S. subsidiary, their original aim (intended strategy) was to focus on selling 250-cc and 350-cc machines to confirmed motorcycle enthusiasts, rather than 50-cc Honda Cubs, which were a big hit in Japan. Their instinct told them that the Honda 50s were not suitable for the U.S. market, where everything was bigger and more luxurious than in Japan.

stored anywhere on the WWW and accessed by anyone with a Web browser that contains a Java interpreter, and the new versions of Netscape Navigator do. Java is indifferent to the operating system of the personal computer on which a Web browser resides. So in theory, someone using a current version of Netscape Navigator can access a word processing program placed somewhere on the Web as and when they need it. Instead of purchasing the program outright for hundreds of dollars, all they need do is pay a few cents for the "run time" during which they use the program.

This represents a potential body blow to Microsoft. It raises the possibility that people will no longer need to purchase expensive applications software from Microsoft and store it on their computers. Nor do they need a machine that utilizes Microsoft's operating system. All they need is a simple and inexpensive machine that is able to run a Netscape browser with a Java interpreter. They can then use this machine to access programs on the Web as and when they need them, using the computing power of a remote server. As Scott Mc-Nealy, the CEO of Sun Microsystems, is fond of saying, in this vision of the future "the network is the computer," while the standard is based not on Microsoft's Windows, but on Netscape and Java.

Microsoft's initial response to this unanticipated threat was to dismiss it. Bill Gates called Netscape's browser technology trivial. However, by late 1995 it was clear that Microsoft had decided to respond to the unexpected threat posed by Netscape and Java by shifting its own strategic focus toward the WWW. Microsoft was to continue to focus on being the dominant software player in the desktop computing business, but its strategy for attaining this objective would start to change. In an all-day Internet conference, Microsoft stated that it would give away its own Web browser and Web server software for free. The company also announced that future software applications produced by Microsoft would contain "browser functions" that would enable users to roam the Web for information. In addition, new versions of its popular word processing program would enable users to convert their documents into HTML format that could be transmitted over the Web. Microsoft also announced that it would license Java from Sun and incorporate Java interpreters into some of its own products. In the weeks that followed, Microsoft also announced an alliance with America Online (AOL), the world's largest on-line service, which would allow AOL's 5 million subscribers to use Microsoft's browser. This was followed by a deal with Intel to develop technology that will make video, voice, and data conferencing via the WWW as commonplace as placing a telephone call. By quickly abandoning its prior strategy and developing a new Internet strategy on the fly in response to an unanticipated threat, Microsoft had suddenly positioned itself as a viable alternative to Netscape.[17]

However, sales of the 250-cc and 350-cc bikes were sluggish, and the bikes themselves were plagued by mechanical failure. It looked as if Honda's strategy was going to fail. At the same time, the Japanese executives were using the Honda 50s to run errands around Los Angeles and attracting a lot of attention doing so. One day they got a call from a Sears, Roebuck buyer who wanted to sell the 50-cc bikes to a broad market of Americans who were not necessarily already motorcycle enthusiasts. The Honda executives were hesitant to sell the small bikes for fear of alienating serious bikers who might then associate Honda with wimpy machines. In the end they were pushed into doing so by the failure of the 250-cc and 350-cc models. The rest is history. Honda had stumbled onto a previously untouched market segment that was to prove huge: the average American who had never owned a motorbike. Honda had also found an untried channel of distribution: general retailers rather than specialty motorbike stores. By 1964 nearly one out of every two motorcycles sold in the United States was a Honda.

FIGURE 1.3

Emergent and
Deliberate Strategies

Source: Reprinted from "Strategy Formation in an Adhocracy," by Henry Mintzberg and Alexandra McGugh, published in *Administrative Science Quarterly,* Vol. 30, No. 2, June 1985, by permission of *Administrative Science Quarterly.*

The conventional explanation of Honda's success is that the company redefined the U.S. motorcycle industry with a brilliantly conceived *intended* strategy. The fact was that Honda's intended strategy was a near disaster. The strategy that *emerged* did so not through planning but through unplanned action taken in response to unforeseen circumstances. Nevertheless, credit should be given to the Japanese management for recognizing the strength of the emergent strategy and for pursuing it with vigor.

The critical point demonstrated by the Honda example is that, in contrast to the view that all strategies are planned, successful strategies can emerge within an organization without prior planning, often in response to unforeseen circumstances. As Mintzberg has noted, strategies can take root in all kinds of strange places, virtually wherever people have the capacity to learn and the resources to support that capacity.

In practice, the strategies of most organizations are probably a combination of the intended (planned) and the emergent. The message for management is that it needs to recognize the process of emergence and to intervene when appropriate, killing off bad emergent strategies but nurturing potentially good ones.[18] To make such decisions, however, managers must be able to judge the worth of emergent strategies. They must be able to think strategically. Even though emergent strategies arise from within the organization without prior planning—that is, without going through the steps illustrated in Figure 1.1 in a *sequential* fashion—top management still has to evaluate emergent strategies. Such evaluation involves comparing each emergent strategy with the organization's goals, external environmental opportunities and threats, and the organization's internal strengths and weaknesses. The objective is to assess whether the emergent strategy fits the organization's needs and capabilities. In addition, Mintzberg stresses that an organization's capability to produce emergent strategies is a function of the kind of corporate culture fostered by the organization's structure and control systems.

In other words, the different components of the strategic management process are just as important from the perspective of emergent strategies as they are from the perspective of intended strategies. The essential differences between the strategic management process for intended and for emergent strategies are illustrated in Figure 1.4. The formulation of intended strategies is basically a top-down-planning-driven process whereas the formulation of emergent strategies is a bottom-up process. In successful organizations both processes are often at work.[19]

FIGURE 1.4
. . . .

FIGURE 1.4
. . . .

The Strategic Management Process for Intended and Emergent Strategies

Intended Strategy

Emergent Strategy

STRATEGIC PLANNING IN PRACTICE

Even the most vocal critics of formal strategic planning concede that it has a role. For example, Mintzberg's model of the strategy-making process, as illustrated in Figure 1.4, maintains a role for formal strategic planning, while simultaneously pointing to the importance of unplanned emergent strategies. Since formal strategic planning is still widely practiced (and rightly so), it is pertinent to ask whether formal planning systems actually help an organization to attain superior performance.

On balance, the research evidence seems to indicate that formal planning systems do help companies make better strategic decisions. For example, a recent study analyzed in detail the results of twenty-six previously published studies of the relationship between strategic planning and a company's performance.[20] The study came to the conclusion that strategic planning does indeed have a positive impact upon a company's performance, suggesting that strategic planning is a valuable activity.

Despite such results, many informed observers have increasingly questioned the use of formal planning systems as an aid to strategic decision making. Thomas J. Peters and Robert H. Waterman, authors of the bestseller *In Search of Excellence*, were among the first to call into question the usefulness of formal planning systems, and the antiplanning rhetoric continues to be a theme in the more recent works of Peters.[21] Similarly, Mintzberg argues that business history is replete with examples of companies that have made poor decisions on the basis of supposedly comprehensive strategic planning.[22] For example, Exxon's decisions to diversify into electrical equipment and office automation and to offset shrinking U.S. oil reserves by investing in shale oil and synthetic fuels resulted from a 1970s planning exercise that was overly pessimistic about the demand for oil-based products. Exxon foresaw ever higher prices for oil and predicted sharp falls in demand as a result. However, oil prices actually tumbled during the 1980s, invalidating one of the basic assumptions of Exxon's plan. In addition, Exxon's diversification failed because of poor acquisitions and management problems in office automation.

Four explanations can be offered as to why formal strategic planning systems do not always produce the desired results. We consider three of them here and take up the fourth, which focuses on decision-making biases among managers, in the next section. The three explanations are as follows: (1) planning under uncertainty; (2) top-down ivory tower planning; and (3) planning for the present, as opposed to the future.

Planning Under Uncertainty

One reason for the poor reputation of strategic planning is that many executives, in their initial enthusiasm for planning techniques, forget that the future is inherently unpredictable. As at Exxon, a common problem is that executives often assume it is possible to forecast the future accurately. However, in the real world, the only constant is change. Even the best-laid plans can fall apart if unforeseen contingencies occur, and, as we noted earlier, in the real world unforeseen contingencies occur all the time. The recognition that in an uncertain world the future cannot be forecast with sufficient accuracy led Royal Dutch/Shell to pioneer the scenario approach to planning discussed in the Strategy in Action 1.3. Rather than try to forecast the fu-

STRATEGY *in* ACTION

Strategic Planning at Royal Dutch/Shell

 Royal Dutch/Shell, the world's largest oil company, is well known for its addiction to strategic planning. Despite the fact that many management gurus and CEOs now consider strategic planning an anachronism, Shell is convinced that long-term strategic planning has served the company well. Part of the reason for this success is that at Shell planning does not take the form of complex and inflexible ten-year plans generated by a team of corporate strategists far removed from operating realities. Rather, the planning process generates a series of "what if" scenarios whose function is to try to get general managers at all levels of the corporation to think strategically about the environment in which they do business.

The strength of Shell's scenario-based planning system was perhaps most evident during the early 1980s. At that time the price of a barrel of oil was hovering around $30. With exploration and development costs running at an industry average of about $11 per barrel, most oil companies were making record profits. Moreover, industry analysts were generally bullish; many were predicting that oil prices would increase to around $50 per barrel by 1990. Shell, however, was mulling over a handful of future scenarios, one of which included the possibility of a breakdown of the OPEC oil cartel's agreement to restrict supply, an oil glut, and a drop in oil prices to $15 per barrel. In 1984 Shell instructed the managers of its operating companies to indicate how they would respond to a $15 per barrel world. This "game" set off some serious work at Shell exploring the question, "What will we do if it happens?"

By early 1986 the consequences of the "game" included efforts to cut exploration costs by pioneering advanced exploration technologies, massive investments in cost-efficient refining facilities, and a process of weeding out the least-profitable service stations. All this planning occurred at a time when most oil companies were busy diversifying outside the oil business rather than trying to improve the efficiency of their core operations. As it turned out, the price of oil was still $27 per barrel in early January 1986. However, the failure of the OPEC cartel to set new production ceilings in 1985, new production from the North Sea and Alaska, and declining demand due to increased conservation efforts had created a growing oil glut. In late January 1986 the dam burst. By February 1 oil was priced at $17 per barrel, and by April the price was $10 per barrel.

Because Shell had already visited the $15-per-barrel world, it had gained a head start over its rivals in its cost-cutting efforts. As a result, by 1989 the company's average oil and gas exploration costs were less than $2 per barrel, compared with an industry average of $4 per barrel. Moreover, in the crucial refining and marketing sector, Shell made a net return on assets of 8.4 percent in 1988, more than double the 3.8 percent average of the other oil majors: Exxon, British Petroleum, Chevron, Mobil, and Texaco.[23]

---

ture, Shell's planners attempt to model the company's environment and use that model to predict a range of possible scenarios. Executives are then asked to devise strategies to cope with the different scenarios. The objective is to get managers to understand the dynamic and complex nature of their environment and to think through problems in a strategic fashion.

The scenario approach to planning seems to have spread quite rapidly among large companies. According to one survey, by the mid 1980s more than 50 percent of the *Fortune* 500 companies used scenario-planning methods.[24] Although a detailed evaluation of the pros and cons of scenario planning has yet to appear, recent work by Paul Schoemaker of the University of Chicago seems to suggest that scenario planning expands people's thinking, and as such it may lead to better plans, as seems to have occurred at Royal Dutch/Shell. However, Schoemaker cautions that forcing planners to consider extreme scenarios that are unbelievable can discredit the approach and cause resistance on the planners' part.

Ivory Tower Planning

A second serious mistake made by many companies in their initial enthusiasm for planning has been to treat planning exclusively as a top-management function. This *ivory tower* approach can result in strategic plans being formulated in a vacuum by planning executives who have little understanding or appreciation of operating realities. As a consequence, strategies are formulated that do more harm than good. For example, when demographic data indicated that houses and families were shrinking, planners at General Electric's appliance group concluded that smaller appliances were the wave of the future. Because the planners had little contact with home builders and retailers, they did not realize that kitchens and bathrooms were the two rooms that were not shrinking. Nor did they appreciate that working women wanted big refrigerators to cut down on trips to the supermarket. The result was that General Electric wasted a lot of time designing small appliances for which there was only limited demand.

The ivory tower concept of planning can also lead to tensions between planners and operating personnel. The experience of General Electric's appliance group is again illuminating. Many of the planners in this group were recruited from consulting firms or from top-flight business schools. Many of the operating managers took this pattern of recruitment to mean that corporate executives did not deem them smart enough to think through strategic problems for themselves. Out of this impression grew an us-versus-them state of mind, which quickly escalated into hostility. As a result, even when the planners were right, operating managers would not listen to them. In the early 1980s the planners correctly recognized the importance of the globalization of the appliance market and the emerging Japanese threat. However, operating managers, who then saw Sears, Roebuck as the competition, paid them little heed.

Correcting the ivory tower approach to planning requires recognizing that, to succeed, strategic planning must encompass managers at *all* levels of the corporation. It is important to understand that much of the best planning can and should be done by operating managers. They are the ones closest to the facts. The role of corporate-level planners should be that of facilitators, who help operating managers do the planning, both by setting the broad strategic goals of the organization and by providing operating managers with the resources required to identify the strategies that might be required to attain those goals.

Planning for the Present

The traditional strategic planning model we reviewed earlier has been characterized as the *fit model* of strategy making, because it tries to achieve a fit between the internal resources and capabilities of an organization, and external environmental opportunities and threats. Gary Hamel and C. K. Prahalad have attacked the fit model as being too static and limiting.[25] They argue that adopting the fit model to strategy formulation leads to a mindset in which management focuses too much on the degree of fit between the *existing* resources of a company and *current* environmental opportunities and not enough upon building *new* resources and capabilities to create and exploit *future* opportunities. Strategies formulated via the fit model, say Hamel and Prahalad, tend to be more concerned with today's problems than with tomorrow's opportunities. As a result, companies that rely exclusively on the fit model as an approach to strategy formulation are unlikely to be able to build and maintain a competitive advantage. This third weakness of formal strategic planning is particularly apparent in a dynamic competitive environment, in which new competitors are continually arising and new ways of doing business are constantly being invented.

As Hamel and Prahalad note again and again, U.S. companies using the fit approach have been surprised by the ascent of foreign competitors that initially seemed to lack the resources and capabilities needed to make them a real threat. This happened to Xerox, which ignored the rise of Canon and Ricoh in the photocopier market until they had become serious global competitors; to General Motors, which initially overlooked the threat posed by Toyota and Honda in the 1970s; and to Caterpillar, which ignored the danger Komatsu posed to its heavy earth-moving business until it was almost too late to respond.

Strategic Intent   The secret of the success of companies such as Toyota, Canon, and Komatsu, according to Hamel and Prahalad, is that they all had bold ambitions that outstripped their existing resources and capabilities. All wanted to achieve global leadership, and they set out to build the resources and capabilities that would enable them to attain this goal. Consequently, the top management of these companies created an obsession with winning at all levels of the organization and then sustained that obsession over a ten- to twenty-year quest for global leadership. It is this obsession that Hamel and Prahalad refer to as **strategic intent**. At the same time, they stress that strategic intent is more than simply unfettered ambition. They argue that strategic intent also encompasses an active management process, which includes "focusing the organization's attention on the essence of winning; motivating people by communicating the value of the target; leaving room for individual and team contributions; sustaining enthusiasm by providing new operational definitions as circumstances change; and using intent consistently to guide resource allocations."[26] Thus, underlying the concept of strategic intent is the notion that strategy formulation should involve setting ambitious goals, which stretch a company, and then finding ways to build the resources and capabilities necessary to attain those goals.

Although Hamel and Prahalad aptly criticize the fit model, they note that in practice the two approaches to strategy formulation are not mutually exclusive. All the components of the strategic management process that we discussed earlier, and that are summarized in Figure 1.1, are important. Managers do have to analyze the external environment to identify opportunities and threats. They do have to analyze the company's resources and capabilities to identify strengths and weaknesses. They need to be familiar with the range of functional-level, business-level, global, and corporate-level strategies that are available to them. They also need to have an appreciation for the structures required to implement different strategies. What Hamel and Prahalad seem to be saying is that the strategic management process should begin with challenging goals, such as attaining global leadership, that stretch the organization. Then, throughout the process the emphasis should be on finding ways (strategies) to develop the resources and capabilities necessary to achieve these goals, rather than on exploiting *existing* strengths to take advantage of *existing* opportunities. The difference between strategic fit and strategic intent, therefore, may just be one of emphasis. Strategic intent is more internally focused and is concerned with building new resources and capabilities. Strategic fit focuses more on matching existing resources and capabilities to the external environment.

IMPROVING STRATEGIC DECISION MAKING

Even the best-designed strategic planning systems will fail to produce the desired results if strategic decision makers do not use the information at their disposal effectively. This is the fourth explanation of why formal planning systems sometimes fail. There is, in fact, a good deal of evidence that many managers are poor strategic decision makers.[27] The reasons why many managers perform so poorly in this regard have to do with two related psychological phenomena: cognitive biases and groupthink. We discuss each of them in turn and then consider techniques for improving decision making.

Cognitive Biases and Strategic Decisions

The rationality of human decision makers is bounded by our own cognitive capabilities.[28] We are not supercomputers, and it is difficult for us to absorb and process large amounts of information effectively. As a result, we tend to fall back on certain rules of thumb, or heuristics, when making decisions. Many of these rules of thumb are actually quite useful, since they help us to make sense out of a complex and uncertain world. However, sometimes they also lead to severe and systematic errors in the decision-making process.[29] Systematic errors are those that appear time and time again. These systematic errors seem to arise from a series of **cognitive biases** in the way that human decision makers process information and reach decisions. Because of cognitive biases, many managers end up making poor strategic decisions.

Figure 1.5 presents five well-known cognitive biases. These biases have been verified repeatedly in laboratory settings, so we can be reasonably sure that they exist and that we are all prone to them.[30] The **prior hypothesis bias** refers to the fact that decision makers who have strong prior beliefs about the relationship between two variables tend to make decisions on the basis of these beliefs, even when presented with evidence that their beliefs are wrong. Moreover, they tend to seek and use information that is consistent with their prior beliefs, while ignoring information that contradicts these beliefs. To put this bias in a strategic context, it suggests that a CEO who has a strong prior belief that a certain strategy makes sense might continue to pursue that strategy, despite evidence that it is inappropriate or failing.

Another well-known cognitive bias is referred to as **escalating commitment**.[31] Escalating commitment occurs when decision makers, having already committed significant resources to a project, commit even more resources if they receive feedback that the project is failing. This may be an irrational response; a more logical response would be to abandon the project and move on (that is, to "cut your losses and run"), rather than escalate commitment. Feelings of personal responsibility for

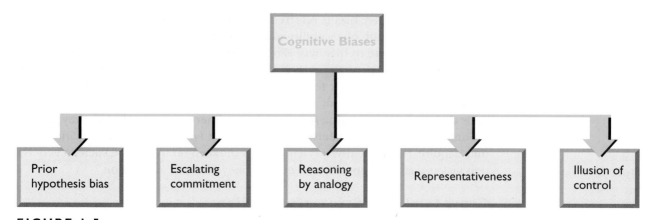

FIGURE 1.5

Five Well-Known Cognitive Biases

a project apparently induce decision makers to stick with a project, despite evidence that it is failing. One of the most famous examples of escalating commitment is the U.S. policy that existed toward the Vietnam War. President Lyndon B. Johnson's reaction to information that U.S. policy in Vietnam was failing was to commit ever more resources to the war.[32] To draw on a business example, during the 1960s and 1970s the response of large U.S. steel makers to cost-efficient competition from minimills and foreign steel makers was to increase their investments in the technologically obsolete steel-making facilities they already possessed, rather than invest in new cutting-edge technology.[33] This was irrational; investments in such obsolete technology would never enable them to become cost efficient.

The bias of **reasoning by analogy** involves the use of simple analogies to make sense out of complex problems. U.S. policy toward Vietnam in the 1960s, for example, was guided by the analogy of falling dominoes. U.S. policymakers believed that if Vietnam fell to the Communists, the rest of Southeast Asia would also fall. The danger of using such analogies is that oversimplifying a complex problem can be misleading. For example, several companies have relied on the analogy of a three-legged stool to justify diversifying into business areas of which they had little prior knowledge. The analogy suggests that a stool with fewer than three legs—and by extension, a company that is active in fewer than three different businesses—is unbalanced. Chrysler applied this analogy to justify its decision in the mid 1980s to diversify into the aerospace industry by acquiring Gulfstream, a manufacturer of executive jets. Five years later Chrysler admitted that the diversification move had been a mistake and divested itself of this activity.

Representativeness is a bias rooted in the tendency to generalize from a small sample, or even a single vivid anecdote. This bias, however, violates the statistical law of large numbers, which says that it is inappropriate to generalize from a small sample, let alone from a single case. An interesting example of representativeness occurred after World War II, when Seawell Avery, the CEO of Montgomery Ward, shelved plans for national expansion to meet competition from Sears because he believed that a depression would follow the war. He based his belief on the fact that there had been a depression after World War I. As it turned out, there was no depression, and Sears went on to become a nationwide retailer, whereas Montgomery Ward did not. Avery's mistake was to generalize from one postwar experience and assume that depressions always follow wars.

The final cognitive bias is referred to as the **illusion of control**. It is the tendency to overestimate one's ability to control events. Top-level managers seem to be particularly prone to this bias. Having risen to the top of an organization, they tend to be overconfident about their ability to succeed. According to Richard Roll, such overconfidence leads to what he has termed the **hubris hypothesis** of takeovers.[34] Roll argues that senior managers are typically overconfident about their abilities to create value by acquiring another company. Hence, they end up making poor acquisition decisions, often paying far too much for the companies they acquire. Subsequently, servicing the debt taken on to finance such an acquisition makes it all but impossible to make money from the acquisition.

Groupthink and Strategic Decisions

The biases just discussed are individual biases. However, most strategic decisions are made by groups, not individuals. Thus, the group context within which decisions are made is clearly an important variable in determining whether cognitive biases will operate adversely to affect the strategic decision-making processes. The psychologist Irvin Janis has argued that many groups are characterized by a process known as groupthink and that as a result many groups do make poor strategic decisions.[35] **Groupthink** occurs when a group of decision makers embarks on a course of action without questioning underlying assumptions. Typically, a group coalesces around a person or policy. It ignores or filters out information that can be used to question the policy and develops after-the-fact rationalizations for its decision. Thus, commitment is based on an emotional, rather than an objective, assessment of the correct course of action. The consequences can be poor decisions.

This phenomenon may explain, at least in part, why companies often make poor strategic decisions in spite of sophisticated strategic management. Janis traced many historical fiascoes to defective policymaking by government leaders who received social support from their in-group of advisers. For example, he suggested that President John F. Kennedy's inner circle suffered from groupthink when the members of this group supported the decision to launch the Bay of Pigs invasion of Cuba, even though available information showed that it would be an unsuccessful venture and would damage U.S. relations with other countries.

Janis has observed that groupthink-dominated groups are characterized by strong pressures toward uniformity, which make their members avoid raising controversial issues, questioning weak arguments, or calling a halt to softheaded thinking. An interesting example of groupthink in a business context, the acquisition of Howard Johnson by the Imperial Group, is highlighted in Strategy in Action 1.4. Note that in this case groupthink seemed to exacerbate a number of other cognitive biases, including the illusion of control and prior hypothesis bias.

Techniques for Improving Decision Making

The existence of cognitive biases and groupthink raises the issue of how to bring critical information to bear on the decision mechanism so that strategic decisions made by the company are realistic and based on thorough evaluation. Two techniques known to counteract groupthink and cognitive biases are devil's advocacy and dialectic inquiry.

I.4	STRATEGY *in* ACTION

Groupthink at Imperial Tobacco

An example of groupthink concerns the 1979 acquisition of Howard Johnson by Britain's Imperial Group. In 1979 Imperial was the third-largest tobacco company in the world, after British American Tobacco and Philip Morris. In the 1970s Imperial began a diversification program designed to reduce its dependence on the declining tobacco market. Part of this program included a plan to acquire a major U.S. company. Imperial spent two years scanning the United States for a suitable acquisition opportunity. It was looking for an enterprise in a high-growth industry that had a high market share, a good track record, and sound growth prospects and that could be acquired at a reasonable price. Imperial scanned more than 30 industries and 200 different companies before deciding on Howard Johnson.

When Imperial announced its plans to buy Howard Johnson for close to $500 million in 1979, the company's shareholders threatened rebellion. They were quick to point out that at $26 per share Imperial was paying double what Howard Johnson had been worth only six months previously, when share prices stood at $13. The acquisition hardly seemed to be at a reasonable price. Moreover, the motel industry was entering a low- rather than a high-growth phase, and growth prospects were poor. Besides, Howard Johnson did not have a good track record. Imperial ignored shareholders' protests and bought the lodging chain. Five years later, after persistent losses, Imperial was trying to divest itself of Howard Johnson. The acquisition had been a complete failure.

What went wrong? Why, after a two-year planning exercise, did Imperial buy a company that so patently did not fit its own criteria? The answer would seem to lie not in the planning but in the quality of strategic decision making. Imperial bought Howard Johnson in spite of its planning, not because of it. The CEO decided independently that Howard Johnson was a good buy. A rather authoritarian figure who was overconfident in his ability (a case of hubris), the CEO surrounded himself with subordinates who agreed with him. In a clear sign that groupthink was at work, once he had made his choice, his advisers concurred with his judgment and shared in developing rationalizations for it. No one questioned the decision itself, even though information was available to show that it was flawed. Instead, strategic planning was used to justify a decision that in practice did not conform with strategic objectives.[36]

Devil's advocacy and dialectic inquiry have been proposed as two means of improving decision making.[37] **Devil's advocacy** requires the generation of both a plan and a critical analysis of the plan. One member of the decision-making group acts as the devil's advocate, bringing out all the reasons that might make the proposal unacceptable. In this way, decision makers can become aware of the possible perils of recommended courses of action. **Dialectic inquiry** is more complex, for it requires the generation of a plan (a thesis) and a counterplan (an antithesis). According to R. O. Mason, one of the early proponents of this method in strategic management, the plan and the counterplan should reflect plausible but conflicting courses of action.[38] Corporate decision makers consider a debate between advocates of the plan and counterplan. The purpose of the debate is to reveal problems with definitions, recommended courses of action, and assumptions. As a result, corporate decision makers and planners are able to form a new and more encompassing conceptualization of the problem, which becomes the final plan (a synthesis).

The two decision-making processes that expose cognitive biases and groupthink are illustrated in Figure 1.6. If either of those processes had been used in the

FIGURE 1.6

Two Decision-Making Processes That Counter- act Cognitive Biases and Groupthink

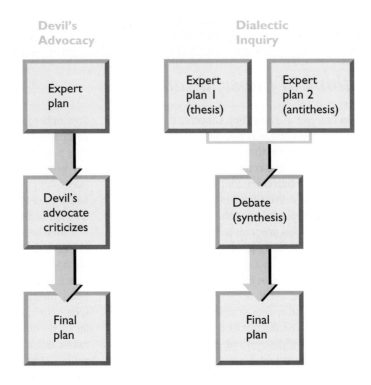

Imperial case, very likely a different (and probably better) decision would have been made. However, there is considerable dispute over which of the two methods is better.[39] Researchers have come to conflicting conclusions, and the jury is still out on this issue. From a practical point of view, however, devil's advocacy is proba- bly the easier method to implement because it involves less commitment in terms of time than dialectic inquiry.

SUMMARY OF CHAPTER

The chapter provides an overview of the strategic management process and examines some of the fac- tors that influence the quality of strategic decisions generated by that process. The role played by strategic leaders in the strategic decision-making process is discussed and the characteristics of strong leaders identified. Besides identifying the main components of the strategic management process, it points out several flaws in the traditional planning systems and the harmful effect that cogni- tive biases and groupthink can have on the quality of strategic decision making. The key points of this chapter are as follows:

✔ A strategy is an action that a company takes to at- tain one or more of its goals.

✔ A central objective of strategic management is to identify why some organizations succeed while others fail.

✔ Traditional definitions of strategy stress that an or- ganization's strategy is the outcome of a rational planning process.

✔ The major components of the strategic manage- ment process include defining the mission and ma- jor goals of the organization; analyzing the external and internal environments of the organization; choosing strategies that align, or fit, the organiza- tion's strengths and weaknesses with external envi- ronmental opportunities and threats; and adopting organizational structures and control systems to implement the organization's chosen strategy.

✔ General managers are individuals who bear re- sponsibility for the overall performance of the organization or for one of its major self-contained divisions. Their overriding strategic concern is for the health of the total organization under their direction.

✔ Functional managers are individuals who bear responsibility for a particular business function. Although they are not in a position to see the big picture, they do have a number of important strategic responsibilities.

✔ The key characteristics of good leaders include vision, eloquence, and consistency; commitment; being well informed; a willingness to delegate and empower; and political astuteness.

✔ A revision of the concept suggests that strategy can emerge from deep within an organization in the absence of formal plans as lower-level managers respond to unpredicted situations.

✔ Strategic planning often fails because executives do not plan for uncertainty and because ivory tower planners lose touch with operating realities.

✔ Hamel and Prahalad have criticized the fit approach to strategy making on the ground that it focuses too much on the degree of fit between existing resources and current opportunities, and not enough on building new resources and capabilities to create and exploit future opportunities.

✔ Strategic intent refers to an obsession with achieving an objective that stretches the company and requires it to build new resources and capabilities.

✔ In spite of systematic planning, companies may adopt poor strategies if their decision-making processes are vulnerable to groupthink and if individual cognitive biases are allowed to intrude into the decision-making process.

✔ Techniques for enhancing the effectiveness of strategic decision making include devil's advocacy and dialectic inquiry.

DISCUSSION QUESTIONS

1. What do we mean by *strategy?*

2. What are the strengths of formal strategic planning? What are its weaknesses?

3. The book *Barbarians at the Gate* by Bryan Burroughs and John Helyar (Harper & Row, 1990) contains a detailed description of the acquisition of RJR Nabisco by KKR. Using the book as your source, evaluate KKR's decision to acquire RJR Nabisco. Do you think cognitive biases were at work here, and would managers at KKR have reached a different decision if they had employed devil's advocacy? Was the acquisition of RJR an intended or an emergent strategy? (Note: Answering this question requires a fair amount of reading.)

4. Evaluate President Bill Clinton against the leadership characteristics discussed in the text. On the basis of this comparison, do you think President Clinton is a good strategic leader?

Practicing Strategic Management

SMALL-GROUP EXERCISE
Designing a Planning System

Break up into groups of three to five people, and discuss the following scenario:

You are a group of senior managers working for a fast-growing computer software company. Your product allows users to play interactive role-playing games over the Internet (World Wide Web). In the last three years your company has gone from being a start-up enterprise with 10 employees and no revenues to a company with 250 employees and revenues of $60 million. The company has been growing so rapidly that you have not had time to create a strategic plan, but now members of your board of directors are telling you that they want to see a plan and they want it to drive decision making and resource allocation at the company. They want you to design a planning process that will have the following attributes:

1. It will be democratic, involving as many key employees as possible in the process.

2. It will help to build a sense of shared vision within the company about how to continue to grow rapidly.

3. It will lead to the generation of three to five key strategies for the company.

4. It will drive the formulation of detailed action plans, and these plans will be subsequently linked to the company's annual operating budget.

Design a planning process for presentation to your board of directors. Think carefully about who should be included in this process. Be sure to outline the strengths and weaknesses of the approach you choose, and be prepared to justify why your approach might be superior to alternative approaches.

EXPLORING THE WEB
Visiting Compaq

Go to the Web site of Compaq Computer (http://www.compaq.com). When there, click on the "Compaq History and Milestones" button. Using the information contained on that page, map out the evolution of strategy at Compaq from its establishment in the early 1980s to the present. To what degree do you think that the evolution of strategy at Compaq was the result of detailed long-term strategic planning, and to what degree was it the result of unplanned actions taken in response to unpredictable circumstances?

Search the Web for a company site where there is sufficient information to map out the evolution of that company's strategy over a significant period of time. What drove the evolution of strategy at this company? To what degree was the evolution of strategy the result of detailed long-term strategic planning, and what degree was it the result of unplanned actions taken in response to unpredictable circumstances?

ARTICLE FILE I

At the end of every chapter in this book, you will find an Article File task. The task requires you to search newspapers or magazines in a library for an example of a real company that satisfies the task question or issue. Your first article file task is to find an example of a company that has recently changed its strategy. Identify whether this change was the outcome of a formal planning process or whether it was an emergent response to unforeseen events occurring in the company's environment.

STRATEGIC MANAGEMENT PROJECT
Module I

To give you a practical insight into the strategic management process, we provide a series of strategic modules, one at the end of every chapter in this book. Each module asks you to collect and analyze information relating to the material discussed in that chapter. By completing these strategic modules, you will gain a clearer idea of the overall strategic management process. The first step in this project is to pick a company to study. We recommend that you focus on the same company throughout the book. Remember also that we will be asking you for information about the corporate and international strategy of your company as well as its structure. We strongly recommend that you pick a company for which such information is likely to be available.

There are two approaches that can be used to select a company to study, and your instructor will tell you which one to follow. The first approach is to pick a well-known company that has a lot of information written about it. For example, large, publicly held companies such as IBM, Microsoft, and Southwest Airlines are routinely covered in the business and financial press. By going to the library at your university, you should be able to locate a great deal of information on such companies. Many libraries now have electronic data search facilities such as *ABI/Inform*, *Wall Street Journal Index*, the *F&S Index*, and *Nexis*. These enable you to identify any article that has been written in the business press on the company of your choice within the last few years. If you do not have electronic data search facilities at your university, we suggest that you ask your librarian about data sources. A number of nonelectronic data sources are available. For example, *F&S Predicasts* publishes an annual list of articles relating to major companies that appeared in the national and international business press. You will also need to collect full financial information on the company that you pick. Again, this can be accessed from electronic databases such as *Compact Disclosure*. Alternatively, your library might have the annual financial reports, 10-K filings, or proxy statements pertaining to the company you pick. Again, ask your librarians; they are the best source of information.

A second approach is to pick a smaller company in your city or town to study. Although small companies are not routinely covered in the national business press, they may be covered in the local press. More importantly, this approach can work well if the management of the company agrees to talk to you *at length*

about the strategy and structure of the company. If you happen to know somebody in such a company or if you yourself have worked there at some point, this approach can be very worthwhile. However, we *do not* recommend this approach unless you can get a *substantial* amount of guaranteed access to the company of your choice. If in doubt, ask your instructor before making a decision. The key issue is to make sure that you have access to enough interesting information to complete the strategic modules.

Your assignment for Strategic Management Project: Module 1 is to choose a company to study and to obtain enough information about that company to carry out the following instructions and answer the questions asked:

1. Give a short account of the history of the company, and trace the evolution of its strategy over time. Try to determine whether the strategic evolution of your company is the product of intended strategies, emergent strategies, or some combination of the two.

2. Identify the mission and major goals of the company.

3. Do a preliminary analysis of the internal strengths and weaknesses of the company and of the opportunities and threats that it faces in its environment. On the basis of this analysis, identify the strategies that you think the company should pursue. (Note: You will need to perform a much more detailed analysis later in the book.)

4. Who is the CEO of the company? Evaluate the CEO's leadership capabilities.

CLOSING CASE

Southwest Airlines

For most of the last fifteen years, the U.S. airline industry has been one of the least attractive to be in. Following the 1978 deregulation of the industry, twenty-nine new airlines entered the industry between 1978 and 1993. This rapid increase in airline carrying capacity led to a situation of overcapacity. As more and more airlines chased passengers, fares were driven down to levels barely sufficient to maintain the profitability of U.S. airlines. Indeed, twice since 1978 the industry has been engulfed in an intense price war—first in the 1981–1983 period and then again in the 1990–1993 period. So intense did the competition become during these two periods that in 1982 the whole industry lost $700 million, while in the 1990–1992 period the industry lost a staggering $7.1 billion, more than had been made during the previous fifty-year history of the industry!

Despite the obviously hostile nature of this industry, one company, Southwest Airlines, has not only been consistently profitable but also has seen its performance improve during years when its competitors were wallowing in red ink. Southwest is a regional airline with a major presence in Texas. In 1992, when every major U.S. airline except Southwest lost money, Southwest actually reported a sharp jump in its net profit to $105.5 million on revenues of $1.68 billion, up from $26.9 million on revenues of $1.31 billion in 1991.

Southwest is profitable because of two factors: its low costs and the loyalty of its customers. Its low costs come from a number of sources. Southwest offers a no-frills approach to customer service. No meals are served on board, and there are no first-class seats. Southwest does not subscribe to the big reservation computers used by travel agents because it deems the booking fees too costly. The airline flies only one type of aircraft, the fuel-efficient Boeing 737, which keeps training and maintenance costs down. Last but not least, the airline has a very productive work force. Southwest employees say that they are willing to work hard because they feel appreciated by the top management. The CEO, Herb Kelleher, has been known to help flight attendants serve drinks and help maintenance engineers service planes. As one flight attendant put it, the airline's employees work hard because "you don't want to let Herb down." In addition, Southwest operates a generous stock option plan that extends to all employees. As a result, about 10 percent of the airline's stock is owned by its employees, which gives them an additional incentive to work hard.

Southwest's customer loyalty also comes from a number of sources. Due to its low cost structure, Southwest can offer its customers low prices, which builds loyalty. Southwest also has a reputation for being the most reliable carrier in the industry. It has the quickest turnaround time in the industry (it takes a Southwest ground crew just fifteen minutes to turn around an incoming aircraft and prepare it for departure), which helps keep flights on time. The company also has a well-earned reputation for listening to its customers. For example, when five Texas medical students who commuted weekly to an out-of-state medical school complained that the flight got them to class fifteen minutes late, Southwest moved the departure time up fifteen minutes. In addition, Southwest's focused route structure (it serves just fifteen states, mostly in the South) has helped it build a substantial regional presence and avoid some of the cutthroat competition that the nationwide airlines have had to grapple with.[40]

Case Discussion Questions

1. What does the success of Southwest Airlines tell you about the relative importance of industry- and company-specific factors in explaining a company's performance?

2. What is the basis of Southwest's competitive advantage? How might it lose that advantage?

CHAPTER 2

Stakeholders and the Corporate Mission

Opening Case: Bill Agee and the Fall of Morrison Knudsen

Overview

Stakeholders

The Mission Statement

Corporate Governance and Strategy

Strategy and Ethics

Closing Case: Body Shop International

OPENING CASE

Bill Agee and the Fall of Morrison Knudsen

Bill Agee is one of the most controversial and colorful figures in corporate America. While still in his early thirties, the Boise, Idaho, native made his name as the financial whiz kid who became the chief financial officer of papermaker Boise Cascade during the 1970s. Agee left Boise Cascade after the company was forced to write down its profits by $250 million due to earlier overstatements of the value of timberland sales. At the time, the write-downs were the largest in corporate history, but this did not stop Agee from being appointed CEO of defense contractor Bendix in 1976 while still only thirty-eight years old. At Bendix, Agee became involved in a famous corporate soap opera that began when he promoted a young manager, Mary Cunnigham, to a senior post at Bendix over the heads of many other more experienced executives. At the time many felt the promotion occurred because the two were romantically involved. Both denied this, but in 1982 Agee divorced his wife and married Cunningham, who by this time had left Bendix.

Agee became CEO of Idaho-based Morrison Knudsen (MK) in 1988. Morrison Knudsen was a seventy-five-year-old construction company that had made its name as the prime contractor on a number of large western construction projects, including the Hoover Dam and the trans-Alaska pipeline. By the time Agee joined the company, MK was perceived as a venerable institution that wasn't quite living up to its performance potential. Agee's strategy for improving performance was to sell off certain of MK's assets and invest the proceeds in the securities of other companies. At the same time, he pushed MK to pursue large construction projects aggressively and to grow its railcar manufacturing business. At one time, the railcar manufacturing business had been a major success story at MK, but in recent years it had fallen on hard times, unable to hold its own in the face of aggressive Japanese competition.

On the surface MK appeared to be prospering under Agee's leadership. In 1993 MK earned $35.8 million, and

Agee proclaimed it a "banner year" and a "watershed period" for the company's drive into railroad and mass-transit industries. Underneath the surface, however, things were unraveling for Bill Agee. For one thing, 62 percent of MK's profits in 1993 came from Agee's financial plays in securities trading and from capital gains on asset sales. Strip out these one-time gains, and it was clear that the operating performance of MK was poor. A prime reason seems to have been Agee's insistence that in order to win new business, MK should be the low bidder on large contracts. For instance, when MK bid on a contract to build eighty transit cars for the Bay Area Rapid Transit District (BART) in Oakland, California, Agee knocked down the bid to $142 million. According to one insider, the result was that "we were looking at a $14 million loss on the contract the day we won it." In the second quarter of 1994, MK announced a $40.5 million loss after taking a $59.4 million charge for underbidding on various transit-car contracts. Similarly, in the third quarter of 1994, MK took a $9.2 million charge against profits for underbidding on a $100 million contract to rebuild locomotives for Southern Pacific.

To compound matters, there had been significant employee opposition to Agee's leadership. In an anonymous letter sent to MK's board in November 1994 by a group of MK executives calling themselves the MK Committee for Excellence, a whole slew of charges were leveled at Agee. The executives claimed that Agee had irked subordinates by removing the portrait of MK's founder from the headquarters and replacing it with a near life-size portrait of him and his wife, Mary Cunningham, paid for by the company. Agee had further estranged insiders by quietly moving the CEO's office to his Pebble Beach estate in California and by scoffing at the company's engineering-oriented culture. Several old hand MK engineering executives, people who had top reputations in their field, had been fired, usually after crossing swords with Agee over his policies.

There was also the matter of Agee's pay and perks. At $2.4 million, Agee's 1993 compensation was equal to 6.8 percent of MK's net income, more than any other CEO of a company with earnings in that range, according to a

Forbes magazine list. According to insiders, MK paid $4 million a year for a corporate jet for Agee, equal to 13 percent of the company's general and administrative budget. The company also paid for landscaping services at Agee's Pebble Beach estate.

Things came to a head on February 1, 1995, when MK's board announced that the company would record a large loss for 1994. The board also announced that Agee would be stepping down as CEO, although initial indications were that he would stay on as chairman of the board. Preliminary figures suggested that MK would have to take a $179.6 million pretax charge in its 1994 fourth quarter, which would result in a net loss of $141 million for the quarter. At the same time, Standard & Poor's downgraded MK's long-term debt to junk bond rating, signaling that a significant risk of default existed.

The announcement gave rise to a blizzard of lawsuits and criticism by shareholders, not only of Agee but also of MK's board for acting so slowly. Many commentators wondered why it took a huge loss and an anonymous letter from MK executives to prod the board into action. Privately, several board members (most of whom were appointees and long-time friends of Agee) indicated that they had been led astray by Agee, who had repeatedly urged them not to worry about poor results. Still, many felt that the audit committee of the board of directors had not done a good job of vetting MK's financial accounts under Agee's leadership. Stung by this criticism, by the growing evidence of massive financial mismanagement under Agee's leadership, and by the downgrade of MK's debt by Standard & Poor's, the board reversed its earlier position and decided to strip Agee of all posts at MK.

The shareholders' lawsuits were settled in September 1995. Under the agreement, MK was to pay $63 million in cash and stock to shareholders. The settlement also required the company to strengthen its board by adding seven new directors over the next two years. As part of the settlement, Agee also agreed to relinquish rights to about $3 million in severance pay and to accept a cut in his MK pension from $303,000 a year for life to $99,750 a year for life.[1]

OVERVIEW

The Opening Case tells the story of how Bill Agee mismanaged Morrison Knudsen (MK) while simultaneously enriching himself and how this brought MK to the edge of bankruptcy. In the process, Agee effectively failed to satisfy the interests of two important groups at MK—the company's stockholders, who saw the value of their stock fall by 90 percent under his leadership, and the company's employees, who as a result of Agee's mismanagement now face an uncertain future. Ultimately, Agee's mismanagement came to the attention of the board of directors, and they terminated his relationship with the company, but only after a great deal of damage had already been done. Two parties can be criticized: Bill Agee for his poor leadership and obvious failure to satisfy the interests of key stakeholders, such as employees and stockholders; and the board of directors for failing to perform its fiduciary duty adequately and to protect the interests of those it is meant to represent, the stockholders.

As the story of Morrison Knudsen suggests, many different kinds of people and groups are affected by the way an organization and its managers behave. If an organization is to survive and prosper, it must pay attention to the interests of these different stakeholder groups. **Stakeholders** are individuals or groups, either within or outside an organization, that have some claim on the organization. Stakeholders include customers, suppliers, employees, and stockholders.

This chapter is concerned with how companies can maintain the support of key stakeholders. We begin by looking at the relationship between stakeholders and a company. Then we move on to consider the corporate mission statement, which is the first key indicator of how an organization views the claims of its stakeholders. The purpose of the mission statement is to establish the guiding principles for strategic decision making. We then explore the issue of corporate governance. By **corporate governance** we mean the mechanisms that are used to "govern" managers and ensure that the actions they take are consistent with the interests of key stakeholder groups. The board of directors is a very important corporate governance mechanism. As we saw in the Opening Case, the board has the ability to remove a CEO who is not satisfying the interests of key stakeholders.

The chapter closes with a look at the ethical dimension of strategic decisions and at the relationship between ethics and the welfare of stakeholders. By the end of this chapter, you will have a good understanding of how stakeholders, corporate governance mechanisms, and ethical considerations all influence the strategies that managers choose for their organizations.

STAKEHOLDERS

A company's **stakeholders** are individuals or groups that have an interest, claim, or stake in the company, in what it does and in how well it performs.[2] Stakeholders can be divided into internal stakeholders and external stakeholders (see Figure 2.1). **Internal stakeholders** are stockholders and employees, including executive officers, other managers, and board members. **External stakeholders** are all other individuals and groups that have some claim on the company. Typically, this group comprises customers, suppliers, governments, unions, local communities, and the general public.

All stakeholders are in an exchange relationship with the company. Each of the stakeholder groups listed in Figure 2.1 supplies the organization with important resources (or contributions), and in exchange each expects its interests to be

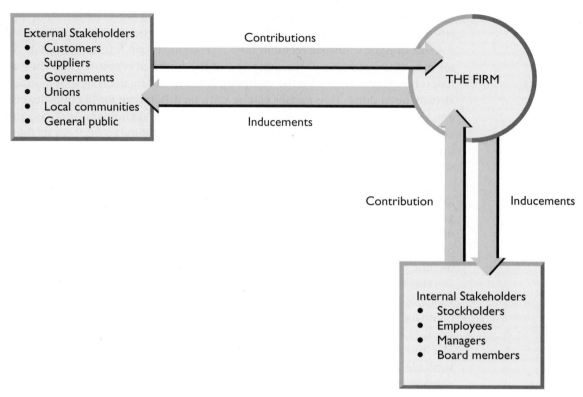

FIGURE 2.1
. . . .

Stakeholders and
the Enterprise

satisfied (by inducements).[3] Stockholders provide the enterprise with capital and in exchange expect an appropriate return on their investment. Employees provide labor and skills and in exchange expect commensurate income, job satisfaction, job security, and good working conditions. Customers provide a company with its revenues, and in exchange they want high-quality reliable products that represent value for money. Suppliers provide a company with inputs, and in exchange they seek revenues and dependable buyers. Governments provide a company with rules and regulations that govern business practice and maintain fair competition, and in exchange they want companies that adhere to these rules. Unions help to provide a company with productive employees, and in exchange they want benefits for their members in proportion to their contributions to the company. Local communities provide companies with local infrastructure, and in exchange they want companies that are responsible citizens. The general public provides companies with national infrastructure, and in exchange it seeks some assurance that the quality of life will be improved as a result of the company's existence.

A company must take these claims into account when formulating its strategies, or else stakeholders may withdraw their support. For example, stockholders may sell their shares, employees may leave their jobs, and customers may buy elsewhere. Suppliers may seek more dependable buyers. Unions may engage in disruptive labor disputes. Communities may oppose the company's attempts to locate its facilities in their area, and the general public may form pressure groups, demanding action against companies that impair the quality of life. Any of these reactions can have a disastrous impact on an enterprise. A detailed example is given in Strategy in Action 2.1, which looks at how Dick Ferris, the former CEO of United Airlines, lost his job because he failed to satisfy the interests of two important stakeholder groups: the company's employees and its stockholders.

A company cannot always satisfy the claims of all stakeholders. The goals of different groups may conflict, and in practice few organizations have the resources to manage all stakeholders.[4] For example, a union's claims for higher wages can conflict with consumers' demands for reasonable prices and stockholders' demands for acceptable returns. Often the company must make choices. To do so, it must identify the most important stakeholders and give highest priority to pursuing strategies that satisfy their needs. Stakeholder impact analysis can provide such identification. Typically, stakeholder impact analysis follows these steps:

1. Identify stakeholders.

2. Identify interests and concerns of stakeholders.

3. Identify what claims stakeholders are likely to make on the organization.

4. Identify the stakeholders who are most important from the organization's perspective.

5. Identify the resulting strategic challenges.[5]

Such an analysis enables a company to identify the stakeholders most critical to its survival and to make sure that the satisfaction of their needs is paramount. Most companies that have gone through this process quickly come to the conclusion that there are three stakeholder groups that must be satisfied if a company is to survive and prosper: customers, employees, and stockholders. Both Bill Agee and Dick Ferris, for example, lost their CEO positions because they failed to satisfy the demands of stockholders for a good return on their investment and those of employees for income, job satisfaction, job security, and good working conditions. More generally, any company that fails to satisfy the needs of its customers will soon see its revenues fall and will ultimately go out of business.

THE MISSION STATEMENT

As we noted earlier, the corporate mission statement is a key indicator of how an organization views the claims of its stakeholders. It describes how a company intends to incorporate the claims of stakeholders into its strategic decision making and thereby reduce the risk of losing their support. The mission statement thus states a company's formal commitment to its stakeholders, and it carries the message that its strategies will be formulated with the claims of those stakeholders in mind

Most corporate mission statements are built around three main elements: (1) a statement of the overall vision, or mission, of the company, (2) a statement that indicates the key philosophical values that managers are committed to and that influence the decisions they make, and (3) the articulation of key goals that

Dick Ferris and United Airlines

 In the early 1980s, Dick Ferris, the CEO of United Airlines, had a vision of the future in which United Airlines was one component of a "worldwide door-to-door travel service." Ferris believed that a company that provided flight, rental car, and hotel services could realize significant synergies. He spoke with zeal about a future in which travel agents around the world would sit in front of their computer screens, coordinating reservations for his airline, his hotels, and his rental cars.

Assembly of the assets for this travel empire had begun in 1970 with the purchase of Westin Hotel. Under Ferris's leadership, United Airlines bought Hertz from RCA in 1985 for $587 million. In March 1987 United bought Hilton International for $980 million. At the same time United Airlines officially changed its name to Allegis Corporation in a symbolic attempt to emphasize the company's rebirth as an integrated travel operation.

The problem with this strategy was that it did not have the support of two major stakeholder groups: the company's airline pilots and its stockholders. Ferris's difficulties with the pilots began in mid 1985, when he demanded wage and productivity concessions from the pilots' union, the Air Line Pilots Association (ALPA), of United Airlines in order to compete with low-cost carriers such as People Express and Continental Airlines. He succeeded in getting the pilots to accept his demands, but only after a twenty-nine-day strike that soured management-labor relations and produced a $92 million quarterly loss. Then, in April 1985 ALPA offered to buy the airline for $4.5 billion. According to F. C. Dubinsky, the ALPA chairman at United, the bid was motivated by the pilots' fear that "the airline is no longer the focus of the company. The management is a hotel management team. We want to return to our core business." The bid was refused by corporate leadership.

While these events were unfolding, a number of corporate raiders were beginning to take an interest in the company. In March 1987 Allegis's stock was trading in the $55 to $60 range. According to stock analysts and many institutional investors, at that price the stock was grossly undervalued. Several investment experts judged that the company would be worth at least $100

per share if its operations were sold separately. In May 1987 Coniston Partners, an investment fund, disclosed that it had purchased 13 percent of Allegis stock. Coniston's intention was to remove the board of directors and sell off the company's constituent businesses.

Ferris's reaction to the takeover bids from ALPA and Coniston was to initiate two takeover defenses. First, as part of a $15 billion jet order, Allegis provided Boeing with new-issue convertible notes valued at $700 million. Should a single investment entity purchase more than 40 percent of Allegis's stock, the interest rates on the notes would increase drastically, thereby severely raising the costs of any hostile takeover attempt. This tactic, however, failed to reassure the majority of Allegis's stockholders, who were becoming increasingly dissatisfied with Ferris. In response, the board of Allegis suggested a massive recapitalization plan that would immediately repay stockholders $60 per share in cash and leave them with stock worth an estimated $28 per share. The drawback, though, was that the plan would add more than $3 billion to the $2.4 billion in long-term debt already on the company's balance sheet. Such a debt load would have been perilous in the competitive airline industry, and the resulting interest payments might have wiped out profits.

Ultimately, Allegis's board could not countenance piling up heavy debt to salvage a master plan that shareholders disliked, nor could it support a CEO who had so clearly alienated both Wall Street investors and many of the company's employees. Consequently, in June 1987 the board ousted Dick Ferris; repudiated his travel supermarket strategy; announced that Westin, Hertz, and Hilton International would all be sold; decided to consider selling a major stake in United Airlines to its employees; and announced plans to change the company's name back to United Airlines. In effect, after supporting Dick Ferris through two difficult years, the board reversed itself under pressure from employees and stockholders. Coniston and ALPA responded by dropping their takeover bids. In the view of both parties, the board was now proposing to do what they had wanted all along.[6]

management believes must be adhered to in order to attain the vision, or mission, and that are consistent with the values to which managers are committed.[7]

An example of a mission statement—that of Seattle City Light, a community-owned electric utility that serves consumers in the Seattle area—is given in Figure 2.2. The vision of Seattle City Light is to become "the most customer-focused, competitive, efficient, innovative, and environmentally responsible community-owned utility in the United States by the year 2000." The mission statement also lists nine key values that management believes should guide decision making within the utility, along with four measurable corporate goals.

Vision, or Mission

The **vision**, or **mission**, of a company is a formal declaration of what the company is trying to achieve over the medium to long term. (In practice the terms *vision* and *mission* are used interchangeably.) Boeing states that its mission is "to be the number one aerospace company in the world and among the premier industrial concerns in terms of quality, profitability, and growth."[8] Intel, the world's largest manufacturer of microprocessors, has articulated its mission as follows: "Intel's mission is to be the preeminent building block supplier to the new computing industry worldwide."[9] In a similar vein, Weyerhaeuser, the world's largest forest products company, has stated that its vision is to simply be "the best forest products company in the world."[10]

What you may notice about these statements is that they all commit the corporation to an ambitious goal. To be "number one," "preeminent," the "best," or the "most customer focused, competitive, efficient, and environmentally responsible." All these mission statements are examples of **strategic intent**.

Strategic Intent We encountered the concept of strategic intent in Chapter 1. As you recall, underlying it is the notion that managers should set an overarching ambitious goal that stretches a company.[11] Often, the vision, or mission, presented in a company's mission statement articulates the company's strategic intent. Thus, Boeing's strategic intent is to remain the number one aerospace company in the world, while Intel's is to become the preeminent supplier of building blocks to the new computer industry. The argument for setting an overarching stretch goal is that (1) it communicates a sense of direction and purpose to those within the company; (2) it helps to drive decision making and resource allocation; and (3) it forces managers within the company to look for significant improvements in the way they run the business, since that is the only way to attain stretch goals. Put differently, as Jack Welsh, the CEO of General Electric, has observed:

> If you don't demand something out of the ordinary, you won't get anything but ordinary results. . . . We used to say nudge the peanut along, moving from, say, 4.73 inventory turns to 4.91. Now we want big stretch results like ten turns or fifteen turns.[12]

However, managers must also ensure that the vision statement does not become so grandiose it is clearly unattainable, thereby losing credibility among employees. A stretch goal is all well and good, but the stretch must be attainable, even if it does require managers to look for extraordinary performance improvements. A detailed

VISION

To be the most customer-focused, competitive, efficient, innovative, and environmentally responsible community-owned utility in the United States by the year 2000.

VALUES

Customer First

Our success depends upon our customers. It is our primary commitment to meet our customers' needs, including reliability, quality, service, and price, in a manner that anticipates and exceeds their expectations.

Investment in Employees

We believe our employees are Seattle City Light's greatest asset. We invest in our employees to be successful in our mission. Our investment through training, employee involvement, and strategic human resource planning is aimed at preparing employees to meet the challenges of today and tomorrow.

Safety

We believe that ensuring the safety of our employees and the public is an overriding responsibility. We express this value through our commitment to complying with regulations, working proactively to reduce workplace hazards and prevent accidents, and training our workers.

Financial Responsibility

We believe in managing City Light in the best long-term interests of our ratepayers through prudent financing and management of our capital assets. We are committed to maintaining low rates consistent with the long-term financial stability of the utility.

Accountability

We believe in taking full responsibility for our performance as individual employees and as an organization. We will be accountable through establishing goals and measuring our performance in achieving those goals.

Community

We believe City Light has an obligation to assist our community in meeting its social and educational needs through fostering partnerships in the community, supporting Combined Charities fundraising, and encouraging the voluntary community efforts of our employees.

Environmental Stewardship

We believe in building, operating, and maintaining our facilities in a manner that is consistent with the long-term sustainability of the ecosystem we affect. We seek to be proactive and innovative in finding solutions to environmental problems. We are committed to promoting and supporting efficient use of electricity to minimize the need for new sources of generation.

FIGURE 2.2

The Mission Statement of Seattle City Light

example of a vision statement that incorporated an attainable stretch goal is given in Strategy in Action 2.2, which looks at how the stretch vision statement articulated by the CEO of 3M back in 1991 has led to significant performance improvements at that company.

Customer Orientation and Business Definition An important first step in the process of formulating a mission statement is to come up with a definition of the organization's business. Essentially, the definition answers these questions: "What is

Excellence

We believe excellence is the standard for all we do and is achieved by serving our customers with quality, reliability, and efficiency. We are committed to continuously seeking and applying new methods and technologies to improve our productivity and our services.

Integrity

It is imperative to our success as a utility for us to conduct business with the highest ethical and legal standards. An excellent reputation is established by honesty, fairness, trustworthiness, and sincerity in all of our activities.

GOALS

Customer Satisfaction

Our goal is to increase the level of customer satisfaction, as measured through customer surveys. The target for 1995 is for 97% of the respondents to rate their level of satisfaction as "highly satisfied" or "totally satisfied."

Employee Satisfaction

Our goal is to improve communication flow and demonstrate increased concern for employees throughout the utility. The target for 1995 is to double the 1993 survey percentage of employees who are satisfied with communication flow and concern shown for people.

Safety

Our goal is to reduce employee injuries and illnesses caused by occupational exposure. The target is to reduce the number of injuries and illnesses by 10% in 1994 and 1995.

Financial Responsibility

Our goal is to maintain City Light's outstanding financial performance. We have a financial responsibility to the customers we serve. And we will work in ways that are cost effective and efficient. Our three targets are to:

- Continue to offer the lowest rates. We will maintain the lowest average electric rates among the 25 largest cities in the United States.
- Keep rates competitive with those of other Northwest utilities. We will maintain City Light's average electric rates at a price no more than 5 percent higher than a sample of other electric utilities in the Pacific Northwest, through 1995.
- Maintain our strong financial position. We will meet the annual target for debt-service coverage of 1.8 adopted by the City Council.

Source: Seattle City Light.

our business? What will it be? What should it be?"[13] The responses guide the formulation of a mission statement.

To answer the first question ("What is our business?"), Derek F. Abell has suggested that a company should define its business in terms of three dimensions: who is being satisfied (what customer groups), what is being satisfied (what customer needs), and how are customers' needs being satisfied (by what skills or distinctive competencies)?[14] Figure 2.3 illustrates these three dimensions.

Abell's approach stresses the need for a **consumer-oriented** rather than a **product-oriented** business definition. A product-oriented business definition

Strategic Intent at 3M

The 3M Company has long had a reputation for being one of the most innovative corporations in the United States. For years the company operated with the seemingly ambitious vision of generating 25 percent of its revenues from products introduced within the last five years, and for years the company consistently attained this stretch goal. The result was a company with sales of $14 billion per annum and a potpourri of more than 60,000 different product offerings.

However, back in 1991 the new CEO of 3M, L. D. DeSimone, decided that this vision had lost its magic. Sales growth had stalled since 1988, while the percentage of revenues being generated from new products had remained essentially flat for three years. DeSimone's solution was to unveil a new vision for 3M. The company was once more to regain its position as an innovator by seeking to generate 30 percent of its sales from products introduced within the last four years. Since new products generally grow revenues faster and have higher profit margins than older products, the CEO argued that this goal would effectively boost 3M's profit performance.

Armed with this new vision, managers at 3M searched for ways to improve its rate of new-product innovation. Pressured by DeSimone to reveal how they would attain the new vision, managers quickly concluded that a major reason for a slowdown in the rate of innovation at 3M was that researchers were wasting far too much time on a large number of products that had only limited market potential and were similar to products 3M already had on the market. Moreover, products were taking far too long—as much as five years—to progress from prototype to full production.

To attain the new vision, DeSimone pushed his managers to concentrate their efforts on a limited number of products that had the potential for big sales. He also insisted that they launch a "pacing program" to identify potential blockbusters in the lab and rush them to market. This new approach helped to break the logjam that had developed in R&D. For example, in 1992 within 3M's $6 billion consumer and industrial goods business, fifty projects were earmarked for the pacing program and put on an accelerated development schedule. By late 1994 more than half these projects had already produced products that were on the market, and the eight largest new-product introductions were targeted to generate sales of around $1 billion by 1998.

One of the most successful of these new products was Scotch-Brite Never Rust soap pads. Ordinary scouring pads are made of steel wool that quickly rusts. In contrast, Never Rust is made from recycled plastic beverage bottles. In January 1992, 3M made Never Rust one of the first products in its pacing program. The result was the fastest product introduction in the company's history. Construction crews broke ground for the manufacturing plant in March 1992, and by November 1992 the plant was completed. Whenever development problems were encountered, experts were called in from all over 3M to try to solve them so that the ambitious schedule could still be met. They were, and the product was introduced in January 1993. In its first eighteen months, Never Rust captured a 22 percent share of the $100 million market. According to DeSimone, this kind of impressive performance would not have been possible had it not been for the stretch goal that focused the attention of managers on the need to break with the old ways of doing things and do extraordinary things in order to accelerate the development process.[15]

focuses just on the products sold and the markets served. Abell maintains that such an approach obscures the company's function, which is to satisfy consumers' needs. A product is only the physical manifestation of applying a particular skill to satisfy a particular need for a particular consumer group. In practice, that need can be

FIGURE 2.3
· · · · · · · · · · ·
Abell's Framework for
Defining the Business

Source: Derek F. Abell, *Defining the Business: The Starting Point of Strategic Planning* (Englewood Cliffs, N.J.: Prentice-Hall, 1980), p. 17.

served in different ways. A broad consumer-oriented business definition that identifies these ways can safeguard companies from being caught unawares by major shifts in demand. Indeed, by helping anticipate demand shifts, Abell's framework can assist companies in capitalizing on the changes in their environment. It can help answer the second question ("What will it [our business] be?").

However, the need to take a customer-oriented view of a company's business has often been ignored. Consequently, history is littered with the wreckage of once-great corporations that did not define their business or that defined it incorrectly. These firms failed to see what their business would become, and ultimately they declined. Theodore Levitt described the fall of the once mighty U.S. railroads in terms of their failure to define their business correctly:

> The railroads did not stop growing because the need for passenger and freight transportation declined. That grew. The railroads are in trouble today not because the need was filled by others (cars, trucks, airplanes, even telephones), but because it was not filled by the railroads themselves. They let others take customers away from them because they assumed themselves to be in the railroad business rather than in the transportation business. The reason they defined their industry wrong was because they were railroad oriented instead of transport oriented; they were product oriented instead of customer oriented.[16]

If the railroads had used Abell's framework, they might have anticipated the impact of technological change and decided that their business was transportation. In that case, they might have transferred their early strength in rail into dominance in today's diversified transport industry. However, most railroads stuck to a product-oriented definition of their business and went bankrupt.

In contrast, for a long time IBM correctly foresaw what its business would be. Originally, IBM was a leader in the manufacture of typewriters and mechanical tabulating equipment using punch card technology. However, IBM defined its business as providing a means for information processing and storage, rather than just supplying mechanical tabulating equipment and typewriters.[17] Given this definition, the company's subsequent moves into computers, software systems, office systems, and printers seem logical. It might also be argued that IBM's problems in the late 1980s and early 1990s arose because the company lost sight of the fact that increasingly consumers' needs for information processing and storage were being satisfied by low-cost personal computers, not by the mainframe computers produced by its core business.

The third question ("What should it [our business] be"?) can also be answered using Abell's framework. Thus, IBM decided that its business should be information processing—that was its vision—and this vision drove its development of computers and office systems, all extensions of its original mechanical tabulating punch card business. A similar kind of consumer-oriented thinking about this third question underlies Intel's mission, "to be the preeminent building block supplier to the new computing industry worldwide." As an increasingly customer-oriented company, Intel has realized that the center of gravity in the computer industry is now shifting from the desktop personal computer, where it has been for a decade, to network-centric computing. At one time Intel saw itself as a supplier of microprocessors for desktop computers, but reflecting the changing competitive environment and changes in the way consumers are now utilizing computers, Intel has recast its mission as a supplier of building blocks (including not just microprocessors but also new products such as motherboards and flash memory devices) to the new (network-centric) computer industry.

Another company that has redefined its mission after taking a close look at the needs of its customers is Kodak. Kodak used to see itself as a supplier of photographic equipment, but under the leadership of its new CEO, George Fisher, it has decided that it is in the "imaging business." By this it means it is in the business of providing any technology that allows customers to capture, process, manipulate, and display images. That includes not only photographic technology based on silver halide applications, which has been the mainstay of Kodak's traditional business, but also new digital imaging technology. Building on this new customer-oriented view of its business, and having asked itself, "What should it [our business] be?" Kodak has recently articulated a new corporate vision, which is to be *the world leader in imaging*.[18]

Values
· · · · ·

The values of a company state how managers within the company intend to conduct themselves, how they intend to do business, and what kind of organization they want to build. Insofar as they help drive behavior within a company, values are increasingly seen as the bedrock of a company's organizational culture and a driver of its competitive advantage. (We discuss the issue of an organization's culture in depth in Chapter 12.) For example, at General Electric CEO Jack Welsh has in recent years repeatedly articulated a set of values that include an emphasis on "boundaryless behavior." In a recent letter to shareholders, he noted that boundaryless behavior, an odd awkward phrase just a few years ago, is increasingly a way of life at GE. It has led to an obsession for finding a better way—a better idea—be its source a colleague, another GE business, or another company across the street or on the other side of the globe that will share its ideas and practices with us.[19]

Stated in this manner, boundaryless behavior is the antithesis of the not-invented-here syndrome (in which managers ignore ideas from outside the organization). It is a value that encourages managers to look outside their own particular function, business, or organization for ideas and solutions to problems. According to Welsh, the institutionalization of boundaryless behavior within GE has shaped the culture of GE and helped improve the competitive position of the enterprise. Welsh gives this example in his letter to shareholders:

> Yokogawa, our partner in the Medical Systems business, has been using "Bullet Train Thinking" to take 30-50% out of product costs over a two year period. This technique, which employs "out-of-the-box" thinking and cross-functional teams dedicated to removing obstacles to cost reduction, is now fully operational in our Aircraft Engines business. This effort should lead this business to double digit profitability growth in 1995, despite less than robust market conditions.[20]

Similarly, many companies articulate a set of values to emphasize their own distinctive outlook on business. The values of Lincoln Electric, for instance, emphasize that productivity increases should be with customers and employees through lower prices and higher wages, respectively. This belief distinguishes Lincoln Electric from many other enterprises and affects its goals and strategies.[21]

Another company whose values are famous is health care giant Johnson & Johnson. Its credo, a statement of its values, is reproduced in Figure 2.4. This credo expresses Johnson & Johnson's belief that the company's first responsibility is to the doctors, nurses, and patients who use Johnson & Johnson products. Next come its employees, the communities in which these employees live and work, and finally the stockholders. The credo is prominently displayed in every manager's office, and, according to the Johnson & Johnson managers, it guides all important decisions. Strong evidence of the credo's influence was apparent in the company's response to the 1982 Tylenol crisis. Seven people in the Chicago area died after taking Tylenol capsules that had been laced with cyanide. Johnson & Johnson immediately withdrew all Tylenol capsules from the U.S. market, at an estimated cost to the company of $100 million. At the same time the company embarked on a comprehensive communication effort targeted at the pharmaceutical and medical communities. By such means, Johnson & Johnson successfully presented itself to the public as a company that was willing to do what was right, regardless of the cost. As a consequence, the Tylenol crisis enhanced rather than tarnished Johnson & Johnson's image. Indeed, because of its actions, the company was able to regain its status as a market leader in painkillers in a matter of months.[22]

A recent study has identified a set of values associated with "high performing organizations" that, through their impact on employees' behavior, help companies achieve superior financial performance.[23] Not surprisingly, these values include respect for the interest of key organizational stakeholders—particularly customers, employees, suppliers, and stockholders. They also include respect and encouragement for the assumption of leadership and entrepreneurial behavior by mid- and

FIGURE 2.4

Johnson & Johnson's
Credo

Our Credo

We believe our first responsibility is to the doctors, nurses and patients,
to mothers and fathers and all others who use our products and services.
In meeting their needs everything we do must be of high quality.
We must constantly strive to reduce our costs
in order to maintain reasonable prices.
Customers' orders must be serviced promptly and accurately.
Our suppliers and distributors must have an opportunity
to make a fair profit.

We are responsible to our employees,
the men and women who work with us throughout the world.
Everyone must be considered as an individual.
We must respect their dignity and recognize their merit.
They must have a sense of security in their jobs.
Compensation must be fair and adequate,
and working conditions clean, orderly and safe.
We must be mindful of ways to help our employees fulfill
their family responsibilities.
Employees must feel free to make suggestions and complaints.
There must be equal opportunity for employment, development
and advancement for those qualified.
We must provide competent management,
and their actions must be just and ethical.

We are responsible to the communities in which we live and work
and to the world community as well.
We must be good citizens — support good works and charities
and bear our fair share of taxes.
We must encourage civic improvements and better health and education.
We must maintain in good order
the property we are privileged to use,
protecting the environment and natural resources.

Our final responsibility is to our stockholders.
Business must make a sound profit.
We must experiment with new ideas.
Research must be carried on, innovative programs developed
and mistakes paid for.
New equipment must be purchased, new facilities provided
and new products launched.
Reserves must be created to provide for adverse times.
When we operate according to these principles,
the stockholders should realize a fair return.

Johnson & Johnson

Source: Courtesy of Johnson & Johnson.

lower-level managers, and respect for and a willingness to support change efforts
within the organization. According to the authors of this study, companies that apparently consistently emphasize such values throughout their organization include
Hewlett Packard, Wal-Mart, and PepsiCo.

The same study also identified the values of poor-performing companies. These values might be expected, although they are *not* articulated in a company's mission statements. They include arrogance, particularly to ideas from outside the company; a lack of respect for key stakeholders such as customers, employees, suppliers, and stockholders; and a history of resisting change efforts and "punishing" mid- and lower-level managers who showed "too much leadership." General Motors was held up as an example of one such organization. According to the authors, mid- and lower-level managers who showed too much leadership and initiative were not promoted!

Goals
. . . . .

Having stated a vision that is founded on a consumer-orientated definition of the company's business and having articulated some key values, the company can take the next step in the formulation of a mission statement—establish major goals. A **goal** is a desired future state that a company attempts to realize. In this context, the purpose of goals is to specify with precision what must be done if the company is to attain its mission. If you look back at the mission statement of Seattle City Light in Figure 2.2, you will see that precise corporate goals are given for customer satisfaction, employee satisfaction, safety, and financial responsibility. For example, the utility committed itself to increasing its customer satisfaction rating from 76 percent in 1993 to 97 percent by 1995. These goals were chosen to help the utility achieve its vision of becoming "the most customer focused, competitive, efficient, innovative, and environmentally responsible community owned utility in the United States by the year 2000."

In a similar vein, consistent with its mission of remaining "the number one aerospace company in the world," the Commercial Aerospace Group of Boeing set itself a number of goals in 1992. The first goal was to maintain a global market share of at least 60 percent in the large commercial jet aircraft business. The second was to cut in half by 1997 the time it took to build an aircraft. The third was to bring down the cost of building an aircraft by 30 percent by the same year.

Goal Characteristics   To be meaningful, goals should have four main characteristics.[24] First, well-constructed goals are *precise and measurable*. If a goal cannot be stated precisely and measured, the company will be unable to assess its progress toward attaining that goal. Measurable goals give managers a yardstick against which they can judge their performance.

A second characteristic of well-constructed goals is that they *address important issues*. To maintain focus, an organization should operate with a limited number of major goals. Thus, the goals that are selected should all be important ones. In Boeing's case, the goals of reducing costs and "build time" focus managerial attention on two issues that are of critical importance if Boeing is to establish a competitive advantage in the commercial aircraft business—costs and customer responsiveness. The goal of a 60 percent minimum market share defines explicitly what it means to be an industry leader in commercial aircraft.

A third characteristic of well-constructed goals is that they should be *challenging but realistic*. Challenging goals give managers an incentive to look for ways to improve the operations of an organization. If a goal is unrealistic in the challenges it poses, employees may give up; if it is too easy, it may fail to motivate managers and other employees.[25] Again, Boeing provides us with an example. Reducing unit costs by 30 percent will require significant improvements in the efficiency of Boeing's operations; thus, this goal is challenging. However, experience at other companies has shown that it is possible to achieve 30 percent unit cost reductions over a six-year period. So, the goal is not unrealistic.[26]

A fourth characteristic of well-constructed goals is that, when appropriate, they should *specify a time period* in which they should be achieved. Thus, Boeing has committed itself to achieving its cost and build time reduction goals by 1997. Time constraints are important because they tell employees that success requires a goal to be attained by a given date, not after that date. Deadlines can inject a sense of urgency into goal attainment and act as a motivator. However, not all goals require time constraints. Boeing's goal of having a market share of at least 60 percent has no time period attached to it because Boeing already has around 60 percent of the market. By articulating this goal, management is saying the Boeing must not let its share slip below this critical level.

Maximizing Stockholders' Returns   Although most profit-seeking organizations operate with a variety of corporate goals, within a *public* corporation (at least in theory) all these goals are directed toward maximizing stockholders' returns. A company's stockholders are its legal owners. Consequently, an overriding goal of most corporations is to maximize stockholders' returns, which means increasing the long-run returns earned by stockholders from owning shares in the corporation.

Stockholders receive returns in two ways: from dividend payments and from capital appreciation in the market value of a share (that is, by increases in stock market prices). A company can best maximize stockholders' returns by pursuing strategies that maximize its own profitability, as measured by the rate of return that the company achieves on its investments in plant, equipment, R&D, and the like—that is, its rate of return on investment (ROI). In general, the more efficient a company, the higher its ROI will be, the better its future prospects look to stockholders, and the greater is its ability to pay dividends. Furthermore, a higher ROI leads to greater demand for a company's shares. Demand bids up the share price and leads to capital appreciation. Thus, for example, Boeing's goals of cutting build time in half and unit costs by 30 percent can be seen as a way of increasing its return on investment and, therefore, of maximizing the returns to those holding shares in the company.

The Short-Term Problem   There is an important danger associated with overemphasizing return on investment as a goal.[27] The overzealous pursuit of ROI can encourage managers to maximize short-run rather than long-run returns. A short-run orientation may encourage such misguided managerial action as cutting expenditures judged to be nonessential in the short run (for instance, expenditures for research and development, marketing, and new capital investments) but that are vital in the long run. Although cutting current expenditures increases current ROI, the resulting underinvestment, lack of innovation, and poor market awareness jeopardize long-run ROI. Despite these negative consequences, managers may make such decisions because the adverse effects of a short-run orientation may not materialize and become apparent to stockholders for several years. By the time long-run performance starts to slip, the management team responsible may have moved on, leaving others to pick up the pieces.

In a now famous *Harvard Business Review* article, Robert H. Hayes and William J. Abernathy argue that historically, the widespread focus on short-run ROI has been a major contributor to the loss of international competitiveness by U.S. companies.[28] MIT economist Lester Thurow likewise faults the short-run orientation of many U.S. businesses for some of their problems. Thurow claims that many U.S. companies are unwilling to make long-run investments for fear of depressing their short-run ROI. He cites declining expenditures for research and development and reduced innovative activity within U.S. enterprises as evidence of this orientation.[29] Similarly, after a detailed study of productivity problems in U.S. industry, the MIT Commission on Industrial Productivity concluded that the short time horizons of many corporations placed them at a competitive disadvantage vis-à-vis their foreign competitors.[30] One of the consequences of short-term horizons, according to the MIT commission, was the loss of U.S. leadership to Japanese companies in the videocassette recorder industry. The videocassette recorder was pioneered in the 1950s by the U.S.-based AMPEX Corporation, primarily for use in the broadcasting industry. AMPEX tried to produce a consumer variant of the product for a mass market but pulled out in 1970, when it decided it could not afford the R&D investment. Similarly, RCA, which also tried to develop a consumer videocassette recorder, pulled out in 1975 in the face of high development costs and manufacturing problems. This left the field open for Sony and Matsushita, both of which had been investing heavily during the 1970s to develop their own technology. Today the videocassette market is a multibillion-dollar market dominated by Matsushita. No U.S. company competes in this market.

As Strategy in Action 2.3 recounts, a similar story of short-term behavior seems to be emerging in the market for active matrix liquid crystal displays (AM-LCDs). The AM-LCD technology, too, was originally developed in the United States, but the market is now dominated by Japanese companies.

Long-Term Goals   To guard against the dangers of short-run behavior, managers need to ensure that they adopt goals whose attainment will increase the long-run performance and competitiveness of their enterprise. Long-term goals are related to such issues as customer satisfaction, employee productivity and efficiency, product quality, and innovation. The thinking is that in order to attain such goals, companies have to make long-term investments in plant, equipment, R&D, people, and processes. Only by doing so can a company improve its customer satisfaction, productivity, product quality, and innovation. Moreover, insofar as the attainment of such goals enhances a company's competitive position and boosts its *long-term* profitability, achieving such goals will help the company maximize the returns to be had from holding its stock.

CORPORATE GOVERNANCE AND STRATEGY

We noted that one of a company's major goals is to give its stockholders a good rate of return on their investment. In most publicly held corporations, however, stockholders delegate the job of controlling the company and selecting its strategies to corporate managers, who become the agents of the stockholders.[31] As the agents of stockholders, managers should pursue strategies that maximize *long-run* returns

Short-Term Emphasis, Long-Term Loss

 Active matrix liquid crystal displays (AM-LCDs) are the flat-topped color displays used in laptop and notebook personal computers. In addition to computer displays, the screens are also critical components in camcorders, medical instruments, high-definition television, auto dashboards, aerospace instruments, factory control devices, and instrumentation for the military. Global sales of AM-LCDs increased from $250 million in 1990 to around $1 billion in 1994, and projections suggest the market will amount to $10 billion plus by the year 2000.

The AM-LCD technology was pioneered during the 1960s at two U.S. companies, RCA and Westinghouse. However, neither company succeeded in commercializing the technology. One reason for this was that corporate management at both companies balked at the development costs and long payback periods, and so they cut funding. The principle Westinghouse researcher, Jim Fergason, subsequently left the company and set up a venture to manufacture AM-LCDs. However, few U.S. companies were willing to utilize the technology, and Fergason found it difficult to raise sufficient capital. Ultimately, Fergason's venture failed.

With no large U.S. company undertaking primary AM-LCD research, it was left to the Japanese to emerge as the major producers. Sharp, NEC, and Toshiba now dominate the market with 95 percent of worldwide production in 1996. Unlike their major U.S. competitors, these firms made massive investments in AM-LCD research and production facilities during the 1980s. Sharp alone reportedly spent more than $1 billion on developing the technology during the 1980s. Although a number of small U.S. companies are in this business, they tend to focus on highly specialized niches (such as supplying the U.S. Department of Defense) and have made investments to support only limited production. With the exception of IBM, which has a joint venture with Toshiba in Japan to manufacture AM-LCDs, no major U.S. company has a presence in this industry, and no U.S. company is capable of mass production.[32]

for stockholders. Although most managers are diligent about doing so, not all act in this fashion. Failure to do so gives rise to the corporate governance problem, wherein managers pursue strategies that are not in the interests of stockholders.

The Corporate Governance Problem

Why should managers want to pursue strategies other than those consistent with maximizing stockholders' returns? Some writers have argued that, like many other people, managers are motivated by desires for status, power, job security, and income.[33] By virtue of their position within the company, certain managers, such as the CEO, can use their authority and control over corporate funds to satisfy these personal desires. For example, CEOs might use their position to invest corporate funds in various perks that enhance their status—executive jets, lavish offices, and expense-paid trips to Hawaii—rather than use those funds in ways that increase stockholders' returns. Economists have termed such behavior **on-the-job consumption**.[34] Bill Agee is an example of a CEO who appeared to engage in excessive on-the-job consumption.

Besides engaging in on-the-job consumption, CEOs, along with other senior managers, might satisfy their desires for greater income by awarding themselves excessive pay increases. Critics of U.S. industry claim that extraordinary pay has now become an endemic problem. They point out that CEOs' pay has been increasing far more rapidly in recent years than the pay of average workers. For example, between 1980 and 1992 the average pay of an engineer doubled, from \$28,486 to \$58,240, while the average pay of 1,000 CEOs of large companies surveyed by *Business Week* increased sixfold, from \$624,996 to \$3,842,247.[35] In 1991 the average U.S. CEO earned 85 to 100 times as much as the average worker. By comparison, in Japan the average CEO earns 17 times as much as the average worker, while in Germany the average CEO earns 23 to 25 times as much.[36]

What rankles critics is the size of some CEOs' pay packages and their apparent lack of relationship to a company's performance.[37] In 1992, for example, Tony O'Reilly, the CEO of H. J. Heinz, received \$115.3 million in salary and stock options, and Roberto Goizueta, the CEO of Coca-Cola, received \$101.1 million. Although both Heinz and Coca-Cola had done well under the leadership of O'Reilly and Goizueta, respectively, many critics felt that the size of these pay awards was out of all proportion to the achievement of the CEOs.[38]

A further concern is that in trying to satisfy a desire for status, security, power, and income, a CEO might engage in "empire building," buying many new businesses in an attempt to increase the size of the company through diversification. Although such growth may do little to enhance the company's profitability, and thus stockholders' returns, it increases the size of the empire under the CEO's control and, by extension, the CEO's status, power, security, and income. (There is a strong relationship between a company's size and a CEO's pay.) To quote Carl Icahn, a famous corporate raider of the 1980s:

> Make no mistake, a strongly knit corporate aristocracy exists in America. The top man, what's more, usually finds expanding his power more important than rewarding owners (stockholders). When Mobil and USX had excess cash, did they enrich shareholders? Of course not. They bought Marcor and Marathon— disastrous investments, but major increases in the size of the manor.[39]

Thus, instead of maximizing stockholders' returns, some senior managers may trade long-run profitability for greater company growth by buying new businesses. Figure 2.5 graphs profitability against a company's growth rate. A company that does not grow is probably missing out on some profitable opportunities.[40] A growth rate of G_0 in Figure 2.5 is not consistent with maximizing profitability ($P_1 < P_{max}$). A moderate growth rate of G_1, on the other hand, does allow a company to maximize profits, producing profits equal to P_{max}. Achieving a growth rate in excess of G_1, however, requires diversification into areas that the company knows little about. Consequently, it can only be achieved by sacrificing profitability. (That is, past G_1 the investment required to finance further growth does not produce an adequate return, and the company's profitability declines.) Yet G_2 may be the growth rate favored by an "empire building" CEO, for it will increase his or her power, status, and income. At this growth rate, profits are only equal to P_2. Because $P_{max} > P_2$, a company growing at this rate is clearly not maximizing its profitability or the wealth of its stockholders. However, a growth rate of G_2 may be consistent with attaining managerial goals of power, status, and income.

Corporate Governance Mechanisms

It must be stressed that by no means do all managers behave in the way just outlined. The vast majority are good stewards, who consciously act to increase

FIGURE 2.5

The Tradeoff Between
Profitability and
Growth Rate

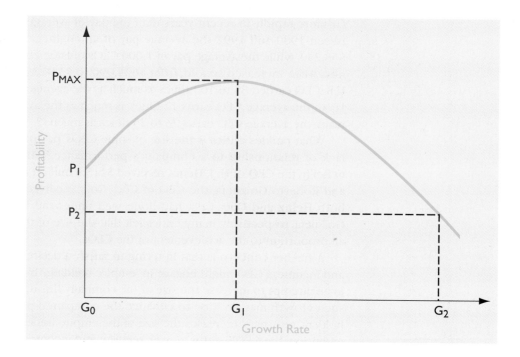

stockholders' returns. However, given that some managers put their own interests first, the problem facing stockholders is how to govern the corporation so that managerial desires for on-the-job consumption, excessive salaries, or empire-building diversification are held in check. There is also a need for mechanisms that allow stockholders to remove incompetent or ineffective managers. A number of **governance mechanisms** allow stockholders to exert some control over managers. They include the board of directors, stock-based compensation schemes, corporate takeovers, and the exchange of equity for debt in a leveraged buyout.

Board of Directors   Stockholders' interests are looked after within a company by the board of directors. Board members are directly elected by stockholders, and under corporate law they represent the stockholders' interests in the company. Thus the board can be held legally accountable for the company's actions. Its position at the apex of decision making within the company allows the board to monitor corporate strategy decisions and ensure that they are consistent with stockholders' interests. If the board's sense is that corporate strategies are not in the best interest of stockholders, it can apply sanctions, such as voting against management's nominations to the board of directors or submitting its own nominees. In addition, the board has the legal authority to hire, fire, and compensate corporate employees, including, most importantly, the CEO.[41] One factor that led to the dismissal of Morrison Knudsen's CEO, Bill Agee, was that his strategies lost the support of board.

The typical board of directors is composed of a mix of inside and outside directors. Inside directors are senior employees of the company, such as the CEO. They are required on the board because they have valuable information about the company's activities. Without such information the board cannot adequately perform its monitoring function. But since insiders are full-time employees of the company, their interests tend to be aligned with those of management. Hence, outside directors are needed to bring objectivity to the monitoring and evaluation processes. Outside directors are not full-time employees of the company. Many of them are full-time professional directors who hold positions on the boards of several companies. The need to maintain a reputation as competent outside directors gives them an incentive to perform their tasks as objectively and effectively as possible.[42]

Critics charge, however, that inside directors may be able to dominate the outsiders on the board. Insiders can use their position within the management hierarchy to exercise control over what kind of company-specific information the board receives. Consequently, insiders can present information in a way that puts themselves in a favorable light. In addition, insiders have the advantage of intimate knowledge of the company's operations. Because superior knowledge and control over information are sources of power (see Chapter 12), insiders may be better positioned to influence boardroom decision making than outsiders. The board may become the captive of insiders and merely rubber-stamp management decisions, instead of guarding stockholders' interests.

Some observers contend that many boards are dominated by the company's CEO, particularly in those cases in which the CEO is also the chairman of the board.[43] To support this view, they point out that both inside and outside directors are often the personal nominees of the CEO. The typical inside director is subordinate to the CEO in the company's hierarchy and therefore unlikely to criticize the boss. Since outside directors are frequently the CEO's nominees as well, they can hardly be expected to evaluate the CEO objectively. Thus, the loyalty of the board may be biased toward the CEO and not the stockholders. Moreover, when the CEO is also chairperson of the board, he or she may be able to control the agenda of the board's discussions in such a manner as to deflect any criticisms of his or her leadership. This was a problem in the case of Bill Agee, who was both CEO and chairman of the board at Morrison Knudsen.

Today there are clear signs that many corporate boards are moving away from merely rubber-stamping top-management's decisions and are beginning to play a much more active role in corporate governance. One catalyst has been an increase in the number of lawsuits filed by stockholders against board members. The trend started in 1985, when a Delaware court ruled that the directors of Trans Union Corporation had been too quick to accept a takeover bid. The court held the directors personally liable for the difference between the offer they accepted and the price the company might have fetched in a sale. The directors then agreed to make up the $23.5 million difference. Since that ruling, a number of major lawsuits have been filed by stockholders against board members. These include suits directed against board members at Holly Farms, Northrup, Lincoln Savings & Loan, Lotus Development, and RJR Nabisco.[44]

Another catalyst has been the growing willingness of some institutional investors, such as the managers of large pension funds or index-linked mutual funds, to use their stockholding in a company, and the voting power it gives them, to gain seats on the board of directors to pressure managers to adopt policies that improve the performance of the company's stock and to pressure the board to replace the CEOs of poorly performing companies. For example, in late 1995 officials of New York City's five major pension funds stated that they would nominate three candidates for seats on the board of Ethyl Corp., a maker of petroleum additives that has performed poorly in recent years. Their objective is to use these board seats to push management harder to improve the performance of Ethyl, and hence the value of their stock in Ethyl.[45]

Spurred on by the threat of legal action and pressures from powerful institutional shareholders, an increasing number of boards has started to assert their independence from company management in general and from corporate CEOs in particular. In recent years boards of directors have engineered the removal or resignation of CEOs at a number of major companies, including American Express, Digital Equipment, General Motors, and IBM. Another trend of some significance is the increasing tendency for outside directors to be made chairperson of the board of directors. By 1997, according to the estimates from the National Association of Corporate Directors, 40 to 50 percent of big companies will name an outside director as chairperson, up from less than half that figure in 1990.[46] Such appointments limit the ability of corporate insiders, particularly the CEO, to exercise control over the board. It is notable that the removal of Robert Stempel as the CEO of General Motors followed the appointment of an outside director, John Smale, as chairperson of the GM board.

Stock-Based Compensation   As another way to align the interests of managers with stockholders, and thus solve the corporate governance problem, stockholders have urged many companies to introduce stock-based compensation schemes for their managers. In addition to their regular salary, managers are given stock options in the company. Stock options give managers the right to buy the company's shares at a predetermined price, which may often turn out to be less than the market price of the stock. The idea behind stock options is to motivate managers to adopt strategies that increase the share price of the company, for in doing so they will also increase the value of their own stock options.

In November 1992, for example, Michael Eisner, the CEO of Walt Disney, exercised stock options that he had been granted some years earlier, when Disney's stock was trading far below its November 1992 market value. His profit from exercising these options was a staggering $197 million. Although critics call such rewards excessive, it should be remembered that under Eisner's leadership Disney's stockholders have reaped substantial benefits. Indeed, had the stock price fallen rather than risen during Eisner's tenure, his stock options would have been worthless. As a counterpoint, consider the case of Paul Lego, CEO of Westinghouse. In 1991 Lego was granted the option to buy 700,000 shares in Westinghouse at $22.28 each. However, by mid 1992 Westinghouse's stock was trading at less than $17 per share, making his options worthless. Shortly afterward Lego resigned as CEO, following pressure from the board, without being able to exercise any of his stock options.[47]

Academic studies seem to confirm that stock-based compensation schemes, such as stock options, for executives can align the interests of management and stockholders. For instance, one study found that managers were more likely to consider the effects of their acquisition decisions on stockholders' returns if they themselves were significant shareholders.[48] According to another study, managers who were significant stockholders were less likely to pursue strategies that would maximize the size of the company rather than its profitability.[49]

For all their attractions, stock-based compensation schemes have yet to be universally adopted by U.S. companies, although the practice is spreading rapidly. Critics argue that the schemes do not always have the desired effect, since stock compensation plans can harm stockholders by diluting their interests and unjustifiably rewarding management for improvements in stock prices. These critics contend that stock price increases are often due to an improving economy rather than managerial effort, and they ask why managers should be rewarded for such increases in share prices. In addition, when stock prices are falling because of factors outside the company's control, such as an economic slump, managers may see the value of their stockholdings decline rapidly. Under such circumstances, stock-based compensation schemes give managers little incentive to align their goals with those of stockholders in general.

Corporate Takeovers   If the board is loyal to management rather than to the stockholders, or if the company has not adopted stock-based compensation schemes, then a corporate governance problem may exist and managers may pursue strategies that are inconsistent with maximizing stockholders' wealth. However, stockholders still have some residual power, for they can always sell their shares. If they start doing so in large numbers, the price of the company's shares will decline. If the share price falls far enough, the company might be worth less on the stock market than the book value of its assets, at which point it may become an attractive acquisition target and runs the risk of being purchased by another enterprise, against the wishes of the target company's management.

The risk of being acquired by another company is known as the **takeover constraint**. The takeover constraint limits the extent to which managers can pursue strategies and take actions that put their own interests above those of stockholders. If they ignore stockholder interests and the company is acquired, senior managers typically lose their independence and probably their jobs as well. So the threat of takeover can constrain management's action.

In recent years the threat of takeover has often been enforced by corporate raiders. **Corporate raiders** are individuals or corporations that buy up large blocks of shares in companies that they think are pursuing strategies inconsistent with maximizing stockholders' wealth. Corporate raiders argue that if these underperforming companies pursued different strategies, they could create more wealth for stockholders. Raiders buy stock in a company either to take over the business and run it more efficiently or to precipitate a change in the top management, replacing the existing team with one more likely to maximize stockholders' returns. Raiders, of course, are motivated not by altruism but by gain. If they succeed in their takeover bid, they can institute strategies that create value for stockholders, including themselves. Even if a takeover bid fails, raiders can still earn millions, for their stockholdings will typically be bought out by the defending company for a hefty premium. Called **greenmail**, this source of gain has stirred much controversy and debate about its benefits. While some claim that the threat posed by raiders has had a salutary effect on an enterprise's performance by pushing corporate management to run their companies better, others claim there is little evidence of this.[50]

Leveraged Buyouts   Whereas in a typical takeover attempt a raider buys enough stock to gain control of a company, in a leveraged buyout (LBO) a company's own managers are often among the buyers. The management group undertaking an LBO raises cash by issuing bonds and then uses that cash to buy the company's stock. In effect, the company replaces its stockholders with creditors (bondholders), transforming the corporation from a public into a private entity. However, often the same institutions that were major stockholders before an LBO are major bondholders afterward. The difference is that as stockholders they were not guaranteed a regular dividend payment from the company; as bondholders they have such a guarantee.

During the 1980s the number and value of LBOs undertaken in the United States increased dramatically. The value of the 76 LBOs undertaken in 1979 totaled $1.4 billion (in 1988 dollars). In comparison, the value of the 214 LBOs undertaken in 1988 exceeded $77 billion. Since then, however, the LBO business in the United States has slowed to a crawl, with only a handful of transactions being executed each year. Its demise, though, may be only temporary. Takeovers tend to go in cycles, and it is quite possible that the next time the United States undergoes a merger boom there will also be a boom in LBOs.

Supporters of the LBO technique, most notably Michael Jensen, claim that the LBO should be viewed as yet another governance mechanism that keeps management's discretion in check.[51] Jensen believes LBOs solve many of the problems created by imperfect corporate governance mechanisms. According to Jensen, a major weakness and source of waste in the public corporation is the conflict between stockholders and managers over the payout of free cash flow. (**Free cash flow** is cash flow in excess of that required to fund all investment projects with positive net present values when discounted at the relevant cost of capital.) Since free cash flow is cash that cannot be profitably reinvested within the company, Jensen argues that it should be distributed to stockholders, but he notes that managers resist such distributions of surplus cash. Instead, for reasons discussed earlier, they tend to invest such cash in empire-building strategies.

Jensen sees LBOs as a solution to this problem. Although management does not have to pay out dividends to stockholders, it must make regular debt payments to bondholders or face bankruptcy. Thus, according to Jensen, the debt used to finance an LBO helps limit the waste of free cash flow by compelling managers to pay out excess cash to service debt rather than spend it on empire-building projects with low or negative returns, excessive staff, indulgent perquisites, and other organizational inefficiencies. Furthermore, Jensen sees debt as a way of motivating managers to seek greater efficiencies; high debt payments can force managers to slash unsound investment programs, reduce overhead, and dispose of assets that are more valuable outside the company. The proceeds generated by these restructurings can then be used to reduce debt to more sustainable levels, creating a more competitive organization.

Not all commentators are as enthusiastic about the potential of LBOs as Jensen. The secretary of labor in the Clinton administration, Robert Reich, is one of the most vocal critics of LBOs.[52] Reich sees two main problems with LBOs. First, he argues that the necessity of paying back large loans forces management to focus on the short term and cut back on long-term investments, particularly in R&D and new capital spending. The net effect is likely to be a decline in the competitiveness of companies that undertake LBOs. Second, Reich believes that the debt taken on to finance an LBO significantly increases the risk of bankruptcy.

The studies that have been done on this issue, although they are limited in number, suggest that LBOs do have some beneficial effects.[53] Companies that undergo an LBO do seem to be more diversified than their peers, suggesting that they had at one time been run by empire-building CEOs. After the LBO, they tend to divest business units and narrow the scope of the company's activities, thereby undoing the excessive diversification of the past. Moreover, there is some evidence that the productivity of a company increases after an LBO, primarily because it sells off poorly performing business units and simplifies its management structures to reduce bureaucracy.

STRATEGY AND ETHICS

Any strategic action taken by a company inevitably affects the welfare of its stakeholders: employees, suppliers, customers, stockholders, the local communities in which it does business, and the general public. While a strategy may enhance the welfare of some stakeholder groups, it may harm others. For example, faced with falling demand and excess capacity, a steel producer may decide to close down a steel-making facility that is the major source of employment in a small town. Although this action might be consistent with maximizing stockholders' returns, it could also result in thousands of people losing employment and the death of a small town. Is such a decision ethical? Is it the right thing to do, considering the likely impact on employees and the community in which they live? Managers must balance these competing benefits and costs. They must decide whether to proceed with the proposed strategy in the light of their assessment not only of its economic benefits but also of its ethical implications, given the potentially adverse effect on some stakeholder groups.[54]

The Purpose of Business Ethics

The purpose of business ethics is not so much to teach the difference between right and wrong as it is to give people the tools for dealing with moral complexity, tools that they can use to identify and think through the moral implications of strategic decisions.[55] Most of us already have a good sense of what is right and wrong. We already know that it is wrong to lie, cheat, and steal. We know that it is wrong to take actions that put the lives of others at risk. Such moral values are instilled into us at an early age through formal and informal socialization. The problem, however, is that although most managers rigorously adhere to such moral principles in their private lives, some fail to apply them in their professional lives, occasionally with disastrous consequences.

The sorry history of Manville Corporation illustrates such failure. Two decades ago Manville (then Johns-Manville) was solid enough to be included among the giants of U.S. industry. By 1989, 80 percent of the equity of Manville was owned by a trust representing people who had sued the company for liability in connection with one of its principal former products, asbestos. More than forty years ago, information began to reach the medical department of Johns-Manville—and through it the company's managers—suggesting that inhalation of asbestos particles was a major cause of asbestosis, a fatal lung disease. Manville's managers suppressed the research. Moreover, as a matter of company policy, they apparently decided to conceal the information from affected employees. The company's medical staff collaborated in the cover-up. Somehow, managers at Manville persuaded themselves that it was more important to cover up the situation than to take steps to improve working conditions and find safer ways to handle asbestos. They calculated that the cost of improving working conditions was greater than the cost of health insurance to cover those who became ill, and so the best "economic" decision was to conceal information from employees.[56]

The key to understanding the Manville story is the realization that the men and women at Manville who participated in the cover-up were not amoral monsters, just ordinary people. Most of them would probably never dream of breaking the law or of physically harming anyone. Yet they consciously made a decision that led directly to great human suffering and death. How could this happen? What seemed to have occurred was that the decision to suppress information was considered on purely economic grounds. Its moral dimension was ignored. Somehow the managers involved at Manville were able to convince themselves that they were engaged in making a rational business decision that should be subjected to an economic cost-benefit analysis. Ethical considerations never entered into this calculation. Such behavior is possible only in an environment in which business decisions are viewed as having no ethical component. However, as the Manville example shows, business decisions *do* have an ethical component.

The task of business ethics, therefore, is to make two central points: (1) business decisions do have an ethical component and (2) managers must weigh the ethical implications of strategic decisions before choosing a course of action. Had managers at Manville been trained to think through the ethical implications of their decision, it is unlikely that they would have chosen the same course of action.

Strategy in Action 2.4 offers another example of the failure to apply business ethics.

Shaping the Ethical Climate of an Organization

To foster awareness that strategic decisions have an ethical dimension, a company must establish an organizational climate that emphasizes the importance of ethics. This requires at least three steps. First, top managers have to use their leadership position to incorporate an ethical dimension into the values they stress. At Hewlett Packard, for example, Bill Hewlett and David Packard, the company's founders, propagated a set of values known as The HP Way. These values, which shape the way business is conducted both within and by the corporation, have an important ethical component. Among other things, they stress the need for confidence in and respect for people, open communication, and concern for the individual employee. Had such values been operational at Manville, they would have helped managers there avoid their catastrophic mistake.

Second, ethical values must be incorporated into the company's mission statement. As noted earlier, Johnson & Johnson's credo helped the company respond to the Tylenol crisis in an ethical manner.

Third, ethical values must be acted on. Top managers have to implement hiring, firing, and incentive systems that explicitly recognize the importance of adhering to ethical values in strategic decision making. At Hewlett Packard, for example, it has been said that although it is difficult to lose your job (because of the concern for individual employees), nothing gets you fired more quickly than violating the ethical norms of the company as articulated in The HP Way.[57]

Thinking Through Ethical Problems

Besides establishing the right kind of ethical climate in an organization, managers must be able to think through the ethical implications of strategic decisions in a sys-

| 2.4 | STRATEGY *in* ACTION |

The Jack-in-the-Box Poisonings—Questionable Ethics?

In January 1993 several hospitals in Seattle started to notice a dramatic increase in the number of cases of E. coli bacterial infections. The E. coli bacteria is found in undercooked meat. The symptoms of infection include severe fever, diarrhea, and vomiting. In the case of young people, the infection can be life threatening. Most of the victims of this outbreak were young, and many were in very serious condition. Epidemiologists quickly found a common element—almost all of the victims had eaten hamburgers at local Jack-in-the-Box restaurants shortly before falling ill.

Foodmaker, the parent company of Jack-in-the-Box, was quick to issue a statement denying that the meat served in its restaurants was undercooked. At the same time, it blamed the outbreak on a batch of bad meat that had been delivered from a supplier. The supplier responded by placing blame on Jack-in-the-Box. While Foodmaker and its supplier traded insults, the number infected rose to 200 and several children became seriously ill. Then Washington State health inspectors revealed that local Jack-in-the-Box restaurants were cooking meat at 140 degrees Fahrenheit, 15 degrees below the 155 degree state standard that had been in force since March 1992. Foodmaker responded by claiming that it had never received notification of the change in standards. When health department officials came up with a copy of the notification that had been sent to local Jack-in-the-Box restaurants, Foodmaker changed its position. According to Robert Nugent, president of Jack-in-the-Box, the company had received the notification but the vice president whose responsibility it was to no-

tify local restaurants hadn't done so. Jack-in-the-Box indicated that it would take disciplinary action against the vice president, whom it refused to name.

Meanwhile, the number of children infected had soared to 450—one had died, several were in comas, and a number of others were listed as being in critical condition. At this stage Jack-in-the-Box offered to pay the hospital costs for those infected. However, there was a catch; in return for paying medical costs, the company's lawyers asked the parents of the infected children to sign forms waiving their rights to file a subsequent lawsuit against Jack-in-the-Box. This request was greeted with outrage, and Jack-in-the-Box once more had to shift its position. This time the company agreed to pay full hospital costs, without requiring a waver.

By February 1993 the worst of the outbreak was over. However, for Foodmaker the impact was only just beginning. Nationwide sales at Jack-in-the-Box restaurants had plunged 35 percent in the first two weeks of February, the company's stock price had lost 30 percent of its value, and the company announced that it had put on hold plans to open up eighty-five new Jack-in-the-Box restaurants for 1993. What seems to have hurt Jack-in-the-Box most was not the outbreak itself, but the company's repeated attempts to shift responsibility for the outbreak onto others and its cynical attempt to link the offer of financial help to victims with lawsuit wavers. As a result, Jack-in-the-Box came out of the crisis with its reputation tarnished and its sales slumping. Compare this to Johnson & Johnson, which came out of the Tylenol crisis with its reputation for ethical behavior enhanced.[58]

tematic way. A number of different frameworks have been suggested as aids to the decision-making process. The four-step model shown in Figure 2.6 is a compilation of the various approaches recommended by several authorities on this subject.[59]

In Step 1, evaluating a proposed strategic decision from an ethical standpoint, managers must identify which stakeholders the decision will affect and in what ways. Most importantly, they need to determine whether the proposed decision would violate the rights of any stakeholders. The term *rights* refers to the fundamental entitlements of a stakeholder. For example, we might argue that the right to information about health risks in the workplace is a fundamental entitlement of employees. It is also an entitlement that Manville ignored.

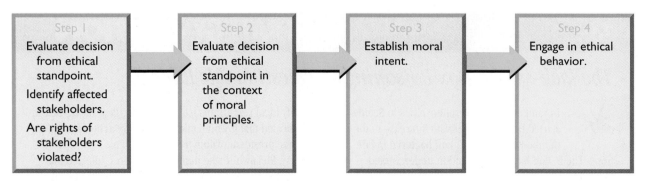

FIGURE 2.6
· · · · · · · · · · · ·
A Model of Ethical
Decision Making

Step 2 involves judging the ethics of the proposed strategic decision, given the information gained in step 1. This judgment should be guided by various moral principles that should not be violated. The principles might be those articulated in a corporate mission statement or other company documents (such as Hewlett Packard's The HP Way). In addition, certain moral principles that we have adopted as members of society, such as the prohibition against stealing, should not be violated. The judgment at this stage will also be guided by the decision rule that is chosen to assess the proposed strategic decision. Although long-run profit maximization is rightly the decision rule that most companies stress, it should be applied subject to the constraint that no moral principles are violated.

Step 3, establishing moral intent, means that the company must resolve to place moral concerns ahead of other concerns in cases in which either the rights of stakeholders or key moral principles have been violated. At this stage input from top management might be particularly valuable. Without the proactive encouragement of top managers, middle-level managers might tend to place the narrow economic interests of the company before the interests of stakeholders. They might do so in the (usually erroneous) belief that top managers favor such an approach.

Step 4 requires the company to engage in ethical behavior. Clearly, Johnson & Johnson fulfilled this requirement during the Tylenol poisoning scare by pulling all its product off retail store shelves at great cost to the company.

Corporate Social Responsibility
· ·

Corporate social responsibility is the sense of obligation on the part of companies to build certain social criteria into their strategic decision making. The concept implies that when companies evaluate decisions from an ethical perspective, there should be a presumption in favor of adopting courses of action that enhance the welfare of society at large. The goals selected might be quite specific, for example, to enhance the welfare of communities in which a company is based, to improve the environment, or to empower employees to give them a sense of self-worth.

In its purest form, social responsibility can be supported for its own sake simply because it is the right way for a company to behave. Less pure but perhaps more practical are the arguments that socially responsible behavior is in a company's self-interest. Economic actions have social consequences affecting a company's outside stakeholders. Therefore, to retain the support of these stakeholders, the company must take those social consequences into account when formulating strategies.

Otherwise, it may generate ill will and opposition. For example, if a community perceives a company as having an adverse impact on the local environment, it may block the company's attempts to build new facilities in the area.

Still, there are those who argue that a company has no business pursuing social goals. Nobel laureate Milton Friedman, for one, insists that considerations of social responsibility should not enter into the decision process.

> What does it mean to say that the corporate executive has a social responsibility in his capacity as a businessman? If this statement is not pure rhetoric, it must mean that he is to act in some way that is not in the interests of his employers. For example . . . that he is to make expenditures on reducing pollution beyond the amount that is in the best interests of the corporation or that is required by law in order to contribute to the social objective of improving the environment. . . . Insofar as his actions in accord with his social responsibility reduce returns to stockholders, he is spending their money. Insofar as his actions raise the price to customers, he is spending the customers' money. Insofar as the actions lower the wages of some employees, he is spending their money.[60]

Friedman's position is that a business has only one kind of responsibility: to use its resources for activities that increase its profits, so long as it stays within the rules of the game, which is to say, so long as it engages in open and free competition without deception or fraud.

On the other hand, Edward H. Bowman of the University of Pennsylvania's Wharton School argues that social responsibility is actually a sound investment strategy.[61] He maintains that a company's social behavior affects the price of its stock; thus, a socially responsible policy can also benefit a company's important inside claimants, the stockholders. According to Bowman, many investors see companies that are not socially responsible as riskier investments. Moreover, many institutional investors, such as churches, universities, cities, states, and mutual funds, pay attention to corporate social behavior and thus influence the market for a company's stock.

Evidence can certainly be found in favor of Bowman's arguments. For example, the withdrawal of U.S. assets from South Africa by companies such as IBM and General Motors in 1986 can at least in part be attributed to a desire to create a favorable impression with investors. At that time, for social and/or political reasons, many investors were selling any stock they held in companies that maintained a substantial presence in South Africa. Similarly, Union Carbide saw its market value plunge more than 37 percent in 1984, in the aftermath of the gas leak at its Bhopal plant in India (which killed 2,000 people and left 150,000 seriously injured) and subsequent revelations concerning poor safety procedures at many Union Carbide plants. For Union Carbide, the consequence was a takeover bid from GAF (which ultimately failed), extended litigation, and a negative image.

SUMMARY OF CHAPTER

● ● ● ● ● ● ● ● ● ● ● ● ● ● ● ● ● ● ●

The primary purpose of this chapter has been to identify the various factors that influence and shape the organizational context within which strategies are formulated. Normally, these factors are explicitly recognized through the corporate mission statement. The mission statement thus sets the boundaries within which strategies must be contained. Specifically, the following points are made:

✔ Stakeholders are individuals or groups, either within or outside an organization, that have some claim on the organization. They include customers, suppliers, employees, and stockholders.

If an organization is to survive and prosper, it must pay attention to the interests of these different stakeholder groups.

✔ The mission statement describes how a company intends to incorporate stakeholders' claims into its strategic decision making and thereby reduce the risk of losing the support of stakeholders.

✔ The mission statement contains three broad elements: (a) a statement of the overall vision of the company, (b) a statement that indicates the key philosophical values that managers are committed to, and (c) the articulation of key goals that management believes must be adhered to in order to fulfill the mission statement.

✔ An important step in the process of formulating a mission statement is to come up with a definition of the organization's business. Defining the business involves focusing on consumer groups to be served, consumer needs to be satisfied, and the technologies by which those needs can be satisfied.

✔ The values of a company state how managers intend to conduct themselves, how they intend to do business, and what kind of organization they want to build. Values can become the bedrock of a company's organizational culture and a driver of its competitive advantage

✔ The goals of a company specify with precision what must be done if the company is to attain its mission. Well-constructed goals are precise and measurable, address important issues, are challenging but realistic, and specify a time period within which they should be achieved.

✔ Stockholders are among a company's most important stakeholders. Maximizing stockholders' wealth is one of the most important goals of a company. A corporate governance problem arises when managers pursue strategies that are not consistent with this goal.

✔ A number of governance mechanisms serve to limit the ability of managers to pursue strategies that are at variance with maximizing stockholders' wealth. These include the board of directors, stock-based compensation schemes, the threat of a takeover, and leveraged buyouts.

✔ Strategic decisions have an ethical dimension. Any action by a company inevitably has an impact on the welfare of its stakeholders.

✔ The purpose of business ethics is not so much to teach the difference between right and wrong but to give people the tools for dealing with moral complexity—for identifying and thinking through the moral implications of strategic decisions.

DISCUSSION QUESTIONS

1. Why is it important for a company to take a consumer-oriented view of its businesses? What are the possible shortcomings of such a view?

2. What are the strategic implications of a focus on short-run returns? Discuss these implications in terms of the impact on product innovation, marketing expenditure, manufacturing, and purchasing decisions.

3. Are corporate raiders a positive or negative influence on the U.S. economy? How can companies reduce the risk of a takeover?

4. "Companies should always behave in an ethical manner, whatever the economic cost." Discuss this statement.

Practicing Strategic Management

SMALL-GROUP EXERCISE
Constructing a Mission Statement

Break up into groups of three to five people, and discuss the following:

1. Define the business of your educational institution.

2. Use this business definition to construct a mission statement for your educational institution. Be sure that the mission statement contains a long-term vision, a set of values, and a number of important, precise, and measurable goals. Be prepared to articulate the logic behind your choice of vision, values, and goals.

3. Take a stab at trying to identify a number of key strategies that your educational institution needs to pursue in order to attain the vision and goals outlined in your mission statement. Be sure that these strategies are consistent with the values you set down in the mission statement.

EXPLORING THE WEB
Visiting Merck

Visit the Web site of Merck, the world's largest pharmaceutical company, at http://www.merck.com. Go to the "Company Overview" of the site, and then look at the mission statement.

1. Evaluate this mission statement in light of the material contained in this chapter. Does the mission state clearly what Merck's basic strategic goal is? Do the values listed here provide a good guideline for managerial action at Merck?

2. Follow the hypertext link "benefits humanity." Read the section on corporate responsibility, and then answer the following questions: How does Merck attempt to balance the goals of providing stockholders with an adequate rate of return on their investment while at the same time developing medicines that benefit humanity and that can be acquired by people in need at an affordable price? Do you think that Merck does a good job of balancing these goals?

ARTICLE FILE 2

Find an example of a company that ran into trouble because it failed to take into account the rights of one of its stakeholder groups when making an important strategic decision.

STRATEGIC MANAGEMENT PROJECT
Module 2

This module deals with the relationships your company has with its major stakeholder groups. With the information you have at your disposal, perform the tasks and answer the questions listed:

1. Does your company has a formal mission statement? Does it define the business, identify major goals, and articulate the corporate philosophy?

2. If your company lacks a mission statement, what do you think its mission statement should be like?

3. If your company has a mission statement, do you see it as appropriate, given the material discussed in this chapter?

4. Identify the main stakeholder groups in your company. What claims do they place on the company? How is the company trying to satisfy those claims?

5. Evaluate the performance of the CEO of your company from the perspective of (a) stockholders, (b) employees, (c) customers, and (d) suppliers. What do you think about the ability of the CEO and the priorities to which he or she is committed?

6. Do the governance mechanisms that operate in your company do a good job of aligning the interests of top managers with those of stockholders?

7. Pick a major strategic decision made by your company in recent years, and try to think through the ethical implications of that decision. Do you think that the company acted correctly?

General Task Using the World Wide Web, find an example of a company's mission statement that you think exemplifies many of the issues discussed here.

Body Shop International

The British based retailer, Body Shop International, is often held up as a prime example of a company that is committed to being ethically and socially responsible in its business dealings. The company's founder and CEO, Anita Roddick, has become an energetic spokesperson for the importance of ethics and social responsibility. The Body Shop competes in the international cosmetics and toiletries market but offers unique products based on natural ingredients. The company has based its success on the claim that none of its products are tested on animals, contain artificial ingredients, or are elaborately packaged. The products appeal to consumers who are concerned about animal rights and the environment. Under a program called "Trade not Aid," The Body Shop claims to purchase many of the ingredients for its products from Third World producers, and the company maintains that it pays its suppliers well. It also makes a point of plowing money back into the communities where its suppliers are based to support a variety of health and educational projects. This commitment to social responsibility helped propel The Body Shop from a single store in 1976 to a global enterprise with 1,100 stores in forty-five countries and annual revenues of more than $700 million in 1995. According to Roddick:

> You can run a business differently from the way most businesses are run, you can share your prosperity with employees, and empower them without being in fear of them. You can rewrite the book in terms of how a company interacts with the community, on third world trade, global responsibility, and the role of educating customers and shareholders, and you can do all this and still play the game according to the City [the British version of Wall Street], still raise money, delight the Institutions and give shareholders a wondrous return on their investment.

This sounds well and good, and Roddick's philosophy helped to turn The Body Shop into the darling of the business ethics community. However, the good feeling was rudely shattered in the fall of 1994 when a journalist, Jon Entine, published an article highly critical of The Body Shop in the *Business Ethics* magazine. Among other things, Entine made the following claims:

- The Body Shop uses many outdated, off-the-shelf product formulas filled with nonrenewable petrochemicals.

- Many of its products are contaminated and contain formaldehyde, an artificial ingredient.

- The Body Shop has used ingredients in its products that have been tested on animals.

- Contrary to the company's claims, The Body Shop sources a tiny amount of ingredients through its Trade not Aid program. Moreover, The Body Shop does not pay "first world wages for third world products" as it claims in its publicity.

- Its charitable contributions and progressive environmental standards fall short of the company's claims. Until 1994 the company never contributed more than 1.24 percent of its pretax profits to charitable organizations.

- The company invented stories about the exotic origins of some of its products.

Entine's article drew a vigorous response from Gordon Roddick, the chairman of Body Shop International. In a ten-page letter sent to all subscribers of *Business Ethics* magazine, Roddick claimed that Entine's article was filled with "many lies, distortions, and gross inaccuracies. . . . I am at a loss to find anything balanced or fair in this article." Roddick went on in the letter to give a detailed rebuttal of Entine's charges. For example, with regard to the Trade not Aid program, Roddick observed that Entine's article

> goes after our Trade not Aid program, building its attack around an utterly irrelevant statistic—the percentage of our ingredients that come from Trade not Aid projects. What is this number supposed to reveal? It certainly tells us nothing about the effectiveness of our efforts. Or the amount of time we have put into nurturing these projects. Or the obstacles we have had to overcome due to the lack of infrastructure in disenfranchised Third World communities. . . . One single ingredient, such as Brazil nut oil or cocoa butter, may take two years or more to source and develop. Believe me, there are much easier ways to do business than by taking on the problems of such projects. . . . We do it because we are asked to help by the disenfranchised communities themselves. The only significant measure of our success is the number of people who are directly beneficially affected by our activities. That

is a number, I am proud to say, that runs into the thousands.

The Body Shop followed up Entine's attack by commissioning an independent "ethics audit" by the New Economics Foundation, a London-based ethics business consultant. Issued in January 1996, the audit reported that 93 percent of The Body Shop's employees feel the company lives up to its mission to be socially and environmentally responsible and that the purchases from suppliers in developing countries and poor communities increased by more than 30 percent during 1995. The audit also noted that less than 2 percent of the company's raw material inputs came from the Trade not Aid program in 1995, although about 17.8 percent of the accessories sold in The Body Shop stores, such as brushes and sponges, came from the program. The company donated 2.3 percent of its pretax profits to charity in 1995.[62]

Case Discussion Questions

1. Is Anita Roddick correct when she claims that it is possible to run a business in a very ethical and socially responsible manner and still "give shareholders a wondrous return on their investment"?

2. Is the percentage of ingredients that come from Trade not Aid projects an irrelevant statistic, as Gordon Roddick claims?

3. Evaluate The Body Shop's claims to be ethically responsible in light of the ethics audit report.

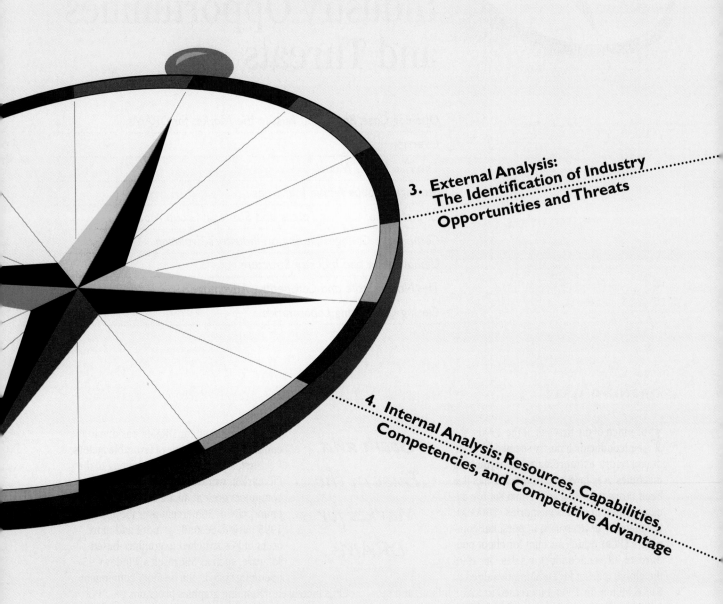

PART TWO

The Nature of Competitive Advantage

3. External Analysis: The Identification of Industry Opportunities and Threats

4. Internal Analysis: Resources, Capabilities, Competencies, and Competitive Advantage

CHAPTER 3

External Analysis: The Identification of Industry Opportunities and Threats

Opening Case: Boom and Bust in the Market for DRAMs

Overview

The Five Forces Model

Strategic Groups Within Industries

Limitations of the Five Forces and Strategic Group Models

Competitive Changes During an Industry's Evolution

Globalization and Industry Structure

The Nation-State and Competitive Advantage

Closing Case: Wang Laboratories

OPENING CASE

For much of the first half of the 1990s, the semiconductor industry seemed like one of the most extraordinary moneymaking machines ever invented. In no case has this been more true than in the market for dynamic random access memories (DRAMs), the memory devices used in personal computers (PCs), which account for about one-third of all semiconductor sales. In 1993 the global market for DRAMs was valued at $13.6 billion. In 1994 it increased to $23.1 billion, and in 1995 it surged to a staggering $55 billion. This rapid in-

Boom and Bust in the Market for DRAMs

crease in demand for DRAMs was due to the confluence of a number of favorable factors.

First, stimulated by price cutting in the PC market, worldwide sales of personal computers grew at an annual average compound rate of 30 percent over the 1990–1995 period. Second, as more and more users of PCs switched to graphics-based software, such as Microsoft's Windows 95 operating system, the memory component of PCs increased. (Running graphics programs on a PC requires a large amount of memory.) Between 1991 and

70

1995, the average amount of DRAM contained in each PC sold increased from 2 megabytes to 12 megabytes. Third, other applications for DRAMs (particularly in telecommunications equipment and cellular phone handsets) also grew rapidly. For example, global shipments of cellular phones increased from 5 million to 50 million between 1991 and 1995.

Not only was demand for DRAMs surging during the 1990–1995 period, supply was also constrained. One reason for the shortage was the reluctance of many semiconductor companies to undertake investments in new semiconductor fabricating plants. By 1995 a new fabrication facility could cost anywhere from $1 billion to $2.5 billion and take eighteen months to construct. Faced with such enormous fixed costs, many companies have been reluctant to undertake the investment, particularly since demand conditions could change significantly in the eighteen months required to bring a new facility on line. Managers in this industry still remember the 1985–1987 period, when a combination of slowing demand and massive capacity expansions by Japanese semiconductor companies led to an excess supply of DRAMs, which plunged prices and resulted in significant financial losses for most of the world's DRAM manufacturers. Indeed, it was during this period that a number of U.S. companies exited the DRAM market, including Intel, the company that invented the DRAM.

The result of surging global demand for DRAMs and constrained supply was that during the 1993–1995 period prices for DRAMs increased dramatically. In 1993 the average selling price for DRAM was $8.89 per megabyte, in 1994 it was $11.69, and by the middle of 1995 it had risen to $14.00. One company that benefited from this situation was Micron Technology of Boise, Idaho. Micron was one of only two U.S. firms that remained in the DRAM market after the debacle of 1985–1987. (The other was Texas Instruments.) In 1990 Micron had sales of less than $300 million and was only just breaking even. Riding the industry wave, by 1994 the company had revenues of $1.63 billion and net income of $400 million. This was followed by 1995 revenues of $2.95 billion and net income of $844 million. Micron's gross profit margin for 1995 was 55 percent—almost unheard of for a DRAM company—compared with 23 percent in 1990. Nor was Micron alone in achieving such impressive profit performance. By 1995 almost every DRAM company in the world was making record profits.

These huge industry profits, however, became a signal for incumbent companies to expand their capacity and for new companies to enter the semiconductor industry. Starting in late 1994, an increasing number of companies announced intentions to invest in semiconductor fabrication facilities. Those jumping on the capacity expansion bandwagon included Micron Technology, which in June 1995 unveiled plans to invest $2.5 billion in a new fabrication facility in Lehi, Utah, that was scheduled to begin production at the end of 1996. When Micron made its announcement, almost 100 new semiconductor fabrication facilities were being constructed around the world, many of which were scheduled to come on line in 1995 and 1996. Moreover, by the end of 1995, plans to build another 100 facilities had been announced.

In the fall of 1995 the other shoe dropped. After four years of rapid growth, there was a sudden slowdown in the growth rate of personal computer sales, particularly in the huge North American market. This slowdown occurred just as the new DRAM capacity was becoming operational. To make matters worse, throughout 1995 manufacturers of personal computers had been building up their inventories of DRAMs, both to hedge against future price increases and to ensure an adequate supply of DRAMs for what they thought would be a very busy Christmas season. When the anticipated surge in Christmas sales of PCs failed to materialize, PC manufacturers found themselves holding too much inventory. They responded by cutting back dramatically on their orders for DRAMs. The result was that DRAM sales volume and prices slumped. Between late 1995 and March 1996, DRAM prices fell from $14 per megabyte to $7 per megabyte. The consequences included falling profit margins for DRAM companies.

Reflecting the widespread perception that a situation of excess demand and rising prices had been replaced in short order by one of excess supply and plunging prices, the Philadelphia Semi-Conductor Index, a measure of the share price of American semiconductor companies, fell by 45 percent between September 1995 and March 1996. In February 1996 Micron Technology responded to this situation by dramatically slowing down the construction schedule for its Lehi facility, pushing out the start date for volume manufacturing another two to five years. Nor was Micron alone; by spring 1996 companies around the world were also announcing that they had put their capacity expansion plans on hold.[1]

OVERVIEW

The Opening Case illustrates the impact that the external environment can have on a company's performance. During the 1992–1995 period, DRAM manufacturers such as Micron Technology did very well because conditions in the semiconductor industry were so favorable. Demand exceeded supply for most of this period, and prices and profits surged. As the case also illustrates, however, toward the end of 1995 industry conditions became much more hostile. The rate of growth in demand for DRAMs slowed significantly, supply increased, and DRAM prices plunged, in the process pulling down the profits of DRAM manufacturers.

Consistent with the theme introduced in the Opening Case, in this chapter we consider the influence of the industry environment in which a company competes on its performance. First, we discuss a number of models that can assist managers in analyzing the environment. The models provide a framework to identify environmental opportunities and threats. **Opportunities** arise when a company can take advantage of conditions in its external environment to formulate and implement strategies that enable it to earn higher profits. **Threats** arise when conditions in the external environment endanger the integrity and profitability of the company's business. Second, we consider the competitive implications that arise when groups of companies within an industry pursue similar strategies. Third, we examine the nature of industry evolution and discuss in detail how the globalization of the world economy is affecting the competitive forces at work in an industry's environment. Finally, we assess the impact of conditions within a nation on competitive advantage. By the end of the chapter, you will understand that to succeed a company either must fit its strategy to the industry environment in which it operates or must be able to reshape the industry's environment to its advantage through its chosen strategy.

THE FIVE FORCES MODEL

An **industry** can be defined as a group of companies offering products or services that are close substitutes for each other. Close substitutes are products or services that satisfy the same basic consumer needs. For example, the metal and plastic body panels used in automobile construction are close substitutes for each other. Despite different production technologies, auto supply companies that manufacture metal body panels are in the same basic industry as companies that manufacture plastic body panels. They serve the same consumer need, that of auto assembly companies for body panels.

The task facing managers is to analyze competitive forces in an industry's environment in order to identify the opportunities and threats confronting a company. Michael E. Porter of the Harvard School of Business Administration has developed a framework that helps managers in this analysis.[2] Porter's framework, known as the **five forces model,** appears in Figure 3.1. This model focuses on five forces that shape competition within an industry: (1) the risk of new entry by potential competitors, (2) the degree of rivalry among established companies within an industry, (3) the bargaining power of buyers, (4) the bargaining power of suppliers, and (5) the threat of substitute products.

FIGURE 3.1

The Five Forces Model

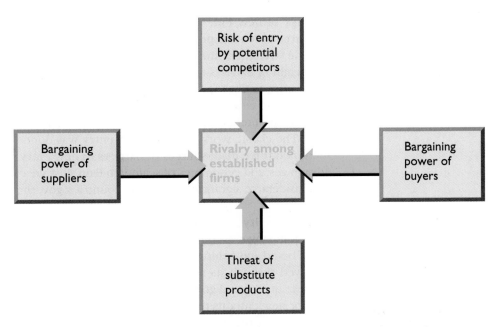

Source: Adapted and reprinted by permission of *Harvard Business Review.* An exhibit from "How Competence Forces Shape Strategy" by Michael E. Porter (March-April 1979). Copyright © 1979 by the President and Fellows of Harvard College; all rights reserved.

Porter argues that the stronger each of these forces is, the more limited is the ability of established companies to raise prices and earn greater profits. Within Porter's framework, for example, a strong competitive force can be regarded as a threat since it depresses profits. A weak competitive force can be viewed as an opportunity, for it allows a company to earn greater profits. The strength of the five forces may change through time as industry conditions change, as illustrated by the Opening Case. The task facing managers is to recognize how changes in the five forces give rise to new opportunities and threats and to formulate appropriate strategic responses. In addition, it is possible for a company, *through its choice of strategy,* to alter the strength of one or more of the five forces to its advantage. This is discussed in the following chapters. In this section, we focus on understanding the impact that each of the five forces has on a company.

Potential Competitors

Potential competitors are companies that are not currently competing in an industry but have the capability to do so if they choose. American Telephone & Telegraph (AT&T), for example, was regarded as a potential competitor in the personal computer industry in the early 1980s, for it had the technology, sales force, and capital necessary to manufacture and sell PCs. AT&T did in fact enter the industry in 1985, although it subsequently failed to secure a strong market position. **Incumbent companies** (those already operating in an industry) try to discourage potential competitors from entering the industry, since the more companies enter, the more difficult it becomes for established companies to hold their share of the market and to generate profits. Thus, a high risk of entry by potential competitors represents a threat to the profitability of established companies. On the other hand, if the risk of new entry is low, incumbent companies can take advantage of this opportunity to raise prices and earn greater returns.

The strength of the competitive force of potential rivals is largely a function of the height of barriers to entry. **Barriers to entry** are factors that make it costly for companies to enter an industry. The greater the costs that potential competitors must bear to enter an industry, the greater are the barriers to entry. High barriers to entry keep potential competitors out of an industry, even when industry returns are high. The classic work on barriers to entry was done by economist Joe Bain, who identified three main sources of barriers to new entry: brand loyalty, absolute cost advantages, and economies of scale.[3] To Bain's list we can add a fourth entry barrier of considerable significance in many countries: governmental regulation.

Brand Loyalty   **Brand loyalty** is buyers' preference for the products of incumbent companies. A company can create brand loyalty through continuous advertising of brand and company names, patent protection of products, product innovation achieved through its research and development programs, an emphasis on high product quality, and good after-sales service. Significant brand loyalty makes it difficult for new entrants to take market share away from established companies. Thus, brand loyalty reduces the threat of entry by potential competitors since they may see the task of breaking down well-established consumer preferences as too costly.

Absolute Cost Advantages   Sometimes incumbent companies have an absolute cost advantage relative to potential entrants. **Absolute cost advantages** can arise from three main sources: (1) superior production operations, due to past experience, patents, or secret processes; (2) control of particular inputs required for production, such as labor, materials, equipment, or management skills; and (3) access to cheaper funds because existing companies represent lower risks than companies that are not yet established. If incumbent companies have an absolute cost advantage, the threat of entry decreases.

Economies of Scale   **Economies of scale** are the cost advantages associated with large company size. Sources of scale economies include cost reductions gained through mass-producing a standardized output, discounts on bulk purchases of raw material inputs and component parts, the advantages gained by spreading fixed costs over a large production volume, and economies of scale in advertising. If these cost advantages are significant, a new entrant faces the dilemma of either entering on a small scale and suffering a significant cost disadvantage or entering on a large scale and bearing the large risk of significant capital costs. A further risk of large-scale entry is that the increased supply of products will depress prices and result in vigorous retaliation by established companies. Thus, when established companies have economies of scale, the threat of entry is reduced.

Governmental Regulation   Historically, governmental regulation has constituted a major entry barrier into many industries. For example, until recently in the United States, government regulation prohibited providers of long-distance telephone service, such as AT&T, MCI, and Sprint, from competing for local telephone service with the Regional Bell Operating Companies (RBOCs) such as US West and Bell Atlantic. Moreover, the RBOCs were prohibited from entering the long-distance telephone market. Other potential providers of telephone service, including cable television service companies such as TCI Communications and Viacom (who could in theory use their cables to carry telephone traffic as well as TV signals), were prohibited from entering the market altogether. These regulatory barriers to entry significantly reduced the level of competition in both the local and long-distance telephone markets, enabling telephone companies to earn higher profits than might otherwise have been the case. All this changed in January 1996 when the United States government deregulated the industry, removing all barriers to entry. In the months that followed this announcement, the RBOCs, long-distance companies, and cable TV companies all announced their intention to enter each other's markets. A significant increase in competitive intensity is to be expected. A similar move toward deregulating telephone service can be seen in many other countries. The member states of the European Union, for example, are set to deregulate their telephone markets on January 1, 1998.

Barriers to Entry and Competition   If established companies have built brand loyalty for their products, have an absolute cost advantage with respect to potential competitors, have significant economies of scale, or enjoy regulatory protection, then the risk of entry by potential competitors is greatly diminished. When this risk is low, established companies can charge higher prices and earn greater profits than would be possible otherwise. Clearly, it is in the interest of companies to pursue strategies consistent with raising barriers to entry. Indeed, empirical evidence suggests that the height of barriers to entry is the most important determinant of profit rates in an industry. [4] Examples of industries in which barriers to entry are considerable include pharmaceuticals, household detergents, and commercial jet aircraft. In the first two cases, product differentiation achieved through substantial expenditures for research and development and for advertising has built brand loyalty, making it difficult for new companies to enter these industries on a significant scale. For example, so successful have the differentiation strategies of Procter & Gamble and Unilever been in household detergents that these two companies dominate the global industry. In the case of the commercial jet aircraft industry, the barriers to entry are primarily due to the enormous fixed costs of product development (it cost Boeing $5 billion to develop its new wide-bodied jetliner, the 777) and the economies of scale enjoyed by the incumbent companies, which enable them to price below a potential entrant's costs of production and still make a significant profit. A more detailed example of barriers to entry is given in Strategy in Action 3.1, which discusses the barriers to entry in the Japanese brewing industry.

Rivalry Among Established Companies

The second of Porter's five competitive forces is the extent of rivalry among established companies within an industry. If this rivalry is weak, companies have an opportunity to raise prices and earn greater profits. If rivalry is strong, significant price competition, including price wars, may result. Price competition limits profitability by reducing the margins that can be earned on sales. Thus, intense rivalry among established companies constitutes a strong threat to profitability. The extent of rivalry among established companies within an industry is largely a function of three factors: (1) the industry's competitive structure, (2) demand conditions, and (3) the height of exit barriers in the industry.

3.1   STRATEGY *in* ACTION

Barriers to Entry in the Japanese Brewing Industry

 In 1565 an English visitor to Japan noted that the Japanese "feed moderately but they drink largely." This is still the case today; the Japanese have one of the highest levels of beer consumption per capita of any country in the world. In 1994, for example, 56 liters of beer were sold for every man, woman, and child in the country, making Japan's per capita level of beer consumption similar to that of big beer-drinking nations such as Australia, Britain, and Germany.

The vast Japanese market is dominated by just four companies: Kirin, Asahi, Sapporo, and Suntory. In 1994 these four had a combined market share of 98 percent. Collectively, these companies enjoy one of the highest profit rates of any industry in Japan. Despite this high level of profitability, however, there has been very little entry into this industry over the last three decades. Suntory is the only successful new entrant in the last thirty years, and its market share stands at no more than 6 percent.

Normally, a lack of new entry into a profitable industry indicates the presence of high barriers to entry, and that is certainly true in this case. As with large brewers all over the world, Japan's big four spend heavily on advertising and promotions. The resulting product differentiation and brand identification have certainly helped to limit the potential for new entry. However, there is more to the story than this. Japan's big brewing companies have also been the beneficiaries of significant regulatory barriers to entry. Brewers in Japan must have a license from the Ministry of Finance (MOF). Prior to 1994, the MOF would not issue a license to any brewer producing less than 2 million liters annually. This restriction represented an imposing hurdle to any potential new entrant. Interestingly enough, the reason for the licensing scheme was bureaucratic convenience rather than a desire to protect brewing

companies from new entry; it is easier to collect tax from 4 companies than from 400.

Another significant barrier to entry has been Japan's distribution system. In Japan there are often close ties between distributors and manufacturers, and this is the case in the brewing industry. Roughly half the beer consumed in Japan is sold in bars and restaurants. Their owners appear to be loyal to the big brewers and reluctant to take on competing brands that might alienate their main suppliers. Small liquor stores are the other main distribution outlet for beer, and they, too, have traditionally maintained close ties with the big brewers and are unwilling to sell the products of new entrants for fear that their main suppliers might "punish" them by denying them access to adequate supplies.

However, it now appears that the barriers to entering Japan's brewing industry are declining. As part of an economic liberalization plan, in 1994 the MOF reduced the production threshold required to gain a license from 2 million liters to 60,000 liters; low enough to allow for the entry of microbreweries using the same technology that is now found in many brew pubs in the United States and Britain. Moreover, regulatory changes have also allowed for the establishment of large new discount stores in Japan. (Until 1994 small retailers could effectively block the establishment of a large discount store in their region by appealing to the local authorities.) Unlike traditional small retailers, large discount retailers are motivated more by price and profit than by loyalties to an established supplier, and they are proving increasingly willing to sell the beer of foreign companies and microbreweries, in addition to that of Japan's big four. Given the decline in traditional barriers to entry, it seems increasingly likely that Japan's big four brewers will have to face up to new competitors, increased competition, and lower profit margins in the years to come.[5]

Competitive Structure   Competitive structure refers to the number and size distribution of companies in an industry. Structures vary from **fragmented** to **consolidated** and have different implications for rivalry. A fragmented industry contains a large number of small or medium-sized companies, none of which is in a position to dominate the industry. A consolidated industry may be dominated by a small

FIGURE 3.2

The Continuum of
Industry Structures

number of large companies (in which case it is referred to as an oligopoly) or, in extreme cases, by just one company (a monopoly). Fragmented industries range from agriculture, video rental, and health clubs, to real estate brokers and sun tanning parlors. Consolidated industries include aerospace, automobiles, and pharmaceuticals. The range of structures is illustrated in Figure 3.2.

Many fragmented industries are characterized by low barriers to entry and commodity-type products that are hard to differentiate. The combination of these traits tends to result in boom-and-bust cycles as industry profits rise and fall. Low barriers to entry imply that whenever demand is strong and profits are high, there will be a flood of new entrants hoping to cash in on the boom. The explosion in the number of video stores, health clubs, and sun tanning parlors during the 1980s exemplifies this situation.

Often the flood of new entrants into a booming fragmented industry creates excess capacity. Once excess capacity develops, companies start to cut prices in order to utilize their spare capacity. The difficulty companies face when trying to differentiate their products from those of competitors can worsen this tendency. The result is a price war, which depresses industry profits, forces some companies out of business, and deters potential new entrants. For example, after a decade of expansion and booming profits, many health clubs are now finding that they have to offer large discounts in order to hold onto their membership. In general, the more commodity-like an industry's product, the more vicious will be the price war. This bust part of the cycle continues until overall industry capacity is brought into line with demand (through bankruptcies), at which point prices may stabilize again.

A fragmented industry structure, then, constitutes a threat rather than an opportunity. Most booms will be relatively short-lived because of the ease of new entry and will be followed by price wars and bankruptcies. Since it is often difficult to differentiate products in these industries, the best strategy for a company to pursue may be cost minimization. This strategy allows a company to rack up high returns in a boom to survive any subsequent bust.

The nature and intensity of rivalry in consolidated industries is much more difficult to predict. In consolidated industries companies are *interdependent,* such that the competitive actions of one company directly affect the profitability of others in the industry. Thus, in a consolidated industry, the competitive action of one company directly affects the market share of its rivals, forcing a response from them. The consequence of such competitive interdependence can be a dangerous competitive spiral, with rival companies trying to undercut each other's prices, pushing industry profits down in the process. The fare wars that wracked the airline industry in the early 1990s provide a good example. When demand for airline travel fell during 1990 as the U.S. economy slipped into a recession, airlines started cutting prices to try to maintain their passenger loads. When one airline serving a particular route cut its prices, its competitors would soon follow. The result was a particularly severe downward price spiral. So intense did price competition become that between 1990 and 1992 the industry lost a staggering $7.1 billion, more than had been made during its previous fifty years, and some long-established carriers, such as Pan American, disappeared into bankruptcy.

Clearly, high rivalry between companies in consolidated industries and the possibility of a price war constitute a major threat. Companies sometimes seek to reduce this threat by following the price lead set by a dominant company in the industry. However, companies must be careful, for explicit price-fixing agreements are illegal, although tacit agreements are not. (A tacit agreement is one arrived at without direct communication.) Instead, companies watch and interpret each other's behavior. Often tacit agreements involve following the price lead set by a dominant company.[6] However, tacit price-leadership agreements often break down under adverse economic conditions, as is beginning to occur in the beer industry. For most of the 1980s, Anheuser-Busch was the acknowledged price leader in this industry. The resulting absence of price competition helped keep industry profits high. However, slow growth in beer consumption during the late 1980s and early 1990s put pressure on the earnings of all beer majors and persuaded Miller Brewing (a division of Philip Morris) and Adolph Coors to break ranks and institute a policy of deep and continuous discounting for most of their beer brands. In 1990 market leader Anheuser-Busch announced that it would start offering similar discounts in order to protect its sales volume. Thus, after the breakdown of a tacit price-leadership agreement, the beer industry seems to be sliding toward a price war.

More generally, when price wars are a threat, companies tend to compete on nonprice factors such as advertising and promotions; brand positioning; and product quality, functionality, and design. This type of competition constitutes an attempt to differentiate the company's product from those of competitors, thereby building brand loyalty and minimizing the likelihood of a price war. The effectiveness of this strategy, however, depends on how easy it is to differentiate the industry's product. Although some products (such as cars) are relatively easy to differentiate, others (such as airline travel) are difficult. Moreover, as Strategy in Action 3.2 demonstrates, in practice nonprice competition in consolidated industries can often be as vigorous, expensive, and damaging as price competition.

Demand Conditions   An industry's demand conditions are another determinant of the intensity of rivalry among established companies. Growing demand from either new customers or additional purchases by existing customers tends to moderate competition by providing greater room for expansion. Growing demand tends to reduce rivalry because all companies can sell more without taking market share away from other companies, and high profits are often the result. The Opening Case, which profiled demand cycles in the DRAM industry, provides a good example of this phenomenon. The DRAM industry is quite fragmented, with no company's accounting for more than 10 percent of the market. Moreover, the product is difficult to differentiate and therefore is sold primarily on price. Other things being equal, both these factors tend to result in vigorous price competition and low industry profits. However, the rapid growth in demand for DRAMs during the 1991–1995 period, when combined with barriers to entry that slowed the rate of new

The Great European Soap War

 The European retail detergents market, like the global detergents market, is dominated by the products of just two companies, Unilever, the Anglo-Dutch concern, and the American consumer products giant, Procter & Gamble (P&G). Both companies sell a broad product line of detergents to consumers; both spend heavily on advertising, promotions, and brand positioning; and both de-emphasize price-based competition. The net result is that historically both companies have benefited from a relatively benign competitive environment that has enabled them to earn higher profit margins than would be the case in a more price-competitive industry.

This cozy situation was rudely shattered in early 1994 following the Pan-European launch of a new detergent by Unilever. The product in question was Omo Power, which Unilever promoted as the biggest technical advance in fabric detergents in fifteen years. According to Unilever, Omo Power contained a powerful cleansing agent that washed clothes cleaner than any other product on the market. Consumers seemed to agree; sales of Omo Power surged in every country in which it was introduced during the first few months of 1994. P&G was alarmed by this development. The introduction of Omo Power seemed to violate a tacit understanding between the two companies that they would share technical information with each other. Moreover, Unilever was gaining market share at P&G's expense for the first time in two decades.

P&G's initial response was to try and discover what the secret ingredient in Omo Power might be. After extensive lab studies, P&G discovered that Unilever had used crystals of manganese. This surprised P&G, for although manganese could speed the bleaching process, it knew from its own research that manganese attacked fabrics, which was why P&G had abandoned work on manganese ten years previously. After submitting Omo Power to its own tests, P&G found that clothes washed repeatedly in the powder did indeed develop holes. Armed with this information, P&G decided to go on the counterattack. Top executives from P&G visited top management at Unilever and stated bluntly that Omo Power was fundamentally flawed and should be pulled off the market. Unilever executives chose to discount this private warning. After two years of market testing with no complaints from consumers, Unilever saw no need to withdraw the product and believed P&G was overstating the problem because it was losing market share. It was at this point that P&G broke with the industry's tradition of not criticizing the products of competitors. P&G went public with the problem, launching a ruthless public relations campaign pointing to the flaws of Omo Power. P&G gave the press a set of color pictures showing clothes purportedly suffering the ill effects of Omo Power, including shots of some tattered boxer shorts that were duly reproduced by the press all over Europe.

Unilever initially tried to dismiss P&G's claims, but a growing number of independent research institutes backed up P&G's findings. After several months of increasingly bitter public recriminations between the two companies, Unilever was eventually forced to concede that there was a problem. Unilever repositioned Omo Power in the marketplace from a product with broad applicability to a niche product for use with white fabrics and low water temperatures (conditions that minimized the damage problems).

In the end, Unilever was forced to admit that its $300 million investment in Omo had been a washout. By the end of 1994, Unilever's market share had fallen back to the level the company had attained prior to the launch of Omo Power. Moreover, executives from both companies admitted that the rules of the game in the industry had changed as a result of the dispute. Gone forever was the cozy agreement of sharing technical information and forbearing from directly attacking the products of a competitor. Nonprice competition in the industry would now be much more difficult than before. P&G fully expected Unilever to try and get its revenge by attacking any new product launch that it might try.[7]

entries into the market, led to an imbalance between demand and supply and an extraordinary profit boom for incumbent companies.

Conversely, declining demand results in more rivalry as companies fight to maintain revenues and market share. Demand declines when consumers leave the marketplace or when each consumer buys less. Under these conditions a company can grow only by taking market share away from other companies. Thus, declining demand constitutes a major threat, for it increases the extent of rivalry between established companies. Moreover, as we saw in the Opening Case, a slowdown in the rate of growth of demand can also create problems. The prices for DRAMs plunged between late 1995 and early 1996, not because demand was declining, but because the *rate of growth* in demand had slowed, while new production capacity had come on stream. The result was that supply was growing faster than demand, reversing the trend that had been in place since 1991. As a result, prices and profits plunged.

Exit Barriers   Exit barriers are economic, strategic, and emotional factors that keep companies in an industry even when returns are low. If exit barriers are high, companies can become locked into an unprofitable industry in which overall demand is static or declining. Excess productive capacity can result. In turn, excess capacity tends to lead to intensified price competition, with companies cutting prices in an attempt to obtain the orders needed to utilize their idle capacity.[8] Common exit barriers include the following:

1. Investments in plant and equipment that have no alternative uses and cannot be sold off. If the company wishes to leave the industry, it has to write off the book value of these assets.

2. High fixed costs of exit, such as severance pay to workers who are being made redundant.

3. Emotional attachments to an industry, as when a company is unwilling to exit from its original industry for sentimental reasons.

4. Economic dependence on the industry, as when a company is not diversified and so relies on the industry for its income.

The experience of the steel industry illustrates the adverse competitive effects of high exit barriers.[9] A combination of declining demand and new low-cost sources of supply created overcapacity in the global steel industry during the late 1980s. U.S. companies, with their high-cost structure, were on the sharp end of this decline. Demand for U.S. steel fell from a 1977 peak of 160 million tons to 70 million tons in 1986. The outcome was excess capacity amounting to an estimated 45 million tons in 1987, or 40 percent of total productive capacity. In order to try to utilize this capacity, many steel companies slashed their prices. As a consequence of the resulting price war, industry profits were low and several of the majors, including LTV Steel and Bethlehem Steel, faced bankruptcy.

Since the steel industry was characterized by excess capacity for most of the 1980s, why did companies not reduce their capacity? The answer is that many tried to, but the costs of exit slowed this process and prolonged the associated price war. For example, in 1983 USX shut down 16 percent of its raw steel-making capacity at a cost of $1.2 billion. USX had to write off the book value of these assets; they could not be sold. In addition, it had to cover pensions and insurance for 15,400 terminated workers. Given such high exit costs, companies such as USX have remained locked into this unprofitable industry. The effect of impeded exit has been more intense price competition than might otherwise be the case. Thus, high exit barriers, by slowing the speed with which companies leave the industry, threaten the profitability of all companies within the steel industry.

The Bargaining Power of Buyers

The third of Porter's five competitive forces is the bargaining power of buyers. A company's buyers may be the customers who ultimately consume its products (its end users), but they may also be the companies that distribute its products to end users, such as retailers and wholesalers. For example, while Unilever sells its detergent to end users, the major buyers of its products are supermarket chains, who then resell the product to the end users. Buyers can be viewed as a competitive threat when they are in a position to demand lower prices from the company or when they demand better service (which can increase operating costs). On the other hand, when buyers are weak, a company can raise its prices and earn greater profits. Whether buyers are able to make demands on a company depends on their power relative to that of the company. According to Porter, buyers are most powerful in the following circumstances:

1. When the supply industry is composed of many small companies and the buyers are few in number and large. These circumstances allow the buyers to dominate supply companies.

2. When the buyers purchase in large quantities. In such circumstances, buyers can use their purchasing power as leverage to bargain for price reductions.

3. When the supply industry depends on the buyers for a large percentage of its total orders.

4. When the buyers can switch orders between supply companies at a low cost, thereby playing off companies against each other to force down prices.

5. When it is economically feasible for the buyers to purchase the input from several companies at once.

6. When the buyers can use the threat to supply their own needs through vertical integration as a device for forcing down prices.

An example of an industry whose buyers are powerful is the auto component supply industry. The buyers here are the large automobile companies, such as General Motors, Ford, and Chrysler. The suppliers of auto components are numerous and typically small in scale. Their buyers, the auto manufacturers, are large in size and few in number. Chrysler, for example, does business with nearly 2,000 different component suppliers and normally contracts with a number of different companies to supply the same part. The auto majors have used their powerful position to play off suppliers against each other, forcing down the price they have to pay for component parts and demanding better quality. If a component supplier objects, then the auto major uses the threat of switching to another supplier as a bargaining tool. Additionally, to keep component prices down, both Ford and General Motors have used the threat of manufacturing a component themselves rather than buying it from auto component suppliers.

Another issue is that the relative power of buyers and suppliers tends to change over time in response to changing industry conditions. For example, due to changes now taking place in the pharmaceutical and health care industries, major buyers of pharmaceuticals (hospitals and health maintenance organizations) are now gaining power over the suppliers of pharmaceuticals and have been able to demand lower prices. The reasons for this change in relative power are explored in Strategy in Action 3.3.

The Bargaining Power of Suppliers

The fourth of Porter's competitive forces is the bargaining power of suppliers. Suppliers can be viewed as a threat when they are able to force up the price that a company must pay for its inputs or reduce the quality of the inputs they supply, thereby depressing the company's profitability. On the other hand, if suppliers are weak, this gives a company the opportunity to force down prices and demand higher input quality. As with buyers, the ability of suppliers to make demands on a company depends on their power relative to that of the company. According to Porter, suppliers are most powerful:

1. When the product that they sell has few substitutes and is important to the company.

2. When the company's industry is not an important customer of theirs. In such instances, the suppliers' health does not depend on the company's industry, and suppliers have little incentive to reduce prices or improve quality.

3. When their respective products are differentiated to such an extent that it is costly for a company to switch from one supplier to another. In such cases, the company depends on its suppliers and cannot play them off against each other.

4. When, to raise prices, they can use the threat of vertically integrating forward into the industry and competing directly with the company.

5. When buying companies cannot use the threat of vertically integrating backward and supplying their own needs as a means to reduce input prices.

Manufacturers of personal computers provide us with an example of an industry that is dependent upon a very powerful supplier. In this case the supplier is Intel, the world's largest manufacturer of microprocessors for personal computers (PCs). The industry standard for personal computers runs on Intel's X86 microprocessor family, such as the Pentium and Pentium Pro microprocessors currently sold in most PCs. So PC manufacturers have little choice but to use an Intel microprocessor as the brains for their machines. Although several companies have tried to produce clones of Intel's microprocessors, their success has been limited, leaving Intel with about 85 percent of the market. This puts Intel in a very powerful position with regard to the PC manufacturers. Because the product it supplies has few substitutes and because switching costs facing the buyers are high, Intel can raise prices above the level that would prevail in a more competitive supply market.[10]

3.3   **STRATEGY** *in* **ACTION**

Changing Buyer-Supplier Relationships in Health Care

For decades pharmaceutical companies, as major suppliers of critical health care products, have been in a powerful position in the health care industry. Pharmaceutical companies spend hundreds of millions of dollars annually to develop new drugs. Although this is a risky process with a low probability of success, the companies that do develop new drugs with important medical applications have historically been in a powerful position. Companies can patent new drugs, which prohibits competitors from producing and marketing products based on the same chemical compound for a seventeen-year period. Protected by patents, pharmaceutical companies have been able to charge very high prices. Since the prescribers of drugs, doctors, do not pay for the drug, they have had no reason to concern themselves with prices. Instead they have been more concerned with medical benefits to patients. As for the patients themselves, since their insurance companies often end up paying for prescription drugs, they, too, have not had a strong incentive to focus on prices. As a result, prices in the pharmaceutical industry have risen rapidly. During the 1980s and early 1990s, drug prices in the United States rose at two to three times the annual inflation rate. In 1992 they rose at an annual rate of 5.7 percent, much faster than the 2.9 percent inflation rate.

There are signs that this situation is changing. Increasingly, powerful buyers are beginning to limit the ability of pharmaceutical companies to raises drug prices. Two factors are at work. The first is the rise of health maintenance organizations (HMOs). HMOs were started in an attempt to control health care costs. Subscribers to HMOs sacrifice freedom of choice in selecting a health care provider for lower insurance costs. HMOs have proved attractive to companies that find it is often cheaper to provide employees with health care

coverage through HMOs than through conventional health insurance. In their attempt to control costs, HMOs negotiate directly with pharmaceutical companies on behalf of all their doctors for attractive prices on key drugs. The larger purchasing power of HMOs has made them powerful buyers. One result has been a marked slowdown in the rate of increase in drug prices.

A second factor slowing down the rise in drug prices is that drug companies are starting to introduce "me-too" drugs to compete with the patented drugs of competitors. Me-too drugs are those that are chemically different from the pioneer's product and, therefore, not covered by a patent but offer similar medical benefits. For example, three companies are now marketing very similar antidepressant drugs: SmithKline Beecham with Paxil, Eli Lilly with Prozac (the pioneer among the three); and Pfizer with Zoloft. The shift to me-too drugs is occurring because pharmaceutical companies have made so many major medical breakthroughs during the last few decades that there are very few therapeutic areas for which there are not already some existing drugs. So in order to maintain their historic growth rates, drug companies are increasingly looking to me-too drugs.

From an HMO's perspective, the recent emergence of me-too drugs suddenly gives them a choice. Thus, for example, if Eli Lilly refuses to reduce the price for Prozac, an HMO can always threaten to use a substitute such as Paxil. The fact that HMOs now have a choice combined with the fact that the pharmaceutical companies are apparently willing to engage in price discounting is beginning to change the power relationship in the health care industry. If the trend continues, the end result is likely to be not only more intense competition and lower drug prices and profits in the pharmaceutical industry but also lower costs for HMOs.[11]

The Threat of Substitute Products

The final force in Porter's model is the threat of substitute products. Substitute products are those of industries that serve consumers' needs in a way that is similar to those being served by the industry being analyzed. For example, companies in the coffee industry compete indirectly with those in the tea and soft drink industries. All three industries serve consumers' need for drinks. The prices that companies in the coffee industry can charge are limited by the existence of substitutes such as tea and soft drinks. If the price of coffee rises too much relative to that of tea or soft drinks, coffee drinkers will switch from coffee to those substitutes. This phenomenon occurred when unusually cold weather destroyed much of the Brazilian coffee crop in 1975–1976. The price of coffee rose to record highs, reflecting the shortage, and consumers began to switch to tea in large numbers.

The existence of close substitutes presents a strong competitive threat, limiting the price a company can charge and thus its profitability. However, if a company's products have few close substitutes (that is, if substitutes are a weak competitive force), then, other things being equal, the company has the opportunity to raise prices and earn additional profits. Consequently, its strategies should be designed to take advantage of this fact.

The Role of the Macroenvironment

So far we have treated industries as self-contained entities. In practice they are embedded in a wider **macroenvironment**—the broader economic, technological, social, demographic, and political environment (see Figure 3.3). Changes in the macroenvironment can have a direct impact on any one of the five forces in Porter's model, thereby altering the relative strength of these forces and, with it, the attractiveness of an industry. We briefly consider the impact that each aspect of these macroenvironmental forces can have on an industry's competitive structure.

The Macroeconomic Environment   The state of the macroeconomic environment determines the general health and well-being of the economy. This in turn affects a company's ability to earn an adequate rate of return. The four most impor-

FIGURE 3.3

The Role of the Macroenvironment

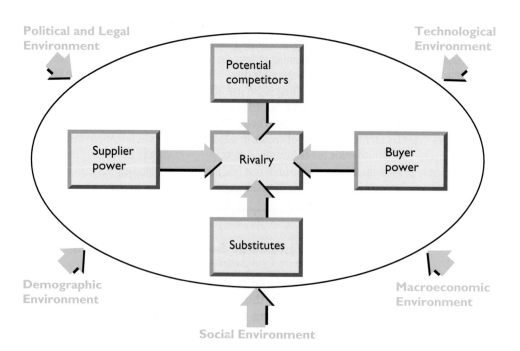

tant factors in the macroeconomy are the growth rate of the economy, interest rates, currency exchange rates, and inflation rates.

Because it leads to an expansion in expenditures by consumers, economic growth tends to produce a general easing of competitive pressures within an industry. This gives companies the opportunity to expand their operations and earn higher profits. Because economic decline leads to a reduction in expenditures by consumers, it increases competitive pressures. Economic decline frequently causes price wars in mature industries.

The level of interest rates can determine the level of demand for a company's products. Interest rates are important whenever consumers routinely borrow money to finance their purchase of these products. The most obvious example is the housing market, in which the mortgage rate directly affects demand, but interest rates also have an impact on the sale of autos, appliances, and capital equipment, to give just a few examples. For companies in such industries, rising interest rates are a threat and falling rates an opportunity.

Currency exchange rates define the value of different national currencies against each other. Movement in currency exchange rates has a direct impact on the competitiveness of a company's products in the global marketplace. For example, when the value of the dollar is low compared with that of other currencies, products made in the United States are relatively inexpensive and products made overseas are relatively expensive. A low or declining dollar reduces the threat from foreign competitors while it creates opportunities for increased sales overseas. For example, the fall in the value of the dollar against the Japanese yen that occurred between 1985 and 1995, when the dollar/yen exchange rate declined from $1 = ¥240 to $1 = ¥85, sharply increased the price of imported Japanese cars, giving U.S. car manufacturers some degree of protection against the Japanese threat.

Inflation can destabilize the economy, producing slower economic growth, higher interest rates, and volatile currency movements. If inflation keeps increasing, investment planning becomes hazardous. The key characteristic of inflation is that it makes the future less predictable. In an inflationary environment, it may be impossible to predict with any accuracy the real value of returns that can be earned from a project five years hence. Such uncertainty makes companies less willing to invest. Their holding back in turn depresses economic activity and ultimately pushes the economy into a slump. Thus, high inflation is a threat to companies.

The Technological Environment   Since World War II, the pace of technological change has accelerated.[12] This has unleashed a process that has been called a "perennial gale of creative destruction."[13] Technological change can make established products obsolete overnight, and at the same time it can create a host of new product possibilities. Thus, technological change is both creative and destructive, both an opportunity and a threat.

One of the most important impacts of technological change is that it can affect the height of barriers to entry and, as a result, radically reshape the structure of an industry. For example, the computer industry of the 1970s was dominated by IBM and a handful of other producers, such as Digital Equipment Corp. (DEC) and Hewlett Packard. However, the invention of the microprocessor in 1971 ultimately led to the birth of the personal computer industry and unleashed a powerful competitive dynamic that is still reshaping the industry. The relatively low cost of the microprocessor allowed small companies with limited capital resources to enter the computer industry and manufacture PCs and computer workstations. Thus, the innovation of the microprocessor lowered barriers to entry in the computer industry and allowed companies such as Intel, Microsoft, Compaq Computer, Dell Computer, and Sun Microsystems to become major players, while old-line companies such as IBM and DEC essentially had to remake themselves in order to survive.

The Social Environment   As with technological change, social change creates opportunities and threats. One of the major social movements of the 1970s and 1980s was the trend toward greater health consciousness. Its impact has been immense, and companies that recognized the opportunities early have often reaped significant gains. Philip Morris, for example, capitalized on the growing trend toward health consciousness when it acquired Miller Brewing and then redefined competition in the beer industry with its introduction of low-calorie beer (Miller Lite). Similarly, Pepsico was able to gain market share from its rival, Coca-Cola, by introducing diet colas and fruit-based soft drinks first. At the same time the health trend has created a threat for many industries. The tobacco industry, for example, is now in decline as a direct result of greater consumer awareness of the health implications of smoking. Similarly, the sugar industry has seen sales decrease as consumers have decided to switch to artificial sweeteners.

The Demographic Environment   The changing composition of the population is another factor in the macroenvironment that can create both opportunities and threats. For example, as the baby-boom generation of the 1960s has aged, it has created a host of opportunities and threats. During the 1980s, many baby boomers were getting married and creating an upsurge in demand for the consumer appliances normally bought by couples marrying for the first time. Companies such as Whirlpool and General Electric capitalized on the resulting upsurge in demand for washing machines, dryers, dishwashers, and the like. The other side of the coin is that industries oriented toward the young, such as the toy industry, have seen their consumer base decline in recent years.

The Political and Legal Environment   Political and legal factors also have a major effect on the level of opportunities and threats in the environment. One of the most significant trends in recent years has been the move toward deregulation. As we noted earlier, by eliminating many legal restrictions, deregulation has lowered barriers to entry and led to intense competition in a number of industries. The deregulation of the airline industry in 1979, for example, created the opportunity to establish low-fare carriers—an opportunity that Southwest Airlines, Value Jet, and others tried to capitalize on. At the same time, the increased intensity of competition created many threats, including, most notably, the threat of prolonged fare wars, which have repeatedly thrown the airline industry into turmoil during the last decade. The United States telecommunications industry is now beginning to experience the same kind of turmoil following the deregulation of that industry in 1996.

For the future, fears about the destruction of the ozone layer, acid rain, and global warming may be near the top of the political agenda. Given these concerns, governments seem increasingly likely to enact tough environmental regulations to limit air pollution. Rather than resist this trend, companies should try to take advantage of it. For example, back in 1974, when ozone depletion was still a theory, E.I. du Pont de Nemours decided to start research into substitutes for ozone-damaging chlorofluorocarbons (CFCs), widely used in aerosols, air conditioners, and refrigeration equipment. At the same time, Du Pont made a pledge to phase out production of CFCs if they were shown to be a threat to public health. In March 1988, in response to data released by the National Aeronautics and Space Administration (NASA), Du Pont honored that commitment and promised to phase out production of CFCs within ten years. Although Du Pont stands to lose the $600 million per year that it was earning from the sale of products using CFCs, since the mid 1970s the company's research has yielded three viable alternatives, each of which is now produced commercially. Thus, by anticipating regulations and undertaking appropriate action, Du Pont has positioned itself well to take a large share of the market for CFC substitutes when the use of CFCs is phased out in the late 1990s.

STRATEGIC GROUPS WITHIN INDUSTRIES

The Concept of Strategic Groups

So far we have said little about how companies in an industry might differ from each other and what implications these differences might have for the opportunities and threats that they face. In practice, companies in an industry often differ from each other with respect to factors such as the distribution channels they use, the market segments they serve, the quality of their products, technological leadership, customer service, pricing policy, advertising policy, and promotions. As a result of these differences within most industries, it is possible to observe groups of companies in which each member follows the same basic strategy as other companies in the group but follows a *different* strategy than that of companies in other groups. These groups of companies are known as **strategic groups.**[14]

Normally, a limited number of groups captures the essence of strategic differences between companies within an industry. For example, in the pharmaceutical industry two main strategic groups stand out (see Figure 3.4).[15] One group, which includes such companies as Merck, Pfizer, and Eli Lilly, is characterized by heavy R&D spending and a focus on developing new proprietary blockbuster drugs. The companies in this *proprietary group* are pursuing a high-risk/high-return strategy. It is a high-risk strategy because basic drug research is difficult and expensive. Bringing a new drug to market can cost $100 million to $200 million in R&D money and a decade of research and clinical trials. The strategy is also a high-return one because a single successful drug can be patented, giving the innovator a seventeen-year monopoly on its production and sale. This lets the innovator charge a very high price for the patented drug, allowing the company to earn millions, if not billions, of dollars over the lifetime of the patent. (For example, in 1992 Glaxo earned $3.44 billion in revenues from a single drug—the antidepressant Zantal).

The second strategic group might be characterized as the *generic group.* This group of companies, which includes Marion Labs, Carter Wallace, and ICN Pharmaceuticals, focuses on the manufacture of generic drugs—low-cost copies of drugs pioneered by companies in the proprietary group whose patents have now expired. The companies in this group are characterized by low R&D spending and an emphasis on price competition. They are pursuing a low-risk, low-return strategy. It

FIGURE 3.4
· · · · · · · · · · ·
Strategic Groups in the
Pharmaceutical Industry

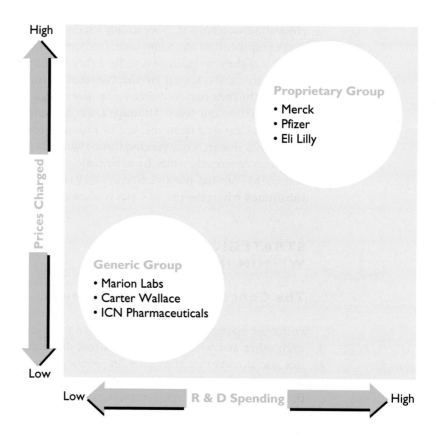

is low risk because they are not investing millions of dollars in R&D. It is low return because they do not charge high prices.

Implications of Strategic Groups
· ·

The concept of strategic groups has a number of implications for the identification of opportunities and threats within an industry. First, a company's closest competitors are those in its strategic group, not those in other strategic groups. Since all the companies in a strategic group pursue similar strategies, consumers tend to view the products of such enterprises as direct substitutes for each other. Thus, a major threat to a company's profitability can come from within its own strategic group.

Second, different strategic groups can have a different standing with respect to each of Porter's five competitive forces. In other words, the risk of new entry by potential competitors, the degree of rivalry among companies within a group, the bargaining power of buyers, the bargaining power of suppliers, and the threat of substitute products can all vary in intensity among different strategic groups within the same industry.

For example, in the pharmaceutical industry, companies in the proprietary group have historically been in a very powerful position vis-à-vis buyers because their products are patented. Besides, rivalry within this group has been limited to competition to be the first to patent a new drug (so-called patent races). Price competition has been rare, although, as indicated in Strategy in Action 3.3, there are signs that this might be changing. Without price competition, companies in this group have been able to charge high prices and earn very high profits. In contrast, companies in the generic group have been in a much weaker position vis-à-vis buyers since they lack patents for their products and since buyers can choose among very similar competing generic drugs. Moreover, price competition among the companies in this group has been quite intense, reflecting the lack of product differentiation. The result is that companies within this group have earned somewhat lower returns than companies in the proprietary group.

It follows that some strategic groups are more desirable than others, for they have a lower level of threats and greater opportunities. Managers must evaluate whether their company would be better off competing in a different strategic group. If the environment of another strategic group is more benign, then moving into that group can be regarded as an opportunity. Yet this opportunity is rarely without costs, mainly because of mobility barriers between groups. **Mobility barriers** are factors that inhibit the movement of companies between groups in an industry. They include both the barriers to entry into a group and the barriers to exit from a company's existing group. For example, Marion Labs would encounter mobility barriers if it attempted to enter the proprietary group in the pharmaceutical industry. These mobility barriers would arise from the fact that Marion lacks the R&D skills possessed by companies in the proprietary group and building these skills would be an expensive proposition. Thus, a company contemplating entry into another strategic group must evaluate the height of mobility barriers before deciding whether the move is worthwhile.

Mobility barriers also imply that companies within a given group may be protected to a greater or lesser extent from the threat of entry by companies based in other strategic groups. If mobility barriers are low, the threat of entry from companies in other groups may be high, effectively limiting the prices companies can charge and the profits they can earn without attracting new competition. If mobility barriers are high, however, the threat of entry is low, and companies within the protected group have an opportunity to raise prices and earn higher returns without attracting entry.

LIMITATIONS OF THE FIVE FORCES AND STRATEGIC GROUP MODELS

The five forces and strategic group models provide useful ways of thinking about and analyzing the nature of competition within an industry to identify opportunities and threats. However, managers need to be aware of their shortcomings. Both models (1) present a static picture of competition that slights the role of innovation and (2) de-emphasizing the significance of individual company differences while overemphasizing the importance of industry and strategic group structure as determinants of company profit rates.

Innovation and an Industry's Structure

Over any reasonable length of time, competition in many industries can be viewed as a process driven by innovation.[16] Companies that pioneer new products, processes, or strategies can often earn enormous profits. This prospect gives companies a strong incentive to seek innovative products, processes, and strategies.

Consider, for example, the explosive growth of Apple Computer, Dell Computer, Toys 'R' Us, and Wal-Mart. In one way or another, all these companies were innovators. Apple pioneered the personal computer, Dell pioneered a whole new way of selling personal computers (by mail order), Toys 'R' Us pioneered a new way of selling toys (through large discount warehouse-type stores), and Wal-Mart pioneered the low-price discount superstore concept.

Successful innovation can revolutionize an industry's structure. In recent decades one of the most common consequences of innovation has been to lower the fixed costs of production, thereby reducing barriers to entry and allowing new and smaller enterprises to compete with large established organizations. Consider the steel industry as an example. Two decades ago the industry was populated by large, integrated steel companies such as U.S. Steel, LTV Steel, and Bethlehem Steel. The industry was a typical oligopoly, dominated by a small number of large producers, in which tacit price collusion was practiced. Then along came a series of efficient minimill producers such as Nucor and Chaparral Steel, which utilized a new technology—electric arc furnaces. Over the last twenty years, they have revolutionized the structure of the industry. What was once a consolidated industry is now much more fragmented and price competitive. The successor company to US Steel, USX, now has only a 15 percent market share, down from 55 percent in the mid 1960s, and both Bethlehem and LTV have been through Chapter 11 bankruptcy proceedings. In contrast, as a group the minimills now hold more than 30 percent of the market, up from 5 percent twenty years ago. Thus, the minimill innovation has reshaped the nature of competition in the steel industry.[17] A five forces model applied to the industry in 1970 would look very different from a five forces model applied in 1997.

In his most recent work, Michael Porter, the originator of the five forces and strategic group concepts, has explicitly recognized the role of innovation in revolutionizing an industry's structure. Porter now talks of innovations as "unfreezing" and "reshaping" an industry's structure. Porter argues that after a period of turbulence triggered by innovation, the structure of an industry once more settles down into a fairly stable pattern. Once the industry stabilizes in its new configuration, the five forces and strategic group concepts can once more be applied.[18] This view of the evolution of industry structure is often referred to as *punctuated equilibrium.*[19] The punctuated equilibrium view holds that long periods of equilibrium, when an industry's structure is stable, are punctuated by periods of rapid change, when an industry's structure is revolutionized by innovation; there is an unfreezing and reshaping process.

Figure 3.5 shows what punctuated equilibrium might look like for one key dimension of industry structure—competitive structure. From time t_0 to t_1, the competitive structure of the industry is a stable oligopoly, with a few companies sharing the market. At time t_1 a major new innovation is pioneered by either an existing company or a new entrant. The result is a period of turbulence between t_1 and t_2. After a while, however, the industry settles down into a new state of equilibrium, but now the competitive structure is far more fragmented. Note that the opposite could have happened. The industry could have become more consolidated, although this seems to be less common. In general, innovations seem to lower barriers to entry; allow more companies into the industry; and, as a result, lead to fragmentation rather than consolidation.

FIGURE 3.5

Punctuated Equilibrium
and Competitive
Structure

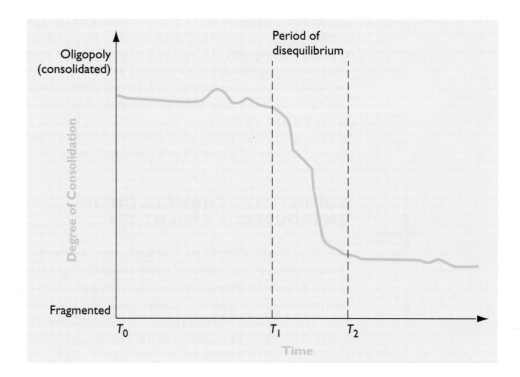

Because the five forces and strategic group models are static, they cannot adequately capture what occurs during periods of rapid change in the environment of an industry, but they are certainly useful tools for analyzing an industry's structure during periods of stability. However, some scholars question the validity of the punctuated equilibrium approach. For example, Richard D'Avani has argued that many industries are **hypercompetitive**.[20] Hypercompetitive industries are characterized by permanent and ongoing innovation. The computer industry is often cited as an example of a hypercompetitive industry. The structure of such industries is constantly being revolutionized by innovation; there are no periods of equilibrium. When this is the case, some might argue that the five forces and strategic group models are of limited value since they represent no more than snapshots of a moving picture.

An Industry's Structure and Company Differences

The second criticism of the five force and strategic group models is that they overemphasize the importance of an industry's structure as a determinant of company performance and underemphasize the importance of differences between companies within an industry or strategic group.[21] As we point out in the next chapter, there can be enormous variance in the profit rates of individual companies within an industry. Recent research by Richard Rumelt, for example, suggests that an industry's structure explains only about 10 percent of the variance in profit rates across companies, the implication being that individual company differences explain much of the remainder.[22] Other studies have put the explained variance closer to 20 percent, which is still not a large figure.[23] Similarly, a growing number of studies has found only very weak evidence of a link between strategic group membership and company profit rates, despite the fact that the strategic group model predicts a strong link.[24] Collectively, these studies suggest that the individual resources and capabilities of a company are far more important determinants of its profitability than is the industry or strategic group of which the company is a member. Although these findings do not make the five forces and strategic group models irrelevant, they do mean that the models have limited usefulness. A company will not be profitable just because it is based in an attractive industry or strategic group. As we discuss in Chapters 4 and 5, more is required.

COMPETITIVE CHANGES DURING AN INDUSTRY'S EVOLUTION

Over time most industries pass through a series of well-defined stages, from growth through maturity and eventually into decline. These stages have different implications for the form of competition. The strength and nature of each of Porter's five competitive forces typically changes as an industry evolves.[25] This is particularly true regarding potential competitors and rivalry, and we focus on these two forces in our discussion. The changes in the strength and nature of these forces give rise to different opportunities and threats at each stage of an industry's evolution. The task facing managers is to *anticipate* how the strength of each force will change with the stage of an industry's development and to formulate strategies that take advantage of opportunities as they arise and that counter emerging threats.

The **industry life cycle model** is a useful tool for analyzing the effects of an industry's evolution on competitive forces. Using the industry life cycle model, we can identify five industry environments, each linked to a distinct stage of an industry's evolution: (1) an embryonic industry environment, (2) a growth industry environment, (3) a shakeout industry environment, (4) a mature industry environment, and (5) a declining industry environment (see Figure 3.6).

FIGURE 3.6

Stages of the Industry Life Cycle

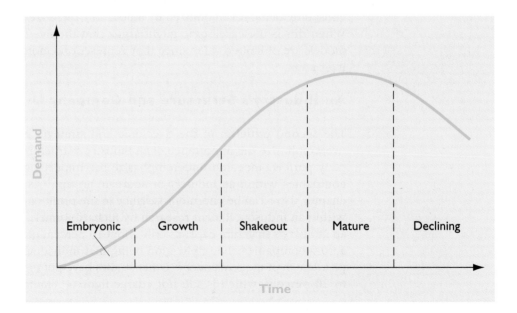

Embryonic Industry Environment

An *embryonic* industry is one that is just beginning to develop (for example, personal computers in 1980). Growth at this stage is slow because of such factors as buyers' unfamiliarity with the industry's product, high prices due to the inability of companies to reap any significant economies of scale, and poorly developed distribution channels. Barriers to entry at this stage in an industry's evolution tend to be based on access to key technological know-how rather than cost economies or brand loyalty. If the core know-how required to compete in the industry is complex and difficult to grasp, barriers to entry can be quite high and incumbent companies will be protected from potential competitors. Rivalry in embryonic industries is based not so much on price as upon educating customers, opening up distribution channels, and perfecting the design of the product. Such rivalry can be intense, and the company that is the first to solve design problems often has the opportunity to develop a significant market position. An embryonic industry may also be the creation of one company's innovative efforts, as happened with personal computers (Apple), vacuum cleaners (Hoover), and photocopiers (Xerox). In such circumstances, the company has a major opportunity to capitalize on the lack of rivalry and build a strong hold on the market.

Growth Industry Environment

Once demand for the industry's product begins to take off, the industry develops the characteristics of a growth industry. In a *growth* industry first-time demand expands rapidly as many new consumers enter the market. Typically, an industry grows when consumers become familiar with the product, when prices fall because experience and economies of scale have been attained, and when distribution channels develop. The U.S. cellular telephone industry was in the growth stage for most of the first half of the 1990s. In 1990 there were only 5 million cellular subscribers in the nation. By 1995, however, this figure had increased to 40 million, and overall demand was still growing at a rate in excess of 25 percent per year.

Normally, the importance of control over technological knowledge as a barrier to entry has diminished by the time an industry enters its growth stage. Because few companies have yet achieved significant economies of scale or differentiated their product sufficiently to guarantee brand loyalty, other barriers to entry tend to be low as well. Thus, the threat from potential competitors generally is highest at this point. Paradoxically, however, high growth usually means that new entrants can be absorbed into an industry without a marked increase in competitive pressure.

During an industry's growth stage, rivalry tends to be low. Rapid growth in demand enables companies to expand their revenues and profits without taking market share away from competitors. A company has the opportunity to expand its operations. In addition, a strategically aware company takes advantage of the relatively benign environment of the growth stage to prepare itself for the intense competition of the coming shakeout industry environment.

Shakeout Industry Environment

Explosive growth of the type experienced by the cellular telephone or personal computer industry in the first half of the 1990s cannot be maintained indefinitely.

Sooner or later the rate of growth slows, and the industry enters the shakeout stage. In a *shakeout* industry, demand approaches the saturation level. In a saturated market, there are few potential first-time buyers left. Most of the demand is limited to replacement demand.

As an industry enters the shakeout stage, rivalry between companies becomes intense. What typically happens is that companies that have become accustomed to rapid growth during an industry's growth phase continue to add capacity at rates consistent with past growth. Managers use historic growth rates to forecast future growth rates, and they plan expansions in productive capacity accordingly. As an industry approaches maturity, however, demand no longer grows at historic rates. The consequence is the emergence of excess productive capacity. This condition is illustrated in Figure 3.7, in which the solid curve indicates the growth in demand over time and the broken curve indicates the growth in productive capacity over time. As you can see, past point t_1 demand growth slows as the industry becomes mature. However, capacity continues to grow until time t_2. The gap between the solid and the broken lines signifies excess capacity. In an attempt to utilize this capacity, companies often cut prices. The result can be a price war, which drives many of the most inefficient companies into bankruptcy. This is itself enough to deter any new entry.

Mature Industry Environment

The shakeout stage ends when the industry enters its mature stage. In a *mature* industry the market is totally saturated and demand is limited to replacement demand. During this stage, growth is low or zero. What little growth there is comes from population expansion bringing new consumers into the market.

As an industry enters maturity, barriers to entry increase and the threat of entry from potential competitors decreases. As growth slows during the shakeout stage, companies can no longer maintain historic growth rates merely by holding on to their market share. Competition for market share develops, driving down prices. Often the result is a price war, as happened in the airline industry during

FIGURE 3.7

Growth in Demand
and Capacity

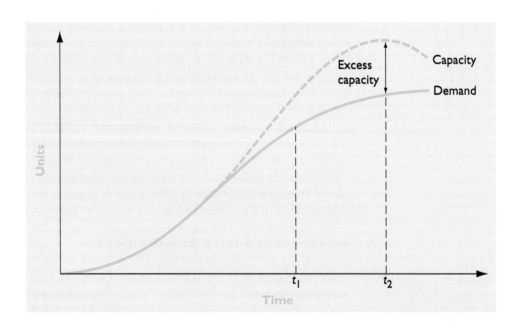

the 1988–1992 shakeout. To survive the shakeout, companies begin to focus both on cost minimization and on building brand loyalty. The airlines, for example, tried to cut operating costs by hiring nonunion labor and to build brand loyalty by introducing frequent-flyer programs. By the time an industry matures, the surviving companies are those that have brand loyalty and low-cost operations. Because both these factors constitute a significant barrier to entry, the threat of entry by potential competitors is greatly diminished. High barriers to entry in mature industries give companies the opportunity to increase prices and profits.

As a result of the shakeout, most industries in the mature stage have consolidated and become oligopolies. In the airline industry, for example, because of the shakeout, the top five companies controlled 80 percent of the industry in 1995, up from only 50 percent in 1984. In mature industries, companies tend to recognize their interdependence and try to avoid price wars. Stable demand gives them the opportunity to enter into price-leadership agreements. The net effect is to reduce the threat of intense rivalry among established companies, thereby allowing greater profitability. However, as noted earlier, the stability of a mature industry is always threatened by further price wars. A general slump in economic activity can depress demand within an industry. As companies fight to maintain their revenues in the face of declining demand, price-leadership agreements break down, rivalry increases, and prices and profits fall. The periodic price wars that occur in the airline industry seem to follow this pattern.

Declining Industry Environment

Eventually, most industries enter a decline stage. In a *declining* industry growth becomes negative for a variety of reasons, including technological substitution (for example, air travel for rail travel), social changes (for example, greater health consciousness hitting tobacco sales), demographics (for example, the declining birthrate hurting the market for baby and child products), and international competition (for example, low-cost foreign competition pushing the U.S. steel industry into decline). Within a declining industry, the degree of rivalry among established companies usually increases. Depending on the speed of the decline and the height of exit barriers, competitive pressures can become as fierce as in the shakeout stage.[26] The main problem in a declining industry is that falling demand leads to the emergence of excess capacity. In trying to utilize this capacity, companies begin to cut prices, thus sparking a price war. As noted earlier, the U.S. steel industry experienced these problems because of the attempt of steel companies to utilize their excess capacity. The same problem occurred in the airline industry in the 1990–1992 period, as companies cut prices to ensure that they would not be flying with half-empty planes (that is, that they would not be operating with substantial excess capacity). Exit barriers play a part in adjusting excess capacity. The greater the exit barriers, the harder it is for companies to reduce capacity and the greater is the threat of severe price competition.

Variations on the Theme

It is important to remember that the industry life cycle model is a generalization. In practice, industry life cycles do not always follow the pattern illustrated in Figure 3.6. In some cases, growth is so rapid that the embryonic stage is very short, as happened in the personal computer industry. In other instances, industries fail to get past the embryonic stage. Industry growth can be revitalized after long periods of decline, either through innovations or through social changes. For example, the health boom brought the bicycle industry back to life after a long period of decline. The time span of the different stages can also vary significantly from industry to industry. Some industries can stay in maturity almost indefinitely if their products become basic necessities of life, as is the case for the automobile industry. Others skip the mature stage and go straight into decline. That is essentially what occurred in the vacuum tube industry. Vacuum tubes were replaced by transistors as a major component in electronic products while the industry was still in its growth stage. Still other industries may go through not one but several shakeouts before they enter full maturity. The Opening Case suggests that this may be occurring in the semiconductor industry.

GLOBALIZATION AND INDUSTRY STRUCTURE

A fundamental change is occurring in the world economy.[27] We seem to be witnessing the globalization of production and of markets. With regard to the **globalization of production,** it has been observed that individual companies are increasingly dispersing parts of their production process to different locations around the globe to take advantage of national differences in the cost and quality of factors of production, such as labor, energy, land, and capital. The objective is to lower costs and boost profits.

For example, Boeing's new commercial jet aircraft, the 777, involves 132,500 engineered parts that are produced around the world by 545 different suppliers. Eight Japanese suppliers make parts of the fuselage, doors, and wings; a supplier in Singapore makes the doors for the nose landing gear; three suppliers in Italy manufacture wing flaps; and so on. Part of Boeing's rationale for outsourcing so much production to foreign suppliers is that these various suppliers are the best in the world at performing their particular activity. Therefore, the result of having foreign suppliers build specific parts is a better final product.[28]

As for the **globalization of markets,** it has been argued that we are moving away from an economic system in which national markets are distinct entities—isolated from each other by trade barriers and barriers of distance, time, and culture—and toward a system in which national markets are merging into one huge global marketplace. According to this view, the tastes and preferences of consumers in different nations are beginning to converge on some global norm. Thus, in many industries it is no longer meaningful to talk about the German market, the U.S. market, or the Japanese market—there is only the global market. The global acceptance of Coca-Cola, Levi's blue jeans, Sony's Walkman, and McDonald's hamburgers exemplifies this trend.[29]

The trend toward the globalization of production and markets has several important implications for competition within an industry. First, it is crucial for companies to recognize that an industry's boundaries do not stop at national borders. Because many industries are becoming global in scope, actual and potential competitors exist not only in a company's home market but also in other national markets. Companies that scan just their home market can be caught unprepared by the entry of efficient foreign competitors. The globalization of production and markets implies that companies around the globe are finding their home markets under attack from foreign competitors. This is true in Japan, where Eastman Kodak has taken market share in the film industry away from Fuji in recent years; in the United States, where Japanese automobile firms have challenged the U.S. trio of GM, Ford, and Chrysler; and in Western Europe, where the once dominant Dutch company, Philips, has seen its market share in the consumer electronics industry taken by Japan's JVC, Matsushita, and Sony.

Second, the shift from national to global markets during the last twenty years has intensified competitive rivalry in industry after industry. National markets that were once consolidated oligopolies, dominated by three or four companies and subjected to relatively little foreign competition, have been transformed into segments of fragmented global industries, in which a large number of companies battle each other for market share in country after country. This rivalry has driven down profit rates and made it all the more critical for companies to maximize their efficiency, quality, customer responsiveness, and innovative ability. The painful restructuring and downsizing that has been going on at companies such as General Motors and Kodak is as much a response to the increased intensity of global competition as it is to anything else. However, not all global industries are fragmented. Many remain consolidated oligopolies, except that now they are consolidated global, rather than national, oligopolies.

Third, as competitive intensity has increased, so has the rate of innovation. Companies strive to gain an advantage over their competitors by pioneering new products, processes, and ways of doing business. The result has been to compress product life cycles and make it vital for companies to stay on the leading edge of technology. In regard to highly competitive global industries, where the rate of innovation is accelerating, the criticism that Porter's five forces model is too static may be particularly relevant.

Finally, even though globalization has increased both the threat of entry and the intensity of rivalry within many formerly protected national markets, it has also created enormous opportunities for companies based in those markets. The steady decline in trade barriers has opened up many once protected markets to companies based outside them. Thus, for example, in recent years U.S. companies have accelerated their investments in the nations of Eastern Europe, Latin America, and Southeast Asia in an attempt to take advantage of growth opportunities in those areas.

THE NATION-STATE AND COMPETITIVE ADVANTAGE

Despite the globalization of production and markets, many of the most successful companies in certain industries are still clustered in a small number of countries. For example, many of the world's most successful biotechnology and computer companies are based in the United States, many of the world's most successful consumer electronics companies are based in Japan, and many of the world's most successful chemical and engineering companies are based in Germany. This suggests that the nation-state within which a company is based may have an important bearing on the competitive position of that company in the global marketplace.

Companies need to understand how national factors can affect competitive advantage, for then they will be able to identify (1) where their most significant competitors are likely to come from and (2) where they might want to locate certain production activities. Thus, seeking to take advantage of U.S. expertise in biotechnology, many foreign companies have set up research facilities in U.S. locations such as San Diego, Boston, and Seattle, where U.S. biotechnology companies tend to be clustered. Similarly, in an attempt to take advantage of Japanese success in consumer electronics, many U.S. electronics companies have set up research and production facilities in Japan, often in conjunction with Japanese partners.

In a study of national competitive advantage, Michael Porter identified four attributes of a nation-state that have an important impact upon the global competitiveness of companies located there.[30] These four attributes are:

- *Factor endowments.* This describes a nation's position in factors of production, such as skilled labor or the infrastructure, that are necessary to compete in a given industry.

- *Demand conditions.* These are the nature of home demand for the industry's product or service.

- *Related and supporting industries.* This attribute refers to the presence or absence in a nation of supplier industries and related industries that are internationally competitive.

- *Strategy, structure, and rivalry.* This attribute describes the conditions in the nation governing how companies are created, organized, and managed and the nature of domestic rivalry.

Porter speaks of these four attributes as constituting *the diamond* (see Figure 3.8). He argues that firms are most likely to succeed in industries or industry segments in which conditions with regard to the four attributes are favorable. He also argues that the diamond's attributes form a mutually reinforcing system in which the effect of one attribute is dependent on the state of others.

Factor Endowments

Porter follows basic economic theory in stressing that **factor conditions**—the cost and quality of factors of production—are a prime determinant of the competitive advantage that certain countries might have in certain industries. Factors of production include **basic factors,** such as land, labor, capital, and raw materials; and **advanced factors,** such as technological know-how, managerial sophistication, and physical infrastructure (that is, roads, railways, and ports). The competitive advantage that the United States enjoys in biotechnology might be explained by the presence of certain advanced factors of production, for example, technological know-how, in combination with some basic factors, which might be a pool of relatively low-cost venture capital that can be used to fund risky start-ups in industries such as biotechnology.

Demand Conditions

Porter emphasizes the role home demand plays in providing the impetus for "upgrading" competitive advantage. Companies are typically most sensitive to the

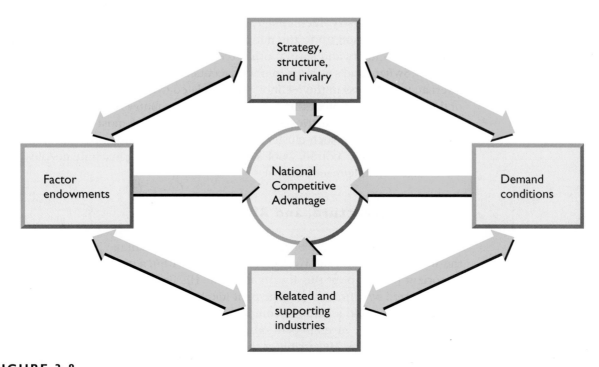

FIGURE 3.8

The Determinants of National Competitive Advantage

needs of their closest customers. Thus, the characteristics of home demand are particularly important in shaping the attributes of domestically made products and in creating pressures for innovation and quality. Porter argues that a nation's companies gain competitive advantage if their domestic consumers are sophisticated and demanding. Sophisticated and demanding consumers pressure local companies to meet high standards of product quality and to produce innovative products. Porter notes that Japan's sophisticated and knowledgeable buyers of cameras helped stimulate the Japanese camera industry to improve product quality and to introduce innovative models. A similar example can be found in the cellular phone equipment industry, in which sophisticated and demanding local customers in Scandinavia helped push Nokia of Finland and Ericsson of Sweden to invest in cellular phone technology long before demand for cellular phones took off in other developed nations. As a result, Nokia and Ericsson, together with Motorola, are today dominant players in the global cellular telephone equipment industry. (The case of Nokia is reviewed in more depth in Strategy in Action 3.4).

Related and Supporting Industries

The third broad attribute of national advantage in an industry is the presence in a country of suppliers or related industries that are internationally competitive. The benefits of investments in advanced factors of production by related and supporting industries can spill over into an industry, thereby helping it achieve a strong competitive position internationally. Swedish strength in fabricated steel products (for example, ball bearings and cutting tools) has drawn on strengths in Sweden's specialty steel industry. Technological leadership in the U.S. semiconductor industry during the period up to the mid 1980s provided the basis for U.S. success in personal computers and several other technically advanced electronic products. Similarly, Switzerland's success in pharmaceuticals is closely related to its previous international success in the technologically related dye industry. One consequence of this process is that successful industries within a country tend to be grouped into "clusters" of related industries. Indeed, this was one of the most pervasive findings of Porter's study. One such cluster is the German textile and apparel sector, which includes high-quality cotton, wool, synthetic fibers, sewing machine needles, and a wide range of textile machinery.

Strategy, Structure, and Rivalry

The fourth broad attribute of national competitive advantage in Porter's model is the strategy, structure, and rivalry of companies within a nation. Porter makes two important points about this fourth attribute. His first is that different nations are characterized by different "management ideologies," which either help them or do not help them build a national competitive advantage. For example, Porter notes the predominance of engineers on the top-management teams of German and Japanese companies. He attributes this to an emphasis in these companies on improving manufacturing processes and product design. In contrast, Porter notes a predominance of people with financial backgrounds on the top-management teams of many U.S. companies. He links this to the lack of attention paid in many U.S. companies to improving manufacturing processes and product design, particularly during the 1970s and 1980s. He also argues that the dominance of finance has led to a corresponding overemphasis on maximizing short-term financial returns. According to Porter, one consequence of these different management ideologies has been a relative loss of U.S. competitiveness in those engineering-based industries in which manufacturing processes and product design issues are all-important (such as automobiles).

Porter's second point is that there is a strong association between vigorous domestic rivalry and the creation and persistence of competitive advantage in an industry. Vigorous domestic rivalry induces companies to look for ways to improve efficiency, which in turn makes them better international competitors. Domestic rivalry creates pressures to innovate, to improve quality, to reduce costs, and to invest in upgrading advanced factors. All this helps to create world-class competitors. As an illustration Porter cites the case of Japan:

> Nowhere is the role of domestic rivalry more evident than in Japan, where it is all-out warfare in which many companies fail to achieve profitability. With goals that stress market share, Japanese companies engage in a continuing struggle to outdo each other. Shares fluctuate markedly. The process is prominently covered in the business press. Elaborate rankings measure which companies are most popular with university graduates. The rate of new product and process development is breathtaking.[31]

A similar point about the stimulating effects of strong domestic competition can be made with regard to the rise of Nokia of Finland to global preeminence in the market for cellular telephone equipment (see Strategy in Action 3.4).

The Rise of Finland's Nokia

The cellular telephone equipment industry is one of the great growth stories of the 1990s. The number of cellular subscribers has been expanding rapidly. By the end of 1994, there were more than 50 million cellular subscribers worldwide, up from less than 10 million in 1990. Three companies currently dominate the global market for cellular equipment (cellular phones, base station equipment, digital switches): Motorola, Nokia, and Ericsson. Of the three, the dramatic rise of Nokia is perhaps the most surprising.

Nokia's roots are in Finland, not normally a country that jumps to mind when we talk about leading-edge technology companies. Back in the 1980s, Nokia was a rambling Finnish conglomerate with activities that embraced tire manufacturing, paper production, consumer electronics, and telecommunications equipment. Today it is a focused $10 billion telecommunications equipment manufacturer with a global reach second only to that of Motorola and with sales and earnings that are growing in excess of 30 percent per annum. How has this former conglomerate emerged to take a global leadership position in cellular equipment? Much of the answer lies in the history, geography, and political economy of Finland and its Nordic neighbors.

The story starts in 1981, when the Nordic nations got together to create the world's first international cellular telephone network. Sparsely populated and inhospitably cold, they had good reason to become pioneers; it cost far too much to lay down a traditional wire line telephone service. Yet the same features that made it difficult make telecommunications all the more valuable there; people driving through the Arctic winter and owners of remote northern houses need a telephone to summon help if things go wrong. As a result, Sweden, Norway, and Finland became the first nations in the world to take cellular telecommunications seriously. They found, for example, that while it cost up to $800 per subscriber to bring a traditional wire line service to remote locations in the far north, the same locations could be linked by wireless cellular for only $500 per person. As a consequence, 12 percent of people in Scandinavia owned cellular phones by 1994, compared with less than 6 percent in the United States, the world's second most developed market.

Nokia, as a long-time telecommunications equipment supplier, was well positioned to take advantage of this development from the start, but there were also other forces at work in Finland that helped Nokia develop its competitive edge. Unlike virtually every other developed nation, Finland has never had a national telephone monopoly. Instead, the country's telephone services have long been provided by about 50 or so autonomous local telephone companies, whose elected boards set prices by referendum (which naturally results in low prices). This army of independent and cost-conscious telephone service providers have prevented Nokia from taking anything for granted in its home country. With typical Finnish pragmatism, its customers have been willing to buy from the lowest-cost supplier, whether that was Nokia, Ericsson, Motorola, or someone else. This situation contrasted sharply with that prevailing in most developed nations up until the late 1980s and early 1990s, in which domestic telephone monopolies typically purchased equipment from a dominant local supplier or made it themselves. Nokia has responded to this competitive pressure by doing everything possible to drive down its manufacturing costs while staying at the leading edge of cellular technology.

The consequences of these forces are clear. While Motorola remains the number one firm in cellular equipment, the once obscure Finnish firm, Nokia, is snapping at its heals. It is Nokia, not Motorola, that is the leader in digital cellular technology, which seems to be the wave of the future. In no small part Nokia has the lead because Scandinavia started switching to digital technology five years before the rest of the world. Moreover, spurred by its cost-conscious customers, Nokia now has the lowest cost structure of any cellular phone equipment manufacturer in the world. The result is that it is a more profitable enterprise than Motorola. Nokia's operating margins in 1994 were 17.7 percent, compared with 14.4 percent at Motorola.[32]

In sum, Porter's argument is that the degree to which a nation is likely to achieve international success in a certain industry is a function of the combined impact of factor endowments, domestic demand conditions, related and supporting industries, and domestic rivalry. He argues that for this "diamond" to affect competitive performance positively, the presence of all four components is usually required (although there are some exceptions). Porter also contends that government can influence each of the four components of the diamond either positively or negatively. Factor endowments can be affected by subsidies, policies toward capital markets, policies toward education, and the like. Government can shape domestic demand through local product standards or with regulations that mandate or influence buyers' needs. Government policy can influence supporting and related industries through regulation, and it can influence rivalry through such devices as capital market regulation, tax policy, and antitrust laws.

As an example of Porter's theory, consider the U.S. computer hardware industry (personal computers, workstations, minicomputers, and mainframes). The existence of a world-class industry in the United States can be explained by the presence of advanced factors of production in the form of technological know-how; an intense rivalry among myriad competing computer companies; a strong local demand for computers (more personal computers have been sold in the United States than in the rest of the world combined); and internationally competitive supporting industries, such as the computer software and microprocessor industries.

Perhaps the most important implication of Porter's framework is the message that it carries about the attractiveness of certain locations for performing certain productive activities. For instance, many Japanese computer companies have moved much of their R&D activity to the United States so that they can benefit from the international competitiveness of the United States in this industry. Most U.S. financial service companies have substantial operations in London so that they can take advantage of London's central position in the world financial services industry. Many international textile companies have design operations in Italy so that they can take advantage of Italian style and design know-how. In all these cases, companies are trying to build a competitive advantage by establishing critical productive activities in the optimal location, as defined by the various elements highlighted in Porter's framework. This is an issue we discuss in depth in Chapter 8.

SUMMARY OF CHAPTER

This chapter details a framework that managers can use to analyze the external environment of their company, enabling them to identify opportunities and threats. The following major points are made in the chapter:

✔ For a company to succeed, either its strategy must fit the environment in which the company operates or the company must be able to reshape this environment to its advantage through its choice of strategy. Companies typically fail when their strategy no longer fits the environment in which they operate.

✔ The main technique used to analyze competition in the industry environment is the five forces model. The five forces are (a) the risk of new entry by potential competitors, (b) the extent of rivalry among established firms within the industry, (c) the bargaining power of buyers, (d) the bargaining power of suppliers, and (e) the threat of substitute products. The stronger each force, the more competitive the industry and the lower the rate of return that can be earned.

✔ The risk of entry by potential competitors is a function of the height of barriers to entry. The higher the barriers to entry, the lower is the risk of entry and the greater are the profits that can be earned in the industry.

✔ The extent of rivalry among established companies is a function of an industry's competitive structure, demand conditions, and barriers to exit. Strong demand conditions moderate the competition among established companies and create opportunities for expansion. When demand is weak, intensive competition can develop, particularly in consolidated industries with high exit barriers.

✔ Buyers are most powerful when a company depends on them for business but they themselves are not dependent on the company. In such circumstances, buyers are a threat.

✔ Suppliers are most powerful when a company depends on them for business but they themselves are not dependent on the company. In such circumstances, suppliers are a threat.

✔ Substitute products are those of companies serving consumers' needs that are similar to the needs served by the industry being analyzed. The more similar the substitute products are to each other, the lower is the price that companies can charge without losing customers to the substitutes.

✔ Most industries are composed of strategic groups. Strategic groups are groups of companies pursuing the same or a similar strategy. Companies in different strategic groups pursue different strategies.

✔ The members of a company's strategic group constitute its immediate competitors. Since different strategic groups are characterized by different opportunities and threats, it may pay a company to switch strategic groups. The feasibility of doing so is a function of the height of mobility barriers.

✔ The five forces and strategic group models have been criticized for presenting a static picture of competition that de-emphasizes the role of innovation. Innovation can revolutionize an industry's structure and completely change the strength of different competitive forces.

✔ The five forces and strategic group models have been criticized for de-emphasizing the importance of individual company differences. A company will not be profitable just because it is based in an attractive industry or strategic group; much more is required.

✔ Industries go through a well-defined life cycle, from an embryonic stage, through growth, shake-out, and maturity, and eventually into decline. Each stage has different implications for the competitive structure of the industry, and each stage gives rise to its own set of opportunities and threats.

✔ A fundamental change is occurring in the world economy: the globalization of production and of markets. The consequences of this change include more intense rivalry, more rapid innovation, and shorter product life cycles.

✔ There is a link between the national environment and the competitive advantage of a company in the global economy.

DISCUSSION QUESTIONS

1. Under what environmental conditions are price wars most likely to occur in an industry? What are the implications of price wars for a company? How should a company try to deal with the threat of a price war?

2. Discuss Porter's five forces model with reference to what you know about the U.S. airline industry. What does the model tell you about the level of competition in this industry?

3. How do you think the trend toward greater globalization is likely to affect the nature and intensity level of competition in the U.S. airline market?

4. Identify a growth industry, a mature industry, and a declining industry. For each industry, identify the following: (a) the number and size distribution of companies, (b) the nature of barriers to entry, (c) the height of barriers to entry, and (d) the extent of product differentiation. What do these factors tell you about the nature of competition in each industry? What are the implications for the company in terms of opportunities and threats?

5. Assess the impact of macroenvironmental factors on the likely level of enrollment at your university over the next decade. What are the implications of these factors for the job security and salary level of your professors?

Practicing Strategic Management

SMALL-GROUP EXERCISE
Entering the Regional Airline Market

Break up into groups of three to five people, and discuss the following scenario:

You are a group of experienced airline pilots who have recently been made redundant by a major airline that is undergoing financial restructuring. You are considering establishing a regional airline to offer service between the medium-sized cities in your region and a large regional airline hub. For example, if you are based in the American Midwest, the regional hub might be Chicago's O'Hare airport, and you would be considering offering a service from surrounding cities to Chicago. You are due to make a presentation to a group of investors who have expressed interest in putting up the funds to enable you to lease six Boeing 737 aircraft that are currently surplus to requirements and parked in the Arizona desert. You know that there are plenty of landing slots available at local airports, and you are confident that you can gain access to landing slots at the regional hub. Before they commit funds, the investors want you to undertake a thorough analysis of the nature of competition in the local market. Accordingly:

1. Use Porter's five forces model to carry out this analysis.

2. On the basis of this analysis, try to predict how your entry into the local market might affect the intensity of competition.

3. Sketch out the basic strategy that you intend to pursue in order to compete in this market.

4. On the basis of the above analysis, if you were one of the investors, would you fund this venture?

EXPLORING THE WEB
Visiting Boeing and Airbus

Visit the Web sites of the Boeing Company (http://www.boeing.com) and Airbus Industrie (http://www.airbus.com). Go to the news features of both sites, and read through the press releases issued by both companies. Also, look at the annual reports and company profile (or history features) contained on both sites. Using this material as your guide:

1. Use Porter's five forces model to analyze the nature of competition in the global commercial jet aircraft market.

2. Assess the likely outlook for competition over the next ten years in this market. Try to establish whether new entry into this industry is likely, whether demand will grow or shrink, how powerful buyers are likely to become, and what the implications of all this are for the nature of competition ten years from now.

General Task

Search the Web for information that allows you to assess the *current* state of competition in the market for DRAMs. Use that information to perform a five forces analysis of the global market. (Hint: Try visiting the Web sites of semiconductor companies and companies that manufacture semiconductor fabrication equipment. Also visit Electronic Business Today at http://www.ebtmag.com).

ARTICLE FILE 3

Find an example of an industry that has become more competitive in recent years. Identify the reasons for the increase in competitive pressure.

STRATEGIC MANAGEMENT PROJECT
Module 3

This module requires you to analyze the environment of the industry in which your company is based. With the information you have at your disposal:

1. Apply the five forces model to the industry in which your company is based. What does this model tell you about the nature of competition in the industry?

2. Are there any changes taking place in the macroenvironment that might have an impact, either positive or negative, upon the industry in which your company is based? If so, what are these changes, and how will they affect the industry?

3. Identify any strategic groups that might exist in the industry. How does the intensity of competition differ across the strategic groups you have identified?

4. How dynamic is the industry in which your company is based? Is there any evidence that innovation is reshaping competition or has done so in the recent past?

5. In what stage of its life cycle is the industry in which your company is based? What are the impli-cations of this for the intensity of competition both now and in the future?

6. Is your company based in an industry that is becoming more global? If so, what are the implications of this change for competitive intensity?

7. Analyze the impact of national context as it pertains to the industry in which your company is based. Does national context help or hinder your company in achieving a competitive advantage in the global marketplace?

CLOSING CASE

Wang Laboratories

Founded in 1951 by a Chinese immigrant, An Wang, in the 1970s, Wang Laboratories was one of a small group of companies that managed to outsmart IBM and carve a profitable niche for itself in the computer industry. In Wang's case the niche was word processing. Back in the early 1970s, Wang developed its own proprietary word-processing software, which it loaded on its own minicomputers, which ran on Wang's proprietary operating system. Word-processing terminals were connected to these minicomputers. The terminals replaced typewriters and moved letter and document writing into a new era.

A story is told that when An Wang was touring the United Nations building, a secretarial pool broke out into spontaneous applause as he passed. "I am the secretaries' friend," he explained to his companion "I have freed them from the tyranny of the typewriter." So it was that Wang Laboratories became one of the high-technology miracle companies of the 1970s. By 1988 the company employed 31,500 people worldwide, generated revenues of more than $3 billion, made $92.7 million in after-tax profits, and was ranked 143 on the *Fortune* 500 list of industrial companies. By August 1992, however, the company had filed for Chapter 11 bankruptcy protection. Revenues had fallen to $1.9 billion, and employment to less than 8,000. The company had lost a total of $1.9 billion since 1988, and the market value of its stock, which once stood at $5.6 billion, had slumped to $70 million. Wang's stock, which traded at $42.50 in 1982, was now trading at $.375 a share.

The reason for Wang's fall was that the company had lost touch with changes going on in the marketplace. Just as it had outflanked IBM in the 1970s, so it in turn was outflanked by a host of personal computer and software companies in the mid 1980s. As personal computers gained in popularity and as inexpensive word-processing software became available, the demand for Wang's expensive minicomputer-based word-processing system declined precipitously. For example, one long-time Wang user explained how he scrapped his $400,000 Wang minicomputer, which had cost $100,000 per year to service, and replaced it with a network of twenty-five personal computers for a total cost of less than $100,000. Faced with this kind of low-cost competition, Wang's market collapsed in the latter half of the 1980s.

The sad aspect of the Wang story, however, was that the company turned down an opportunity to get into the personal computer industry during its infancy. In March 1984 the company considered a partnership with Apple Computer, which had just released the Macintosh. The objective was to combine Wang's word-processing software with Apple's graphic user interface and applications, taking market share from the systems based on MS-DOS, such as IBM's original PC. Apple's president, John Sculley, recognizing the value of Wang's word-processing application, was reported to be very eager for the deal. Apple even talked about licensing its Macintosh operating system to Wang, which would have enabled Wang to manufacture PCs. However, Wang rejected the proposal. According to internal memos, senior managers at Wang felt that "office automation is *our* business— Apple could decide to move in and use Wang to enter the market. . . . Apple is a young, volatile, ego-driven company. Should Wang be associated with such an unpredictable company?" Wang also scoffed at word-processing programs developed by the likes of

WordStar and WordPerfect. As a $2 billion company, Wang failed to see small start-ups such as WordPerfect as viable competitors. In addition, Wang was reportedly reluctant to sell its software separately from its hardware. The company felt that if it sold its word-processing software separately, no one would buy its hardware. This might have been true, but today no one buys either its software or hardware, and applications such as WordPerfect and Microsoft Word have far surpassed Wang's word-processing software in sales.[33]

Case Discussion Questions

1. What does the story of Wang tell companies about the importance of scanning the external environment?

2. With hindsight, what steps could Wang have taken that might have averted the disaster that befell the company in the early 1990s?

CHAPTER 4

Internal Analysis: Resources, Capabilities, Competencies, and Competitive Advantage

Opening Case: The Rise of Intel

Overview

Competitive Advantage: Value Creation, Low Cost, and Differentiation

The Generic Building Blocks of Competitive Advantage

Business Functions, the Value Chain, and Value Creation

Distinctive Competencies, Resources, and Capabilities

The Durability of Competitive Advantage

Why Do Companies Fail?

Avoiding Failure and Sustaining Competitive Advantage

Closing Case: Marks & Spencer

OPENING CASE

Founded in 1968, Intel in 1971 invented the microprocessor, or "computer on a chip," and was rewarded for its efforts in 1980 when IBM picked Intel's 8086 microprocessor as the central component of its original IBM PC. Since the introduction of the PC in 1981, Intel and Microsoft, whose MS-DOS and Windows operating systems are designed to run on Intel's microprocessors, have created the technical standard for the personal computer industry. Most popular applications software, such as word processors, will only run on one of Microsoft's operating systems, and until recently Microsoft's operating systems ran exclusively on micro-

The Rise of Intel

processors that were compatible with Intel's X86 series, such as the 486 and Pentium processors. This symbiotic relationship between Intel and Microsoft has helped propel Intel to a staggering 80 to 85 percent share of the global market for personal computer microprocessors. As a result, in 1995 the California-based company recorded a net profit of $3.5 billion on sales of $16.2 billion.

It would be wrong to attribute Intel's monopoly position simply to its role in setting the industry's standards. Intel's monopoly position is continually being challenged by a host of competitors, including Advanced Micro

Devices (AMD), NextGen, and Cyrix. All three of these companies make Intel-compatible microprocessors, or clones, that are capable of interfacing flawlessly with Microsoft's MS-DOS and Windows operating systems. The reason that Intel has been able to acquire and hold on to such a staggering market share (despite the best efforts of competitors) is that the company's success is based upon competencies that its rivals lack.

First, Intel has proved repeatedly that it has world-class product development capabilities. Since 1978, when it introduced the 8086 microprocessor, Intel has released five subsequent microprocessor platforms—the 286, 386, 486, Pentium, and Pentium Pro—each significantly more powerful than its predecessor. Within each of these platforms, the company has produced a number of derivative products, each of which is also more powerful than its predecessor. Thus, while the first Pentium processors had a clock speed of 75 megahertz, within a year the company was shipping Pentiums with clock speeds of 150 megahertz. (Higher clock speed translates into faster performance.) Each successive microprocessor generation has involved a quantum leap in the number of transistors crammed onto a single, small silicon chip that is less than 1 inch square.

Designing such microcircuitry requires magnificent microengineering and software capabilities, and the evidence suggests that Intel has a substantial edge over its competitors in this regard. Intel has consistently beaten its competitors to market with new generations of the X86 series and with ever more powerful derivative products within each generation. For example, it took more than one year after the introduction of the Pentium before Intel's major competitor, AMD, was able to produce its own version of the Pentium, the K5 processor. By the time the K5 hit the market, Intel had already introduced its subsequent processor, the Pentium Pro. Thus, it is in part its rapid product development, which allows the company to stay one step ahead of competitors, that has enabled Intel to sustain its monopoly in leading-edge processors.

Second, Intel is also a world-class manufacturing company. The manufacture of microprocessors entails substantial fixed costs (including more than $1 billion for a fabrication facility) but relatively small ongoing production costs. The result is that as production volume in-

creases, unit costs fall steeply once the manufacturer starts to realize substantial economies of scale. Intel's rapid product development has allowed the company to start volume production of leading-edge microprocessors ahead of competitors. Consequently, when competitors do enter the market, Intel's huge economies of scale give the company a substantial cost advantage. In turn, this allows Intel to price its offerings below those of competitors and still make significant profits.

Intel's manufacturing advantage is not based just on economies of scale. Working together with equipment suppliers, Intel has also proved adept at pushing out the technical limits of manufacturing microprocessors, and its competitors cannot match its manufacturing expertise. In 1996, for example, Intel doubled the number of microprocessor chips that it could place on a single 8-inch silicon wafer, which increased its revenues per wafer from $90,000 to $382,500.

Despite its impressive competencies in product design and leading-edge high volume manufacturing, Intel is not immune to making mistakes. In the early 1990s Intel began its "Intel Inside" campaign. This campaign was designed to create "pull through" demand for its microprocessors by building brand loyalty for Intel processors among the end users of computers by stressing the superior quality of Intel's processors. The idea was that end users would purchase computers with Intel's microprocessors inside, as opposed to those produced by AMD or Cyrix. The campaign worked well until late 1994, when a U.S. mathematician revealed a flaw in the Pentium processor that led to a small error in the calculation of certain complex numbers. Intel responded that the problem was irrelevant for most end users, since it occurred too rarely to concern any but the most demanding scientists. Furthermore, the company offered to replace flawed Pentiums only if an end user could demonstrate that it affected his or her work. While Intel may have been correct in categorizing the problem as "irrelevant for most users," it was caught off guard by the storm of criticism that its apparent lack of customer responsiveness unleashed among end users and the media. After weeks of controversy, an embarrassed Intel was forced to reverse its original position and offer a free replacement for any Pentium processor that contained the fault.[1]

OVERVIEW

In Chapter 3 we discuss the elements of the external environment that determine an industry's attractiveness and examine how an industry's structure explains why some industries are more profitable than others. However, an industry's structure is not the only force that affects a company's profits. Within any given industry, some companies are more profitable than others. For example, in the global auto industry, Toyota has consistently outperformed General Motors for most of the last twenty years. In the steel industry, Nucor has consistently outperformed US Steel. In the U.S. retail clothing industry, The Gap has consistently outperformed J.C. Penney, while in the semiconductor industry, as detailed in the Opening Case, Intel has consistently outperformed competitors such as AMD. The question, therefore, is why within a particular industry do some companies outperform others? What is the basis of their competitive advantage?

Intel provides some clues as to the sources of competitive advantage, that is, a company's ability to outperform its competitors. The Opening Case shows how the competitive advantage of Intel is based upon the company's superior product development and manufacturing capabilities. Its product development capabilities allow Intel to stay one step ahead of rivals in the race to produce ever more powerful microprocessors. In turn, this capability gives Intel a temporary monopoly in the supply of leading-edge microprocessors, which allows the company to charge a high price during that time period when rivals have yet to introduce a comparable product. In other words, Intel has an advantage over its rivals when it comes to product innovation. Moreover, Intel's volume manufacturing capabilities allow the company to achieve production efficiencies that its rivals can only dream of. As a result, when imitators do produce clones of Intel's latest generation microprocessor, Intel is able to bring down prices for that particular product and still make substantial profits due to its lower cost structure.

As this chapter makes clear, *efficiency* and *innovation* can be regarded as two of the main building blocks, or dimensions, of competitive advantage. To these building blocks we add two others, *quality* and *customer responsiveness*. As the Opening Case demonstrates, Intel's score on these two dimensions is less than perfect. The quality of its Pentium processor was compromised by design errors, while the company's reputation for customer responsiveness was tarnished by the hamfisted way in which Intel handled the resulting controversy. Still, Intel has such profound strengths in manufacturing efficiency and innovation that the company's competitive position was not fundamentally damaged by its relative weaknesses with regard to product quality and customer responsiveness. Moreover, there are signs that Intel has now learned from its problems with the Pentium processor and as a result has improved its quality and customer responsiveness. Indeed, as we argue in this chapter, the ability to learn and continually improve the efficiency, innovative capability, product quality, and customer responsiveness of an organization is itself a fundamental prerequisite for a sustained competitive advantage.

In this chapter and the next we look inside an organization at the strengths and weaknesses that determine the efficiency, innovative capability, product quality, and customer responsiveness of an organization. We explore how the strengths of an organization are grounded in its resources, capabilities, and competencies, and we discuss how these help a company to attain a competitive advantage based on superior efficiency, innovation, quality, and customer responsiveness. We also discuss three critical questions. First, once it is obtained, what factors influence the durability of competitive advantage? Second, why do successful companies lose their competitive advantage? Third, how can companies avoid competitive failure and sustain their competitive advantage over time? By the time you have finished this chapter, you will have a good understanding of the nature of competitive advantage. This understanding will help you to make better strategic decisions as a manager.

COMPETITIVE ADVANTAGE: VALUE CREATION, LOW COST, AND DIFFERENTIATION

We say that a company has a *competitive advantage* when its profit rate is higher than the average for its industry, and it has a *sustained competitive advantage* when it is able to maintain this high profit rate over a number of years. Profit rate is normally defined as some ratio, such as return on capital employed (ROK). Figure 4.1 graphs the return on capital employed earned by four companies active in the personal computer industry between 1986 and 1994.[2] Their profit rates are shown *relative to* the mean ROK earned by all companies active in the industry. If we look at just one year, for example, 1986, we might conclude that Dell Computer enjoyed a competitive advantage and that the other three players shown were at a competitive disadvantage. However, this single year's perspective is misleading. Over the whole period it was Apple Computer that seemed to enjoy the most pronounced competitive advantage with above-average returns from 1987 through 1993. Apple clearly had a sustained competitive advantage over this period, although its competitive position got progressively weaker from 1988 until 1994, when it appears to have lost its advantage. By the same token, AST Research seems to have been at a sustained competitive *disadvantage* for almost all the 1986 to 1994 period, with the exception of 1991, its one year of above-average returns. Compaq and Dell, on the other hand, each had good years and bad years. Although they both enjoyed a competitive advantage in certain years, neither company was a consistent performer over the whole period.

Two basic conditions determine a company's profit rate and hence whether it has a competitive advantage: first, the amount of value customers place on the company's goods or services; second, the company's costs of production. In general, the more value customers place on a company's products, the higher the price the company can charge for those products. Note, however, that the price a company charges for a good or service is typically less than the value placed on that good or service by the customer. This is so because the customer captures some of that value in the form of what economists call a consumer surplus.[3] The customer is able to do this because the company is competing with other companies for the customer's business, so the company must charge a lower prices than it could were it a monopoly supplier. Moreover, it is normally impossible to segment the market to such a degree that the company can charge each customer a price that reflects that individual's assessment of the value of a product, which economists refer to as a customer's reservation price. For these reasons the price that gets charged tends to be less than the value placed on the product by many customers.

These concepts are illustrated in Figure 4.2. There you can see that the value of a product to a consumer may be *V*, the price that the company can charge for that

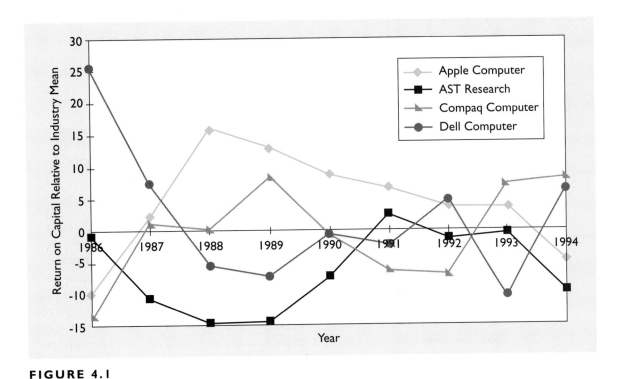

FIGURE 4.1

Personal Computer Companies: Return on Capital Employed Relative to Industry Means, 1986–1994

product given competitive pressures may be P, and the costs of producing that product are C. The company's profit margin is equal to $P - C$, while the consumer surplus is equal to $V - P$. The company makes a profit so long as $P > C$, and its profit rate will be greater the lower C is *relative* to P. Bear in mind that the difference between V and P is in part determined by the intensity of competitive pressure in the marketplace. The lower the intensity of competitive pressure, the higher the price that can be charged relative to V.[4]

Note also that the value created by a company is measured by the difference between V and C ($V - C$). A company creates value by converting inputs that cost C into a product on which consumers place a value of V. A company can create more value for its customers either by lowering C or by making the product more attractive through superior design, functionality, quality, and the like, so that consumers place a greater value on it (V increases) and, consequently, are willing to pay a high price (P increases). This discussion suggests that a company has high profits, and thus a competitive advantage, when it creates more value for its customers than do rivals. Put differently, *the concept of value creation lies at the heart of competitive advantage.*[5]

For a more concrete example, consider again the case of the personal computer industry. In 1994 Compaq Computer was selling its top-of-the-line personal computers for about $2,600 each ($P$), while all of the costs associated with producing these computers (C)—including material costs, administrative costs, manufacturing costs, marketing costs, R&D costs, and capital costs—amounted to $2,300 per computer, giving Compaq a net profit margin (net of all costs) of $300 per computer. In contrast, AST was only able to charge $2,300 for its equivalent personal computer, while the cost of producing these machines was $2,400, giving AST a net loss of $100 per computer.

FIGURE 4.2

Value Creation

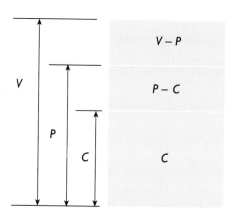

V = Value to consumer
P = Price
C = Costs of production
$V - P$ = Consumer surplus
$P - C$ = Profit margin

This comparison shows how a company's profit rate is jointly determined by the price it can charge for its products and by its cost structure. Compaq made more profit per computer than AST in 1994 because it could charge a higher price for its machines *and* because it had a lower cost structure. Compaq's lower cost structure came primarily from manufacturing efficiencies that AST lacked. (Compaq is renowned for its efficient manufacturing process.) As for its higher price, Compaq could command a higher price for its computers because consumers placed a higher value on a Compaq machine than on an AST machine, and therefore they were willing to pay more for a Compaq computer. Why did consumers place more value on Compaq machines? The main reason is that they perceived Compaq's products to be of a superior quality, functionality, and design relative to AST's products. Put differently, Compaq had succeeded in differentiating its computers from those of AST (and various other producers) in the eyes of consumers. Thus, Compaq's competitive advantage in 1994 came from a combination of low costs and differentiation. As a consequence of its superior cost and differentiation position, Compaq created more value for consumers than AST ($V - C$ was greater for Compaq than for AST). So one could say that Compaq's competitive advantage over AST was based upon superior value creation.

We should note that superior value creation does not necessarily require a company to have the lowest cost structure in an industry or to create the most valuable product in the eyes of consumers, but it does require that the gap between perceived value (V) and costs of production (C) be greater than the gap attained by competitors. If we look again at Figure 4.1, we can see that between 1988 and 1992, Apple Computer had a clear competitive advantage in the personal computer industry, as demonstrated by its persistently high return on capital. Although Apple had a relatively high cost structure, it was able to create more value because it successfully differentiated its products in the eyes of consumers so that consumers assigned a higher V to Apple machines. This perception of superior value was based upon the functionality of Apple machines (they were easier to use and had superior graphics and multimedia capabilities), and it allowed Apple to charge a much higher price (P) for its machines than Compaq, AST, or Dell. The higher price translated into a greater profit margin ($P - C$). Apple's problems in the mid 1990s were based on the fact that its competitors improved the functionality of their machines, which increased the value consumers assigned to the products of Apple's competitors and limited Apple's ability to charge a premium price.

Michael Porter has argued that low cost and differentiation are two basic strategies for creating value and attaining a competitive advantage in an industry.[6] According to Porter, competitive advantage (and higher profits) goes to those companies that can create superior value, and the way to create superior value is to drive down the cost structure of the business and/or differentiate the product in some way so that consumers value it more and are prepared to pay a premium price. This is all well and good, but it rather begs the question of exactly how a company can drive down its cost structure and differentiate its product offering from that of competitors so that it can create superior value. In this chapter and the next, we explain just how companies can do these two things. We return to Porter's notions of low cost and differentiation strategies in Chapter 6, in which we examine his idea in significantly more depth.

THE GENERIC BUILDING BLOCKS OF COMPETITIVE ADVANTAGE

We've seen that four factors build competitive advantage: efficiency, quality, innovation, and customer responsiveness. They are the generic building blocks of competitive advantage that any company can adopt, regardless of its industry or the products or services it produces (see Figure 4.3). Although we discuss each separately in the text that follows, they are highly interrelated. For example, superior quality can lead to superior efficiency, while innovation can enhance efficiency, quality, and customer responsiveness.

FIGURE 4.3

Generic Building Blocks of Competitive Advantage

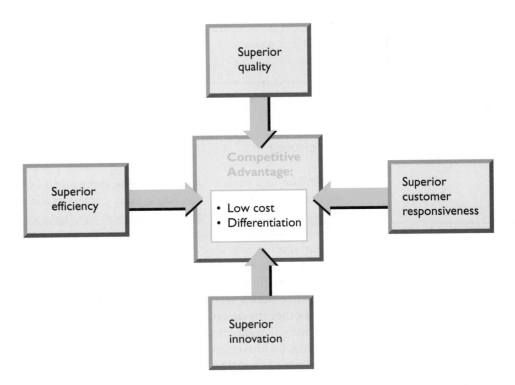

Productivity in the Automobile Industry

Every year since 1980, Harbor Associates, a consulting company founded by former Chrysler executive James Harbor, has issued a report on the level of productivity in assembly plants of U.S.-based volume manufacturers of automobiles. Until 1993 the report focused on just the big three U.S. companies—General Motors, Ford, and Chrysler—but now it also includes data on the U.S.-based assembly operations of Nissan and Toyota, both of which have a significant manufacturing presence in the country. The following table shows the amount of labor hours that it took to assemble a car at each of these companies in 1988, 1993, and 1994.

This table suggests that Nissan and Toyota are the most efficient volume producers in the United States, while General Motors is the least efficient. The higher labor productivity of Nissan and Toyota is attributed to their lean production systems, which are based upon a large number of productivity-enhancing management techniques. For example, both companies make extensive use of self-managing work teams. Each team is given the responsibility for performing a major assembly task, and the teams are also set challenging productivity and quality goals. At the same time, the teams are empowered to find ways to improve their productivity

and quality control and are rewarded through the use of incentive pay if they exceed their productivity or quality goals. While the big three U.S. companies have also tried to introduce self-managing teams into the workplace, diffusion of the technique has been held back by a long history of adversarial labor relations at these companies, which has made it difficult for management and labor to cooperate to introduce new concepts.

Another source of the superior labor productivity enjoyed by Nissan and Toyota is product design. Both

Hours of Labor Taken to Assemble a Car

Company	1988	1993	1994
General Motors	39.02	31.52	30.26
Chrysler	36.64	28.16	27.80
Ford	26.00	23.92	25.00
Toyota	Not Available	19.52	19.30
Nissan	Not Available	18.30	17.60

Efficiency

A company is a device for transforming inputs into outputs. Inputs are basic factors of production such as labor, land, capital, management, and technological know-how. Outputs are the goods and services that a company produces. The simplest measure of efficiency is the quantity of inputs that it takes to produce a given output; that is, Efficiency = outputs/inputs. The more efficient a company, the fewer the inputs required to produce a given output. For example, if it takes General Motors thirty hours of employee time to assemble a car and it takes Ford twenty-five hours, we can say that Ford is more efficient than GM. Moreover, so long as other things are equal, such as wage rates, we can assume from these data that Ford will have a lower cost structure than GM. Thus, efficiency helps a company attain a low-cost competitive advantage. In the Opening Case you saw how Intel attained superior efficiency by pioneering new production techniques that these companies have long adhered to a design-for-manufacturing philosophy, whose central principle has been to design cars in a way that makes them less complex to assemble. In turn, this has helped boost labor productivity, which translates into a cost-based competitive advantage.

Having said this, we must recognize that the big three U.S. companies have made rapid improvements in their productivity in recent years. Between 1988 and 1994, GM improved its labor productivity by 22.5 percent, while Chrysler did so by more than 24 percent, primarily because both companies are doing their best to imitate the lean production techniques utilized by their Japanese rivals. If this trend continues at its current rate, the productivity-based competitive advantage currently enjoyed by Toyota and Nissan may disappear by early next century.

Moreover, Chrysler in particular claims that the data given in the preceding table presents an incomplete picture of productivity, primarily because it ignores that company's low product development costs. According to Chrysler, these are a source of superior productivity not recognized in the Harbor report. Until the early 1990s, it took Chrysler at least four years and 1,400 design engineers to design a new car, or 5,600 engineer years. The Chrysler Neon, however, was designed in just thirty-three months and required only 740 design engineers, which translates into 2,035 engineer years, a more than 50 percent improvement in productivity and a saving in design costs of $45 million. Chrysler estimates that the design for its next major car project can be completed in two years by just 540 design engineers. James Harbor, the author of the Harbor report, agrees that Chrysler's superior design capabilities are an important source of superior productivity. In his 1995 report he concluded that when design costs are added to assembly costs, Chrysler emerges as the most productive automobile company in the United States.

How has Chrysler done this? Primarily by forming teams of design engineers, component suppliers, manufacturing personnel, and marketing staff to oversee the design process. These teams make sure that there is very tight integration in the design process between suppliers, engineering, manufacturing, and marketing. Cars are now designed for ease of manufacturing, and with input upfront from marketing, while suppliers are brought into the process early to ensure that their design for component parts interfaces well with Chrysler's design for the finished car. The result is a dramatic reduction in the amount of redesign work that has to be undertaken, and a corresponding reduction in the design cycle time from four to six years to less than three.[7]

allowed it to double the output from a silicon wafer, which lowered the company's costs of production.

The most important component of efficiency for many companies is employee productivity, which is usually measured by output per employee. Holding all else constant, the company with the highest employee productivity in an industry will typically have the lowest costs of production. In other words, that company will have a cost-based competitive advantage. Strategy in Action 4.1 looks at the level of employee productivity attained by volume manufacturers of automobiles based in the United States. These data suggest that in their assembly operations, Japanese manufacturers still enjoy a productivity-based competitive advantage relative to their U.S. counterparts, although the gap has closed significantly since the late 1980s. Moreover, it would seem that Chrysler in particular has realized huge productivity gains in its product design process, which, when added to its assembly process, may make Chrysler the most efficient volume manufacturer in the United States.

The interesting issue, of course, is how to achieve superior productivity. In later chapters we examine in detail how a company can achieve high productivity (and quality, innovation, and customer responsiveness). For now, we just note that to achieve high productivity, a company must adopt the appropriate strategy, structure, and control systems.

Quality

Quality products are goods and services that are reliable in the sense that they do the job they were designed for and do it well. This concept applies whether we are talking about a Toyota automobile, clothes designed and sold by The Gap, or the customer service department of Citibank. The impact of high product quality on competitive advantage is twofold.[8] First, providing high-quality products increases the value of those products in the eyes of consumers. In turn, this enhanced perception of value allows the company to charge a higher price for its products. In the automobile industry, for example, Japanese companies such as Toyota not only have had a productivity-based cost advantage over many of their U.S. and European competitors but also charge a higher price for their cars because of the higher quality of their products. Thus, compared with a company such as General Motors, Toyota has had both lower costs and the ability to charge higher prices. As a result, historically Toyota has operated with a bigger profit margin than GM.

The second impact of high quality on competitive advantage comes from the greater efficiency and the lower unit costs it brings. Less employee time is wasted making defective products or providing substandard services, and less time has to be spent fixing mistakes, which translates into higher employee productivity and lower unit costs. Thus high product quality lets a company not only charge higher prices for its product but also lower its costs (see Figure 4.4).

The importance of quality in building competitive advantage has increased dramatically in recent years. Indeed, so crucial is the emphasis placed on quality by many companies that achieving high product quality can no longer be viewed as just one way of gaining a competitive advantage. In many industries, it has become an absolute imperative for survival.

Innovation

Innovation can be defined as anything new or novel about the way a company operates or the products it produces. Innovation includes advances in the kinds of products, production processes, management systems, organizational structures, and strategies developed by a company. Intel's development of the microprocessor, Toys 'R' Us's discounting strategy in the retail toy business, Toyota's lean production system for manufacturing automobiles, and Sony's development of the Walkman can all be viewed as innovations.

Innovation is perhaps the single most important building block of competitive advantage. In the long run, competition can be viewed as a process driven by innovation. Although not all innovations succeed, those that do can be a major source of competitive advantage because, by definition, they give a company something **unique**, something its competitors lack (until they imitate the innovation). Uniqueness can allow a company either to differentiate itself from its rivals

FIGURE 4.4

The Impact of Quality
on Profits

and charge a premium price for its product or to reduce its unit costs far below those of competitors.

As with efficiency and quality, we explore the issue of innovation more fully later in the book. A few examples, however, can highlight the importance of innovation. Consider Xerox's development of the photocopier, Intel's development of new microprocessors, Hewlett Packard's development of the laser printer, NIKE's development of high-tech athletic shoes, Bausch & Lomb's development of contact lenses, and Sony's development of the Walkman. All these product innovations helped build a competitive advantage for the pioneering companies. In each case the company, by virtue of being the sole supplier of a new product, could charge a premium price. By the time competitors succeeded in imitating the innovator, the innovating company had built up such strong brand loyalty that its position proved difficult for imitators to attack. Sony is still known for its Walkman, and Hewlett Packard for its laser printers.

Customer Responsiveness

To achieve superior customer responsiveness, a company must be able to do a better job than competitors of identifying and satisfying the needs of its customers. Consumers will then place more value on its products, creating a differentiation-based competitive advantage. Improving the quality of a company's product offering is consistent with achieving customer responsiveness, as is developing new products with features that existing products lack. In other words, achieving superior quality and innovation is an integral part of achieving superior customer responsiveness.

Another factor that stands out in any discussion of customer responsiveness is the need to customize goods and services to the unique demands of individual customers or customer groups. For example, the proliferation of different types of soft drinks and beers in recent years can be viewed partly as a response to this trend. Automobile companies, too, have become more adept at customizing cars to the demands of individual customers. For instance, following the lead of Toyota, the Saturn division of General Motors builds cars to order for individual customers, letting them choose from a wide range of colors and options.

An aspect of customer responsiveness that has drawn increasing attention is **customer response time,** which is the time that it takes for a good to be

STRATEGY *in* ACTION

4.2

Time-Based Competition and Customer Responsiveness at Citicorp

During the 1980s Citicorp moved from being a small player in the mortgage-lending industry to being a major force. In 1982 mortgage originations from Citicorp were running at an annual rate of $756 million. By 1987 the annual rate had increased to $14.8 billion. Moreover, although Citicorp still only accounted for 3.3 percent of all mortgage originations in the United States in 1987, it could claim 37 percent more originations than its largest competitor, H. F. Ahmanson.

The core of Citicorp's success has been a strategy that achieves superior customer responsiveness by emphasizing quick response time and highly competent mortgage officers. Citicorp also realized that the borrower is only one of the customers that the lender must serve. The real estate agent is also a customer. The borrower often asks the agent which lending institution in the area has money at the most attractive rates. Which lending institution is the real estate agent going to recommend? Citicorp reasoned that because realtors want to close a deal as quickly as possible, they will recommend lending institutions that are quick at processing loan applications and that are staffed by responsive and competent loan officers.

Traditionally, loan applications take about forty-five days to approve, give or take two weeks. As anyone who has purchased real estate knows, these forty-five days can be a stressful and uncertain time. The stress is compounded when late in the approval process an ill-prepared mortgage company requires more documentation, or clarification, from the borrower. Against this background, Citicorp decided to reduce the time taken to approve a loan to just fifteen days. To achieve this goal, Citicorp created a program called MortgagePower. Real estate agents pay an annual subscription fee of $2,500 to join MortgagePower. The real estate agents then qualify their buyers for Citicorp in return for a one-half to one-and-a-half point discount and the promise of a loan decision within fifteen days. The realtor can do whatever is allowed by state regulations with the discount—either give it all to the buyer or, in some states, keep the discount by charging the buyer a fee for arranging the financing. The results for Citicorp have been dramatic.[9]

delivered or a service to be performed.[10] For a manufacturer of machinery, response time is the time it takes to fill customers' orders. For a bank, it is the time it takes to process a loan or the time that customers must stand in line to wait for a free teller. For a supermarket, it is the time that customers must stand in checkout lines. Customer survey after customer survey has shown slow response time to be a major source of customer dissatisfaction.[11] The way in which Citicorp changed its loan practices to reduce the time it took to process mortgage applications illustrates how reducing response time can build competitive advantage (see Strategy in Action 4.2).

Besides quality, customization, and response time, other sources of enhanced customer responsiveness are superior design, superior service, and superior after-sales service and support. All these factors enhance customer responsiveness and allow a company to differentiate itself from its less responsive competitors. In turn, differentiation enables a company to build brand loyalty and to charge a premium price for its products. For example, consider how much more people are prepared to pay for next-day delivery of Express Mail, as opposed to delivery in three to four days. In 1996 a two-page letter sent by overnight Express Mail within the United States cost about $10, compared with $.32 for regular mail. Thus, the price pre-

FIGURE 4.5
• • • • • • • • • •
The Impact of Efficiency,
Quality, Customer Re-
sponsiveness, and Inno-
vation on Unit Costs
and Prices

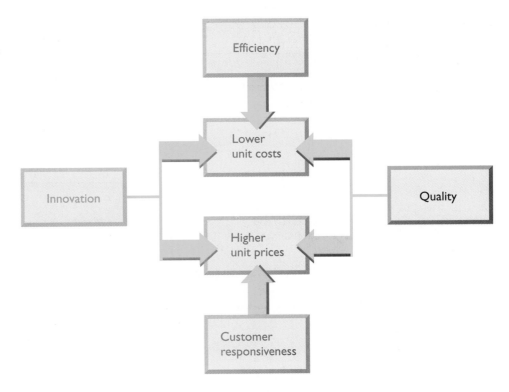

mium for express delivery (reduced response time) was $9.68, or a premium of
3,025 percent more than the regular price!

Summary
• • • • • • • •

Efficiency, quality, customer responsiveness, and innovation are all important elements in obtaining a competitive advantage. Superior efficiency enables a company
to lower its costs; superior quality lets it both charge a higher price and lower its
costs; superior customer responsiveness allows it to charge a higher price; and superior innovation can lead to higher prices or lower unit costs (see Figure 4.5). Together, these four factors help a company to create more value by lowering costs or
differentiating its products from those of competitors, which enables the company
to outperform its competitors.

BUSINESS FUNCTIONS, THE VALUE CHAIN, AND VALUE CREATION
• •

In this section we examine the role played by the different functions of a company—such as production, marketing, R&D, service, materials management, and
human resources—in the value creation process. Specifically, we briefly review
how the different functions of a company can help in the process of driving down
costs and increasing the perception of value through differentiation. As a first step

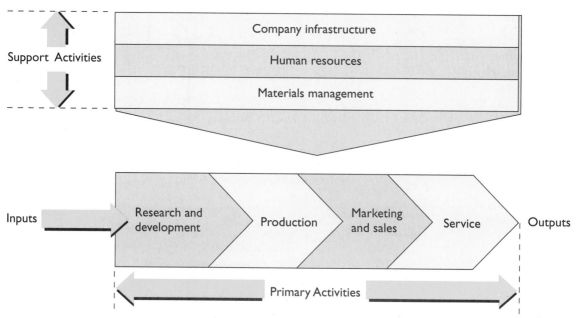

FIGURE 4.6
. . . .
The Value Chain

toward doing this, consider the concept of the value chain, which is illustrated in Figure 4.6.[12] The term *value chain* refers to the idea that a company is a chain of activities for transforming inputs into outputs that customers value. The process of transforming inputs into outputs is composed of a number of primary activities and support activities. Each activity adds value to the product.

Primary Activities
. . . .

Primary activities have to do with the design, creation, and delivery of the product as well as its marketing and its support and after-sales service. In the value chain illustrated in Figure 4.6, the primary activities are broken down into four functions; research and development, production, marketing and sales, and service.

    Research and development (R&D) is concerned with the design of products and production processes. Although we tend to think of R&D as being associated with the design of physical products and production processes in manufacturing enterprises, many service companies also undertake R&D. For example, banks compete with each other by developing new financial products and new ways of delivering those products to customers. On-line banking and smart debit cards are two recent examples of the fruits of new product development in the banking industry. Earlier examples of innovation in the banking industry include ATM machines, credit cards, and debit cards.

    By superior product design, R&D can increase the functionality of products, which makes them more attractive to consumers. Alternatively, the work of R&D may result in more efficient production processes, thereby lowering production costs. Either way, the R&D function of an enterprise can create value. At Intel, for example, which we profile in the Opening Case, R&D creates value both by developing ever more powerful microprocessors and by helping to pioneer ever more efficient manufacturing processes (in conjunction with equipment suppliers).

Production is concerned with the creation of a good or service. For physical products, *production* generally has to do with manufacturing. For services such as banking or retail operations, production typically takes place when the service is actually delivered to the customer. For example, when a bank originates a loan for a customer, it is engaged in production of the loan. The production function of a company creates value by performing its activities efficiently so that lower costs result. Thus, as suggested by the data contained in Strategy in Action 4.1, the efficient production operations of Nissan and Toyota help those automobile companies to create more value relative to competitors such as General Motors. Production can also create value by performing its activities in a way that is consistent with high product quality, which leads to differentiation and to lower costs, both of which increase the value created by a company.

There are several ways in which the **marketing and sales** functions of a company can help to create value. Through brand positioning and advertising, the marketing function can increase the value that consumers perceive to be contained in a company's product. Insofar as these help to create a favorable impression of the company's product in the minds of consumers, they increase value. For example, in the 1980s the French company Perrier did a wonderful job of persuading U.S. consumers that slightly carbonated bottled water was worth $1.50 per bottle, rather than a price closer to the $.50 that it actually cost to collect, bottle, and distribute the water. Perrier's marketing function essentially increased the perception of value that consumers ascribed to the product.

Marketing and sales can also create value by discovering consumer needs and communicating them back to the R&D function of the company, which can then design products that better match those needs. For another example of value creation by the marketing function of an enterprise, see Strategy in Action 4.3, which looks at how the sales force of Pfizer increased the perception of the value associated with one of that company's main pharmaceuticals, Zoloft.

The role of the **service** function of an enterprise is to provide after-sales service and support. This function can create a perception of superior value in the minds of consumers by solving customers' problems and supporting customers after they have purchased the product. For example, Caterpillar, the U.S.-based manufacturer of heavy earthmoving equipment, can get spare parts to any point in the world within twenty-four hours, thereby minimizing the amount of downtime its customers have to suffer if their Caterpillar equipment malfunctions. This is an extremely valuable support capability in an industry where downtime is very expensive. It has helped to increase the value that customers associate with Caterpillar products and, thus, the price that Caterpillar can charge for its products.

Support Activities

The **support activities** of the value chain provide inputs that allow the primary activities to take place (see Figure 4.6). The **materials management** function controls the transmission of physical materials through the value chain, from procurement through production and into distribution. The efficiency with which this is carried out can significantly lower cost, thereby creating more value. Wal-Mart, the U.S. retailing giant, reportedly has the most efficient materials management setup in the retail industry. By tightly controlling the flow of goods from its suppliers through its stores and into the hands of consumers, Wal-Mart has eliminated the

Value Creation at Pfizer

The antidepressant drug Prozac, introduced by Eli Lilly in 1988, has been one of the most lucrative mental-health drugs in history. In 1995 U.S. consumers alone filled almost 19 million prescriptions for Prozac, hoping to mitigate the effects of a wide range of mental disorders including chronic depression, bulimia, and obsessive disorders. Worldwide sales of the drug topped $2 billion in 1995, making it a gold mine for Lilly.

However, Prozac's market position is now under attack from an aggressive marketing and sales campaign by rival pharmaceutical company Pfizer. In 1992 Pfizer introduced its own antidepressant, Zoloft. According to medical experts, the differences between Prozac and Zoloft are slight at best. Both drugs function in the same basic manner, by boosting serotonin, a chemical in the brain believed to be in short supply in many depressed people. Both drugs also have a similar list of possible side effects. Prozac's label cites nausea, nervousness, anxiety, insomnia, and drowsiness as possible side effects; Zoloft's label lists nausea and other stomach problems, diarrhea, sexual dysfunction, and sleepiness. As one expert noted, "these drugs are so similar that you have to be kidding yourself if you think one drug is going to be consistently superior to the other in treating patients."

Despite the similarity between the two products, however, Pfizer has been gaining share from Lilly in the market for antidepressant drugs. By 1995 Zoloft accounted for 33.5 percent of the market, up from little more than 0 percent in 1992. The main reason for the success of Zoloft seems to be an aggressive marketing and sales campaign by Pfizer that has created an impression in the eyes of physicians that Zoloft is a safer drug. Pfizer salespeople bill their product as a kind of "Prozac Lite": just as effective but without Prozac's occasional downside, anxiety. The reference to anxiety seems carefully designed to remind doctors of a spate of failed lawsuits alleging that Prozac caused suicides and violent acts. Pfizer's sales force has also logged more "face time" with physicians than Lilly's. According to Scott-Levin and Associates, in 1995 Zoloft sales representatives made 660,000 sales visits to doctors, 70,000 more than the Prozac sales force logged. About three-quarters of the visits by Zoloft representatives were not to psychiatrists but to basic primary care physicians, who increasingly prescribe antidepressants but presumably are less familiar with their subtler properties. Doctors also claim that Pfizer salespeople play up Prozac's clinical reputation for being more agitating than Zoloft. They also emphasize that unlike Zoloft, Prozac remains in the bloodstream for weeks after a patient stops taking it, raising the possibility of adverse drug interaction if a patient switches to other medications.

The important point here is that Pfizer is using its marketing staff and sales force to alter physicians' perceptions of the relative value of Prozac and Zoloft. For Pfizer the payoff has come in terms of rapidly increasing revenues and market share and, of course, a greater return on the company's investment in developing Zoloft.[13]

need to hold large inventories of goods. Lower inventories mean lower costs and, hence, greater value creation. Moreover, by utilizing state-of-the-art information systems, Wal-Mart's materials management function is able to track the sale of individual items very closely. This has enabled Wal-Mart to optimize its product mix and pricing strategy. Wal-Mart is rarely left with unwanted merchandise on its hands, which saves on costs, and the company is able to provide the right mix of goods to consumers, which increases the perception of value that consumers associate with Wal-Mart.

Similarly, there are a number of ways in which the **human resource** function can help an enterprise create more value. The human resource function ensures that the company has the right mix of skilled people to perform its value creation activities effectively. It is also the job of the human resource function to ensure that people are adequately trained, motivated, and compensated to perform their value creation tasks.

The final support activity is the **company infrastructure**. This has a somewhat different character from the other support activities. *Infrastructure* has to do with the companywide context within which all the other value creation activities take place. The infrastructure includes the organizational structure, control systems, and culture of the company. Since top management can exert considerable influence in shaping these aspects of a company, top management should also be viewed as part of the infrastructure of a company. Indeed, through strong leadership top management can consciously shape the infrastructure of a company, and through that the performance of all other value creation activities that take place within it.

Cross-Functional Goals

Achieving superior efficiency, quality, innovation, and customer responsiveness requires strategies that embrace several distinct value creation activities. Indeed, these goals can be regarded as *goals that cut across the different value creation functions of a company*; they are goals whose attainment requires substantial cross-functional integration. We look in more detail at how to achieve cross-functional integration in Chapter 11 of this text.

DISTINCTIVE COMPETENCIES, RESOURCES, AND CAPABILITIES

A **distinctive competency** is a unique strength that allows a company to achieve superior efficiency, quality, innovation, or customer responsiveness and thereby to create superior value and attain a competitive advantage. A firm with a distinctive competency can differentiate its products or achieve substantially lower costs than its rivals. Consequently, it creates more value than its rivals and will earn a profit rate substantially above the industry's average.

For example, it can be argued that Toyota has distinctive competencies in the development and operation of manufacturing processes. Toyota has pioneered a whole range of manufacturing techniques, such as just-in-time (JIT) inventory systems, self-managing teams, and reduced setup times for complex equipment. These competencies have helped Toyota attain superior efficiency and product quality, which are the basis of its competitive advantage in the global automobile industry.[14]

Resources and Capabilities

The distinctive competencies of an organization arise from two complementary sources: its **resources** and **capabilities** (see Figure 4.7).[15] The financial, physical, human, technological, and organizational resources of the company can be divided into **tangible resources** (land, buildings, plant, and equipment) and **intangible resources** (brand names, reputation, patents, and technological or marketing know-how). To give rise to a distinctive competency, a company's resources must be both *unique* and *valuable*. A unique resource is one that no other company has. For example, Polaroid's distinctive competency in instant photography was based

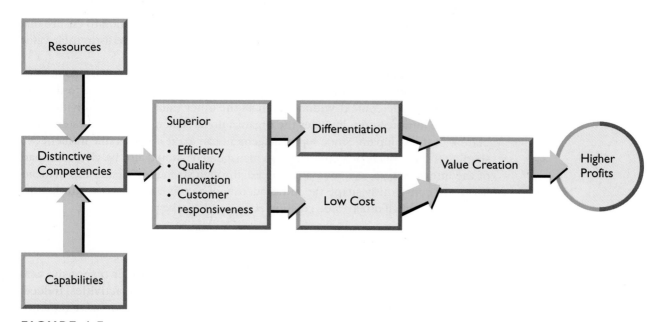

FIGURE 4.7

The Roots of Competitive Advantage

on a unique intangible resource: technological know-how in instant film processing, protected from imitation by a thicket of patents. A resource is valuable if it in some way helps create strong demand for the company's products. Thus, Polaroid's technological know-how was valuable because it created strong demand for its photographic products.

Capabilities refer to a company's skills at coordinating its resources and putting them to productive use. These skills reside in an organization's routines, that is, in the way a company makes decisions and manages its internal processes in order to achieve organizational objectives. More generally, a company's capabilities are the product of its organizational structure and control systems. They specify how and where decisions are made within a company, the kind of behaviors the company rewards, and the company's cultural norms and values. (We discuss how organizational structure and control systems help a company obtain capabilities in Chapters 11 and 12, respectively.) It is important to keep in mind that capabilities are, by definition, intangible. They reside not so much in individuals as in the way individuals interact, cooperate, and make decisions within the context of an organization.[16]

The distinction between resources and capabilities is critical to understanding what generates a distinctive competency. A company may have unique and valuable resources, but unless it has the capability to use those resources effectively it may not be able to create or sustain a distinctive competency. It is also important to recognize that a company may not need unique and valuable resources to establish a distinctive competency so long as it has capabilities that no competitor possesses. For example, the steel minimill operator Nucor is widely acknowledged to be the most cost-efficient steel maker in the United States. However, Nucor's distinctive competency in low-cost steel making does not come from any unique and valuable resources. Nucor has the same resources (plant, equipment, skilled employees, know-how) as many other minimill operators. What distinguishes Nucor is its unique capability to manage its resources in a highly productive way. Specifically,

FIGURE 4.8

The Relationship Among
Strategies, Resources,
and Capabilities

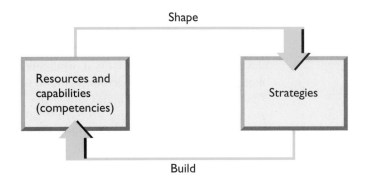

Nucor's structure, control systems, and culture promote efficiency at all levels within the company.

In sum, for a company to have a distinctive competency, it must at a minimum have either (1) a unique and valuable resource and the capabilities (skills) necessary to exploit that resource (as illustrated by Polaroid) or (2) a unique capability to manage common resources (as exemplified by Nucor). A company's distinctive competency is strongest when it possesses *both* unique and valuable resources as well as unique capabilities to manage those resources.

Strategy and Competitive Advantage

The primary objective of strategy is to achieve a competitive advantage. Attaining this goal demands a two-pronged effort. A company needs to pursue strategies that build on its existing resources and capabilities (its competencies) as well as strategies that build additional resources and capabilities (that is, develop new competencies) and thus enhance the company's long-run competitive position.[17] Figure 4.8 illustrates the relationship between a firm's strategies and its resources and capabilities. It is important to note that by *strategies* we mean *all* types of strategy—functional-level strategies, business-level strategies, corporate-level strategies, global strategies, or, more typically, some combination of them. We discuss the various strategies available to a company in detail throughout the next six chapters. What needs stressing here is that successful strategies often either build on a company's existing distinctive competencies or help a company develop new ones.

The history of The Walt Disney Company during the 1980s exemplifies the need to pursue strategies that build on a firm's resources and capabilities. In the early 1980s Disney suffered a string of poor financial years. This culminated in a 1984 management shakeup, when Michael Eisner was appointed CEO. Four years later Disney's sales had increased from $1.66 billion to $3.75 billion, its net profits from $98 million to $570 million, and its stock market valuation from $1.8 billion to $10.3 billion. What brought about this transformation was the company's deliberate attempt to exploit its existing resources and capabilities more aggressively. These resources and capabilities included Disney's enormous film library, its brand name, and its in-house filmmaking skills, particularly in animation. Under Eisner, many old Disney classics were rereleased, first in movie theaters and then on video, earning the company millions in the process. Disney also started a cable television channel, the Disney Channel, to utilize this library and capitalize on the firm's brand name. In addition, under Eisner the filmmaking arm of Disney flourished, first with a string of low-budget box-office hits under the Touchstone label and then with the reintroduction of the product that had originally made Disney famous, the full-length animated feature. Putting together its brand name and in-house animation capabilities, Disney produced three major box-office hits in four years: *The Little Mermaid, Beauty and the Beast,* and *Aladdin.*[18] In sum, Disney's transformation was based primarily upon strategies that exploited the company's existing resource base.

Other companies that have successfully exploited their resources and capabilities to create profitable opportunities include 3M (which has exploited its distinctive competency in sticky tape to create products as diverse as Post-it Notes, pressure-sensitive tapes, and coated abrasives) and Honda (which has exploited its distinctive competency in the design and manufacture of high-powered lightweight engines to move from motorcycles to cars, lawn mowers, and four-wheel off-road buggies). By the same token, some of the most striking strategic failures of recent years have occurred at companies that have strayed too far from their distinctive competencies. For example, Exxon, which has distinctive competencies in oil exploration, extraction, and refining, spent much of the 1970s diversifying into areas such as office automation equipment, in which it had no capabilities. The effort failed, and Exxon sold off these diversified businesses during the 1980s.

As for the process of building resources and capabilities through strategies, consider Xerox. During the late 1970s, its market share in the photocopier business slumped by 50 percent because its main Japanese competitors, Canon and Ricoh, were paying close attention to their distinctive competencies whereas Xerox was not. As a result, by the early 1980s Canon and Ricoh were selling high-quality, technologically superior copiers at a price that was approximately equivalent to Xerox's. To recapture its lost market share, Xerox had to fundamentally rethink the way it did business. It launched a series of functional-level strategies designed to improve quality and product design, eliminate unnecessary inventory, and reduce new product development time (cycle time). In essence, the goal of these strategies was to develop the kind of resources and capabilities that had enabled Canon and Ricoh to take market share away from Xerox. So successful was Xerox in this process that it became the first major U.S. company to recapture market share from Japanese competitors. Its share of the U.S. copier market increased from a low of 10 percent in 1985 to 18 percent in 1991.[19] Xerox's renaissance, in other words, was built upon the successful implementation of functional-level strategies to build new distinctive competencies.

The Role of Luck

A number of scholars have argued that luck plays a critical role in determining competitive success and failure.[20] In its most extreme version, the luck argument devalues the importance of strategy altogether. Instead, it states that in the face of uncertainty some companies just happen to pick the correct strategy. Put another way, they just happen to develop or possess the right kind of resources and capabilities by accident rather than design.

Although luck may be the reason for a company's success in particular cases, it is an unconvincing explanation for the persistent success of a company. Recall our argument that the generic building blocks of competitive advantage are superior ef-

Lucky Microsoft

The product that launched Microsoft into its leadership position in the software industry was MS-DOS, the operating system for IBM and IBM-compatible PCs. The original DOS program, however, was not developed by Microsoft. Instead, it was developed by a company called Seattle Computer, where it was known as Q-DOS (which stood for "quick and dirty operating system"). When IBM was looking for an operating system to run its original PC, it made contact with a number of software companies, including Microsoft, asking them whether they could develop such a system. IBM did not, however, make contact with Seattle Computer. Bill Gates, a player in the emerging Seattle computer community, knew that Seattle Computer had already developed a disk operating system. He borrowed $50,000 from his father, a senior partner in a prominent Seattle law company. Gates then went to see the CEO of Seattle Computer and offered to purchase the rights to the company's Q-DOS system. Gates did not, of course, tell him that IBM was looking for a

disk operating system. Since Seattle Computer was short of cash, the CEO quickly agreed. Gates then renamed the system MS-DOS, upgraded it somewhat, and licensed it to IBM. The rest, as they say, is history.

So, was Microsoft lucky? Of course it was. It was lucky that Seattle Computer had not heard about IBM's request. It was lucky that IBM had approached Microsoft. It was lucky that Gates had known about Seattle Computer's operating system. It was also lucky that Gates had a father wealthy enough to lend him $50,000 on short notice. On the other hand, to attribute all of Microsoft's subsequent success to luck would be wrong. While MS-DOS gave Microsoft a tremendous head start in the industry, it did not guarantee that Microsoft would continue to enjoy the kind of worldwide success that it has. To do that, Microsoft had to build the appropriate set of resources and capabilities required to produce a continual stream of innovative software, which is precisely what Gates did with the cash generated from MS-DOS.[21]

ficiency, quality, innovation, and customer responsiveness. Keep in mind also that competition is a process in which companies are continually trying to outdo each other in their ability to achieve high efficiency, quality, innovation, and customer responsiveness. It is possible to imagine a company getting lucky and coming into possession of resources that allow it to achieve excellence on one or more of these dimensions, but it is difficult to imagine how *sustained* excellence on any of these four dimensions could be produced by anything other than conscious effort, that is, by strategy. Luck may indeed play a role in success, and Strategy in Action 4.4 discusses the lucky beginnings of Microsoft. However, to argue that success is entirely a matter of luck is to strain credibility.

THE DURABILITY OF COMPETITIVE ADVANTAGE

The question that we now need to address is, how long will a competitive advantage last once it has been created? What is the durability of competitive advantage given that other companies are also seeking to develop distinctive competencies that will give them a competitive advantage? The answer depends upon three factors: barriers to imitation, the capability of competitors, and the general dynamism of an industry's environment.

Barriers to Imitation
● ● ● ● ● ● ● ● ● ● ● ● ● ● ● ● ● ● ●

A company with a competitive advantage will earn higher-than-average profits. These profits send a signal to rivals that the company is in possession of some valuable distinctive competency that allows it to create superior value. Naturally, its competitors will try to identify and imitate that competency. Insofar as they are successful, they may ultimately surpass the company's superior profits.[22] How quickly will rivals imitate a company's distinctive competencies? This is an important question, because the speed of imitation has a bearing upon the durability of a company's competitive advantage. Other things being equal, the more rapidly competitors imitate a company's distinctive competencies, the less durable its competitive advantage will be and the more important it is that the company continually improve its competencies to stay one step ahead of the imitators. It is important to stress at the outset that ultimately almost any distinctive competency can be imitated by a competitor. The critical issue is *time*. The longer it takes competitors to imitate a distinctive competency, the greater the opportunity the company has to build a strong market position and reputation with consumers, which is then more difficult for competitors to attack. Moreover, the longer it takes to achieve an imitation, the greater is the opportunity for the imitated company to improve on its competency or build other competencies, thereby staying one step ahead of the competition.

Barriers to imitation are a primary determinant of the speed of imitation. **Barriers to imitation** are factors that make it difficult for a competitor to copy a company's distinctive competencies. The greater the barriers to such imitation, the more sustainable is a company's competitive advantage.[23]

Imitating Resources   In general, the easiest distinctive competencies for prospective rivals to imitate tend to be those based on possession of unique and valuable tangible resources, such as buildings, plant, and equipment. Such resources are visible to competitors and can often be purchased on the open market. For example, if a company's competitive advantage is based on its sole possession of efficient-scale manufacturing facilities, competitors may move fairly quickly to establish similar facilities. Although Ford gained a competitive advantage over General Motors in the 1920s by being the first to adopt an assembly line manufacturing technology to produce automobiles, General Motors quickly imitated that innovation, surpassing Ford's distinctive competence in the process. A similar process is occurring in the auto industry at present, as companies try to imitate Toyota's famous production system, which formed the basis for much of its competitive advantage during the 1970s and 1980s. GM's Saturn plant, for instance, is GM's attempt to replicate Toyota's production system.

Intangible resources can be more difficult to imitate. This is particularly true of brand names. Brand names are important because they symbolize a company's reputation. In the heavy earthmoving equipment industry, for example, the Caterpillar brand name is synonymous with high quality and superior after-sales service and support. Similarly, the St. Michael's brand name used by Marks & Spencer, Britain's largest retailer and one of the world's most profitable, symbolizes high-quality, reasonably priced clothing. Customers will often display a preference for the products of such companies because the brand name is an important guarantee of high quality. Although competitors might like to imitate well-established brand names, the law prohibits them from doing so.

Marketing and technological know-how are also important intangible resources. Unlike brand names, however, company-specific marketing and technological know-how can be relatively easy to imitate. In the case of marketing know-how, the movement of skilled marketing personnel between companies may facilitate the general dissemination of know-how. For example, in the 1970s Ford was acknowledged as the best marketer among the big three U.S. auto companies. In 1979 it lost a lot of its marketing know-how to Chrysler when its most successful marketer, Lee Iacocca, joined Chrysler. Iacocca subsequently hired many of Ford's top marketing people to work with him at Chrysler. More generally, successful marketing strategies are relatively easy to imitate because they are so visible to competitors. Thus, Coca-Cola quickly imitated Pepsico's Diet Pepsi brand with the introduction of its own brand, Diet Coke. In a similar example, Compaq Computer recently imitated Dell Computer's successful marketing strategy of selling personal computers through mail order.

With regard to technological know-how, in theory, the patent system should make technological know-how relatively immune to imitation. Patents give the inventor of a new product a seventeen-year exclusive production agreement. Thus, for example, pharmaceutical giant Merck patented a cholesterol-reducing drug that is marketed under the brand name Mevacor. Approved by the Food and Drug Administration (FDA) in August 1987, Mevacor generated sales of $430 million in 1988 and annual sales of more than $1 billion in 1992. However, whereas it is relatively easy to use the patent system to protect a chemical compound from imitation, this is not true of many other inventions. In electrical and computer engineering, for example, it is often possible to "invent around" patents. One study found that 60 percent of patented innovations were successfully invented around in four years.[24] This suggests that, in general, distinctive competencies based on technological know-how can be relatively short-lived.

Imitating Capabilities   Imitating a company's capabilities tends to be more difficult than imitating its tangible and intangible resources, chiefly because a company's capabilities are often invisible to outsiders. Since capabilities are based on the way in which decisions are made and processes managed deep within a company, by definition it is hard for outsiders to discern them. Thus, for example, outsiders may have trouble identifying precisely why 3M is so successful at developing new products or why Nucor is such an efficient steel producer.

Taken alone, the invisible nature of capabilities would not be enough to halt imitation. In theory, competitors could still gain insights into how a company operates by hiring people away from that company. However, a company's capabilities rarely reside in a single individual. Rather, they are the product of numerous individuals interacting within a unique organizational setting. It is possible that no one individual within a company may be familiar with the totality of a company's internal operating routines and procedures. In such cases, hiring people away from a successful company in order to imitate its key capabilities may not be helpful.

Consider a football team. Its success is the product not of any one individual but of the way individuals work together as a team and the unwritten, or tacit, understanding between them. Therefore, the transfer of a star player from a winning to a losing team may not be enough to improve the performance of the losing team. However, suppose you buy the whole team. This is what almost happened in 1993 to the German subsidiary of General Motors. It had to obtain an injunction from the German government to prevent Ignacio Lopez de Arriortua, the former GM vice president of operations and the new CEO of Volkswagen, from poaching forty of GM's managers by offering them very high salaries. His intent was to take all the managers who were expert in low-cost production to Volkswagen, which is desperately trying to reduce its costs to compete with the Japanese. Clearly, he was trying to imitate GM's new-found competency in efficiency by buying GM's capabilities through buying its managers.

To sum up, since resources are easier to imitate than capabilities, a distinctive competency based on a company's unique capabilities is probably more durable (less imitable) than one based on its resources. It is more likely to form the foundation for a long-run competitive advantage.

Capability of Competitors

According to work by Pankaj Ghemawat, a major determinant of the capability of competitors to imitate a company's competitive advantage rapidly is the nature of the competitors' prior strategic commitments.[25] By *strategic commitment,* Ghemawat means a company's commitment to a particular way of doing business—that is, to developing a particular set of resources and capabilities. Ghemawat's point is that once a company has made a strategic commitment it will find it difficult to respond to new competition if doing so requires a break with this commitment. Therefore, when competitors already have long-established commitments to a particular way of doing business, they may be slow to imitate an innovating company's competitive advantage. Its competitive advantage will thus be relatively durable.

The U.S. automobile industry offers an example. From 1945 to 1975 the industry was dominated by the stable oligopoly of General Motors, Ford, and Chrysler, all of whom geared their operations to the production of large cars. When the market shifted from large cars to small, fuel-efficient ones during the late 1970s, U.S. companies lacked the resources and capabilities required to produce these cars. Their prior commitments had built the wrong kind of skills for this new environment. As a result, foreign producers, and particularly the Japanese, stepped into the market breach by providing compact, fuel-efficient, high-quality, and low-cost cars. The failure of U.S. auto manufacturers to react quickly to the distinctive competency of Japanese auto companies gave the latter time to build a strong market position and brand loyalty, which are now proving difficult to attack.

Industry Dynamism

A dynamic industry environment is one that is changing rapidly. We examined the factors that determine the dynamism and intensity of competition in an industry in Chapter 3, in which we discuss the external environment. The most dynamic industries tend to be those with a very high rate of product innovation, for instance, the consumer electronics industry and the personal computer industry. In dynamic industries, the rapid rate of innovation means that product life cycles are short and that competitive advantage can be very transitory. A company that has a competitive advantage today may find its market position outflanked tomorrow by a rival's innovation.

In the personal computer industry, for example, the rapid increase in computing power during the last two decades has contributed to a high degree of innovation and a turbulent environment. Reflecting the persistence of innovation, in the late 1970s and early 1980s, Apple Computer had an industrywide competitive advantage due to its innovation. Then in 1982 the advantage was seized by IBM with its introduction of its first personal computer. By the mid 1980s, however, IBM had lost its competitive advantage to high-power clone manufacturers such as Compaq, which had beaten IBM in the race to introduce a computer based upon Intel's 386 chip. In turn, in the late 1980s and early 1990s, Compaq subsequently lost its competitive advantage to companies such as Dell, which pioneered new low-cost ways of delivering computers to consumers (mail order) and in this way were able to undercut Compaq's price. Later Dell found it difficult to hold on to its competitive advantage in the face of rapid imitation of its strategy by rivals, including Compaq and Gateway 2000, which are also selling computers via mail order.

Summary

The durability of a company's competitive advantage depends on three factors: the height of barriers to imitation, the capability of competitors to imitate its innovation, and the general level of dynamism in the industry's environment. When barriers to imitation are low, capable competitors abound and the environment is very dynamic, with innovations being developed all the time, and competitive advantage is likely to be transitory. On the other hand, even within such industries, companies can build a more enduring competitive advantage if they are able to make investments that build barriers to imitation. During the 1980s Apple Computer built a competitive advantage based on the combination of a proprietary disk operating system and an intangible product image (as noted earlier, intangible resources are difficult to imitate). The resulting brand loyalty enabled Apple to carve out a fairly secure niche in an industry in which competitive advantage has otherwise proven to be very fleeting. However, by the mid 1990s its strategy had been imitated, primarily due to the introduction of Microsoft's Windows 95 operating system, which imitated most of the features that had enabled Apple to build brand loyalty. The result was that by 1996 Apple was in deep financial trouble, providing yet another example that no competitive advantage lasts forever. Ultimately, anything can be imitated.

WHY DO COMPANIES FAIL?

In this section we take the issue of why a company might lose its competitive advantage one step further and ask, Why do companies fail? We define a failing company as one whose profit rate is substantially lower than the average profit rate of its competitors. A company can lose its competitive advantage but still not fail. It may just earn average profits. Failure implies something more drastic. Failing companies typically earn low or negative profits; in other words, they are at a competitive disadvantage.

The question is particularly pertinent since some of the most successful companies of the twentieth century have seen their competitive position deteriorate in recent years. Companies such as IBM, General Motors, American Express, and Digital Equipment, which were once held up as examples of managerial excellence, have all registered large losses in recent years, although after several difficult years, a number of these companies have managed to put together impressive turnarounds. We explore three related reasons for failure: inertia, prior strategic commitments, and the Icarus paradox.

Inertia

The inertia argument says that companies find it difficult to change their strategies and structures in order to adapt to changing competitive conditions.[26] IBM is a classic example of this problem. For thirty years it was widely viewed as the world's most successful computer company. Then, in the space of a few short years, its success turned into a disaster, with a loss of $5 billion in 1992 leading to layoffs of more than 100,000 employees. IBM's troubles were caused by a dramatic decline in the cost of computing power as a result of innovations in microprocessors. With the advent of powerful low-cost microprocessors, the locus of the computer market shifted from mainframes to small, low-priced personal computers. This left IBM's huge mainframe operations with a much diminished market. Even though IBM had, and still has, a significant presence in the personal computer market, it had failed to shift the focus of its efforts away from mainframes and toward personal computers. This failure meant deep trouble for one of the most successful companies of the twentieth century.

Why do companies find it so difficult to adapt to new environmental conditions? One factor that seems to stand out is the role of an organization's capabilities in causing inertia. Earlier in the chapter, we argue that organizational capabilities can be a source of competitive advantage; the downside, however, is that they are difficult to change. Recall that capabilities are the way a company makes decisions and manages its processes. IBM always emphasized close coordination between different operating units and favored decision processes that stressed consensus among interdependent operating units as a prerequisite for a decision to go forward.[27] This capability was a source of advantage for IBM during the 1970s, when coordination among its worldwide operating units was necessary to develop, manufacture, and sell complex mainframes. But the slow-moving bureaucracy that it had spawned was a source of failure in the 1990s, when organizations had to adapt readily to rapid environmental change.

Capabilities are difficult to change because a certain distribution of power and influence is embedded within the established decision-making and management processes of an organization. Those who play key roles in a decision-making process clearly have more power. It follows that changing the established capabilities of an organization means changing its existing distribution of power and influence, and those whose power and influence would diminish resist such change. Proposals for change trigger turf battles. This power struggle and the political resistance associated with trying to alter the way in which an organization makes decisions and manages its process—that is, trying to change its capabilities—bring on inertia. This is not to say that companies cannot change. However, because change is so often resisted by those who feel threatened by it, in most cases change has to be induced by a crisis. By then the company may already be failing, as happened at IBM.

Prior Strategic Commitments

Ghemawat has argued that a company's prior strategic commitments not only limit its ability to imitate rivals but may also cause competitive disadvantage.[28] IBM, for instance, had made major investments in the mainframe computer business. As a result, when the market shifted, it was stuck with significant resources that were specialized to that particular business. The company had manufacturing facilities geared to the production of mainframes, research organizations that were similarly specialized, and a mainframe sales force. Since these resources were not well suited to the newly emerging personal computer business, IBM's difficulties in the early 1990s were in a sense inevitable. Its prior strategic commitments locked IBM into a business that was shrinking. Shedding these resources was bound to cause hardship for all of the organization's stakeholders.

The Icarus Paradox

In his book, Danny Miller postulated that the roots of competitive failure can be found in what he termed the Icarus paradox.[29] Icarus is a figure in Greek mythology who used a pair of wings, made for him by his father, to escape from an island where he was being held prisoner. He flew so well that he went higher and higher, ever closer to the sun, until the heat of the sun melted the wax that held his wings together and he plunged to his death in the Aegean Sea. The paradox is that his greatest asset, his ability to fly, caused his demise. Miller argues that the same paradox applies to many once successful companies. According to Miller, many companies become so dazzled by their early success that they believe more of the same type of effort is the way to future success. As a result, however, a company can become so specialized and inner-directed that it loses sight of market realities and the fundamental requirements for achieving a competitive advantage. Sooner or later this leads to failure.

Miller identified four major categories among the rising and falling companies. The "craftsmen," such as Texas Instruments and Digital Equipment Corporation (DEC) achieved early success through engineering excellence. However, the companies then became so obsessed with engineering details that they lost sight of market realities. (The story of DEC's demise is summarized in Strategy in Action 4.5.) Then there are the "builders," for instance, Gulf & Western and ITT. Having built successful, moderately diversified companies, they then became so enchanted with diversification for its own sake that they continued to diversify far beyond the point at which it was profitable to do so. Miller's third group are the "pioneers," such as Wang Laboratories. Enamored of their own originally brilliant innovations, they continued to search for additional brilliant innovations but ended up producing novel but completely useless products. The final category is composed of the "salesmen," exemplified by Procter & Gamble and Chrysler. They became so convinced of their ability to sell anything that they paid scant attention to product development and manufacturing excellence and, as a result, spawned a proliferation of bland, inferior products.

STRATEGY *in* ACTION

The Road to Ruin at DEC

DEC's original success was founded upon the minicomputer, a cheaper, more flexible version of its mainframe cousins that Ken Olson and his brilliant team of engineers invented in the 1960s. Olson and his staff improved their original minis until they absolutely could not be beat for quality and reliability. In the 1970s their VAX series of minicomputers was widely regarded as the most reliable computer ever produced. DEC was rewarded by high profit rates and rapid growth. By 1990 DEC was number twenty-seven on the *Fortune* 500 list of the largest corporations in America.

However, buoyed up by its own success, DEC turned into an engineering monoculture. Its engineers became idols; its marketing and accounting staffs were barely tolerated. Component specs and design standards were all that senior managers understood. Technological fine-tuning became such an obsession that the needs of customers for smaller, more economical, user-friendly computers were ignored. DEC's personal computers, for example, bombed because they were so out of touch with the needs of consumers, while the company failed to respond to the threat to its core market presented by the rise of computer workstations and client/server architecture. Indeed, Ken Olson was known for dismissing such new products. He once said, "We always say that customers are right, but they are not always right." Perhaps; but DEC, blinded by its own early success, failed to remain responsive to its customers and to changing market conditions.

By the early 1990s DEC was a company in deep trouble. Olson was forced out of DEC in July 1992, and the company lost billions of dollars between 1992 and 1995. The company returned to profitability in 1996, primarily because of the success of a turnaround strategy aimed at reorienting the company to serve precisely those areas that Olson had dismissed.[30]

AVOIDING FAILURE AND SUSTAINING COMPETITIVE ADVANTAGE

How can a company avoid the traps that have snared so many once successful companies? How can it build a sustainable competitive advantage? We do not give a complete answer here, since much of the remaining text deals with these issues. However, a number of key points can be made at this juncture.

Focus on the Building Blocks of Competitive Advantage

First, maintaining a competitive advantage requires a company to continue focusing on the four generic building blocks of competitive advantage—efficiency, quality, innovation, and customer responsiveness—and to develop distinctive competencies that contribute to superior performance in these areas. One of the messages of Miller's Icarus paradox is that many successful companies become unbalanced in their pursuit of distinctive competencies. DEC, for example, focused on engineering quality at the expense of almost everything else, including, most importantly, customer responsiveness. Other companies forget to focus on any distinctive competency. This was certainly the case at ITT, where an empire-building CEO, Harold Geneen, focused on diversification but lost sight of the need to focus on achieving excellence in efficiency, quality, innovation, and customer responsiveness at the level of business units within ITT.

Institute Continuous Improvement and Learning

The only constant in the world is change. Today's source of competitive advantage may soon be rapidly imitated by capable competitors, or it may be made obsolete by the innovations of a rival. In such a dynamic and fast-paced environment, the only way that a company can maintain a competitive advantage over time is to improve its efficiency, quality, innovation, and customer responsiveness continually. The way to do this is to recognize the importance of learning within the organization.[31] The most successful companies are not those that stand still, resting on their laurels. They are those that continually seek out ways of improving their operations, and in the process they are constantly upgrading the value of their distinctive competencies or creating new ones. Companies such as Motorola and Toyota have a reputation for being learning organizations. What this means is that they are continually analyzing the processes that underlie their efficiency, quality, innovation, and customer responsiveness. Their objective is to learn from prior mistakes and to seek out ways to improve their processes over time. This has enabled Toyota, for example, to upgrade its employee productivity and product quality continually, allowing the company to stay one step ahead of imitators.

Track Best Industrial Practice and Use Benchmarking

One of the best ways to develop distinctive competencies that contribute toward superior efficiency, quality, innovation, and customer responsiveness is to identify **best industrial practice** and to adopt it. Only by so doing will a company be able to build and maintain the resources and capabilities that underpin excellence in efficiency, quality, innovation, and customer responsiveness. What constitutes best industrial practice is an issue we discuss in some depth in Chapter 5. However, it requires tracking the practice of other companies, and perhaps the best way to do so is through **benchmarking**. This is the process of measuring the company against the products, practices, and services of some of its most efficient global competitors. For example, when Xerox was in trouble in the early 1980s, it decided to institute a policy of benchmarking as a means of identifying ways to improve the efficiency of its operations. Xerox benchmarked L.L. Bean for distribution procedures, Deere & Company for central computer operations, Procter & Gamble for marketing, and Florida Power & Light for total quality management (TQM) processes. By the early 1990s Xerox was benchmarking 240 functions against comparable areas in other companies. This process has been credited with helping Xerox dramatically improve the efficiency of its operations.[32]

Overcome Inertia

A further reason for failure is an inability to adapt to changing conditions because of organizational inertia. Overcoming the barriers to change within an organization is one of the key requirements for maintaining a competitive advantage, and we devote a whole chapter, Chapter 14, to this issue. Suffice it to say here that identifying barriers to change is an important first step. Once this step has been taken, implementing change requires good leadership, the judicious use of power, and appropriate changes in organizational structure and control systems. All these issues are discussed later in the book.

SUMMARY OF CHAPTER

The principal objective of this chapter is to identify the basis of competitive advantage—examining why, within a given industry, some companies outperform others. Competitive advantage is the product of at least one of the following: superior efficiency, superior quality, superior innovation, and superior customer responsiveness. Achieving superiority requires that a company develop appropriate distinctive competencies, which in turn are a product of the kind of resources and capabilities that a company possesses. The chapter also examines issues related to the durability of competitive advantage. This durability is determined by the height of barriers to imitation, the capability of competitors to imitate a company's advantage, and the general level of environmental turbulence. Finally, the discussion of why companies fail and what they can do to avoid failure indicates that failure is due to factors such as organizational inertia, prior strategic commitments, and the Icarus paradox. Avoiding failure requires that a company constantly try to upgrade its distinctive competencies in accordance with best industrial practice and take steps to overcome organizational inertia. The main points made in this chapter can be summarized as follows:

✔ The source of a competitive advantage is superior value creation.

✔ To create superior value, a company must lower its costs, differentiate its product so that it can charge a higher price, or do both simultaneously.

✔ The four generic building blocks of competitive advantage are efficiency, quality, innovation, and customer responsiveness.

✔ Superior efficiency enables a company to lower its costs; superior quality allows it both to charge a higher price and to lower its costs; and superior customer service lets it charge a higher price. Superior innovation can lead to higher prices, particularly in the case of product innovations; or it can lead to lower unit costs, particularly in the case of process innovations.

✔ Distinctive competencies are the unique strengths of a company. Valuable distinctive competencies enable a company to earn a profit rate that is above the industry's average.

✔ The distinctive competencies of an organization arise from its resources and capabilities.

✔ Resources refer to the financial, physical, human, technological, and organizational assets of a company.

✔ Capabilities refer to a company's skills at coordinating and putting resources to productive use.

✔ In order to achieve a competitive advantage, companies need to pursue strategies that build on the existing resources and capabilities of an organization (its competencies) and they need to formulate strategies that build additional resources and capabilities (develop new competencies).

✔ The durability of a company's competitive advantage depends on the height of barriers to imitation, the capability of competitors, and environmental dynamism.

✔ Failing companies typically earn low or negative profits. Three factors seem to contribute to failure: organizational inertia in the face of environmental change, the nature of a company's prior strategic commitments, and the Icarus paradox.

✔ Avoiding failure requires a constant focus on the basic building blocks of competitive advantage, continuous improvement and learning, identification and adoption of best industrial practice, and victory over inertia.

DISCUSSION QUESTIONS

1. What are the main implications of the material discussed in this chapter for strategy formulation?

2. When is a company's competitive advantage most likely to endure over time?

3. Which is more important in explaining the success and failure of companies, strategy or luck?

Practicing Strategic Management

SMALL GROUP EXERCISE
Analyzing Competitive Advantage

Break into a group of three to five people and reread the Opening Case to this chapter, which profiled Intel. You are a team of consultants that has been hired by AMD, a competitor to Intel in the market for microprocessors. AMD has asked you to evaluate Intel's competitive position and to suggest a strategy that will enable AMD to beat Intel at its own game. Prepare some brief statements for AMD's management that:

1. Identify the source of Intel's competitive advantage.

2. Highlight the barriers to imitation that protect Intel's competitive advantage from rivals such as AMD.

3. Describe and justify the main elements of your recommended strategy for AMD.

EXPLORING THE WEB
Visiting Johnson & Johnson

Visit the Web site of Johnson & Johnson (http://www.jnj.com). Read through the material contained on the site, paying particular attention to the features on the company's history, its credo, innovations, and company news. On the basis of this information, answer the following questions:

1. Do you think that Johnson & Johnson has a distinctive competence?

2. What is the nature of this competence? How does it help the company to attain a competitive advantage?

3. What are the resources and capabilities that underlie this competence? Where do these resources and capabilities come from?

4. How imitable is Johnson & Johnson's distinctive competence?

   Search the Web for a company site that goes into depth about the history, products, and competitive position of that company. On the basis of the information you collect, answer the following questions:

1. Does the company have a distinctive competence?

2. What is the nature of this competence? How does it help the company to attain a competitive advantage?

3. What are the resources and capabilities that underlie this competence? Where do these resources and capabilities come from?

4. How imitable is the company's distinctive competence?

ARTICLE FILE 4

Find an example of a company that has sustained its competitive advantage for more than ten years. Identify the source of the competitive advantage, and describe why it has lasted so long.

STRATEGIC MANAGEMENT PROJECT
Module 4

This module deals with the competitive position of your company. With the information you have at your disposal, perform the tasks and answer the questions listed here:

1. Identify whether your company has a competitive advantage or disadvantage in its primary industry. (Its primary industry is the one in which it has the most sales.)

2. Evaluate your company against the four generic building blocks of competitive advantage: efficiency, quality, innovation, and customer responsiveness. How does this exercise help you understand the performance of your company relative to that of its competitors?

3. What are the distinctive competencies of your company?

4. What role have prior strategies played in shaping the distinctive competencies of your company? What has been the role of luck?

5. Do the strategies currently pursued by your company build on its distinctive competencies? Are they an attempt to build new competencies?

6. What are the barriers to imitating the distinctive competencies of your company?

7. Is there any evidence that your company finds it difficult to adapt to changing industry conditions? If so, why do you think this is the case?

Marks & Spencer

Marks & Spencer (M&S) is a British re-tailing institution. Founded in 1884 by Michael Marks, a Polish Jew who had emigrated to England, the company has been a national chain since the early 1900s. By 1926 the company had a branch in every major town in the country and had become Britain's largest retailer, a position it still held in 1996. Primarily a supplier of clothing and foodstuffs, M&S is one of the world's most profitable retailers. In 1992 M&S's 280 United Kingdom stores had sales of $7.5 billion. M&S accounted for 15.0 percent of all retail clothing sales in the United Kingdom, and 4.6 percent of all food sales. According to the *Guinness Book of Records*, in 1991 the company's flagship store at Marble Arch in London had a turnover of $3,700 per square foot, more than any other department store in the world.

M&S provides a selective range of clothing and food items aimed at rapid turnover. The firm sells all its products under its own St. Michael's label. M&S offers high-quality products at moderate rather than low prices. This combination of high quality and reasonable price encourages customers to associate M&S with value for money, and the firm's ability to deliver this combination consistently over the years has built up enormous goodwill from customers in Britain. In fact, so strong is M&S's reputation among British consumers that the company does no advertising in that market.

To achieve the combination of moderate prices and high quality, M&S works very closely with its suppliers, many of whom have been selling a major portion of their output to M&S for generations. The focus on quality is reinforced by M&S's practice of having its technical people work closely with suppliers on product design. Suppliers are more than willing to respond to the firm's demands, for they know that M&S is loyal to its suppliers and as it grows so do they. The sales volume generated by M&S's strategy of providing only a selective range of clothing and food enables M&S's suppliers to realize substantial economies of scale from large production runs. These cost savings are then passed on to M&S in the form of lower prices. In turn, M&S passes on part of the savings to the consumer.

Crucial to M&S's effectiveness is a clear focus on the customer. The tone is set by top management. Each senior manager makes a habit of wearing M&S clothes and eating M&S food. Thus managers develop an understanding of what it is that customers want and like about M&S products; by staying close to the customer, they can improve the quality and design of the products they offer. The focus on the customer is reinforced at the store level by store managers who monitor sales volume and quickly identify lines that are selling and those that are not. Then store managers can transmit this information to suppliers, which have the capacity to modify their production quickly, increasing the output of lines that are selling well and reducing the output of lines that are not moving.

Another central feature of M&S is its pioneering approach to human relations. Long before it became fashionable to do so, M&S had developed a commitment to the well-being of its employees. M&S has always viewed itself as a family business with a broad responsibility for the welfare of its employees. M&S offers employees medical and pension plans with benefits that are well above the average within the industry. Likewise, the company pays its employees at a rate that is well above the average within the industry, and it makes a practice of promoting employees from within, rather than hiring from outside. Furthermore, there are a series of in-store amenities for employees, including subsidized cafeterias, medical services, recreation rooms, and hairdressing salons. The reward for M&S is the trust and loyalty of its employees and, ultimately, high employee productivity.

Also vital is the company's commitment to simplifying its operating structure and strategic control systems. M&S has a very flat hierarchy; there is little in the way of intervening management layers between store managers and top management. The firm utilizes just two profit margins, one for foodstuff and one for clothing. This practice reduces bureaucracy and frees its store managers from worrying about pricing issues. Instead, they are encouraged to focus on maximizing sales volume. A store's performance is assessed by its sales volume. Control is achieved partly through formal budgetary procedures and partly through an informal probing process, in which top management drops in unannounced at stores and quizzes managers there about the store. In a typical year, just about every store in Britain will receive at least one unannounced visit from top management. This keeps store managers on their toes and constantly alert to the need to provide the kind of value-for-money products that customers have come to associate with M&S.[33]

Case Discussion Questions

1. What do you think is the source of Marks & Spencer's competitive advantage?

2. Marks & Spencer has managed to maintain its competitive advantage in British retailing for more than fifty years. Why, do you think, have rival firms found Marks & Spencer's competitive position so difficult to attack?

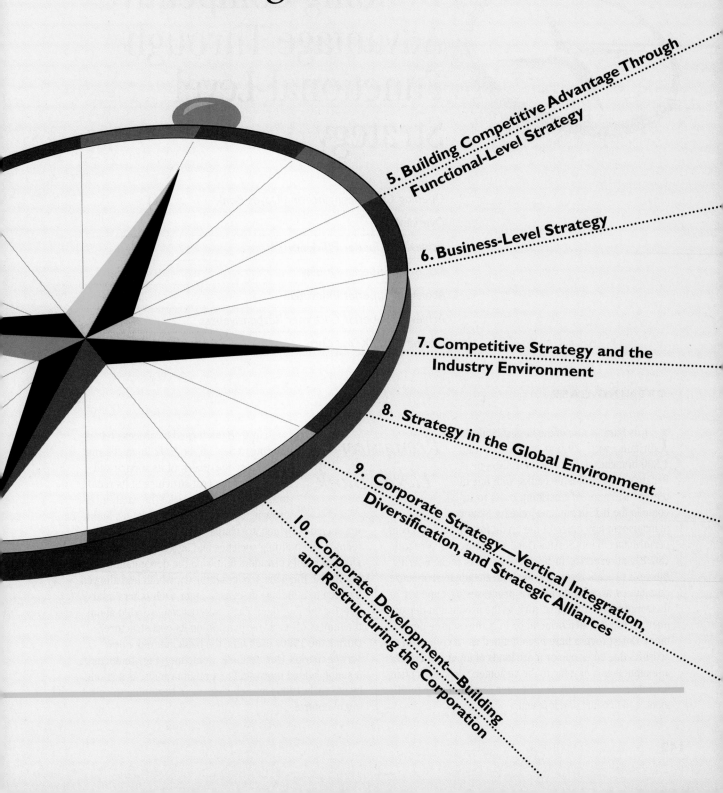

PART THREE

Strategies

5. Building Competitive Advantage Through Functional-Level Strategy

6. Business-Level Strategy

7. Competitive Strategy and the Industry Environment

8. Strategy in the Global Environment

9. Corporate Strategy—Vertical Integration, Diversification, and Strategic Alliances

10. Corporate Development—Building and Restructuring the Corporation

Building Competitive Advantage Through Functional-Level Strategy

Opening Case: Reengineering Lloyds Bank

Overview

Achieving Superior Efficiency

Achieving Superior Quality

Achieving Superior Innovation

Achieving Superior Customer Responsiveness

Closing Case: Xerox Corp.

OPENING CASE

Reengineering Lloyds Bank

Lloyds Bank is one of the largest banks in Britain, with 29,000 employees and 1,800 branches nationwide. It is also one of Britain's most profitable banks, with one of the lowest ratios of operating costs to income in the British banking industry. Senior management lays much of the credit for the bank's recent performance on its Service Quality Improvement Program (SQIP), an exercise in business process reengineering. Business process reengineering is an attempt to reorganize companies around their core processes as opposed to their traditional functions, such as the production department, marketing department, or human resource department. Core process have been defined as "a collection of activities that takes one or more kinds of input and creates an output that is of value to the customer." Processes often include activities such as customer service, order fulfillment, and product development.

Lloyds Bank turned to process reengineering in September 1992 in an attempt to increase the quality of its service and drive down the cost structure of its retail branch banking network. The catalyst was growing competition from Britain's building societies (which are similar to U.S. savings and loans). The building societies had aggressively pursued Lloyds's retail customers following the deregulation of the British financial services industry, which had allowed banks and building societies to enter each others' markets for the first time. The bank was also worried about the impact of service expansion on its cost structure. During the 1980s each time the bank entered a new service market (for example, home mortgage financing), it simply added more staff to a retail branch. As a result, by the early 1990s branch costs were beginning to spiral out of control.

Under the traditional system at Lloyds, staff were given narrowly defined functional responsibilities within the context of a rigid hierarchical structure. One set of people would be responsible for managing checking accounts, another for reviewing a customer's credit, another for issuing credit cards, and so on. One consequence was that countless people and bits of paper were involved in what, from the customers' point of view, was a single process. For example, under the old system for opening an account at a Lloyds branch, an application form could spend a month wandering from desk to desk as different staff ordered bank cards, reviewed credit details, ordered checkbooks, opened savings accounts, and so on. Under the new system, a single person is now responsible for a largely paperless "quality welcome" process that entails reviewing the customer's credit history; setting up an account; and issuing credit cards, ATM cards, and checkbooks. Under the new process it usually takes less than a week for a new account to be fully functional.

In addition to the "quality welcome" process, Lloyds identified five other core processes within its branches including "lending control," "periodic payments," and "customer retention." Each process was assigned a process owner, whose job it was to make sure that the process was reengineered to achieve Lloyds's goals of driving down costs and increasing the quality of customer service. The processes were initially tested in a make-believe branch before being introduced across the bank's network of retail branches in a series of waves starting in July 1993. The early indications are that SQIP is having the desired effect. Lloyds' managers claim that the reengineering project has comfortably cleared the 12 percent return on capital hurdle required of business ideas. For example, the number of faulty checkbook orders fell by 30 percent in the first two months of the program, producing savings large enough to pay for the computers that monitor this activity under the new process. There is also evidence that the bank is meeting its central aim of improving customer service. Lloyds's own measure of customer satisfaction rose from 73 percent in mid 1993, when the project began, to 80 percent by mid 1995, putting the bank comfortably ahead of its two largest British rivals. Having said that, however, a 7 percent improvement in customer satisfaction is less than stunning.

Also on the downside, Lloyds has had to deal with morale problems in many of its branches, where the reengineering process is often perceived to be a subtle way of cutting jobs and, in some cases, closing branches altogether. The bank closed 300 branches between 1990 and 1995, although management claims that this effort is independent of the reengineering process, which focuses on what is happening within branches. Management does not question the fact that 200 jobs have been lost as a result of the reengineering process, but it points out that all these losses were voluntary. In point of fact, those hit hardest by the reengineering effort seem to be middle-level managers, as opposed to branch employees. Between mid 1993 and mid 1995, the bank reduced the number of area directors from eighty to forty-one, largely because the reengineering effort enabled the bank to do more with less. Whatever the true cause of the job losses, there are concerns that employee morale problems are inhibiting the ability of Lloyds to realize the full benefits of its reengineering efforts.[1]

OVERVIEW

In Chapter 4 we discuss the central role played by efficiency, quality, innovation, and customer responsiveness in building and maintaining a competitive advantage. In this chapter we look at what managers can do at the level of functions, or operations, within a company to attain superior efficiency, quality, innovation, and customer responsiveness. Functional-level strategies are those directed at improving the effectiveness of basic operations within a company, such as production, marketing, materials management, research and development, and human resources. Even though these strategies may be focused on a given function, as often as not they embrace two or more functions and require close cooperation among functions to attain companywide efficiency, quality, innovation, and customer responsiveness goals.

For example, the Opening Case describes how Lloyds Bank is utilizing a reengineering approach to drive down its cost structure and hold onto customers in the face of competition from Britain's building societies. In terms of the framework developed in the last chapter, Lloyds is using business process reengineering as a tool to increase the efficiency, quality, and customer responsiveness of its retail branch banking network. By reengineering activities, Lloyds has found that it can "do more with less," which implies increased efficiency. Moreover, the Opening Case suggests that Lloyds has increased its product quality, as demonstrated by the fall in errors for new checkbooks. This increase in product quality is no doubt one factor that has helped the bank to become more customer responsive, as measured by the rise in its customer satisfaction rating between 1993 and 1995.

We might also note that the focus of Lloyds's efforts is not upon individual business functions, such as credit control or account management, but upon processes that cut across functions. Lloyds's focus is consistent with the argument made in the last chapter that efficiency, quality, innovation, and customer responsiveness are goals that cut across the traditional functions of most enterprises. In fact, their attainment frequently requires intense cross-functional coordination. Focusing upon business processes, as opposed to functions, is one way of achieving such coordination, although as we shall see later in this book (Chapter 12), there are other ways of achieving cross-functional coordination.

To explore the issue of functional-level strategies further, in this chapter we look at how companies can increase their efficiency, quality, innovation, and customer responsiveness. Although in some cases we focus upon the contribution of a given function toward attaining these goals, such as production or marketing, we also emphasize the importance of strategies and policies that cut across functions. By the time you have finished this chapter, you should have a much clearer understanding of the actions that managers can take at the operating level to attain superior efficiency, quality, innovation, and customer responsiveness.

ACHIEVING SUPERIOR EFFICIENCY

A company is a device for transforming inputs into outputs. Inputs are basic factors of production such as labor, land, capital, management, technological know-how, and so on. Outputs are the goods and services that a company produces. The simplest measure of efficiency is the quantity of inputs that it takes to produce a given output; that is, Efficiency = outputs/inputs. The more efficient a company, the fewer the inputs required to produce a given output and, therefore, the lower its cost structure will be. Put another way, an efficient company has higher productivity than its rivals and, therefore, lower costs.

In this section we review the various steps that companies can take at the functional level to boost their efficiency and, accordingly, lower their unit costs. We start with the primary functions of production and marketing before moving on to look at the various support functions of the enterprise. We should emphasize that achieving superior quality plays a major role in achieving superior efficiency. However, we delay discussion of how to achieve superior quality until the next section.

Production and Efficiency: Economies of Scale

Economies of scale are unit-cost reductions associated with a large scale of output. One source of economies of scale is the ability to spread fixed costs over a large production volume. Fixed costs are those that must be incurred to produce a product whatever the level of output; they include the costs of purchasing machinery, the costs of setting up machinery for individual production runs, the costs of facilities, and the costs of advertising and R&D. Another source of economies of scale is the ability of companies producing in large volumes to achieve a greater division of labor and specialization. Specialization, in turn, is said to have a favorable impact on productivity, mainly because it enables employees to become very skilled at performing a particular task.

The classic example of such economies is Ford's Model T automobile. The world's first mass-produced car, the Model T Ford was introduced in 1923. Until then Ford had made cars using an expensive hand-built "craft production" method. By introducing mass production techniques, the company achieved greater division of labor (that is, it split assembly into small, repeatable tasks) and specialization, which boosted employees' productivity. Ford was also able to spread the fixed costs of developing an automobile and setting up production machinery over a large volume of output. As a result of these economies, the cost of manufacturing a car at Ford fell from $3,000 to less than $900 (in 1958 dollars).[2]

In many other situations, economies of scale lower costs. Du Pont, for example, was able to reduce the cost of rayon fiber from $.53 per pound to $.17 per pound in less than two decades, mainly through economies of scale. Nor are economies of scale relevant just to manufacturing enterprises such as Ford and Du Pont. Many service companies also benefit from the realization of substantial economies of scale. An example is given in Strategy in Action 5.1, which looks at the economies of scale that might be realized from the merger between two money center New York banks, Chemical Bank and Chase Manhattan Bank.

It is important to note that the scope for realizing economies of scale is ultimately limited. Indeed, many experts argue that after a certain minimum efficient scale (MES) of output is reached, there are few, if any, additional economies of scale to be had from expanding volume.[3] (**Minimum efficient scale** is the minimum plant size necessary to gain significant economies of scale.) In other words, as shown in Figure 5.1, the long-run unit-cost curve of a company is L-shaped. At outputs beyond MES in Figure 5.1, additional cost reductions are hard to come by. Another point worth bearing in mind is that diseconomies of scale can arise when large enterprises build up a substantial corporate bureaucracy that increases corporate overhead without reducing unit costs.

Production and Efficiency: Learning Effects

Learning effects are cost savings that come from learning by doing. Labor, for example, learns by repetition how best to carry out a task. In other words, labor productivity increases over time, and unit costs fall as individuals learn the most efficient way to perform a particular task. Equally important, in new manufacturing facilities management typically learns over time how best to run the new operation. Hence, production costs decline because of increasing labor productivity and management efficiency.

STRATEGY in ACTION

Chemical and Chase Banks Merge to Realize Economies of Scale

In August 1995 two of the world's largest banks, Chemical Bank and Chase Manhattan Bank, both of New York, announced their intention to merge. The merger was officially completed on March 31, 1996. The combined bank, which goes under the Chase name, has more than $300 billion in assets, making it the largest bank in the United States and the fourth largest in the world. The new Chase is capitalized at $20 billion and is number one or two in the United States in numerous segments of the banking business, including loan syndication, trading of derivatives, currency and securities trading, global custody services, luxury auto financing, New York City retail banking, and mortgaging services.

The prime reason given for the merger was anticipated cost savings of more than $1.7 billion per year, primarily through the realization of economies of scale. The newly merged bank has good reason for thinking that these kinds of cost savings are possible. In a 1991 merger between Chemical and Manufacturers Hanover, another New York-based bank, cost savings of $750 million per year were realized from the elimination of duplicated assets, including physical facilities, information systems, and personnel.

The cost savings in the Chase-Chemical combination have several sources. First, significant economies of scale are possible from combining the 600 retail branches of the original banks. Closing down excess branches and consolidating its retail business into a smaller number of branches should allow the new bank to increase the capacity utilization of its retail banking network significantly. The combined bank will be able to generate the same volume of retail business from fewer branches. The fixed costs associated with retail branches—including rents, personnel, equipment, and utility costs—will drop, which translates into a substantial reduction in the unit cost required to serve the average customer.

A second source of scale-based cost savings arises from the combination of a whole array of "back-office" functions. For example, the combined bank now only has to operate one computer network, instead of two. By getting greater utilization out of a fixed computer infrastructure—including mainframe computers, servers, and the associated software—the combined bank should be able to drive down its fixed cost structure even further. Substantial savings will also arise from the combination of management functions. For example, the new Chase bank has doubled the number of auto loans and mortgage originations it issues, but because of office automation it can manage the increased volume with less than twice the management staff. This saving implies a big reduction in fixed costs and a corresponding fall in the unit costs of servicing the average auto loan or mortgage customer.[4]

Learning effects tend to be more significant when a technologically complex task is repeated, since there is more to learn. Thus, learning effects are more significant in an assembly process involving 1,000 complex steps than in an assembly process involving 100 simple steps. Although learning effects are normally associated with manufacturing processes, as with economies of scale there are reasons to believe that they are just as important in many service industries. For example, one famous study of learning in the context of the health care industry found that more experienced medical providers posted significantly lower mortality rates for a number of common surgical procedures, suggesting that learning effects are at work in surgery.[5] The authors of this study used the evidence to argue for the establishment of regional referral centers for the provision of highly specialized medical care. These centers would perform many specific surgical procedures (for example, heart surgery), replacing local facilities with lower volumes and presumably higher mortality rates.

FIGURE 5.1

A Typical Long-Run
Unit-Cost Curve

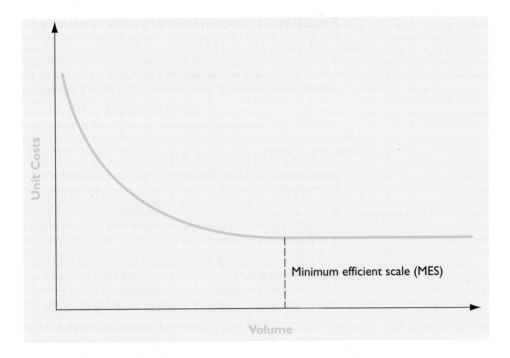

In terms of the long-run average cost curve of a company, while economies of scale imply a movement along the curve (for example, from *A* to *B* as shown in Figure 5.2), the realization of learning effects implies a downward shift of the entire curve (as shown from *B* to *C* in Figure 5.2) as both labor and management become more efficient over time at performing their tasks at each and every level of output. No matter how complex the task, however, learning effects typically die out after a limited period of time. Indeed, it has been suggested that they are really important only during the start-up period of a new process and cease after two or three years.[6]

FIGURE 5.2

Economies of Scale and
Learning Effects

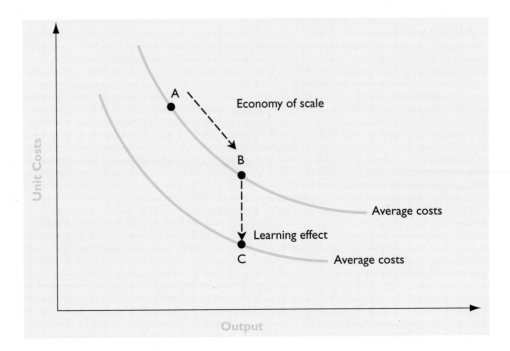

Production and Efficiency: The Experience Curve

The experience curve refers to systematic unit-cost reductions that have been observed to occur over the life of a product.[7] According to the experience curve concept, unit manufacturing costs for a product typically decline by some characteristic amount each time accumulated output of the product is doubled. (Accumulated output is the total output of a product since its introduction.) The relationship was first observed in the aircraft industry, where it was found that each time accumulated output of airframes was doubled unit costs declined to 80 percent of their previous level.[8] Thus, the fourth airframe typically costs only 80 percent of the second airframe to produce, the eighth airframe only 80 percent of the fourth, the sixteenth only 80 percent of the eighth, and so on. The outcome of this process is a relationship between unit manufacturing costs and accumulated output similar to that illustrated in Figure 5.3.

Economies of scale and learning effects underlie the experience curve phenomenon. Put simply, as a company increases the accumulated volume of its output over time, it is able to realize both economies of scale (as volume increases) and learning effects. Consequently, unit costs fall with increases in accumulated output.

The strategic significance of the experience curve is clear. It suggests that increasing a company's product volume and market share will also bring cost advantages over the competition. Thus, company *A* in Figure 5.3, because it is further down the experience curve, has a clear cost advantage over company *B*. The concept is perhaps most important in those industries in which the production process involves the mass production of a standardized output (for example, the manufacture of semiconductor chips). If a company wishes to become more efficient, and thereby attain a low-cost position, it must try to ride down the experience curve as

FIGURE 5.3

A Typical
Experience Curve

5.2   STRATEGY *in* ACTION

Too Much Experience at Texas Instruments

Texas Instruments (TI) was an early user of the experience curve concept. TI was a technological innovator, first in silicon transistors and then in semiconductors. The company discovered that with every doubling of accumulated production volume of a transistor or semiconductor, unit costs declined to 73 percent of their previous level. Building on this insight, when TI first produced a new transistor or semiconductor, it would slash the price of the product to stimulate demand. The goal was to drive up the accumulated volume of production and so drive down costs through the realization of experience curve economies. As a result, during the 1960s and 1970s, TI hammered its competitors in transistors, moved on to prevail in semiconductors, and ultimately dominated in hand-held calculators and digital watches. Indeed, for the twenty years up until 1982, TI enjoyed rapid growth, with sales quadrupling between 1977 and 1981 alone.

However, after 1982 things began to go wrong for TI. The company's single-minded focus on cost reductions, an outgrowth of its strategic reliance on the ex-

perience curve, left it with a poor understanding of consumers' needs and market trends. Competitors such as Casio and Hewlett Packard began to make major inroads into TI's hand-held calculator business by focusing upon additional features that consumers demanded, rather than on cost and price. TI was slow to react to this trend and lost substantial market share as a result. In the late 1970s, TI also decided to focus on semiconductors for watches and calculators, where it had gained substantial experience curve-based cost economies, rather than develop metal-oxide semiconductors for computer memories and advanced semiconductors. As it turned out, however, with the growth in minicomputers and personal computers in the early 1980s, the market shifted toward high-power metal-oxide semiconductors. Consequently, TI soon found itself outflanked by Intel and Motorola. In sum, TI's focus on realizing experience curve economies initially benefited the company, but then it seems to have contributed toward a myopia that was to cost the company dearly.[9]

quickly as possible. This means constructing efficient scale manufacturing facilities even before the company has the demand and aggressively pursuing cost reductions from learning effects. The company might also need to adopt an aggressive marketing strategy, cutting prices to the bone and stressing heavy sales promotions in order to build up demand, and hence accumulated volume, as quickly as possible. Once down the experience curve, because of its superior efficiency, the company is likely to have a significant cost advantage over its competitors. For example, it has been argued that the early success of Texas Instruments was based on exploiting the experience curve (see Strategy in Action 5.2 for details), that Japanese semiconductor companies aggressively used such tactics to ride down the experience curve and gain a competitive advantage over their U.S. rivals in the market for DRAM chips, and that one reason Matsushita came to dominate the global market for VHS videotape recorders is that it based its strategy on the experience curve.[10]

However, the company furthest down the experience curve must not become complacent about its cost advantage. Strategy in Action 5.2 explains how obsession with the experience curve at Texas Instruments may have harmed the company in the long run. More generally, there are three reasons why companies should not become complacent about their efficiency-based cost advantages derived from experience effects. First, since neither learning effects nor economies of scale go on forever, the experience curve is likely to bottom out at some point; indeed, it must do so by definition. When this occurs, further unit-cost reductions from learning effects and economies of scale will be hard to come by. Thus, in time, other companies can catch up with the cost leader. Once this happens, a number of low-cost companies can have cost parity with each other. In such circumstances, a sustainable competitive advantage must rely on other strategic factors besides the minimization of production costs by utilizing existing technologies—factors such as better customer responsiveness, product quality, and innovation.

Second, cost advantages gained from experience effects can be made obsolete by the development of new technologies. For example, the price of television picture tubes followed the experience curve pattern from the introduction of television in the late 1940s until 1963. The average unit price dropped from $34 to $8 (in 1958 dollars) during that time period. The advent of color television interrupted the experience curve. Manufacturing picture tubes for color televisions required a new manufacturing technology, and the price for color TV tubes shot up to $51 by 1966. Then the experience curve reasserted itself. The price dropped to $48 in 1968, $37 in 1970, and $36 in 1972.[11] In short, technological change can alter the rules of the game, requiring that former low-cost companies take steps to reestablish their competitive edge.

A third reason for avoiding complacency is that high volume does not necessarily give a company a cost advantage. Some technologies have different cost functions. For example, the steel industry has two alternative manufacturing technologies: an integrated technology, which relies on the basic oxygen furnace, and a minimill technology, which depends on the electric arc furnace. As illustrated in Figure 5.4, the minimum efficient scale (MES) of the electric arc furnace is located at relatively low volumes, whereas the MES of the basic oxygen furnace is located at relatively high volumes. Even when both operations are producing at their most efficient output levels, steel companies with basic oxygen furnaces do not have a cost advantage over minimills.

FIGURE 5.4

Unit Production Costs in an Integrated Steel Mill and a Minimill

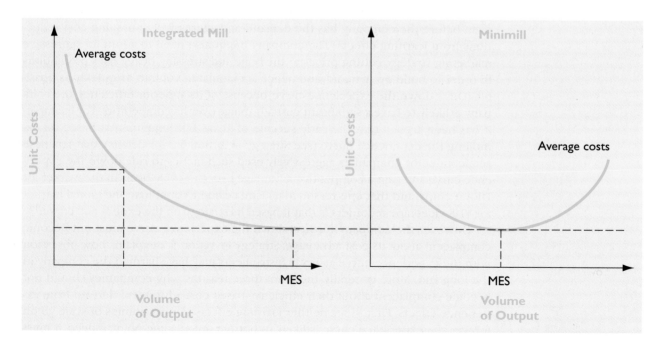

Consequently, the pursuit of experience economies by an integrated company using basic oxygen technology may not bring the kind of cost advantages that a naive reading of the experience curve phenomenon would lead the company to expect. Indeed, in recent years integrated companies have not been able to get enough orders to run at optimum capacity. Hence their production costs have been considerably higher than those of minimills.[12] More generally, as we discuss next, in many industries new flexible manufacturing technologies hold out the promise of allowing small manufacturers to produce at unit costs comparable to those of large assembly line operations.

Production and Efficiency: Flexible Manufacturing

Central to the concept of economies of scale is the idea that the best way to achieve high efficiency, and hence low unit costs, is through the mass production of a standardized output. The tradeoff implicit in this idea is between unit costs and product variety. Producing greater product variety from a factory implies shorter production runs, which in turn implies an inability to realize economies of scale. That is, wide product variety makes it difficult for a company to increase its production efficiency and thus reduce its unit costs. According to this logic, one way to increase efficiency and drive down unit costs is to limit product variety and produce a standardized product in large volumes (see Figure 5.5a).

This view of production efficiency has been challenged by the rise of flexible manufacturing technologies. The term *flexible manufacturing technology*—or *lean production,* as it is often called—covers a range of manufacturing technologies designed to (1) reduce setup times for complex equipment, (2) increase the utilization of individual machines through better scheduling, and (3) improve quality

FIGURE 5.5

The Tradeoff Between Costs and Product Variety

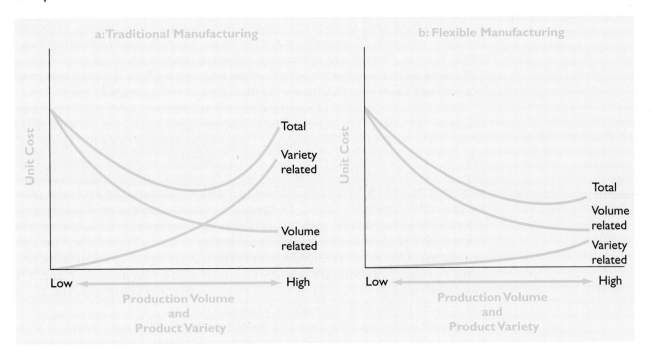

a: Traditional Manufacturing

Unit Cost

Total
Variety related
Volume related

Low ← → High

Production Volume and Product Variety

b: Flexible Manufacturing

Unit Cost

Total
Volume related
Variety related

Low ← → High

Production Volume and Product Variety

control at all stages of the manufacturing process.[13] Flexible manufacturing technologies (see Figure 5.5b) allow the company to produce a wider variety of end products at a unit cost that at one time could only be achieved through the mass production of a standardized output. Indeed, recent research suggests that the adoption of flexible manufacturing technologies may both increase efficiency and lower unit costs relative to what can be achieved by the mass production of a standardized output, as well as enable the company to customize its product offering to a much greater extent than was once thought possible. The term ***mass customization*** has been coined to describe the ability of companies to use flexible manufacturing technology to reconcile two goals that were once thought to be incompatible—low cost and product customization.[14]

Flexible manufacturing technologies vary in their sophistication and complexity. One of the most famous examples of a flexible manufacturing technology, Toyota's production system, is relatively unsophisticated, but it has been credited with making Toyota the most efficient auto company in the global industry. Toyota's flexible manufacturing system is profiled in Strategy in Action 5.3. **Flexible machine cells** are another common flexible manufacturing technology. A flexible machine cell is a grouping of various types of machinery, a common materials handler, and a centralized cell controller (computer). Each cell normally contains four to six machines capable of performing a variety of operations. The typical cell is dedicated to the production of a family of parts or products. The settings on machines are computer controlled, which allows each cell to switch quickly between the production of different parts or products.

Improved capacity utilization and reductions in work-in-progress (that is, stockpiles of partly finished products) and in waste are major efficiency benefits of flexible machine cells. Improved capacity utilization arises from the reduction in setup times and from the computer-controlled coordination of production flow between machines, which eliminates bottlenecks. The tight coordination between machines also reduces work-in-progress. Reductions in waste are due to the ability of computer-controlled machinery to identify ways to transform inputs into outputs while producing a minimum of unusable waste material. Whereas freestanding machines might be in use 50 percent of the time, the same machines when grouped into a cell can be used more than 80 percent of the time and produce the same end product with half the waste. This increases efficiency and results in lower costs.

The efficiency benefits of installing flexible manufacturing technology can be dramatic. W. L. Gore, a privately owned company that manufactures a wide range of products from high-tech computer cables to its famous Gore-Tex fabric, has adopted flexible cells in several of its forty-six factories. In its cable-making facilities, the effect has been to cut the time taken to make computer cables by 50 percent, to reduce stock by 33 percent, and to shrink the space taken up by the plant by 25 percent. Similarly, Compaq Computer, the manufacturer of personal computers, recently replaced three of the sixteen assembly lines in its Houston factory with twenty-one cells. As a result, employee productivity rose by 25 percent and the cost of converting the three assembly lines to cells was recouped in six months. Lexmark, a producer of computer printers, has also converted 80 percent of its 2,700-employee factories in Lexington, Kentucky, to flexible manufacturing cells, and it too has seen productivity increase by around 25 percent.[15]

Besides improving efficiency and lowering costs, flexible manufacturing technologies also enable companies to customize products to the unique demands of

5.3

STRATEGY *in* ACTION

Toyota's Lean Production System

Toyota's flexible manufacturing system was developed by one of the company's engineers, Ohno Taiichi. After working at Toyota for five years and visiting Ford's U.S. plants, Ohno became convinced that the mass-production philosophy for making cars was flawed. He saw numerous problems, including three major drawbacks. First, long production runs created massive inventories, which had to be stored in large warehouses. This was expensive, both because of the cost of warehousing and because inventories tied up capital in unproductive uses. Second, if the initial machine settings were wrong, long production runs resulted in the production of a large number of defects (that is, waste). Third, the mass-production system was unable to accommodate consumers' preferences for product diversity.

Ohno looked for ways to make shorter production runs economical. He developed a number of techniques designed to reduce setup times for production equipment (a major source of fixed costs). By using a system of levers and pulleys, he was able to reduce the time required to change dies on stamping equipment from a full day in 1950 to three minutes by 1971. This made small production runs economical, which in turn allowed Toyota to respond better to consumers' demands for product diversity. Small production runs also eliminated the need to hold large inventories, thereby reducing warehousing costs. Furthermore, small product runs and the lack of inventory meant that defective parts were only produced in small numbers and entered the assembly process immediately. This reduced waste and made it easier to trace defects to their source and fix the problem. In sum, Ohno's innovations enabled Toyota to produce a more diverse product range at a lower unit cost than was possible with conventional mass production.[16]

small consumer groups, at a cost that at one time could be achieved only by mass-producing a standardized output. Thus, these technologies help a company to achieve mass customization, which increases its customer responsiveness. For example, Compaq Computer plans to build all its computers to the specifications laid down by customers or retailers. With its plan for 100 or so cells at its Houston plant, the company figures that it will be able to build a wide variety of different models and to increase or decrease production of individual models in line with demand. With sixteen production lines, such flexibility and product customization would not be cost efficient, but with 100 cells it apparently is.[17]

Marketing and Efficiency

The marketing strategy that a company adopts can have a major impact upon the efficiency and cost structure of an enterprise. *Marketing strategy* refers to the position that a company takes with regard to pricing, promotion, advertising, product design, and distribution. It can play a major role in boosting a company's efficiency. Some of the steps leading to greater efficiency are fairly obvious. For example, we have already discussed how riding down the experience curve to gain a low-cost position can be facilitated by aggressive pricing, promotions, and advertising—all of which are the task of the marketing function. However, there are other aspects of marketing strategy that have a less obvious but no less important impact on efficiency. One important aspect is the relationship between customer defection rates and unit costs.[18]

FIGURE 5.6
• • • • • • • • • • •

The Relationship
Between Average Unit
Costs and Customer
Defection Rates

Customer defection rates are the percentage of a company's customers that defect every year to competitors. Defection rates are determined by customers' loyalty, which in turn is a function of the ability of a company to satisfy its customers. Because acquiring a new customer entails certain one-time fixed costs for advertising, promotions, and the like, there is a direct relationship between defection rates and costs. The longer a company holds on to a customer, the greater is the volume of customer-generated unit sales that can be set against these fixed costs and the lower the average unit cost of each sale. Thus, lowering customer defection rates allows a company to achieve substantial cost economies. This is illustrated in Figure 5.6, which shows that high defection rates imply high average unit costs (and vice versa).

One consequence of the relationship summarized in Figure 5.6 is a relationship, illustrated in Figure 5.7, between the length of time that a customer stays with the company and profit per customer. Because of the fixed costs of acquiring new customers, serving customers who stay with the company only for a short time before switching to competitors can often yield a negative profit. However, the longer a customer stays with the company, the more the fixed costs of acquiring that customer can be spread out over repeat purchases, which boosts the profit per customer. Thus, as shown in Figure 5.7, there is a positive relationship between the length of time that a customer stays with a company and profit per customer.

For an example of this phenomenon, consider the credit card business.[19] In 1990 most credit card companies spent an average of $51 to recruit a customer and set up a new account. These costs came from the advertising required to attract new customers, from credit checks required for each customer, and from the mechanics of setting up an account and issuing a card. These one-time fixed costs can be recouped only if a customer stays with the company for at least two years. More-

FIGURE 5.7

The Relationship Between Customer Loyalty and Profit per Customer

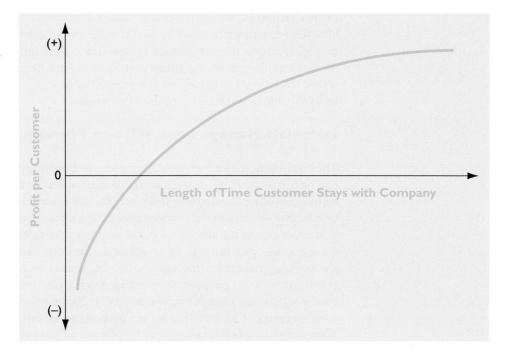

over, when customers stay a second year, they tend to increase their use of the credit card, which raises the volume of revenues generated by each customer over time. As a result, the average profit per customer in the credit card business increases from minus $51 in year 1 (that is, a loss of $51), to $44 in year 3, and $55 in year 6.

Another economic benefit of long-time loyalty by customers is the free advertising that customers provide for a company. Loyal customers do a lot of talking, and they can dramatically increase the volume of business through referrals. A striking example of this is the British clothing and food retailer Marks & Spencer. Marks & Spencer is Britain's largest and most profitable retailer. Its success is built upon a well-earned reputation for providing its customers with high-quality goods at a reasonable price. The company has generated such customer loyalty that it does not need to do any advertising in Britain, which translates into a major source of cost saving.

The key message, then, is that reducing customer defection rates and building their loyalty can be a major source of cost saving. Because it leads to lower unit costs, reducing customer defection rates by just 5 percent can increase profits per customer anywhere from 25 to 85 percent, depending on the industry. For example, a 5 percent reduction in customer defection rates leads to the following increases in profits per customer over the average customer life: a 75 percent increase in profit per customer in the credit card business, a 50 percent increase in profit per customer in the insurance brokerage industry, a 45 percent increase in profit per customer in the industrial laundry business, and a 35 percent increase in profit per customer in the computer software industry.[20]

How can a company reduce customer defection rates? It can do so by building brand loyalty, which in turn requires that the company be responsive to the needs of its customers. We consider the issue of customer responsiveness later in the chapter. For now, note that a central component of developing a strategy to reduce defection rates is to spot customers who defect, find out why they defected, and act on that information so that other customers do not defect for similar reasons in the future. To take these measures, the marketing function must have information systems capable of tracking customers' defections.

Materials Management, JIT, and Efficiency

The contribution of materials management to boosting the efficiency of a company can be just as dramatic as the contribution of production and marketing. **Materials management** encompasses the activities necessary to get materials to a production facility (including the costs of purchasing material inputs), through the production process, and out through a distribution system to the end user.[21] The potential for reducing costs through more efficient materials management is enormous. For the average manufacturing enterprise, the materials and transportation costs account for 50 to 70 percent of revenues. Even a small reduction in these costs can have a substantial impact on profitability. According to one estimate, for a company with revenues of $1 million, a return on investment rate of 5 percent, and materials management costs that amount to 50 percent of sales revenues (including purchasing costs), increasing total profits by $15,000 would require either a 30 percent increase in sales revenues or a 3 percent reduction in materials costs.[22] In a saturated market, it would be much easier to reduce materials costs by 3 percent than to increase sales revenues by 30 percent.

Improving the efficiency of the materials management function typically requires the adoption of just-in-time (JIT) inventory systems. The basic philosophy behind JIT is to economize on inventory holding costs by having materials arrive at a manufacturing plant just in time to enter the production process, and not before. The major cost saving comes from increasing inventory turnover, which reduces inventory holding costs, such as warehousing and storage costs. For example, Ford's switch to JIT systems in the early 1980s reportedly brought the firm a huge one-time saving of $3 billion. At Ford minimal inventory now turns over nine times a year instead of the former six, while carrying costs have been reduced by one-third.

More recently, the JIT concept has been adopted by a number of service companies, often with great success. For example, Wal-Mart uses JIT systems to replenish the stock in its stores at least twice a week. Many stores receive daily deliveries. The typical competitor—Kmart or Sears—replenishes its stock every two weeks. Compared with these competitors, Wal-Mart can maintain the same service levels with one-fourth the inventory investment, which is a major source of cost saving. Thus, faster inventory turnover has helped Wal-Mart achieve an efficiency-based competitive advantage in the retailing industry.[23]

The drawback of JIT systems is that they leave a firm without a buffer stock of inventory. Although buffer stocks of inventory are expensive to store, they can help tide a firm over shortages on inputs brought about by disruption among suppliers (for instance, a labor dispute at a key supplier). Buffer stocks can also help a firm respond quickly to increases in demand. However, there are ways around these limitations. For example, to reduce the risks linked to dependence on just one supplier for an important input, it might pay the firm to source inputs from multiple suppliers.

R&D Strategy and Efficiency

The role of superior research and development in helping a company achieve greater efficiency is twofold. First, the R&D function can boost efficiency by designing products that are easy to manufacture. By cutting down on the number of parts that make up a product, R&D can dramatically decrease the required assembly time, which translates into higher employee productivity and lower unit costs. For example, after Texas Instruments redesigned an infrared sighting mechanism that it supplies to the Pentagon, the company found that it had reduced the number of parts from 47 to 12, the number of assembly steps from 56 to 13, the time spent fabricating metal from 757 minutes per unit to 219 minutes per unit, and unit assembly time from 129 minutes to 20 minutes. The result was a substantial decline in production costs. Design for manufacturing requires close coordination between the production and R&D functions of the company, of course. This is best achieved by cross-functional teams that contain production and R&D personnel, so that they can work on the problem jointly.

The second way in which the R&D function can help a company achieve greater efficiency is by pioneering process innovations. A process innovation is an innovation in the way production processes operate that improves their efficiency. Process innovations have often been a major source of competitive advantage. For example, in the automobile industry, Toyota's competitive advantage is based partly on the company's invention of new flexible manufacturing processes, which dramatically reduced setup times. This process innovation enabled Toyota to obtain efficiency gains associated with flexible manufacturing systems years ahead of its competitors.

Human Resource Strategy and Efficiency

Employee productivity is one of the key determinants of an enterprise's efficiency and cost structure. The more productive the employees, the lower the unit costs. The challenge for a company's human resource function is to devise ways to increase employees' productivity. There are three main choices: employee training, self-managing teams, and pay for performance.

Employee Training   Individuals are a major input into the production process. A company that employs individuals with high skills is likely to be more efficient than one employing less skilled personnel. Individuals who are highly skilled can perform tasks faster and more accurately and are more likely to learn the complex tasks associated with many modern production methods than individuals with lesser skills. Training can upgrade the skill levels of employees, bringing the firm productivity-related efficiency gains.[24]

Work done by the MIT Commission on Industrial Productivity in the 1980s indicated that one major source of the competitive advantage that many Japanese companies enjoyed over their European and U.S. rivals was their commitment to improving the skill level of their employees through ongoing training programs.[25] These training programs have four main components. First, rotating employees through various departments lets them acquire general skills. For example, all new workers hired at Sanyo, the Japanese electronics company, must spend time in sales and in rotations between research and manufacturing. Second, many Japanese companies have extensive off-the-job training. For instance, of Sanyo's 30,000 employees, 10,000 pass through the Sanyo Corporate Educational Training Center each year, with every person spending at least three days at the center. Third, many Japanese companies encourage their employees to develop skills through correspondence courses, whose costs the employers often reimburse on completion of the program. Finally, participation in team activities that focus on improving the company's performance results in a general upgrading of employees' skills. Non-Japanese companies that wish to enhance the skills of their employees might consider taking similar steps.

Self-Managing Teams   Self-managing teams are a relatively recent phenomenon in U.S. industry. Few companies used them until the mid 1980s, but since then they have spread rapidly. The growth of flexible manufacturing cells, which group workers into teams, has undoubtedly facilitated the spread of self-managing teams among manufacturing enterprises. The typical team comprises five to fifteen employees, who produce an entire product or undertake an entire task. Team members learn all team tasks and rotate from job to job. A more flexible work force is one result. Team members can fill in for absent coworkers. Teams also take over managerial duties, such as work and vacation scheduling, ordering materials, and hiring new members. The greater responsibility thrust on team members and the empowerment it implies are seen as motivators. (Empowerment is the process of giving lower-level employees decision-making power.) People often respond well to being given greater autonomy and responsibility. Performance bonuses linked to team production and quality targets work as an additional motivator.

The net effect of introducing self-managing teams is reportedly an increase in productivity of 30 percent or more and a substantial increase in product quality. Further cost savings arise from eliminating supervisors and creating a flatter organizational hierarchy. In manufacturing enterprises perhaps the most potent combination is that of self-managing teams and flexible manufacturing cells. The two seem designed for each other. For example, after the introduction of flexible manufacturing technology and work practices based on self-managing teams in 1988, a General Electric plant in Salisbury, North Carolina, increased productivity by 250 percent compared with other GE plants that produced the same products in 1984.[26] Still, teams are no panacea; in manufacturing enterprises, self-managing teams may fail to live up to their potential unless they are integrated with flexible manufacturing technology. More generally, teams thrust a lot of management responsibilities on team members, and helping the members to cope with these responsibilities often requires substantial training. This is a fact that many companies often forget in their rush to drive down costs, with the result that the teams don't work out as well as planned.[27]

Pay for Performance   People work for money, so it is hardly surprising that linking pay to performance can help increase employee productivity. However, the issue is not quite so simple as just introducing incentive pay systems; it is also important to define what kind of performance is to be rewarded and how. Some of the most efficient companies in the world, mindful that cooperation among employees is necessary to realize productivity gains, do not link pay to individual performance. Instead they link pay to group or team performance. For example, at Nucor, which is widely viewed as one of the most efficient steel makers in the world, the work force is divided into teams of thirty or so. Bonus pay, which can amount to 30 percent of base pay, is linked to the ability of the team to meet productivity and quality goals. This link creates a strong incentive for individuals to cooperate with each other in pursuit of team goals; that is, it facilitates teamwork.

Infrastructure and Efficiency

Because the infrastructure sets the context within which all other value creation activities take place, it follows that the infrastructure can help in achieving efficiency goals. Above all, the infrastructure can foster a companywide commitment to efficiency and can promote cooperation among different functions in pursuit of efficiency goals.

A companywide commitment to efficiency is built through the leadership of top management. The leadership task is to articulate a vision that recognizes the need for all functions of the company to focus on improving their efficiency. It is not enough just to improve the efficiency of production, or marketing, or R&D. Achieving superior efficiency requires a companywide commitment to this goal, and this commitment can be articulated only by top management.

A further leadership task is to facilitate cross-functional cooperation needed to achieve superior efficiency. For example, designing products that are easy to manufacture requires that production and R&D personnel communicate; integrating JIT systems with production scheduling requires close communication between materials management and production; designing self-managing teams to perform production tasks requires close cooperation between human resources and production; and so on.

Summary: Achieving Superior Efficiency

Table 5.1 summarizes the primary roles that various functions must take in order to achieve superior efficiency. Bear in mind that achieving superior efficiency is not something that can be tackled on a function-by-function basis. It requires an organizationwide commitment and an ability to ensure close cooperation among

TABLE 5.1

The Primary Roles of Different Value Creation Functions in Achieving Superior Efficiency

Value Creation Function	Primary Roles
Infrastructure (Leadership)	1. Provide companywide commitment to efficiency. 2. Facilitate cooperation among functions.
Production	1. Where appropriate, pursue economies of scale and learning economics. 2. Implement flexible manufacturing systems.
Marketing	1. Where appropriate, adopt aggressive marketing to ride down the experience curve. 2. Limit customer defection rates by building brand loyalty.
Materials Management	1. Implement JIT systems.
R&D	1. Design products for ease of manufacture. 2. Seek process innovations.
Human Resources	1. Institute training programs to build skills. 2. Implement self-managing teams. 3. Implement pay for performance.

functions. Top management, by exercising leadership and influencing the infrastructure, plays a major role in this process.

ACHIEVING SUPERIOR QUALITY

We noted in Chapter 4 that superior quality gives a company two advantages. The enhanced reputation for quality lets the company charge a premium price for its product, and the elimination of defects from the production process increases efficiency and hence lowers costs. In this section, we examine the means a company can use to achieve superior quality. The main one is **total quality management** (TQM), a management philosophy that focuses on improving the quality of a company's products and services and stresses that all company operations should be oriented toward this goal.[28] A companywide philosophy, it requires the cooperation of all the different functions if it is to be implemented successfully. We first consider the total quality management concept and then discuss the various steps needed to implement TQM programs. Throughout, we highlight the roles that different functions must play in this process.

The TQM Concept

The total quality management concept was first developed by a number of U.S. consultants, including W. Edwards Deming, Joseph Juran, and A. V. Feigenbaum.[29] Originally, these consultants won few converts in the United States. In contrast, the Japanese embraced them enthusiastically and even named their premier annual prize for manufacturing excellence after Deming. The philosophy underlying TQM, as articulated by Deming, is based on the following five-step chain reaction:

1. Improved quality means that costs decrease because of less rework, fewer mistakes, fewer delays, and better use of time and materials.

2. As a result, productivity improves.

3. Better quality leads to higher market share and allows the company to raise prices.

4. This increases the company's profitability and allows it to stay in business.

5. Thus, the company creates more jobs.[30]

   Deming has identified fourteen steps that should be part of any TQM program; they are summarized in Table 5.2. (Deming continually changed these points in line with his belief in the importance of continuous quality improvement; those given here are the latest—1990—version.) In essence, Deming urges a company to have a definite strategic plan for where it is going and how it is going to get there. He argues that management should embrace the philosophy that mistakes, defects, and poor-quality materials are not acceptable and should be eliminated. Quality of supervision should be improved by allowing more time for supervisors to work with employees and by giving them appropriate skills for the job. Furthermore, management should create an environment in which no employee will fear reporting problems or recommending improvements. Deming also believes that work standards should not only be defined as numbers or quotas but should

TABLE 5.2

Deming's Fourteen Points to Quality

1. Create constancy of purpose toward improvement of product and service, with the aim to become competitive and to stay in business, and to provide jobs.

2. Adopt the new philosophy. We are in a new economic age. Western management must awaken to the challenge, must learn their responsibilities, and take on leadership for change.

3. Cease dependence on inspection to achieve quality. Eliminate the need for inspection on a mass basis by building quality into the product in the first place.

4. End of practice of awarding business on the basis of price tag. Instead, minimize total cost.

5. Improve constantly and forever the system of production and service, to improve quality and productivity, and thus constantly decrease costs.

6. Institute training on the job.

7. Institute leadership. The aim of leadership should be to help people and machines and gadgets do a better job. Leadership of management is in need of an overhaul, as well as leadership of production workers.

8. Drive out fear, so that everyone may work effectively for the company.

9. Break down barriers between departments. People in research, design, sales, and production must work as a team, to foresee problems of production and in use that may be encountered with the product or service.

10. Eliminate slogans, exhortations, and targets for the work force asking for zero defects and new levels of productivity. Such exhortations only create adversarial relationships. The bulk of the causes of low quality and low productivity belong to the system and thus lie beyond the power of the work force.

11. (a) Eliminate work standards on the factory floor. Substitute leadership. (b) Eliminate management by objective. Eliminate management by numbers, numerical goals. Substitute leadership.

12. (a) Remove barriers that rob hourly workers of their right to pride of workmanship. The responsibility of supervisors must be changed from sheer numbers to quality. (b) Remove barriers that rob people in management and in engineering of their right to pride of workmanship.

13. Institute a vigorous program of education and self-improvement.

14. Put everybody in the company to work to accomplish the transformation. The transformation is everybody's job.

"Demming's 14 Points to Quality" from Gaber, Andrea, *The Man Who Discovered Quality: Howard W. Edwards Demming Brought the Quality Revolution to America—The Stories of Ford, Xerox, & GM,* 1990, Random House.

also include some notion of quality to promote the production of defect-free output. He argues that management has the responsibility to train employees in new skills to keep pace with changes in the workplace and that achieving better quality requires the commitment of everyone in the company.

It took the rise of Japan to the top rank of economic powers to alert western business to the importance of the TQM concept. Since the early 1980s, TQM practices have spread rapidly throughout western industry. Strategy in Action 5.4 offers some examples of the impact that TQM programs can have on quality. However, despite such instances of spectacular success, TQM practices are still not universally

| 5.4 | STRATEGY *in* ACTION |

The Impact of TQM Programs on Quality

- In 1987 Motorola's semiconductor business was producing 6,000 defects per million parts. By 1992 this figure had been reduced to 40 per million. Between 1987 and 1994 Motorola figures that it has saved an estimated $6.5 billion in manufacturing costs as a result of its TQM programs.[31]

- Since it first adopted an aggressive TQM program in 1978, Hitachi has seen the number of defects reported by customers of its software business drop from 100 per thousand computers to fewer than 2 per thousand by 1992.[32]

- In 1978 Yokogawa Hewlett Packard (YHP) adopted a TQM program. At that time the defect rate in its soldering process was 4,000 parts per million. By 1982 YHP had reduced its defect rate to 3 parts per million. Over the same time period, employees' productivity rose 91 percent, costs fell 42 percent, and profits increased 177 percent.[33]

- When Xerox first introduced a TQM program in conjunction with its suppliers in 1983, its suppliers were producing about 25,000 defective parts per million. By 1992 the defect rate on parts from suppliers was less than 300 per million.[34]

accepted. A 1992 study by the American Quality Foundation found that only 20 percent of U.S. companies regularly review the consequences of quality performance, compared with 70 percent of Japanese companies.[35] Another study by Arthur D. Little of 500 American companies using TQM found that only 36 percent believed that TQM was increasing their competitiveness.[36] A prime reason for this, according to the study, was that many companies had not fully understood or embraced the TQM concept.

Implementing TQM

Among companies that have successfully adopted TQM, certain imperatives stand out.[37] We discuss them in the order in which they are usually tackled in companies implementing TQM programs, and we highlight the role that the various functions play in regard to each precept. What cannot be stressed enough, however, is that implementing TQM requires close cooperation among all functions in the pursuit of the common goal of improving quality; it is a process that cuts across functions. The role played by the different functions in implementing TQM is summarized in Table 5.3. Strategy in Action 5.5, at the end of this section, describes the efforts of a service company to put TQM into practice and the benefits it has gained.

Build Organizational Commitment to Quality There is evidence that TQM will do little to improve the performance of a company unless it is embraced by everyone in the organization.[38] For example, when Xerox launched its quality program in 1983, its first step was to educate its entire work force, from top management down, in the importance and operation of the TQM concept. It did so by forming groups, beginning with a group at the top of the organization that included

TABLE 5.3

The Role Played by Different Functions in Implementing TQM

Value Creation Function	Primary Roles
Infrastructure (Leadership)	1. Provide leadership and commitment to quality. 2. Find ways to measure quality. 3. Set goals and create incentives. 4. Solicit input from employees. 5. Encourage cooperation among functions.
Production	1. Shorten production runs. 2. Trace defects back to source.
Marketing	1. Focus on the customer. 2. Provide customers' feedback on quality.
Materials Management	1. Rationalize suppliers. 2. Help suppliers implement TQM. 3. Trace defects back to suppliers.
R&D	1. Design products that are easy to manufacture.
Human Resources	1. Institute TQM training programs. 2. Organize employees into quality teams.

the CEO. The top group was the first to receive basic TQM training. Each member of this group was then given the task of training a group at the next level in the hierarchy, and so on down throughout the organization until all 100,000 employees had received basic TQM training. Both top management and the human resource function of the company play a major role in this process. Top management has the responsibility of exercising the leadership required to make a commitment to quality an organizationwide goal. The human resource function must take responsibility for companywide training in TQM techniques.

Focus on the Customer   TQM practitioners see a focus on the customer as the starting point, and indeed, the raison d'être of the whole quality philosophy.[39] The marketing function, because it provides the primary point of contact with the customer, should play a major role in this effort. It needs to identify what the customers want from the good or service that the company provides; what the company actually provides to customers; and the gap between what customers want and what they actually get, which could be called the quality gap. Then, together with the other functions of the company, it needs to formulate a plan for closing the quality gap.

Find Ways to Measure Quality   Another imperative of any TQM program is to create some metric that can be used to measure quality. This is relatively easy in manufacturing companies, where quality can be measured by criteria such as defects per million parts. It tends to be more difficult in service companies, but with a little creativity suitable metrics can be devised. For example, one of the metrics

Florida Power & Light uses to measure quality is meter reading errors per month. Another is the frequency and duration of power outages. L.L. Bean, the Freeport, Maine, mail-order retailer of outdoor gear, uses the percentage of orders that are correctly filled as one of its quality measures. For some banks, the key measures are the number of customer defections per year and the number of statement errors per thousand customers. The common theme that runs through all these examples is identifying what quality means from a *customer's* perspective and devising a method to gauge this. Top management should take primary responsibility for formulating different metrics to measure quality, but to succeed in this effort, it must receive input from various other functions of the company.

Set Goals and Create Incentives   Once a metric has been devised, the next step is to set a challenging quality goal and to create incentives for reaching that goal. Xerox again provides us with an example. When it first introduced its TQM program, Xerox's initial goal was to reduce defective parts from 25,000 per million to 1,000 per million. One way of creating incentives to attain such a goal is to link rewards, such as bonus pay and promotional opportunities, to the goal. Thus, within many companies that have adopted self-managing teams, the bonus pay of team members is determined in part by their ability to attain quality goals. The task of setting goals and creating incentives is one of the key tasks of top management.

Solicit Input from Employees   Employees can be a vital source of information regarding the sources of poor quality. Therefore, some framework must be established for soliciting employees' suggestions as to the improvements that can be made. Quality circles, which are meetings of groups of employees, have often been used to achieve this goal. Other companies have utilized self-managing teams as forums for discussing quality improvement ideas. Whatever the forum, soliciting input from lower-level employees requires that management be open to receiving and acting on bad news and criticism from employees. According to Deming, one problem with U.S. management is that it has grown used to "killing the bearer of bad tidings." He argues, to the contrary, that managers who are committed to the quality concept must recognize that bad news is a gold mine of information.[40]

Identify Defects and Trace Them to Source   Product defects most often occur in the production process. TQM preaches the need to identify defects during the work process, trace them to their source, find out what caused them, and make corrections so that they do not recur. Production and materials management typically have primary responsibility for this task.

To uncover defects, Deming advocates the use of statistical procedures to pinpoint variations in the quality of goods or services. Deming views variation as the enemy of quality.[41] Once variations have been identified, they must be traced to their source and eliminated. One technique that helps greatly in tracing defects to their source is reducing lot sizes for manufactured products. With short production runs, defects show up immediately. Consequently, they can be quickly traced to the source, and the problem can be fixed. Reducing lot sizes also means that when defective products are produced, their number will not be large, thus decreasing waste. Flexible manufacturing techniques, discussed earlier, can be used to reduce lot sizes without raising costs. Consequently, adopting flexible manufacturing techniques is an important aspect of a TQM program.

STRATEGY *in* **ACTION**

Total Quality Management at Intermountain Health Care

Intermountain Health Care is a nonprofit chain of twenty-four hospitals operating in Idaho, Utah, and Wyoming. Intermountain first adopted TQM for certain sections of its system in the mid 1980s, and in 1990 it adopted TQM system-wide. The goal of TQM was to find and eliminate inappropriate variations in medical care—to provide the patient with better health care and, in the process, to reduce costs. The starting point was to identify variations in practice across physicians, particularly with regard to the cost and success rate of treatments. These data were then shared among physicians within the Intermountain system. The next step was for the physicians to take these data and use them to eliminate poor practices and to upgrade generally the quality of medical care.

The results have been quite striking. One early improvement was an attempt by Intermountain's hospital in Salt Lake City to lower the rate of postoperative wound infections. Before the effort began in 1985, the hospital's postoperative infection rate was 1.8 percent; this was 0.2 points below the national average, but still unacceptably high from a TQM perspective. By using a bedside computer system to make sure that antibiotics were given to patients two hours before surgery, the hospital dropped the infection rate in half, to 0.9 percent, within a year. Since then the postoperative infection rate has dropped further still, to 0.4 percent compared with the current national average of 2 percent. Given that the average postoperative infection adds $14,000 to a hospital bill, this constitutes a big cost saving.

Intermountain is now focusing on dozens of problems, including situations in which the wrong type or dose of medication is given, the top cause of poor medical care. Intermountain expects its efforts in this area to eliminate quickly at least 60 percent of such mistakes and to reduce medical related costs by up to $2 million a year per hospital.[42]

Just-in-time (JIT) inventory systems also play a part. Under a JIT system, defective parts enter the manufacturing process immediately; they are not warehoused for several months before use. Hence, defective inputs can be quickly spotted. The problem can then be traced to the supply source and corrected before more defective parts are produced. Under a more traditional system, the practice of warehousing parts for months before they are used may mean that large numbers of defects are produced by a supplier before they enter the production process.

Build Relationship with Suppliers A major source of poor-quality finished goods is poor-quality component parts. To decrease product defects, a company has to work with its suppliers to improve the quality of the parts they supply. The primary responsibility in this area falls on the materials management function, since it is the function that interacts with suppliers.

To implement JIT systems with suppliers and to get suppliers to adopt their own TQM programs, two steps are necessary. First, the number of suppliers has to be reduced to manageable proportions. Second, the company must commit to building a cooperative long-term relationship with the suppliers that remain. Asking suppliers to invest in JIT and TQM systems is asking them to make major investments that tie them to the company. For example, in order to implement a JIT system fully, the company may ask a supplier to relocate its manufacturing plant so that it is next door to the company's assembly plant. Suppliers are likely to be hesitant about making such investments unless they feel that the company is committed to an enduring, long-term relationship with them.

Design for Ease of Manufacture   The more assembly steps a product requires, the more opportunities there are for making mistakes. Designing products with fewer parts should make assembly easier and result in fewer defects. Both R&D and manufacturing need to be involved in designing products that are easy to manufacture.

Break Down Barriers Among Functions   Implementing TQM requires organizationwide commitment and substantial cooperation among functions. R&D has to cooperate with production to design products that are easy to manufacture, marketing has to cooperate with production and R&D so that customers' problems identified by marketing can be acted on, human resource management has to cooperate with all the other functions of the company in order to devise suitable quality training programs, and so on. The issue of achieving cooperation among subunits within a company is explored in Chapter 11. What needs stressing at this point is that ultimately it is the responsibility of top management to ensure that such cooperation occurs.

ACHIEVING SUPERIOR INNOVATION

In many ways innovation is the single most important building block of competitive advantage. Successful innovation of products or processes gives a company something unique that its competitors lack. This uniqueness may allow a company to charge a premium price or lower its cost structure below that of its rivals. Competitors, however, will try to imitate successful innovations. Often they will succeed, although high barriers to imitation can slow down the speed of imitation. Therefore, maintaining a competitive advantage requires a continuing commitment to innovation.

Many companies have established a track record for successful innovation. Among them are Du Pont, which has produced a steady stream of successful innovations such as cellophane, nylon, Freon (used in all air conditioners), and Teflon (used to coat cooking pans); Sony, whose successes include the Walkman and the compact disk; Merck, the drug company that during the 1980s produced seven major new drugs; 3M, which has applied its core competency in tapes and adhesives to developing a wide range of new products; and Intel, which has consistently managed to lead in the development of innovative new microprocessors to run personal computers.

The High Failure Rate of Innovation

Although innovation can be a source of competitive advantage, the failure rate of innovative new products is high. One study of product development in sixteen companies in the chemical, drug, petroleum, and electronics industries suggested that only about 20 percent of R&D projects ultimately result in a commercially successful product or process.[43] Another in-depth case study of product development in three companies (one in chemicals and two in drugs) reported that about 60 percent of R&D projects reached technical completion, 30 percent were commercialized, and only 12 percent earned an economic profit that exceeded the company's cost of capital.[44] Similarly, a study by the consulting division of Booz, Allen, & Hamilton found that more than one-third of 13,000 consumer and industrial products introduced between 1976 and 1981 failed to meet company-specific financial and strategic performance criteria.[45] A more recent study found that 45 percent of new products introduced into the marketplace did not meet their profitability goals.[46] In sum, this evidence suggests that many R&D projects do not result in a commercial product and that between 33 and 60 percent of all new products that do reach the marketplace fail to generate an adequate economic return. Two well-publicized product failures are Apple Computer's Newton, a personal digital assistant, and Sony's Betamax format in the video player and recorder market. While many reasons have been advanced to explain why so many new products fail to generate an economic return, five explanations for failure appear on most lists: uncertainty, poor commercialization, poor positioning strategy, technological myopia, and a lack of speed in the development process.[47]

Uncertainty   New-product development is an inherently risky process. It requires testing a hypothesis whose answer is impossible to know prior to market introduction—namely, is there sufficient market demand for this new technology? Although good market research can minimize the uncertainty about likely future demand for a new technology, the uncertainty cannot be eradicated altogether. A certain failure rate is to be expected.

We would expect that failure rate to be higher for quantum innovations than for incremental innovations. A **quantum innovation** represents a radical departure from existing technology—the introduction of something that is new to the world. The development of the World Wide Web can be considered a quantum innovation in communications technology. Other quantum innovations include the development of the first photocopier by Xerox, the first videocassette recorder by AMPEX, and the first contact lenses by Bausch & Lomb. **Incremental innovation** refers to an extension of existing technology. For example, Intel's Pentium Pro microprocessor is an incremental innovation because it builds upon the existing microprocessor architecture of Intel's X86 series.

The uncertainty of future demand for a new product is much greater if that product represents a quantum innovation than if it is an incremental innovation, designed to replace an established product whose demand profile is already well known. Consequently, the failure rate tends to be higher for quantum innovations.

Poor Commercialization   A second reason frequently cited to explain the high failure rate of new-product introductions is **poor commercialization**. This condition occurs when there is an intrinsic demand for a new technology, but the technology is not well adapted to consumers' needs because of factors such as poor design and poor quality. For instance, many of the early personal computers failed to sell because the user practically needed to be a computer programmer. It took Steve Jobs at Apple Computer to understand that if the technology could be made user-friendly (if it could be commercialized), there would be an enormous market for it. Hence, the original personal computers marketed by Apple incorporated little in the way of radically new technology; instead, they made existing technology accessible to the average person. The failure of Apple Computer to establish a market for the Newton, the Personal Digital Assistant, or the hand-held computer that Apple introduced in the summer of 1993 can be traced to poor commercialization of a potentially attractive technology. Apple predicted a $1 billion market for the Newton, but sales failed to materialize when it became clear that the Newton's software could not adequately recognize messages written on the Newton's message pad. Despite this failure, many companies believe that there is an intrinsic demand for this kind of technology, but only if the product can be better commercialized.

Poor Positioning Strategy   Poor positioning strategy, a third reason for new-product failures, arises when a company introduces an intrinsically attractive new product, but sales fail to materialize because it is poorly positioned in the marketplace. **Positioning strategy** is the position a company adopts for a product on four main dimensions of marketing—price, distribution, promotion and advertising, and product features. Apart from poor product quality, another reason for the failure of Apple's Newton was poor positioning strategy. The Newton was introduced at such a high initial price (close to $1,000) that there would probably have been few takers even if the technology had been adequately commercialized. Poor positioning strategy may have also affected the recent introduction of the digital compact cassette (DCC), which is profiled in Strategy in Action 5.6. The DCC suffered from high prices, poor promotion, and a failure by the innovating companies to produce products for the portable and car markets.

Technological Myopia   A fourth reason why many new-product introductions fail is that companies often make the mistake of marketing a technology for which there is not enough consumer demand. **Technological myopia** occurs when a company gets blinded by the wizardry of a new technology and fails to examine whether there is consumer demand for the product. This problem may have been a factor in the failure of the desktop computer introduced by NeXT in the late 1980s. (NeXT was founded by Steve Jobs, the founder of Apple Computer.) Technologically, NeXT's machines were clearly ahead of their time, with advanced software and hardware features that would not be incorporated into most personal computers for another decade. However, acceptance by consumers was very slow, primarily because of the complete lack of applications software, such as spreadsheet and word-processing programs, to run on the machines. Management at NeXT was so enthused by the technology incorporated in their new computer that they ignored this basic market reality. After several years of slow sales, NeXT eventually withdrew the machines from the marketplace.

Slow to Market   Finally, companies fail when they are slow to get their products to market. The longer the time between initial development and final marketing—that is, the slower the "cycle time"—the more likely that someone else will beat the firm to market and gain a first-mover advantage.[48] By and large, slow innovators update their products less frequently than fast innovators. Consequently, they can be perceived as technical laggards relative to the fast innovators. In the automobile industry, General Motors has suffered from being a slow innovator. Its product development cycle has been about five years, compared with two to three years at Honda, Toyota, and Mazda, and three to four years at Ford. Because they are based on five-year-old technology and design concepts, GM cars are already out-of-date

Whatever Happened to the Digital Compact Cassette?

The digital compact cassette (DCC) was developed by Philips, the Dutch consumer electronics company. The DCC is a recordable audio digital technology that offers sound qualities superior to those of analog cassette technology. The DCC was designed to replace analog cassette tapes in much the same way that digital compact disks have replaced analog long-playing records. An attractive feature of the technology was a design that allowed users to play their existing analog cassette tapes on the DCC in addition to DCC digital tapes. The thinking at Philips was that this feature would make the product very attractive to users, who would not have to replace their existing collection of analog cassette tapes when they purchased a DCC player. To try to ensure initial acceptance of the technology, Philips lined up a number of recording companies—including MCA, Polygram, EMI, and Warner—all of whom agreed to issue prerecorded DCC tapes in conjunction with the launch by Philips of the tapes players.

Introduced in 1993, the DCC was hailed in the press as the biggest new-product introduction in the consumer electronics industry since the introduction of the compact disk a decade earlier. However, as initial demand failed to materialize, retailers with unsold DCC tapes and decks on their hands refused to keep devoting valuable shelf space to DCC products, and recording companies soon stopped issuing prerecorded DCC tapes. It was clear within a year that the product was essentially stillborn in the marketplace.

Why did the DCC fail to gain market acceptance despite its apparently attractive features? Poor positioning strategy is probably part of the explanation. Philips introduced the technology at a very high price—around $1,000 for a basic home deck—out of the reach of most consumers. Moreover, Philips failed to introduce a portable model (to compete with Sony's Walkman) or a model for cars (to replace the analog tape players most consumers still have in their cars). To make matters worse, the original promotional advertising failed to mention one of the most attractive features of the technology, the fact that DCC tape drives could play existing analog tapes. Finally, Philips implemented a very abstract advertising campaign that left most consumers confused about the nature of the new technology.

Another reason for the poor market acceptance was the limited value placed on the technology by many consumers. Most consumers did not see the DCC as a big advance over CD players. True, CD technology did not have recording capability, but CD players were increasingly turning up in cars, and Sony had marketed a very successful portable version of the CD (the Discman)—both market niches that were natural targets for the DCC. Given this, few consumers valued the technology enough to pay more than $1,000 for a player. Whether Philips would have been able to build sales for the DCC had it entered the market at a lower price, with better advertising, and with a broader range of models remains an open question, but success would probably have been more likely under such a scenario.[49]

when they reach the market. Another example of the consequences of slow innovation, the demise of Apollo Computer at the hands of Sun Microsystems, is given in Strategy in Action 5.7.

Building Competencies in Innovation

Companies can take a number of steps in order to build a competency in innovation and avoid failure. Three of the most important steps seem to be (1) building skills in basic and applied scientific research, (2) developing a good process for project selection and project management, and (3) achieving close integration among

Slow Cycle Time at Apollo Computer

In 1980 Apollo Computer created the market for engineering computer workstations (high-powered, freestanding minicomputers). Apollo was rewarded with rapid growth and a virtual monopoly position. Its first real competitor, Sun Microsystems, did not introduce a competing product until 1982. However, by 1988 Apollo had lost its lead in the workstation market to Sun. While Apollo was generating revenues of $600 million in 1988, Sun's revenues were more than $1 billion. Between 1984 and 1988, Sun's revenues from workstations grew at an annual rate of 100 percent per year, compared with Apollo's growth rate of 35 percent per annum.

The cause of Apollo's slower growth was a slow cycle time. In the computer industry, innovations in microprocessor technology proceed at a furious pace. In order to stay abreast of new microprocessor technology, any manufacturer of computers must be continually updating its product. However, while Sun had succeeded in introducing a new product every twelve months and in doubling the power of its workstations every eighteen months on average, Apollo's product development cycle had stretched out to more than two years. As a result, Apollo's products were regularly superseded by the more technologically advanced products introduced by Sun, and Apollo was falling further and further behind. Consequently, while Sun had increased its market share from 21 to 33 percent between 1985 and 1988, Apollo's fell from 41 percent to less than 20 percent. In 1989, facing mounting problems, Apollo was acquired by Hewlett Packard.[50]

the different functions of the company through cross-functional product development teams and partly parallel development processes.[51] Following is a discussion of what each of these entails.

Basic and Applied Research   Building skills in basic and applied research requires the employment of research scientists and engineers and the establishment of a work environment that fosters creativity. A number of top companies try to achieve this by setting up university-style research facilities, in which scientists and engineers are given time to work on their own research projects in addition to projects that are linked directly to ongoing company research. At Hewlett Packard, for example, the company labs are open to engineers around the clock. Hewlett Packard even encourages its corporate researchers to devote 10 percent of company time to exploring their own ideas—and does not penalize them if they fail. Similarly, at 3M there is a "15 percent rule," which allows researchers to spend 15 percent of the workweek researching any topic they want to investigate, as long as there is the potential of a payoff for the company. The most famous outcome of this policy is the ubiquitous yellow Post-it Notes. The idea for them evolved from a researcher's desire to find a way to keep the bookmark from falling out of his hymn book. Post-it Notes are now a major 3M consumer business, with 1988 revenues of around $300 million.

Project Management   Project management is the overall management of the innovation process, from generation of the original concept, through development, and into final production and shipping. Project management requires three impor-

FIGURE 5.8
....

The Development
Funnel

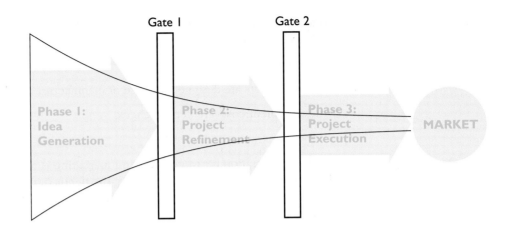

tant skills: the ability to encourage as much idea generation as possible, the ability to select among competing projects at an early stage of development so that the most promising receive funding and potential costly failures are killed off, and the ability to minimize time to market. The concept of the development funnel, illustrated in Figure 5.8, summarizes what is required to build these skills.[52]

As Figure 5.8 shows, the development funnel is divided into three phases. The objective in phase 1 is to widen the mouth of the funnel to encourage as much idea generation as possible. To this end, a company should solicit input from all its functions, as well as from customers, competitors, and suppliers.

At gate 1 the funnel narrows. At this stage, ideas are reviewed by a cross-functional team of managers who were not involved in the original concept development. Those concepts that are ready to proceed then move on to phase 2 of the funnel, which is the stage at which the details of the project proposal are worked out. Note that gate 1 is not a go/no-go evaluation point. At this point, ideas may be sent back for further concept development to be resubmitted for evaluation.

During phase 2, which typically lasts only one or two months, the data and information developed during phase 1 are put into a form that will enable senior management to evaluate proposed projects against competing projects. Normally this requires the development of a careful project plan, complete with details of the proposed target market, attainable market share, likely revenues, development costs, production costs, key milestones, and the like. The next big selection point, gate 2, is a go/no-go evaluation point. Senior managers are brought in to review the various projects under consideration. Their task is to select those projects that seem likely winners and that make most sense from a strategic perspective, given the long-term goals of the enterprise. The overriding objective at this gate is to select projects whose successful completion will help to maintain or build a competitive advantage for the company. A related objective is to ensure that the company does not spread its scarce capital and human resources too thinly over too many projects and instead concentrates resources on those projects for which the probability of success and potential returns are most attractive. Any project selected to go forward at this stage will be funded and staffed, the expectation being that it will be carried through to market introduction. In phase 3 the project development proposal is executed by a cross-functional product development team.

Cross-Functional Integration   Tight cross-functional integration between R&D, production, and marketing can help a company to ensure that

1. product development projects are driven by customer needs

2. new products are designed for ease of manufacture

3. development costs are kept in check

4. time to market is minimized.

Close integration between R&D and marketing is required to ensure that product development projects are driven by the needs of customers. A company's customers can be one of its primary sources of new product ideas. Identification of customers' needs, and particularly unmet needs, can set the context within which successful product innovation takes place. As the point of contact with customers, the marketing function of a company can provide valuable information in this regard. Moreover, integration of R&D and marketing is crucial if a new product is to be properly commercialized. Without integration of R&D and marketing, a company runs the risk of developing products for which there is little or no demand.

The case of Techsonic Industries illustrates the benefits of integrating R&D and marketing. This Alabama company manufactures depth finders—electronic devices used by anglers to measure the depth of water beneath a boat and to track their prey. Techsonic had weathered nine new-product failures in a row before 1985. Then the company decided to interview anglers across the country to identify what it was they needed. They discovered an unmet need for a depth finder with a gauge that could be read in bright sunlight, so that is what Techsonic developed. In the year after the $250 depth finder hit the market, Techsonic's sales tripled to $80 million and its market share surged to 40 percent.[53]

Integration between R&D and production can help a company ensure that products are designed with manufacturing requirements in mind. Designing with an eye to manufacturing lowers manufacturing costs and leaves less room for mistakes. The result is lower costs and increased product quality.

Integrating R&D and production can also help lower development costs and speed products to market. If a new product is not designed with manufacturing capabilities in mind, it may prove too difficult to build, given existing manufacturing technology. In that case, the product will have to be redesigned, and both overall development costs and the time it takes to bring the product to market may increase significantly. For example, making design changes during product planning could increase overall development costs by 50 percent and add 25 percent to the time it takes to bring the product to market.[54] Moreover, many quantum product innovations require new processes to manufacture them, which makes it all the more important to achieve close integration between R&D and production, since minimizing time to market and development costs may require the simultaneous development of new products and new processes.[55]

Product Development Teams   One of the best ways to achieve cross-functional integration is to establish cross-functional product development teams. These are teams composed of representatives from R&D, marketing, and production. The objective of a team should be to take a product development project through from the initial concept development to market introduction. A number of attributes seem to be important in order for a product development team to function effectively and to meet all its development milestones.[56]

First, the team should be led by a "heavyweight" project manager who has high status within the organization and who has the power and authority required to get the financial and human resources that the team needs to succeed. The "heavyweight" leader should be dedicated primarily, if not entirely, to the project. The leader should be someone who believes in the project (a champion) and who is skilled at integrating the perspectives of different functions and at helping personnel from different functions work together for a common goal. The leader should also be able to act as an advocate of the team to senior management.

Second, the team should be composed of at least one member from each key function. The team members should have a number of attributes including an ability to contribute functional expertise, high standing within their function, a willingness to share responsibility for team results, and an ability to put functional advocacy aside. It is generally preferable if core team members are 100 percent dedicated to the project for its duration. This makes sure that their focus is on the project, not on the ongoing work of their function.

Third, the team members should be physically colocated to create a sense of camaraderie and to facilitate communication.

Fourth, the team should have a clear plan and clear goals, particularly with regard to critical development milestones and development budgets. The team should have incentives to attain those goals, for example, pay bonuses when major development milestones are hit.

Fifth, each team needs to develop its own processes for communication and conflict resolution. For example, one product development team at Quantum Corporation, a California-based manufacturer of disk drives for personal computers, instituted a rule that all major decisions would be made and conflicts resolved at meetings that were held every Monday afternoon. This simple rule helped the team to meet its development goals.[57]

Partly Parallel Development Processes   One way in which a product development team can compress the time it takes to develop a product and bring it to market is to utilize a partly parallel development process. Traditionally, product development processes have been organized on a sequential basis, as illustrated in Figure 5.9a. A problem with this kind of process is that product development proceeds without manufacturing issues in mind. Most significantly, since the basic design of a product is completed prior to the design of a manufacturing process and full-scale commercial production, there is no early warning system to indicate manufacturability. As a consequence, the company may find that it cannot manufacture the product in a cost-efficient manner and must send it back to the design stage for redesign. The result is that the cycle time lengthens as the product iterates back and forth between stages.

To solve this problem, companies typically use a process similar to that illustrated in Figure 5.9b. In the partly parallel development process, development stages overlap so that, for example, work starts on the development of the production process before the product design is finalized. By reducing the need for expensive and time-consuming product redesigns, such a process can significantly reduce the time it takes to develop a new product and bring it to market.

FIGURE 5.9
· · · · · · · · · · · ·
Sequential and Partly
Parallel Development
Processes

a: A Sequential Process

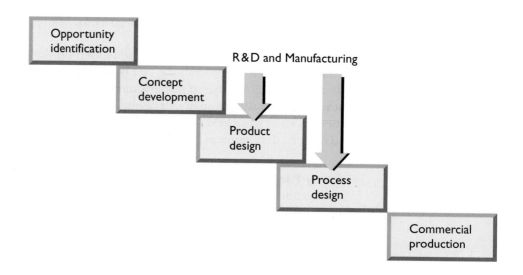

b: A Partly Parallel Process

For an example, consider what occurred after Intel introduced its 386 micro-processor in 1986. A number of companies, including IBM and Compaq, were racing to be the first to introduce a 386-based personal computer. Compaq beat IBM by six months and gained a major share of the high-powered market, mainly because it used a cross-functional team and a partly parallel process to develop the product. The team included people from engineering (R&D), marketing, production, and finance. Each function worked in parallel rather than sequentially. While engineers were designing the product, production people were setting up the manufacturing facilities, marketing people were working on distribution and planning marketing campaigns, and the finance people were working on funding for the project.

TABLE 5.4

The Role Played by Various Functions in Achieving Superior Innovation

Value Creation Function	Primary Roles
Infrastructure (Leadership)	1. Manage overall project (i.e., manage the development function). 2. Facilitate cross-functional cooperation.
Production	1. Cooperate with R&D on designing products that are easy to manufacture. 2. Work with R&D to develop process innovations.
Marketing	1. Provide market information to R&D. Work with R&D to develop new products.
Materials Management	No primary responsibility.
R&D	1. Develop new products and processes. 2. Cooperate with other functions, particularly marketing and manufacturing, in the development process.
Human Resources	1. Hire talented scientists and engineers.

Summary: Achieving Superior Innovation

The primary role that the various functions play in achieving superior innovation is summarized in Table 5.4. Two points in particular should be noted. First, top management bears primary responsibility for overseeing the whole development process. This entails both managing the development funnel and facilitating cooperation between functions. Second, while R&D plays a central role in the innovation process, the effectiveness of R&D in developing new products and processes depends on its ability to cooperate with marketing and production.

ACHIEVING SUPERIOR CUSTOMER RESPONSIVENESS

To achieve superior customer responsiveness a company must give customers what they want when they want it—so long as the company's long-term profitability is not compromised in the process. The more responsive a company is to the needs of its customers, the greater the brand loyalty the company can command. In turn, strong brand loyalty may allow a company to charge a premium price for its products or to sell more goods and services to customers. Either way, the company that is responsive to its customers' needs will have a competitive advantage.

Achieving superior customer responsiveness means giving customers value for money, and steps taken to improve the efficiency of a company's production process and the quality of its output should be consistent with this aim. In addition, giving customers what they want may require the development of new products with new features. In other words, achieving superior efficiency, quality, and innovation is all part of achieving superior customer responsiveness. There are two other prerequisites for attaining this goal. The first is to focus on the company's customers and their needs, and the second is to find ways to better satisfy those needs.

Focusing on the Customer

A company cannot be responsive to its customers' needs unless it knows what those needs are. Thus, the first step in building superior customer responsiveness is to motivate the whole company to focus on the customer. The means to this end are demonstrating leadership, shaping employee attitudes, and using mechanisms for bringing customers into the company.

Leadership   Focusing on the customer must start at the top of the organization. A commitment to superior customer responsiveness brings attitudinal changes throughout a company that can ultimately be built only through strong leadership. A mission statement (see Chapter 2) that puts customers first is one way to send a clear message to employees about the desired focus. Another avenue is top management's own actions. For example, Tom Monaghan, the founder of Domino's Pizza, stays close to the customer by visiting as many stores as possible every week, running some deliveries himself, insisting that other top managers do the same, and eating Domino's pizza regularly.[58]

Employee Attitudes   Achieving a superior customer focus requires that all employees see the customer as the focus of their activity. Leadership alone is not enough to attain this goal. All employees must be trained to focus on the customer, whether their function is marketing, manufacturing, R&D, or accounting. The objective should be to make employees think of themselves as customers—that is, to put themselves in the customers' shoes. This will better enable employees to identify ways to improve the quality of a customer's experience with the company.

To reinforce this mindset, incentive systems within the company should reward employees for satisfying customers. For example, senior managers at the Four Seasons hotel chain, who pride themselves on their customer focus, like to tell the story of Roy Dyment, a doorman in Toronto who neglected to load a departing guest's briefcase into his taxi. The doorman called the guest, a lawyer, in Washington, D.C., and found that he desperately needed the briefcase for a morning meeting. Dyment hopped on a plane to Washington and returned it—without first securing approval from his boss. Far from punishing Dyment for making the mistake and for not checking with management before going to Washington, the Four Seasons responded by naming Dyment Employee of the Year.[59] This action sent a powerful message to Four Seasons employees about the importance of satisfying customers' needs.

Bringing Customers into the Company   "Know thy customer" is one of the keys to achieving superior customer responsiveness. Knowing the customer not only requires that employees think like customers themselves but also demands that they listen to what their customers have to say, and, as much as possible, bring them into the company. While this may not involve physically bringing customers into the company, it does mean bringing in customers' opinions by soliciting feedback from customers on the company's goods and services and by building information systems that communicate the feedback to the relevant people.

For an example, consider mail-order clothing retailer Lands' End. Through its catalog and customer service telephone operators, Lands' End actively solicits comments from its customers about the quality of its clothing and the kind of merchandise they want Lands' End to supply. Indeed, it was customers' insistence that prompted the company to move into the clothing segment. Lands' End used to supply equipment for sailboats through mail-order catalogs. However, it received so many requests from customers to include outdoor clothing in its offering that it responded by expanding the catalog to fill this need. Soon clothing became the main business, and Lands' End dropped the sailboat equipment. Today the company still pays close attention to customers' requests. Every month a computer printout of customers' requests and comments is given to managers. This feedback helps the company to fine-tune the merchandise it sells. Indeed, frequently new lines of merchandise are introduced in response to customers' requests.[60]

Now many companies are trying actively to bring customers into their new-product development process. You have already seen an example of this effort in the section on innovation: Techsonic's development of depth finders. Another example is Boeing's new 777 jetliner, the design of which was finalized only after intensive consultations with potential airline customers.[61]

Satisfying Customers' Needs

Once a focus on the customer has been achieved, the next task is to satisfy the customers' needs that have been identified. As already noted, efficiency, quality, and innovation all are crucial to satisfying those needs. Beyond that, companies can provide a higher level of satisfaction if they customize the product, as much as possible, to the requirements of individual customers and if they minimize the time it takes to respond to customers' demands.

Customization   **Customization** is varying the features of a good or service to tailor it to the unique needs of groups of customers or, in the extreme case, individual customers. It used to be thought that customization raised costs. However, as we noted earlier in this chapter, the development of flexible manufacturing technologies has made it possible to produce a far greater variety of products than previously without suffering a substantial cost penalty. Companies can now customize their products to a much greater extent than was feasible ten to fifteen years ago.[62] The following examples illustrate the effects of flexible manufacturing technologies:

- Panasonic Bicycle Company of Japan is able to turn out more than 11,000 variations of bicycle designs according to each customer's height, size, and color preferences—all without any downtime in the factory.

- Ingersoll Milling Machine Company can produce 25,000 part designs, mostly in lots of one and many one of a kind, to support its world dominance in the market for specialized production machinery.

- Because of its flexible production systems, Toshiba can manufacture nine different word processors on the same assembly line and twenty different varieties of laptop computer on an adjacent line, with only a limited increase in unit costs relative to manufacturing a single product.[63]

The trend toward customization has fragmented many markets, particularly consumer markets, into ever smaller niches. An example of this fragmentation occurred in Japan in the early 1980s, when Honda dominated the motorcycle market there.

Materials Management and Information Systems Help Bose Improve Its Customer Responsiveness

The Massachusetts-based Bose Corporation manufactures some of the world's best-known high-fidelity speakers. Indeed, Bose speakers are bestsellers in Japan, the world leader in consumer electronics. The company attributes much of its success to a tightly coordinated materials management function that allows it to respond quickly to customers' demands. Bose purchases most of the electronic and nonelectronic components that go into its speakers from independent suppliers. Roughly 50 percent of its purchases are from foreign suppliers, the majority of whom are found in the Far East. Bose's problem is to coordinate this globally dispersed supply chain so that materials holding and transportation costs can be minimized. This requires that component parts arrive at the Massachusetts assembly plant just in time to enter the production process, and not before. At the same time, Bose has to remain responsive to customers' demands. Most of all, this requires that the company respond quickly to increases in customers' demands for certain speakers. If Bose does not respond quickly, it can lose a big order to competitors. Since the company does not want to hold extensive inventories at its Massachusetts plant, the need to remain responsive to customers' demands requires that Bose's supply chain respond rapidly to increased demand for component parts.

The responsibility for coordinating the supply chain to minimize transportation and inventory holding costs, while simultaneously remaining able to respond

Second-place Yamaha decided to go after Honda's lead. In 1981 it announced the opening of a new factory that, when operating at full capacity, would make Yamaha the world's largest manufacturer of motorcycles. Honda responded by proliferating its product line and stepping up its rate of new-product introduction. At the start of what became known as the "motorcycle wars," Honda had 60 motorcycles in its product line. Over the next eighteen months Honda rapidly increased its range to 113 models, customizing them to ever smaller niches. Honda was able to accomplish this without bearing a significant cost penalty because it was a flexible manufacturer. The flood of Honda's customized models pushed Yamaha out of much of the market, effectively stalling its bid to overtake Honda.[64]

Response Time   Giving customers what they want when they want it requires speed of response. To gain a competitive advantage, a company must often respond to consumers' demands very quickly, whether the transaction is a furniture manufacturer's delivery of a product once it has been ordered, a bank's processing of a loan application, an automobile manufacturer's delivery of a spare part for a car that broke down, or the wait in a supermarket checkout line. We live in a fast-paced society, where time is a valuable commodity. Companies that can satisfy customers' demands quickly can build brand loyalty and set a higher price for the product or service.

Increased speed lets a company charge a significant premium, as the mail delivery industry illustrates. The air express niche of the mail delivery industry is based on the notion that customers are often willing to pay considerably more for quickly to customers' demands, falls upon Bose's materials management function. The materials management function achieves coordination through a sophisticated logistics operation. Most of Bose's imports from the Far East come via ships to the West coast and then across North America to its Massachusetts plant via train. Most of the company's exports also move by ocean freight, although Bose uses air freight if goods are needed in a hurry.

To control this supply chain, Bose has established a relationship with W. N. Procter, a Boston-based freight forwarder and customs broker. Procter handles customs clearance and shipping from suppliers to Bose and offers Bose up-to-the-minute electronic data interchange (EDI) capabilities through a system known as ProcterLink. This gives Bose the information needed to track parts as they move through the global supply chain and to fine-tune its production scheduling so that supplies enter the production process just in time.

Procter is also electronically tied into the U.S. customs system so it can electronically clear freight as much as five days before a ship arrives at a U.S. port or hours before an international airfreight shipment touches down. This can save several days in getting goods to Bose's manufacturing plant.

Just how well this system can work was illustrated recently when one Japanese customer doubled its order for Bose speakers. Bose had to gear up its manufacturing in a hurry, but many of its components were stretched out across long distances. By using Procter-Link, Bose was able to locate the needed parts in its supply chain. It then broke them out of the normal delivery chain and moved them by airfreight to get them to the manufacturing line in time for the accelerated schedule. As a result, Bose was able to meet the request of its Japanese customer.[65]

overnight Express Mail, as opposed to regular mail. Another example of the value of rapid response is Caterpillar, the manufacturer of heavy earthmoving equipment, which can get a spare part to any point in the world within twenty-four hours. Since downtime for heavy construction equipment is very costly, Caterpillar's ability to respond quickly in the event of equipment malfunction is of prime importance to its customers. As a result, many of them have remained loyal to Caterpillar despite the aggressive low-priced competition from Komatsu of Japan.

In general, reducing response time requires (1) a marketing function that can quickly communicate customers' requests to production, (2) production and materials management functions that can quickly adjust production schedules in response to unanticipated customers' demands, and (3) information systems that can help production and marketing in this process. Strategy in Action 5.8 provides a detailed example of the role materials management and information systems can play in achieving superior customer responsiveness. Note that the combination of flexible manufacturing systems, just-in-time inventory systems, and information systems is needed for a quick response to customers' demands.

Summary: Achieving Superior Customer Responsiveness

Table 5.5 summarizes the steps different functions must take if a company is to achieve superior customer responsiveness. Although marketing plays the critical role in helping a company attain this goal, primarily because it represents the point of contact with the customer, Table 5.5 shows that the other functions also have

TABLE 5.5
....

The Primary Role of Different Functions in Achieving Superior Customer Responsiveness

Value Creation Function	Primary Roles
Infrastructure (Leadership)	1. Through leadership by example, build a companywide commitment to customer responsiveness.
Production	1. Achieve customization through implementation of flexible manufacturing. 2. Achieve rapid response through flexible manufacturing.
Marketing	1. Know the customer. 2. Communicate customer feedback to appropriate functions.
Materials Management	1. Develop logistics systems capable of responding quickly to unanticipated customer demands (JIT).
R&D	1. Bring customers into the product development process.
Human Resources	1. Develop training programs that get employees to think like customers themselves.

major roles to perform. Moreover, as with achieving superior efficiency, quality, and innovation, achieving superior customer responsiveness requires top management to lead in building a customer orientation within the company.

SUMMARY OF CHAPTER
....

This chapter discusses the role that functional-level strategies play in achieving efficiency, quality, innovation, and customer responsiveness; reviews in detail the different steps that lead to this end; and makes the following main points:

✔ A company can increase efficiency through a number of steps. These include exploiting economies of scale and learning effects, adopting flexible manufacturing technologies, reducing customer defection rates, implementing just-in-time systems, getting the R&D function to design products that are easy to manufacture, upgrading the skills of employees through training, introducing self-managing teams, linking pay to performance, building a companywide commitment to efficiency through strong leadership, and designing structures that facilitate cooperation among different functions in pursuit of efficiency goals.

✔ Superior quality can help a company both to lower its costs and to differentiate its product and charge a premium price.

✔ Achieving superior quality demands an organizationwide commitment to quality and a clear focus on the customer. It also requires metrics to measure quality goals and incentives that emphasize quality, input from employees regarding ways in which quality can be improved, a methodology for tracing defects to their source and correcting the problems that produce them, rationalization of the company's supply base, cooperation with the suppliers that remain to implement TQM programs, products that are designed for ease of manufacturing, and substantial cooperation among functions.

✔ The failure rate of new-product introductions is high due to factors such as uncertainty, poor commercialization, poor positioning strategy, technological myopia, and slow cycle time.

✔ To achieve superior innovation, a company must build skills in basic and applied research; design good processes for managing development projects; and achieve close integration among the different functions of the enterprise, primarily through the adoption of cross-functional product development teams and partly parallel development processes.

✔ To achieve superior customer responsiveness often requires that the company achieve superior efficiency, quality, and innovation.

✔ To achieve superior customer responsiveness, a company needs to give customers what they want when they want it. It must ensure a strong customer focus, which can be attained through leadership; training employees to think like customers; bringing customers into the company through superior market research; customizing the product to the unique needs of individual customers or customer groups; and responding quickly to customers' demands.

DISCUSSION QUESTIONS

1. How are the four generic building blocks of competitive advantage related to each other?

2. What role can top management play in helping a company achieve superior efficiency, quality, innovation, and customer responsiveness?

3. In the long run, will adoption of TQM practices give a company a competitive advantage, or will it be required just to achieve parity with competitors?

4. In what sense might innovation be called the single most important building block of competitive advantage?

Practicing Strategic Management

SMALL GROUP EXERCISE
Identifying Excellence

Break up into groups of three to five people. You are the management team of a start-up company that will produce disk drives for the personal computer industry. You will sell your product to manufacturers of personal computers (original equipment manufacturers). The disk drive market is characterized by rapid technological change, product life cycles of only six to nine months, intense price competition, high fixed costs for manufacturing equipment, and substantial manufacturing economies of scale. Your customers—the original equipment manufacturers—issue very demanding technological specifications with which your product must comply. The original equipment manufacturers also pressure you to deliver your product on time so that it fits in with their own product introduction schedule. In this industry, what functional competencies are the most important for you to build? How will you design your internal processes to ensure that those competencies are built within the company?

EXPLORING THE WEB
Visiting Applied Materials

Applied Materials is the world's largest manufacturer of semiconductor fabrication equipment. Visit its Web site (www.appliedmaterials.com). Go to the section titled "About Applied Materials," and read the company's mission statement. What does this mission statement tell you about the kind of competitive advantage Applied Materials is trying to build? How important are efficiency, quality, innovation, and customer responsiveness to this company?

Now go to the sections of Applied's Web site that detail the company's financial results, products, and press releases. Read through these sections to establish how successful Applied has been at meeting the objectives set down in its mission statement. What do you think the company has done at the functional level to increase its efficiency, customer responsiveness, innovative ability, and product quality?

Search the Web for a company whose home page describes in some detail its approach to achieving one of the following: superior productivity, product quality, customer service, or innovation. Using this information, document the company's functional-level strategy, and assess whether the strategy makes sense given what you have learned so far in this book.

ARTICLE FILE 5

Find an example of a company that is widely regarded as excellent. Identify the source of its excellence, and relate it to the material discussed in this chapter. Pay particular attention to the role played by the various functions in building excellence.

STRATEGIC MANAGEMENT PROJECT
Module 5

This module deals with the ability of your company to achieve superior efficiency, quality, innovation, and customer responsiveness. With the information you have at your disposal, answer the questions and perform the tasks listed:

1. Is your company pursuing any of the efficiency-enhancing practices discussed in this chapter?

2. Is your company pursuing any of the quality-enhancing practices discussed in this chapter?

3. Is your company pursuing any of the practices designed to enhance innovation discussed in this chapter?

4. Is your company pursuing any of the practices designed to increase customer responsiveness discussed in this chapter?

5. Evaluate the competitive position of your company in the light of your answers to questions 1–4. Explain what, if anything, the company needs to do to improve its competitive position.

CLOSING CASE

Xerox Corp.

In 1960 Xerox shipped its first 914 copier, beginning one of the most successful new-product introductions in history. For the next fifteen years, Xerox dominated the photocopier market. However, by 1980 the company was facing problems. Two Japanese companies, Canon and Ricoh, had emerged as significant global competitors and were selling high-quality copiers at a price equivalent to Xerox's cost for producing comparable products. Because of high costs and high prices, Xerox's market share had fallen by half and its return on assets had slumped to 8 percent.

Xerox learned firsthand how far it had fallen behind when it began to produce and market a copier in the United States that had been designed by its Japanese affiliate, Fuji-Xerox. Xerox found that the reject rate for Fuji-Xerox parts was only a fraction of the reject rate for American-produced parts. Visits to Fuji-Xerox revealed another important truth—quality in manufacturing does not increase costs; it decreases costs by reducing the number of defective products and service costs.

These developments forced Xerox to rethink the way it did business. In 1982 the company launched the first of a series of initiatives that over the next decade transformed the way it ran its operations. In 1981 Xerox had more than 5,000 individual suppliers worldwide. The Xerox management realized that by consolidating the company's worldwide supply base, it could achieve three goals:

1. By simplifying the purchasing process, it could cut overhead in purchasing.

2. By having a single supplier produce a single part for all of Xerox's worldwide operations, it would enable the supplier to achieve economies of scale in production; these cost savings could be passed on to Xerox in the form of lower prices.

3. By cutting down the number of suppliers, Xerox would find it easier to work with its suppliers to improve the quality of component parts.

Toward this end, in 1982 Xerox created "commodity teams," which included buyers, engineers, costing experts, and quality-control personnel. Their first task was to decrease Xerox's supplier base from more than 5,000 to less than 500; they reduced it to 325 suppliers. Because the consolidation of suppliers simplified the purchasing process, overhead rates fell from 9 percent of total costs for materials in 1982 to about 3 percent in 1992.

Next, Xerox launched a quality training effort with its suppliers. Its goal was to reduce the number of defective parts coming from suppliers to less than 1,000 per million. At that time some suppliers had defect rates as high as 25,000 per million parts. The company soon met its quality goal of 1,000 defects per million parts. Indeed, by 1992 the defect rate for parts was less than 300 per million.

In 1983 Xerox introduced its Leadership Through Quality program. Groups were formed throughout the company, from top management down to the factory floor. Each group received training in quality improvement programs. Emphasis was placed on identifying quality shortfalls, determining the root causes of poor quality, developing solutions, and implementing them. The training program began with the top-tier groups and then cascaded down throughout the organization, spreading worldwide to some 100,000 employees.

In 1985 and 1986 Xerox began to focus on its new-product development process. One goal was to design products that, while customized to market conditions in different countries, also contained a large number of globally standardized parts. Another goal was to reduce the time it took to design new products and bring them to market. To achieve these goals, Xerox established multifunctional, multinational new-product development teams. Each team managed the design, component sources, manufacturing, distribution, and follow-up customer service on a worldwide basis. The use of design teams cut as much as one year from the overall product development cycle and saved millions of dollars.

One consequence of the new approach to product development was the 5100 copier. This was the first product designed jointly by Xerox and Fuji-Xerox for the worldwide market. The 5100 is manufactured in U.S. plants. It was launched in Japan in November 1990 and in the United States the following February. The 5100's global design reportedly reduced the overall time to market and saved the company more than $10 million in development costs.

In 1989 Xerox calculated that it could eliminate $1 billion in inventory and $200 million in inventory-related costs by linking worldwide customer orders more closely with production. It formed a multinational organization called Central Logistics and Assets Management, whose aim is to achieve tight integration between individual customer's orders and plant production levels, thereby reducing the need to hold excessive inventory to serve demand.

As a result of these steps, Xerox's position improved markedly during the 1980s. Thanks to its improved quality, lower costs, and shorter product development time, Xerox was able to regain market share from its competitors and to boost its profits and revenues. Xerox's share of the U.S. copier market increased from a low of 10 percent in 1985 to 18 percent in 1991.[66]

Case Discussion Questions

1. Identify how the changes that Xerox undertook after 1982 helped the company to improve its efficiency, quality, innovation, and customer responsiveness.
2. To what extent were the changes undertaken by Xerox after 1982 the result of functions working together to achieve a common goal?

CHAPTER 6

Business-Level Strategy

Opening Case: Ford's Difficult Balancing Act

Overview

What Is Business-Level Strategy?

Choosing a Generic Business-Level Strategy

Strategic Groups and Business-Level Strategy

Choosing an Investment Strategy at the Business Level

Closing Case: Liz Claiborne, Inc.

OPENING CASE

Ford's Difficult Balancing Act

In the 1990s Alex Trotman, Ford Motor's current CEO, has faced the problem of how best to compete in an increasingly competitive car industry. On the one hand, Ford, like other large U.S. carmakers, has been forced to find ways to reduce costs to compete effectively against low-priced competitors from Japan and Europe. On the other hand, Ford has to differentiate its cars and make them stand out so that customers will be attracted to them and will buy them rather than the cars of its rivals.

To reduce costs, Ford has forged ahead with a global cost-cutting plan called Ford 2000. The plan includes producing very similar models of cars and trucks that can be sold globally to customers in all the countries of the world in which Ford does business. It also means centralizing all car design activities at five global design centers to reduce costs. Finally, the plan reduces the number of different car platforms (the frames on which the car models are based) and the number of component parts, again to reduce costs. For example, Ford used to use more than thirty different kinds of car horns. Now it employs only three, which it buys in bigger volume from a few manufacturers. Ford projects a $1 billion saving in engineering costs and $11 billion in reduced plant investment costs from this plan.[1]

To make Ford's products unique, CEO Trotman also authorized a radically new program of car styling. Throughout the 1970s and 1980s, Ford had been known for the big, boxy, plain look of its cars, a look that had changed little in decades. From the mid 1980s on, Ford began to re-style all its cars. Trotman's multibillion-dollar program culminated in the radical redesign of the best-selling car in the United States, the Ford Taurus, which Ford launched in the fall of 1995. The accentuated curves and oval shape of the Taurus reflected the redesign of Ford's other cars, such as the Lincoln Continental, the Mustang, and the Mondeo, Ford's first world car.

By 1996, however, it became clear to Trotman and other top Ford executives that the dual push to reduce costs on a global level while launching a whole new series of redesigned global cars was not working. The enormous development costs of the new cars had raised costs dramatically and forced up car prices. The typical well-equipped Taurus, for example, was retailing for more than $20,000, more than $3,000 above the old model, and customers were experiencing sticker shock. In essence, all the cost savings brought about by the Ford 2000 plan were being eaten up by the high costs associated with its push to produce a radically new, differentiated line of cars. By mid 1996 the Honda Accord had once again become the best-selling car in the United States, Ford's profits had plunged 58 percent, its stock price was flat, and many analysts were worried that Ford's new strategy was not working.[2]

In May 1996 Trotman announced a new plan to bring together the cost and differentiation sides of Ford's business-level strategy. Trotman argued that Ford's basic strategy was correct and that all the benefits of the launch of new cars and the saving in costs would be reaped well into the next century. In the short term, however, to boost sales Ford announced that it would bring out stripped-down models of the Taurus and other cars to reduce price and attract more customers. Furthermore, recognizing that its new cars were costing too much to develop, Ford announced that it would close down two of its global design centers and further consolidate its design program to reduce development costs. Trotman and his top management team have continued to search for ways to align both the cost and differentiation sides of the business-strategy equation to provide Ford's customers with a well-designed car at a price they are willing to pay. By the fall of 1996, there were signs that this was paying off, as sales of Ford's cars rose sharply.

OVERVIEW

As the Ford case suggests, this chapter examines how a company can compete effectively in a business or industry and scrutinizes the various strategies that it can adopt to maximize competitive advantage and profitability. Chapter 3, on the external industry environment, provides concepts for analyzing industry opportunities and threats. Chapters 4 and 5 discuss how a company develops functional-level strategies to build internal strengths and distinctive competencies to achieve a competitive advantage. The purpose of this chapter is to consider the business-level strategies that a company can use to exploit its competitive advantage and compete effectively in an industry. By the end of this chapter, you will be able to identify and distinguish between the principal kinds of business-level strategies that strategic managers can develop to give their companies a competitive advantage over their rivals.

WHAT IS BUSINESS-LEVEL STRATEGY?

Business-level strategy refers to the plan of action that strategic managers adopt to use a company's resources and distinctive competencies to gain a competitive advantage over its rivals in a market or industry. In Chapter 2 we discuss Derek F. Abell's view that the process of business definition entails decisions about (1) customers' needs, or *what* is to be satisfied; (2) customer groups, or *who* is to be satisfied; and (3) distinctive competencies, or *how* customer needs are to be satisfied.[3] These three decisions are the basis of the choice of a business-level strategy because they determine how a company will compete in a business or industry. Consequently, we need to look at the ways in which a company makes these three decisions to gain a competitive advantage over its rivals.

Customers' Needs and Product Differentiation

Customers' needs are desires, wants, or cravings that can be satisfied by means of the characteristics of a product or service. For example, a person's craving for something sweet can be satisfied by a carton of Ben & Jerry's ice cream, a Snickers bar, or a spoonful of sugar. **Product differentiation** is the process of creating a competitive advantage by designing products—goods or services—to satisfy customers' needs. All companies must differentiate their products to a certain degree in order to attract customers and satisfy some minimal level of need. However, some companies differentiate their products to a much greater degree than others, and this difference can give them a competitive edge.

Some companies offer the customer a low-priced product without engaging in much product differentiation. Others seek to create something unique about their product so that they satisfy customers' needs in ways that other products cannot. The uniqueness may relate to the physical characteristics of the product, such as quality or reliability, or it may lie in the product's appeal to customers' psychological needs, such as the need for prestige or status.[4] Thus, a Japanese car may be differentiated by its reputation for reliability, and a Corvette or a Porsche may be differentiated by its ability to satisfy customers' needs for status.

Customer Groups and Market Segmentation

Market segmentation is the way a company decides to group customers, based on important differences in their needs or preferences, in order to gain a competitive advantage.[5] For example, General Motors groups its customers according to the amount of money they want and can afford to spend to buy a car, and for each group it builds different cars, which range from the low-priced GEO Metro to the high-priced Cadillac Seville.

In general, a company can adopt three alternative strategies toward market segmentation.[6] First, it can choose not to recognize that different groups of customers have different needs and instead adopt the approach of serving the average customer. Second, a company can choose to segment its market into different constituencies and develop a product to suit the needs of each. For example, in a recent catalog Sony offered twenty-four different 19-inch color television sets, each targeted at a different market segment. Third, a company can choose to recognize that the market is segmented but concentrate on servicing only one market segment, or niche, such as the luxury-car niche pursued by Mercedes-Benz.

Why would a company want to make complex product/market choices and create a different product tailored to each market segment rather than create a single product for the whole market? The answer is that the decision to provide many products for many market niches allows a company to satisfy customers' needs better. As a result, customers' demand for the company's products rises and generates more revenue than would be the case if the company offered just one product for the whole market.[7] Sometimes, however, the nature of the product or the nature of the industry does not allow much differentiation, which is the case, for example, with bulk chemicals or cement.[8] In these industries, there is little opportunity for obtaining a competitive advantage through product differentiation and market segmentation because there is little opportunity for serving customers' needs and customer groups in different ways. Instead, price is the main criterion used by customers to evaluate the product, and the competitive advantage lies with the company that has superior efficiency and can provide the lowest-priced product.

Distinctive Competencies

The third issue in business-level strategy is to decide which distinctive competencies to pursue to satisfy customers' needs and customer groups.[9] As we discussed in Chapter 4, there are four ways companies can obtain a competitive advantage: superior efficiency, quality, innovation, and responsiveness to customers. The Four Seasons hotel chain, for example, attempts to do all it can to provide its customers with the highest-quality accommodations and the best customer service possible. In making business strategy choices, a company must decide how to organize and combine its distinctive competencies to gain a competitive advantage. The source of these distinctive competencies is examined at length in Chapter 5.

CHOOSING A GENERIC BUSINESS-LEVEL STRATEGY

Companies pursue a business-level strategy to gain a competitive advantage that allows them to outperform rivals and achieve above-average returns. They can choose from three basic generic competitive approaches: cost leadership, differentiation, and focus, although as we will see these can be combined in different ways.[10] These strategies are called *generic* because all businesses or industries can pursue them regardless of whether they are manufacturing, service, or not-for-profit enterprises. Each of the generic strategies results from a company's making consistent choices on product, market, and distinctive competencies—choices that reinforce each other. Table 6.1 summarizes the choices appropriate for each of the three generic strategies.

Cost-Leadership Strategy

A company's goal in pursuing a **cost-leadership strategy** is to outperform competitors by doing everything it can to produce goods or services at a cost lower than theirs. Two advantages accrue from a cost-leadership strategy. First, because of

TABLE 6.1

Product/Market/Distinctive-Competency Choices and Generic Competitive Strategies

	Cost Leadership	*Differentiation*	*Focus*
Product Differentiation	Low (principally by price)	High (principally by uniqueness)	Low to high (price or uniqueness)
Market Segmentation	Low (mass market)	High (many market segments)	Low (one or a few segments)
Distinctive Competency	Manufacturing and materials management	Research and development, sales and marketing	Any kind of distinctive competency

its lower costs, the cost leader is able to charge a lower price than its competitors yet make the same level of profit. If companies in the industry charge similar prices for their products, the cost leader still makes a higher profit than its competitors because of its lower costs. Second, if rivalry within the industry increases and companies start to compete on price, the cost leader will be able to withstand competition better than the other companies because of its lower costs. For both these reasons, cost leaders are likely to earn above-average profits.

How does a company become the cost leader? It achieves this position by means of the product/market/distinctive-competency choices that it makes to gain a low-cost competitive advantage (see Table 6.1).

Strategic Choices   The cost leader chooses a low level of product differentiation. Differentiation is expensive; if the company expends resources to make its products unique, then its costs rise.[11] The cost leader aims for a level of differentiation not markedly inferior to that of the differentiator (a company that competes by spending resources on product development), but a level obtainable at low cost.[12] The cost leader does not try to be the industry leader in differentiation; it waits until customers want a feature or service before providing it. For example, a cost leader does not introduce stereo sound in television sets. It adds stereo sound only when it is obvious that consumers want it.

The cost leader also normally ignores the different market segments and positions its product to appeal to the average customer. The reason the cost leader makes this choice is, again, that developing a line of products tailored to the needs of different market segments is an expensive proposition. A cost leader normally engages in only a limited amount of market segmentation. Even though no customer may be totally happy with the product, the fact that the company normally charges a lower price than its competitors attracts customers to its products.

In developing distinctive competencies, the overriding goal of the cost leader must be to increase its efficiency and lower its costs compared with its rivals. The development of distinctive competencies in manufacturing and materials management is central to achieving this goal. Companies pursuing a low-cost strategy may attempt to ride down the experience curve so that they can lower their manufacturing costs.

Achieving a low-cost position may also require that the company develop skills in flexible manufacturing and adopt efficient materials-management techniques. (As you may recall, Table 5.1 outlines the ways in which a company's functions can be used to increase efficiency.) Consequently, the manufacturing and materials-management functions are the center of attention for a company pursuing a cost-leadership strategy, and the other functions shape their distinctive competencies to meet the needs of manufacturing and materials management.[13] For example, the sales function may develop the competency of capturing large, stable sets of customers' orders. In turn, this allows manufacturing to make longer production runs and so achieve economies of scale and reduce costs. The human resource function may focus on instituting training programs and compensation systems that lower costs by enhancing employees' productivity, and the research and development function may specialize in process improvements to lower the manufacturing costs. The way in which Nissan developed its mid-sized car, the Altima, is discussed in Strategy in Action 6.1, which provides a good illustration of a company that decides to pursue a cost-leadership strategy.

Nissan's Cost-Leadership Strategy

Nissan, the Japanese automaker, had watched its U.S. sales slide 35 percent from their peak in 1985. The reason was that the quality and design of its cars simply did not keep up with those of other Japanese competitors, such as Honda, Mazda, and Toyota. While these companies had been innovators in introducing stylish, new rounded-car designs and cars such as the Miata and the Previa for new market segments, Nissan plodded along with its boxy Stanzas and Maximas, which were at least as expensive as the cars of its rivals. As sales and profits declined, the company realized that it needed to rethink its U.S. strategy. As part of a companywide shakeup, Nissan appointed Earl J. Hesterberg as vice president and general manager of the U.S. Nissan division and gave him wide authority to turn the U.S. division's fortunes around.

Recognizing that Nissan was now far behind its rivals in terms of its reputation for product innovation and design, Hesterberg decided on a new strategy for introducing the new Nissan mid-sized car: a cost-leadership strategy. The mid-sized cars of Nissan's rivals—the Toyota Camry, Honda Accord, and Mazda 626—had increased steadily in size and price with each new model. A well-equipped Camry or Accord, for example, had a sticker price of more than $19,000. Hesterberg decided that Nissan would not increase the size of its car and hence would keep its cost and price low. Nissan's designers were instructed to aim for a car that would be cheap to produce but of a quality comparable to that of other Japanese manufacturers. The result was the Nissan Altima, whose four-door base model lists for $14,000 and the better-equipped one costs thousands less than the Camry or Accord. Nissan kept costs low by deliberately restricting the number of different models to these two, an approach that both Ford and Toyota, among others, have copied.[14]

Another part of Hesterberg's strategy was to concentrate most of Nissan's marketing budget (more than $100 million) on the Altima and the Nissan Quest, its minivan, and to focus on building a large market share for these cars in order to build sales revenues. In its marketing, Nissan was careful to emphasize the value of the Altima by comparing its quality with that of the Toyota Lexus, which costs more than three times as much.

The results of this low-cost strategy were astounding. Nissan hoped to sell 100,000 cars in its first year; it sold more than 140,000. Although the profit margin on each car was lower than it was for the Accord or the Camry, the extra sales volume brought Nissan a huge profit. Its pursuit of a low-cost, low-price strategy in the mid-sized car segment has been very successful and has hurt its competitors. For example, for the first time in its history, Honda was forced to offer discounts on its Accord, and sales of the Toyota Camry and Mazda 626 were below projections. Clearly, a low-cost strategy can pay big dividends.[15]

The cost leader gears all its strategic product/market/distinctive-competency choices to the single goal of squeezing out every cent of costs to provide a competitive advantage. A company such as H. J. Heinz is another excellent example of a cost leader. Because beans and canned vegetables do not permit much of a markup, the profit comes from the large volume of cans sold. Therefore Heinz goes to extraordinary lengths to try to reduce costs—by even one-twentieth of a cent per can—because this will lead to large cost savings and thus bigger profits over the long run. As you will see in the chapters in Part IV on strategy implementation, another source of cost savings in pursuing cost leadership is the design of the organizational structure to match this strategy, since structure is a major source of a company's costs. As we discuss in Chapter 12, a low-cost strategy usually implies tight production controls and rigorous use of budgets to control the production process.

Advantages and Disadvantages The advantages of each generic strategy are best discussed in terms of Porter's five forces model, which is introduced in Chapter 3.[16] The five forces are threats from competitors, powerful suppliers, powerful buyers, substitute products, and new entrants. The cost leader is protected from *industry competitors* by its cost advantage. Its lower costs also mean that it will be less affected than its competitors by increases in the price of inputs if there are *powerful suppliers* and less affected by a fall in the price it can charge for its products if there are *powerful buyers*. Moreover, since cost leadership usually requires a big market share, the cost leader purchases in relatively large quantities, increasing its bargaining power over suppliers. If *substitute products* start to come into the market, the cost leader can reduce its price to compete with them and retain its market share. Finally, the leader's cost advantage constitutes a *barrier to entry*, since other companies are unable to enter the industry and match the leader's costs or prices. The cost leader is, therefore, relatively safe as long as it can maintain its cost advantage, and price is the key for a significant number of buyers.

The principal dangers of the cost-leadership approach lurk in competitors' ability to find ways to produce at lower cost and beat the cost leader at its own game. For instance, if technological change makes experience-curve economies obsolete, new companies may apply lower-cost technologies that give them a cost advantage over the cost leader. The steel minimills discussed in Chapter 5 gained this advantage. Competitors may also draw a cost advantage from labor-cost savings. Foreign competitors in the Third World have very low labor costs; for example, wage costs in the United States are roughly 600 percent more than they are in Malaysia, China, or Mexico. Many U.S. companies now assemble their products abroad as part of their low-cost strategy; many are forced to do so simply to compete.

Competitors' ability to imitate the cost leader's methods easily is another threat to the cost-leadership strategy. For example, the ability of IBM-clone manufacturers to produce IBM-compatible products at costs similar to IBM's (but, of course, to sell them at a much lower price) was a major factor contributing to IBM's troubles.

Finally, the cost-leadership strategy carries a risk that the cost leader, in its single-minded desire to reduce costs, may lose sight of changes in customers' tastes. Thus, a company might make decisions that decrease costs but drastically affect demand for the product. For example, Joseph Schlitz Brewing lowered the quality of its beer's ingredients, substituting inferior grains to reduce costs. Consumers immediately caught on, with the result that demand for the product dropped dramatically. As mentioned earlier, the cost leader cannot abandon product differentiation, and even low-priced products, such as Timex watches, cannot be too inferior to the more expensive watches made by Seiko if the low-cost, low-price policy is to succeed.

Differentiation Strategy

The objective of the generic **differentiation strategy** is to achieve a competitive advantage by creating a product (good or service) that is perceived by customers to be *unique* in some important way. The differentiated company's ability to satisfy a customer's need in a way that its competitors cannot means that it can charge a *premium price* (a price considerably above the industry's average). The ability to increase revenues by charging premium prices (rather than by reducing costs as the cost leader does) allows the differentiator to outperform its competitors and gain above-average profits. The premium price is usually substantially above the price charged by the cost leader, and customers pay it because they believe the product's differentiated qualities are worth the difference. Consequently, the product is priced on the basis of what the market will bear.[17]

Thus, Mercedes-Benz cars are much more expensive in the United States than in Europe because they confer more status here. Similarly, a BMW is not a lot more expensive to produce than a Honda, but its price is determined by customers who perceive that the prestige of owning a BMW is something worth paying for. Similarly, Rolex watches do not cost much to produce; their design has not changed very much for years, and their gold content represents only a fraction of the price. Customers, however, buy a Rolex because of the unique quality they perceive in it: its ability to confer status on its wearer. In stereos, the name Bang & Olufsen of Denmark stands out; in jewelry, Tiffany; in airplanes, Learjets. All these products command premium prices because of their differentiated qualities.

Strategic Choices   As Table 6.1 shows, a differentiator chooses a high level of product differentiation to gain a competitive advantage. Product differentiation can be achieved in three principal ways, which are discussed in detail in Chapter 4: quality, innovation, and responsiveness to customers. For example, Procter & Gamble claims that its product quality is high and that Ivory soap is 99.44 percent pure. Maytag stresses reliability and the best repair record of any washer on the market. IBM promotes the quality service provided by its well-trained sales force.

Innovation is very important for technologically complex products, for which new features are the source of differentiation, and many people pay a premium price for new and innovative products, such as a state-of-the-art computer, stereo, or car.

When differentiation is based on responsiveness to customers, a company offers comprehensive after-sales service and product repair. This is an especially important consideration for complex products such as cars and domestic appliances, which are likely to break down periodically. Companies such as Maytag, Dell Computer, and BMW all excel in responsiveness to customers. In service organizations, quality-of-service attributes are also very important. Why can Neiman Marcus, Nordstrum, and Federal Express charge premium prices? They offer an exceptionally high level of service. Similarly, firms of lawyers or accountants stress the service aspects of their operations to clients: their knowledge, professionalism, and reputation.

Finally, a product's appeal to customers' psychological desires can become a source of differentiation. The appeal can be to prestige or status, as it is with BMWs and Rolex watches; to patriotism, as with Chevrolet; to safety of home and family, as with Prudential Insurance; or to value for money, as with Sears and J.C. Penney. Differentiation can also be tailored to age groups and to socioeconomic groups. Indeed, the bases of differentiation are endless.

A company that pursues a differentiation strategy strives to differentiate itself along as many dimensions as possible. The less it resembles its rivals, the more it is protected from competition and the wider is its market appeal. Thus, BMWs do not just offer prestige. They also offer technological sophistication; luxury; reliability; as well as good, although very expensive, repair service. All these bases of differentiation help increase sales.

Generally, a differentiator chooses to segment its market into many niches. Now and then a company offers a product designed for each market niche and decides to be a **broad differentiator**, but a company might choose to serve just those niches in which it has a specific differentiation advantage. For example, Sony produces twenty-four models of television, filling all the niches from mid-priced to high-priced sets. However, its lowest-priced model is always priced about $100 above that of its competitors, bringing into play the premium-price factor. You have to pay extra for a Sony. Similarly, although Mercedes-Benz has filled niches below its old high-priced models with its S and C series, until recently it made no attempt to produce a car for every market segment. In 1996, however, it announced that it was planning to introduce a new line of less expensive cars to appeal to a wider market, and analysts were at once concerned that this would affect its differentiated appeal.

Finally, in choosing which distinctive competency to pursue, a differentiated company concentrates on the organizational function that provides the sources of its differentiation advantage. Differentiation on the basis of innovation and technological competency depends on the R&D function, as discussed in Chapter 5. Efforts to improve service to customers depend on the quality of the sales function. A focus on a specific function does not mean, however, that the control of costs is not important for a differentiator. A differentiator does not want to increase costs unnecessarily and tries to keep them somewhere near those of the cost leader. However, since developing the distinctive competency needed to provide a differentiation advantage is often expensive, a differentiator usually has higher costs than the cost leader.

Still, it must control all costs that do not contribute to its differentiation advantage so that the price of the product does not exceed what customers are willing to pay. Since bigger profits are earned by controlling costs and by maximizing revenues, it pays to control costs, though not to minimize them to the point of losing the source of differentiation.[18] The owners of the famous Savoy Hotel in London, England, faced just this problem in the 1990s. The Savoy's reputation has always been based on the incredibly high level of service it offers its customers. Three hotel employees service the needs of each guest, and in every room a guest can summon a waiter, maid, or valet by pressing a button at the bedside. The cost of offering this level of service has been so high that the hotel makes less than 1 percent net profit every year.[19] Its owners are trying to find ways to reduce costs to increase profits. However, their problem is that if they reduce the number of hotel staff (the main source of the Savoy's high costs) they may destroy the main source of its differentiated appeal!

Advantages and Disadvantages   The advantages of the differentiation strategy can now be discussed in the context of the five forces model. Differentiation safeguards a company against competitors to the degree that customers develop *brand loyalty* for its products. Brand loyalty is a very valuable asset because it protects the company on all fronts. For example, *powerful suppliers* are rarely a problem because the differentiated company's strategy is geared more toward the price it can charge than toward the costs of production. Thus, a differentiator can tolerate moderate increases in the prices of its inputs better than the cost leader can. Differentiators are unlikely to experience problems with *powerful buyers* because the differentiator offers the buyer a unique product. Only it can supply the product, and it commands brand loyalty. Differentiators can pass on price increases to customers because customers are willing to pay the premium price. Differentiation and brand loyalty also create a *barrier to entry* for other companies seeking to enter the industry. New companies are forced to develop their own distinctive competency to be able to compete, and doing so is very expensive.

Finally, the threat of *substitute products* depends on the ability of competitors' products to meet the same customers' needs as the differentiator's products and to break customers' brand loyalty. This can happen, as when IBM-clone manufacturers captured a large share of the home computer market, but many people still want an IBM, even though there are many IBM clones available. The issue is, how much of a premium price a company can charge for uniqueness before customers switch products. The Opening Case discussed how Ford found that it could increase the prices of its models such as the Taurus only by so much before customers would switch to less expensive alternatives such as the Nissan Altima, for example.

The main problems with a differentiation strategy center on the company's long-term ability to maintain its perceived uniqueness in customers' eyes. We have seen in the last ten years how quickly competitors move to imitate and copy successful differentiators. This has happened in many industries, such as computers, autos, and home electronics. Patents and first-mover advantages (the advantages of being the first to market a product or service) last only so long, and as the overall quality of products produced by all companies goes up, brand loyalty declines. The story of the way American Express lost its competitive advantage, told in Strategy in Action 6.2, highlights many of the threats that face a differentiator.

A strategy of differentiation, then, requires the firm to develop a competitive advantage by making choices about its product, market, and distinctive competency that reinforce each other and together increase the value of a good or service in the eyes of consumers. When a product has uniqueness in customers' eyes, differentiators can charge a premium price. However, the disadvantages of a differentiation strategy are the ease with which competitors can imitate a differentiator's product and the difficulty of maintaining a premium price. When differentiation stems from the design or physical features of the product, differentiators are at great risk because imitation is easy. The risk is that over time products such as VCRs or stereos become *commoditylike* products, for which the importance of differentiation diminishes as customers become more price sensitive. When differentiation stems from quality of service or reliability or from any *intangible source*, such as Federal Express's guarantee or the prestige of a Rolex, a company is much more secure. It is difficult to imitate intangibles, and the differentiator can reap the benefits of this strategy for a long time. Nevertheless, all differentiators must watch out for imitators and be careful that they do not charge a price higher than the market will bear.

Cost Leadership *and* Differentiation

Recently, changes in production techniques—in particular, the development of flexible manufacturing technologies (discussed in Chapter 5)—have made the choice between cost-leadership and differentiation strategies less clear-cut. With technological developments, companies have found it easier to obtain the benefits of both strategies. The reason is that the new flexible technologies allow firms to pursue a

Who Wants an American Express Card?

American Express Company's green, gold, and platinum credit cards used to be closely linked with high status and prestige. Obtaining an American Express (AmEx) card required a high income, and obtaining a gold or platinum card required an even higher one. AmEx carefully differentiated its product by using famous people to advertise the virtues—exclusivity and uniqueness—of possessing its card. Consumers were willing to pay the high yearly fee to possess the card, even though every month they were required to pay off the debit balance they had accumulated. AmEx's cards were a premium product that allowed the company to charge both customers and merchants more because it offered quality service and conferred status on the user. For many years its credit card operation was the money spinner of AmEx's Travel Related Services (TRS) division, and the company's stock price soared as its profits reached more than $200 million by 1990.[20]

AmEx's differentiated strategy has been suffering in the 1990s, however. Rival companies such as Master-Card and Visa have demonstrated how their cards can be used at locations where AmEx's cannot. Moreover, as they make clear, anybody can own a MasterCard or a Visa gold card; it is not just for the fortunate elite. In addition, various companies and banks have banded together to offer the consumer many other benefits of using their particular credit cards. For example, banks and airlines have been forming alliances that allow con-

sumers to use a bank's credit card to accumulate miles toward the purchase of an airline's tickets. Moreover, large companies such as AT&T and General Motors have issued their own credit cards that offer customers savings on their products, often without a yearly fee.

The emergence of all these new credit cards has broken the loyalty of AmEx customers and shattered the card's unique image. It has now lost its differentiated appeal and become one more credit card in an overcrowded market. By 1992 more than 2 million of its users had deserted AmEx, and the firm took a one-year loss of more than $100 million.

AmEx is trying to fight back and restore profitability to its division. To reduce costs, it announced a layoff of more than 5,000 employees in the TRS division, it started its own airline mileage program to try to attract its users back, and it has made its card more available to potential users. It has also tried to increase the number of outlets that accept the card by lowering the fees it makes merchants pay. For example, the card can now be used at Kmart. Finally, it hired a new advertising agency to try to restore its differentiated appeal. These moves have had some success in attracting customers, and in 1996 Visa and MasterCard fought hard to prevent banks that issue their cards from issuing AmEx cards as well. However, in making its cards more accessible, AmEx has reduced the card's differentiated appeal and if anybody can use the card and use it anywhere, why choose AmEx?[21]

differentiation strategy at a low cost; that is, companies can combine these two generic strategies.

Traditionally, differentiation was obtainable only at high cost, because the necessity of producing different models for different market segments meant that firms had to have short production runs, which raised manufacturing costs. In addition, the differentiated firm had to bear higher marketing costs than the cost leader because it was servicing many market segments. As a result, differentiators had higher costs than cost leaders, which produced large batches of standardized products. However, flexible manufacturing may enable a firm pursuing differentiation to manufacture a range of products at a cost comparable to that of the cost leader. The use of robots and flexible manufacturing cells reduces the costs of retooling the production line and the costs associated with small production runs. Indeed, a factor promoting the current trend toward market fragmentation and niche marketing in many consumer goods industries, such as mobile phones, computers, and appliances, is the substantial reduction of the costs of differentiation by flexible manufacturing.

Another way that a differentiated producer may be able to realize significant economies of scale is by standardizing many of the component parts used in its end products. For example, in the 1990s Chrysler began to offer more than twenty different models of cars and minivans to different segments of the auto market. However, despite their different appearances, all twenty models were based on only three different platforms. Moreover, most of the cars used many of the same components, including axles, drive units, suspensions, and gear boxes. As a result, Chrysler was able to realize significant economies of scale in the manufacture and bulk purchase of standardized component parts.

A company can also reduce both production and marketing costs if it limits the number of models in the product line by offering packages of options rather than letting consumers decide exactly what options they require. It is increasingly common for auto manufacturers, for example, to offer an economy auto package, a luxury package, and a sports package to appeal to the principal market segments. Package offerings substantially lower manufacturing costs because long production runs of the various packages are possible. At the same time, the firm is able to focus its advertising and marketing efforts on particular market segments so that these costs are also decreased. Once again, the firm is getting gains from differentiation and from low cost at the same time.

Just-in-time inventory systems can also help reduce costs and improve the quality and reliability of a company's products. This benefit is important to differentiated firms, for whom quality and reliability are essential ingredients of the product's appeal. Rolls-Royces, for example, are never supposed to break down. Improved quality control enhances a company's reputation and thus allows it to charge a premium price, which is one object of TQM programs.

Taking advantage of the new production and marketing developments, some firms are managing to reap the gains from cost-leadership and differentiation strategies simultaneously. Since they can charge a premium price for their products compared with the price charged by the pure cost leader and since they have lower costs than the pure differentiator, they are obtaining at least an equal, and probably a higher, level of profit than firms pursuing only one of the generic strategies. Hence, the combined strategy is the most profitable to pursue, and companies are quickly moving to take advantage of the new production, materials-management, and marketing techniques. Indeed, U.S. companies must take advantage of them if they are to regain a competitive advantage, for the Japanese pioneered many of these new developments. This explains why firms such as Toyota and Sony are currently much more profitable than their U.S. counterparts, General Motors and Zenith, respectively. However, American firms such as McDonald's, Apple Computer, Intel, and Motorola are pursuing both strategies simultaneously with great success.

Focus Strategy

The third generic competitive strategy, the **focus strategy**, differs from the other two chiefly because it is directed toward serving the needs of a *limited customer group or segment*. A focus strategy concentrates on serving a particular market

FIGURE 6.1

Types of Business-Level
Strategies

	Offers products to only one group of customers	Offers products to many kinds of customers
Offers low-priced products to customers	Focused Cost-Leadership Strategy	Cost-Leadership Strategy
Offers unique or distinctive products to customers	Focused Differentiation Strategy	Differentiation Strategy

niche, which can be defined geographically, by type of customer, or by segment of the product line.[22] For example, a geographic niche can be defined by region or even by locality. Selecting a niche by type of customer might mean serving only the very rich, the very young, or the very adventurous. Concentrating only on a segment of the product line means focusing only on vegetarian foods, on very fast automobiles, on designer clothes, or sunglasses. In following a focus strategy, a company is *specializing* in some way.

Once it has chosen its market segment, a company pursues a focus strategy through either a differentiation or a low-cost approach. Figure 6.1 shows these two different kinds of focused strategies and compares them with a pure cost-leadership or differentiation strategy.

In essence, a focused company is a specialized differentiator *or* a cost leader. If a company uses a focused low-cost approach, it competes against the cost leader in the market segments in which it has no cost disadvantage. For example, in local lumber or cement markets, the focuser has lower transportation costs than the low-cost national company. The focuser may also have a cost advantage because it is producing complex or custom-built products that do not lend themselves easily to economies of scale in production and, therefore, offer few experience-curve advantages. With a focus strategy, a company concentrates on small-volume custom products, for which it has a cost advantage, and leaves the large-volume standardized market to the cost leader.

If a company uses a focused differentiation approach, then all the means of differentiation that are open to the differentiator are available to the focused company. The point is that the focused company competes with the differentiator in only one or in just a few segments. For example, Porsche, a focused company, competes against General Motors in the sports car segment of the car market, not in other market segments. Focused companies are likely to develop differentiated product qualities successfully because of their knowledge of a small customer set (such as sports car buyers) or knowledge of a region.

Furthermore, concentration on a small range of products sometimes allows a focuser to develop innovations faster than a large differentiator can. However, the focuser does not attempt to serve all market segments because doing so would bring it into direct competition with the differentiator. Instead, a focused company concentrates on building market share in one market segment and, if successful, may begin to serve more and more market segments and chip away at the differentiator's

STRATEGY *in* ACTION

Finding a Niche in the Outsourcing Market

Outsourcing occurs when one company contracts with another company to perform one of the value creation functions on its behalf. Increasingly, many companies are finding it very difficult to keep up with the pace of technological change in the computer software industry and are outsourcing their data-processing needs to specialized software companies. For example, Electronic Data Systems (EDS), founded by Ross Perot, has grown into a $15 billion computer services giant that manages other companies' data-processing operations using its own proprietary software. IBM is another large company trying to exploit this developing market.

As you can imagine, however, different kinds of organizations, such as universities, banks, insurance agencies, local governments, and utilities, have different kinds of data-processing needs and problems. Consequently, each kind of company requires a specialized kind of software system that can be customized to its specific needs. As a result, it is difficult for any one software company to service the needs of a wide range of different companies, and the outsourcing market in data processing is very fragmented. Large companies such as EDS have only a small market share; for exam-

ple, EDS had just 18 percent market share in 1996. Consequently, opportunities abound.

Increasingly, small, specialized software companies are springing up to manage the needs of particular kinds of clients. An example is Systems & Computer Technology, based in Malvern, Pennsylvania, which went head-to-head with EDS to secure a seven-year $35 million outsourcing contract to service the data-processing needs of Dallas County. The company has yearly revenues of only $200 million, compared with EDS's $15 billion, but it won the contract because it specializes in servicing the needs of local government and institutions of higher education.[23] It could show Dallas County its twelve ongoing contracts with municipal clients, whereas EDS could offer its experience with only one, a hospital. The focused company won out over the differentiator.

Other focused companies are also springing up—for instance, the Bisys Group and Systematics Company, which serves the needs of banks and universities. It appears that in the data-processing industry, small, focused companies are strong competitors because of their ability to provide specialized, personal service to specific clients in a way that large differentiators cannot.[24]

competitive advantage. The way in which small software companies have emerged to take advantage of specialized niches in the outsourcing market, discussed in Strategy in Action 6.3, illustrates how focused companies can obtain a competitive advantage.

Strategic Choices   Table 6.1 illustrates the specific product/market/distinctive-competency choices made by a focused company. Differentiation can be high or low because the company can pursue a low-cost or a differentiation approach. As for customer groups, a focused company chooses specific niches in which to compete rather than going for a whole market, as a cost leader does, or filling a large number of niches, as a broad differentiator does. The focused firm can pursue any distinctive competency because it can seek any kind of differentiation or low-cost advantage. Thus, it might find a cost advantage and develop a superior efficiency in low-cost manufacturing within a region. Alternatively, it might develop superior skills in responsiveness to customers, based on its ability to serve the needs of regional customers in ways that a national differentiator would find very expensive.

The many avenues a focused company can take to develop a competitive advantage explain why there are so many small companies in relation to large ones. A focused company has enormous opportunity to develop its own niche and compete against low-cost and differentiated enterprises, which tend to be larger. A focus strategy provides an opportunity for an entrepreneur to find and then exploit a gap in the market by developing an innovative product that customers cannot do without.[25] The steel minimills discussed in Chapter 5 are a good example of how focused companies specializing in one market can grow so efficient that they become the cost leaders. Many large companies started with a focus strategy, and, of course, one means by which companies can expand is to take over other focused companies. For example, Saatchi & Saatchi DFS Compton, a specialist marketing company, grew by taking over several companies that were also specialists in their own markets, such as Hay Associates, the management consultants.

Advantages and Disadvantages   A focused company's competitive advantages stem from the source of its distinctive competency—efficiency, quality, innovation, or responsiveness to customers. The firm is protected from *rivals* to the extent that it can provide a product or service they cannot. This ability also gives the focuser power over its *buyers* because they cannot get the same thing from anyone else. With regard to *powerful suppliers*, however, a focused company is at a disadvantage, because it buys in small volume and thus is in the suppliers' power. However, as long as it can pass on price increases to loyal customers, this disadvantage may not be a significant problem. *Potential entrants* have to overcome the loyalty from customers the focuser has generated, and the development of customers' loyalty also lessens the threat from *substitute products*. This protection from the five forces allows the focuser to earn above-average returns on its investment. Another advantage of the focus strategy is that it permits a company to stay close to its customers and to respond to their changing needs. The difficulty a large differentiator sometimes experiences in managing a large number of market segments is not an issue for a focuser.

Since a focuser produces a small volume, its production costs often exceed those of a low-cost company. Higher costs can also reduce profitability if a focuser is forced to invest heavily in developing a distinctive competency, such as expensive product innovation, in order to compete with a differentiated firm. However, once again, flexible manufacturing systems are opening up new opportunities for focused firms because small production runs become possible at a lower cost. Increasingly, small specialized firms are competing with large companies in specific market segments in which their cost disadvantage is much reduced.

A second problem is that the focuser's niche can suddenly disappear because of technological change or changes in consumers' tastes. Unlike the more generalist differentiator, a focuser cannot move easily to new niches, given its concentration of resources and competency in one or a few niches. For example, a clothing manufacturer that focuses on heavy metal enthusiasts would find it difficult to shift to other segments if heavy metal loses its appeal, and a Mexican restaurant would find it difficult to move to Chinese food if customers' tastes change. The disappearance of niches is one reason that so many small companies fail.

Finally, there is the prospect that differentiators will compete for a focuser's niche by offering a product that can satisfy the demands of the focuser's customers; for example, GM's and Ford's new luxury cars are aimed at Lexus, BMW, and

Mercedes-Benz buyers. A focuser is vulnerable to attack and, therefore, has to defend its niche constantly.

Stuck in the Middle
. . . .

Each generic strategy requires a company to make consistent product/market/distinctive-competency choices to establish a competitive advantage. In other words, a company must achieve a fit among the three components of business-level strategy. Thus, for example, a low-cost company cannot strive for a high level of market segmentation, as a differentiator does, and provide a wide range of products because doing so would raise production costs too much and the company would lose its low-cost advantage. Similarly, a differentiator with a competency in innovation that tries to reduce its expenditures on research and development or one with a competency in responsiveness to customers through after-sales service that seeks to economize on its sales force to decrease costs is asking for trouble because it will lose its competitive advantage as its distinctive competency disappears.

Choosing a business-level strategy successfully means giving serious attention to all elements of the competitive plan. Many companies, through ignorance or through mistakes, do not do the planning necessary for success in their chosen strategy. Such companies are said to be **stuck in the middle** because they have made product/market choices in such a way that they have been unable to obtain or sustain a competitive advantage.[26] As a result, they have no consistent business-level strategy, experience below-average performance, and suffer when industry competition intensifies.

Some stuck-in-the-middle companies may have started out pursuing one of the three generic strategies but then made wrong resource allocation decisions or experienced a hostile, changing environment. It is very easy to lose control of a generic strategy unless strategic managers keep close track of the business and its environment, constantly adjusting product/market choices to suit changing conditions within the industry. The experience of Holiday Inns in the 1980s, described in Strategy in Action 6.4, shows how a company can become stuck in the middle because of environmental changes.

As the experience of Holiday Inns suggests, there are many paths to being stuck in the middle. Quite commonly, a focuser can get stuck in the middle when it becomes overconfident and starts to act like a broad differentiator. People Express, the defunct airline, exemplified a company in this situation. It started out as a specialized air carrier serving a narrow market niche: low-priced travel on the eastern seaboard. In pursuing this focus strategy based on cost leadership, it was very successful, but when it tried to expand to other geographic regions and began taking over other airlines to gain a larger number of planes, it lost its niche. People Express became one more carrier in an increasingly competitive market, in which it had no special competitive advantage against the other national carriers. The result was financial troubles. People Express was swallowed up by Texas Air and incorporated into Continental Airlines. By contrast, Southwest Airlines, the focused low-cost company, has continued to focus on this strategy and has grown successfully.

Differentiators, too, can fail in the market and end up stuck in the middle if competitors attack their markets with more specialized or low-cost products that blunt their competitive edge. This happened to IBM in the large-frame computer market as personal computers became more powerful and able to do the job of the much

6.4

STRATEGY *in* ACTION

Holiday Inns Makes a Comeback

The history of the Holiday Inns motel chain is one of the great success stories in U.S. business. Its founder, Kemmons Wilson, vacationing in the early 1950s, found existing motels to be small, expensive, and of unpredictable quality. This discovery, along with the prospect of unprecedented highway travel that would come with the new interstate highway program, triggered a realization: There was an unmet customer need, a gap in the market for quality accommodations. Holiday Inns was founded to meet that need.

From the beginning, Holiday Inns set the standard for offering motel features such as air conditioning and icemakers while keeping room rates reasonable. These amenities enhanced the motels' popularity, and motel franchising, Wilson's invention, made rapid expansion possible. By 1960 Holiday Inns' motels dotted the U.S. landscape; they could be found in virtually every city and on every major highway. Before the 1960s ended, more than 1,000 of them were in full operation and occupancy rates averaged 80 percent. The concept of mass accommodation had arrived.[27]

By the 1970s, however, the motel chain was in trouble. The service offered by Holiday Inns appealed to the average traveler, who wanted a standardized product (a room) at an average price. In essence, Holiday Inns had been targeting the middle of the hotel-room market. The problem was that travelers were beginning to make different demands on hotels and motels. Some wanted luxury and were willing to pay higher prices for better accommodations and service. Others sought low prices and accepted rock-bottom quality and service in exchange. Although the market had fragmented into different groups of customers with different needs, Holiday Inns was still offering an undifferentiated, average-cost, average-quality product.[28]

Holiday Inns missed the change in the market and thus failed to respond appropriately to it, but the competition did not. Companies such as Hyatt siphoned off the top end of the market, where quality and service sold rooms. Chains such as Motel 6 and Days Inns captured the basic-quality, low-price end of the market. In between were many specialty chains that appealed to business travelers, families, or self-caterers (people who want to be able to cook in their hotel rooms). Holiday Inns' position was attacked from all sides. The company's earnings declined as occupancy rates dropped drastically, and marginal Holiday Inns motels began to close as competition increased.

Wounded but not dead, Holiday Inns began a counterattack. The original chain was upgraded to suit quality-oriented travelers. At the same time, to meet the needs of different kinds of travelers, Holiday Inns created new hotel and motel chains, including the luxury Crowne Plazas; the Hampton Inns, which serve the low-priced end of the market; and the all-suite Embassy Suites. Holiday Inns attempted to meet the demands of the many niches, or segments, of the hotel market that have emerged as customers' needs have changed over time.[29]

more expensive mainframes. The increasing movement toward flexible manufacturing systems aggravates the problems faced by cost leaders and differentiators. Many large firms will become stuck in the middle unless they make the investment needed to pursue both strategies simultaneously. No company is safe in the jungle of competition, and each must be constantly on the lookout to exploit competitive advantages as they arise and to defend the advantages it already has.

To sum up, successful management of a generic competitive strategy requires strategic managers to attend to two main matters. First, they need to ensure that the product/market/distinctive-competency decisions they make are oriented toward one specific competitive strategy. Second, they need to monitor the environment so that they can keep the firm's sources of competitive advantage in tune with changing opportunities and threats.

STRATEGIC GROUPS AND BUSINESS-LEVEL STRATEGY

As implied by the preceding discussion, companies in an industry can pursue many different kinds of business-level strategies that differ from each other with respect to factors such as the choice of market segments to serve, product quality, technological leadership, customer service, pricing policy, and advertising policy. As a result, within most industries, strategic groups emerge, each of which is composed of companies pursuing the same generic strategy.[30] Thus, for example, all the companies inside an industry pursuing a low-cost strategy form one strategic group, while all those seeking to pursue a broad differentiation strategy constitute another strategic group, while all those companies pursing a focus-differentiation strategy or a focused low-cost strategy form yet other strategic groups.

In the pharmaceutical industry, for example, which we discuss in Chapter 3, there are two main strategic groups.[31] One group includes such companies as Merck, Eli Lilly, and Pfizer (see Figure 3.4), which pursue a differentiation strategy characterized by heavy R&D spending and a focus on developing new proprietary blockbuster drugs. The second strategic group in the pharmaceutical industry might be characterized as the *low-cost strategic group* because it focuses on the manufacture of low-priced generic drugs. Companies in this group are pursuing a low-cost strategy because they are not investing millions of dollars in R&D, and, as a result, they cannot expect to charge a premium price.

The concept of strategic groups has a number of implications for business-level strategy. First, a company's immediate competitors are those companies pursuing the same strategy in its strategic group. Consumers tend to view the products of such enterprises as being direct substitutes for each other. Thus, a major threat to a company's profitability may arise primarily from within its own strategic group, not necessarily from the other companies in the industry pursuing different generic business-level strategies. For example, the main competition for Toyota comes from Honda, Ford, and GM, not from Rolls-Royce.

Second, different strategic groups can have a different standing with respect to each of Porter's five competitive forces because, as already discussed, the five forces affect companies in different ways. In other words, the risk of new entry by potential competitors, the degree of rivalry among companies within a group, the bargaining power of buyers, the bargaining power of suppliers, and the competitive force of substitute products can all vary in intensity among different strategic groups within the same industry.

In the pharmaceutical industry, for example, companies in the differentiation strategic group have historically been in a very powerful position vis-à-vis buyers because their products are patented. Besides, rivalry within this group has been limited to competition to be the first to patent a new drug and achieve a first-mover advantage, the advantage that a company that is first to market a new product is said to possess. In contrast, companies in the low-cost group have been in a much weaker position, since they lack patents for their products and buyers can choose among very similar competing generic drugs. Moreover, price competition among the companies in this group has been quite intense, reflecting the lack of product differentiation. Thus, companies within this group have earned somewhat lower returns than companies in the proprietary group.

As discussed in Chapter 3, mobility barriers are factors that inhibit the movement of companies between groups in an industry. The relative height of mobility barriers determines how successfully companies in one group can compete with companies in another group. For example, can a differentiation strategic group also pursue a low-cost strategy and thus achieve the low cost-differentiation strategy previously discussed? To the degree that companies in one group can develop or obtain the functional and financial resources they need to either lower their costs or embark on a major R&D expansion, they may be able to compete successfully with companies in another strategic group. In effect, they have created yet another strategic group—a combined low-cost and differentiation strategic group, which, as we have seen, has the strongest competitive advantage and the greatest ability to earn above-average profits. In fact, the need to pursue a simultaneous global low-cost/differentiation strategy has been the major driving force behind the wave of merger activities among the large drug companies that has happened in the 1990s. In 1995, for example, the U.S. company Upjohn merged with the Swedish company Pharmacia to pursue a global low-cost/differentiation strategy. Thus, the strategic group map in the pharmaceutical industry is changing dramatically as firms fight to survive in the rapidly consolidating global pharmaceutical industry. So far, Pfizer, Merck, and Eli Lilly still pursue a pure differentiated strategy, but the other merged companies are moving quickly to reposition themselves as low-cost differentiators.

CHOOSING AN INVESTMENT STRATEGY AT THE BUSINESS LEVEL

We have been discussing business-level strategy in terms of making product/market/ distinctive-competency choices to gain a competitive advantage. There is a second major choice to be made at the business level, however—the choice of which type of investment strategy to pursue in support of the competitive strategy.[32]

An **investment strategy** sets the amount and type of resources—human, functional, and financial—that must be invested to gain a competitive advantage. Generic competitive strategies provide competitive advantages, but they are expensive to develop and maintain. A simultaneous differentiation/cost-leadership strategy is the most expensive, because it requires that a company invest resources not only in functions such as R&D, sales, and marketing to develop distinctive competencies but also in functions such as manufacturing and materials management to find ways to reduce costs. Differentiation is the next most expensive generic strategy and then cost leadership, which is less expensive to maintain once the initial investment in a manufacturing plant and equipment has been made. Cost leadership does not require such sophisticated research and development or marketing efforts as a differentiation strategy. The focus strategy is cheapest because fewer resources are needed to serve one market segment than to serve the whole market.

In deciding on an investment strategy, a company must evaluate the potential returns from investing in a generic competitive strategy against the cost. In this way, it can determine whether it is likely to be profitable to pursue a certain strategy and how profitability will change as competition within the industry changes. Two factors are crucial in choosing an investment strategy: the strength of a company's position in an industry relative to its competitors and the stage of the industry's life cycle in which the company is competing.[33]

Competitive Position

Two attributes can be used to determine the strength of a company's relative competitive position. First, the larger a company's *market share*, the stronger is its competitive position and the greater are the potential returns from future investment. A large market share provides experience-curve economies and suggests that the company has earned brand loyalty. One of the main reasons a wave of mergers has taken place in the pharmaceutical industry, for example, is that the merging of two or more different companies creates a much larger customer base that can be more efficiently served by one global sales force rather than the two global sales forces that previously existed. Thus, large market share may help an organization to lower its costs on a global, as well as a national, basis.

The uniqueness, strength, and number of a company's *distinctive competencies* are the second measure of competitive position. If it is difficult to imitate a company's research and development expertise, its manufacturing and marketing skills, its knowledge of particular customer segments, and its unique reputation or brand name capital, the company's relative competitive position is strong and its returns from the generic strategy increase. Once again, an attempt to build new and improved distinctive competences has been a principal reason for the merger of pharmaceutical companies. Ciba-Geigy and Sandoz, two giant Swiss pharmaceutical companies, for example, recently merged because they were developing complementary kinds of drugs for treating the same broad range of diseases. By pooling their skills and abilities, they have created the second largest pharmaceutical company in the world, and they hope to use their combined distinctive competencies to compete head-to-head with U.S. companies such as Pfizer and Merck.

In general, companies with the largest market share and the strongest distinctive competencies are in the best position to build and sustain their competitive advantage. A unique distinctive competency leads to increased demand for the company's products, and as a result of the revenues obtained from larger market share, the company has more resources to invest in developing its distinctive competency. These two attributes reinforce one another and explain why some companies get stronger and stronger over time. Companies with a smaller market share and little potential for developing a distinctive competency are in a much weaker competitive position.[34]

Life Cycle Effects

The second main factor influencing the investment attractiveness of a generic strategy is the *stage of the industry's life cycle.* Each life cycle stage is accompanied by a particular industry environment, presenting different opportunities and threats. Each stage, therefore, has different implications for the investment of resources needed to obtain a competitive advantage. Competition is strongest in the shakeout stage of the life cycle and least important in the embryonic stage, for example. The risks of pursuing a strategy change over time. The difference in risk explains why the potential returns from investing in a competitive strategy depend on the life cycle stage.

Choosing an Investment Strategy

Table 6.2 summarizes the relationship among the stage of the life cycle, the competitive position, and the investment strategy at the business level.

TABLE 6.2
· · · · · · · · · · ·
Choosing an Investment Strategy at the Business Level

Stage of Industry Life Cycle	*Strong Competitive Position*	*Weak Competitive Position*
Embryonic	Share building	Share building
Growth	Growth	Market concentration
Shakeout	Share increasing	Market concentration or harvest/liquidation
Maturity	Hold-and-maintain or profit	Harvest or liquidation/ divestiture
Decline	Market concentration or harvest (asset reduction)	Turnaround, liquidation, or divestiture

Embryonic Strategy   In the embryonic stage, all companies, weak and strong, emphasize the development of a distinctive competency and a product/market policy. During this stage, investment needs are great because a company has to establish a competitive advantage. Many fledgling companies in the industry are seeking resources to develop a distinctive competency. Thus, the appropriate business-level investment strategy is a **share-building strategy**. The aim is to build market share by developing a stable and unique competitive advantage to attract customers who have no knowledge of the company's products.

Companies require large amounts of capital to build research and development competencies or sales and service competencies. They cannot generate much of this capital internally. Thus, a company's success depends on its ability to demonstrate a unique competency to attract outside investors, or venture capitalists. If a company gains the resources to develop a distinctive competency, it will be in a relatively stronger competitive position. If it fails, its only option may be to exit the industry. In fact, companies in weak competitive positions at all stages in the life cycle may choose to exit the industry to cut their losses.

Growth Strategies   At the growth stage, the task facing a company is to consolidate its position and provide the base it needs to survive the coming shakeout. Thus, the appropriate investment strategy is the **growth strategy**. The goal is to maintain a company's relative competitive position in a rapidly expanding market and, if possible, to increase it—in other words, to grow with the expanding market. However, other companies are entering the market and catching up with the industry's innovators. As a result, first movers require successive waves of capital infusion to maintain the momentum generated by their success in the embryonic stage. For example, differentiators need to engage in massive research and development to maintain their technological lead, and cost leaders need to invest in state-of-the-art machinery and computers to obtain new experience-curve economies. All this investment is very expensive.

The growth stage is also the time when companies attempt to consolidate existing market niches and enter new ones so that they can increase their market share. Increasing the level of market segmentation to become a broad differentiator is expensive as well. A company has to invest resources to develop a new sales and marketing competency. Consequently, at the growth stage, companies fine-tune their competitive strategy (which we discuss at length in the next chapter) and make business-level investment decisions about the relative advantages of a differentiation, low-cost, or focus strategy, given financial needs and relative competitive position. If one company has emerged as the cost leader, for example, while some companies may decide to compete head-to-head with it and enter this strategic group, others will not. Instead, they will pursue a growth strategy using a differentiation or focus approach and invest resources in developing unique competencies. As a result, strategic groups start to develop in an industry as each company seeks the best way to invest its scarce resources to maximize its competitive advantage.

Companies must spend a lot of money just to keep up with growth in the market, and finding additional resources to develop new skills and competencies is a difficult task for strategic managers. Consequently, companies in a weak competitive position at this stage engage in a **market concentration strategy** to consolidate their position. They seek to specialize in some way and may adopt a focus strategy and move to a focused strategic group to reduce their investment needs. If very weak, they may also choose to exit the industry and sell out to a stronger competitor.

Shakeout Strategies By the shakeout stage, demand increases slowly and competition by price or product characteristics becomes intense. Companies in strong competitive positions need resources to invest in a **share-increasing strategy** to attract customers from weak companies that are exiting the market. In other words, companies attempt to maintain and increase market share despite fierce competition. The way companies invest their resources depends on their generic strategy.

For cost leaders, because of the price wars that can occur, investment in cost control is crucial if they are to survive the shakeout stage, and they must do all they can to reduce costs. Differentiators in a strong competitive position choose to forge ahead and become broad differentiators. Their investment is likely to be oriented toward marketing, and they are likely to develop a sophisticated after-sales service network. They also widen the product range to match the range of customers' needs. Differentiators in a weak position reduce their investment burden by withdrawing to a focused strategy—the **market concentration strategy**—to specialize in a particular niche or product. Weak companies exiting the industry engage in a **harvest or liquidation strategy**, both of which are discussed later in this chapter.

Maturity Strategies By the maturity stage, a relatively stable strategic group structure has emerged in the industry, and companies have learned how their competitors will react to their competitive moves. At this point, companies want to reap the rewards of their previous investments in developing a generic strategy. Until now profits have been reinvested in the business, and dividends have been small. Investors in strong companies have obtained their rewards through the appreciation of the value of their stock, because the company has reinvested most of its capital to maintain and increase market share. As market growth slows in the maturity stage, a company's investment strategy depends on the level of competition in the industry and the source of the company's competitive advantage.

In environments in which competition is high because technological change is occurring or where barriers to entry are low, companies need to defend their competitive position. Strategic managers need to continue to invest heavily in maintaining the company's competitive advantage. Both low-cost companies and differentiators adopt a **hold-and-maintain strategy** to support their generic strategies. They expend resources to develop their distinctive competency so as to remain the market leaders. For example, differentiated companies may invest in improved after-sales service, and low-cost companies may invest in the latest production technologies, such as robotics.

It is at this point, however, that companies realize they must begin to pursue both a low-cost and a differentiation strategy if they are to protect themselves from aggressive competitors (both at home and abroad) who are watching for any opportunity or perceived weakness to take the lead in the industry. Differentiators take advantage of their strong position to develop flexible manufacturing systems to reduce their production costs. Cost leaders move to start differentiating their products to expand their market share by serving more market segments. For example, Gallo moved from the bulk-wine segment and began marketing premium wines and wine coolers to take advantage of its low production costs. In 1996 Gallo's new premium brand, Falling Leaf, became the best-selling chardonnay in the United States. Similarly, in the fast-food industry in the 1990s, McDonald's experienced intense competition to lower its costs after Taco Bell began to offer its $.99 tacos. In response, McDonald's sought to find new ways to lower its costs and widen its menu to respond to these competitive attacks.

Historically, however, many companies have felt protected from competition within the industry in the maturity stage and decide to exploit their competitive advantage to the fullest by engaging in a **profit strategy**. A company pursuing this strategy attempts to maximize the present returns from its previous investments. Typically, it reinvests proportionally less in improving its functional resources and increases returns to shareholders. The profit strategy works well only as long as competitive forces remain relatively constant, so that a company can maintain the profit margins developed by its competitive strategy. However, a company must be alert to threats from the environment and must take care not to become complacent and unresponsive to changes in it.

All too often market leaders fail to exercise vigilance in managing the environment, imagining that they are impervious to competition. General Motors, for example, felt secure against foreign-car manufacturers until changes in oil prices precipitated a crisis. Kodak, which had profited for so long from its strengths in film processing, was slow to respond to the threat of electronic imaging techniques. Paradoxically, the most successful companies often fail to sense changes in the market. As Strategy in Action 6.5 shows, Campbell Soup is another example of a company that over time failed to pursue a hold-and-maintain strategy to manage the competitive environment.

Decline Strategies   The decline stage of an industry's life cycle begins when demand for the industry's product starts to fall. There are many possible reasons for decline, including foreign competition and the loss of a company's distinctive

Campbell Soup Heats Up

The name Campbell Soup is closely linked with its well-known soups, and for many years they have been the source of the company's profitability. However, during the 1980s the company's fortunes declined as its top executives failed to manage the business and keep it abreast of changes in the environment. While competitors such as Heinz and Nestlé were innovating products and introducing new cost-saving machinery, Campbell was content to do business the way it had always done, even though its costs were rising and its sales were stagnant. This state of affairs changed in 1990, when David W. Johnson arrived from Gerber Products to revitalize the company.

Johnson moved immediately to reduce costs and to increase profits. He closed twenty inefficient plants, including Campbell's famous multistory Camden, New Jersey, factory, where it had made soup in the traditional way in large copper pans. Moreover, he fired 16 percent of Campbell's work force and divested many of Campbell's unprofitable businesses. All these actions were part of his turnaround strategy to move Campbell back to a hold-and-maintain position in the food industry in order to redeploy its resources so that it could compete for market share against its more efficient rivals. His actions were successful, and the company's stock price doubled in one year as profits rebounded.

Although analysts have applauded his efforts, they became concerned that Johnson might be pursuing his cost-cutting strategy a little too vigorously and at the expense of new-product development. Normally, a hold-and-maintain strategy includes investing resources in developing new products that build and maintain market share. However, Johnson killed many of the company's new product lines because they were unprofitable and seemed reluctant to invest much in new-product development.[35] It soon became clear that the pause in product development was just to give Johnson and his top management team time to study the situation carefully. By 1996 Campbell was making record profits and was once again in a very strong situation after having brought out a large number of successful new products.[36]

competency as its rivals enter with new or more efficient technologies. Thus, a company must decide what investment strategy to adopt in order to deal with new circumstances within its industry. Table 6.2 lists the strategies that companies can resort to when their competitive position is declining.[37]

The initial strategies that companies can adopt are market concentration and asset reduction.[38] With a **market concentration strategy**, a company attempts to consolidate its product and market choices. It narrows its product range and exits marginal niches in an attempt to redeploy its resources more effectively and improve its competitive position. Reducing customer groups served may also allow a company to pursue a focus strategy in order to survive the decline stage. (As noted earlier, weak companies in the growth stage tend to adopt this strategy.) That is what International Harvester did as the demand for farm machinery fell. It now produces only medium-sized trucks under the Navistar name.

An **asset reduction strategy** requires a company to limit or decrease its investment in a business and to extract, or milk, the investment as much as it can. This approach is sometimes called a **harvest strategy** because a company will exit the industry once it has harvested all the returns it can. It reduces to a minimum the assets it employs in the business and forgoes investment for the sake of immediate profits.[39] A market concentration strategy, on the other hand, generally indicates that a company is trying to turn around its business so that it can survive in the long run.

Low-cost companies are more likely to pursue a harvest strategy simply because a smaller market share means higher costs and they are unable to move to a focus strategy. Differentiators, in contrast, have a competitive advantage in this stage if they can move to a focus strategy.

At any stage of the life cycle, companies that are in weak competitive positions may apply **turnaround strategies**.[40] The questions that a company has to answer are whether it has the resources available to develop a viable business-level strategy to compete in the industry and how much it will cost. If a company is stuck in the middle, for example, it must assess the investment costs of developing a low-cost or differentiation strategy. Perhaps a company pursuing a low-cost strategy has not made the right product or market choices, or perhaps a differentiator has been missing niche opportunities. In such cases, the company can redeploy resources and change its strategy.

Sometimes a company's loss of competitiveness may be due to poor strategy implementation. If so, the company must move to change its structure and control systems rather than its strategy. For example, Dan Schendel, a prominent management researcher, found that 74 percent of the turnaround situations he and his colleagues studied were due to inefficient strategy implementation. The strategy-structure fit at the business level is thus very important in determining competitive strength.[41] We discuss it in detail in Chapter 13.

If a company decides that turnaround is not possible, either for competitive or for life cycle reasons, then the two remaining investment alternatives are **liquidation** and **divestiture**. As the terms imply, the company moves to exit the industry either by liquidating its assets or by selling the whole business. Both can be regarded as radical forms of harvesting strategy, because the company is seeking to get back as much as it can from its investment in the business. Often, however, it can only exit at a loss and take a tax write-off. Timing is important, because the earlier a company senses that divestiture is necessary, the more it can get for its assets. There are many stories about companies that buy weak or declining companies, thinking they can turn them around, and then realize their mistake as the new acquisitions become a drain on their resources. Often the acquired companies have lost their competitive advantage, and the cost of regaining it is too great. However, there have also been spectacular successes, such as that achieved by Lee Iacocca, who engaged in a low-cost strategy at Chrysler that set the scene for its success in the 1990s.

SUMMARY OF CHAPTER

The purpose of this chapter is to discuss the factors that must be considered if a company is to develop a business-level strategy that allows it to compete effectively in the marketplace. The formulation of business-level strategy means matching the opportunities and threats in the environment to the company's strengths and weaknesses by making choices about products, markets, distinctive competencies, and the investments necessary to pursue the choices. All companies, from one-person operations to the strategic business units of large corporations, must develop a business strategy if they are to compete effectively and maximize their long-term profitability. The chapter makes the following main points:

✔ Business-level strategy refers to the way strategic managers devise a plan of action to use a company's resources and distinctive competencies to gain a competitive advantage over rivals in a market or industry.

✔ At the heart of developing a generic business-level strategy are choices concerning product differentiation, market segmentation, and distinctive competency.

✔ The combination of those three choices results in the specific form of generic business-level strategy employed by a company.

✔ The three pure generic competitive strategies are cost leadership, differentiation, and focus. Each has advantages and disadvantages. A company must constantly manage its strategy; otherwise, it risks being stuck in the middle.

✔ Increasingly, developments in manufacturing technology are allowing firms to pursue both a cost-leadership and a differentiation strategy and thus obtain the economic benefits of both strategies simultaneously. Technical developments also allow small firms to compete with large firms on an equal footing in particular market segments and hence increase the number of firms pursuing a focus strategy.

✔ Companies can also adopt two forms of focus strategy, a focused low-cost strategy and a focused differentiation strategy.

✔ Most industries are composed of strategic groups. Strategic groups are groups of companies pursuing the same or a similar business-level strategy. The members of a strategic group constitute its immediate competitors.

✔ Since different strategic groups are characterized by different opportunities and threats, it may pay a company to switch strategic groups. The feasibility of doing so is a function of the height of mobility barriers.

✔ The second choice facing a company is an investment strategy for supporting the competitive strategy. The choice of investment strategy depends on two main factors: (a) the strength of a company's competitive position in the industry and (b) the stage of the industry's life cycle.

✔ The main types of investment strategy are share building, growth, share increasing, hold-and-maintain, profit, market concentration, asset reduction, harvest, turnaround, liquidation, and divestiture.

DISCUSSION QUESTIONS

1. Why does each generic competitive strategy require a different set of product/market/distinctive-competency choices? Give examples of pairs of companies in (a) the computer industry and (b) the auto industry that pursue different competitive strategies.

2. How can companies pursuing a cost-leadership, differentiation, or focus strategy become stuck in the middle? In what ways can they regain their competitive advantage?

3. Over an industry's life cycle, what investment strategy choices should be made by (a) differentiators in a strong competitive position and (b) differentiators in a weak competitive position?

4. How do technical developments affect the generic strategies pursued by firms in an industry? How might they do so in the future?

5. Why is it difficult for a company in one strategic group to change to a different strategic group?

Practicing Strategic Management

SMALL-GROUP EXERCISE
Finding a Strategy for a Restaurant

Break up into groups of three to five people, and discuss the following scenario:

You are a group of partners contemplating opening a new restaurant in your city. You are trying to decide what business-level strategy can provide your restaurant with the best competitive advantage to make it as profitable as possible.

1. Create a strategic group of the restaurants in your city, and define their generic strategies.

2. Identify which restaurants you think are the most profitable and why.

3. On the basis of this analysis, decide what kind of restaurant you want to open and why.

EXPLORING THE WEB
Visiting the Luxury-Car Market

Enter the Web sites of three luxury-car makers such as Lexus (www.lexususa.com), BMW (www.bmwusa.com), or Cadillac (www.cadillac.com), all of which compete in the same strategic group. Scan the sites to determine the key features of each company's business-level strategy. In what ways are their strategies similar and different? Which of these companies do you think has a competitive advantage over the others? Why?

Search the Web for a company pursuing a low-cost strategy, a differentiation strategy, or both. What product/market/distinctive-competency choices has the company made to pursue this strategy? How successful has the company been in its industry using this strategy?

ARTICLE FILE 6

Find an example (or several examples) of a company pursuing one or more of the three generic business-level strategies. Which strategy is it? What product/market/distinctive-competency choices is it based on? What are its advantages and disadvantages?

STRATEGIC MANAGEMENT PROJECT
Module 6

This part of the project focuses on the nature of your company's business-level strategy. If your company operates in more than one business, concentrate on either its core, or most central, business or on its most important businesses. Using all the information you have collected on your company, answer the following questions:

1. How differentiated are the products/services of your company? What is the basis of their differentiated appeal?

2. What is your company's strategy toward market segmentation? If it segments its market, on what basis does it do so?

3. What distinctive competencies does your company have? (Use the information from the module on functional-level strategy in the last chapter to answer this question.) Is efficiency, quality, innovation, responsiveness to customers, or a combination of these factors the main driving force in your company?

4. Based on these product/market/distinctive-competency choices, what generic business-level strategy is your company pursuing?

5. What are the advantages and disadvantages associated with your company's choice of business-level strategy?

6. How could you improve its business-level strategy to strengthen its competitive advantage?

7. Is your company a member of a strategic group in an industry? If so, which one?

8. What investment strategy is your company pursuing to support its generic strategy? How does this match the strength of its competitive position and the stage of its industry's life cycle?

CLOSING CASE

Liz Claiborne, Inc.

Designer Liz Claiborne founded her company in 1976 with the help of three partners. By 1990 her company had more than $2 billion in annual sales, and its stock had become a Wall Street favorite. The secret of the company's success was Liz Claiborne's decision to focus on the rapidly growing professional women's segment of the clothing market. By 1976 women were entering the work force in rapidly increasing numbers, but relatively few companies were producing clothes for this segment. Those that did cater to it were very high-priced firms such as Ellen Tracy, Donna Karan, and Anne Klein. Liz Claiborne decided to find out what kinds of clothing professional women wanted. Then she used her considerable talents to create a design team to focus on providing attractively designed clothing for professional women at reasonable prices. In doing so she tapped an unmet customer need, and the result was dramatic as sales boomed.

To protect her firm's image, Liz Claiborne sold her clothing through established retailers, such as Macy's, Bloomingdale's, and Dillard's. Retailers were required to buy at least $50,000 worth of her collection, and the company controlled the way its suits and dresses were sold in each store, for example, the way clothes were hung and displayed. This attention to detail was part of her strategy of focusing on the upscale professional clothing niche. To promote its growth, the company then started to find new outlets for its clothes and opened a chain of Liz Claiborne boutiques and factory outlets. The Liz Claiborne team also used its design skills to produce a line of men's sportswear and to develop new products such as perfume, shoes, and accessories. By 1988 the Liz Claiborne name had become famous.

However, by 1990 the company's growth had slowed, and the company was in trouble. Competitors, recognizing the niche pioneered by Liz Claiborne, had begun to offer their own lines of professional women's clothing. Expensive designers such as Anne Klein and Donna Karan had new lines of cheaper clothing, priced to compete directly with Liz Claiborne. In addition, low-cost manufacturers had begun to produce clothing lines that undercut Liz Claiborne's prices, often using look-alike designs. This competition from both the top and the bottom end of the market took sales away from the company.

Another problem for Liz Claiborne came from the retail end. Many of the company's best customers, retailers such as Macy's, were in deep financial difficulty and were cutting back on purchases to reduce their debt. At the same time, cost-conscious consumers were buying more and more clothing from stores such as Casual Corner and J.C. Penney and even from discount stores such as Kmart and Wal-Mart, which do not sell the Liz Claiborne line but carry the low-priced lines of competitors. As customers switched to both cheaper stores and cheaper lines, Liz Claiborne's sales suffered.

Given this deteriorating situation, the company moved quickly to change its strategy. Jerry Chazen, who replaced Liz Claiborne as CEO of the company on her retirement, decided to broaden the company's product line and produce low-cost lines of clothing. To do so and at the same time protect the Liz Claiborne brand name, he bought Russ Togs, a clothing maker that produces three brands of women's clothing: Crazy Horse, The Villager, and Red Horse. As part of the company's new strategy, each of these clothing makers' lines will be redesigned and targeted at a different price range in the women's clothing market. For example, Russ Togs, a sportswear line, is to be upgraded and will sell a new line of clothing for 20 to 30 percent less than the Liz Claiborne line. Moreover, this clothing will be sold through discount merchandisers such as Wal-Mart and in low-priced department stores such as Sears and J.C. Penney. In this way, the Liz Claiborne company will begin to serve the general women's clothing market, not just the professional women's clothing niche.[42]

Top management hopes that this new strategy will bolster the company's sagging sales and lead to a new period of growth and expansion in the late 1990s. They believe that there is wide scope for the company to take its existing design skills and capabilities and apply them in new market segments. However, the company will now be going head-to-head with low-cost producers and will have to find new ways to reduce its costs in order to compete. In 1996 the company reported increased operating profits due to a growth in sales in its main product lines. It appears that Liz Claiborne has turned the corner and will remain a major player in the volatile women's clothing industry.[43]

Case Discussion Questions

1. What factors led to Liz Claiborne, Inc.'s, success?

2. What changes has the company recently made in its strategy? Why?

CHAPTER 7

Competitive Strategy and the Industry Environment

Opening Case: The Burger Wars

Overview

Strategies in Fragmented Industries

Strategies in Embryonic and Growth Industries

Strategy in Mature Industries

Strategies to Deter Entry in Mature Industries

Strategies to Manage Rivalry in Mature Industries

Supply-and-Distribution Strategy in Mature Industries

Strategies in Declining Industries

Closing Case: The Goodyear Tire & Rubber Company

OPENING CASE

The Burger Wars

During the 1990s in the mature and saturated fast-food industry, competition for customers between the different hamburger chains has been intense. McDonald's, the industry leader, has been under pressure to maintain its profit margins, because, as the price of fast food has fallen, price wars have periodically broken out. Taco Bell started a major price war when it introduced its $.99 taco, for instance, which pushed McDonald's and other burger chains such as Burger King and Wendy's to find ways to lower their costs and prices. As a result of price competition, all the burger chains were forced to learn how to make a cheaper hamburger, and they have been able to lower their prices.

With most fast-food restaurants now offering comparable prices, the focus of competition between the burger chains has shifted to other aspects of their products. First, the major chains are all introducing bigger burger patties. The battle was started by Burger King, which is still waging an aggressive campaign to increase its market share at the expense of McDonald's. In 1994 Burger King added a full ounce of beef to its 1.8 ounce regular patty and followed this with an intense advertising campaign based on the slogan, "Get Your Burger's Worth," directed at McDonald's burger, which was more than 40 percent lighter. The campaign worked for Burger King, and the chain's market share rose by 18 percent in 1995. As a result, in May 1996 McDonald's announced that it would enlarge its regular patty by 25 percent to beat back the challenge from Burger King and from Wendy's, which has always offered a larger burger (and whose "Where's the Beef?" slogan helped it gain market share in the 1980s).[1]

Developing bigger burgers is only one part of competitive strategy in the fast-food industry, however. The main burger chains are constantly experimenting with new and improved kinds of burgers to appeal to customers—burgers that add cheese, bacon, different kinds of vegetables, and exotic sauces. They are also trying whole-meal offerings, such as McDonald's "value meals," to provide a competitive package to attract customers.

Finally, recognizing the competition from other kinds of fast-food chains such as those specializing in chicken or Mexican food, the burger chains have moved to broaden their menus. McDonald's, for example, offers chicken dishes, pizza, and salads and also allows restaurants to customize their menus to suit the tastes of customers in the region in which they are located. For example, McDonald's restaurants in New England have lobster on the menu, and those in Japan serve sushi. Product development is a major part of competitive strategy in the industry.

Another major competitive strategy that Burger King and McDonald's have adopted is market penetration, opening up new restaurants to attract customers. Because all the big chains have thousands of restaurants each, many analysts thought that the market was saturated, meaning that it would not be profitable to open more restaurants. However, McDonald's in particular has opened hundreds of restaurants in new locations such as gas stations and large retail stores (for example, Wal-Mart), all of which are profitable and have helped it protect its market share and maintain its margins.

Finally, a major aspect of the burger chains' competitive strategy has been to take their core competencies and apply them on an international level by building global restaurant empires. Indeed, so important have global operations become that both McDonald's and Burger King earn a significant part of their profits from their foreign operations. In the mature fast-food industry, developing new competitive strategies to fend off attacks by other companies within the industry and to protect and enhance competitive advantage is a never-ending task for strategic managers.

OVERVIEW

Chapter 6 examined the different kinds of generic business-level strategies that companies can adopt to obtain a competitive advantage and outperform their rivals. If strategic managers do succeed in developing a successful generic business-level strategy, they still face another crucial issue: how to choose appropriate competitive tactics, gambits, and maneuvers to position their company to sustain its competitive advantage over time in different kinds of industry environments. As our discussion of competition in the fast-food industry suggests, this chapter examines this issue.

First, we focus on how companies in *fragmented industries* try to develop competitive strategies that support their generic strategies. Second, we consider the challenges of developing a competitive advantage in *embryonic and growth industries.* Third, we probe the nature of competitive relations in *mature industries*. Here, we concentrate on how a set of companies that have been pursuing successful generic competitive strategies (such as the major burger chains) can use a variety of competitive tactics and gambits to manage the high level of competitive interdependence found in such industries. Finally, we assess the problems of managing a company's generic competitive strategy in *declining industries*, in which rivalry between competitors is high because market demand is slowing or falling. By the end of this chapter, you will understand how the successful pursuit of a generic strategy depends on the selection of the right competitive strategy to manage the industry environment.

STRATEGIES IN FRAGMENTED INDUSTRIES

A **fragmented industry** is one composed of a large number of small and medium-sized companies. The video-rental industry is still very fragmented, for example, as are the restaurant industry, the health-club industry, and the legal-services industry. There are several reasons why an industry may consist of many small companies rather than a few large ones.[2] In some industries there are few economies of scale, so large companies do not have an advantage over smaller enterprises. Indeed, in some industries there are diseconomies of scale. Many home buyers, for example, have a preference for dealing with local real estate agents, whom they perceive as having better local knowledge than national chains. Similarly in the restaurant business, many customers prefer the unique style of a local restaurant. In addition, because of the lack of economies of scale, many fragmented industries are characterized by low barriers to entry (and new entry keeps the industry fragmented). The restaurant industry exemplifies this situation. The costs of opening a restaurant are very moderate and can be borne by a single entrepreneur. High transportation costs, too, can keep an industry fragmented, for regional production may be the only efficient way to satisfy customers' needs, as in the cement business. Finally, an industry may be fragmented because customers' needs are so specialized that only small job lots of products are required, and thus there is no room for a large mass-production operation to satisfy the market.

For some fragmented industries, these factors dictate the competitive strategy to pursue, and the *focus strategy* stands out as a principal choice. Companies may specialize by customer group, customer need, or geographic region, so that many small specialty companies operate in local or regional market segments. All kinds of custom-made products—furniture, clothing, hats, boots, and so on—fall into this category, as do all small service operations that cater to particular customers' needs, such as laundries, restaurants, health clubs, and furniture-rental stores. Indeed, service companies make up a large proportion of the enterprises in fragmented industries because they provide personalized service to clients and, therefore, need to be responsive to their needs.

Strategic managers, however, are eager to gain the cost advantages of pursuing a low-cost strategy or the sales/revenue-enhancing advantages of differentiation by circumventing the problems of a fragmented industry. Because the returns from consolidating a fragmented industry are often huge, during the last thirty years many companies have developed competitive strategies to consolidate fragmented industries. These companies include large retailers such as Wal-Mart, Sears, and J.C. Penney; fast-food chains such as McDonald's and Burger King; video-rental chains such as Blockbuster Entertainment with its Blockbuster Video stores; and chains of health clubs, repair shops, and even lawyers and consultants. To grow, consolidate their industries, and become the industry leaders, these companies utilize three main competitive strategies: (1) chaining, (2) franchising, and (3) horizontal merger.

Chaining

Companies such as Wal-Mart and Midas International pursue a **chaining** strategy to obtain the advantages of cost leadership. They establish networks of linked merchandising outlets that are so interconnected they function as one large business entity. The amazing buying power that these companies possess through their nationwide store chains allows them to negotiate large price reductions with their suppliers, which in turn promotes their competitive advantage. They overcome the barrier of high transportation costs by establishing sophisticated regional distribution centers, which can economize on inventory costs and maximize responsiveness to the needs of stores and customers. (This is Wal-Mart's specialty.) Last but not least, they realize economies of scale from sharing managerial skills across the chain and from placing nationwide, rather than local, advertising.

Franchising

For differentiated companies in fragmented industries, such as McDonald's or Century 21 Real Estate, the competitive advantage comes from a business strategy that employs franchise agreements. In **franchising** the franchisor (parent) grants the franchisee the right to use the parent's name, reputation, and business skills at a particular location or area. If the franchisee also acts as the manager, he or she is strongly motivated to control the business closely and make sure that quality and standards are consistently high so that customers' needs are always satisfied. Such motivation is particularly critical in a strategy of differentiation, for which it is important for a company to maintain its uniqueness. One reason industries fragment is the difficulty of maintaining control over the many small outlets that must be operated while at the same time retaining their uniqueness. Franchising solves this problem.[3] In addition, franchising lessens the financial burden of swift expansion and so permits rapid growth of the company. Finally, a differentiated large company can reap the advantages of large-scale advertising, as well as economies in purchasing, management, and distribution, as McDonald's does very efficiently. Indeed, McDonald's is able to pursue cost leadership and differentiation simultaneously only because franchising allows costs to be controlled locally and differentiation to be achieved by marketing on a national level.

Horizontal Merger

Companies such as Anheuser-Busch, Dillard Department Stores, and Blockbuster Entertainment have been choosing a business-level strategy of **horizontal merger** to consolidate their respective industries. For example, Dillard arranged the merger of regional store chains in order to form a national company. By pursuing horizontal merger, companies are able to obtain economies of scale or secure a national market for their product. As a result, they are able to pursue a cost-leadership or a differentiation strategy, or both.

The challenge in a fragmented industry is to choose the most appropriate means—franchising, chaining, or horizontal merger—of overcoming a fragmented market so that the competitive advantages associated with the different business-level strategies can be realized. It is difficult to think of any major service activities—from consulting and accounting firms to businesses satisfying the smallest consumer need, such as beauty parlors and car-repair shops—that have not been merged or consolidated by chaining or franchising.

STRATEGIES IN EMBRYONIC AND GROWTH INDUSTRIES

Embryonic industries are typically created by the innovations of pioneering companies that become the first movers in a new market. For example, Apple single-handedly created the market for personal computers, Xerox created the market for photocopiers, and McDonald's created the market for fast food. In most cases, the pioneering company can initially earn enormous profits from its innovation because it is the only company in the industry for a time. For example, before the entry of IBM into the personal computer market in 1981, Apple enjoyed a virtual monopoly. Similarly, during the seventeen years before its patents expired, Xerox enjoyed a monopoly in the market for photocopiers, earning enormous profits as a result.[4]

However, innovators' high profits also attract potential imitators and second movers, as the companies who enter the market later are known. Typically, second movers enter during the growth stage of an industry and may cause the pioneering, first-mover company to lose its commanding competitive position. Figure 7.1 shows how the profit rate enjoyed by the innovator in an embryonic industry can decline as imitators crowd into the market during its growth stage. Thus, Apple's onetime monopoly position was competed away as hordes of other personal computer makers entered the market in the early and mid 1980s, trying to share in Apple's success. Once its patents expired, Xerox, too, faced many imitators, and some of them, such as Canon and Ricoh, were ultimately very successful in the photocopier market. In the fast-food market, the early success of McDonald's drew imitators, including Burger King; Wendy's; and Foodmaker, with its Jack-in-the-Box restaurants.

Although their market share has declined since their early days, companies such as Xerox and McDonald's are still major competitors. Other early innovators were not so lucky. For example, in the mid 1970s EMI pioneered the development of the CAT scanner. Widely regarded as the most important advance in radiology since the x-ray, the CAT scanner takes three-dimensional x-ray pictures of the body. Despite being the pioneer, however, EMI soon saw imitators such as General Electric capture the market. EMI itself withdrew from the CAT market in the early 1980s. Similarly, Bowman invented the pocket calculator, only to see Texas Instruments reap the long-run rewards of the innovation, and Royal Crown Cola pioneered the introduction of diet colas, but it was Coca-Cola and PepsiCo that made enormous profits from the concept. Thus, first movers often lose out to second movers as competition in an industry becomes intense.

Given the inevitability of imitation, the key issue for an innovating company in an embryonic industry is how to exploit its innovation and build an enduring long-run competitive advantage based on low cost or differentiation. Three strategies are available to the company: (1) to develop and market the innovation itself, (2) to develop and market the innovation jointly with other companies through a strategic alliance or joint venture, and (3) to license the innovation to others and let them develop the market.

The optimal choice of strategy depends on the answers to three questions. First, does the innovating company have the *complementary assets* to exploit its innovation and obtain a competitive advantage? Second, how difficult is it for imitators to copy the company's innovation, in other words, what is the *height of barriers to imitation*? And third, are there *capable competitors* that could rapidly imitate the

FIGURE 7.1
• • • • • • • • •
How an Innovator's
Profits Can Be
Competed Away

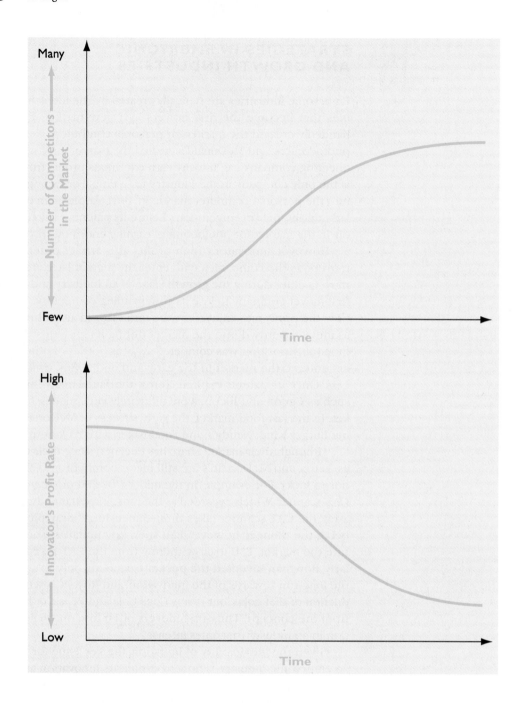

innovation? Before we discuss the optimal choice of innovation strategy, we need to examine the answers to these three questions.

Complementary Assets
• • • • • • • • • • • • • • • • • • • •

Complementary assets are those required to exploit a new innovation and gain a competitive advantage successfully.[5] Among the most important complementary assets are competitive manufacturing facilities capable of handling rapid growth in customers' demand while maintaining high product quality. State-of-the-art manufacturing facilities enable the innovator to move quickly down the experience curve without encountering production bottlenecks and/or problems with the quality of the product. The inability to satisfy demand because of these problems, however, creates the opportunity for imitators to enter the marketplace. For example, Compaq Computer was able to grow rapidly in the market for MS-DOS personal computers during the 1990s at the expense of the product's pioneer, IBM, largely because IBM lacked the state-of-the-art manufacturing facilities to build low-cost computers that Compaq possessed.

Complementary assets also include marketing know-how, an adequate sales force, access to distribution systems, and an after-sales service and support network. All these assets can help an innovator build brand loyalty. They also help the innovator achieve market penetration more rapidly.[6] In turn, the resulting increases in volume facilitate more rapid movement down the experience curve.

Developing such complementary assets is expensive, and embryonic companies often need large infusions of capital for this purpose. That is the reason first movers often lose out to late movers that are large, successful companies, often established in other industries, with the resources to develop a presence in the new industry quickly. Hewlett Packard and 3M exemplify companies that can move quickly to capitalize on the opportunities arising when other companies open up new product markets, such as compact disks or floppy disks. In 1995, for example, Hewlett Packard began to produce personal computers that competed directly with those of Compaq, IBM, and Apple, the early movers.

Height of Barriers to Imitation

Barriers to imitation are introduced in Chapter 4, in the discussion of the durability of competitive advantage. As you may recall, **barriers to imitation** are factors that prevent rivals from imitating a company's distinctive competencies. Barriers to imitation also prevent rivals, particularly second or late movers, from imitating a company's innovation. Although ultimately any innovation can be copied, the higher the barriers, the longer it takes for rivals to imitate.

Barriers to imitation give an innovator time to establish a competitive advantage and build more enduring barriers to entry in the newly created market. Patents, for example, are among the most widely used barriers to imitation. By protecting its photocopier technology with a thicket of patents, Xerox was able to delay any significant imitation of its product for seventeen years. However, patents are often easy to "invent around." For example, one study found that this happened to 60 percent of patented innovations within four years.[7] If patent protection is weak, a company might try to slow imitation by developing new products and processes in secret. The most famous example of this approach is Coca-Cola, which has kept the formula for Coke a secret for generations. But Coca-Cola's success in this regard is an exception. A study of 100 companies has estimated that proprietary information about a company's decision to develop a major new product or process is known to its rivals within about twelve to eighteen months of the original development decision.[8]

Capable Competitors

Capable competitors are companies that can move quickly to imitate the pioneering company. Competitors' capability to imitate a pioneer's innovation depends primarily on two factors: (1) R&D skills and (2) access to complementary assets. In general, the greater the number of capable competitors with access to the R&D skills and complementary assets needed to imitate an innovation, the more rapid is imitation likely to be.

In this context, R&D skills refers to the ability of rivals to reverse engineer an innovation in order to find out how it works and quickly develop a comparable product. As an example, consider the CAT scanner. GE bought one of the first CAT scanners produced by EMI, and its technical experts reverse engineered it. Despite the product's technological complexity, GE developed its own version of it, which allowed GE to imitate EMI quickly and ultimately to replace EMI as the major supplier of CAT scanners.

With regard to complementary assets, the access that rivals have to marketing, sales know-how, or manufacturing capabilities is one of the key determinants of the rate of imitation. If would-be imitators lack critical complementary assets, not only do they have to imitate the innovation, they may also have to imitate the innovator's complementary assets. This is expensive, as AT&T discovered when it tried to enter the personal computer business in 1984. AT&T lacked the marketing assets (sales force and distribution systems) necessary to support personal computer products. The lack of these assets and the time it takes to build them partly explain why four years after it originally entered the market AT&T had lost $2.5 billion and still had not emerged as a viable contender.

Three Innovation Strategies

The way in which these three factors—complementary assets, height of barriers to imitation, and the capability of competitors—influence the choice of innovation strategy is summarized in Table 7.1. The competitive strategy of *developing and marketing the innovation alone* makes most sense when (1) the innovator has the complementary assets necessary to develop the innovation, (2) the barriers to imitating a new innovation are high, and (3) the number of capable competitors is limited. Complementary assets allow rapid development and promotion of the innovation. High barriers to imitation buy the innovator time to establish a competitive advantage and build enduring barriers to entry through brand loyalty and/or experience-based cost advantages. The fewer the capable competitors, the less likely it is that any one of them will succeed in circumventing barriers to imitation and quickly imitating the innovation.

TABLE 7.1

Strategies for Profiting from Innovation

Strategy	Does Innovator Have All Required Complementary Assets?	Likely Height of Barriers to Imitation	Number of Capable Competitors
Go it alone	Yes	High	Few
Enter into alliance	No	High	Limited
License innovation	No	Low	Many

The Body Shop Opens Too Late

In 1976 Anita Roddick, a former flower child and the owner of a small hotel in southern England, had an idea. Rising sentiment against the use of animals in testing cosmetics and a wave of environmentalism that focused on "natural" products gave her the idea for a range of skin creams, shampoos, and lotions made from fruit and vegetable oils rather than animal products. Her products, moreover, would not be tested on animals. Roddick began to sell her line of new products from a small shop in Brighton, a seaside town, and the results surpassed her wildest expectations. Her line of cosmetics was an instant success, and to capitalize on it, she began to franchise the right to open stores called The Body Shop to sell her products. By 1993 there were more than 700 of these stores around the world, with combined sales of more than $250 million.

In Britain and Europe, to speed the growth of the company, Roddick mainly franchised her stores through alliances with other individuals and companies. In her push to enter the U.S. market in 1988, however, she decided to own her own stores and forgo the rapid expansion that franchising would have made possible. This was a costly mistake. Large U.S. cosmetic companies such as Estée Lauder and entrepreneurs such as Leslie Wexner of The Limited were quick to see the opportunities that Roddick had opened up in this rapidly growing market segment. They moved fast to imitate her product lines, which was not technically difficult to do, and began to market their own natural cosmetics. For example, Estée Lauder brought out its Origins line of cosmetics, and Wexner opened the Bath and Body Works to sell his own line of natural cosmetics. Both these ventures have been very successful and have gained a large share of the market.

Realizing the competitive threat from imitators, in 1990 Roddick began to move quickly to franchise The Body Shop in the United States, and by 1993 more than 150 stores had opened. Although the stores have been successful, the delay in opening them gave Roddick's competitors the opportunity to establish their own brand names and robbed her enterprise of the uniqueness that its products enjoy throughout Europe. Given that the United States is by far the world's biggest cosmetics market and natural cosmetics are its fastest-growing segment, this mistake has cost The Body Shop billions of dollars in lost revenues, and Roddick has acknowledged that her strategy was a mistake. When an innovation is easy to imitate and there are many capable competitors, entering into an alliance with others can speed the development of a new product.[9]

The competitive strategy of *developing and marketing the innovation jointly with other companies through a strategic alliance or joint venture* makes most sense when (1) the innovator lacks complementary assets, (2) barriers to imitation are high, and (3) there are several capable competitors. In such circumstances, it makes sense to enter into an alliance with a company that already has the complementary assets, in other words, with a capable competitor. Theoretically, such an alliance should prove to be mutually beneficial, and each partner can share in high profits that neither could earn on its own. The attempt by Body Shop International, described in Strategy in Action 7.1, to go it alone in the effort to enter the U.S. market rather than to form an alliance with U.S. partners illustrates the benefit of alliances in quickly exploiting an innovation.

The third strategy, *licensing*, makes most sense when (1) the innovating company lacks the complementary assets, (2) barriers to imitation are low, and (3) there are many capable competitors. The combination of low barriers to imitation and many capable competitors makes rapid imitation almost certain. The innovator's lack of complementary assets further suggests that an imitator will soon capture the innovator's competitive advantage. Given these factors, since rapid diffusion of the innovator's technology through imitation is inevitable, by licensing out its technology the innovator can at least share in some of the benefits of this diffusion.[10]

STRATEGY IN MATURE INDUSTRIES

As a result of fierce competition in the shakeout stage, an industry becomes consolidated, and so a mature industry is often dominated by a small number of large companies. Although a mature industry may also contain many medium-sized companies and a host of small specialized ones, the large companies determine the nature of the industry's competition because they can influence the five competitive forces. Indeed, these are the companies that developed the most successful generic business-level strategies in the industry.

By the end of the shakeout stage, strategic groups of companies pursuing similar generic competitive strategies have emerged in the industry. As we discussed in Chapter 6, for example, all the companies pursuing a low-cost strategy can be viewed as comprising one strategic group; all those pursuing differentiation constitute another, and the focusers form a third. Companies in an industry constantly analyze each other's business-level strategies, and they know that if they move to change their strategies, their actions are likely to stimulate a competitive response from rivals in their strategic group and from companies in other groups that may be threatened by the change in strategy.

For example, a differentiator that starts to lower its prices because it has adopted a more cost-efficient technology not only threatens other differentiators in its group, it also threatens low-cost companies, which see their competitive edge being eroded. These other companies may now change their strategies in response, most likely by reducing their prices, too, as is currently occurring in the personal computer industry. Thus, the way one company changes or fine-tunes its business-level strategy over time affects the way the other companies in the industry pursue theirs. Hence, by the mature stage of the industry life cycle, companies have learned just how *interdependent* their strategies are.

In fact, the main issue facing companies in a mature industry is to adopt a competitive strategy that *simultaneously* allows each individual company to protect its competitive advantage while preserving industry profitability. No generic strategy will generate above-average profits if competitive forces in an industry are so strong that companies are at the mercy of each other, potential entrants, powerful suppliers, powerful customers, and so on. As a result, in mature industries, competitive strategy revolves around understanding how large companies try *collectively* to reduce the strength of the five forces of industry competition to preserve both company and industry profitability.

Interdependent companies can help protect their competitive advantage and profitability by adopting competitive moves and tactics to reduce the threat of each competitive force. In the next sections, we examine the various price and nonprice competitive moves and tactics that companies use—first, to deter entry into an industry, and second, to reduce the level of rivalry within an industry. We then discuss methods that companies can employ to gain more control over suppliers and buyers.

STRATEGIES TO DETER ENTRY IN MATURE INDUSTRIES

Companies can utilize three main methods to deter entry by potential rivals and hence maintain and increase industry profitability. As Figure 7.2 shows, these methods are product proliferation, price cutting, and excess capacity.

Product Proliferation

Companies seldom produce just one product. Most commonly, they produce a range of products aimed at different market segments so that they have broad product lines. Sometimes, to reduce the threat of entry, companies expand the range of products they make to fill a wide variety of niches. This creates a barrier to entry because potential competitors now find it harder to break into an industry in which all the niches are filled.[11] This strategy of pursuing a broad product line to deter entry is known as **product proliferation**.

Because the large U.S. carmakers were so slow to fill the small-car niches (they did *not* pursue a product proliferation strategy), they were vulnerable to the entry of the Japanese into these market segments in the United States. U.S. carmakers really had no excuse for this situation, for in their European operations they had a long history of small-car manufacturing. They should have seen the opening and filled it ten years earlier, but their view was that small cars meant small profits. In the breakfast-cereal industry, on the other hand, competition is based on the production of new kinds of cereal to satisfy or create new desires by consumers. Thus the number of breakfast cereals proliferates, making it very difficult for prospective entrants to attack a new market segment.

Figure 7.3 indicates how product proliferation can deter entry. It depicts product space in the restaurant industry along two dimensions: (1) atmosphere, which ranges from fast food to candlelight dining; and (2) quality of food, which ranges from average to gourmet. The circles represent product spaces filled by restaurants located along the two dimensions. Thus, McDonald's is situated in the average quality/fast-food area. A gap in the product space gives a potential entrant or an existing rival an opportunity to enter the market and make inroads. The shaded unoccupied product space represents areas where new restaurants can enter the market. Filling all the product spaces, however, creates a barrier to entry and makes it much more difficult for a new company to gain a foothold in the market and differentiate itself.

FIGURE 7.2

Strategies for Deterring Entry of Rivals

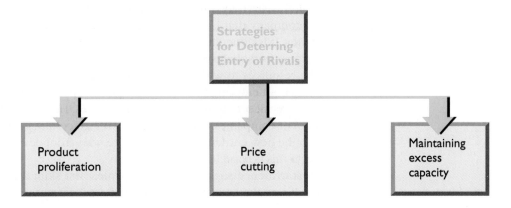

FIGURE 7.3
● ● ● ● ● ● ● ● ● ●

Product Proliferation in
the Restaurant Industry

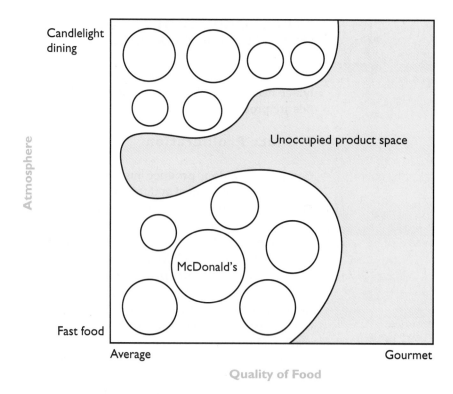

Price Cutting
● ● ● ● ● ● ● ● ● ● ●

In some situations, pricing strategies involving **price cutting** can be used to deter entry by other companies, thus protecting the profit margins of companies already in an industry. One price-cutting strategy, for example, is to charge a high price initially for a product and seize short-term profits but then to cut prices aggressively in order to build market share *and* deter potential entrants simultaneously.[12] The incumbent companies thus signal to potential entrants that if they enter the industry, the incumbents will use their competitive advantage to drive down prices to a level at which new companies will be unable to cover their costs.[13] This pricing strategy also allows a company to ride down the experience curve and obtain substantial economies of scale. Since costs fall with prices, profit margins could still be maintained.

Still, this strategy is unlikely to deter a strong potential competitor, an established company that is trying to find profitable investment opportunities in other industries. It is difficult, for example, to imagine 3M's being afraid to enter an industry because companies there threaten to drive down prices. A company such as 3M has the resources to withstand any short-term losses. Hewlett Packard also had few worries about entering the highly competitive personal computer industry because of its powerful set of distinctive competencies. Hence, it may be in the interests of incumbent companies to accept new entry gracefully, giving up market share gradually to the new entrants to prevent price wars from developing, and thus save their profits, if this is feasible.

Most evidence suggests that companies first skim the market and charge high prices during the growth stage, maximizing short-run profits.[14] Then they move to originated as a market signal by one company that was quickly copied by all other companies in the industry. In sum, price signaling allows companies to give one another information that enables them to understand each other's competitive product/market strategy and make coordinated, competitive moves.

Price Leadership

Price leadership, the taking on by one company of the responsibility for setting industry prices, is a second tactic used to enhance the profitability of companies in a mature industry.[18] Formal price leadership, or price setting by companies jointly, is illegal under antitrust laws, so the process of price leadership is often very subtle. In the auto industry, for example, auto prices are set by imitation. The price set by the weakest company, that is, the one with the highest costs, is often used as the basis for competitors' pricing. Thus, U.S. carmakers set their prices, and Japanese carmakers then set theirs with reference to the U.S. prices. The Japanese are happy to do this because they have lower costs than U.S. companies and are making higher profits than U.S. carmakers without competing with them by price. Pricing is done by market segment. The prices of different auto models in the model range indicate the customer segments that the companies are aiming for and the price range they believe the market segment can tolerate. Each manufacturer prices a model in the segment with reference to the *prices* charged by its competitors, not by reference to competitors' costs. Price leadership allows differentiators to charge a premium price and also helps low-cost companies by increasing their margins.

Although price leadership can stabilize industry relationships by preventing head-to-head competition and thus raise the level of profitability within an industry, it has its dangers. Price leadership helps companies with high costs, allowing them to survive without becoming more productive or more efficient. Thus, it may foster complacency; companies may keep extracting profits without reinvesting any to improve their productivity. In the long term, such behavior will make them vulnerable to new entrants that have lower costs because they have developed new productive techniques. That is what happened in the U.S. auto industry after the Japanese entered the market. After years of tacit price fixing, with General Motors as the leader, the carmakers were subjected to growing low-cost Japanese competition, to which they were unable to respond. Indeed, many U.S. auto companies have survived into the 1990s only because the Japanese carmakers were foreign firms. Had the foreign firms been new U.S. entrants, the government would probably not have taken steps to protect Chrysler, Ford, or General Motors, and they would be much smaller companies today.

Nonprice Competition

A third very important aspect of product/market strategy in mature industries is the use of **nonprice competition** to manage rivalry within an industry. Using various tactics and maneuvers to try to prevent costly price cutting and price wars does not preclude competition by product differentiation. Indeed, in many industries, product differentiation is the principal competitive tactic used to prevent competitors from obtaining access to a company's customers and attacking its market share. In other words, companies rely on product differentiation to deter potential entrants and manage rivalry within their industry. Product differentiation allows industry

FIGURE 7.4

Four Nonprice
Competitive Strategies

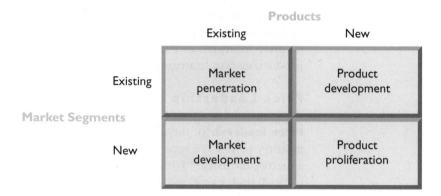

rivals to compete for market share by offering products with different or superior features or by applying different marketing techniques. In Figure 7.4, product and market segment dimensions are used to identify four nonprice competitive strategies based on product differentiation. (Notice that this model applies to new market segments, not new markets.)[19]

Market Penetration   When a company concentrates on expanding market share in its existing product markets, it is engaging in a strategy of **market penetration**.[20] Market penetration involves heavy advertising to promote and build product differentiation. In a mature industry, the thrust of advertising is to influence consumers' brand choice and create a brand-name reputation for the company and its products. In this way, a company can increase its market share by attracting the customers of its rivals. Because brand-name products often command premium prices, building market share in this situation is very profitable.

In some mature industries—for example, soap and detergent, disposable diapers, and brewing—a market-penetration strategy becomes a way of life.[21] In these industries, all companies engage in intensive advertising and battle for market share. Each company fears that by not advertising it will lose market share to rivals. Consequently, in the soap and detergent industry, for instance, Procter & Gamble spends more than 20 percent of sales revenues on advertising, with the aim of maintaining and perhaps building market share. These huge advertising outlays constitute a barrier to entry for prospective entrants. As Strategy in Action 7.3 details, Toys 'R' Us rose to prominence in the retail toy market by pursuing a market-penetration strategy.

Product Development   **Product development** is the creation of new or improved products to replace existing ones, such as occurs in the fast-food industry discussed in the Opening Case.[22] The wet-shaving industry is another industry that depends on product replacement to create successive waves of consumer demand, which then create new sources of revenue for companies in the industry. Gillette, for example, periodically comes out with a new and improved razor, such as the Sensor shaving system, which often gives a massive boost to its market share. Similarly, in the car industry each major car company replaces its models every three to five years to encourage customers to trade in their old models and buy the new one.

Product development is important for maintaining product differentiation and building market share.[23] For instance, the laundry detergent Tide has gone through

7.3 **STRATEGY** *in* **ACTION**

Warfare in Toyland

Toys 'R' Us, based in Paramus, New Jersey, grew at an astonishing 25 percent annual rate throughout the 1980s and today holds a 20 percent share of the $15 billion retail toy market, which makes it the industry leader. To reach its dominant position, the company used a strategy of market penetration based on developing a nationwide chain of retail outlets and a cost-leadership strategy. To lower costs, Toys 'R' Us developed efficient materials-management techniques for ordering and distributing toys to its stores. It also provided only a low level of customer service. Together, these moves allowed it to obtain a very low expense-to-sales ratio of 17 percent. Toys 'R' Us then used its low costs to promote a philosophy of everyday low pricing. The company deliberately set out to undercut the prices of its rivals, and it succeeded. In fact, its two largest competitors in the 1980s, Child World and Lionel, went bankrupt.[24] Pursuing a market-penetration strategy based on low cost thus brought spectacular results for Toys 'R' Us.

In the 1990s, however, the company's commanding position is being threatened by a new set of rivals, which are also pursuing market-penetration strategies. Companies such as Wal-Mart, Kmart, and Target Stores are rapidly expanding the number of their stores and trying to beat Toys 'R' Us at its own game by selling toys at prices that are often below those of Toys 'R' Us. Indeed, Wal-Mart has more than doubled its share of the toy market (to more than 13 percent), and both Kmart's and Target's toy sales are rapidly increasing. This new competition is squeezing profits for Toys 'R' Us, and the company is turning to nonprice competition to attract customers. For example, Toys 'R' Us is promoting its wide range of products as a competitive advantage; it carries more than 16,000 items versus 2,000 at a typical discount store. It has also decided to increase the level of customer service by offering customers more personalized attention. By emphasizing quality and customer responsiveness, as well as low price, the company seeks to fend off the new challenge from the discount stores and maintain its growth in the 1990s.[25]

---

more than fifty different changes in formulation during the past forty years to improve its performance. The product is always advertised as Tide, but it is a different product each year. The battle over diet colas is another interesting example of competitive product differentiation by product development. Royal Crown Cola developed Diet Rite, the first diet cola. However, Coca-Cola and PepsiCo responded quickly with their versions of the diet drink, and by massive advertising they soon took over the market. Refining and improving products is an important competitive tactic in defending a company's generic competitive strategy in a mature industry, but this kind of competition can be as vicious as a price war because it is very expensive and raises costs dramatically.

Market signaling to competitors can also be an important part of a product development strategy. One company may let the others know that it is proceeding with product innovations that will provide a competitive advantage the others will be unable to imitate effectively because their entry into the market will be too late. For example, software companies such as Microsoft often announce new operating systems years in advance. The purpose of such an announcement is to deter prospective competitors from making the huge investments needed to compete with the industry leaders and to let its customers know that the company still has the competitive edge so important to retaining customers' loyalty. However, preemptive signaling can backfire, as IBM found out when it announced that its PS/2 operating system would not be compatible with the operating systems presently standard in the industry. Other companies in the industry collectively signaled to IBM and IBM's customers that they would band together to protect the existing operation systems, thus preserving industry standards and preventing IBM from obtaining a competitive advantage from its new technology. IBM subsequently backed down. If a preemptive move is to succeed, competitors must believe that a company will act according to its signals and stick to its position. If the threat is not credible, the signaling company weakens its position.

Market Development   **Market development** finds new market segments for a company's products. A company pursuing this strategy wants to capitalize on the brand name it has developed in one market segment by locating new market segments in which to compete. In this way, it can exploit the product differentiation advantages of its brand name. The Japanese auto manufacturers provide an interesting example of the use of market development. When they first entered the market, each Japanese manufacturer offered a car, such as the Toyota Corolla and the Honda Accord, aimed at the economy segment of the auto market. However, the Japanese upgraded each car over time, and now each is directed at a more expensive market segment. The Accord is a leading contender in the mid-sized car segment, while the Corolla fills the small-car segment that used to be occupied by the Celica, which is now aimed at a sportier market segment. By redefining their product offerings, Japanese manufacturers have profitably developed their market segments and successfully attacked their industry rivals, wresting market share from these companies. Although the Japanese used to compete primarily as low-cost producers, market development has allowed them to become differentiators as well. Toyota is an example of a company that has used market development to pursue simultaneously a low-cost and a differentiation strategy.

Product Proliferation   **Product proliferation** can be used to manage rivalry within an industry and to deter entry. The strategy of product proliferation generally means that large companies in an industry all have a product in each market segment or niche and compete head-to-head for customers. If a new niche develops, such as sports utility vehicles, designer sunglasses, or Internet Web sites, then the leader gets a first-mover advantage, but soon all the other companies catch up, and once again competition is stabilized and rivalry within the industry is reduced. Product proliferation thus allows the development of stable industry competition based on product differentiation, not price—that is, nonprice competition based on the development of new products. The battle is over a product's perceived quality and uniqueness, *not* over its price.

Capacity Control

Although nonprice competition helps mature industries avoid the cutthroat price cutting that reduces both company and industry levels of profitability, in some industries price competition does periodically break out. This occurs most commonly when there is industry overcapacity, that is, when companies collectively produce too much output so that reducing price is the only way to dispose of it. If one company starts to cut prices, then the others quickly follow because they fear that the

FIGURE 7.5
· · · · · · · · · · ·
Changes in Industry
Capacity and Demand

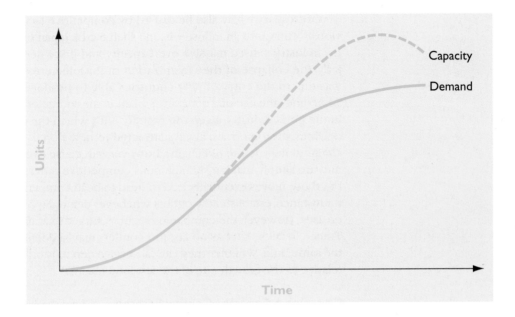

price cutter will be able to sell all its inventory and they will be left holding unwanted goods. **Capacity control** strategies are the last set of competitive tactics and maneuvers for managing rivalry within an industry that we discuss in this chapter.

Excess capacity may be caused by a shortfall in demand, as when a recession lowers the demand for cars and causes car companies to give customers price incentives to purchase a new car. In this situation, companies can do nothing except wait for better times. By and large, however, excess capacity results from companies within an industry simultaneously responding to favorable conditions: they all invest in new plants to be able to take advantage of the predicted upsurge in demand. Paradoxically, each individual company's effort to outperform the others means that collectively the companies create industry overcapacity, which hurts them all. Figure 7.5 illustrates this situation. Although demand is rising, the consequence of each company's decision to increase capacity is a surge in industry capacity, which drives down prices.

To prevent the accumulation of costly excess capacity, companies must devise strategies that let them control, or at least benefit from, capacity expansion programs. Before we examine these strategies, however, we need to consider in greater detail the factors that cause excess capacity.[26]

Factors Causing Excess Capacity   The problem of excess capacity often derives from technological factors. Sometimes new, low-cost technology is the culprit because, to prevent being left behind, all companies introduce it simultaneously. Excess capacity occurs because the new technology can produce more than the old. In addition, new technology is often introduced in large increments, which generate overcapacity. For instance, an airline that needs more seats on a route must add another plane, thereby adding hundreds of seats even though only fifty are needed. To take another example, a new chemical process may operate efficiently only at the rate of 1,000 gallons a day, whereas the previous process was efficient at 500 gallons a day. If all companies within an industry change technologies, industry capacity may double and enormous problems can result.

Overcapacity may also be caused by competitive factors within an industry. Obviously, entry into an industry is one such factor. Japan's entry into the semiconductor industry caused massive overcapacity and price declines for microchips. Similarly, the collapse of the Organization of Petroleum Exporting Countries (OPEC) was due to the entry of new countries able to produce oil at competitive prices. Sometimes the age of a company's plant is the source of the problem. For example, in the hotel industry, given the rapidity with which the quality of hotel furnishings declines, customers are always attracted to new hotels. The building of new hotel chains alongside the old chains, however, can cause excess capacity. Often companies are simply making simultaneous competitive moves based on industry trends, but those moves eventually lead to head-to-head competition. Most fast-food chains, for instance, establish new outlets whenever demographic data show population increases. However, the companies seem to forget that all chains use the same data. Thus, a locality that has no fast-food outlets may suddenly see several being built at the same time. Whether they can all survive depends on the growth rate of demand relative to the growth rate of the fast-food chains.

Choosing a Capacity-Control Strategy   Given the various ways in which capacity can expand, companies clearly need to find some means of controlling it. If they are always plagued by price cutting and price wars, companies will be unable to recoup the investments in their generic strategies. Low profitability within an industry caused by overcapacity forces not just the weakest companies but sometimes the major players as well to exit the industry. In general, companies have two strategic choices. Either (1) each company individually must try to preempt its rivals and seize the initiative, or (2) the companies collectively must find indirect means of coordinating with each other so that they are all aware of the mutual effects of their actions.

To *preempt* rivals, a company must forecast a large increase in demand in the product market and then move rapidly to establish large-scale operations that will be able to satisfy the predicted demand. By achieving a first-mover advantage, the company may deter other firms from entering the market since the preemptor will usually be able to move down the experience curve, reduce its costs and therefore its prices as well, and threaten a price war if necessary.

This strategy, however, is extremely risky, for it involves investing resources in a generic strategy before the extent and profitability of the future market are clear. Wal-Mart, with its strategy of locating in small rural towns to tap an underexploited market for discount goods, preempted Sears and Kmart. Wal-Mart has been able to engage in market penetration and market expansion because of the secure base it established in its rural strongholds.

A preemptive strategy is also risky if it does not deter competitors and they decide to enter the market. If the competitors have a stronger generic strategy or more resources, such as AT&T or IBM, they can make the preemptor suffer. Thus, for the strategy to succeed, the preemptor must generally be a credible company with enough resources to withstand a possible price war.

To *coordinate* with rivals as a capacity-control strategy, caution must be exercised since collusion on the timing of new investments is illegal under antitrust law. However, tacit coordination is practiced in many industries as companies attempt to understand and forecast the competitive moves of each other. Generally, companies use market signaling and engage in a kind of tit-for-tat strategy to secure coordination. They make announcements about their future investment decisions in trade journals and newspapers. In addition, they share information about their production levels and their forecasts of demand within the industry to bring supply and demand into equilibrium. Thus, a coordination strategy reduces the risks associated with investment in the industry.

SUPPLY-AND-DISTRIBUTION STRATEGY IN MATURE INDUSTRIES

As you saw in Chapter 3, when an industry becomes consolidated and comprises a few large companies, it gains strength over its suppliers and customers. Suppliers become dependent on the industry for buying their inputs and on customers for obtaining the industry's outputs. By the mature stage, to protect their market share and improve product quality, many companies want to take over more of the distribution of their products and control the source of inputs crucial to the production process. When they seek ownership of supply or distribution operations, they are pursuing a strategy of *vertical integration*, which is considered in detail in Chapter 9. In this chapter we discuss how the way a company controls its supplier and distributor relationships protects its generic strategy and develops a competitive advantage.

By controlling supplier and distributor relationships, a company can safeguard its ability to dispose of its outputs or acquire inputs in a timely, reliable manner. This, in turn, can reduce costs and improve product quality. One way to analyze the issues involved in choosing a distribution/supplier strategy is to contrast the situation that exists between a company and its suppliers and distributors in Japan with the situation that exists in the United States.

In the United States it is common for a company and its suppliers and distributors to have an anonymous relationship in which each party tries to strike the best bargain to make the most profit. Often purchasing and distribution personnel are routinely rotated to prevent kickbacks. In contrast, the relationship between a company and its suppliers and distributors in Japan is based on long-term personal relationships and trust. Suppliers in Japan are sensitive to the needs of the company, respond quickly to changes in the specification of inputs, and adjust supply to meet the requirements of a company's just-in-time inventory system. The results of this close relationship are lower costs and the ability to respond to unexpected changes in customers' demand. Developing close supplier/distributor relationships is a tactic that supports Japanese companies' generic strategies. Clearly, it pays a company to develop a long-term relationship with its suppliers and distributors, and more and more U.S. companies such as Xerox, Motorola, Kodak, McDonald's, and Wal-Mart have formed close linkages with their suppliers.

A company has many options to choose from in deciding on the appropriate way to distribute its products to gain a competitive advantage. It may distribute its products to an independent distributor, which in turn distributes them to retailers. Alternatively, a company might distribute directly to retailers or even to the final customer. As Strategy in Action 7.4 illustrates, companies may also need to change their distribution strategies as the industry changes.

In general, the *complexity of a product* and the *amount of information* needed about its operation and maintenance determine the distribution strategy chosen.

Compaq and Dell Go Head-to-Head in Distribution

As new developments in technology alter the nature of competition in the personal computer industry, the distribution strategies of its major players are also changing. These changes are evident in the struggle between Dell Computer and Compaq Computer for domination of the personal computer market. Founded by a team of engineers, Compaq has from the start emphasized the engineering and research side of the PC business. For example, it was the first company to bring out a computer using Intel's new 486 chip. Its differentiation strategy was to produce high-end PCs based on the newest technology, which would command a premium price. Compaq specialized in the business market, and it developed a sophisticated dealer network to distribute, sell, and service its expensive PCs.[27]

Dell, on the other hand, focused from the beginning on the marketing and distribution end of the PC business. Its low-cost strategy was to assemble a PC and then sell it directly to consumers through mail-order

outlets, cutting out the dealer in order to offer a rock-bottom price. The company was viewed by its managers primarily as a distribution or mail-order company, and not as an engineering one.

As computers increasingly became commodity products and prices fell drastically, Compaq realized that its strategy of selling only though high-priced dealers would mean disaster. It changed its strategy to produce a low-cost computer and in 1993 began its own mail-order distribution, offering its machines directly to consumers. Its new low-cost distribution strategy has been very successful. The result is that Compaq is now battling Dell for the same customers. To compete, each company is advertising its ability to serve customers more quickly and efficiently than the other. For example, each offers next-day delivery and installation of computers as well as extended warranties. For both companies, distribution and sales strategies have become a vital part of the competitive game.[28]

Car companies, for example, use franchisees rather than "car supermarkets" to control the distribution of their autos. The reason is the high level of after-sales service and support needed to satisfy customers. Carmakers are able to penalize franchisees by withholding cars from a dealership if customers' complaints rise, giving them effective control over franchisees' behavior.

On the other hand, large electronics manufacturers and producers of consumer durables such as appliances generally prefer to use a network of distributors to control distribution. To enhance market share and control the way products are sold and serviced, manufacturers choose five or six large distributors per state to control distribution. The distributors are required to carry the full line of a company's products and invest in after-sales service facilities. The result is that the manufacturer receives good feedback on how its products are selling, and the distributor becomes knowledgeable about a company's products and thus helps the company maintain and increase its control over the market. The company is able to discipline its distributors if they start to discount prices or otherwise threaten the company's reputation or generic strategy.

Large manufacturers such as Johnson & Johnson, Procter & Gamble, and General Foods typically sell directly to a retailer and avoid giving profits to a distributor or wholesaler. They do so in part because they have lower profit margins than the makers of electronic equipment and consumer durables. However, this strategy also allows them to influence a retailer's behavior directly. For example, they can refuse to supply a particular product that a retailer wants unless the retailer stocks the entire range of the company's products. In addition, the companies are assured of shelf space for new products. Coca-Cola and PepsiCo are two companies that are able to influence retailers to reduce the shelf space given to competing products or even to exclude them. They can do so because soft drinks have the highest profit margins of any product sold in supermarkets. Gallo is one of the few winemakers that controls the distribution and retailing of its own products. This is one reason Gallo is so consistently profitable.

In sum, devising the appropriate strategy for acquiring inputs and disposing of outputs is a crucial part of competitive strategy in mature industry environments. Companies can gain a competitive advantage through the way they choose to control their relationships with distributors and suppliers. By choosing the right strategy, they are able to control their costs, their price and nonprice strategies, their reputation, and product quality. These are crucial issues in mature industries.

STRATEGIES IN DECLINING INDUSTRIES

Sooner or later many industries enter into a decline stage, in which the size of the total market starts to shrink. Examples include the railroad industry, the tobacco industry, and the steel industry. Industries start declining for a number of reasons, including technological change, social trends, and demographic shifts. The railroad and steel industries began to decline when technological changes brought viable substitutes for the products these industries manufactured. The advent of the internal combustion engine drove the railroad industry into decline, and the steel industry fell into decline with the rise of plastics and composite materials. As for the tobacco industry, changing social attitudes toward smoking, which are themselves a product of growing concerns about the health effects of smoking, have caused decline.

There are four main strategies that companies can adopt to deal with decline: (1) a **leadership strategy**, by which a company seeks to become the dominant player in a declining industry; (2) a **niche strategy**, which focuses on pockets of demand that are declining more slowly than the industry as a whole; (3) a **harvest strategy**, which optimizes cash flow; and (4) a **divestment strategy**, by which a company sells off the business to others. Before we examine each of these strategies in detail, it is important to note that the choice of strategy depends in part on the *intensity* of the competition.

The Severity of Decline

When the size of the total market is shrinking, competition tends to intensify in a declining industry and profit rates tend to fall. The intensity of competition in a declining industry depends on four critical factors, which are indicated in Figure 7.6. First, the intensity of competition is greater in industries in which decline is rapid as opposed to industries, such as tobacco, in which decline is slow and gradual.

Second, the intensity of competition is greater in declining industries in which exit barriers are high. As you recall from Chapter 3, high exit barriers keep companies locked into an industry even when demand is falling. The result is the emergence of excess productive capacity, and hence an increased probability of fierce price competition.

FIGURE 7.6

Factors That Determine the Intensity of Competition in Declining Industries

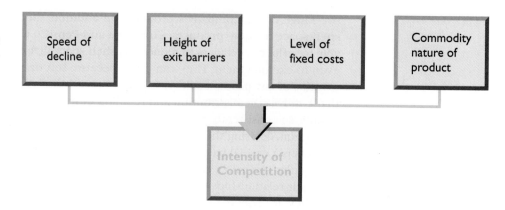

Third, and related to the previous point, the intensity of competition is greater in declining industries in which fixed costs are high (as in the steel industry). The reason is that the need to cover fixed costs, such as the costs of maintaining productive capacity, can make companies try to utilize any excess capacity they have by slashing prices, an action that can trigger a price war.

Finally, the intensity of competition is greater in declining industries in which the product is perceived as a commodity (as it is in the steel industry) in contrast to industries in which differentiation gives rise to significant brand loyalty, as was true until very recently of the declining tobacco industry.

Not all segments of an industry typically decline at the same rate. In some segments, demand may remain reasonably strong, despite decline elsewhere. The steel industry illustrates this situation. Although bulk steel products, such as sheet steel, have suffered a general decline, demand has actually risen for specialty steels, such as those used in high-speed machine tools. Vacuum tubes provide another example. Although demand for them collapsed when transistors replaced them as a key component in many electronics products, for years afterward vacuum tubes still had some limited applications in radar equipment. Consequently, demand in this vacuum tube segment remained strong despite the general decline in the demand for vacuum tubes. The point, then, is that there may be *pockets of demand* in an industry in which demand is declining more slowly than in the industry as a whole or not declining at all. Price competition thus may be far less intense among the companies serving such pockets of demand than within the industry as a whole.

Choosing a Strategy

As already noted, four main strategies are available to companies in a declining industry: a leadership strategy, a niche strategy, a harvest strategy, and a divestment strategy. Figure 7.7 provides a simple framework for guiding strategic choice. Note that intensity of competition in the declining industry is measured on the vertical axis and that a company's strengths *relative* to remaining pockets of demand are measured on the horizontal axis.

Leadership Strategy   A leadership strategy aims at growing in a declining industry by picking up the market share of companies that are leaving the industry. A leadership strategy makes most sense (1) when the company has distinctive

FIGURE 7.7

Strategy Selection in a
Declining Industry

strengths that allow it to capture market share in a declining industry and (2) when
the speed of decline and the intensity of competition in the declining industry are
moderate. Philip Morris has pursued such a strategy in the tobacco industry. By aggressive marketing, Philip Morris has increased its market share in a declining industry and earned enormous profits in the process.

The tactical steps companies might use to achieve a leadership position include
aggressive pricing and marketing to build market share; acquiring established competitors to consolidate the industry; and raising the stakes for other competitors, for
example, by making new investments in productive capacity. Such competitive tactics signal to other competitors that the company is willing and able to stay and
compete in the declining industry. These signals may persuade other companies to
exit the industry, which would further enhance the competitive position of the industry leader. Strategy in Action 7.5 offers an example of a company, Richardson
Electronics, that has prospered by taking a leadership position in a declining industry. It is one of the last companies in the vacuum tube business.

Niche Strategy A niche strategy focuses on those pockets of demand in the industry in which demand is stable or declining less rapidly than the industry as a
whole. The strategy makes sense when the company has some unique strengths relative to those niches where demand remains relatively strong. As an example, consider Naval, a company that manufactures whaling harpoons and small guns to fire
them and makes money doing so. This might be considered rather odd, since whaling has been outlawed by the world community. However, Naval survived the ter-
minal decline of the harpoon industry by focusing on the one group of people who

How to Make Money in the Vacuum Tube Business

 At its peak in the early 1950s, the vacuum tube business was a major industry in which companies such as Westinghouse, General Electric, RCA, and Western Electric had a large stake. Then along came the transistor, making most vacuum tubes obsolete, and one by one all the big companies exited the industry. One company, however, Richardson Electronics, not only stayed in the business but also demonstrated that high returns are possible in a declining industry. Primarily a distributor (although it does have some manufacturing capabilities), Richardson bought the remains of a dozen companies in the United States and Europe as they exited the vacuum tube industry. Richardson now has a warehouse that stocks more than 10,000 different types of vacuum tubes. The company is now the world's only supplier of many of them, which helps explain why its gross margin is in the 35 to 40 percent range.

Richardson survives and prospers because vacuum tubes are vital parts of some older electronic equipment that would be costly to replace with solid-state equipment. In addition, vacuum tubes still outperform semiconductors in some limited applications, including radar and welding machines. The U.S. government and General Motors are big customers of Richardson.

Speed is the essence of Richardson's business. The company's Illinois warehouse offers overnight delivery to some 40,000 customers, processing 650 orders a day, whose average price is $550. Customers such as GM don't really care whether a vacuum tube costs $250 or $350; what they care about is the $40,000 to $50,000 downtime loss that they face when a key piece of welding equipment isn't working. By responding quickly to the demands of such customers and by being the only major supplier of many types of vacuum tubes, Richardson has placed itself in a position that many companies in growing industries would envy—a monopoly position. As a result, its sales tripled to $101 million during the second half of the 1980s, while its profits quadrupled to $8.5 million and are still rising.[29]

are still allowed to hunt whales, although only in very limited numbers—North American Eskimos. Eskimos are permitted to hunt bowhead whales, provided that they do so only for food and not for commercial purposes. Naval is the sole supplier of small harpoon whaling guns to Eskimo communities, and its monopoly position allows it to earn a healthy return in this small market.[30]

Harvest Strategy   As we note in Chapter 6, a harvest strategy is the best choice when a company wishes to get out of a declining industry and perhaps optimize cash flow in the process. This strategy makes the most sense when the company foresees a steep decline and intense future competition or when it lacks strengths relative to remaining pockets of demand in the industry. A harvest strategy requires the company to cut all new investments in capital equipment, advertising, R&D, and the like. As illustrated in Figure 7.8, the inevitable result is that the company will lose market share, but because it is no longer investing in this business, initially its positive cash flow will increase. Essentially, the company is taking cash flow in exchange for market share. Ultimately, however, cash flows will start to decline, and at this stage it makes sense for the company to liquidate the business. Although this strategy is very appealing in theory, it can be somewhat difficult to put into practice. Employee morale in a business that is being run down may suffer. Furthermore, if customers catch on to what the company is doing, they may defect rapidly. Then market share may decline much faster than the company expected.

FIGURE 7.8
. . . .
A Harvest Strategy

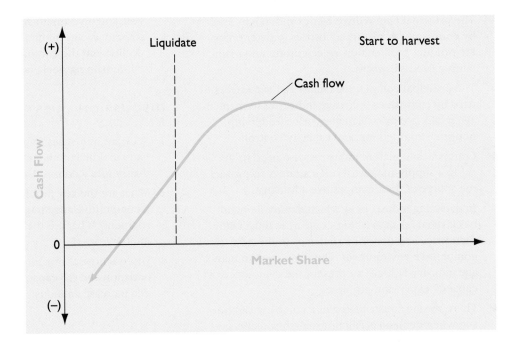

Divestment Strategy   A divestment strategy rests on the idea that a company can maximize its net investment recovery from a business by selling it early, before the industry has entered into a steep decline. This strategy is appropriate when the company has few strengths relative to whatever pockets of demand are likely to remain in the industry and when the competition in the declining industry is likely to be intense. The best option may be to sell out to a company that is pursuing a leadership strategy in the industry. The drawback of the divestment strategy is that it depends for its success on the ability of the company accurately to spot its industry's decline before it becomes serious and to sell out while the company's assets are still valued by others.

SUMMARY OF CHAPTER
. . . .

The purpose of this chapter is to discuss the competitive strategies that companies can use in different industry environments to protect and enhance their generic business-level strategies. Developing a generic competitive strategy and an investment strategy is only the first part, albeit a crucial one, of business-level strategy. Choosing industry-appropriate competitive tactics, gambits, and maneuvers is the second part of successful strategy formulation at the business level. Companies must always be on the alert for changes in conditions within their industry and in the competitive behavior of their rivals if they are to respond to these changes in a timely manner. The chapter makes the following main points:

✔ In fragmented industries composed of a large number of small and medium-sized companies, the principal forms of competitive strategy are chaining, franchising, and horizontal merger.

✔ In embryonic and growth industries, developing a strategy to profit from technical innovations is a crucial aspect of competitive strategy. The three strategies a company can choose from are (1) to develop and market the technology itself, (2) to do so jointly with another company, or (3) to license the technology to existing companies.

✔ Mature industries are composed of a few large companies whose actions are so highly interdependent that the success of one company's strategy depends on the responses of its rivals.

✔ The principal competitive tactics and moves used by companies in mature industries to deter entry are product proliferation, price cutting, and maintaining excess capacity.

✔ The principal competitive tactics and maneuvers used by companies in mature industries to manage rivalry are price signaling, price leadership, nonprice competition, and capacity control.

✔ Companies in mature industries also need to develop a supply-and-distribution strategy to protect the source of their competitive advantage.

✔ In declining industries in which market demand has leveled off or is falling, companies must tailor their price and nonprice strategies to the new competitive environment. They also need to manage industry capacity to prevent the emergence of capacity expansion problems.

✔ There are four main strategies a company can pursue when demand is falling: leadership, niche, har- vest, and divestment strategies. The choice of strategy is determined by the severity of industry decline and the company's strengths relative to the remaining pockets of demand.

DISCUSSION QUESTIONS

1. Why are industries fragmented? What are the main ways in which companies can turn a fragmented industry into a consolidated one?

2. What are the key problems involved in maintaining a competitive advantage in a growth industry environment? What are the dangers associated with being the leader?

3. Discuss how companies can use (a) product differentiation and (b) capacity control to manage rivalry and increase an industry's profitability.

Practicing Strategic Management

SMALL-GROUP EXERCISE
How to Keep the Hot Sauce Hot

Break up into groups of three to five people, and discuss the following scenario:

You are the managers of a company that has pioneered a new kind of hot sauce for chicken that has taken the market by storm. The hot sauce's differentiated appeal has been based on a unique combination of spices and packaging that allows you to charge a premium price. Within the last three years, your hot sauce has achieved a national reputation, and now major food companies such as Kraft and Nabisco, seeing the potential of this market segment, are beginning to introduce hot sauces of their own, imitating your product.

1. Describe the generic business-level strategy you are pursuing.

2. Describe the industry's environment in which you are competing.

3. What kinds of competitive tactics and maneuvers could you adopt to protect your generic strategy in this kind of environment?

4. What do you think is the best strategy for you to pursue in this situation?

EXPLORING THE WEB
Visiting Wal-Mart

Enter the Web site of retailer Wal-Mart (www.wal.mart.com/). Click on "Corporate Information," and then click on "Corporate Timeline." Study the events in Wal-Mart's timeline, and from them outline the way Wal-Mart's competitive strategy in the retailing industry has developed over time.

Search the Web for a company that has recently changed its competitive strategy in some way. What precipitated the change in its strategy? What were the strategy changes the company made?

ARTICLE FILE 7

Find examples of the ways in which a company or group of companies has adopted a competitive strategy to protect or enhance its business-level strategy.

STRATEGIC MANAGEMENT PROJECT
Module 7

This part of the project continues the analysis of your company's business-level strategy and considers how conditions in the industry's environment affect the company's competitive strategy.

1. In what kind of industry environment (for example, embryonic, mature) does your company operate? (Use the information from Strategic Management Project: Module 3 to answer this question.)

2. Discuss how your company has attempted to develop a competitive strategy to protect its business-level strategy. For example, if your company is operating in an embryonic industry, discuss the ways it has attempted to increase its competitive advantage over time. If it operates in a mature industry, discuss how it has tried to manage the five forces of industry competition.

3. What new strategies would you advise your company to pursue to increase its competitive advantage? For example, what kinds of strategy toward buyers or suppliers should it adopt? How should it attempt to differentiate its products in the future?

4. Based on this analysis, do you think your company will be able to maintain its competitive advantage in the future? Why or why not?

CLOSING CASE

The Goodyear Tire & Rubber Company

By the end of 1992 Goodyear Tire & Rubber, the largest tire manufacturer in the United States, posted a profit of more than $340 million on record sales of more than $11 billion. This was a far cry from the situation in 1991, when the company had a record loss. For a while it looked as if Goodyear, languishing under a debt of more than $3.7 billion, might go bankrupt. What altered its fortunes was a combination of a new CEO, who restored the company's competitive advantage, and a change in the nature of competition within the industry.

Throughout the 1980s Goodyear's sales had fallen as the company lost market share to its two main competitors, Michelin of France and Bridgestone of Japan. These companies had expanded rapidly into the United States, launching an aggressive strategy to build market share and penetrate the market. Their entry started a price war in the U.S. tire market, which especially hurt Goodyear because of the company's high costs. Goodyear also had a poor record in product innovation and had been slow to bring out new products that would attract its customers back. After the company's huge losses in 1991, its board of directors forced out the CEO, Tom Barrett, and replaced him with Stanley Gault, who had been the CEO of Rubbermaid. Gault immediately began to change the way Goodyear operated to restore its competitive advantage.

First, he embarked on a strategy of massively reducing operating costs. Gault's predecessor, Barrett, had started this process by investing more than $4 billion in the 1980s in new, more efficient plant and equipment and by decreasing the size of the work force by more than 20 percent. By 1991 output per worker had climbed 51 percent.[31] However, Gault took this process much further and began to slash costs everywhere. By example, he showed managers how to reduce costs. He began by eliminating limousines for top executives and replacing them with family sedans. He sold off three of the five corporate jets and eliminated the Goodyear blimp, based in Houston, Texas. He even removed most of the light bulbs from his office to demonstrate his commitment to lower costs. The other Goodyear managers followed his lead and systematically began their cost-cutting efforts, with the spectacular results previously noted.

To increase market share, Gault also worked to increase innovation, quality, and the speed at which the company introduced new products. Goodyear had had many tires in development for years, including one named the Aquatread, a tire that performed very well on wet road surfaces. However, it had been slow to bring them to the market. In 1991 Gault decided on a bold strategy: Goodyear would introduce four new tires at once, including the Aquatread. Each tire was directed at a different market segment. For example, the Aquatread was aimed at the safety-conscious consumer, whereas another tire was constructed to lower gas costs. These moves were very successful. Goodyear's new tires, which had higher profit margins than its older tires, restored customers' perceptions that the firm was a premium tire manufacturer, and sales of the new tires, particularly the Aquatread, surged. Indeed, Goodyear sold more than 1 million Aquatreads in one year, 20 percent more than its forecast. Gault's combined strategy of reducing costs and raising the differentiated appeal of the company's products paid off in the form of a huge increase in profits.

By 1991, the same year Goodyear recorded its record loss, U.S. tire manufacturers had grown weary of the rounds of price cutting and price wars that had plagued the industry and diminished their profits. Tire manufacturers started to support each other's attempts to keep prices up and avoid price cutting. They also began searching for new ways to compete that did not reduce the industry's profitability. One strategy they adopted was to develop new kinds of tires and aggressively market them to customers. Gault's strategy of developing innovative products coincided with this change in the industry from price to nonprice competition and helped promote Goodyear's turnaround and increased sales. Goodyear and its competitors have all benefited from their new strategy of nonprice competition, which has been maintained throughout the 1990s. In 1996 Goodyear introduced a new tire that has a lifetime warranty, and its profits continue to increase as it pioneers ever better kinds of tires.[32]

Case Discussion Questions

1. How did the nature of competition in the tire industry cause problems for Goodyear?

2. What strategies did Gault develop to turn the company around?

CHAPTER 8

Strategy in the Global Environment

Opening Case: IKEA

Overview

Profiting from Global Expansion

Pressures for Cost Reductions and Local Responsiveness

Strategic Choice

The Choice of Entry Mode

Global Strategic Alliances

Making Strategic Alliances Work

Closing Case: The Ford-Mazda Alliance

OPENING CASE

Originally established in the 1940s in Sweden by Ingvar Kamprad, IKEA has grown rapidly in recent years to become one of the world's largest retailers of home furnishings. In its initial push to expand globally, IKEA largely ignored the retailing rule that international success requires closely tailoring product lines to national tastes and preferences. Instead, IKEA stuck with the vision, articulated by Kamprad, that the company should sell a basic product range that is "typically Swedish" wherever it ventures in the world. The company also remained primarily production oriented; that is, the Swedish management and design group decided what it was going to sell and then presented it to the worldwide public, often with very little research as to what the public actually wanted. Moreover, the company emphasized its Swedish roots in its international advertising, even going as far as to insist on a "Swedish" blue and yellow color scheme for its stores.

Despite breaking some key rules of international retailing, the formula of selling Swedish-designed products

IKEA

in the same manner everywhere seemed to work. Between 1974 and 1994 IKEA expanded from a company with 10 stores, only 1 of which was outside Scandinavia, and annual revenues of $210 million, to a group with 125 stores in twenty-six countries and sales of close to $5 billion. In 1994 only 11 percent of its sales were generated in Sweden. Of the balance, 29.6 percent came from Germany, 42.5 percent from the rest of Western Europe, and 14.2 percent from North America. IKEA's expansion in North America is its most recent international venture.

The foundation of IKEA's success has been to offer consumers good value for money. IKEA's approach starts with a global network of suppliers, which now numbers 2,700 firms in sixty-seven countries. A supplier for IKEA gains long-term contracts, technical advice, and leased equipment from the company. In return, IKEA demands an exclusive contract and low prices. IKEA's designers work closely with suppliers to build savings into the products from the outset by designing products that can be produced at a low cost. IKEA displays its enormous range of more than 10,000 products in cheap out-of-town stores. It sells most of its furniture as knocked-down kits for customers to take home and assemble themselves. The firm reaps huge economies of scale from the size of each store and from the big production runs made possible by selling the same products all over the world. This strategy allows IKEA to match its rivals on quality but undercut them by up to 30 percent on price, while maintaining a healthy after-tax return on sales of around 7 percent.

This strategy worked well until 1985, when IKEA entered the North American market. Between 1985 and 1990 IKEA opened six stores in North America. However, unlike the company's stores across Europe, the new stores did not quickly become profitable. Instead, by 1990 it was clear that IKEA's North American operations were in trouble. IKEA's unapologetically Swedish products, which had sold so well across Europe, jarred with U.S. tastes and sometimes physiques. For example, Swedish beds were narrow and measured in centimeters. IKEA did not sell the matching bedroom suites that U.S. consumers liked. Its kitchen cupboards were too narrow for the large dinner plates needed for pizza. Its glasses were too small for a nation that added ice to everything. And the drawers in IKEA's bedroom chests were too

shallow for American consumers, who tend to store sweaters in them.

In 1990 the company's top management realized that if the company were going to succeed in North America, it would have to customize its product offerings. As a result, the company set about redesigning its product range. For example, the drawers on bedroom chests were designed to be two inches deeper, and sales immediately increased by 30 to 40 percent. IKEA now sells U.S.-style king- and queen-sized beds, measured in inches, and it sells them as part of complete bedroom suites. Currently it is redesigning its entire range of kitchen furniture and kitchenware to appeal better to U.S. tastes. The company has also boosted the amount of products being sourced locally from 15 percent in 1990 to 45 percent in 1994, a move that makes the company far less vulnerable to adverse movements in exchange rates.

This break with IKEA's traditional strategy has paid off. Between 1990 and 1994 IKEA's North American sales tripled to $480 million, and the company claims that it has been making a profit in North America since early 1993 (although it admits that profit margins are still lower in North America than in Europe). By 1995 the company had also expanded the number of North American stores to fifteen.[1]

OVERVIEW

In this chapter we look at the strategies companies adopt when they expand outside their domestic marketplace and start to compete on a global basis. One option is for companies to pursue the same basic strategy worldwide, which is referred to as a global strategy. This was the strategy adopted by IKEA during its initial expansion from Sweden into neighboring European nations. As we noted in the Opening Case, IKEA's strategy was initially very successful. Selling the same basic product the same way in every nation allowed the company to realize substantial cost savings from greater economies of scale. These cost savings were passed on to consumers in the form of lower prices, enabling IKEA to gain market share from competitors in each market in which it competed. However, IKEA's strategy started to unravel when it entered the North American market. To succeed in its newest marketplace, IKEA has found that it had to customize its product offerings to cater to the tastes and preferences of local consumers, becoming more locally responsive. While this helped IKEA boost sales in North America, the shorter production runs associated with such a strategy have also raised the costs of competing in the North American market and lowered IKEA's profit margins.

As we shall see, the desire to offer a standardized product worldwide, thereby realizing substantial economies of scale and building a cost-based competitive advantage, often conflicts with the need to customize products to the tastes and preference of consumers in different marketplaces, precisely because customization tends to raise costs. The tension between how much to standardize and how much to customize is one of the fundamental conflicts that global companies have to resolve. In this chapter we explore the nature of this conflict, and we suggest some guidelines that companies can use to identify the best strategy, given their resources and capabilities and the nature of the markets in which they compete. Toward this end, we consider the different strategies that companies use to compete in the global marketplace and discuss the advantages and disadvantages of each. In this chapter we also examine the different means that companies employ to enter foreign markets—including exporting, licensing, setting up a joint venture, and setting up a wholly owned subsidiary. The chapter closes with a discussion of the benefits and costs of entering into strategic alliances with global competitors. By the time you have completed this chapter, you will have a good understanding of the various strategic issues companies face when they decide to expand their operations outside of their home country.

PROFITING FROM GLOBAL EXPANSION

Expanding globally allows companies, large or small, to increase their profitability in ways not available to purely domestic enterprises. Companies that operate internationally can (1) earn a greater return from their distinctive competencies; (2) realize what we refer to as location economies by dispersing individual value creation activities to those locations where they can be performed most efficiently; and (3) ride down the experience curve ahead of competitors, thereby lowering the costs of value creation.

Transferring Distinctive Competencies

The concept of distinctive competencies was first considered in Chapter 4. *Distinctive competencies* are defined there as "unique strengths that allow a company to achieve superior efficiency, quality, innovation, or customer responsiveness." Such strengths typically find their expression in product offerings that other companies find difficult to match or imitate. Thus, distinctive competencies form the bedrock of a company's competitive advantage. They enable a company to lower the costs of value creation and/or to perform value creation activities in ways that lead to differentiation and premium pricing.

Companies with valuable distinctive competencies can often realize enormous returns by applying those competencies and the products they produce to foreign markets, where indigenous competitors lack similar competencies and products. For example, as described in Strategy in Action 8.1, McDonald's has expanded rapidly overseas in recent years to exploit its distinctive competencies in managing fast-food operations. These competencies have proved to be just as valuable in countries as diverse as France, Russia, China, Germany, and Brazil as they have been in the United States. Before McDonald's entry, none of these countries had U.S.-style fast-food chains, so McDonald's was bringing in unique skills and a unique product. The lack of indigenous competitors with similar competencies and products has greatly enhanced the profitability of this strategy for McDonald's.

In an earlier era U.S. companies such as Kellogg, Coca-Cola, H. J. Heinz, and Procter & Gamble expanded overseas to exploit their distinctive competencies in

It's a McWorld

During the 1980s McDonald's had to face the problem that after three decades of rapid growth, the U.S. fast-food market was beginning to show signs of market saturation. McDonald's response to the slowdown was to expand abroad rapidly. In 1980, 28 percent of the chain's new restaurant openings were abroad; in 1986 the figure was 40 percent; in 1990 it was close to 60 percent; and in 1994 it hit 66 percent. By 1994 the firm had 4,700 restaurants in seventy-two countries outside of the United States. Together they generated $3.4 billion (46 percent) of the firm's $7.4 billion in revenues. Moreover, McDonald's shows no signs of slowing down. Management notes that there is still only one McDonald's restaurant for every 600,000 people in the seventy-two foreign countries in which it currently does business. This compares to one McDonald's restaurant for every 25,000 people in the United States. The firm's plans call for this foreign expansion to continue at a rapid rate. In England, France, and Germany combined, the firm plans to open 500 more restaurants by 1997, increasing its number of restaurants in those countries by 37 percent. During the same period McDonald's is expected to double to 800 the number of its restaurants in the Caribbean, Mexico, Central America, and South America. The firm also

plans to enter another twnty-five to thirty countries by the end of the century.

One of the keys to the firm's successful foreign expansion is detailed planning. When McDonald's enters a foreign country, it does so only after very careful preparation. What happened in Poland is a typical pattern. Before McDonald's opened its first Polish restaurant in 1992, the firm spent eighteen months establishing essential contacts and getting to know the local culture. Locations, real estate, construction, suppliers, personnel, and legal and governmental relationships were all worked out in advance. In June 1992 a team of fifty employees from the United States, Russia, Germany, and Britain went to Poland to help with the opening of the first four resturants. One of their primary objectives was to hire and train local personnel. By mid 1994 all these employees except one had returned to their home country. They were replaced by Polish nationals who had been brought up to the skill level required to run a McDonald's operation.

Another key to the firm's international strategy is the export of the management skills (not just its fast-food products) that spurred its growth in the United States. McDonald's U.S. success was built on a formula of close relationships with suppliers, the power of na-

developing and marketing branded consumer products. These competencies and the resulting products, which were developed in the U.S. market during the 1950s and 1960s, yielded enormous returns when applied to European markets, where most indigenous competitors lacked similar marketing skills and products. Their near monopoly on consumer marketing skills allowed these U.S. companies to dominate many European consumer product markets during the 1960s and 1970s. Similarly, in the 1970s and 1980s many Japanese companies were expanding globally to exploit their distinctive competencies in production, materials management, and new product development—competencies that many of their indigenous U.S. and European competitors seemed to lack.

Realizing Location Economies

Location economies are those that arise from performing a value creation activity in the optimal location for that activity, wherever in the world that might be (transportation costs and trade barriers permitting). Locating a value creation activity in the optimal location for that activity can have one of two effects. It can (1) *lower* tionwide marketing, tight control over store-level operating procedures, and a franchising system that encourages entrepreneurial individual franchisees. Although this system has worked flawlessly in the United States, some modifications had to be made in other countries. One of the firm's biggest challenges has been to infuse each store with the same enthusiasm for the corporate culture and standardized operating procedures that have been the hallmark of its success in the United States. To aid in this task, in many countries McDonald's has enlisted the help of large partners through joint ventures. The partners play a key role in learning and transplanting the organization's values to local employees.

Foreign partners have also played a key role in helping McDonald's adapt its marketing methods and menu to local conditions. Although U.S.-style fast food remains the staple fare on the menu, local products have been added. In Brazil, for example, McDonald's sells a soft drink made from the guarana, an Amazonian berry. Patrons of McDonald's in Malaysia, Singapore, and Thailand savor milk shakes flavored with durian, a foul-smelling (to U.S. tastes, at least) fruit considered an aphrodisiac by the locals. In addition to their help in product adaptation, these partners can steer the firm away from potentially expensive marketing pitfalls. In Japan, for example, Den Fujita, president of McDonald's in Japan, avoided the suburban locations typical in the United States and stressed urban sites that consumers could walk to.

McDonald's biggest problem, however, has been to replicate its U.S. supply chain in other countries. McDonald's maintains very rigorous specifications for all the raw ingredients it uses, the key to its consistency and quality control. Its U.S. suppliers are fiercely loyal to McDonald's; they must be, because their fortunes are closely linked to those of McDonald's. Outside the United States, however, McDonald's has found suppliers far less willing to make the investments required to meet its specifications. In Britain, for example, McDonald's had problems getting local bakeries to produce the hamburger bun. After experiencing quality problems with two local bakeries, McDonald's built its own bakery to supply its stores there. In a more extreme case, when McDonald's decided to open a store in Russia, it found that local suppliers lacked the capability to produce goods of the quality it demanded. The firm was forced to integrate vertically through the local food industry on a heroic scale, importing potato seeds and bull semen and indirectly managing dairy farms, cattle ranches, and vegetable plots. It also had to construct the world's largest food-processing plant, at a cost of $40 million. The restaurant itself cost only $4.5 million.[2]

the costs of value creation, helping the company achieve a low-cost position or (2) enable a company to differentiate its product offering and charge a premium price. Thus, efforts to realize location economies are consistent with the generic business-level strategies of low cost and differentiation. In theory, a company that realizes location economies by dispersing each of its value creation activities to its optimal location should have a competitive advantage over a company that bases all its value creation activities at a single location. It should be better able to differentiate its product offering and lower its cost structure than its single-location competitor. In a world in which competitive pressures are increasing, such a strategy may well become an imperative for survival.

For an example of location economies, consider Swan Optical, a U.S.-based manufacturer and distributor of eyewear. With sales revenues only in the $20 million to $30 million range, Swan is hardly a giant, yet it manufactures its eyewear in low-cost factories in Hong Kong and China that it jointly owns with a Hong Kong-based partner. Swan also has a minority stake in eyewear design houses in Japan, France, and Italy. What we see in the Swan Optical story is a company that has dispersed its manufacturing and design processes to different locations around the world to take advantage of the favorable skill base and cost structure found in other countries. Investments in Hong Kong and subsequently China have helped Swan to lower its cost structure, while investments in Japan, France, and Italy have helped it to produce differentiated designer eyewear for which it can charge a premium price. The critical point is that by dispersing its manufacturing and design activities in this manner, Swan has been able to establish a competitive advantage for itself in the global marketplace for eyewear.[3]

For another example, consider Boeing's strategy for manufacturing its new commercial jet aircraft, the 777. The 777 uses 132,500 engineered parts produced around the world by 545 different suppliers. For example, 8 Japanese suppliers make parts of the fuselage, doors, and wings; a supplier in Singapore makes the doors for the nose landing gear; and 3 suppliers in Italy manufacture wing flaps. Part of Boeing's rationale for outsourcing so much production to foreign suppliers is that these various suppliers are the best in the world at performing their particular activity when measured on the basis of cost and quality. Therefore, the result of having foreign suppliers build specific parts is a better final product and a competitive advantage for Boeing in the global marketplace.[4]

Moving Down the Experience Curve

As you recall from Chapter 5, the experience curve refers to the systematic decrease in production costs that has been observed to occur over the life of a product. In Chapter 5 we point out that learning effects and economies of scale underlie the experience curve and that moving down the experience curve allows a company to lower the costs of value creation. The company that moves down the experience curve most rapidly will have a cost advantage over its competitors. Moving down the experience curve is, therefore, consistent with the business-level strategy of cost leadership.

Many of the underlying sources of experience-based cost economies are to be found at the plant level. This is true of most learning effects and of the economies of scale derived from spreading the fixed costs of building productive capacity over a large output. It follows that the key to riding down the experience curve as rapidly as possible is to increase the accumulated volume *produced by a plant* as quickly as possible. Since global markets are larger than domestic markets, companies that serve a global market *from a single location* are likely to build up accumulated volume faster than companies that focus primarily on serving their home market or on serving multiple markets from multiple production locations. Thus, serving a global market from a single location is consistent with moving down the experience curve and establishing a low-cost position.

In addition, to get down the experience curve quickly, companies need to price and market very aggressively so that demand expands rapidly. They also need to build production capacity capable of serving a global market. Another point to bear in mind is that the cost advantages of serving the world market from a single location will be all the more significant if that location is also the optimal one for performing that value creation activity; that is, if the company is *simultaneously* realizing cost economies from experience-curve effects *and* from location economies.

One company that has excelled in the pursuit of such a strategy is Matsushita. Along with Sony and Philips NV, in the 1970s Matsushita was in the race to develop a commercially viable VCR. Although Matsushita initially lagged behind both Philips and Sony, it was ultimately able to get its VHS format accepted as the world standard and to reap enormous experience- curve cost economies in the process. This cost advantage subsequently constituted a formidable barrier to new competition. Matsushita's strategy was to build global volume as rapidly as possible. To ensure that it could accommodate worldwide demand, it increased production capacity thirty-threefold, from 205,000 units in 1977 to 6.8 million units by 1984. By serving the world market from a single location in Japan, Matsushita was able to realize significant learning effects and economies of scale. These allowed it to drop its prices by 50 percent within five years of selling its first VHS-formatted VCR. As a result, by 1983 Matsushita was the world's major VCR producer, accounting for approximately 45 percent of world production and enjoying a significant cost advantage over its major competitors. The next largest company, Hitachi, accounted for only 11.1 percent of world production in 1983.[5]

Global Expansion and Business-Level Strategy

It is important to recognize that the different ways of profiting from global expansion are all linked to the generic *business-level strategies* of cost leadership and differentiation. Companies that transfer distinctive competencies to other countries are trying to realize greater gains from their low-cost or differentiation-based competitive advantage. Companies such as Swan Optical that attempt to realize location economies are trying to lower their costs and/or increase value added so that they can better differentiate themselves from their competitors. Furthermore, companies that serve a global market in order to ride more quickly down the experience curve are trying to build a competitive advantage based on low cost, as Matsushita did with its VHS-formatted VCRs.

PRESSURES FOR COST REDUCTIONS AND LOCAL RESPONSIVENESS

Companies that compete in the global marketplace typically face two types of competitive pressures: *pressures for cost reductions* and *pressures to be locally responsive* (see Figure 8.1).[6] As we noted with regard to IKEA, these competitive pressures place conflicting demands on a company. Responding to pressures for cost reductions requires that a company try to minimize its unit costs. To attain this goal, a company may have to base its productive activities at the most favorable low-cost location, wherever in the world that might be. It may also have to offer a standardized product to the global marketplace in order to ride down the experience curve as quickly as possible. On the other hand, responding to pressures to be locally responsive requires that a company differentiate its product offering and marketing strategy from country to country in an effort to accommodate the diverse demands arising from national differences in consumers' tastes and preferences, business practices, distribution channels, competitive conditions, and governmental policies. Because differentiation across countries can involve significant duplication and a lack of product standardization, it may raise costs.

While some companies, such as company A in Figure 8.1, face high pressures for cost reductions and low pressures for local responsiveness and others, such as

FIGURE 8.1

Pressures for Cost
Reduction and Local
Responsiveness

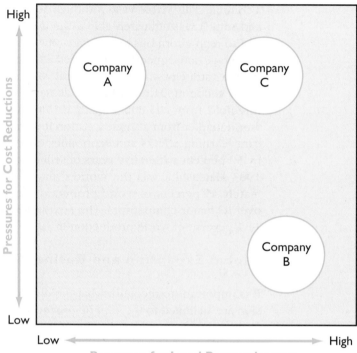

company B, face low pressures for cost reductions and high pressures for local responsiveness, many companies are in the position of company C. They face high pressures for *both* cost reductions and local responsiveness. Dealing with these conflicting and contradictory pressures is a difficult strategic challenge for a company, primarily because being locally responsive tends to raise costs. In the remainder of this section, we consider the sources of pressures for cost reductions and local responsiveness. In the next section we examine the strategies that companies adopt in order to deal with these pressures.

Pressures for Cost Reductions

Increasingly, international companies must cope with pressures for cost reductions. Pressures for cost reductions can be particularly intense in industries producing commodity-type products, for which meaningful differentiation on nonprice factors is difficult and price is the main competitive weapon. Products that serve universal needs tend to fall into this category. Universal needs exist when the tastes and preferences of consumers in different nations are similar, if not identical. This obviously applies to conventional commodity products such as bulk chemicals, petroleum, steel, sugar, and the like. It also tends to be true for many industrial and consumer products, for instance, hand-held calculators, semiconductor chips, and personal computers. Pressures for cost reductions are also intense in industries in which major competitors are based in low-cost locations, in which there is persistent excess capacity, and in which consumers are powerful and face low switching costs. Many commentators have also argued that the liberalization of the world trade and investment environment in recent decades has generally increased cost pressures by facilitating greater international competition.[7]

Pressures for cost reductions have been intense in the global tire industry in recent years. Tires are essentially a commodity product for which differentiation is difficult and price is the main competitive weapon. The major buyers of tires, automobile companies, are powerful and face low switching costs, so they have been playing tire companies off against each other in an attempt to get lower prices. Furthermore, the decline in global demand for automobiles in the early 1990s has created a serious situation of excess capacity in the tire industry, with as much as 25 percent of world capacity standing idle. The result has been a worldwide price war, with almost all tire companies suffering heavy losses in the early 1990s. In response to the cost pressures, most tire companies are now trying to rationalize their operations in a way consistent with the attainment of a low-cost position. They are moving production to low-cost facilities and offering globally standardized products in an attempt to realize experience-curve economies.[8]

Pressures for Local Responsiveness

Pressures for local responsiveness arise from differences in consumers' tastes and preferences, differences in infrastructure and traditional practices, differences in distribution channels, and the demands of the host government.

Differences in Consumers' Tastes and Preferences Strong pressures for local responsiveness emerge when consumers' tastes and preferences differ significantly between countries, as they may for historic or cultural reasons. In such cases, the product and marketing messages have to be customized to appeal to the tastes and preferences of local consumers. This typically creates pressures for the delegation of production and marketing functions to national subsidiaries.

In the automobile industry, for example, there is a strong demand among North American consumers for pickup trucks. This is particularly true in the South and West, where many families have a pickup truck as a second or third car. In contrast, in European countries pickup trucks are seen purely as utility vehicles and are purchased primarily by companies rather than individuals. Consequently, the marketing message needs to be tailored to the different nature of demand in North America and Europe. For another example, consider again the story of IKEA. Initially, IKEA's stores in North America failed to meet expectations precisely because the company failed to appreciate that the tastes and preferences of North American consumers were different from those of Western European consumers.

As a counterpoint, in a now famous article, Professor Theodore Levitt of the Harvard Business School argued that consumers' demands for local customization are on the decline worldwide.[9] According to Levitt, modern communications and transport technologies have created the conditions for a convergence of the tastes and preferences of consumers from different nations. The result is the emergence of enormous global markets for standardized consumer products. Levitt cites worldwide acceptance of McDonald's hamburgers, Coca-Cola, Levi Strauss blue jeans, and Sony television sets, all of which are sold as standardized products, as evidence of the increasing homogeneity of the global marketplace.

Levitt's argument, however, has been characterized as extreme by many commentators. For example, Christopher Bartlett and Sumantra Ghoshal have observed that in the consumer electronics industry buyers reacted to an overdose of standardized global products by showing a renewed preference for products that are differentiated to local conditions.[10] They note that Amstrad, the fast-growing British computer and electronics company, got its start by recognizing and responding to the needs of local consumers. Amstrad captured a major share of the British audioplayer market by moving away from the standardized inexpensive music centers marketed by global companies such as Sony and Matsushita. Amstrad's product was encased in teak rather than metal cabinets, with a control panel tailor-made to appeal to British consumers' preferences. In response, Matsushita had to reverse its earlier bias toward standardized global design and place more emphasis on local customization.

Differences in Infrastructure and/or Traditional Practices   Pressures for local responsiveness arise from differences in infrastructure and/or traditional practices among countries, creating a need to customize products accordingly. Fulfilling this need may require the delegation of manufacturing and production functions to foreign subsidiaries. For example, in North America consumer electric systems are based on 110 volts, whereas in some European countries 240-volt systems are standard. Thus, domestic electric appliances have to be customized to take this difference in infrastructure into account. Traditional practices also often vary across nations. For example, in Britain people drive on the left-hand side of the road, creating a demand for right-hand-drive cars, whereas in France people drive on the right-hand side of the road and therefore want left-hand-drive cars. Obviously, automobiles have to be customized to take this difference in traditional practice into account.

Differences in Distribution Channels   A company's marketing strategies may have to be responsive to differences in distribution channels among countries. This may necessitate the delegation of marketing functions to national subsidiaries. In the pharmaceutical industry, for example, the British and Japanese distribution system is radically different from the U.S. system. British and Japanese doctors do not accept or respond favorably to a U.S.-style, high-pressure sales force. Thus, pharmaceutical companies have to adopt different marketing practices in Britain and Japan compared with those in the United States; they have to switch from a hard sell to a soft sell.

Demands of Host Government   Economic and political demands imposed by host governments may necessitate a degree of local responsiveness. For example, the politics of health care around the world requires that pharmaceutical companies manufacture in multiple locations. Pharmaceutical companies are subject to local clinical testing, registration procedures, and pricing restrictions, all of which make it necessary that the manufacturing and marketing of a drug should meet local requirements. Moreover, since governments and governmental agencies control a significant proportion of the health care budget in most countries, they are in a powerful position to demand a high level of local responsiveness. More generally, threats of protectionism, economic nationalism, and local content rules (which dictate that a certain percentage of a product should be manufactured locally) all dictate that international businesses manufacture locally. Part of the motivation for

Japanese auto companies setting up U.S. production, for example, is to counter the threat of protectionism increasingly voiced by the U.S. Congress.

Implications Pressures for local responsiveness imply that it may not be possible for a company to realize the full benefits from experience-curve effects and location economies. For example, it may not be possible to serve the global marketplace from a single low-cost location, producing a globally standardized product and marketing it worldwide to achieve experience-curve cost economies. In practice, the need to customize the product offering to local conditions may work against the implementation of such a strategy. Automobile companies, for instance, have found that Japanese, U.S., and European consumers demand different kinds of cars, which means customizing products for local markets. In response, companies such as Honda, Ford, and Toyota are pursuing a strategy of establishing top-to-bottom design and production facilities in each of these regions so that they can better serve local demands. Although such customization brings benefits, it also limits the ability of a company to realize significant experience-curve cost economies and location economies. In addition, pressures for local responsiveness imply that it may not be possible to transfer wholesale from one nation to another the skills and products associated with a company's distinctive competencies. Concessions often have to be made to local conditions. For an example, look again at Strategy in Action 8.1. It describes some of the concessions to local conditions that McDonald's has had to make in different national markets.

STRATEGIC CHOICE

Companies use four basic strategies to enter and compete in the international environment: an international strategy, a multidomestic strategy, a global strategy, and a transnational strategy.[11] Each of these strategies has its advantages and disadvantages. The appropriateness of each varies with the extent of pressures for cost reductions and local responsiveness. Figure 8.2 illustrates when each of these strategies is most appropriate. In this section we describe each strategy, identify when it is appropriate, and discuss its pros and cons.

International Strategy

Companies that pursue an international strategy try to create value by transferring valuable skills and products to foreign markets where indigenous competitors lack those skills and products. Most international companies have created value by transferring differentiated product offerings developed at home to new markets overseas. Accordingly, they tend to centralize product development functions (for instance, R&D) at home. However, they also tend to establish manufacturing and marketing functions in each major country in which they do business. Although they may undertake some local customization of product offering and marketing strategy, this tends to be rather limited in scope. Ultimately, in most international companies the head office retains tight control over marketing and product strategy.

International companies include such enterprises as Toys 'R' Us, McDonald's, IBM, Kellogg, and Procter & Gamble. Indeed, the majority of U.S. companies that

FIGURE 8.2

Four Basic Strategies

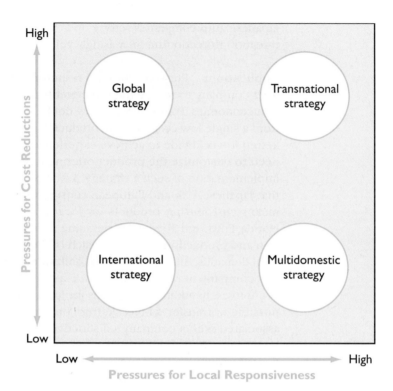

expanded abroad in the 1950s and 1960s fall into this category. As an example, consider Procter & Gamble, which is profiled in Strategy in Action 8.2. Traditionally, Procter & Gamble has had production facilities in all its major markets outside of the United States, including Britain, Germany, and Japan. These facilities, however, manufactured differentiated products that had been developed by the U.S. parent company and that were often marketed using the marketing message developed in the United States. Historically at least, local responsiveness on the part of Procter & Gamble has been quite limited, which is now causing problems, as Strategy in Action 8.2 explains.

An international strategy makes sense if a company has a valuable distinctive competency that indigenous competitors in foreign markets lack and if the company faces relatively weak pressures for local responsiveness and cost reductions. In such circumstances, an international strategy can be very profitable. However, when pressures for local responsiveness are high, companies pursuing this strategy lose out to companies that place a greater emphasis on customizing the product offering and market strategy to local conditions. Moreover, because of the duplication of manufacturing facilities, companies that pursue an international strategy tend to incur high operating costs. Hence, this strategy is often inappropriate in industries in which cost pressures are high.

Multidomestic Strategy

Companies pursuing a multidomestic strategy orient themselves toward achieving maximum local responsiveness. As with companies pursuing an international strategy, they tend to transfer skills and products developed at home to foreign markets. However, unlike international companies, multidomestic ones extensively customize both their product offering and their marketing strategy to different national conditions. Consistent with this approach, they also tend to establish a complete set of value creation activities—including production, marketing, and R&D—in each major national market in which they do business. As a result, they generally cannot realize value from experience-curve effects and location economies and, therefore, often have a high cost structure.

A multidomestic strategy makes most sense when there are high pressures for local responsiveness and low pressures for cost reductions. The high cost structure associated with the duplication of production facilities makes this strategy inappropriate in industries in which cost pressures are intense. Another weakness of this strategy is that many multidomestic companies have developed into decentralized federations in which each national subsidiary functions in a largely autonomous manner. Consequently, after a time they begin to lose the ability to transfer the skills and products derived from distinctive competencies to their various national subsidiaries around the world. In a famous case that illustrates the problems this can cause, the failure of Philips NV to establish its V2000 VCR format as the dominant design in the VCR industry during the late 1970s, as opposed to Matsushita's VHS format, was due to the refusal of its U.S. subsidiary company to adopt the V2000 format. Instead, the subsidiary bought VCRs produced by Matsushita and put its own label on them.

Global Strategy

Companies that pursue a global strategy focus on increasing profitability by reaping the cost reductions that come from experience-curve effects and location economies. That is, they are pursuing a low-cost strategy. The production, marketing, and R&D activities of companies pursuing a global strategy are concentrated in a few favorable locations. Global companies tend not to customize their product offering and marketing strategy to local conditions. This is because customization raises costs since it involves shorter production runs and the duplication of functions. Instead, global companies prefer to market a standardized product worldwide so that they can reap the maximum benefits from the economies of scale that underlie the experience curve. They also tend to use their cost advantage to support aggressive pricing in world markets. Prior to its strategic shift in North America, IKEA provides an example of a retailing company that pursued a global strategy (see Opening Case).

This strategy makes most sense in those cases in which there are strong pressures for cost reductions and where demands for local responsiveness are minimal. Increasingly, these conditions prevail in many industrial goods industries. In the semiconductor industry, for example, global standards have emerged, creating enormous demands for standardized global products. Accordingly, companies such as Intel, Texas Instruments, and Motorola all pursue a global strategy. However, as noted earlier, these conditions are not found in many consumer goods markets, where demands for local responsiveness remain high (as in the markets for audio players, automobiles, and processed food products). The strategy is inappropriate when demands for local responsiveness are high.

Transnational Strategy

Christopher Bartlett and Sumantra Ghoshal argue that in today's environment, competitive conditions are so intense that in order to survive in the global marketplace companies *must exploit experience-based cost economies and location economies, transfer distinctive competencies within the company, and at the same*

8.2   STRATEGY *in* ACTION

Procter & Gamble

Procter & Gamble (P&G), the large U.S. consumer products company, has a well-earned reputation as one of the world's best marketers. With more than eighty major brands, P&G generates more than $20 billion in revenues worldwide. Together with Unilever, P&G is a dominant global force in laundry detergents, cleaning products, and personal-care products. P&G expanded abroad in the post-World War II years by pursuing an international strategy that transferred brands and marketing policies developed in the United States to Western Europe, initially with considerable success. During the next thirty years, this policy resulted in the development of a classic international firm in which new product development and marketing strategies were pioneered in the United States and only then transferred to other countries. Although some adaptation of marketing policies to accommodate country differences was pursued, by and large this adaptation was fairly minimal.

The first signs that this strategy was flawed began to emerge in the 1970s, when P&G suffered a number of major setbacks in Japan. By 1985, after thirteen years in Japan, P&G was still losing $40 million a year there.

After initially introducing disposable diapers into Japan and at one time commanding an 80 percent share of the market, by the early 1980s P&G had seen its share slip to a miserable 8 percent. In P&G's place, three major Japanese consumer products firms dominated the market. P&G's problem was that its diapers, developed in the United States, were too bulky for the tastes of Japanese consumers. With this in mind, the Japanese consumer products firm, Kao, developed a line of trim-fit diapers that appealed more to the tastes of Japanese consumers. Kao supported the introduction of its product with a marketing blitz. The company was quickly rewarded with a 30 percent share of the market. As for P&G, only belatedly did it realize that it had to modify its diapers to accommodate the tastes of Japanese consumers. Now the company has increased its share of the Japanese market to 30 percent. Moreover, in an example of global learning, P&G's trim-fit diapers, originally developed for the Japanese market, have now become a bestseller in the United States.

P&G's experience with disposable diapers in Japan prompted the company to rethink its new product development and marketing philosophy. The company has

time pay attention to pressures for local responsiveness.[12] Moreover, they note that in the modern multinational enterprise, distinctive competencies do not reside just in the home country but can develop in any of the company's worldwide operations. Thus, they maintain that the flow of skills and product offerings should not be all one way, from home company to foreign subsidiary, as in the case of companies pursuing an international strategy. Rather, the flow should also be from foreign subsidiary to home country, and from foreign subsidiary to foreign subsidiary, a process Bartlett and Ghoshal refer to as **global learning**. They term the strategy pursued by companies that are trying to achieve all of these objectives simultaneously a **transnational strategy**.

A transnational strategy makes sense when a company faces high pressures for cost reductions and high pressures for local responsiveness. In essence, *companies that pursue a transnational strategy are trying to achieve low-cost and differentiation advantages simultaneously.* As attractive as this sounds, in practice it is a difficult strategy to pursue. As mentioned earlier, pressures for local responsiveness and cost reductions place conflicting demands on a company. Being locally responsive raises costs, which obviously makes cost reductions difficult to achieve. How, then, can a company effectively pursue a transnational strategy?

now admitted that its U.S.-centered way of doing business will no longer work. Since the late 1980s P&G has been attempting to delegate far more responsibility for new product development and marketing strategy to its major subsidiary firms in Japan and Europe. The result has been the creation of a company that is more responsive to local differences in consumers' tastes and preferences and more willing to admit that good new products can be developed outside the United States.

Despite the apparent changes at P&G, it is still not clear that P&G has achieved the revolution in thinking that is required to alter its long-established practices. P&G's recent venture into the Polish shampoo market perhaps illustrates that the company still has some way to go. In the summer of 1991, P&G entered the Polish market with its Vidal Sasson Wash & Go, an all-in-one shampoo and conditioner that is a bestseller in the United States and Europe. The product launch was supported by a U.S.-style marketing blitz on a scale never before seen in Poland. At first the campaign seemed to be working, as P&G captured more than 30 percent of the market for shampoos in Poland, but in early 1992 sales suddenly plummeted. Then came the rumors—Wash & Go caused dandruff and hair loss—allegations P&G has strenuously denied. Next came the jokes. One

doing the rounds in Poland runs as follows: "I washed my car with Wash & Go, and the tires went bald." When President Lech Walesa proposed earlier that year that he also become prime minister, critics derided the idea as a "two in one solution, just like Wash & Go."

Where did P&G go wrong? The most common theory is that it promoted Wash & Go too hard in a country that has little enthusiasm for brash American-style advertising. A poll by Pentor, a private market research company in Warsaw, found that almost three times as many Poles disliked P&G's commercials as liked them. Pentor also argues that the high-profile marketing campaign backfired because years of Communist Party propaganda have led Polish consumers to suspect that advertising is simply a way to shift goods that nobody wants. Some also believe that Wash & Go, which was developed for U.S. consumers who shampoo daily, was far too sophisticated for Polish consumers who are less obsessed with personal hygiene. Underlying all these criticisms seems to be the idea that P&G was once again stumbling because it had transferred a product and marketing strategy wholesale from the United States to another country without modification to accommodate the tastes and preferences of local consumers.[13]

Some clues can be derived from the case of Caterpillar. The need to compete with low-cost competitors such as Komatsu of Japan has forced Caterpillar to look for greater cost economies. However, variations in construction practices and government regulations across countries mean that Caterpillar also has to be responsive to local demands. Therefore, as illustrated in Figure 8.3, Caterpillar confronts significant pressures for cost reductions and for local responsiveness.

To deal with cost pressures, Caterpillar redesigned its products to use many identical components and invested in a few large-scale component manufacturing facilities, sited at favorable locations, to fill global demand and realize economies of scale. At the same time, the company augments the centralized manufacturing of components with assembly plants in each of its major global markets. At these plants, Caterpillar adds local product features, tailoring the finished product to local needs. In this way Caterpillar is able to realize many of the benefits of global manufacturing and react to pressures for local responsiveness by differentiating its product among national markets.[14]

Unilever provides another example. Once a company that used a classic multidomestic strategy, in recent years Unilever has had to shift more toward using a transnational strategy. A rise in low-cost competition, which increased cost

FIGURE 8.3
● ● ● ● ● ● ● ● ● ● ●

Cost Pressures and
Pressures for Local
Responsiveness Facing
Caterpillar

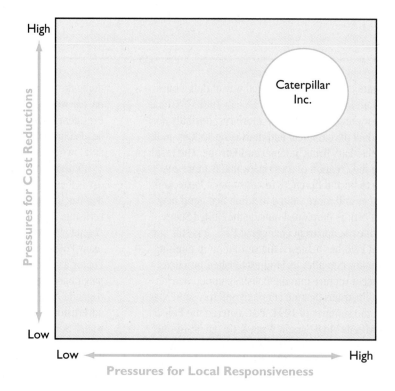

pressures, has forced Unilever to look for ways of rationalizing its detergents business. During the 1980s Unilever had seventeen different and largely self-contained detergents operations in Europe alone, an enormous duplication in terms of assets and marketing. Moreover, because Unilever was so fragmented, it could take as long as four years for the company to introduce a new product across Europe. Now Unilever is trying to weld its European operation into a single entity, with detergents manufactured in a handful of cost-efficient plants and with standard packaging and advertising used across Europe. According to the company's estimates, the result could be an annual cost saving of more than $200 million. Unilever recognizes, however, that because of national differences in distribution channels and brand awareness, it must still remain locally responsive, even as it strives to realize economies from consolidating production and marketing at the optimal locations.[15]

Despite such examples as Caterpillar and Unilever, Bartlett and Ghoshal admit that building an organization capable of supporting a transnational strategic posture is a complex and difficult task. The core of the problem is that simultaneously trying to achieve cost efficiencies, global learning, and local responsiveness places contradictory demands on an organization. Exactly how a company can deal with the dilemmas posed by such difficult organizational issues is a topic that we return to and discuss in more detail in Chapter 13, where we examine the structure of international business. For now it is important to note that the organizational problems associated with pursuing what are essentially conflicting objectives constitute a major impediment to implementing a transnational strategy. Companies that

TABLE 8.1
. . . .

The Advantages and Disadvantages of Different Strategies for Competing Globally

Strategy	Advantages	Disadvantages
International	• Transfer of distinctive competencies to foreign markets	• Lack of local responsiveness • Inability to realize location economies • Failure to exploit experience-curve effects
Multidomestic	• Ability to customize product offerings and marketing in accordance with local responsiveness	• Inability to realize location economies • Failure to exploit experience-curve effects • Failure to transfer distinctive competencies to foreign markets
Global	• Ability to exploit experience-curve effects • Ability to exploit location economies	• Lack of local responsiveness
Transnational	• Ability to exploit experience-curve effects • Ability to exploit location economies • Ability to customize product offerings and marketing in accordance with local responsiveness • Reaping benefits of global learning	• Difficulties in implementation because of organizational problems

attempt to pursue a transnational strategy can become bogged down in an organizational morass that only leads to inefficiencies.

It might also be noted that, by presenting it as the only viable strategy, Bartlett and Ghoshal may be overstating the case for using a transnational strategy. Although doubtless in some industries the company that can adopt such a strategy will have a competitive advantage, in other industries global, multidomestic, and international strategies remain viable. In the global semiconductor industry, for example, pressures for local customization are minimal and competition is purely a cost game, making a global strategy optimal. Indeed, this is the case in many industrial goods markets in which the product serves universal needs. On the other hand, the argument can be made that to compete in certain consumer goods markets, such as the consumer electronics industry, a company has to try to adopt a transnational strategy.

Summary
. . . .

The advantages and disadvantages of each of these four strategies are summarized in Table 8.1. Although a transnational strategy appears to offer the most advantages, it should not be forgotten that implementing it raises difficult organizational issues. More generally, as already shown in Figure 8.2, the appropriateness of each strategy depends on the relative strength of pressures for cost reductions and for local responsiveness.

THE CHOICE OF ENTRY MODE

Considering entry into a foreign market raises the question of the best mode of such entry. There are five main choices: exporting, licensing, franchising, entering into a joint venture with a host country company, and setting up a wholly owned subsidiary in the host country. Each entry mode has its advantages and disadvantages, and managers must weigh these carefully when deciding which mode to use.[16]

Exporting

Most manufacturing companies begin their global expansion as exporters and only later switch to one of the other modes for serving a foreign market. Exporting has two distinct advantages. First, it avoids the costs of establishing manufacturing operations in the host country, which are often substantial. Second, it may be consistent with realizing experience-curve cost economies and location economies. By manufacturing the product in a centralized location and then exporting it to other national markets, the company may be able to realize substantial economies of scale from its global sales volume. That is how Sony came to dominate the global television market, how Matsushita came to dominate the VCR market, and how many Japanese auto companies originally made inroads into the U.S. auto market.

On the other hand, there are a number of drawbacks to exporting. First, exporting from the company's *home* base may not be appropriate if there are lower-cost locations for manufacturing the product abroad (that is, if the company can realize location economies by moving production elsewhere). Thus, particularly in the case of a company pursuing a global or transnational strategy, it may pay to manufacture in a location where conditions are most favorable from a value creation perspective and then to export from that location to the rest of the globe. This, of course, is not so much an argument against exporting as an argument against exporting from the company's *home* country. For example, many U.S. electronics companies have moved some of their manufacturing to Asia because low-cost but highly skilled labor is available there. They export from that location to the rest of the globe, including the United States.

A second drawback is that high transport costs can make exporting uneconomical, particularly in the case of bulk products. One way of getting around this problem is to manufacture bulk products on a regional basis. Such a strategy enables the company to realize some economies from large-scale production and at the same time limit transport costs. Thus, many multinational chemical companies manufacture their products on a regional basis, serving several countries in a region from one facility.

Third, tariff barriers can make exporting uneconomical, and the threat to impose tariff barriers by the government of a country the company is exporting to can make the strategy very risky. Indeed, the implicit threat from Congress to impose tariffs on Japanese cars imported into the United States led directly to the decision by many Japanese auto companies to set up manufacturing plants in the United States.

Finally, a common practice among companies that are just beginning to export also poses risks. A company may delegate marketing activities in each country in which it does business to a local agent, but there is no guarantee that the agent will act in the company's best interest. Often foreign agents also carry the products of competing companies and thus have divided loyalties. Consequently, they may not do as good a job as the company would do if it managed marketing itself. One way to solve this problem is to set up a wholly owned subsidiary in the host country to handle local marketing. By so doing, the company can both reap the cost advantages that arise from manufacturing the product in a single location and exercise tight control over marketing strategy in the host country.

Licensing

International licensing is an arrangement whereby a foreign licensee buys the rights to produce a company's product in the licensee's country for a negotiated fee (normally, royalty payments on the number of units sold) The licensee then puts up most of the capital necessary to get the overseas operation going.[17]

The advantage of licensing is that the company does not have to b ar the development costs and risks associated with opening up a foreign market. Licensing, therefore, can be a very attractive option for companies that lack the capital to develop operations overseas. It can also be an attractive option for companies that are unwilling to commit substantial financial resources to an unfamiliar or politically volatile foreign market in which risks are particularly high.

Licensing has three serious drawbacks, however. First, it does not give a company the tight control over manufacturing, marketing, and strategic functions in foreign countries that it needs to have in order to realize experience-curve cost economies and location economies, as companies pursuing both global and transnational strategies try to do. Each licensee typically sets up its own manufacturing operations. Hence, the company stands little chance of realizing experience-curve cost economies and location economies by manufacturing its product in a centralized location. When these economies are likely to be important, lic nsing may not be the best way to expand overseas.

Second, competing in a global marketplace may make it necessary for a company to coordinate strategic moves across countries so that the profits earned in one country can be used to support competitive attacks in another. Licensing, by its very nature, severely limits a company's ability to coordinate strategy in this way. A licensee is unlikely to let a multinational company take its profits (beyond those due in the form of royalty payments) and use them to support an entirely different licensee operating in another country.

A third problem with licensing is the risk associated with licensing technological know-how to foreign companies. For many multinational companies, technological know-how forms the basis of their competitive advantage, and they would want to maintain control over the use to which it is put. By licensing its technology, a company can quickly lose control over it. RCA, for instance, once licensed its color television technology to a number of Japanese companies. The Japanese companies quickly assimilated RCA's technology and then used it to enter the U.S. market. Now the Japanese have a bigger share of the U.S. market than the RCA brand. Similar concerns surfaced over the 1989 decision by Congress to allow Japanese companies to produce the advanced FSX fighter under license from McDonnell Douglas. Critics of this decision fear that the Japanese will use the FSX technology to support the development of a commercial airline industry that will compete with Boeing and McDonnell Douglas in the global marketplace.

On the other hand, it is worth noting that there are ways to reduce this risk. One is to enter into a cross-licensing agreement with a foreign firm. Under a **cross-licensing agreement**, a firm might license some valuable intangible property to a foreign partner, but in addition to a royalty payment, the firm might also request that the foreign partner license some of its valuable know-how to the firm. Such agreements are reckoned to reduce the risks associated with licensing technological know-how, since the licensee realizes that if it violates the spirit of a licensing contract (by using the knowledge obtained to compete directly with the licensor), the licensor can do the same to it. Put differently, cross-licensing agreements enable firms to hold each other "hostage," which thereby reduces the probability that they will behave opportunistically toward each other.[18] Such cross-licensing agreements are increasingly common in high-technology industries. For example, the U.S. biotechnology firm Amgen has licensed one of its key drugs, Nuprogene, to Kirin, the Japanese pharmaceutical company. The license gives Kirin the right to sell Nuprogene in Japan. In return, Amgen receives a royalty payment, and through a licensing agreement it has the right to sell certain of Kirin's products in the United States.

Franchising

Whereas licensing is a strategy pursued primarily by manufacturing companies, franchising, which resembles it in some respects, is a strategy employed chiefly by service companies. For example, both McDonald's and Hilton Hotels have expanded internationally by franchising.[19] In franchising, the company sells to franchisees limited rights to use its brand name in return for a lump-sum payment and a share of the franchisee's profits. However, unlike the parties to most licensing agreements, franchisees have to agree to abide by strict rules as to how they do business. When McDonald's enters into a franchising agreement with a foreign company, it expects that company to run its restaurants in the same way that McDonald's restaurants elsewhere in the world are run.

The advantages of franchising are similar to those of licensing. Specifically, the franchiser does not have to bear the development costs and risks of opening up a foreign market on its own, for the franchisee typically assumes those costs and risks. Thus, using a franchising strategy, a service company can build up a global presence quickly and at a low cost.

The disadvantages, however, are less pronounced than in the case of licensing. Since franchising is a strategy used by service companies, a franchiser does not have to consider the need to coordinate manufacturing in order to achieve experience-curve effects and location economies. Nevertheless, franchising may inhibit a company's ability to achieve global strategic coordination.

A more significant disadvantage of franchising is the lack of quality control. The foundation of franchising arrangements is the notion that the company's brand name conveys a message to consumers about the quality of the company's product. Thus, a business traveler booking into a Hilton International hotel in Hong Kong can reasonably expect the same quality of room, food, and service as he or she would receive in New York. The Hilton brand name is a guarantee of the consistency of product quality. However, foreign franchisees may not be as concerned about quality as they should be, and poor quality may mean not only lost sales in the foreign market but also a decline in the company's worldwide reputation. For example, if the business traveler has a bad experience at the Hilton in Hong Kong, he or she may never go to another Hilton hotel and may steer colleagues away as well. The geographic distance separating it from its foreign franchisees and the sheer number of individual franchisees (tens of thousands in the case of McDonald's) can make it difficult for the franchiser to detect poor quality. Consequently, quality problems may persist.

To obviate this drawback, a company can set up a subsidiary in each country or region in which it is expanding. The subsidiary might be wholly owned by the company or a joint venture with a foreign company. The subsidiary then assumes the rights and obligations to establish franchisees throughout that particular country or region. The combination of proximity and the limited number of independent franchisees that have to be monitored reduces the problem of quality control. Besides, since the subsidiary is at least partly owned by the company, the company can place its own managers in the subsidiary to ensure the kind of quality monitoring it wants. This organizational arrangement has proved very popular in practice. It has been used by McDonald's, Kentucky Fried Chicken, and Hilton Hotels to expand their international operations, to name just three examples.

Joint Ventures

Establishing a joint venture with a foreign company has long been a favored mode for entering a new market. One of the most famous long-term joint ventures, the Fuji-Xerox joint venture to produce photocopiers for the Japanese market, is profiled in Strategy in Action 8.3. The most typical form of joint venture is a 50/50 venture, in which each party takes a 50 percent ownership stake and operating control is shared by a team of managers from both parent companies (as is the case with the Fuji-Xerox joint venture). Some companies, however, have sought joint ventures in which they have a majority shareholding (for example, a 51/49 ownership split). This permits tighter control by the dominant partner.[20]

Joint ventures have a number of advantages. First, a company may feel that it can benefit from a local partner's knowledge of a host country's competitive conditions, culture, language, political systems, and business systems. (See Strategy in Action 8.1 for an example of how McDonald's benefited from this.) Second, when the development costs and risks of opening up a foreign market are high, a company might gain by sharing these costs and risks with a local partner. Third, in many countries political considerations make joint ventures the only feasible entry mode.[21] For example, historically many U.S. companies have found it much easier to get permission to set up operations in Japan if they went in with a Japanese partner than if they tried to enter on their own. Indeed, this was a prime motivation behind the establishment of the Fuji-Xerox joint venture (see Strategy in Action 8.3).

Despite these advantages, joint ventures can be difficult to establish and run because of two main drawbacks. First, as in the case of licensing, a company that enters into a joint venture risks losing control over its technology to its venture partner. To minimize this risk, a company can seek a majority ownership stake in the joint venture, for as the dominant partner it would be able to exercise greater control over its technology. The trouble with this strategy is that it may be difficult to find a foreign partner willing to accept a minority ownership position.

The second disadvantage is that a joint venture does not give a company the tight control over its subsidiaries that it might need in order to realize experience-curve effects or location economies (as both global and transnational companies try to do) or to engage in coordinated global attacks against its global rivals. Consider the entry of Texas Instruments (TI) into the Japanese semiconductor market. When TI established semiconductor facilities in Japan, its sole purpose was to limit

Fuji-Xerox

Originally established in 1962, today Fuji-Xerox is structured as a 50/50 joint venture between the Xerox Corp., the U.S. maker of photocopiers, and Fuji Photo Film, Japan's largest manufacturer of film products. With 1995 sales of more than $8 billion, Fuji-Xerox provides Xerox with more than 20 percent of its worldwide revenues. A prime motivation for the initial establishment of the joint venture was the fact that in the early 1960s the Japanese government did not allow foreign companies to set up wholly owned subsidiaries in Japan. The joint venture was originally conceived as a marketing organization to sell xerographic products that would be manufactured by Fuji Photo under license from Xerox. However, when the Japanese government refused to approve the establishment of a joint venture intended solely as a sales company, the joint venture agreement was revised to give Fuji-Xerox manufacturing rights. Day-to-day management of the venture was placed in the hands of a Japanese management team that was given autonomy to develop its own operations and strategy, subject to oversight by a board of directors that contained representatives from both Xerox and Fuji Photo.

Initially, Fuji-Xerox followed the lead of Xerox in manufacturing and selling the large high-volume copiers developed by Xerox in the United States. These machines were sold at a premium price to the high end

of the market. However, Fuji-Xerox noticed that in the Japanese market new competitors, such as Canon and Ricoh, were making significant inroads by building small low-volume copiers and focusing on the mid- and low-priced segments of the market. This led to Fuji-Xerox's development of its first "homegrown" copier, the FX2200, which at the time was billed as the world's smallest copier. Introduced in 1973, the FX2200 hit the market just in time to allow Fuji-Xerox to hold its own against a blizzard of new competition in Japan that followed the expiration of many of Xerox's key patents.

Around the same time, Fuji-Xerox also embarked upon a total quality control (TQC) program. The aims of the program were to speed up the development of new products, reduce waste, improve quality, and lower manufacturing costs. The first fruit of this program was the FX3500, introduced in 1977. By 1979 the FX3500 had broken the Japanese record for the number of copiers sold in one year. Partly because of the success of the FX3500, in 1980 the company won Japan's prestigious Deming Prize. The success of the FX3500 was all the more notable because at the same time Xerox was canceling a series of programs to develop low- to mid-level copiers and instead reaffirming its commitment to serving the high end of the market.

By the early 1980s Fuji-Xerox was number two in the Japanese copier market with a share in the 20 to

---

Japanese manufacturers' market share and the amount of cash available to them to invade TI's global market. In other words, TI was engaging in global strategic coordination. To implement this strategy, TI's Japanese subsidiary had to be prepared to take instructions from the TI corporate headquarters regarding competitive strategy. The strategy also required that the Japanese subsidiary be run at a loss if necessary. Clearly, a Japanese joint venture partner would have been unlikely to accept such conditions since they would have meant a negative return on investment. Thus, in order to implement this strategy, TI set up a wholly owned subsidiary in Japan instead of entering this market through a joint venture.

Wholly Owned Subsidiaries

A **wholly owned subsidiary** is one in which the parent company owns 100 percent of the subsidiary's stock. To establish a wholly owned subsidiary in a foreign market, a company can either set up a completely new operation in that country or

22 percent range, just behind that of market leader Canon. In contrast, Xerox was running into all sorts of problems in the U.S. market. As Xerox's patents had expired, a number of companies, including Canon, Ricoh, Kodak, and IBM, began to take market share from Xerox. Canon and Ricoh were particularly successful by focusing upon that segment of the market that Xerox had ignored—the low end. As a result, Xerox's market share in the Americas fell from 35 percent in 1975 to 10 percent in 1985, while its profitability slumped.

In an attempt to recapture share, Xerox began to sell Fuji-Xerox's FX3500 copier in the United States. Not only did the FX3500 help Xerox halt the rapid decline in its share of the U.S. market, it also opened Xerox's eyes to the benefits of Fuji-Xerox's TQC program. Xerox found that the reject rate for Fuji-Xerox parts was only a fraction of that for U.S. parts. Visits to Fuji-Xerox revealed another important truth: quality in manufacturing doesn't increase real costs, it reduces costs, by reducing defective products and service costs. These developments forced Xerox to rethink the way it did business.

From being the main provider of products, technology, and management know-how to Fuji-Xerox, in the 1980s Xerox became the willing pupil of Fuji-Xerox. In 1983 Xerox introduced its Leadership Through Quality program, which was based upon Fuji-Xerox's TQC program. As part of this effort, Xerox launched a quality-training effort with its suppliers and was rewarded when the number of defective parts from suppliers subsequently fell from 25,000 per million in 1983 to 300 per million by 1992.

In 1985 and 1986 Xerox began to focus upon its new-product development process. One goal was to design products that, while customized to market conditions in different countries, contained a large number of globally standardized parts. Another goal was to reduce the time it took to design new products and bring them to market. To achieve these goals, Xerox set up joint product development teams with Fuji-Xerox. Each team managed the design, component sources, manufacturing, distribution, and follow-up customer service on a worldwide basis. The use of design teams cut as much as one year from the overall product development cycle and saved millions of dollars.

One consequence of the new approach to product development was the 5100 copier. Manufactured in U.S. plants, this was the first product designed jointly by Xerox and Fuji-Xerox for the worldwide market. It was launched in Japan in November 1990 and in the United States the following February. The 5100's global design reportedly reduced overall time to market and saved the company more than $10 million in development costs.

Due to the skills and products acquired from Fuji-Xerox, Xerox's position improved markedly during the latter part of the 1980s. Xerox was able to gain market share back from its competitors and to boost its profits and revenues. Xerox's share of the U.S. copier market increased from a low of 10 percent in 1985 to 18 percent in 1991.[22]

acquire an established host country company and use it to promote its products in the host market.

Setting up a wholly owned subsidiary offers three advantages. First, when a company's competitive advantage is based on its control of a technological competency, a wholly owned subsidiary is normally the preferred entry mode, since it reduces the company's risk of losing this control. Consequently, many high-tech companies prefer wholly owned subsidiaries to joint ventures or licensing arrangements. Wholly owned subsidiaries tend to be the favored entry mode in the semiconductor, electronics, and pharmaceutical industries. Second, a wholly owned subsidiary gives a company the kind of tight control over operations in different countries that it needs if it is going to engage in global strategic coordination—taking profits from one country to support competitive attacks in another. Third, a wholly owned subsidiary may be the best choice if a company wants to realize location economies and experience-curve effects. As you saw earlier, when cost pressures are intense, it may pay a company to configure its value chain in such a way that value added at each stage is maximized. Thus, a national subsidiary may specialize in manufacturing only part of the product line or certain components of the end product, exchanging parts and products with other subsidiaries in the company's global system. Establishing such a global production system requires a high degree of control over the operations of national affiliates. Different national operations have to be prepared to accept centrally determined decisions as to how they should produce, how much they should produce, and how their output should be priced for transfer between operations. A wholly owned subsidiary would, of course, have to comply with these mandates, whereas licensees or joint venture partners would most likely shun such a subservient role.

On the other hand, establishing a wholly owned subsidiary is generally the most costly method of serving a foreign market. The parent company must bear all the costs and risks of setting up overseas operations. This is in contrast to joint ventures, in which the costs and risks are shared, and to licensing, in which the licensee bears most of the costs and risks. However, the risks of learning to do business in a new culture diminish if the company acquires an established enterprise in the host country. Acquisitions, though, raise a whole set of additional problems, such as trying to marry divergent corporate cultures, and these problems may more than offset the benefits. (The problems associated with acquisitions are discussed in Chapter 10.)

Choosing Among Entry Modes

The advantages and disadvantages of the various entry modes are summarized in Table 8.2. Inevitably, there are tradeoffs in choosing one entry mode over another. For example, when considering entry into an unfamiliar country with a track record of nationalizing foreign-owned enterprises, a company might favor a joint venture with a local enterprise. Its rationale might be that the local partner will help it establish operations in an unfamiliar environment and will speak out against nationalization should the possibility arise. But if the company's distinctive competency is based on proprietary technology, entering into a joint venture might mean risking loss of control over that technology to the joint venture partner, which would make this strategy unattractive. Despite such hazards, some generalizations can be offered about the optimal choice of entry mode.

Distinctive Competencies and Entry Mode   When companies expand internationally to earn greater returns from their distinctive competencies, transferring the skills and products derived from their competencies to foreign markets where indigenous competitors lack those skills, the companies are pursuing an international strategy. The optimal entry mode for such companies depends to some degree on the nature of their distinctive competency. In particular, we need to distinguish between companies with a distinctive competency in technological know-how and those with a distinctive competency in management know-how.

If a company's competitive advantage—that is, its distinctive competency—derives from its control of proprietary *technological know-how*, licensing and joint venture arrangements should be avoided, if possible, in order to minimize the risk of losing control of that technology. Thus, if a high-tech company is considering setting up operations in a foreign country in order to profit from a distinctive compe-

TABLE 8.2
• • • • • • • • • •

The Advantages and Disadvantages of Different Entry Modes

Entry Mode	Advantages	Disadvantages
Exporting	• Ability to realize location and experience-curve economies	• High transport costs • Trade barriers • Problems with local marketing agents
Licensing	• Low development costs and risks	• Inability to realize location and experience-curve economies • Inability to engage in global strategic coordination • Lack of control over technology
Franchising	• Low development costs and risks	• Inability to engage in global strategic coordination • Lack of control over quality
Joint ventures	• Access to local partner's knowledge • Shared development costs and risks • Political acceptability	• Inability to engage in global strategic coordination • Inability to realize location and experience-curve economies • Lack of control over technology
Wholly owned subsidiaries	• Protection of technology • Ability to engage in global strategic coordination • Ability to realize location and experience-curve economies	• High costs and risks

tency in technological know-how, it should probably do so through a wholly owned subsidiary.

However, this rule should not be viewed as a hard and fast one. For instance, a licensing or joint venture arrangement might be structured in such a way as to reduce the risks of a company's technological know-how being expropriated by licensees or joint venture partners (as was the case with the Fuji-Xerox venture). We consider this kind of arrangement in more detail later in the chapter when we discuss the issue of structuring strategic alliances. To take another exception to the rule, a company may perceive its technological advantage as being only transitory and expect rapid imitation of its core technology by competitors. In such a case, the company might want to license its technology as quickly as possible to foreign companies in order to gain global acceptance of its technology before imitation occurs.[23] Such a strategy has some advantages. By licensing its technology to competitors, the company may deter them from developing their own, possibly superior, technology. It also may be able to establish its technology as the dominant design in the industry (as Matsushita did with its VHS format for VCRs), ensuring a steady stream of royalty payments. Such situations apart, however, the attractions of licensing are probably outweighed by the risks of losing control of technology, and, therefore, licensing should be avoided.

The competitive advantage of many service companies, such as McDonald's or Hilton Hotels, is based on *management know-how*. For such companies, the risk of losing control of their management skills to franchisees or joint venture partners is not that great. The reason is that the valuable asset of such companies is their brand name, and brand names are generally well protected by international laws pertaining to trademarks. Given this fact, many of the issues that arise in the case of technological know-how do not arise in the case of management know-how. As a result, many service companies favor a combination of franchising and subsidiaries to control franchisees within a particular country or region. The subsidiary may be wholly owned or a joint venture. In most cases, however, service companies have found that entering into a joint venture with a local partner in order to set up a controlling subsidiary in a country or region works best because a joint venture is often politically more acceptable and brings a degree of local knowledge to the subsidiary.

Pressures for Cost Reduction and Entry Mode   The greater the pressures for cost reductions, the more likely it is that a company will want to pursue some combination of exporting and wholly owned subsidiaries. By manufacturing in the locations where factor conditions are optimal and then exporting to the rest of the world, a company may be able to realize substantial location economies and experience-curve effects. The company might then want to export the finished product to marketing subsidiaries based in various countries. Typically, these subsidiaries are wholly owned and have the responsibility for overseeing distribution in a particular country. Setting up wholly owned marketing subsidiaries is preferable to a joint ventures arrangement or to using a foreign marketing agent, because it gives the company the tight control over marketing that might be required to coordinate a globally dispersed value chain. In addition, tight control over a local operation enables the company to use the profits generated in one market to improve its competitive position in another. Hence, companies pursuing global or transnational strategies prefer to establish wholly owned subsidiaries.

GLOBAL STRATEGIC ALLIANCES

Strategic alliances are cooperative agreements between companies that may also be competitors. In this section we deal specifically with strategic alliances between companies from different countries. Strategic alliances run the range from formal joint ventures, in which two or more companies have an equity stake, to short-term contractual agreements, in which two companies may agree to cooperate on a particular problem (such as developing a new product). There is no doubt that collaboration between competitors is in fashion. Recent years have seen a virtual explosion in the number of strategic alliances. Examples include a cooperative arrangement between Boeing and a consortium of Japanese companies to produce the 767 and 777 wide-bodied commercial jets; an alliance between Eastman Kodak and Canon of Japan under which Canon manufactures a line of medium-volume copiers for sale under Kodak's name; an agreement between Texas Instruments and Kobe Steel of Japan to make logic semiconductors in Japan; and an agreement between Motorola and Toshiba to pool their technological know-how and manufacture microprocessors.

Advantages of Strategic Alliances

Companies enter into strategic alliances with actual or potential competitors in order to achieve a number of strategic objectives.[24] First, as noted earlier in this chapter, strategic alliances may be a way of facilitating entry into a foreign market. For example, Motorola initially found it very difficult to gain access to the Japanese cellular telephone market. In the mid 1980s the company complained loudly about formal and informal Japanese trade barriers. The turning point for Motorola came in 1987, when it formed its alliance with Toshiba to build microprocessors. As part of the deal, Toshiba provided Motorola with marketing help, including some of its best managers. This aided Motorola in the political game of winning government approval to enter the Japanese market and obtaining allocations of radio frequencies for its mobile communications systems. Since then Motorola has played down the importance of Japan's informal trade barriers. Although privately the company still admits they exist, with Toshiba's help Motorola has become skilled at getting around them.[25]

Second, many companies have entered into strategic alliances in order to share the fixed costs (and associated risks) that arise from the development of new products or processes. For example, Motorola's alliance with Toshiba was partly motivated by a desire to share the high fixed costs associated with setting up an operation to manufacture microprocessors. The microprocessor business is so capital intensive (it cost Motorola and Toshiba close to $1 billion to set up their facility) that few companies can afford the costs and risks of going it alone.

Third, many alliances can be seen as a way of bringing together complementary skills and assets that neither company could easily develop on its own. For example, in 1990 AT&T struck a deal with NEC of Japan to trade technological skills. Under the agreement AT&T transferred some of its computer-aided design technology to NEC. In return, NEC gave AT&T access to the technology underlying NEC advanced-logic computer chips. Such equitable trading of distinctive competencies seems to underlie many of the most successful strategic alliances.

Finally, it may make sense to enter into an alliance if it helps the company set technological standards for its industry and if those standards benefit the company. For example, in 1992 the Dutch electronics company, Philips, entered into an alliance with its global competitor, Matsushita, to manufacture and market the digital compact cassette (DCC) system pioneered by Philips. The motive for this action was that linking up with Matsushita would help Philips establish the DCC system as a new technological standard in the recording and consumer electronics industries. The issue is an important one because Sony has developed a competing minicompact disk technology, which Sony hopes to establish as a new technical standard. Since the two technologies do very similar things, there is probably room for only one new standard. The technology that becomes the new standard will be the one to succeed. The loser in this race will in all probability have to write off an investment worth billions of dollars. Philips sees the alliance with Matsushita as a tactic for winning the race, for it ties a potential major competitor into its standard.

Disadvantages of Strategic Alliances

The various advantages just discussed can be very significant. Nevertheless, some commentators have criticized strategic alliances on the grounds that they give competitors a low-cost route to gain new technology and market access. For example,

Robert Reich and Eric Mankin have argued that strategic alliances between U.S. and Japanese companies are part of an implicit Japanese strategy to keep higher-paying, higher-value-added jobs in Japan while gaining the project-engineering and production-process skills that underlie the competitive success of many U.S. companies.[26] They have viewed Japanese success in the machine tool and semiconductor industries as largely built on U.S. technology acquired through various strategic alliances. Futhermore, they have asserted that increasingly U.S. managers are aiding the Japanese in achieving their goals by entering into alliances that channel new inventions to Japan and provide a U.S. sales and distribution network for the resulting products. Although such deals may generate short-term profits, in the long run, according to Reich and Mankin, the result is to "hollow out" U.S. companies, leaving them with no competitive advantage in the global marketplace.

Reich and Mankin have a point; alliances do have risks. Unless it is careful, a company can give away more than it gets in return. On the other hand, there are so many examples of apparently successful alliances between companies, including alliances between U.S. and Japanese companies, that Reich and Mankin's position seems more than a little extreme. For example, it is difficult to see how the Motorola-Toshiba alliance, the Ford-Mazda alliance, or the twenty-five-year-old Fuji-Xerox venture to build and market photocopiers in Asia fits their thesis. In all these cases, both partners seemed to have gained from the alliance. Since Reich and Mankin undoubtedly do have a point, the question becomes, *why do some alliances benefit a company, whereas in others it can end up giving away technology and market access and get very little in return?* The next section provides an answer to this question.

MAKING STRATEGIC ALLIANCES WORK

The benefits that a company derives from a strategic alliance seem to be a function of three factors: partner selection, alliance structure, and the way in which the alliance is managed. We look at each of these issues in turn.

Partner Selection

One of the keys to making a strategic alliance work is to select the right kind of partner. A good partner has three principal characteristics. First, a good partner helps the firm achieve its strategic goals, whether they be achieving market access, sharing the costs and risks of new product development, or gaining access to critical core competencies. In other words, the partner must have capabilities that the company lacks and that it values.

Second, a good partner shares the firm's vision for the purpose of the alliance. If two companies approach an alliance with radically different agendas, the chances are great that the relationship will not be harmonious and will end in divorce. This seems to have been the case with the alliance between GM and Daewoo (see Strategy in Action 8.4 for details). GM's agenda was to use Daewoo as a source of cheap labor to produce cars for the Korean and U.S. markets, whereas Daewoo wanted to use GM's know-how and distribution systems to grow Daewoo's business, not just

General Motors and Daewoo

In June 1984 General Motors and Daewoo of Korea signed an agreement that called for each to invest $100 million in a Korean-based 50/50 joint venture, Daewoo Motor Company, that would manufacture a subcompact car, the Pontiac LeMans, based upon GM's popular German-designed Opel Kadett. (Opel is the German subsidiary of GM.) The day-to-day management of the alliance was to be placed in the hands of Daewoo executives, with managerial and technical advice being provided by a few GM executives. Initially the alliance was seen as a smart move for both companies. GM doubted that a small car could be built profitably in the United States because of high labor costs, and it saw enormous advantages in this marriage of German technology and cheap Korean labor. Roger Smith, then GM's chairman, told Korean reporters that GM's North American operation would probably end up importing 80,000 to 100,000 cars a year from Daewoo Motor. As for Daewoo, it saw itself getting access to the superior engineering skills of GM and an entrée into the world's largest car market—the United States.

Eight years of financial losses later, the joint venture collapsed in a blizzard of mutual recriminations between Daewoo and General Motors. From the perspective of GM, things started to go seriously wrong in 1987, just as the first LeMans was rolling off Daewoo's production line. Korea had lurched toward democracy, and workers throughout the country demanded better wages. Daewoo was hit by a series of bitter strikes that repeatedly halted production of the LeMans. To calm the labor troubles, Daewoo Motor more than doubled workers' wages, and suddenly it was cheaper to build Opels in Germany. (German wages were still higher, but German productivity was also much higher, which translated into lower labor costs.)

Equally problematic was the poor quality of the cars rolling off the Daewoo production line. Electrical systems often crashed on the LeMans, and the braking system had a tendency to fail after just a few thousand miles. The LeMans soon gained a reputation for poor quality, and U.S. sales plummeted to 37,000 vehicles in 1991, down 86 percent from their 1988 high point. Hurt by the LeMan's reputation as a lemon, Daewoo's share of the rapidly growing Korean car market also slumped from a high of 21.4 percent in 1987 to 12.3 percent in 1991.

If GM was disappointed in Daewoo, that was nothing compared to Daewoo's frustration with GM. The chairman of Daewoo, Kim Woo Choong, complained that GM executives were arrogant and treated him shabbily. Mr. Kim was angry that GM had tried to prohibit him from expanding the market for Daewoo's cars. In late 1988 he negotiated a deal to sell 7,000 Daewoo Motor's cars in Eastern Europe. GM executives immediately tried to kill the deal, telling Mr. Kim that Europe was the territory of GM's German subsidiary, Opel. To make matters worse, when Daewoo developed a new sedan car and asked GM to sell it in the United States, GM said no. By this point Mr. Kim's frustrations at having his expansion plans in Eastern Europe and the United States held back by GM was clear to all. Daewoo's management also believed that the poor sales of the LeMans in the United States were not due to quality problems but to the poor marketing efforts of GM.

Events came to a head in 1991 when Daewoo asked GM to agree to expand the manufacturing facilities of the joint venture. The plan called for each partner to put in another $100 million and for Daewoo to double its output. GM refused on the grounds that increasing output would not help Daewoo Motor unless the venture could first improve its product quality. The matter festered until late 1991, when GM delivered a blunt proposal to Daewoo—either GM would buy out Daewoo's stake or Daewoo would buy out GM's stake in the joint venture. Much to GM's surprise, Daewoo agreed to buy out GM's stake. The divorce was completed in November 1992 with an agreement by Daewoo to pay GM $170 million over three years for its 50 percent stake in Daewoo Motor Company.[27]

in Korea and the United States, but also in Europe. Different perceptions over the strategic role of the venture ultimately contributed to the dissolution of the alliance.

Third, a good partner is unlikely to try to exploit the alliance opportunistically for its own ends, that is, to expropriate the company's technological know-how while giving away little in return. In this respect, firms that want to maintain their reputations for fair play probably make the best partners. For example, IBM is involved in so many strategic alliances that it would not pay the company to ride roughshod over individual alliance partners. Such actions would tarnish IBM's hard-won reputation of being a good partner and would make it more difficult for IBM to attract alliance partners in the future. Similarly, their reputations make it less likely that such Japanese companies as Sony, Toshiba, and Fuji, which have histories of alliances with non-Japanese firms, would opportunistically exploit an alliance partner.

To select a partner with these three characteristics, a company needs to conduct some comprehensive research on potential alliance candidates. To increase the probability of selecting a good partner, the firm should collect as much pertinent, publicly available information about potential allies as possible; collect data from informed third parties, including companies that have had alliances with the potential partners, investment bankers who have had dealings with them, and some of their former employees; and get to know potential partners as well as possible before committing to an alliance. This last step should include face-to-face meetings between senior managers (and perhaps middle-level managers) to ensure that the chemistry is right.

Alliance Structure

Having selected a partner, the alliance should be structured so that the company's risk of giving too much away to the partner is reduced to an acceptable level. Figure 8.4 depicts the four safeguards against opportunism by alliance partners that we discuss here. (Opportunism includes the "theft" of technology and/or markets that Reich and Mankin describe.) First, alliances can be designed to make it difficult (if not impossible) to transfer technology not meant to be transferred. Specifically, the design, development, manufacture, and service of a product manufactured by an alliance can be structured so as to "wall off" sensitive technologies to prevent their leakage to the other participant. In the alliance between General Electric and Snecma to build commercial aircraft engines, for example, GE reduced the risk of "excess transfer" by walling off certain sections of the production process. The modularization effectively cut off the transfer of what GE regarded as key competitive technology, while permitting Snecma access to final assembly. Similarly, in the alliance between Boeing and the Japanese to build the 767, Boeing walled off research, design, and marketing functions considered central to its competitive position, while allowing the Japanese to share in production technology. Boeing also walled off new technologies not required for 767 production.[28]

Second, contractual safeguards can be written into an alliance agreement to guard against the risk of opportunism by a partner. For example, TRW has three strategic alliances with large Japanese auto component suppliers to produce seat belts, engine valves, and steering gears for sale to Japanese-owned auto assembly plants in the United States. TRW has clauses in each of its alliance contracts that bar the Japanese firms from competing with TRW to supply U.S.-owned auto compa-

FIGURE 8.4

Structuring Alliances to
Reduce Opportunism

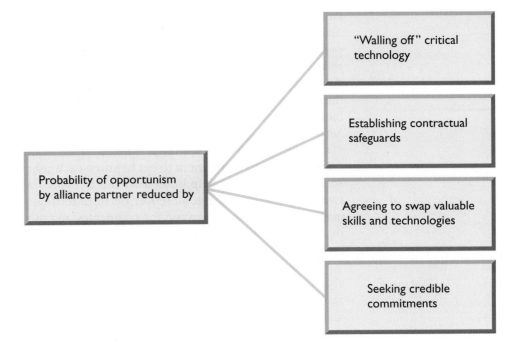

nies with component parts. By doing this, TRW protects itself against the possibility that the Japanese companies are entering into the alliances merely as a means of gaining access to the North American market to compete with TRW in its home market.

Third, both parties to an alliance can agree in advance to swap skills and technologies, thereby ensuring a chance for equitable gain. Cross-licensing agreements are one way to achieve this goal. For example, in the alliance between Motorola and Toshiba, Motorola has licensed some of its microprocessor technology to Toshiba, and in return Toshiba has licensed some of its memory-chip technology to Motorola.

Fourth, the risk of opportunism by an alliance partner can be reduced if the firm extracts a significant credible commitment from its partner in advance. The long-term alliance between Xerox and Fuji to build photocopiers for the Asian market perhaps best illustrates this. Rather than enter into an informal agreement or some kind of licensing arrangement (which Fuji Photo initially wanted), Xerox insisted that Fuji invest in a 50/50 joint venture to serve Japan and East Asia. This venture constituted such a significant investment in people, equipment, and facilities that Fuji Photo was committed from the outset to making the alliance work in order to earn a return on its investment. By agreeing to the joint venture, Fuji essentially made a credible commitment to the alliance. Given this, Xerox felt secure in transferring its photocopier technology to Fuji (see Strategy in Action 8.3 for details).[29]

Managing the Alliance

Once a partner has been selected and an appropriate alliance structure agreed on, the task facing the company is to maximize the benefits from the alliance. One important ingredient of success appears to be a sensitivity to cultural differences.

Differences in management style can often be attributed to cultural differences. Managers need to make allowances for such differences when dealing with their partner. In addition, managing an alliance successfully means building interpersonal relationships among managers from the different companies, a lesson that can be drawn from the successful strategic alliance between Ford and Mazda (see the Closing Case at the end of the chapter). This partnership has resulted in the development of such best-selling cars as the Ford Explorer and the Mazda Navajo. Ford and Mazda have set up a framework of meetings within which managers from Ford and Mazda not only discuss matters pertaining to the alliance but also have sufficient nonwork time to allow them to get to know each other better. The resulting personal friendships can help build trust and facilitate harmonious relationships between the two companies. Moreover, personal relationships can create an informal management network between the companies, and this network can then be used to help solve problems that arise in more formal contexts, such as joint committee meetings between personnel from both firms.

A major factor determining how much a company gains from an alliance is its ability to learn from alliance partners. Gary Hamel, Yves Doz, and C. K. Prahalad reached this conclusion after a five-year study of fifteen strategic alliances between major multinationals. They focused on a number of alliances between Japanese companies and western (European or American) partners. In every case in which a Japanese company emerged from an alliance stronger than its western partner, the Japanese company had made a greater effort to learn. Indeed, few western companies seemed to want to learn from their Japanese partners. They tended to regard the alliance purely as a cost-sharing or risk-sharing device, rather than as an opportunity to learn how a potential competitor does business.[30] As a counterpoint, however, it is worth noting that Xerox clearly used the Fuji-Xerox joint venture to learn about Japanese manufacturing practices, such as total quality manufacturing and design for manufacturing (see Strategy in Action 8.3).

For an example of an alliance in which there was a clear learning asymmetry, consider the agreement between General Motors and Toyota to build the Chevrolet Nova. This alliance is structured as a formal joint venture, called New United Motor Manufacturing Inc., in which both parties have a 50 percent equity stake. The venture owns an auto plant in Fremont, California. According to one of the Japanese managers, Toyota achieved most of its objectives from the alliance. "We learned about U.S. supply and transportation. And we got the confidence to manage U.S. workers." All that knowledge was then quickly transferred to Georgetown, Kentucky, where Toyota opened a plant of its own in 1988. By contrast, although General Motors got a new product, the Chevrolet Nova, some GM managers complained that their new knowledge was never put to good use inside GM. They say that they should have been kept together as a team to educate GM's engineers and workers about the Japanese system. Instead they were dispersed to different GM subsidiaries.[31]

When entering an alliance, a company must take some measures to ensure that it learns from its alliance partner and then put that knowledge to good use within its own organization. One suggested approach is to educate all operating employees about the partner's strengths and weaknesses and make clear to them how acquiring particular skills will bolster their company's competitive position. For such learning to be of value, the knowledge acquired from an alliance has to be diffused throughout the organization, which did not happen at GM. To spread this knowledge, the managers involved in an alliance should be used as a resource in familiarizing others within the company about the skills of an alliance partner.

SUMMARY OF CHAPTER

In this chapter we examine the various ways in which companies can profit from global expansion, and we review the strategies that companies engaged in global competition can adopt. We also discuss the optimal choice of entry mode to serve a foreign market and explore the issue of strategic alliances. The following points have been made:

✔ For some companies, international expansion represents a way of earning greater returns by transferring the skills and product offerings derived from their distinctive competencies to markets in which indigenous competitors lack those skills.

✔ Because of national differences, it pays a company to base each value creation activity it performs at the location where factor conditions are most conducive to the performance of that activity. We refer to this strategy as focusing on the attainment of location economies.

✔ By building sales volume rapidly, international expansion can assist a company in the process of moving down the experience curve.

✔ The best choice of strategy for a company to pursue is affected by two kinds of pressures: pressures for cost reductions and pressures for local responsiveness. Pressures for cost reductions are greatest in industries producing commodity-type products, for which price is the main competitive weapon. Pressures for local responsiveness arise from differences in consumers' tastes and preferences in national infrastructure and/or traditional practices, in distribution channels, and in demands by host governments.

✔ Companies pursuing an international strategy transfer the skills and products derived from distinctive competencies to foreign markets and at the same time undertake some limited local customization.

✔ Companies pursuing a multidomestic strategy customize their product offering, marketing strategy, and business strategy to national conditions.

✔ Companies pursuing a global strategy focus on reaping the cost reductions that come from experience-curve effects and location economies.

✔ Many industries are now so competitive that companies must adopt a transnational strategy. This involves a simultaneous focus on reducing costs, transferring skills and products, and local respon-

siveness. Implementing such a strategy, however, may not be easy.

✔ There are five different ways of entering a foreign market—exporting, licensing, franchising, entering into a joint venture, and setting up a wholly owned subsidiary. The optimal choice among entry modes depends on the company's strategy.

✔ Strategic alliances are cooperative agreements between actual or potential competitors. The advantages of alliances are that they facilitate entry into foreign markets, enable partners to share the fixed costs and risks associated with new products and processes, facilitate the transfer of complementary skills between companies, and help companies establish technical standards.

✔ The drawbacks of a strategic alliance are that the company risks giving away technological know-how and market access to its alliance partner while getting very little in return.

✔ The disadvantages associated with alliances can be reduced if the company selects partners carefully, paying close attention to reputation, and structures the alliance so as to avoid unintended transfers of know-how.

DISCUSSION QUESTIONS

1. Plot the position of the following companies on Figure 8.1: Procter & Gamble, IBM, Coca-Cola, Dow Chemical, USX, and McDonald's. In each case, justify your answer.

2. Are the following global industries or multidomestic industries: bulk chemicals, pharmaceuticals, branded food products, moviemaking, television manufacture, personal computers, and airline travel?

3. Discuss how the need for control over foreign operations varies with the strategy and distinctive competencies of a company. What are the implications of this relationship for the choice of entry mode?

4. Licensing proprietary technology to foreign competitors is the best way to give up a company's competitive advantage. Discuss.

5. What kind of companies stand to gain the most from entering into strategic alliances with potential competitors? Why?

Practicing Strategic Management

SMALL-GROUP EXERCISE
Developing a Global Strategy

Break into a group of three to five people, and discuss the following scenario:

You work for a company in the soft drink industry that has developed a line of carbonated fruit-based beverages. You have already established a significant presence in your home market, and now you are planning the global strategy development of the company in the soft drink industry. You need to decide the following:

1. What overall strategy should you pursue—a global strategy, a multidomestic strategy, an international strategy, or a transnational strategy?

2. What entry strategy should you pursue (for example, franchising, joint venture, wholly owned subsidiary)?

What information do you need in order to make these kinds of decisions? On the basis of what you do know, what strategies would you recommend?

EXPLORING THE WEB
Visting IBM

Visit the Web site of IBM at http://www.ibm.com. Go to the "IBM Planetwide" button on the page. Select and visit the Web sites of the following IBM subsidiaries: IBM Australia, IBM Hong Kong, IBM United Kingdom. At each Web site, read the section that outlines the history of the local unit. On the basis of this information, try to establish how IBM first entered each foreign market and how its involvement there subsequently evolved. Be sure to think through the strategic rationale for IBM's choices of entry strategy. In retrospect, does the entry strategy of IBM in each of these countries make sense?

ARTICLE FILE 8

Find an example of a multinational company that in recent years has switched its strategy from a multidomestic, an international, or a global strategy to a transnational strategy. Identify why the company made the switch and any problems that the company may be encountering while it tries to change its strategic orientation.

STRATEGIC MANAGEMENT PROJECT
Module 8

This module requires you to identify how your company might profit from global expansion, the strategy that your company should pursue globally, and the entry mode that it might favor. With the information you have at your disposal, answer the questions regarding the following two situations:

Your Company Is Already Doing Business in Other Countries

1. Is your company creating value or lowering the costs of value creation by realizing location economies, transferring distinctive competencies abroad, or realizing cost economies from the experience curve? If not, does it have the potential to?

2. How responsive is your company to differences between nations? Does it vary its product and marketing message from country to country? Should it?

3. What are the cost pressures and pressures for local responsiveness in the industry in which your company is based?

4. What strategy is your company pursuing to compete globally? In your opinion, is this the correct strategy, given cost pressures and pressures for local responsiveness?

5. What major foreign market does your company serve, and what mode has it used to enter this market? What are the advantages and disadvantages of using this mode? Might another mode be preferable?

Your Company Is Not Yet Doing Business in Other Countries

1. What potential does your company have to add value to its products or lower the costs of value creation by expanding internationally?

2. On the international level, what are the cost pressures and pressures for local responsiveness in the

industry in which your company is based? What implications do these pressures have for the strategy that your company might pursue if it chose to expand globally?

3. What foreign market might your company enter, and what entry mode should it use to enter this market? Justify your answer.

General Task

Search the Web for a company site where there is a good description of that company's international operations. On the basis of this information, try to establish how the company enters foreign markets and what overall strategy it is pursuing (global, international, multidomestic, or transnational).

CLOSING CASE

The Ford–Mazda Alliance

During the 1980s the global auto industry was swept by a wave of strategic alliances between competitors. The number of alliances among the twenty-three largest competitors increased from ten in 1978 to fifty-two in 1988. By 1990 almost all of the world's carmakers were linked to at least one other company in this web of alliances. One factor responsible for this trend is the growing cost of developing a new car—it can be as much as $2 billion. By entering into alliances, auto companies can share the fixed costs of new-product development and, at the same time, gain access to new markets, manufacturing, and technological know-how.

One of the most successful and enduring of these alliances is the one between Ford and Mazda. Ford and Mazda began to cooperate in 1971 when Ford started purchasing Mazda trucks for sale in Asia. That same year Henry Ford II approached Mazda about buying a stake in the company but was rebuffed. Then came the oil crisis of 1973. At that time Mazda was using a gas-hungry rotary engine in most of its cars, and its sales slumped. Throughout the 1970s Mazda struggled to recover. Reeling under a string of financial losses, Mazda approached Ford in 1977 to see whether the U.S. company was still interested in a relationship. Ford was not, but the two companies kept talking. Then in 1979 the second oil crisis hit, and Ford saw Mazda as an attractive partner because Mazda was manufacturing the type of small, fuel-efficient cars that were likely to sell well in a high-oil-price environment. As a result, Ford purchased a 25 percent stake in the Japanese company for $130 million. In 1991 this stake earned Ford dividends of $14.3 million. However, the benefits of the alliance far exceed this return on Ford's initial investment.

For Ford some of the benefits of the alliance have been in the form of sales in Japan. Ford is now the most popular foreign nameplate in Japan; the company sells more than 72,000 cars and trucks a year through a dealer network it owns jointly with Mazda. Ford also benefits from access to Mazda's manufacturing and engineering skills and from its ability to share the costs of developing new models with Mazda. When Ford built an assembly plant in Hermosillo, Mexico, in the mid 1980s, it used Mazda's superefficient Hofu (Japan) factory as the blueprint. The Hermosillo plant has become one of Ford's top-ranking plants for quality and productivity and is now serving as a model in the renovation of many of Ford's older European and U.S. facilities. As for new product development, Ford and Mazda have worked together on ten new models, usually with Ford doing most of the styling and Mazda making many key engineering contributions. For Ford these cars include the Escort, the Mercury Tracer, the Festiva, the Probe, the Mercury Capri, and the Explorer. The Ford-aided Mazda models are the MX-6, the 323, the Protégé, and the Navajo.

From Mazda's perspective, in addition to the initial injection of cash, the benefits of the alliance include access to the North American market through Ford's dealer network, access to Ford's styling and marketing skills, and a partner with whom to share the costs of developing new car models.

Both partners view the alliance as a success, but it has not been all smooth sailing. Differences in national and corporate cultures have often stood in the path of harmonious relationships and communications. To reduce the possibility of conflicts arising out of misunderstandings, Ford and Mazda have held a series of meetings between the two companies' top- and middle-level managers. The purposes of those meetings have been to coordinate activities and also to help facilitate the growth of enduring interpersonal relationships between managers at Ford and Mazda.

Nevertheless, at times the competitive squabbles have been fierce. For example, Ford wanted Mazda's rotary engine for use in a sports car, but Mazda refused to share the design. On another occasion, Ford refused to let Mazda copy an innovative window design in one of its models. More recently, Mazda wanted access to the design of the four-door Ford Explorer, which Mazda intended to use as a blueprint for a four-door Navajo, but Ford refused. Mazda, too, likes to keep certain models for itself. For instance, Mazda refuses to allow Ford to produce its own version of Mazda's best-selling sports car, the Miata. Over the years, however, disagreements and conflict have become increasingly rare. Initially, the top management at Mazda and Ford were continually having to arbitrate disagreements between their middle managers. The need for such arbitration is less common now, and the companies are able to assist each other in many ways. For example, seeing how Mazda benefited from many small ideas contributed by its workers, Ford instituted a similar employee suggestion program. At its Hermosillo plant, Ford followed Mazda's practice of building a stamping plant nearby. This facilitated the introduction of a just-in-time inventory system and helped Ford boost quality control.

The ideas have also flowed the other way. Ford gave Mazda access to some sophisticated computer programs for measuring noise and vibrations and some electronic systems for helping control engine emissions. Mazda also hopes to profit from Ford's marketing know-how. While working together on the Navajo and Explorer, Mazda got a close look at the customer surveys Ford had collected on the old Bronco II, the Explorer's predecessor. The surveys showed Ford engineers which components and vehicle systems are most important to consumers. Mazda came away so impressed that it adopted Ford's system wholesale.[32]

Case Discussion Questions

1. What are the main strategic benefits of the Ford-Mazda alliance?

2. What risks is Ford running by entering into this alliance with Mazda? What risks is Mazda running?

3. Compare and contrast the Ford-Mazda alliance with the one between General Motors and Daewoo that was profiled in Strategy in Action 8.4. Why do you think the Ford-Mazda alliance has worked so well, while the GM-Daewoo alliance failed?

Corporate Strategy—Vertical Integration, Diversification, and Strategic Alliances

Opening Case: Rockwell International

Overview

Concentration on a Single Business

Vertical Integration

Alternatives to Vertical Integration: Cooperative Relationships and Strategic Outsourcing

Diversification

Strategic Alliances as an Alternative to Diversification

Closing Case: Daimler-Benz

OPENING CASE

In recent years diversification has become decidedly unfashionable, with many once diversified companies selling off businesses acquired in an earlier period of expansion in order to refocus on their "strategic core." Sears, for example, recently sold off its insurance, real estate, and financial services businesses in order to refocus on its core retailing operation. In contrast to this trend, Rockwell International has continued to pursue a strategy of diversification into business areas that at first glance seem to bear little relationship to its original operations. Once primarily known as an aerospace defense contractor, since the mid 1980s a driving force behind Rockwell's diversification strategy has been the relative decline in military spending, which has forced the company

Rockwell International

to look for other sources of income. The most recent example of Rockwell's diversification was its 1995 acquisition for $1.5 billion of Reliance Electric, a supplier of components to the automotive industry. As of 1995 Rockwell generated revenues of $13 billion from a grab bag of businesses ranging from space rocket engines, printing presses, truck axles, factory automation, semiconductors, and aircraft parts. So disparate did Rockwell's collection of businesses seem that Robert Anderson, predecessor to the current CEO, Donald Beall, once described the company as "the most ill-conceived company ever conceived."

Despite pursuing an unfashionable strategy, in recent years Rockwell's financial performance has been impressive. While revenues rose by a moderate 19 percent over the 1992 to 1995 period, reflecting the slowdown in defense spending, net income and earnings per share rose by 54 percent and 58 percent, respectively, while return on equity increased from 17.6 to 20.8 percent during the same period. According to the company, a prime reason for this performance has been its ability to create value for its customers and shareholders by leveraging managerial and technological know-how across a group of businesses that have more in common than first meets the eye.

CEO Donald Beall believes that Rockwell's "new-technology" businesses in semiconductors and aerospace are able to transfer leading-edge electronics and communications know-how to its "old-technology" industrial automotive and printing press businesses, enabling the "old-technology" units to upgrade their existing products and, just as importantly, create new ones. An example is the company's automotive parts division, which, in addition to selling traditional products such as drive systems and vehicle transmissions, is now selling electronic car components such as autonavigation devices to help drivers navigate around strange cities and regulators for power windows that retract if you forget to pull in your hand while the window is closing. Another example of the cross-fertilization of know-how is Rockwell's Fleetmaster product. Fleetmaster uses satellite communications to allow trucking companies to track the position of every vehicle in their fleet. The system was derived from hand-held global positioning devices

initially developed for the military by Rockwell's aerospace business. The military devices originally cost around $50,000 per unit. However, by reducing circuitry size and ramping up production volume to serve a mass consumer market, prices have been reduced to $500 per unit, making it economical for trucking companies to install units in each of their vehicles. High-technology electronic know-how has also been transferred to Rockwell's printing business. As a result, the electronic content, by value, of one of Rockwell's printing presses has increased from 10 to 20 percent over the last decade.

Rockwell also tries to leverage other kinds of know-how across its various business units. Back in 1985 Rockwell acquired Allen-Bradley, a leader in the fast-growing field of computerized factory automation. Since then Rockwell has used Allen-Bradley's skills to upgrade the efficiency of its own factories. Rockwell has also worked hard to identify "best practices" in product development, quality management, and productivity enhancement within its various businesses. It has then leveraged those practices across business units to benefit the company as a whole. For example, the company has used the product development processes developed in its aerospace business to improve the effectiveness of new-product development within its automotive business. So long as Rockwell can continue to leverage such technological and managerial know-how across businesses, Beall maintains that the company is more than the sum of its various parts, and its diversification will help to create value for both customers and shareholders.[1]

OVERVIEW

The principal concern of corporate strategy is identifying the business areas in which a company should participate in order to maximize its long-run profitability. In choosing business areas to compete in, a company has several options. It can focus on just one business; it can diversify into a number of different business areas as Rockwell has (see the Opening Case); or it can integrate vertically, either upstream to produce its own inputs or downstream to dispose of its own outputs. In this chapter we explore these options in depth and examine their pros and cons. We also look at strategic alliances as alternatives to vertical integration and diversification.

The Opening Case describes the corporate strategy of Rockwell International. Originally an aerospace defense contractor, Rockwell recently has built a substantial business in commercial electronics and automotive components. The catalyst behind this strategy has been a desire to reduce the company's dependence upon the defense sector, in which spending has been declining since the end of the Cold War. What is notable about Rockwell is the close attention the company has paid to *creating value* by leveraging technological and managerial know-how across various business units, raising their performance in the process. As discussed later in this chapter, Rockwell's achievements in this regard are significant, for the corporate-level strategies pursued by many other companies seem to have dissipated rather than created value.

In this chapter we repeatedly stress that to succeed, corporate-level strategies should *create value*. To understand what this means, we have to go back to the concept of value creation and the value chain, introduced in Chapter 4. *To create value, a corporate strategy should enable a company, or one or more of its business units, to perform one or more of the value creation functions at a lower cost or perform one or more of the value creation functions in a way that allows for differentiation and a premium price.* Thus, a company's *corporate* strategy should help in the process of establishing a distinctive competency and a competitive advantage *at the business level.* There is, therefore, a very important link between corporate-level strategy and competitive advantage at the business level. It is a link, however, that many companies appear to have lost sight of.

CONCENTRATION ON A SINGLE BUSINESS

For many companies the appropriate corporate-level strategy does not involve vertical integration or diversification. Instead, corporate strategy entails concentrating on competing successfully within the confines of a single business (that is, focusing upon a single industry or market). Examples of companies that currently pursue such a strategy include McDonald's, with its focus on the fast-food restaurant business; Coca-Cola, with its focus on the soft drink business; and Sears, with its focus on department store retailing. Interestingly enough, both Coca-Cola and Sears at one time pursued a diversification strategy. Coca-Cola once owned Columbia Pictures and a wine-producing business, while Sears owned Allstate Insurance, Caldwell Banker (a real estate operation), and Dean Witter (a financial services enterprise). However, both companies came to the conclusion that diversification dissipated rather than created value, and in recent years they divested their diverse businesses and refocused on a single operation. They have done this because there are clear advantages to concentrating on just one business area.

One advantage is that it allows the company to focus its total managerial, financial, technological, and physical resources and capabilities on competing successfully in just one area. This strategy can be important in fast-growing industries in which demands on the company's resources and capabilities are likely to be substantial but in which the long-term profits that flow from establishing a competitive advantage are also likely to be very significant. For example, it would make little sense for a company such as America Online to pursue a diversification strategy while the on-line industry still has many years of rapid growth ahead of it and while competing successfully in that marketplace is placing significant demands upon the managerial, financial, and technological resources and capabilities of America Online. If it did diversify, America Online would probably run the risk of starving its fast-growing core business of necessary resources, which could quickly result in the decline of that operation.

Nor is it just fast-growing companies that benefit from focusing an organization's resources and capabilities on one business activity. Some diversified companies active in more mature businesses have also stretched scarce resources too thinly over too many activities, and their performance has declined as a consequence. Sears, for example, found that its diversification into financial services and real estate diverted top management's attention away from its core retailing business, which helped to contribute to a decline in the profitability of that activity. Similarly, Coca-Cola's decision to divest Columbia Pictures was in part driven by a realization that running an entertainment business was diverting the attention of valuable top management from its core soft drink operation.

Another advantage of concentration on a single business is that the company thereby "sticks to its knitting."[2] What this means is that the company sticks to doing what it knows best and does not make the mistake of diversifying into areas that it knows little about and where its existing resources and capabilities add little value. Companies that do undertake such diversification are prone to discover after the event that they are involved in a business they do not understand, one in which their uninformed decision making may have a serious and perhaps detrimental effect. For example, in 1991 the Japanese consumer electronics concern Matsushita acquired the U.S. movie and music group MCA. The senior executives at Matsushita, however, soon discovered that they knew very little about either the music or movie business. Matsushita's hamfisted attempts to give strategic guidance to top managers at MCA alienated those managers, several of whom left the organization. Others engaged in what amounted to "open rebellion," ignoring attempts by Japanese executives to intervene in the running of MCA. At one time it was rumored in the financial press that as many as 100 top MCA managers were considering defecting from the organization. This proved to be very damaging in a business in which one of the prime assets is people. Matsushita soon found itself trying to fix managerial problems in a business it did not understand. In 1995 it divested itself of MCA, admitting at the time it had made an expensive mistake. (Matsushita reportedly lost $2 billion on the deal.)[3]

On the other hand, concentrating on just one business area has disadvantages as well. As we shall see in the next section, a certain amount of vertical integration may be necessary to create value and establish a competitive advantage within a company's core business. Moreover, companies that concentrate on just one business may be missing out on opportunities to create value and make greater profits by leveraging their resources and capabilities to other activities. Thus, as we saw in the Opening Case, by allowing the company to leverage valuable resources and capabilities across businesses, Rockwell's diversification has helped it create value.

VERTICAL INTEGRATION

A strategy of **vertical integration** means that a company is producing its own inputs (backward, or upstream, integration) or is disposing of its own outputs (forward, or downstream, integration). A steel company that supplies its iron ore needs from company-owned iron ore mines exemplifies backward (upstream) integration. An automaker that sells its cars through company-owned distribution outlets illustrates forward (downstream) integration. Figure 9.1 illustrates four *main* stages in a

Upstream ←———————————————————————————————→ *Downstream*

FIGURE 9.1

Stages in the Raw
Material to Consumer
Value Chain

typical raw-material-to-consumer production chain. For a company based in the assembly stage, backward integration means moving into intermediate manufacturing and raw materials production. Forward integration means moving into distribution. At each stage in the chain, *value is added* to the product. What this means is that a company at that stage takes the product produced in the previous stage and transforms it in some way so that it is worth more to a company at the next stage in the chain and, ultimately, to the end user.

As an example of the value-added concept, consider the production chain in the personal computer industry, illustrated in Figure 9.2. In the personal computer industry, the raw materials companies include the manufacturers of specialty ceramics, chemicals, and metals such as Kyocera of Japan, which manufactures the ceramic substrate for semiconductors. These companies sell their output to the manufacturers of intermediate products. The intermediate manufacturers, which include companies such as Intel and Motorola, transform the ceramics, chemicals, and metals they purchase into computer components such as microprocessors, memory chips, and disk drives. In doing so they *add value* to the raw materials they purchase. These components are then sold to assembly companies such as Apple and Compaq, which take these components and transform them into personal computers—that is, *add value* to the components they purchase. Many of the completed personal computers are then sold to distributors such as Bizmart and Computer World, which in turn sell them to final customers. The distributors also *add value* to the product by making it accessible to customers and by providing service and support. Thus, value is added by companies at each stage in the raw materials-to-consumer chain.

Viewed this way, vertical integration presents companies with a choice about which value-added stages of the raw material-to-consumer chain to compete in. In the personal computer industry, most companies have not integrated into adjacent stages. However, there are some major exceptions. For example, IBM and Digital Equipment operate in both the intermediate manufacturer and assembly stages of

FIGURE 9.2

The Raw Material to
Consumer Value Chain
in the Personal
Computer Industry

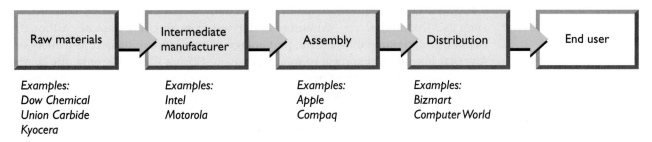

Examples:
Dow Chemical
Union Carbide
Kyocera

Examples:
Intel
Motorola

Examples:
Apple
Compaq

Examples:
Bizmart
Computer World

FIGURE 9.3

Full and Taper
Integration

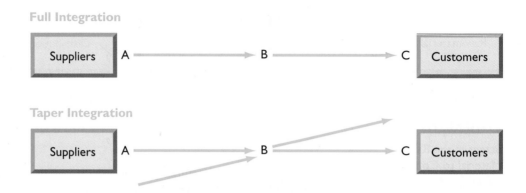

the industry. They are vertically integrated enterprises. In contrast, many of their competitors in the end-user market, such as Compaq and Apple, are not vertically integrated.

Finally, note that besides forward and backward integration, it is also possible to distinguish between **full integration** and **taper integration** (see Figure 9.3).[4] A company achieves full integration when it produces all of a particular input needed for its processes or when it disposes of all its output through its own operations. Taper integration occurs when a company buys from independent suppliers in addition to company-owned suppliers or when it disposes of its output through independent outlets in addition to company-owned outlets. The advantages of taper integration over full integration are discussed later in the chapter.

Creating Value Through Vertical Integration

A company pursuing vertical integration is normally motivated by a desire to strengthen the competitive position of its original, or core, business.[5] There are four main arguments for pursuing a vertical-integration strategy. Vertical integration (1) enables the company to build barriers to new competition, (2) facilitates investments in efficiency-enhancing specialized assets, (3) protects product quality, and (4) results in improved scheduling.

Building Barriers to Entry   By vertically integrating backward to gain control over the source of critical inputs or vertically integrating forward to gain control over distribution channels, a company can build barriers to new entry into its industry. To the extent that this strategy is effective, it limits competition in the company's industry, thereby enabling the company to charge a higher price and make greater profits than it could otherwise.[6] To grasp this argument, consider a famous example of this strategy from the 1930s.

At that time commercial smelting of aluminum was pioneered by companies such as Alcoa and Alcan. Aluminum is derived from smelting bauxite. Although bauxite is a common mineral, the percentage of aluminum in bauxite is usually so low that it is not economical to mine and smelt. During the 1930s only one large-scale deposit of bauxite had been discovered in which the percentage of aluminum in the mineral made smelting economical. This deposit was on the Caribbean island of Jamaica. Alcoa and Alcan vertically integrated backward and acquired ownership of this deposit. This action created a barrier to entry into the aluminum industry.

Potential competitors were deterred from entry because they could not get access to high-grade bauxite; it was all owned by Alcoa and Alcan. Because they had to use lower-grade bauxite, those that did enter the industry found themselves at a cost disadvantage. This situation persisted until the 1950s, when new high-grade deposits were discovered in Australia and Indonesia.

More recently, a similar strategy has been pursued by vertically integrated companies in the computer industry, such as IBM and Digital Equipment. These companies manufacture the main computer components such as microprocessors and memory chips, design and assemble the computers, produce the software that runs the computers, and sell the final product directly to end users. The original rationale behind this strategy was that many of the key components and software used in computers contained proprietary elements. These companies reasoned that by producing the proprietary technology in-house they could limit rivals' access to it, thereby building barriers to entry. Thus, when IBM introduced its PS/2 personal computer system in the mid 1980s, it announced that certain component parts incorporating proprietary technology would be manufactured in-house by IBM.

While this strategy worked well from the 1960s until the early 1980s, it has been failing since then. In the early 1990s the worst performers in the computer industry were precisely the companies that pursued a vertical integration strategy: IBM and Digital Equipment. What seems to have happened is that the shift to open standards in computer hardware and software has nullified the advantages for computer companies of being extensively vertically integrated. In addition, new personal computer companies such as Compaq found that they could quickly reverse engineer and duplicate the proprietary components that companies such as IBM placed in their computers, effectively circumventing this barrier to entry.

Facilitating Investments in Specialized Assets   A specialized asset is one that is designed to perform a specific task and whose value is significantly reduced in its next best use.[7] A specialized asset may be a piece of equipment that has very specialized uses, or it may be the know-how or skills that an individual or company has acquired through training and experience. Companies (and individuals) invest in specialized assets because these assets allow them to lower the costs of value creation and/or to differentiate their product offering more effectively from that of competitors, thereby facilitating premium pricing. A company might invest in specialized equipment because that enables it to lower its manufacturing costs and increase its quality, or it might invest in developing highly specialized technological knowledge because doing so lets it develop better products than its rivals. Thus, specialization can be the basis for achieving a competitive advantage at the business level.

In this section we look at why a company may find it very difficult to persuade other companies in *adjacent* stages in the raw materials-to-consumer production chain to undertake investments in specialized assets. To realize the economic gains associated with such investments, the company may have to integrate vertically into such adjacent stages and make the investments itself. As an illustration, imagine that Ford has developed a new, high-performance, high-quality, and uniquely designed carburetor. The carburetor will increase fuel efficiency, which in turn will help differentiate Ford's cars from those of its rivals—that is, it will give Ford a competitive advantage. Ford has to decide whether to make the carburetor in-house (vertical integration) or contract out manufacturing to an independent supplier (outsourcing).

Manufacturing these carburetors requires substantial investments in equipment that can be used only for this purpose. Because of its unique design, the equipment cannot be used to manufacture any other type of carburetor for Ford or any other auto firm. Thus, the investment in this equipment constitutes an investment in specialized assets.

First, consider this situation from the perspective of an independent supplier that has been asked by Ford to make this investment. The supplier might reason that once it has made the investment, it will become dependent on Ford for business *since Ford is the only possible customer for the output of this equipment.* The supplier perceives this as putting Ford in a strong bargaining position and worries that Ford might use this position to squeeze down prices for the carburetors. Given this risk, the supplier declines to make the investment in specialized equipment.

Now, consider Ford's position. Ford might reason that if it contracts out production of these carburetors to an independent supplier, it might become too dependent on that supplier for a vital input. Since specialized equipment is required to produce the carburetors, Ford cannot easily switch its orders to other suppliers that lack the equipment. Ford perceives this as increasing the bargaining power of the supplier and worries that the supplier might use its bargaining strength to demand higher prices.

The situation of *mutual dependence* that would be created by the investment in specialized assets makes Ford hesitant to contract out manufacturing and makes any potential suppliers hesitant to undertake the investments in specialized assets required to produce the carburetors. The real problem here is a lack of trust. Neither Ford nor the supplier completely trusts the other to play fair in this situation. The lack of trust arises from the **risk of holdup,** that is, of being taken advantage of by a trading partner after the investment in specialized assets has been made.[8] Because of this risk, Ford might reason that the only safe way to get the new carburetors is to manufacture them itself.

To generalize from this example, when achieving a competitive advantage requires one company to make investments in specialized assets in order to trade with another, the risk of holdup may serve as a deterrent, and the investment may not take place. Consequently, the potential for competitive gains from specialization would be lost. To prevent such loss, companies integrate vertically into adjacent stages in the value chain. This consideration has driven automobile companies to integrate vertically backward into the production of component parts, steel companies to integrate vertically backward into the production of iron, computer companies to integrate vertically backward into chip production, and aluminum companies to integrate vertically backward into bauxite mining. The rationale underlying vertical integration in the aluminum industry is explored in greater detail in Strategy in Action 9.1.

Protecting Product Quality   By protecting product quality, vertical integration enables a company to become a differentiated player in its core business. The banana industry illustrates this situation. Historically, a problem facing food companies that import bananas was the variable quality of delivered bananas, which often arrived on the shelves of American stores either too ripe or not ripe enough. To correct this problem, major U.S. food companies such as General Foods have integrated backward to gain control over supply sources. Consequently, they have been able

STRATEGY *in* ACTION

Specialized Assets and Vertical Integration in the Aluminum Industry

For an example of how an investment in a specialized asset can lead to vertical integration, consider the case of an aluminum-refining company. Aluminum refineries are designed to refine bauxite ore and produce aluminum. The metal content and chemical composition of bauxite ore vary from deposit to deposit. Each type of ore requires a specialized refinery; that is, the refinery must be designed for a particular type of ore. Running one type of bauxite through a refinery designed for another type reportedly increases production costs by 20 to 100 percent.[9] Thus, the value of an investment in a specialized aluminum refinery and the cost of the output produced by that refinery depend upon its receiving the right kind of bauxite ore.

Imagine that an aluminum company has to decide whether to invest in an aluminum refinery that is designed to refine a certain type of ore. Assume further that this ore is only produced by a bauxite company at a single bauxite mine. Using a different type of ore would raise production costs by 50 percent. Therefore, the value of the aluminum company's investment is dependent on the price it must pay the bauxite company for this bauxite. Recognizing this, once the aluminum company has made the investment in a new refinery, what is to stop the bauxite company from raising bauxite prices? The answer is nothing; once it has made the investment, the aluminum company is locked into its relationship with its bauxite supplier. The bauxite company can increase bauxite prices, secure in the knowledge that so long as the resulting increase in the total production costs of the aluminum company are less than 50 percent, the aluminum company will continue to buy from it. Thus, once the aluminum company has made the investment, the bauxite company can hold up the aluminum company.

How can the aluminum company reduce the risk of holdup? The answer is by purchasing the bauxite company. If the aluminum company can purchase the bauxite company or that company's bauxite mine, it need no longer fear that bauxite prices will be increased after the investment in an aluminum refinery has been made. In other words, it makes economic sense for the aluminum company contemplating the investment to engage in vertical integration. Vertical integration, by eliminating the risk of holdup, makes the specialized investment worthwhile. In practice it has been argued that these kinds of considerations have driven aluminum companies to pursue vertical integration to such a degree that, according to one study, 91 percent of the total volume of bauxite is transferred within vertically integrated aluminum companies.[10]

to distribute bananas of a standard quality at the optimal time for consumption. Knowing they can rely on the quality of these brands, consumers are willing to pay more for them. Thus, by vertically integrating backward into plantation ownership, the banana companies have built consumer confidence, which enables them in turn to charge a premium price for their product. Similarly, when McDonald's decided to open its first restaurant in Moscow, it found, much to its initial dismay, that in order to serve food and drink indistinguishable from that served in McDonald's restaurants elsewhere, it had to vertically integrate backward and supply its own needs. The quality of Russian-grown potatoes and meat was simply too poor. Thus, to protect the quality of its product, McDonald's set up its own dairy farms, cattle ranches, vegetable plots, and a food-processing plant within the Soviet Union.

The same kind of considerations can result in forward integration. Ownership of distribution outlets may be necessary if the required standards of after-sales service for complex products are to be maintained. For example, in the 1920s Kodak owned retail outlets for distributing photographic equipment. The company felt that few established retail outlets had the skills necessary to sell and service its photographic equipment. By the 1930s, however, Kodak decided that it no longer needed to own its retail outlets because other retailers had begun to provide satisfactory distribution and service for Kodak products. The company then withdrew from retailing.

Improved Scheduling   It is sometimes argued that strategic advantages arise from the easier planning, coordination, and scheduling of adjacent processes made possible in vertically integrated organizations.[11] Such advantages can be particularly important to companies trying to realize the benefits of just-in-time inventory systems, discussed in detail in Chapter 5. For example, in the 1920s Ford profited from the tight coordination and scheduling that is possible with backward vertical integration. Ford integrated backward into steel foundries, iron ore shipping, and iron ore mining. Deliveries at Ford were coordinated to such an extent that iron ore unloaded at Ford's steel foundries on the Great Lakes was turned into engine blocks within twenty-four hours. Thus, Ford substantially lowered its cost structure by eliminating the need to hold excessive inventories.

The enhanced scheduling that vertical integration makes feasible may also enable a company to respond better to sudden changes in demand conditions or to get its product into the marketplace faster. A situation in the microprocessor industry of the early 1990s illustrates this point. Demand for microprocessors was running at an all-time high, and most microprocessor manufacturing plants were operating at full capacity. At that time several microprocessor companies that specialized in chip design but contracted out manufacturing found themselves at a strategic disadvantage. For example, in 1991 Chips & Technologies succeeded in designing a clone of Intel's 386 microprocessor. Chips & Technologies sent its clone design to Texas Instruments (TI) to be manufactured, only to find that it had to wait fourteen weeks until TI could schedule time to manufacture that item. In that short span prices for 386 microprocessors fell from \$112 to \$50. By the time TI produced the 386 clone for Chips & Technologies, the company had missed the best part of the market. Had Chips & Technologies been vertically integrated into manufacturing, this loss would not have occurred.[12]

Arguments Against Vertical Integration

Vertical integration has its disadvantages. Most important among them are (1) cost disadvantages, (2) disadvantages that arise when technology is changing fast, and (3) disadvantages that arise when demand is unpredictable. These disadvantages imply that the benefits of vertical integration are not always as substantial as they might seem initially.

Cost Disadvantages   Although often undertaken to gain a production cost advantage, vertical integration can raise costs if a company becomes committed to purchasing inputs from company-owned suppliers when low-cost external sources of supply exist. For example, during the early 1990s General Motors made 68 percent of the component parts for its vehicles in-house, more than any other major automaker. (At Chrysler the figure is 30 percent, and at Toyota it is 28 percent.)

That vertical integration has caused GM to be the highest-cost producer among the world's major car companies. In 1992 GM was paying $34.60 an hour in United Auto Workers wages and benefits to its employees at company-owned suppliers for work that rivals could get done by independent nonunionized suppliers at half these rates.[13] Thus, vertical integration can be a disadvantage when a company's own sources of supply have higher operating costs than those of independent suppliers.

Company-owned suppliers might have high operating costs compared with independent suppliers because company-owned suppliers know that they can always sell their output to other parts of the company. Not having to compete for orders lessens the incentive to minimize operating costs. Indeed, the managers of the supply operation may be tempted to pass on any cost increases to other parts of the company in the form of higher transfer prices, rather than look for ways to lower those costs. Thus, the lack of incentive to reduce costs can raise operating costs. The problem may be less serious, however, when the company pursues taper, rather than full, integration, since the need to compete with independent suppliers can produce downward pressure on the cost structure of company-owned suppliers.

Technological Change   When technology is changing fast, vertical integration poses the hazard of tying a company to obsolescent technology.[14] Consider a radio manufacturer that in the 1950s integrated backward and acquired a manufacturer of vacuum tubes. When in the 1960s transistors replaced vacuum tubes as a major component in radios, this company found itself tied to a technologically obsolescent business. Switching to transistors would have meant writing off its investment in vacuum tubes. Therefore, the company was reluctant to change and instead continued to use vacuum tubes in its radios while its nonintegrated competitors were rapidly switching to the new technology. Since it kept making an outdated product, the company rapidly lost market share. Thus, vertical integration can inhibit a company's ability to change its suppliers or its distribution systems to match the requirements of changing technology.

Demand Uncertainty   Vertical integration can also be risky in unstable or unpredictable demand conditions. When demand is stable, higher degrees of vertical integration might be managed with relative ease. Stable demand allows better scheduling and coordination of production flows among different activities. When demand conditions are unstable or unpredictable, achieving close coordination among vertically integrated activities may be difficult.

The problem is to balance capacity among different stages of a process. For example, an auto manufacturer might vertically integrate backward to acquire a supplier of carburetors that has a capacity exactly matching the auto manufacturer's needs. However, if demand for autos subsequently falls, the automaker will find itself locked into a business that is running below capacity. Clearly, this would be uneconomical. The auto manufacturer could avoid this situation by continuing to buy carburetors on the open market rather than making them itself. If demand conditions are unpredictable, taper integration might be somewhat less risky than full integration. When a company obtains only part of its total input requirements from company-owned suppliers, in times of low demand it can keep its in-house suppliers running at full capacity by ordering exclusively from them.

Bureaucratic Costs and the Limits of Vertical Integration

As already noted, although vertical integration can create value, it may also result in substantial costs caused by a lack of incentive on the part of company-owned suppliers to reduce their operating costs, by a possible lack of strategic flexibility in times of changing technology, or by uncertain demand. Together, these costs form a major component of what we refer to as the **bureaucratic costs** of vertical integration. Bureaucratic costs are those involved in running an organization. They include the costs that stem from bureaucratic inefficiencies, such as those we have just discussed. Bureaucratic costs place a limit on the amount of vertical integration that can be profitably pursued: it makes sense for a company to integrate vertically only if the value created by such a strategy exceeds the bureaucratic costs associated with expanding the boundaries of the organization to incorporate additional upstream or downstream activities.

Common sense reasoning suggests that not all vertical integration opportunities have the same potential for value creation. Although vertical integration may initially have a favorable impact, the value created by additional integration into areas more distant from a company's core business is likely to become increasingly marginal. The more marginal the value created by a vertical integration move, the more likely it is that the bureaucratic costs associated with expanding the boundaries of the organization into new activities will outweigh the value created. Once this occurs, a limit to profitable vertical integration has been reached.[15]

However, it is worth bearing in mind that the pursuit of taper integration rather than full integration may decrease the bureaucratic costs of vertical integration. This occurs because taper integration creates an incentive for in-house suppliers to reduce their operating costs and increases the company's ability to respond to changing demand conditions. Hence, it reduces some of the organizational inefficiencies that raise bureaucratic costs.

ALTERNATIVES TO VERTICAL INTEGRATION: COOPERATIVE RELATIONSHIPS AND STRATEGIC OUTSOURCING

The disadvantages associated with vertical integration raise the question of whether it is possible to reap the benefits of vertical integration without having to bear the same level of bureaucratic costs. Can the benefits associated with vertical integration be captured through outsourcing activities to other companies? The answer seems to be a qualified yes. Under certain circumstances, companies can realize the gains linked with vertical integration without having to bear the bureaucratic costs if they enter into long-term cooperative relationships with their trading partners. Such long-term relationships are typically referred to as strategic alliances. However, companies will generally be unable to realize the gains associated with vertical integration if they enter into short-term contracts with their trading partners. To see why this is so, we first discuss the problems associated with short-term contracts. Then we look at strategic alliances and long-term contracts as an alternative to vertical integration and discuss how companies can build enduring, long-term relationships with their trading partners.

Short-Term Contracts and Competitive Bidding

A short-term contract is one that lasts for a year or less. Many companies use short-term contracts to structure the purchasing of their inputs or the sale of their outputs. A classic example is the automobile company that uses a **competitive bidding strategy** to negotiate the price for a particular part produced by component suppliers. For example, General Motors often solicits bids from a number of different suppliers for producing a component part and awards a one-year contract to the supplier submitting the lowest bid. At the end of the year, the contract is put out for competitive bid again. Thus, there is no guarantee the company that won the contract one year will hold on to it the next.

The benefit of this strategy is that it forces suppliers to keep down their prices. However, GM's lack of long-term commitment to individual suppliers may make them very hesitant to undertake the type of investments in specialized assets that may be needed to improve the design or quality of component parts or to improve scheduling between GM and its suppliers. Indeed, with no guarantee that it would remain a GM supplier the following year, the supplier may refuse to undertake investments in specialized assets. GM then may have to integrate vertically backward in order to realize the gains associated with specialization.

In other words, using a strategy of short-term contracting and competitive bidding, *because it signals a lack of long-term commitment to its suppliers on the part of a company,* makes it very difficult for that company to realize the gains associated with vertical integration. This is not a problem when there is minimal need for close cooperation between the company and its suppliers to facilitate investments in specialized assets, improve scheduling, or improve product quality. In such cases competitive bidding may be optimal. However, when this need is significant, a competitive bidding strategy can be a serious drawback.

Interestingly enough, there are signs that GM, by adopting a competitive bidding stance with regard to its suppliers, has placed itself at a competitive disadvantage. In 1992 the company instructed its parts suppliers to cut their prices by 10 percent, regardless of prior pricing agreements. In effect, GM tore up existing contracts and tried to force through its policy by threatening to weed out suppliers that did not agree to the price reduction. Although such action may yield short-term benefits for GM, there is a long-term cost to be borne: the loss of trust and the hostility created between the company and its suppliers. According to press reports, several suppliers have claimed that they are cutting back on research for future GM parts. They have also indicated that they will impart new ideas to Chrysler or Ford, both of which have recently taken a more cooperative approach to forging long-term relationships with suppliers.[16]

Strategic Alliances and Long-Term Contracting

Long-term contracts are long-term cooperative relationships between two companies. Such agreements are often referred to in the popular press as **strategic alliances.** Typically in these arrangements, one company agrees to supply the other, and the other company agrees to continue purchasing from that supplier; both make a commitment to seek jointly ways of lowering the costs or raising the quality of inputs into the downstream company's value creation process. If it is achieved, such a stable long-term relationship lets the participating companies share the value that might be created by vertical integration and at the same time avoid many of the bureaucratic costs linked with ownership of an adjacent stage in the raw material-to-consumer production chain. Thus, long-term contracts can substitute for vertical integration.

Consider the cooperative relationships that many Japanese auto companies have with their component-parts suppliers (the *keiretsu* system), which exemplify successful long-term contracting. These relationships often go back decades. Together, the auto companies and their suppliers work out ways to add value—for instance, by implementing just-in-time inventory systems or by cooperating on designs for component parts to improve quality and lower assembly costs. As part of this process, the suppliers make substantial investments in specialized assets in order to serve the needs of the auto companies better. Thus, the Japanese automakers have been able to capture many of the benefits of vertical integration without having to bear the associated bureaucratic costs. The suppliers of component parts also benefit from these relationships, for they grow with the company they supply and share in its success.[17]

In contrast to their Japanese counterparts, U.S. auto companies have historically tended to pursue formal vertical integration. General Motors manufactures 68 percent of its own component parts and Ford 47 percent, compared with less than 30 percent among most Japanese auto companies.[18] According to several studies, the increased bureaucratic costs of managing extensive vertical integration have helped place GM and Ford at a competitive disadvantage relative to their Japanese competition.[19] Moreover, when U.S. auto companies decide not to integrate vertically, they do not necessarily enter into cooperative long-term relationships with independent component suppliers. Instead, they have tended to use their powerful position to pursue an aggressive competitive bidding strategy, playing off component suppliers against each other. Although Ford and Chrysler have now backed away from such a policy, it remains in force at GM, as noted earlier. For details on how Chrysler has attempted to build long-term cooperative relationships with suppliers, see Strategy in Action 9.2.

Building Long-Term Cooperative Relationships

The interesting question raised by the preceding section is how a company can achieve a stable long-term strategic alliance with another, given the lack of trust and the fear of holdup that arises when one company has to invest in specialized assets in order to trade with another. How have companies such as Toyota managed to develop such enduring relationships with their suppliers?

Companies can take some specific steps to ensure that a long-term cooperative relationship can work and to lessen the chances of a partner's reneging on an agreement. One of those steps is for the company making investments in specialized assets to demand a hostage from its partner. Another is to establish a credible commitment on both sides to build a trusting long-term relationship.[20]

Hostage Taking   Hostage taking is essentially a means of guaranteeing that a partner will keep its side of the bargain. The cooperative relationship between Boeing and Northrop Grumman illustrates this type of situation. Northrop Grumman is a major subcontractor for Boeing's commercial airline division, providing many com-

9.2   STRATEGY *in* ACTION

Chrysler Builds an American Keiretsu

As with many U.S. companies, Chrysler for most of its history managed suppliers through a competitive bidding process in which suppliers were selected on the basis of their ability to supply Chrysler with components at the lowest possible cost. A supplier's track record on performance and quality was relatively unimportant in this process. Contracts were renegotiated every two years with little or no commitment from Chrysler to continuing to do business with a particular supplier. As a result, the typical relationship between Chrysler and its suppliers was characterized by mutual distrust, suspicion, and a reluctance on the part of suppliers to invest too much in their relationship with Chrysler.

Since the early 1990s, however, Chrysler has systematically reorganized its dealings with suppliers in an attempt to build stable long-term relationships. The aim of this new approach has been to try and get suppliers to help Chrysler in the process of developing new products and improving its production processes. To encourage suppliers to cooperate and to make investments that are specific to Chrysler's needs, the company has moved sharply away from its old adversarial approach. The average contract with suppliers has been lengthened from two years to more than four and a half years. Furthermore, Chrysler has given 90 percent of its suppliers oral commitments that business will be extended for at least the life of a model, if not beyond that. The company has also committed itself to share with suppliers the benefits of any process improvements they might suggest. The basic thinking behind offering suppliers such credible commitments is to align incentives between Chrysler and its suppliers—to create a sense of shared destiny—that encourages mutual cooperation to increase the size of the financial pie available to both.

The fruits of this new approach are beginning to appear. By involving suppliers early in product development and giving them greater responsibility for design

and manufacturing, Chrysler has substantially compressed its product development cycle and also taken a lot of cost out of product development. For example, Chrysler has reduced the time it takes to develop a new vehicle from 234 weeks during the mid 1980s to about 160 weeks in 1996. The total cost of developing a new vehicle has also fallen by 20 to 40 percent, depending on the model. With development costs in the automobile industry running between $1 billion and $2 billion per model, that translates into a huge financial saving. Many of these savings are the direct result of engineering improvements suggested by suppliers or of improved coordination between Chrysler and suppliers in the design process. To facilitate this process, the number of resident engineers from suppliers who work side by side with Chrysler engineers in cross-company design teams has increased from 30 in 1989 to more than 300 by 1996.

Beginning in 1990, Chrysler has also implemented a program known internally as the Supplier Cost Reduction Effort (or SCORE). SCORE focuses upon cooperation between Chrysler and suppliers to identify opportunities for process improvements. In its first two years of operation, SCORE generated 875 ideas from suppliers that were worth $170.8 million in annual savings. In 1994 suppliers submitted 3,786 ideas that produced $504 million in annual savings. By December 1995 Chrysler had implemented a total of 5,300 ideas that have generated more than $1.7 billion in annual savings. One supplier alone, Magna International, had submitted 214 proposals by December 1995, 129 of which Chrysler adopted for a total cost saving of $75.5 million. Many of the ideas themselves have a relatively small financial impact. For example, a Magna suggestion to change the type of decorative wood grain used on minivans saved $0.5 million per year. However, the cumulative impact of thousands of such ideas has had a very significant impact upon Chrysler's bottom line.[21]

ponent parts for the 747 and 767 aircraft. To serve Boeing's special needs, Northrop Grumman has had to make substantial investments in specialized assets. In theory, because of the sunk costs associated with such investments, Northrop Grumman is dependent on Boeing, and Boeing is in a position to renege on previous agreements and use the threat to switch orders to other suppliers as a way of driving down prices. However, in practice Boeing is unlikely to do so since the company is also a major supplier to Northrop Grumman's defense division, providing many parts for the Stealth bomber. Boeing has had to make substantial investments in specialized assets in order to serve Northrop Grumman's needs. Thus, the companies are *mutually dependent.* Boeing, therefore, is unlikely to renege on any pricing agreements with Northrop Grumman, since it knows that Northrop Grumman could respond in kind. Each company holds a hostage that can be used as insurance against the other company's unilateral reneging on prior pricing agreements.

Credible Commitments   A credible commitment is a believable commitment to support the development of a long-term relationship between companies. To understand the concept of credibility in this context, consider the relationship between General Electric and IBM. GE is one of the major suppliers of advanced semiconductor chips to IBM, and many of the chips are customized to IBM's own requirements. To meet IBM's specific needs, GE has had to make substantial investments in specialized assets that have little other value. As a consequence, GE is dependent on IBM and faces the risk that IBM will take advantage of this dependence to demand lower prices. Theoretically, IBM could back up its demand with the threat to switch to another supplier. However, GE reduced this risk by having IBM enter into a contractual agreement that committed IBM to purchase chips from GE until the end of the 1990s. In addition, IBM agreed to share in the costs of developing the customized chips, thereby reducing GE's investments in specialized assets. Thus, by publicly committing itself to a long-term contract and by putting some money into the development of the customized chips, IBM has essentially made a credible commitment to continue purchasing those chips from GE.

Maintaining Market Discipline   A company that has entered into a long-term relationship can become too dependent on an inefficient partner. Since it does not have to compete with other organizations in the marketplace for the company's business, the partner may lack the incentive to be cost efficient. Consequently, a company entering into a cooperative long-term relationship must be able to apply some kind of market discipline to its partner.

The company holds two strong cards. First, even long-term contracts are periodically renegotiated, generally every four to five years. Thus, a partner knows that if it fails to live up to its commitments, the company may refuse to renew the contract. Second, some companies engaged in long-term relationships with suppliers use a **parallel sourcing policy**—that is, they enter into a long-term contract with two suppliers for the same part (as is the practice at Toyota, for example).[22] This arrangement gives the company a hedge against a defiant partner, for each supplier knows that if it fails to comply with the agreement, the company can switch all its business to the other. This threat is rarely made explicit, since that would be against the spirit of building a cooperative long-term relationship. However, the mere awareness of parallel sourcing serves to inject an element of market discipline into the relationship, signaling to suppliers that if the need arises, they can be replaced at short notice.

Summary   By establishing credible commitments or by taking hostages, companies may be able to use long-term contracts to realize much of the value associated with vertical integration without its bureaucratic costs. As a general point, note that the growing importance of just-in-time inventory systems as a way of reducing costs and enhancing quality is increasing the pressure on companies to enter into long-term agreements in a wide range of industries. These agreements thus might become much more popular in the future. However, when such agreements cannot be reached, formal vertical integration may be necessary.

Strategic Outsourcing and the Virtual Corporation

The opposite of vertical integration is **outsourcing** value creation activities to subcontractors. In recent years there has been a clear move among many enterprises to outsource noncore activities.[23] This process typically begins with a company's identifying those value creation activities that form the basis of its competitive advantage (its distinctive, or core, competencies). The idea is to keep performing these core value creation activities within the company. The remaining activities are then reviewed to see whether they can be performed more effectively and efficiently by independent suppliers. If they can, these activities are outsourced to those suppliers. The relationships between the company and those suppliers are then often structured as long-term contractual relationships, although in some instances it may make sense to manage relationships on the basis of competitive bidding. The term **virtual corporation** has been coined to describe companies that have pursued extensive strategic outsourcing.[24]

In recent years Xerox has placed greater reliance on strategic outsourcing. The corporation has determined that its distinctive competencies are to be found in the design and manufacture of photocopying systems. In an attempt to reduce the cost of performing noncore value creation activities, Xerox has outsourced the responsibility for performing many of them to other companies. For example, Xerox has a $3.2 billion contract with Electronic Data Systems (EDS) under which EDS runs all of Xerox's internal computer and telecommunications networks. As part of this relationship, 1,700 Xerox employees have been transferred to EDS. Since the relationship involves substantial investments in specialized assets on the part of EDS, Xerox has structured it as a long-term cooperative alliance.[25] In another case, NIKE, the world's largest manufacturer of athletic shoes, has outsourced all its manufacturing operations to Asian partners but kept its core product design and marketing capabilities in-house. For another example of strategic outsourcing, see Strategy in Action 9.3.

There are several advantages of strategic outsourcing.[26] First, by outsourcing a noncore activity to a supplier that is more efficient at performing that particular activity, the company may be able to reduce its own cost structure. As you can see from Strategy in Action 9.3, this has been a major factor behind recent outsourcing decisions at Boeing.

Second, by outsourcing a noncore value creation activity to a supplier that has a distinctive competency in that particular activity, the company may also be able to differentiate its final product better. For example, Cincinnati Bell has developed a distinctive competency in the customer care function. (Customer care includes activating accounts, billing customers, and dealing with customers' inquiries.) Accordingly, several other telephone companies, including AT&T Wireless and MCI Long Distance, outsource their customer care function to Cincinnati Bell. Both companies believe that Cincinnati Bell can provide a better customer care service than

Strategic Outsourcing at Boeing

 Boeing is the world's largest manufacturer of commercial jet aircraft, with a 60 percent share of the global market. Despite its large market share, in recent years Boeing has found it tough going competitively. The company's problems are twofold. First, Boeing faces a very aggressive competitor in Europe's Airbus Industrie. The dog fight between Boeing and Airbus for market share has enabled major airlines to play the two companies off against each other in an attempt to bargain down the price for commercial jet aircraft. Second, as if this weren't bad enough, the world's major airlines have been through some very rough years recently, with many airlines racking up massive financial losses. As a result, many now lack the financial resources required to purchase new aircraft. Instead, they are holding on to their used aircraft for much longer than has typically been the case. Thus, while the average service life of a Boeing 737 was once reckoned to be about fifteen years, many airlines are now making the aircraft last as long as twenty-five years. This translates into lower orders for new aircraft. Indeed, in 1994 Boeing and Airbus only gained orders for 150 new aircraft, down from nearly 700 orders in 1989 at the peak of the last order boom. Confronted with this new reality, Boeing has come to the conclusion that the only way it can persuade cash-starved airlines to replace their used aircraft with new ones is to be very aggressive with regard to pricing.

Thus, Boeing has recently had to face up to the fact that its ability to raise prices for commercial jet aircraft, which was once quite strong, has now been severely limited. Indeed, if anything, falling prices might now be the norm. If prices are going to come under constant pressure, the only way that Boeing can continue to make a profit ts to drive down its cost structure. With this in mind, in 1994 Boeing undertook a companywide review of its make-or-buy decisions. The objective was to try to identify activities that could be outsourced to subcontractors, both in the United States and abroad, in order to drive down production costs.

When making these decision, Boeing applied a number of criteria. First, Boeing looked at the *basic*

economics of the outsourcing decision. The central issue was whether an activity could be performed more cost effectively by an outside manufacturer or by Boeing. Second, Boeing considered the *strategic risk* associated with outsourcing an activity. Boeing decided that it would not outsource any activity that it deemed to be part of its long-term competitive advantage. For example, the company decided not to outsource the production of wings, because it believed that doing so might give away valuable technology to potential competitors. Third, Boeing looked at the *operational risk* associated with outsourcing an activity. The basic objective was to make sure that Boeing did not become too dependent upon a single outside supplier for critical components. Boeing's philosophy is to hedge operational risk by purchasing from two or more suppliers. Finally, Boeing considered whether it made sense to outsource certain activities to a supplier in a given country in order to help secure orders for commercial jet aircraft from that country. This practice, known as *offsetting,* is common not only in this industry but also in many others. For example, Boeing has decided to outsource the production of certain components to China. This decision was influenced by current forecasts that suggest the Chinese will purchase more than $100 billion worth of commercial jets over the next twenty years. Boeing's hope is that pushing some subcontracting work China's way will help it gain a larger share of this market than its global competitor, Airbus.

One of the first decisions to come out of this process was the one to outsource the production of insulation blankets for 737 and 757 aircraft to suppliers in Mexico. Insulation blankets are wrapped around the inside of the fuselage of an aircraft to keep the interior warm at high altitudes. Boeing has traditionally made these blankets in-house, but it found that it can save $50 million per year by outsourcing production to a Mexican supplier. In total, Boeing reckons that outsourcing will cut its cost structure by $600 million per year between 1994 and 1997. By the time the outsourcing is complete, the amount of an aircraft that Boeing builds will have shrunk 4 percent, from 52 to 48 percent.[27]

they can. Thus, outsourcing helps AT&T Wireless and MCI Long Distance to differentiate their service offerings better.

A third advantage of strategic outsourcing is that it enables the company to concentrate scarce human, financial, and physical resources on further strengthening its core or distinctive competencies. Thus, AT&T Wireless can devote all its energies to building wireless networks, secure in the knowledge that Cincinnati Bell can look after the customer care functions.

Finally, it has been argued that strategic outsourcing enables a company to be more flexible and responsive to changing market conditions. The belief is that, unencumbered by commitments to internal suppliers, a company can switch more easily between providers of noncore value creation activities in response to changing market conditions than can a comparable company that undertakes those activities itself.

Having said this, we must also recognize some clear disadvantages associated with strategic outsourcing. One is that a company that outsources an activity loses both the ability to learn from that activity and the opportunity to transform that activity into a distinctive competence of the company. Thus, while outsourcing customer care activities to Cincinnati Bell may make sense right now for AT&T Wireless, one potential problem with this strategy is that AT&T Wireless will fail to build a valuable internal competency in customer care. Ultimately there is a risk that this lack may place AT&T Wireless at a competitive disadvantage relative to other wireless providers that have such a competency, particularly if customer care becomes an important feature of competition in the marketplace. A second drawback of outsourcing is that the company may become too dependent upon a particular supplier. In the long run, this may hurt the company if the performance of that supplier starts to deteriorate, or if the supplier starts to use its power to demand higher prices from the company. A third concern is that in its enthusiasm for strategic outsourcing, a company might go too far and outsource value creation activities that are central to the maintenance of its competitive advantage. By doing so, the company may lose control over the future development of a competency, with the result that its performance might ultimately decline. None of this is meant to imply that strategic outsourcing should not be pursued, but it does indicate that managers should carefully weigh the pros and cons of the strategy before pursuing it.

DIVERSIFICATION

Up until this point we have been dealing with vertical integration and its alternatives. It is now time to consider diversification. There are two major types of diversification: related diversification and unrelated diversification. **Related diversification** is diversification into a new business activity that is linked to a company's existing business activity or activities by commonality between one or more components of each activity's value chain. Normally, these linkages are based on manufacturing, marketing, or technological commonalties. The diversification of Philip Morris into the brewing industry with the acquisition of Miller Brewing is an example of related diversification because there are marketing commonalties between the brewing and tobacco business. (Both are consumer product businesses in which competitive success depends on brand-positioning skills.) **Unrelated diversification** is diversification into a new business area that has no obvious connection with any of the company's existing areas.

In this section, we first consider how diversification can create value for a company, and then we examine some reasons why so much diversification apparently dissipates rather than creates value. We also take into account the bureaucratic costs of diversification. Finally, we discuss some of the factors that determine the choice between the strategies of related and unrelated diversification.

Creating Value Through Diversification

Most companies first consider diversification when they are generating financial resources *in excess* of those necessary to maintain a competitive advantage in their original, or core, business.[28] The question they must tackle is how to invest the excess resources in order to create value. The diversified company can create value in three main ways: (1) by acquiring and restructuring poorly run enterprises, (2) by transferring competencies among businesses, and (3) by realizing economies of scope.

Acquiring and Restructuring   An acquiring and restructuring strategy rests on the presumption that an efficiently managed company can create value by acquiring inefficient and poorly managed enterprises and improving their efficiency.[29] This approach is considered a form of diversification because the acquired company does not have to be in the same industry as the acquiring company for the strategy to work.

Improvements in the efficiency of an acquired company can come from a number of sources. First, the acquiring company usually replaces the top management team of the acquired company with a more aggressive one. Second, the new top management team is encouraged to sell off any unproductive assets, such as executive jets and elaborate corporate headquarters, and to reduce staffing levels. Third, the new top management team is also encouraged to intervene in the running of the acquired businesses to seek out ways of improving the unit's efficiency, quality, innovativeness, and customer responsiveness. Fourth, to motivate the new top management team and other employees of the acquired unit to undertake such actions, increases in their pay may be linked to increases in the performance of the acquired unit. In addition, the acquiring company often establishes performance goals for the acquired company that cannot be met without significant improvements in operating efficiency. It also makes the new top management aware that failure to achieve performance improvements consistent with these goals within a given amount of time will probably result in their losing their jobs. This system of rewards and punishments established by the acquiring company gives the new managers of the acquired enterprise every incentive to look for ways of improving the efficiency of the unit under their charge.

There are some good examples of how successful a restructuring strategy can be in terms of its impact upon a company's profitability. For instance, the British conglomerates BTR and Hanson both grew by pursuing such a strategy. To a lesser extent, General Electric has also done so.[30] However, the strategy has its critics. Some contend that constant pressures to meet challenging performance objectives within such companies can lead to short-run profit maximization and risk avoidance by managers of business units.[31] Moreover, the arms-length relationship between corporate headquarters and the managers of the business unit, which is common in such enterprises, allows this type of behavior to go undetected until a good deal of damage has been done. The poor performance of portfolio diversifiers, such as Gulf & Western, Consolidated Foods, and ITT—all of which have now been broken up into smaller businesses—lends weight to these criticisms. More than anything else, the conflicting examples suggest that the strategy is difficult to implement.

Transferring Competencies   Companies that base their diversification strategy on transferring competencies seek out new businesses related to their existing business by one or more value creation functions, such as manufacturing, marketing, materials management, and R&D. They may want to create value by drawing on distinctive skills in one or more of their existing value creation functions in order to improve the competitive position of the new business. Alternatively, they may acquire a company in a different business area in the belief that some of the skills of the acquired company can improve the efficiency of their existing value creation activities. If successful, such competency transfers can lower the costs of value creation in one or more of a company's diversified businesses or enable one or more of a company's diversified businesses to undertake their value creation functions in a way that leads to differentiation and a premium price.

An example is Rockwell International, which is profiled in the Opening Case. As we have already noted, Rockwell is seeking to create value by transferring technological skills from its "new technology" businesses, such as aerospace and semiconductors, to its "old technology" businesses, such as automotive components. So far, the results of this exercise seem to be very successful. Philip Morris's transfer of marketing skills to Miller Brewing, discussed earlier, is perhaps one of the classic examples of how value *can* be created by competency transfers. Drawing on its marketing and brand-positioning skills, Philip Morris pioneered the introduction of Miller Lite, the product that redefined the brewing industry and moved Miller from number six to number two in the market.

For such a strategy to work, the competencies being transferred must involve activities that are important for establishing a competitive advantage. All too often companies assume that any commonality is sufficient for creating value. The acquisition of Hughes Aircraft by General Motors, made simply because autos and auto manufacturing were going electronic and Hughes was an electronics concern, demonstrates the folly of overestimating the commonalities among businesses. To date, the acquisition has failed to realize any of the anticipated gains for GM, whose competitive position has only worsened.

Realizing Economies of Scope   **Economies of scope** arise when two or more business units share resources such as manufacturing facilities, distribution channels, advertising campaigns, R&D costs, and so on. Each business unit that shares resources has to invest less in the shared functions.[32] For example, the costs of General Electric's advertising, sales, and service activities in major appliances are low because they are spread over a wide range of products. In addition, such a strategy can utilize the capacity of certain functions better. For example, by producing the components for the assembly operations of two distinct businesses, a component-manufacturing plant may be able to operate at greater capacity, thereby realizing *economies of scale* in addition to economies of scope. Thus, a diversification strategy based on economies of scope can help a company attain a low-cost position in each of the businesses in which it operates. Diversification to realize economies of scope can, therefore, be a valid way of supporting the generic business-level strategy of cost leadership.

However, as with competency transfers, diversification to realize economies of scope is possible only when there are significant commonalities between one or more of the value creation functions of a company's existing and new activities. Moreover, managers need to be aware that the bureaucratic costs of coordination necessary to achieve economies of scope within a company often outweigh the value that can be created by such a strategy.[33] Consequently, the strategy should be pursued only when sharing is likely to generate a *significant* competitive advantage in one or more of a company's business units.

Procter & Gamble's disposable diaper and paper towel businesses offer one of the best examples of the successful realization of economies of scope. These businesses share the costs of procuring certain raw materials (such as paper) and developing the technology for new products and processes. In addition, a joint sales force sells both products to supermarket buyers, and both products are shipped by means of the same distribution system. This resource sharing has given both business units a cost advantage that has enabled them to undercut their less diversified competitors.[34]

Bureaucratic Costs and the Limits of Diversification

While diversification can create value for a company, it often ends up doing just the opposite. For example, in a study that looked at the diversification of thirty-three major U.S. corporations between 1950 and 1986, Michael Porter observed that the track record of corporate diversification has been dismal.[35] Porter found that most of the companies had divested many more diversified acquisitions than they had kept. He concluded that the corporate diversification strategies of most companies have dissipated value instead of created it. More generally, a large number of academic studies support the conclusion that *extensive* diversification tends to depress rather than improve a company's profitability.[36]

One reason for the failure of diversification to achieve its aims is that all too often the *bureaucratic costs* of diversification exceed the value created by the strategy. The level of bureaucratic costs in a diversified organization is a function of two factors: (1) the number of businesses in a company's portfolio and (2) the extent of coordination required among the different businesses of the company in order to realize value from a diversification strategy.

Number of Businesses   The greater the number of businesses in a company's portfolio, the more difficult it is for corporate management to remain informed about the complexities of each business. Management simply does not have the time to process all the information needed to assess the strategic plan of each business unit objectively. This problem began to occur at General Electric in the 1970s. As then CEO Reg Jones commented,

> I tried to review each plan in great detail. This effort took untold hours and
> placed a tremendous burden on the corporate executive office. After a while I

> began to realize that no matter how hard we would work, we could not achieve the necessary in-depth understanding of the 40-odd business unit plans.[37]

The information overload in extensively diversified companies may lead corporate-level management to base important resource allocation decisions on only the most superficial analysis of each business unit's competitive position. Thus, for example, a promising business unit may be starved of investment funds, while other business units receive far more cash than they can profitably reinvest in their operations. Furthermore, the lack of familiarity with operating affairs on the part of corporate-level management increases the chances that business-level managers might deceive corporate-level managers. For instance, business-unit managers might blame poor performance on difficult competitive conditions, even when it is the consequence of poor management. Thus, information overload can result in substantial inefficiencies within extensively diversified companies that cancel out the value created by diversification. These inefficiencies include the suboptimal allocation of cash resources within the company and a failure by corporate management to successfully encourage and reward aggressive profit-seeking behavior by business-unit managers.

The inefficiencies arising from information overload can be viewed as one component of the bureaucratic costs of extensive diversification. Of course, these costs can be reduced to manageable proportions if a company limits the scope of its diversification. Indeed, a desire to decrease these costs lay behind the 1980s and 1990s divestments and strategic concentration strategies of highly diversified conglomerates created in the 1960s and 1970s, such as Esmark, General Electric, ITT, Textron, Tenneco, and United Technologies. For example, under the leadership of Jack Welch, GE switched its emphasis from forty main business units to sixteen contained within three clearly defined sectors.

Coordination Among Businesses   The coordination required to realize value from a diversification strategy based on competency transfers or economies of scope can also be a source of bureaucratic costs. Both the transfer of distinctive competencies and the achievement of economies of scope demand close coordination among business units. It is the bureaucratic mechanisms needed for this coordination that give rise to bureaucratic costs. (We discuss the mechanisms for achieving coordination in Chapter 12.)

A more serious matter, however, is that substantial bureaucratic costs can result from a firm's inability to identify the unique profit contribution of a business unit that is sharing resources with another unit in an attempt to realize economies of scope. Consider a company that has two business units—one producing household products (such as liquid soap and laundry detergent) and another producing packaged food products. The products of both units are sold through supermarkets. In order to lower the costs of value creation, the parent company decides to pool the marketing and sales functions of each business unit. Pooling allows the business units to share the costs of a sales force (one sales force can sell the products of both divisions) and gain cost economies from using the same physical distribution system. The organizational structure required to achieve this might be similar to that illustrated in Figure 9.4. The company is organized into three divisions: a household products division, a food products division, and a marketing and sales division.

FIGURE 9.4
●●●●●●●●●●●

Structure of a
Company Sharing
Marketing Between
Two Business Units

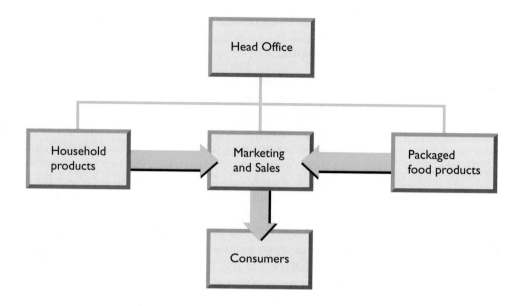

Although such an arrangement may create value, it can also give rise to substantial control problems and hence bureaucratic costs. For example, if the performance of the household products business begins to slip, identifying who is to be held accountable—the management of the household products division or the management of the marketing division—may prove difficult. Indeed, each may blame the other for poor performance: The management of the household products division might blame the marketing policies of the marketing division, and the management of the marketing division might blame the poor quality and high costs of products produced by the household products division. Although this kind of problem can be resolved if corporate management directly audits the affairs of both divisions, doing so is costly in terms of both the time and the effort that corporate management must expend.

Now imagine the situation within a company that is trying to create value by sharing marketing, manufacturing, and R&D resources across ten businesses rather than just two. Clearly, the accountability problem could become far more severe in such a company. Indeed, the problem might become so acute that the effort involved in trying to tie down accountability might create a serious information overload for corporate management. When this occurs, corporate management effectively loses control of the company. If accountability cannot be sorted out, the consequences may include poor resource allocation decisions, a generally high level of organizational slack, and an inability by corporate management to encourage and reward aggressive profit-seeking behavior by business-unit managers. All these inefficiencies can be considered part of the bureaucratic costs of diversification to realize economies of scope.

Limits of Diversification   Thus, although diversification can create value for a company, it inevitably involves bureaucratic costs. As is the case with vertical integration, the existence of bureaucratic costs places a limit on the amount of diversification that can profitably be pursued. It makes sense for a company to diversify only as long as the value created by such a strategy exceeds the bureaucratic costs associated with expanding the boundaries of the organization to incorporate additional business activities.

Remember that the greater the number of business units within a company and the greater the need for coordination among those business units, the larger the bureaucratic costs are likely to be. Hence, a company that has twenty businesses, all of which are trying to share resources, incurs much larger bureaucratic costs than a company that has ten businesses, none of which are trying to share resources. The implications of this relationship are quite straightforward. Specifically, the greater the number of businesses already in a company's portfolio and the greater the need for coordination among those businesses, the more probable it is that the value created by a diversification move will be outweighed by the resulting increase in bureaucratic costs. Once this occurs, a profitable limit to the diversified scope of the enterprise will be reached. However, many companies continue to diversify past this limit, and their performance declines. To solve this problem, a company must reduce the scope of the enterprise through divestments. Strategy in Action 9.4 discusses ICI, a company that overdiversified and subsequently had to divest itself of previously acquired businesses. In Chapter 10 we look at a number of other companies that have made the same mistake.

Diversification That Dissipates Value

Another reason so much diversification fails to create value is that many companies diversify for the wrong reasons. This is particularly true of diversification to pool risks or to achieve greater growth, both of which are often given by company managers as reasons for diversification.

Consider diversification to pool risks. The benefits of risk pooling are said to come from merging imperfectly correlated income streams to create a more stable income stream. An example of risk pooling might be USX's diversification into the oil and gas industry in an attempt to offset the adverse effects of cyclical downturns in the steel industry. According to advocates of risk pooling, the more stable income stream reduces the risk of bankruptcy and is in the best interests of the company's stockholders.

However, this simple argument ignores two facts. First, stockholders can easily eliminate the risks inherent in holding an individual stock by diversifying their own portfolios, and they can do so at a much lower cost than the company can. Thus, far from being in the best interests of stockholders, attempts to pool risks through diversification represent an unproductive use of resources. Second, research on this topic suggests that corporate diversification is not a very effective way to pool risks.[38] The business cycles of different industries are not easy to predict and, in any case, tend to be less important in terms of their impact on profits than a general economic downturn, which hits all industries simultaneously. International Harvester illustrates the point. By 1979 International Harvester had diversified into three major businesses: agricultural equipment, construction equipment, and trucks. These businesses were supposed to follow different business cycles, cushioning the company against severe fluctuations. In the early 1980s, however, all these businesses suffered a downturn at the same time, cumulating a $2.9 billion loss for Harvester.

Now consider diversification to achieve greater growth. Such diversification is not a coherent strategy because growth on its own does not create value. Growth

Diversification and Divestments at ICI

Formed in 1926 by the merger of a number of chemical concerns, Britain's Imperial Chemical Industries (ICI) has always been a diverse company, but in the 1980s ICI embarked upon a new wave of diversified acquisitions aimed at expanding its presence in a broad range of high-value-added specialty chemicals operations. By the early 1980s ICI was already involved in such markets as bulk chemicals, explosives, fertilizers, paints, commodity plastics, and pharmaceuticals. It added to this portfolio in 1985 with the purchase of the advanced plastics materials operations of the U.S. company Beatrice Company for $750 million. In 1986 it bought Glidden, another American company, for $580 million. This acquisition made ICI the world's biggest paint manufacturer. This was followed by the 1987 acquisition of American Stauffer Chemical for $1.7 billion. ICI retained American Stauffer's specialty agrochemical business, but sold off the rest. As a result, by the end of the 1980s, ICI was Britain's largest manufacturing enterprise and the world's fourth largest chemical company.

Unfortunately, this expansion in the scope of ICI's business activities did little for the company's bottom line. In 1990 ICI saw its pretax profits drop by 36 percent to $1.7 billion on sales of $23 billion. Meanwhile, ICI's specialty chemicals operations did not do as well as the company had hoped. Paints and other specialty products enjoyed a profit margin of only 2.8 percent that year, compared with a margin of 5.7 percent in the company's more traditional bulk chemical operations.

In May 1991 these financial problems attracted the attention of Hanson PLC, one of Britain's best-known corporate raiders. Hanson has thrived by purchasing conglomerates such as ICI and then breaking them up and selling the parts off to other companies, typically for a substantial profit. Hanson purchased a 4.1 percent stake in ICI and threatened to make a full takeover bid. Although the full bid never materialized and Hanson subsequently sold off its stake for a handsome profit, the threatened takeover started a debate in ICI as to the rationale behind its diversification strategy.

After much consideration ICI's top management came to two main conclusions. First, although many of ICI's businesses were linked in some way to the chemical industry, there were far fewer synergies between its operations than management had initially thought. In the final analysis, ICI's top management concluded that there was little commonality between bulk chemicals and pharmaceuticals, between plastics and paint, and between explosives and advanced materials. Second, the company had become so diverse that top management found itself spread too thinly over too many different businesses. The company simply wasn't able to give the kind of top-management attention and financial resources that many of its businesses required. In other words, the value created by the strategy of diversification was questionable, while the bureaucratic costs of managing a large and complex diversified entity were substantial. Thus, diversification at ICI dissipated rather than created value.

Accordingly, in 1992 ICI's top management decided to start breaking up the company into its constituent parts. The first stage in this process was completed in March of 1993, when ICI was split into two parts. One part, which kept the name ICI, is made up of industrial chemicals, paints, and explosives. According to the company, bits of this operation will probably be sold off in the future. The other part, which is now called Zeneca, has taken ICI's drugs, pesticides, seeds, and specialty chemicals businesses. ICI believes that the two companies will do better on their own than they did as part of a larger enterprise.[39]

should be the *byproduct,* not the objective, of a diversification strategy. However, companies sometimes diversify for reasons of growth alone, rather than the attainment of any carefully thought-out strategic advantage. ITT under the leadership of Harold Geneen took this path. Geneen turned ITT from an international telecommunications company into a broadly based conglomerate consisting of more than 100 separate businesses, with interests in such diverse areas as baking, car rental, defense electronics, fire hydrants, insurance, hotels, paper products, and telecommunications. The strategy had more to do with Geneen's desire to build an empire than with maximizing the company's value. Following Geneen's departure in 1979, ITT's management divested many of the businesses acquired under his leadership in order to concentrate on insurance and financial services. This process reached its logical conclusion in 1996, when the remaining three businesses of ITT were spun off as independent entities.

Related Versus Unrelated Diversification

One issue a company must resolve is whether to diversify into totally new businesses or businesses related to its existing business by value chain commonalities. The distinction is between related diversification and unrelated diversification. By definition, a related company can create value by resource sharing and by transferring competencies between businesses. It can also carry out some restructuring. In contrast, since there are no commonalities between the value chains of unrelated businesses, an unrelated company cannot create value by sharing resources or transferring competencies. Unrelated diversifiers can create value only by pursuing an acquisition and restructuring strategy.

Since related diversification can create value in more ways than unrelated diversification can, you might think that related diversification is the preferred strategy. In addition, related diversification is normally perceived as involving fewer risks because the company is moving into business areas about which top management already has some knowledge. Probably because of these considerations, most diversified companies display a preference for related diversification.[40] However, research suggests that the average related company is, at best, only marginally more profitable than the average unrelated company.[41] How can this be if related diversification is associated with more benefits than unrelated diversification?

The answer is quite simple. Bureaucratic costs arise from (1) the number of businesses in a company's portfolio and (2) the extent of coordination required among the different businesses in order to realize value from a diversification strategy. Because an unrelated company does not have to achieve coordination between business units, it has to cope only with the bureaucratic costs that arise from the number of businesses in its portfolio. In contrast, a related diversified company has to achieve coordination between business units if it is to realize the value that comes from skill transfers and resource sharing. Consequently, it has to cope with the bureaucratic costs that arise *both* from the number of business units in its portfolio *and* from coordination among business units. Thus, although it is true that related diversified companies can create value in more ways than unrelated companies, they have to bear higher bureaucratic costs in order to do so. These higher costs may cancel out the higher benefits, making the strategy no more profitable than one of unrelated diversification. Table 9.1 lists the sources of value and costs for each strategy.

How then is a company to choose between these strategies? The choice depends on a comparison of the relative value added and the bureaucratic costs associated with each strategy. In making this comparison, note that the opportunities for creating value from related diversification are a function of the extent of commonalities between the skills required to compete in the company's core business and the skills required to compete in other industrial and commercial areas. Some

TABLE 9.1

Comparing Related and Unrelated Diversification

Strategy	Ways of Creating Value	Source of Bureaucratic Costs
Related diversification	• Restructuring • Transferring skills • Economies of scope	• Number of businesses • Coordination among businesses
Unrelated diversification	• Restructuring	• Number of businesses

companies' skills are so specialized that they have few applications outside the core businesses. For example, since the commonalities between steel making and other industrial or commercial operations are few, most steel companies have diversified into unrelated industries (for example, LTV into defense contracting, USX into oil and gas). When companies have less specialized skills, they can find many more related diversification opportunities outside the core business. Examples include chemical companies (such as Dow Chemical and Du Pont) and electrical engineering companies (such as General Electric). Consequently, the opportunities available to them to create value from related diversification are much greater.

Thus, it pays a firm to concentrate on related diversification when (1) the company's core skills are applicable to a wide variety of industrial and commercial situations and (2) the bureaucratic costs of implementation do not exceed the value that can be created through resource sharing or skill transfers. The second condition is likely to hold only for companies that are moderately diversified. At high levels of related diversification, the bureaucratic costs of additional diversification are likely to outweigh the value created by that diversification, and the strategy may become unprofitable.

By the same logic, it may pay a company to concentrate on unrelated diversification when (1) the company's core functional skills are highly specialized and have few applications outside the company's core business, (2) the company's top management is skilled at acquiring and turning around poorly run businesses (and many are not), and (3) the bureaucratic costs of implementation do not exceed the value that can be created by pursuing a restructuring strategy. However, the third condition is *unlikely* to hold for companies that are highly diversified. Thus, regardless of whether a company pursues a related or an unrelated diversification strategy, the existence of bureaucratic costs suggests that there are very real limits to the profitable diversification of the company.

STRATEGIC ALLIANCES AS AN ALTERNATIVE TO DIVERSIFICATION

Diversification can be unprofitable because of the bureaucratic costs associated with implementing the strategy. One way of trying to realize the value associated with diversification without having to bear the same level of bureaucratic costs is to enter into a strategic alliance with another company to start a new business venture.

In this context, strategic alliances are essentially agreements between two or more companies to share the costs, risks, and benefits associated with developing new business opportunities. Many strategic alliances are constituted as formal joint ventures in which each party has an equity stake. Other alliances take the form of a long-term contract between companies in which they agree to undertake some joint activity that benefits both. Agreements to work together on joint R&D projects often take this form.

Strategic alliances seem to be a particularly viable option when a company wishes to create value from transferring competencies or sharing resources between diversified businesses in order to realize economies of scope. Alliances offer companies a framework within which to share the resources required to establish a new business. Alternatively, alliances enable companies to swap complementary skills to produce a new range of products. For example, consider the alliance between United Technologies and Dow Chemical to build plastic-based composite parts for the aerospace industry. United Technologies was already involved in the aerospace industry (it built Sikorsky helicopters), and Dow Chemical had skills in the development and manufacture of plastic-based composites. The alliance called for United Technologies to contribute its advanced aerospace skills and for Dow to contribute its skills in developing and manufacturing plastic-based composites to a joint venture in which each company would have a 50 percent equity stake. The joint venture was to undertake the task of developing, manufacturing, and marketing a new line of plastic-based composite parts for the aerospace industry. Through the alliance, both companies would become involved in new activities. They would, in short, be able to realize some of the benefits associated with related diversification without having to merge activities formally or bear the costs and risks of developing the new products on their own.

Bureaucratic costs have been reduced because neither Dow nor United Technologies actually expanded its own organization, nor did either company have to coordinate internal skill transfers. Rather, since incorporation, the joint venture has been operating as an independent company, and both Dow and United Technologies receive payment in the form of dividends.

Of course, there is a downside to such alliances. For one thing, profits must be split with an alliance partner, whereas with full diversification a company gets to keep all the profits. Another problem is that when a company enters into an alliance, it always runs the risk that it might give away critical know-how to its alliance partner, who might then use that know-how to compete directly with the company in the future. For example, having gained access to Dow's expertise in plastic-based composites, United Technologies might dissolve the alliance and produce these materials on its own. However, such risk can be minimized if Dow gets a *credible commitment* from United Technologies. By entering into a formal joint venture, rather than a loosely structured alliance, United Technologies has given such a commitment because it has had to invest substantial amounts of capital. Thus, if United Technologies tried to produce plastic-based composites on its own, it would essentially be competing against itself.

SUMMARY OF CHAPTER

The purpose of this chapter is to examine the different corporate-level strategies that companies pursue in order to maximize their value.

✔ Corporate strategies should *add value* to a corporation, enabling it, or one or more of its business units, to perform one or more of the value creation functions at a lower cost or in a way that allows for differentiation and a premium price.

✔ Concentrating on a single business allows a company to focus its total managerial, financial, technological, and physical resources and capabilities on competing successfully in just one area. It also ensures that the company sticks to doing what it knows best.

✔ The company that concentrates on a single business may be missing out on the opportunity to create value through vertical integration and/or diversification.

✔ Vertical integration can enable a company to achieve a competitive advantage by helping build barriers to entry, facilitating investments in specialized assets, protecting product quality, and helping improve scheduling between adjacent stages in the value chain.

✔ The disadvantages of vertical integration include cost disadvantages if a company's internal source of supply is a high-cost one and lack of flexibility when technology is changing fast or when demand is uncertain.

✔ Entering into a long-term contract can enable a company to realize many of the benefits associated with vertical integration without having to bear the same level of bureaucratic costs. However, to avoid the risks associated with becoming too dependent on its partner, a company entering into a long-term contract needs to seek a credible commitment from its partner or establish a mutual hostage-taking situation.

✔ The strategic outsourcing of noncore value creation activities may allow a company to lower its costs, differentiate its product offering better, make better use of scarce resources, and enable it to respond rapidly to changing market conditions. However, strategic outsourcing may have a detrimental effect if the company outsources important value creation activities or if it becomes too dependent on key suppliers of those activities.

✔ Diversification can create value through the pursuit of a restructuring strategy, competency transfers, and the realization of economies of scope.

✔ The bureaucratic costs of diversification are a function of the number of independent business units within the company and the extent of coordination among those business units.

✔ Diversification motivated by a desire to pool risks or achieve greater growth is often associated with the dissipation of value.

✔ Related diversification is preferred to unrelated diversification because it enables a company to engage in more value creation activities and is less risky. If a company's skills are not transferable, the company may have no choice but to pursue unrelated diversification.

✔ Strategic alliances can enable companies to realize many of the benefits of related diversification without having to bear the same level of bureaucratic costs. However, when entering into an alliance, a company does run the risk of giving away key technology to its partner. The risk of this occurring can be minimized if a company gets a credible commitment from its partner.

DISCUSSION QUESTIONS

1. Why was it profitable for General Motors and Ford to integrate backward into component-parts manufacturing in the past, and why are both companies now trying to buy more of their parts from outside companies?

2. Under what conditions might concentration on a single business be inconsistent with the goal of maximizing stockholder wealth? Why?

3. General Motors integrated vertically in the 1920s, diversified in the 1930s, and expanded overseas in the 1950s. Explain these developments with reference to the profitability of pursuing each strategy. Why do you think vertical integration is normally the first strategy to be pursued after concentration on a single business?

4. What value creation activities should a company outsource to independent suppliers? What are the risks involved in outsourcing these activities?

5. When is a company likely to choose related diversification and when unrelated diversification? Discuss with reference to an electronics manufacturer and an ocean shipping company.

Practicing Strategic Management

SMALL-GROUP EXERCISE
Comparing Vertical Integration Strategies

Break into a small group of three to five people. Then read the following description of the activities of Quantum and Seagate Technologies, both of which manufacture computer disk drives. On the basis of this description, outline the pros and cons of a vertical integration strategy. Which strategy do you think makes more sense in the context of the computer disk drive industry?

Quantum Corporation and Seagate Technologies are both major producers of disk drives for personal computers and workstations. The disk drive industry is characterized by sharp fluctuations in the level of demand, intense price competition, rapid technological change, and product life cycles of no more than twelve to eighteen months. In recent years Quantum and Seagate have pursued very different vertical integration strategies. Quantum specializes in design and outsources most of its manufacturing to a number of independent suppliers including, most importantly, Matsushita Kotobuki Electronics (MKE) of Japan. Quantum makes only its newest and most expensive products in-house. Once a new drive is perfected and ready for large-scale manufacturing, Quantum turns over manufacturing to MKE. MKE and Quantum have cemented their partnership over eight years. At each stage in designing a new product, Quantum's engineers send the newest drawings to a production team at MKE. MKE examines the drawings and constantly proposes changes that make the new disk drives easier to manufacture. When the product is ready for manufacture, eight to ten of Quantum's engineers travel to MKE's plant in Japan for at least a month to work on production ramp up. Seagate is a vertically integrated manufacturer of disk drives, both designing and manufacturing the bulk of its own disk drives.

EXPLORING THE WEB
Visiting Motorola

Visit the Web site of Motorola (http://www.motorola.com). Review the various business activities of Motorola. Using this information, answer the following questions:

1. To what extent is Motorola vertically integrated?

2. Does vertical integration help Motorola establish a competitive advantage, or does it put the company at a competitive disadvantage?

3. How diversified is Motorola? What diversification strategy is Motorola pursuing—related or unrelated diversification?

4. How, if at all, does Motorola's diversification strategy create value for the company's stockholders?

General Task

Search the Web for an example of a company that has pursued a diversification strategy. Describe that strategy, and assess whether the strategy creates or dissipates value for the company.

ARTICLE FILE 9

Find an example of a company whose vertical integration or diversification strategy appears to have dissipated rather than created value. Identify why this has been the case and what the company should do to rectify the situation.

STRATEGIC MANAGEMENT PROJECT
Module 9

This module requires you to assess the vertical integration and diversification strategy being pursued by your company. With the information you have at your disposal, answer the following questions and perform the tasks listed:

1. How vertically integrated is your company? If your company does have vertically integrated operations, is it pursuing a strategy of taper or full integration?

2. How diversified is your company? If your company is already diversified, is it pursuing a related diversification strategy, an unrelated diversification strategy, or some mix of the two?

3. Assess the potential for your company to create value through vertical integration. In reaching

your assessment, also consider the bureaucratic costs of managing vertical integration.

4. On the basis of your assessment in question 3, do you think your company should (a) outsource some operations that are currently performed in-house or (b) bring some operations in-house that are currently outsourced? Justify your recommendations.

5. Is your company currently involved in any long-term cooperative relationships with suppliers or buyers? If so, how are these relationships structured? Do you think that these relationships add value to the company? Why?

6. Is there any potential for your company to enter into (additional) long-term cooperative relationships with suppliers or buyers? If so, how might these relationships be structured?

7. Assess the potential for your company to create value through diversification. In reaching your as-

sessment, consider the bureaucratic costs of managing diversification.

8. On the basis of your assessment in question 7, do you think your company should (a) sell off some diversified operations or (b) pursue additional diversification? Justify your recommendations.

9. Is your company currently trying to transfer skills or realize economies of scope by entering into strategic alliances with other companies? If so, how are these relationships structured? Do you think that these relationships add value to the company? Why?

10. Is there any potential for your company to transfer skills or realize economies of scope by entering into (additional) strategic alliances with other companies? If so, how might these relationships be structured?

CLOSING CASE

Daimler-Benz

For years Germany's Daimler-Benz enjoyed a well-earned reputation as one of the world's premier makers of high-quality luxury cars. During the mid 1980s, however, under the leadership of a new CEO, Edzard Reuter, Daimler-Benz embarked on a dramatic strategic change. Reuter transformed Daimler-Benz from a focused company producing luxury cars and trucks under the Mercedes-Benz label into Germany's largest industrial conglomerate, with annual revenues in the $60 billion range. He achieved this by acquiring a number of major German companies, including electronics and consumer goods manufacturer AEG and the aerospace companies Dornier Aircraft and Messerschmitt-Boelkow-Blohm (MBB). Daimler-Benz subsequently combined Dornier and MBB into Deutsche Aerospace. Deutsche Aerospace is now the effective owner of Germany's 37.9 percent stake in the European Airbus Industrie consortium, which is competing head-to-head with Boeing in the world commercial jet aircraft market.

The logic underlying Reuter's diversification strategy was based on a number of factors. First, he believed that the intensity of rivalry in the global automobile industry would increase. Japanese competitors were beginning to move up market into Mercedes-Benz's territory, making it

more difficult for Daimler-Benz to hold on to its differential advantage. Second, Reuter reasoned that in this new competitive environment, the companies that would come out on top would be those able to incorporate leading-edge technology into their cars before rivals did. Third, he believed that by acquiring electronics and aerospace businesses, Daimler-Benz could gain access to just such leading-edge technological know-how. In short, Reuter believed that technological developments were creating enormous opportunities for sharing know-how across the aerospace, automobile, and electronics businesses.

However, Reuter's ambitious plans have yet to bring the gains he so boldly predicted. Since the mid 1980s the company's profits have stagnated. A prime reason has been the poor performance of Daimler-Benz's new businesses. AEG was losing money when Daimler-Benz bought it. According to analysts, AEG has yet to show a profit. Similarly, MBB has turned out to be a perennial money loser. As a result, by the early 1990s the Mercedes-Benz car business, even though it made up only 40 percent of Daimler-Benz's total revenues, accounted for 90 percent of profits. To make matters worse, there are signs that the car business may be running into trouble. In 1992, for the first time ever, Daimler-Benz's archrival, BMW, sold more cars than Daimler-Benz. BMW sold an estimated 590,000 cars around the world in 1992, well ahead of the 530,000 Mercedes-Benz cars that were sold.

Reuter claims that these problems are short-run ones and that in the long run the diversification strategy will pay off. Others are not so sure. Many analysts always thought that Reuter had an exaggerated view of the potential for sharing technology among the aerospace, automobile, and electronic businesses. They were also puzzled as to why a diversified conglomerate had to be built to share such know-how, particularly at a time when many other companies were sharing know-how through strategic alliances. Critics of Reuter's policies also point to serious morale problems that have begun to emerge within the enlarged group. For example, managers at AEG were apparently unhappy about being ordered to hand over their lucrative aerospace division to Deutsche Aerospace.

The Dornier-MBB combination has also run into problems. The two aerospace companies had radically different cultures and were old rivals before their marriage enforced by Daimler-Benz. Now MBB's Munich-based managers apparently resent having to report to the Deutsche Aerospace head office in Stuttgart, which is staffed primarily by old Dornier personnel. Furthermore, managers at Mercedes-Benz resent having most of their company's profits used to finance money-losing business units such as AEG and MBB, and Mercedes-Benz's engineers dislike being lumped together with companies they perceive to be inferior. In addition, there is the perception that Reuter's focus on diversification has sapped capital and diverted top management's attention from the company's core car-making business, which has resulted in Mercedes-Benz's recent loss of leadership in the German automobile industry to BMW.[42]

Case Discussion Questions

1. Evaluate critically the logic underlying Daimler-Benz's diversification strategy. How might this strategy add value to Daimler-Benz's established automobile business?

2. Identify ways in which Daimler-Benz's diversification strategy might have destroyed rather than created value.

3. Do you think that Daimler-Benz needed to diversify in order to gain access to leading-edge technological know-how? What approach other than diversification might the company have used?

CHAPTER 10

Corporate Development— Building and Restructuring the Corporation

Opening Case: Breaking Up AT&T

Overview

Reviewing the Corporate Portfolio

Internal New Venturing as an Entry Strategy

Acquisitions as an Entry Strategy

Joint Ventures as an Entry Strategy

Restructuring

Turnaround Strategies

Closing Case: Restructuring Xerox

OPENING CASE

On September 20, 1995, AT&T, the world's largest telecommunications company with annual revenues of $75 billion, announced that it would split itself into three independent companies. The largest of these, which was to retain the AT&T name, would manage the company's long-distance, international, and wireless telecommunications businesses. The new AT&T would retain its position as the largest provider of telecommunications service in the world, with 1995 revenues in excess of $50 billion. Sec-

Breaking Up AT&T

ond in size of the new companies was to be the network equipment business. Renamed Lucent Technologies, this business generated 1995 revenues of $21 billion and ranked as the third largest provider of telecommunication network equipment in the world after Germany's Alcatel and Motorola of the United States. The smallest of the new companies was AT&T's Global Information Solutions business, a manufacturer of computer systems with annual revenues of $9 billion. Global Information Solutions was built around

NCR, a computer company that AT&T had acquired in 1991 for $7.5 billion.

The decision to break up AT&T into three parts was the result of a number of factors that came to a head in the mid 1990s. First was the impending deregulation of the U.S. telecommunications industry. After deregulation, local and long-distance telephone companies would be free to enter each other's markets. AT&T would face more competition in its core long-distance business as the Regional Bell Operating Companies (RBOCs) tried to enter this market. At the same time, AT&T would be able to enter the local phone business and compete directly against the RBOCs. Second was the privatization of state-owned telephone companies around the world and the deregulation of many foreign telephone markets. These developments created enormous opportunities for AT&T, which for the first time saw the possibility of building a truly global telephone network by forming alliances with newly privatized telephone companies and by entering foreign markets. Third was rapid change in the telecommunications business as new technologies, such as wireless communications and the Internet, created significant opportunities and threats for AT&T. Faced with such changes in its operating environment, AT&T's management realized that it needed to focus all its energies and resources on the company's core telecommunications business, unencumbered by the distractions presented by the network equipment and computer businesses.

There was also an understanding on the part of AT&T's management that the performance of the computer and network equipment businesses had suffered as a result of its association with AT&T. The equipment business was trying to sell products to companies that competed directly against AT&T, such as MCI and Sprint, or would compete against AT&T after deregulation, such as the RBOCs. These potential customers were increasingly reluctant to purchase equipment from a supplier that was also a competitor. For example, just before the breakup was announced, Motorola beat AT&T to a $800 million order for wireless telecommunications equipment from GTE. GTE had long been one of AT&T's largest equipment customers, but now it faced the threat of competing against AT&T in the local phone business. Freed from its association with AT&T, the network equipment business would have a greater chance of capturing business from other telephone service providers.

As for the computer business, this was forecast to lose around $1 billion in 1995. Although AT&T had always had some significant computer skills (after all, many network equipment products, such as digital switches, are essentially specialized computers), it had never been able to establish a profitable computer operation. During the 1980s AT&T lost billions of dollars trying to establish a presence in the personal computer market through an internal new venture. Moreover, its 1991 acquisition of NCR, which was an attempt to strengthen this venture, turned out to be a disaster, partly because the computer market shifted away from the kind of customized equipment provided by NCR and partly because there was a clash between the management cultures of the two companies that led to high management turnover in the acquired unit. Many now felt that AT&T's deep pockets had kept the computer operation in markets that it should have exited years ago, such as the personal computer market. They believed that an independent computer operation might be more responsive to market demands. Moreover, an independent computer operation would not be burdened by the clashing cultural heritage of AT&T and NCR.[1]

OVERVIEW

Chapter 9 discussed the corporate-level strategies that companies pursue in order to become multibusiness enterprises. This chapter builds on Chapter 9 by addressing central issues of corporate development. **Corporate development** is concerned with identifying *which* business opportunities a company should pursue, *how* it should pursue those opportunities, and *how* it should exit from businesses that do not fit with the company's strategic vision. The Opening Case touched on all these issues. During the 1980s and early 1990s, AT&T believed that it should pursue business opportunities in the computer industry. Its vehicles for pursuing those opportunities included an internal new computer venture and, in 1991, the acquisition of NCR. By 1995, however, AT&T had altered its strategy. It decided that changes taking place in its operating environment gave rise to significant new business opportunities in its core telecommunications business, such as the opportunity to create wireless and global telephone networks. Accordingly, AT&T decided to restructure the company, focusing on telecommunications services and exiting from the computer and network equipment businesses by spinning off these operations to independent investors.

We begin this chapter by looking at approaches a company can take in reviewing its portfolio of businesses. The objectives of such a review are to help determine which of its existing businesses a company should continue to participate in, which it should exit from, and whether the company should consider entering any new business areas. Having done this, we turn our attention to the different *vehicles,* or means, a company can use to enter and develop new business areas. The choice is between acquisitions, internal new ventures, and joint ventures. **Acquisitions** involve buying an existing business, **internal new ventures** start a new business from scratch, and **joint ventures** typically establish a new business with the assistance of a partner.

The chapter closes with a look at restructuring and exit strategy. For reasons that we first touched on in Chapter 9 and discuss further in this chapter, during the 1970s and 1980s many companies became too diversified or too vertically integrated. In recent years there has been a notable shift away from these strategies, with companies selling off many of their diversified activities and refocusing on their core businesses.

REVIEWING THE CORPORATE PORTFOLIO

A central concern of corporate development is identifying which business opportunities a company should pursue. A common starting point is to review a company's existing portfolio of businesses activities. The purpose of such a review is to help determine which of its existing businesses a company should continue to participate in, which it should exit from, and whether the company should consider entering any new business areas. In this section we discuss two different approaches to undertaking such a review.

The first approach utilizes a set of techniques known as portfolio planning matrices.[2] Developed primarily by management consultants, this set of techniques is meant to compare the competitive position of the different businesses in a company's portfolio against each other on the basis of common criteria. Below we argue that these techniques contain some flaws and their application has produced some bad decisions.

The second approach we consider has been championed by Gary Hamel and C. K. Prahalad. This approach reconceptualizes a company as a portfolio of core competencies, as opposed to a portfolio of businesses.[3] Corporate development is oriented toward maintaining existing competencies, building new competencies, and leveraging competencies by applying them to new business opportunities. For example, according to Hamel and Prahalad, the success of a company such as 3M in creating new business has come from its ability to apply its core competency in adhesives to a wide range of businesses opportunities, from Scotch Tape to Post-it Notes.

Portfolio Planning

One of the most famous portfolio planning matrices is referred to as the growth-share matrix. This was developed by the Boston Consulting Group (BCG), principally to help senior managers identify the cash flow requirements of different businesses in their portfolio and to help determine whether they need to change the mix of businesses in the portfolio. We review the growth-share matrix in order to illustrate both the value and limitations of portfolio planning tools. The growth-share matrix has three main steps: (1) dividing a company into strategic business units (SBUs); (2) assessing the prospects of each SBU and comparing them against each other by means of a matrix; and (3) developing strategic objectives for each SBU.

Identifying SBUs   According to the BCG, a company must create an SBU for each economically distinct business area in which it competes. Normally, a company defines its SBUs in terms of the product markets they compete in. For example, Ciba-Geigy, Switzerland's largest chemical and pharmaceutical company and an active user of portfolio planning techniques, has identified thirty-three strategic business units in areas such as proprietary pharmaceuticals, generic pharmaceuticals, seed treatments, reactive dyes, detergents, resins, paper chemicals, diagnostics, and composite materials. (See Strategy in Action 10.1 for details.)

Assessing and Comparing SBUs   Having identified SBUs, top managers then assess each according to two criteria: (1) the SBU's relative market share and (2) the growth rate of the SBU's industry. **Relative market share** is the ratio of an SBU's market share to the market share held by the largest rival company in its industry. If SBU X has a market share of 10 percent and its largest rival has a market share of 30 percent, SBU X's relative market share is 10/30, or 0.3. Only if an SBU is a market leader in its industry will it have a relative market share greater than 1.0. For example, if SBU Y has a market share of 40 percent and its largest rival has a market share of 10 percent, then SBU Y's relative market share is 40/10, or 4.0. According to the BCG, market share gives a company cost advantages from economies of scale and learning effects. An SBU with a relative market share greater than 1.0 is assumed to be farther down the experience curve and, therefore, to have a significant cost advantage over its rivals. By similar logic, an SBU with a relative market share smaller than 1.0 is assumed to lack the economies of scale and low-cost position of the market leader.

The growth rate of an SBU's industry is assessed according to whether it is faster or slower than the growth rate of the economy as a whole. BCG's position is that high-growth industries offer a more favorable competitive environment and better long-term prospects than slow-growth industries.

Given the relative market share and industry growth rate for each SBU, management compares SBUs against each other by way of a matrix similar to that illustrated in Figure 10.1. The horizontal dimension of this matrix measures relative market share; the vertical dimension measures industry growth rate. The center of each circle corresponds to the position of an SBU on the two dimensions of the matrix. The size of each circle is proportional to the sales revenue generated by each business in the company's portfolio. The bigger the circle, the larger the SBU relative to total corporate revenues.

FIGURE 10.1
· · · · · · · · · · · ·
The BCG Matrix

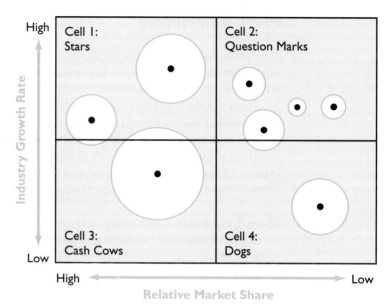

Source: *Perspectives*, No. 66, "The Product Portfolio." Adapted by permission from The Boston Consulting Group, Inc., 1970.

The matrix is divided into four cells. SBUs in cell 1 are defined as stars, in cell 2 as question marks, in cell 3 as cash cows, and in cell 4 as dogs. BCG argues that these different types of SBUs have different long-term prospects and different implications for cash flows.

- *Stars.* The leading SBUs in a company's portfolio are the stars. Stars have a high relative market share and are based in high-growth industries. Accordingly, they offer attractive long-term profit and growth opportunities.

- *Question marks.* Question marks are SBUs that are relatively weak in competitive terms (they have low relative market shares) but are based in high-growth industries and thus may offer opportunities for long-term profit and growth. A question mark can become a star if nurtured properly. To become a market leader, a question mark requires substantial net injections of cash; it is cash hungry. The corporate head office has to decide whether a particular question mark has the potential to become a star and is therefore worth the capital investment necessary to achieve stardom.

- *Cash cows.* SBUs that have a high market share in low-growth industries (i.e., a strong competitive position in mature industries) are cash cows. Their competitive strength comes from being farthest down the experience curve. They are the cost leaders in their industries. BCG argues that this position enables such SBUs to remain very profitable. However, low growth implies a lack of opportunities for future expansion. As a consequence, BCG argues that the capital investment requirements of cash cows are not substantial, and, thus, they are depicted as generating a strong positive cash flow.

- *Dogs.* SBUs that are in low-growth industries but have a low market share are dogs. They have a weak competitive position in unattractive industries and, thus, are viewed as offering few benefits to a company. BCG suggests that such SBUs are unlikely to generate much in the way of a positive cash flow and indeed may become cash hogs. Though offering few prospects for future growth in returns, dogs may require substantial capital investments just to maintain their low market share.

Developing Strategic Objectives   The objective of the BCG portfolio matrix is to identify how corporate cash resources can best be used to maximize a company's future growth and profitability. BCG recommendations include the following:

■ The cash surplus from any cash cows should be used to support the development of selected question marks and to nurture stars. The long-term objective is to consolidate the position of stars and to turn favored question marks into stars, thus making the company's portfolio more attractive.

■ Question marks with the weakest or most uncertain long-term prospects should be divested to reduce demands on a company's cash resources.

■ The company should exit from any industry in which the SBU is a dog.

■ If a company lacks sufficient cash cows, stars, or question marks, it should consider acquisitions and divestments to build a more balanced portfolio. A portfolio should contain enough stars and question marks to ensure a healthy growth and profit outlook for the company and enough cash cows to support the investment requirements of the stars and question marks.

Limitations of Portfolio Planning

Though portfolio planning techniques may sound reasonable, if we take the BCG matrix as an example, there at least four main flaws. First, the model is simplistic. An assessment of an SBU in terms of just two dimensions, relative market share and industry growth, is bound to be misleading, for a host of other relevant factors should be taken into account. Although market share is undoubtedly an important determinant of an SBU's competitive position, companies can also establish a strong competitive position by differentiating their product to serve the needs of a particular segment of the market. A business having a low market share can be very profitable and have a strong competitive position in certain segments of a market. The auto manufacturer BMW is in this position, yet the BCG matrix would classify BMW as a dog because it is a low-market-share business in a low-growth industry. Similarly, industry growth is not the only factor that determines industry attractiveness. Many factors besides growth determine competitive intensity in an industry and thus its attractiveness.

Second, the connection between relative market share and cost savings is not as straightforward as BCG suggests. High market share does not always give a company a cost advantage. In some industries (for example, the U.S. steel industry) low-market-share companies using a low-share technology (such as minimills) can have lower production costs than high-market-share companies using a high-share technology (such as integrated mills). The BCG matrix would classify minimill operations as the dogs of the U.S. steel industry, whereas in fact their performance over the last decade has characterized them as star businesses.

Portfolio Planning at Ciba-Geigy

Ciba-Geigy is a large Swiss-based company with interests in chemicals and pharmaceuticals and with annual revenues in excess of $25 billion. Since 1984 the company has been using portfolio planning techniques as a tool to assist corporate management in the process of strategic planning, resource allocation, and performance assessment. Although the company looked closely at the growth-share matrix devised by the Boston Consulting Group, it decided to develop a customized portfolio planning tool that would better suit its needs.

Ciba has divided the company into thirty-three separate strategic business units, such as proprietary pharmaceuticals, generic pharmaceuticals, seed treatments, reactive dyes, detergents, resins, paper chemicals, diagnostics, and composite materials. At Ciba each SBU is assessed according to two main criteria: the likely future growth rate of its industry and the competitive position of the SBU relative to its rivals. In deriving a measure of competitive position, Ciba looks at relative market share, but unlike the original BCG growth-share matrix, the company also considers a range of other competitive factors, such as cost structure, product quality, core competencies, and relative profitability.

Using these data, Ciba classifies its SBUs into one of five categories: development, growth, pillar, niche, and core. Development businesses are in the early stage of their life cycle and usually require substantial R&D investments. Growth businesses are competitive SBUs based in large and/or growing markets. Ciba will commit substantial funds in order to build the competitive position of such a business. Pillar businesses are market leaders that are based in attractive industries, such as Ciba's pharmaceutical businesses. They typically receive a high priority in R&D funding and resource allo-

cation in order to maintain their pillar status. Niche businesses are market leaders that are constrained because they serve a relatively small market. (Ciba's animal health business, for example, is defined as a niche business.) Core businesses are large SBUs that compete in mature industries. (Ciba's dyes, polymers, and pigments SBUs are all classified as core.) Core businesses are seen as generating excess cash that can be used to fund investments elsewhere within the company.

What is interesting about Ciba's approach is that these classifications are not taken as gospel. The company is quite willing to violate the investment rules associated with the different categories if that seems appropriate. For example, in 1994 Ciba committed itself to major new investments in its pigments SBU to upgrade its U.S. production facilities, even though its portfolio planning categories suggest that this was a mature low-growth core business that should be used to generate funds for investment elsewhere within the company. Ciba's view appears to be that the utility of portfolio planning lies not so much in its role as a guide to resource allocation as it does in helping top managers set reasonable strategic expectations and objectives for the different SBUs within the company. Thus, Ciba's corporate managers assign very different strategic and financial objectives to SBUs classified as growth businesses compared with those classified as pillars. Pillars are expected to earn a higher return on assets, generate greater cash flow, and contribute more of their earnings to the corporate bottom line than a growth business. By the same token, however, growth businesses are expected to grow their revenues and earnings at a faster rate than pillars. The performance of managers running these SBUs is then compared against these different expectations.[4]

Third, a high market share in a low-growth industry does not necessarily result in the large positive cash flow characteristic of cash cow businesses. The BCG matrix would classify General Motors' auto operations as a cash cow. However, the capital investments needed to remain competitive are so substantial in the auto industry that the reverse is more likely to be true. Low-growth industries can be very competitive, and staying ahead in such an environment can require substantial cash investments.

FIGURE 10.2
. . . .
The McKinsey Matrix

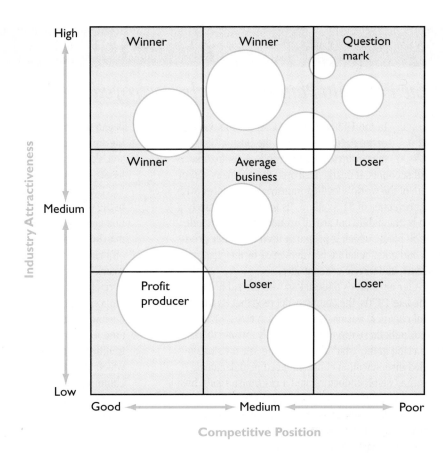

To be fair, several companies and management consulting enterprises have recognized the limitations of the BCG approach and developed alternative approaches that address the weaknesses noted above. For example, Ciba-Geigy, whose use of portfolio planning technique is reviewed in Strategy in Action 10.1, has devised a planning approach that recognizes a wider range of competitive factors needed to be taken into consideration when assessing an SBUs position. Similarly, the management consultants McKinsey and Company developed a portfolio matrix that uses a much wider range of factors to assess the attractiveness of an industry in which an SBU competes, as well as the competitive position of an SBU (see Figure 10.2). Included in the assessment of an industry's attractiveness are factors such as industry size, growth, cyclicality, competitive intensity, and technological dynamism. The assessment of competitive position relies upon factors such as market share and an SBU's relative position with regard to production costs, product quality, price competitiveness, distribution, and innovation.

However, while there is no doubt that the approach adopted by Ciba and McKinsey represents a distinct improvement over the original BCG model, in general all portfolio planning techniques suffer from significant flaws. Most importantly perhaps, they fail to pay attention to the source of value creation from diversification. They treat business units as independent, whereas in fact they may be linked by the need to transfer skills and competencies or to realize economies of scope. Moreover, portfolio planning approaches tend to trivialize the process of managing a large diversified company. They suggest that success is simply a matter of putting

STRATEGY *in* ACTION

10.2

How Portfolio Planning Nearly Destroyed the Cabot Corporation

In the 1970s the Cabot Corporation was one of the eager adopters of the Boston Consulting Group's (BCG) portfolio planning matrix. By all accounts, it nearly destroyed the company. Cabot is one of the world's leading industrial companies, with 1992 revenues of $1.5 billion. Its products are rarely seen by the public but are all around us. They include carbon black, which is primarily used in rubber products and inks, tantalum powders used by the electronics industry, and plastic concentrates.

After an analysis undertaken with the aid of the BCG in the late 1970s, the company decreed that its traditional chemical businesses were "cash cows." The plan was to milk these divisions for cash that would then be reinvested in the "star" divisions. The star divisions included diversification efforts in metal manufacturing, ceramics, semiconductors, and a gas transmission business. The result, however, was to throw good chemical earnings into businesses in which Cabot had no experience and to which Cabot could add little value. In the meantime, Cabot's chemical operations were starved of the capital that they needed to keep them operating efficiently. Moreover, morale in the chemical operations

began to slide as managers realized that funds were being siphoned off to support other operations. As a result, throughout much of the 1980s Cabot's return on assets declined.

Ultimately the Cabot family, which owns 30 percent of the stock, woke up to what was going on and brought in a new CEO, Sam Bodman, to run the business. Bodman spent his first few years restructuring Cabot, selling off many businesses that the BCG had designated as "stars" and redirecting funds toward the company's core chemical operations. He spent more than $500 million refurbishing and expanding the long-ignored chemical plants and building five new ones. At the same time, research efforts were redirected toward Cabot's traditional areas of expertise—organic chemicals—in which the emphasis was upon adding value to Cabot's commodity products.

The result is that Cabot's operating costs have fallen dramatically and the development of a new generation of specialty chemicals has allowed the company to widen its margins. After years of financial malaise, in 1992 Cabot's earning surged 55 percent ahead of the 1991 figures on flat revenues (reflecting divestments).[5]

together the right portfolio of businesses, whereas in reality it comes from managing a diversified portfolio to *create value,* whether by leveraging distinctive competencies across business units, by sharing resources to realize economies of scope, or by achieving superior governance. By diverting top management's attention away from these vital tasks and by legitimizing underinvestment in core business areas designated as cash cows, portfolio management techniques may have done a great disservice to the corporations that have adopted them. For instance, as Strategy in Action 10.2 recounts, the active application of portfolio planning techniques nearly destroyed Cabot Corporation. This is not to say that such techniques should not be used, but it does suggest that they should be employed with caution.

The Corporation as a Portfolio of Core Competencies

According to Gary Hamel and C. K. Prahalad, a more fruitful approach toward identifying the different business opportunities open to a company is to reconceptualize the company as a portfolio of core competencies (as opposed to a portfolio of businesses) and then consider how those competencies might be developed to sustain existing businesses and leveraged to create new business opportunities.[6] We

FIGURE 10.3
· · · · · · · · · · · · ·
Establishing the Core
Competence Agenda

Source: G. Hamel and C. K. Prahalad, *Competing for the Future* (Cambridge, Mass.: Harvard Business School Press, 1994), p. 227.

introduced the concept of a *competence* in Chapter 4, where we discussed how distinctive competencies can form the bedrock of a company's competitive advantage. According to Hamel and Prahalad, a **core competence** is a central *value-creating capability* of an organization—a core skill. They argue, for example, that Canon, the Japanese concern best known for its cameras and photocopiers, has core competencies in precision mechanics, fine optics, microelectronics, and electronic imaging.

Hamel and Prahalad maintain that the identification of *current* core competencies constitutes the first step for a company that is engaged in the process of deciding which business opportunities to pursue. Once a company has identified its core competencies, Hamel and Prahalad advocate using a matrix similar to that illustrated in Figure 10.3 to establish an agenda for building and leveraging core competencies to create new business opportunities. This matrix distinguishes between existing and new competencies, and between existing and new-product markets. Each quadrant in the matrix has a title, the strategic implications of which are discussed in the following paragraphs.

Fill in the Blanks   The lower-left quadrant represents the company's existing portfolio of competencies and products. Ten years ago, for example, Canon had competencies in precision mechanics, fine optics, and microelectronics and was active in two basic businesses—the production of cameras and photocopiers. The competencies in precision mechanics and fine optics were used in the production of basic mechanical cameras. These two competencies plus an additional competence in microelectronics were required to produce plain-paper copiers. The term *fill in the blanks* refers to the opportunity to improve the company's competitive position in existing markets by leveraging existing core competencies. So, for example, Canon was able to improve the position of its camera business by leveraging microelectronics skills from its copier business to support the development of cameras with electronic features, such as autofocus capabilities.

Premier Plus 10   The upper-left quadrant is referred to as premier plus 10. The title is meant to suggest an important question: What new core competencies must be built today to ensure that the company remains a *premier* provider of its existing products in *ten* years time? Canon, for example, decided that in order to maintain a competitive edge in its copier business, it was going to have to build a new competence in electronic imaging (which refers to the ability to capture and store images in a digital format, as opposed to using more traditional chemical-based photographic processes). In turn, this new competence has subsequently helped Canon to extend its product range to include laser copiers, color copiers, and digital cameras.

White Spaces   The lower-right quadrant is referred to as "white spaces." The question to be addressed here is how best to fill the "white space" by creatively redeploying or recombining current core competencies. In Canon's case, the company has been able to recombine its established core competencies in precision mechanics, fine optics, and its recently acquired competence in electronic imaging to enter the market for fax machines and bubble jet printers.

Mega-Opportunities   Opportunities represented by the upper-right quadrant of Figure 10.3 do not overlap with the company's current market position or its current competence endowment. Nevertheless, a company may choose to pursue such opportunities if they are seen to be particularly attractive, significant, or relevant to the company's existing business opportunities. For example, in 1979 Monsanto was primarily a manufacturer of chemicals, including fertilizers. However, the company saw that there were enormous opportunities in the emerging field of biotechnology. Specifically, senior research scientists at Monsanto felt that it might be possible to produce genetically engineered crop seeds that would produce their own "organic" pesticides. In that year the company embarked upon a massive investment that ultimately amounted to several hundred million dollars to build a world-class competence in biotechnology. This investment was funded by cash flows generated from Monsanto's core chemical operations. The investment began to bear fruit in the mid 1990s, when Monsanto introduced a series of genetically engineered crop seeds, including Bollgard, a cotton seed that is resistant against many common pests, such as the bollworm, and a resistant soybean seed, and Roundup. (Roundup is a herbicide produced by Monsanto. The soybean seeds are resistant to Roundup.)[7]

As with more traditional tools for reviewing a corporate portfolio, such as the portfolio planning matrices discussed earlier, the framework advocated by Hamel and Prahalad helps to identify business opportunities and holds out clear implications for resource allocation (as exemplified by the Monsanto case just discussed). However, the great advantage of Hamel and Prahalad's framework is that it focuses explicitly on how a company can *create value* by building new competencies or by recombining existing competencies to enter new business areas (as Canon did with fax machines and bubble jet printers). While traditional portfolio tools treat businesses as independent, Hamel and Prahalad's framework recognizes the interdependencies between businesses and focuses upon the opportunities for creating value by building and leveraging competencies. In this sense, their framework is far more "strategic" than the frameworks once advocated by the Boston Consulting Group and the like.

Entry Strategy

Having reviewed the different businesses in the company's portfolio, corporate management might decide to enter a new business area, as Monsanto did when it decided in 1979 to enter the biotechnology field. There are three vehicles that companies use to enter new business areas: internal ventures, acquisition, and joint ventures. Over the next three sections, we review the benefits and risks associated with each entry mode, and we look at how those risks can be minimized. Then we discuss the factors that influence the choice among these three modes in a given situation.

INTERNAL NEW VENTURING AS AN ENTRY STRATEGY

Attractions of Internal New Venturing

Internal new venturing is typically employed as an entry strategy when a company possesses a set of valuable competencies (resources and capabilities) in its existing businesses that can be leveraged or recombined to enter a new business area. For example, in 1981 IBM leveraged its core competencies in computer design, sales, and after-sales service and support to enter the personal computer business. (Until 1981 IBM had produced only mainframe and mid-range computers.)

As a rule, science-based companies that use their technology to create market opportunities in related areas tend to favor internal new venturing as an entry strategy. Du Pont, for example, has created whole new markets with products such as cellophane, nylon, Freon, and Teflon—all internally generated innovations. Another company, 3M, has a near-legendary knack for shaping new markets from internally generated ideas. Intel provides us with yet another example of a company that has leveraged its core competencies to enter new markets. Intel started off as a manufacturer of dynamic random access memory (DRAM) devices but it subsequently built upon its core competencies in semiconductor design and fabrication to enter the microprocessor business and then the flash memory business. Interestingly enough, Intel exited the DRAM business in the late 1980s, but it remains the world's largest producer of microprocessors and flash memories.

Even if it lacks the competencies required to compete in a new business area, a company may pursue an internal venturing strategy when it is entering a newly emerging or embryonic industry in which there are no established players that possess the competencies required to compete in that industry. In such a case, the option of acquiring an established enterprise that possesses those competencies is ruled out, and the company may have no choice but to enter through an internal new venture. This was the position that Monsanto found itself in in 1979, when it contemplated entering the biotechnology field to produce herbicides and pest-resistant crop seeds. The biotechnology field was young at that time, and there were no incumbent companies focused on applying biotechnology to agricultural products. Accordingly, Monsanto established an internal new venture to enter the field, even though at the time it lacked the required competencies. Indeed, Monsanto's whole venturing strategy was built around the notion that it needed to build competencies ahead of other potential competitors, thereby gaining a strong competitive lead in this newly emerging field.

Pitfalls of Internal New Venturing

Despite the popularity of the internal new venturing, its failure rate is reportedly very high. The evidence on the failure rate of new products indicates the scope of the problem, since most internal new ventures are associated with new product offerings. Somewhere between 33 and 60 percent of all new products that reach the marketplace fail to generate an adequate economic return.[8] Three reasons are often given to explain the relatively high failure rate of internal new ventures: (1) market entry on too small a scale, (2) poor commercialization of the new venture product, and (3) poor corporate management of the venture process.[9]

Scale of Entry Too Small   Research suggests that *on average* large-scale entry into a new business is often a critical precondition of new-venture success. Although in the short run large-scale entry means significant development costs and substantial losses, in the long run (which can be as long as five to twelve years depending on the industry) it brings greater returns than small-scale entry.[10] The reasons for this include the ability of large-scale entrants to realize economies of scale more rapidly, build brand loyalty, and gain access to distribution channels, all of which increase the probability of a new venture's succeeding. In contrast, small-scale entrants may find themselves handicapped by high costs due to a lack of economies of scale and a lack of market presence that limits their ability to build brand loyalties and gain access to distribution channels. These scale effects are probably particularly significant when a company is entering an established industry in which incumbent companies exist that possess economies of scale, brand loyalties, and access to distribution channels and in which the new entrant often has to match these in order to succeed.

Figure 10.4 plots the relationships among scale of entry, profitability, and cash flow over time for successful small- and large-scale ventures. The figure shows that successful small-scale entry incurs lower initial losses, but in the long run large-scale entry generates greater returns. However, perhaps because of the costs of large-scale entry and the potential losses if the venture fails, many companies prefer a small-scale entry strategy. Acting on this preference can be a mistake, for the company fails to build up the market share necessary for long-term success.

Poor Commercialization   Many internal new ventures are high-technology operations. To be commercially successful, science-based innovations must be developed with market requirements in mind. Many internal new ventures fail when a company ignores the basic needs of the market. A company can become blinded by the technological possibilities of a new product and fail to analyze market opportunities properly. Thus, a new venture may fail because of a lack of commercialization or because it is marketing a technology for which there is no demand.

For example, consider the desktop computer marketed by NeXT, the company started by the founder of Apple, Steven Jobs. The NeXT system failed to gain market share because the computer incorporated an array of expensive technologies that consumers simply did not want, such as optical disk drives and hi-fi sound. The optical disk drives, in particular, turned off customers because they made it tough to switch work from a PC with a floppy drive to a NeXT machine with an optical drive. In other words, NeXT failed because its founder was so dazzled by leading-edge technology that he ignored customers' needs.

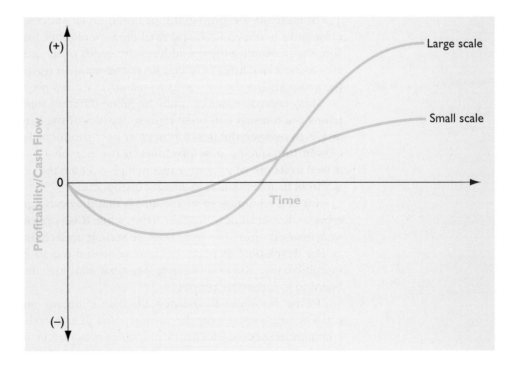

Poor Implementation   Managing the new-venture process raises difficult organizational issues.[11] Although we deal with the specifics of implementation in later chapters, we must note some of the most common mistakes here.[12] The shotgun approach of supporting many different internal new ventures can be a major error, for it places great demands on a company's cash flow and can result in the best ventures being starved of the cash they need for success.

A second common mistake is failure by corporate management to set the strategic context within which new-venture projects should be developed. Simply taking a team of research scientists and allowing them to do research in their favorite field may produce novel results, but these results may have little strategic or commercial value. It is necessary to be very clear about the strategic objectives of the venture and to understand how the venture will seek to establish a competitive advantage.

Failure to anticipate the time and costs involved in the venture process constitutes a third mistake. Many companies have unrealistic expectations regarding the time frame involved. Reportedly, some companies operate with a philosophy of killing new businesses if they do not turn a profit by the end of the third year—clearly an unrealistic view, given the evidence that it can take five to twelve years before a venture generates substantial profits.

Guidelines for Successful Internal New Venturing
. . . .

To avoid the pitfalls just discussed, a company should adopt a structured approach to managing internal new venturing. New venturing typically begins with R&D. To make effective use of its R&D capacity, a company must first spell out its strategic objectives and then communicate them to its scientists and engineers. Research, after all, makes sense only when it is undertaken in areas relevant to strategic goals.[13]

To increase the probability of commercial success, a company should foster close links between R&D and marketing personnel, for this is the best way to ensure that research projects address the needs of the market. The company should also foster close links between R&D and manufacturing personnel to ensure that the company has the capability to manufacture any proposed new products.

Many companies successfully integrate different functions by setting up project teams. Such teams comprise representatives of the various functional areas; their task is to oversee the development of new products. For example, Compaq's success in introducing new products in the personal computer industry has been linked to its use of project teams, which oversee the development of a new product from its inception to its market introduction.

Another advantage of such teams is that they can significantly reduce the time it takes to develop a new product. Thus, while R&D personnel are working on the design, manufacturing personnel can be setting up facilities, and marketing personnel can be developing its plans. Because of such integration, Compaq needed only six months to take the first portable personal computer from an idea on the drawing board to a marketable product.

To use resources to the best effect, a company must also devise a selection process for choosing only the ventures that demonstrate the greatest probability of commercial success. Picking future winners is a tricky business, since by definition new ventures have an uncertain future. One study found the uncertainty surrounding new ventures to be so great that it usually takes a company four to five years after launching the venture to reasonably estimate the venture's future profitability.[14] Nevertheless, a selection process is necessary if a company is to avoid spreading its resources too thinly over too many projects.

Once a project has been selected, management needs to monitor the progress of the venture closely. Evidence suggests that the most important criterion for evaluating a venture during its first four to five years is market share growth rather than cash flow or profitability. In the long run, the most successful ventures are those that increase their market share. A company should have clearly defined market share objectives for an internal new venture and decide to retain or kill it in its early years on the basis of its ability to achieve market share goals. Only in the medium term should profitability and cash flow begin to take on greater importance.

Finally, the association of large-scale entry with greater long-term profitability suggests that a company can increase the probability of success for an internal new venture by thinking big. Thinking big means the construction of efficient-scale manufacturing facilities in advance of demand, large marketing expenditures to build a market presence and brand loyalty, and a commitment by corporate management to accept initial losses as long as market share is expanding.

ACQUISITIONS AS AN ENTRY STRATEGY

Attractions of Acquisitions

Companies typically use acquisition to enter a business area that is new to them when they lack important competencies (resources and capabilities) required to compete in that area but can purchase an incumbent company that has those competencies and do so at a reasonable price. The thinking behind AT&T's acquisition of NCR, for example, was that NCR would bring to AT&T a set of competencies that AT&T lacked and help AT&T compete better in the computer business (although, as noted in the Opening Case, the acquisition failed to produce the anticipated gains).

Companies also have a preference for acquisitions as an entry mode when they feel the need to move fast. As discussed above, building a new business through internal venturing can be a relatively slow process. In contrast, acquisition is a much quicker way to establish a significant market presence and generate profitability. A company can purchase a market leader in a strong cash position overnight, rather than spend years building up a market-leadership position through internal development. Thus, when speed is important, acquisition is the favored entry mode.

Acquisitions are also often perceived to be somewhat less risky than internal new ventures, primarily because they involve less uncertainty. Due to the nature of internal new ventures, large uncertainties are associated with projecting future profitability, revenues, and cash flows. In contrast, when a company makes an acquisition, it is acquiring known profitability, known revenues, and known market share, all of which reduce uncertainty. An acquisition allows a company to buy an established business with a track record, and for this reason many companies favor acquisitions as a method of entry into new business areas.

Finally, acquisitions may be the preferred entry mode when the industry to be entered is well established and incumbent enterprises enjoy significant protection from barriers to entry. As you recall from Chapter 3, barriers to entry arise from factors associated with product differentiation (brand loyalty), absolute cost advantages, and economies of scale. When such barriers are substantial, a company finds entering an industry through internal new venturing difficult. To enter, a company may have to construct an efficient-scale manufacturing plant, undertake massive advertising to break down established brand loyalties, and quickly build up distribution outlets—all hard-to-achieve goals likely to involve substantial expenditures. In contrast, by acquiring an established enterprise, a company can circumvent most barriers to entry. It can purchase a market leader, which already benefits from substantial economies of scale and brand loyalty. Thus, the greater the barriers to entry, the more likely it is that acquisitions will be the favored entry mode. (We should note that the attractiveness of an acquisition is predicated upon the assumption that an incumbent company can be acquired for less than it would cost to enter the same industry via an internal new venture. As we shall see in the next section, the validity of this assumption is often questionable.)

Pitfalls of Acquisitions

For the reasons just noted, acquisitions have long been a popular vehicle for expanding the scope of the organization into new business areas. However, despite this popularity, there is ample evidence that many acquisitions fail to add value for the acquiring company and, indeed, often end up dissipating value. For example, a study by Mercer Management Consulting looked at 150 acquisitions worth more than $500 million each that were undertaken between January 1990 and July 1995.[15] The Mercer study concluded that 50 percent of these acquisitions ended up eroding, or substantially eroding, shareholder value, while another 33 percent created only marginal returns. Only 17 percent of these acquisitions were judged to be successful.

More generally, there is a wealth of evidence from academic research suggesting that many acquisitions fail to realize their anticipated benefits.[16] In a major study of the postacquisition performance of acquired companies, during the 1960s and 1970s, David Ravenscraft and Mike Scherer concluded that many good companies were acquired during this period and, on average, their profits and market shares declined following acquisition.[17] They also noted that a smaller but substantial subset of those good companies experienced traumatic difficulties, which ultimately led to their being sold off by the acquiring company. In other words, Ravenscraft and Scherer's evidence suggests that many acquisitions destroy rather than create value.

Why do so many acquisitions apparently fail to create value? There appear to be four major reasons: (1) companies often experience difficulties when trying to integrate divergent corporate cultures, (2) companies overestimate the potential economic benefits from an acquisition, (3) acquisitions tend to be very expensive, and (4) companies often do not adequately screen their acquisition targets.

Difficulty with Postacquisition Integration   Having made an acquisition, the acquiring company has to integrate the acquired business into its own organizational structure. Integration can entail the adoption of common management and financial control systems, the joining together of operations from the acquired and the acquiring company, or the establishment of linkages to share information and personnel. When integration is attempted, many unexpected problems can occur. Often they stem from differences in corporate cultures. After an acquisition, many acquired companies experience high management turnover, possibly because their employees do not like the acquiring company's way of doing things.[18] Recent research evidence suggests that the loss of management talent and expertise, to say nothing of the damage from constant tension between the businesses, can materially harm the performance of the acquired unit.[19] For an example of what can occur, see Strategy in Action 10.3, which examines the high management turnover at The Boston Company after it was acquired by Mellon Bank in 1993.

Overestimating Economic Benefits   Even when companies achieve integration, they often overestimate the potential for creating value by joining together different businesses. They overestimate the strategic advantages that can be derived from the acquisition and thus pay more for the target company than it is probably worth. Richard Roll has attributed this tendency to hubris on the part of top management. According to Roll, top managers typically overestimate their ability to create value from an acquisition, primarily because rising to the top of a corporation has given them an exaggerated sense of their own capabilities.[20]

Coca-Cola's 1975 acquisition of a number of medium-sized winemaking companies illustrates the situation in which a company overestimates the economic benefits from an acquisition. Reasoning that a beverage is a beverage, Coca-Cola wanted to use its distinctive competence in marketing to dominate the U.S. wine industry. However, after buying three wine companies and enduring seven years of marginal profits, Coca-Cola finally conceded that wine and soft drinks are very different products, with different kinds of appeal, pricing systems, and distribution networks. In 1983 it sold the wine operations to Joseph E. Seagram & Sons for $210 million, the price Coca-Cola had paid and a substantial loss when adjusted for inflation.[21]

One Big Unhappy Family at Mellon Bank

In the early 1990s Frank Cahouet, the CEO of Philadelphia-based Mellon Bank, conceived of a corporate strategy that would reduce the vulnerability of Mellon's earnings to changes in interest rates. Cahouet's solution was to diversify into financial services to gain access to a steady flow of fee-based income from money management operations. As part of this strategy, in 1993 Mellon acquired The Boston Company for $1.45 billion. Boston is a high-profile money management company that manages investments for major institutional clients, such as state and corporate pension funds. In 1994 Mellon followed up its Boston acquisition with the acquisition of Dreyfus, a mutual fund provider, for $1.7 billion. As a result, by 1995 almost half of Mellon's income was generated from fee-based financial services.

However, in 1993 Mellon hit some serious bumps on the road in its attempt to become a money market powerhouse. Problems at Boston began to surface soon after its acquisition by Mellon. From the start there was a clear clash of cultures. At Mellon, many managers arrive at their mundane offices by 7 A.M. and put in twelve-hour days for pay that is modest by banking industry standards. They are also accustomed to a firm management hierarchy that is carefully controlled by Frank Cahouet, whose management style emphasizes cost containment and frugality. Boston managers also put in twelve-hour days, but they expect considerable autonomy, flexible work schedules, high pay, ample perks, and large performance bonuses. In most years, the top twenty executives at Boston earn between $750,000 and $1 million each. Mellon executives who visited The Boston Company unit were dumbstruck by the country club atmosphere and opulence they saw. In its move to streamline Boston, Mellon insisted that Boston cut expenses and introduced new regulations for restricting travel, entertainment, and perks.

Things started to go wrong in October 1993, when the Wisconsin state pension fund complained to Mellon of lower returns on a portfolio run by Boston. In November Mellon liquidated the portfolio, taking a $130 million charge against earnings. Mellon also fired the portfolio manager, who it claimed was making "unau-thorized trades." At Boston, however, many managers saw Mellon's action as violating guarantees of operating autonomy that Mellon had given Boston at the time of the acquisition. They blamed Mellon for prematurely liquidating a portfolio whose strategy, they claimed, Mellon executives had approved and that, moreover, could still prove a winner if interest rates fell (which they subsequently did).

Infuriated by Mellon's interference in the running of Boston, in March seven managers at Boston's Asset Management unit, including the unit's CEO, Desmond Heathwood, proposed a management buyout to Mellon. This unit was one of the gems in Boston's crown, with more than $26 billion in assets under management. Heathwood had been openly disdainful of Mellon's bankers, believing that they were out of their league in the investment business. In April Mellon rejected the buyout proposal, and Heathwood promptly left to start his own investment management company. A few days later Mellon asked employees at Boston to sign employment contracts that limited their ability to leave and work for Heathwood's competing business. Another thirteen senior employees refused to sign. These thirteen all quit in order to join Heathwood's new money management operation.

The defection of Heathwood and his colleagues was followed by a series of high-profile client defections. The Arizona state retirement system, for example, pulled $1 billion out of Mellon and transferred it to Heathwood's firm, while the Fresno County retirement system transferred $400 million in assets to Heathwood. As one client stated, "We have a relationship with The Boston Co. that goes back over 30 years, and the people who worked on the account are the people who left—so we left too."

Reflecting on the episode, Frank Cahouet noted that "we've clearly been hurt. . . . But this episode is very manageable. We are not going to lose our momentum." Others weren't so sure. In this incident they saw yet another example of how difficult it can be to merge two divergent corporate cultures and how the management turnover that results can deal a serious blow to any attempt to create value from an acquisition.[22]

The Expense of Acquisitions   Acquisitions of companies whose stock is publicly traded tend to be very expensive. When a company bids to acquire the stock of another enterprise, the stock price frequently gets bid up in the acquisition process. This is particularly likely to occur in the case of contested bids, in which two or more companies simultaneously bid for control of a single target company. Thus, the acquiring company must often pay a premium over the current market value of the target. In the early 1980s acquiring companies paid an average premium of 40 to 50 percent over current stock prices for an acquisition. Between 1985 and 1988, when takeover activity was at its peak, premiums of 80 percent were not uncommon. Indeed, in the giant contested takeover bid for RJR Nabisco during late 1988, the stock price of RJR was bid up from $45 per share prior to the takeover attempt to $110 per share by the time RJR was sold—a premium of more than 200 percent! By the first half of the 1990s, the takeover premium was once more in the 40 to 50 percent range.

The debt taken on to finance such expensive acquisitions can later become a noose around the acquiring company's neck, particularly if interest rates rise. Moreover, if the market value of the target company prior to an acquisition was a true reflection of that company's worth under its management at that time, a premium of 50 percent over this value means that the acquiring company has to improve the performance of the acquired unit by just as much if it is to reap a positive return on its investment. Such performance gains, however, can be very difficult to achieve.

Inadequate Preacquisition Screening   After researching acquisitions made by twenty different companies, a study by Philippe Haspeslagh and David Jemison came to the conclusion that one reason for the failure of acquisitions is management's inadequate attention to preacquisition screening.[23] They found that many companies decide to acquire other firms without thoroughly analyzing the potential benefits and costs. After the acquisition has been completed, many acquiring companies discover that instead of buying a well-run business, they have purchased a troubled organization. That was Xerox's experience when it purchased the Crum and Forster insurance business in the early 1980s. Only after the acquisition was completed did Xerox learn that Crum and Forster was a high-cost and inefficient provider of insurance. Xerox subsequently divested itself of the business for a significant financial loss.

Guidelines for Successful Acquisitions

To avoid pitfalls and make successful acquisitions, companies need to take a structured approach with three main components: (1) target identification and preacquisition screening, (2) bidding strategy, and (3) integration.[24]

Screening   Thorough preacquisition screening increases a company's knowledge about potential takeover targets, leads to a more realistic assessment of the problems involved in executing an acquisition and integrating the new business into the company's organizational structure, and lessens the risk of purchasing a potential problem business. The screening should begin with a detailed assessment of the strategic rationale for making the acquisition and identification of the kind of enterprise that would make an ideal acquisition candidate.

Next, the company should scan a target population of potential acquisition candidates, evaluating each according to a detailed set of criteria, focusing on (1) financial position, (2) product market position, (3) competitive environment, (4) management capabilities, and (5) corporate culture. Such an evaluation should enable the company to identify the strengths and weaknesses of each candidate, the extent of potential economies of scope between the acquiring and the acquired companies, potential integration problems, and the compatibility of the corporate cultures of the acquiring and the acquired companies.

The company should then reduce the list of candidates to the most favored ones and evaluate them further. At this stage, it should sound out third parties, such as investment bankers, whose opinions may be important and who may be able to give valuable insights about the efficiency of target companies. The company that leads the list after this process should be the acquisition target.

Bidding Strategy   The objective of bidding strategy is to reduce the price that a company must pay for an acquisition candidate. The essential element of a good bidding strategy is timing. For example, Hanson PLC, one of the most successful takeover machines of the 1980s, always looked for essentially sound businesses that were suffering from short-term problems due to cyclical industry factors or from problems localized in one division. Such companies are typically undervalued by the stock market and thus can be picked up without payment of the standard 40 or 50 percent premium over current stock prices. With good timing, a company can make a bargain purchase.

Integration   Despite good screening and bidding, an acquisition will fail unless positive steps are taken to integrate the acquired company into the organizational structure of the acquiring one. Integration should center on the source of the potential strategic advantages of the acquisition—for instance, opportunities to share marketing, manufacturing, procurement, R&D, financial, or management resources. Integration should also be accompanied by steps to eliminate any duplication of facilities or functions. In addition, any unwanted activities of the acquired company should be sold. Finally, if the different business activities are closely related, they will require a high degree of integration. In the case of a company such as Hanson PLC, the level of integration can be minimal, for the company's strategy is one of unrelated diversification. However, a company such as Philip Morris requires greater integration because its strategy is one of related diversification.

JOINT VENTURES AS AN ENTRY STRATEGY

Attractions of Joint Ventures

A company may prefer internal new venturing to acquisition as an entry strategy into new business areas yet hesitate to commit itself to an internal new venture because of the risks and costs of building a new operation up from the ground floor. Such a situation is most likely to occur when a company sees the possibility of establishing a new business in an embryonic or growth industry, but the risks and costs associated with the project are more than it is willing to assume on its own. In these circumstances, the company may decide to enter into a joint venture with another company and use the joint venture as a vehicle for entering the new business area. Such an arrangement enables the company to share the substantial risks and costs involved in a new project.

For example, in 1990 IBM and Motorola set up a joint venture whose purpose was to provide a service that allowed computer users to communicate over radio waves. Customers buying the service can use hand-held computers, made by Motorola, to communicate by means of a private network of radio towers that IBM has built across the United States. The venture is aimed at the potentially enormous market of people who could benefit from using computers in the field, such as people who repair equipment in offices and insurance claims adjusters. Analysts estimate that the market for such a service is currently in the tens of millions of dollars but could reach the billions over the next decade.[25]

Because of the embryonic nature of the industry, the venture faces substantial risks. A number of competing technologies are on the horizon. For example, laptop computers are being fitted with modems that can communicate with host computers through cellular telephone networks. Although cellular networks are more crowded and less reliable than radio networks, that state of affairs could change. Given this uncertainty, it makes sense for IBM and Motorola to combine in a joint venture and share the risks associated with building up this business.

In addition, a joint venture makes sense when a company can increase the probability of successfully establishing a new business by joining forces with another company. For a company that has some of the skills and assets necessary to establish a successful new venture, teaming up with another company that has complementary skills and assets may increase the probability of success.

Again, the venture between IBM and Motorola provides an example. Motorola dominates the market for mobile radios and already manufactures hand-held computers, but it lacks a nationwide radio network through which users of hand-held computers might communicate with each other. IBM lacks radio technology, but it does have a private network of radio towers (originally built for communicating with 20,000-plus IBM service people in the field), which covers more than 90 percent of the country. Combining Motorola's skills in radio technology with IBM's radio network in a single joint venture increases significantly the probability of establishing a successful new business.

Pitfalls of Joint Ventures

There are three main pitfalls to joint ventures. First, a joint venture allows a company to share the risks and costs of developing a new business, but it also requires the sharing of profits if the new business succeeds. Second, a company that enters into a joint venture always runs the risk of giving critical know-how away to its partner, which might use that know-how to compete directly with the company in the future. However, as we point out in the discussion of global strategic alliances in Chapter 8, joint ventures can be structured to minimize this risk. Third, the venture partners must share control. If the partners have different business philosophies, time horizons, or investment preferences, substantial problems can arise. Conflicts over how to run the joint venture can tear it apart and result in business failure.

In sum, although joint ventures often have a distinct advantage over internal new venturing as a means of establishing a new business operation, they also have certain drawbacks. When deciding whether to go it alone or cooperate with another company in a joint venture, strategic managers need to assess carefully the pros and cons of the alternatives.

RESTRUCTURING

So far we have focused on strategies for expanding the scope of a company into new business areas. We turn now to a discussion of the opposite side of the coin: strategies for reducing the scope of the company by *exiting* business areas. In recent years reducing the scope of a company through restructuring has become an increasingly popular strategy, particularly among the companies that diversified their activities during the 1960s, 1970s, and 1980s. In most cases companies that are engaged in restructuring are divesting themselves of diversified activities in order to concentrate on their core businesses.[26] The Opening Case, you recall, describes how AT&T decided to restructure the company, focusing on telecommunications services and exiting the computer and network equipment businesses by spinning off these operations to independent investors. Other large, diversified, well-known companies have pursued similar strategies. They include General Electric, which began restructuring when Jack Welch became its CEO, and Sears, which sold off Allstate Insurance, Coldwell Banker Real Estate, and the brokerage Dean Witter Reynolds in order to focus more on its core retailing operations. (For details of restructuring at Sears, see Strategy in Action 10.4.)

The first question that must be asked is, why are so many companies restructuring at this particular time? After answering it, we examine the different strategies that companies adopt for exiting from business areas. Then we discuss the various turnaround strategies that companies employ to revitalize their core business area.

Why Restructure?

One reason for so much restructuring in recent years is overdiversification. There is plenty of evidence that in the heyday of the corporate diversification movement, which began in the 1960s and lasted until the early 1980s, many companies overdiversified.[27] More precisely, the bureaucratic inefficiencies created by expanding the scope of the organization outweighed the additional value that could be created, and company performance declined. As performance declined, the stock price of many of these diversified companies fell, and they found themselves vulnerable to hostile takeover bids. Indeed, a number of diversified companies were acquired in the 1980s and subsequently broken up. This is what happened to U.S. Industries and SCM, two diversified conglomerates that were acquired and then broken up by Hanson PLC. Similarly, after the diversified consumer products business RJR Nabisco was acquired by Kohlberg, Kravis & Roberts in a 1988 leveraged buyout, RJR sold off many of its diversified businesses to independent investors or to other companies.

A second factor driving the current restructuring trend is that in the 1980s and 1990s many diversified companies found their core business areas under attack from new competition. For example, due to deregulation AT&T now faces a much

The Restructuring of Sears

In 1981 Sears, which was then the largest retailer in the United States, announced in a single week that it would acquire Dean Witter Reynolds, the country's fifth largest brokerage, and Coldwell Banker, the nation's biggest real estate broker, for a total of $800 million. The idea was to team these two financial service operations with Allstate Insurance, which Sears had acquired in 1934 and which was then the world's second largest personal property and casualty insurer. At the heart of Sears's strategy was a desire to leverage its fabled "bond of trust" with the consumer into the fast-growing financial services industry, a strategy its CEO, Edward Brennan, often referred to as "socks to stocks." Sears felt that its retail customers would be strongly attracted to financial services providers that were owned by Sears. Indeed, the company planned to locate offices for its financial services operations in Sears department stores and to use its catalog mailing list as a channel for selling financial services.

However, the 1980s and early 1990s were not kind to Sears. While the financial services operations of the company did well, its core retailing operation ran into serious problems. During most of the 1980s, the earnings of Sears's retail group fell at an annual rate of 7 to 8 percent and its market share slumped. The share of department store merchandise accounted for by Sears fell from 9 percent in 1982 to 6 percent in 1992. More significantly, Sears did little to keep up with the growth of discount and niche retailers such as Wal-Mart, Costco, The Home Depot, and Toys 'R' Us, all of which ate into Sears's blue-collar clientele. Critics charged that senior executives at Sears seemed more interested in new ventures and the potential for synergy than in the basic business of running Sears's stores. As a result, Sears was slow to respond to new competition, and its sales stagnated.

The problems in Sears's retail operations attracted the scorn of Wall Street and at least one abortive takeover attempt in early 1988, when rumors of a $50.2 billion takeover bid by Revlon's Chairman Ronald O. Perelman were making the rounds on Wall Street. Sears responded by announcing a decision to sell off its Chicago headquarters and introducing an "everyday low pricing" strategy at its stores. Both moves failed. After a year Sears abandoned attempts to sell the Sears Tower. Furthermore, it never could convince consumers that it had the lowest prices in town—probably because it didn't!

Meanwhile the stock continued to slump. To make matters worse, in 1992 Sears's fabled "bond of trust" with consumers was blown apart when it was revealed that its automobile services operation had been systematically overcharging consumers for repair services. At the same time Moody's Investors Service, noting Sears's growing burden of debt, lowered its bond rating on the company. The stock slumped further, and investors pushed the company to take drastic action. In September 1992 Sears announced plans to sell Dean Witter Reynolds and Coldwell Banker and to spin off 20 percent of Allstate to independent investors. In effect, Sears was turning its back on thirteen years of diversification and an investment of billions of dollars in order that top management could devote more time to revitalizing its troubled retailing arm. The change in strategy was a humiliating admission by Sears's top management, and particularly CEO Brennan, that it had mishandled the strategic direction of the company.[28]

more competitive environment in its core long-distance business, which helped to drive its decision to exit from noncore activities. Similarly, Sears still faces profound competitive challenges in the retailing industry, where demand is shifting from department stores such as Sears to low-cost discounters such as Costco or niche stores such as The Gap. (See Strategy in Action 10.4 for details.) The top management of these companies found that in order to devote the necessary attention to their troubled core business, it had to shed its diversified activities, which had become an unwelcome distraction.

A final factor of some importance is that innovations in management processes and strategy have diminished the advantages of vertical integration or diversification. In response, companies have reduced the scope of their activities through restructuring and divestments. For example, ten years ago there was little understanding of how long-term cooperative relationships between a company and its suppliers could be a viable alternative to vertical integration. Most companies considered only two alternatives for managing the supply chain: vertical integration or competitive bidding. As we note in Chapter 9, however, if the conditions are right, a third alternative for managing the supply chain, *long-term contracting,* can be a superior strategy to both vertical integration and competitive bidding. As with vertical integration, long-term contracting facilitates investments in specialization. However, unlike vertical integration, it does not involve high bureaucratic costs, nor does it dispense with market discipline. As this strategic innovation has spread throughout the business world, the relative advantages of vertical integration have declined.

Exit Strategies

Companies can choose from three main strategies for exiting business areas: divestment, harvest, and liquidation. You have already encountered all three in Chapter 7, where we discuss strategies for competing in declining industries. We review them briefly here.

Divestment   Of the three main strategies, divestment is usually favored. It represents the best way for a company to recoup as much of its initial investment in a business unit as possible. The idea is to sell the business unit to the highest bidder. Three types of buyers are independent investors, other companies, and the management of the unit to be divested. Selling off a business unit to independent investors is normally referred to as a **spinoff.** A spinoff makes good sense when the unit to be sold is profitable and when the stock market has an appetite for new stock issues (which is normal during market upswings, but *not* during market downswings). Thus, for example, in 1992 the timber products company Weyerhaeuser successfully spun off its Paragon Trade Brands to independent investors. Investors snapped up the stock of the new issue, which makes "own label" disposable diapers for supermarket chains and is highly profitable. However, spinoffs do not work if the unit to be spun off is unprofitable and unattractive to independent investors or if the stock market is slumping and unresponsive to new issues.

Selling off a unit to another company is a strategy frequently pursued when a unit can be sold to a company in the same line of business as the unit. In such cases, the purchaser is often prepared to pay a considerable amount of money for the opportunity to substantially increase the size of its business virtually overnight. For example, in 1987 Hanson PLC sold off its Glidden paint subsidiary, which it had acquired six months earlier in the takeover of SCM, to Imperial Chemical Industries (ICI). Glidden was the largest paint company in the United States, and ICI was the largest manufacturer of paint outside the United States, so the match made a good deal of sense from ICI's perspective, and Hanson was able to get a substantial price for the sale.

Selling off a unit to its management is normally referred to as a **management buyout (MBO).** MBOs are very similar to leveraged buyouts (LBOs), discussed in Chapter 2. In an MBO, the unit is sold to its management, which often finances the purchase through the sale of high-yield bonds to investors. The bond issue is normally arranged by a buyout specialist, such as Kohlberg, Kravis & Roberts, which, along with management, will typically hold a sizable proportion of the shares in the MBO. MBOs often take place when financially troubled units have only two other options: a harvest strategy or liquidation.

An MBO can be very risky for the management team involved, since its members may have to sign personal guarantees to back up the bond issue and may lose everything if the MBO ultimately fails. On the other hand, if the management team succeeds in turning around the troubled unit, its reward can be a significant increase in personal wealth. Thus, an MBO strategy can be characterized as a *high risk–high return strategy* for the management team involved. Faced with the possible liquidation of their business unit, many management teams are willing to take the risk. However, the viability of this option depends not only on a willing management team but also on enough buyers of high-yield/high-risk bonds—so-called junk bonds—to be able to finance the MBO. In recent years, the general slump in the junk bond market has made the MBO strategy a more difficult one for companies to follow.

Harvest and Liquidation Since the pros and cons of harvest and liquidation strategies are discussed in detail in Chapter 7, we note just a few points here. First, a harvest or liquidation strategy is generally considered inferior to a divestment strategy since the company can probably best recoup its investment in a business unit by divestment. Second, a harvest strategy means halting investment in a unit in order to maximize short-to-medium-term cash flow from that unit before liquidating it. Although this strategy seems fine in theory, it is often a poor one to apply in practice. Once it becomes apparent that the unit is pursuing a harvest strategy, the morale of the unit's employees, as well as the confidence of the unit's customers and suppliers in its continuing operation, can sink very quickly. If this occurs, as it often does, then the rapid decline in the unit's revenues can make the strategy untenable. Finally, a liquidation strategy is the least attractive of all to pursue since it requires the company to write off its investment in a business unit, often at a considerable cost. However, for a poorly performing business unit for which a selloff or spinoff is unlikely and for which an MBO cannot be arranged, it may be the only viable alternative.

TURNAROUND STRATEGIES

Many companies restructure their operations, divesting themselves of their diversified activities because they wish to focus more on their core business area. As in the case of Sears, this often occurs because the core business area is itself in trouble and needs top management's attention. An integral part of restructuring, therefore, is the development of a strategy for turning around the company's core or remaining business areas. In this section, we review in some detail the various steps that companies take to turn around troubled business areas. We first look at the causes of corporate decline and then discuss the main elements of successful turnaround strategies.

The Causes of Corporate Decline

Seven main causes stand out in most cases of corporate decline: poor management, overexpansion, inadequate financial controls, high costs, the emergence of powerful new competition, unforeseen shifts in demand, and organizational inertia.[29] Normally several, if not all, of these factors are present in a decline. For example, IBM's decline in the early 1990s was brought on by a high-cost structure, powerful new low-cost competition from personal computer makers, a shift in demand away from mainframe computers (IBM's main business), and IBM's slow response to these factors due to organizational inertia.

Poor Management   Poor management covers a multitude of sins, ranging from sheer incompetence to neglect of core businesses to an insufficient number of good managers. Although not necessarily a bad thing, one-person rule often seems to be at the root of poor management. One study found that the presence of a dominant and autocratic chief executive with a passion for empire-building strategies often characterizes many failing companies.[30] Another study of eighty-one turnaround situations found that in thirty-six cases troubled companies suffered from an autocratic manager who tried to do it all and, in the face of complexity and change, could not.[31] In a review of the empirical studies of turnaround situations, Richard Hoffman identified a number of other managerial defects commonly found in declining companies.[32] These included a lack of balanced expertise at the top (for example, too many engineers), a lack of strong middle management, a failure to provide for orderly management succession by a departing CEO (which may result in an internal succession battle), and a failure by the board of directors to monitor management's strategic decisions adequately.

Overexpansion   The empire-building strategies of autocratic CEOs often involve rapid expansion and extensive diversification. Much of this diversification tends to be poorly conceived and adds little value to a company. As already pointed out in this chapter and in Chapter 9, the consequences of too much diversification include loss of control and an inability to cope with recessionary conditions. Moreover, companies that expand rapidly tend to do so by taking on large amounts of debt financing. Adverse economic conditions can limit a company's ability to meet its debt requirements and can thus precipitate a financial crisis.

Inadequate Financial Controls   The most common aspect of inadequate financial controls is a failure to assign profit responsibility to key decision makers within the organization. A lack of accountability for the financial consequences of their actions can encourage middle-level managers to employ excess staff and spend resources beyond what is necessary for maximum efficiency. In such cases, bureaucracy may balloon and costs spiral out of control. This is precisely what happened at Chrysler during the 1970s. As Lee Iacocca later noted, Jerry Greenwald, whom Iacocca brought in to head the finance function in 1980, "had a hell of a time finding anybody who could be identified as having specific responsibility for anything. They would tell him, 'Well, everyone is responsible for controlling costs.' Jerry knew very well what that meant—in the final analysis nobody was."[33]

High Costs   Inadequate financial controls can lead to high costs. Beyond this, the most common cause of a high-cost structure is low labor productivity. It may stem from union-imposed restrictive working practices (as in the case of the auto and steel industries); management's failure to invest in new labor-saving technologies; or, more often, a combination of both. Other common causes include high wage rates (a particularly important factor for companies competing on costs in the global marketplace) and a failure to realize economies of scale because of low market share.

New Competition   Competition in capitalist economies is a process characterized by the continual emergence of new companies' championing new ways of doing business. In recent years few industries and few established companies have been spared the competitive challenge of powerful new competition. Indeed, many established businesses have failed or run into serious trouble because they did not respond quickly enough to such threats. Powerful new competition is a central cause of corporate decline. IBM has been hammered by powerful new competition from personal computer makers, and Sears has been hard hit by powerful new competition from discount and niche stores (see Strategy in Action 10.4). In both these cases, the established company failed to appreciate the strength of new competitors until it was in serious trouble.

Unforeseen Demand Shifts   Unforeseen, and often unforeseeable, shifts in demand can be brought about by major changes in technology, in economic or political conditions, and in social and cultural norms. Although such changes can open up market opportunities for new products, they also threaten the existence of many established enterprises, necessitating restructuring. A recent example is the rapid rise of the Internet and World Wide Web which, among other things, blind-sided Microsoft, the dominant software company in the personal computer market. Although Microsoft has since responded to the rise of the Internet, doing so required the company to remake its strategy.

Organizational Inertia   On their own, the emergence of powerful new competition and unforeseen shifts in demand might not be enough to cause corporate decline. What is also required is an organization that is slow to respond to such environmental changes. As you saw in Chapter 4, where we first touched on the issue of corporate decline, organizational inertia stands out as a major reason why companies are often so slow to respond to new competitive conditions.

The Main Steps of Turnaround

There is no standard model of how a company should respond to a decline. Indeed, there can be no such model because every situation is unique. However, in most successful turnaround situations, a number of common features are present. They include changing the leadership; redefining the company's strategic focus; divesting or closure of unwanted assets; taking steps to improve the profitability of remaining operations; and, occasionally, making acquisitions to rebuild core operations.

Changing the Leadership   Since the old leadership bears the stigma of failure, new leadership is an essential element of most retrenchment and turnaround situations. For example, as the first step in implementing a turnaround, IBM replaced

CEO John Akers with an outsider, Lou Gerstner. To resolve a crisis, the new leader should be someone who is able to make difficult decisions, motivate lower-level managers, listen to the views of others, and delegate power when appropriate.

Redefining Strategic Focus   For a single-business enterprise, redefining strategic focus involves a reevaluation of the company's business-level strategy. A failed cost leader, for example, may reorient toward a more focused or differentiated strategy. For a diversified company, redefining strategic focus means identifying the businesses in the portfolio that have the best long-term profit and growth prospects and concentrating investment there.

Divesting or Closure of Assets   Having redefined its strategic focus, a company should divest as many unwanted assets as it can find buyers for and liquidate whatever remains. It is important not to confuse unwanted assets with unprofitable assets. Assets that no longer fit with the redefined strategic focus of the company may be very profitable. Their sale can bring the company much needed cash, which it can invest in improving the operations that remain.

Improving Profitability   Improving the profitability of the operations that remain after asset sales and closures takes a number of steps to improve efficiency, quality, innovation, and customer responsiveness. We discuss many of the functional-level strategies that companies can pursue to achieve these ends in Chapter 5, so you may want to review that chapter for details. Note, though, that improving profitability typically involves one or more of the following: (1) laying off white- and blue-collar employees; (2) investing in labor-saving equipment; (3) assigning profit responsibility to individuals and subunits within the company, by a change of organizational structure if necessary; (4) tightening financial controls; (5) cutting back on marginal products; (6) reengineering business processes to cut costs and boost productivity; and (7) introducing total quality management processes.

Making Acquisitions   A somewhat surprising but quite common turnaround strategy is to make acquisitions, primarily to strengthen the competitive position of a company's remaining core operations. For example, Champion International used to be a very diversified company, manufacturing a wide range of paper and wood products. After years of declining performance, in the mid 1980s Champion decided to focus on its profitable newsprint and magazine paper business. The company divested itself of many of its other paper and wood products businesses, but at the same time it paid $1.8 billion for St. Regis, one of the country's largest manufacturers of newsprint and magazine paper.

SUMMARY OF CHAPTER

This chapter has built on the material in Chapter 9 by addressing central issues of corporate development. **Corporate development** is concerned with identifying *which* business opportunities a company should pursue, *how* it should pursue those opportunities, and *how* it should exit from businesses that do not fit with the company's strategic vision. The following points have been made in this chapter.

✔ A common starting point for identifying which business opportunities to pursue is to review a company's existing portfolio of businesses activities. One approach to undertaking such a review utilizes a set of techniques known as portfolio planning matrices. The purpose of these techniques is to compare the competitive position of the different businesses in a company's portfolio against each other on the basis of common criteria.

✓ A second approach to the corporate development process championed by Gary Hamel and C. K. Prahalad reconceptualizes a company as a portfolio of core competencies, as opposed to a portfolio of businesses. In this approach, corporate development is oriented toward maintaining existing competencies, building new competencies, and leveraging competencies by applying them to new business opportunities.

✓ The advantage of Hamel and Prahalad's framework is that it focuses explicitly on how a company can *create value* by building new competencies or by recombining existing competencies to enter new business areas. While traditional portfolio planning matrices treat businesses as independent, Hamel and Prahalad's framework recognizes the interdependencies between businesses and focuses upon the opportunities for creating value by building and leveraging competencies.

✓ There are three vehicles that companies use to enter new business areas: internal ventures, acquisitions, and joint ventures.

✓ Internal new venturing is typically employed as an entry strategy when a company possesses a set of valuable competencies in its existing businesses that can be leveraged or recombined to enter a new business area.

✓ Many internal ventures fail because of entry on too small a scale, poor commercialization, and poor corporate management of the internal venture process. Guarding against failure involves a structured approach toward project selection and management, integration of R&D and marketing to improve commercialization of a venture idea, and entry on a significant scale.

✓ Acquisitions are often favored as an entry strategy when the company lacks important competencies (resources and capabilities) required to compete in an area, but when it can purchase an incumbent company that has those competencies and do so at a reasonable price. Acquisitions also tend to be favored when the barriers to entry into the target industry are high and when the company is unwilling to accept the time frame, development costs, and risks of internal new venturing.

✓ Many acquisitions fail because of poor postacquisition integration, overestimation of the value that can be created from an acquisition, the high cost of acquisition, and poor preacquisition screening. Guarding against acquisition failure requires structured screening, good bidding strategies, and positive attempts to integrate the acquired company into the organization of the acquiring one.

✓ Joint ventures may be the preferred entry strategy when (a) the risks and costs associated with setting up a new business unit are more than the company is willing to assume on its own and (b) the company can increase the probability of successfully establishing a new business by teaming up with another company that has skills and assets that complement its own.

✓ The current popularity of restructuring is due to (a) overdiversification by many companies in the 1970s and 1980s, (b) the rise of competitive challenges to the core business units of many diversified enterprises, and (c) innovations in the management process that have reduced the advantages of vertical integration and diversification.

✓ Exit strategies include divestment, harvest, and liquidation. The choice of exit strategy is governed by the characteristics of the relevant business unit.

✓ The causes of corporate decline include poor management, overexpansion, inadequate financial controls, high costs, the emergence of powerful new competition, unforeseen shifts in demand, and organizational inertia.

✓ Responses to corporate decline include changing the leadership, redefining the company's strategic focus, divesting or closure of unwanted assets, taking steps to improve the profitability of the operations that remain, and occasionally, making acquisitions to rebuild core operations.

DISCUSSION QUESTIONS

1. Under what circumstances might it be best to enter a new business area by acquisition, and under what circumstances might internal new venturing be the preferred entry mode?

2. IBM has decided to diversify into the cellular telecommunication business. What entry strategy would you recommend the company pursue? Why?

3. Review the change in the composition of GE's portfolio of businesses under the leadership of Jack Welch (1981 to the present). How has GE's portfolio been reorganized? From the perspective of value creation, what is the logic underlying this reorganization?

Practicing Strategic Management

SMALL-GROUP EXERCISE
Dun & Bradstreet

Break into small groups of three to five people. Then read the following news release from Dun & Bradstreet. On the basis of this information, identify the strategic rationale for the split, and evaluate how the split might affect the performance of three successor companies. If you were a stockholder in the old Dun & Bradstreet, would you approve of this split? Why?

D&B TRANSFORMED INTO THREE
INDEPENDENT PUBLIC COMPANIES

WILTON, CONN., Jan. 9, 1996—Dun & Bradstreet CEO Robert E. Weissman today announced a sweeping strategy that will transform the 155-year-old business information giant into three publicly traded, global corporations.

"This important action is designed to increase shareholder value by unlocking D&B's substantial underlying franchise strengths," said Weissman.

Building on preeminent Dun & Bradstreet businesses, the reorganization establishes three independent companies focused on high-growth information markets, financial information services, and consumer-product market research.

"Since the 1800s, D&B has grown by effectively managing a portfolio of businesses and gaining economies of scale," stated Weissman, "but the velocity of change in information markets has dramatically altered the rules of business survival. Today, market focus and speed are the primary drivers of competitive advantage. This plan is our blueprint for success in the twenty-first century," said Weissman.

The plan, approved today at a special meeting of D&B's board of directors, calls for D&B to create three separate companies by spinning off two of its businesses to shareholders. "D&B is the leader in business information," said Weissman. "By freeing our companies to focus tightly on our core vertical markets, we can more rapidly leverage this leadership position into emerging growth areas."

The three new companies are:

- Cognizant Corporation, a new high-growth company, which includes IMS International, the lead-

ing global supplier of marketing information to the pharmaceutical and health care industries; Nielsen Media Research, the leader in audience measurement for electronic media; and Gartner Group, the premier provider of advisory services to high-tech users, vendors, and suppliers, in which Cognizant will hold a majority interest

- The Dun & Bradstreet Corporation, consisting of Dun & Bradstreet Information Services, the world's largest source of business-to-business marketing and commercial-credit information; Moody's Investors Service, a global leader in rating debt; and Reuben H. Donnelley, a premier provider of Yellow Pages marketing and publishing

- A. C. Nielsen, the global leader in marketing information for the fast-moving consumer packaged goods industry

"These three separate companies will tailor their strategies to the unique demands of their markets, determining investments, capital structures, and policies that will strengthen their respective global capabilities. This plan also clarifies D&B from an investor's perspective by grouping the businesses into three logical investment categories, each with distinct risk/reward profiles," said Weissman.

The Dun & Bradstreet Corporation is the world's largest marketer of information, software, and services for business decision making, with worldwide revenue of $4.9 billion in 1994.

EXPLORING THE WEB
Visiting General Electric

Visit the Web site of General Electric (http://www.ge.com). Using the information contained on that Web site, answer the following questions. (Make sure to visit the "Inside GE" section of the Web site.)

1. Review GE's portfolio of major businesses. Does this portfolio make sense from a value creation perspective? Why?

2. What (if any) changes would you make to GE's portfolio of businesses? Why would you make these changes?

3. What (if any) core competencies do you think are held in common by one or more of GE's major business units? Is there any evidence that GE creates new businesses by leveraging its core competencies?

General Task   By searching through information sources on the Web, find an example of a company that has recently restructured its portfolio of businesses. Identify and evaluate the strategic rationale behind this restructuring. Does it make sense?

• •

ARTICLE FILE 10

Find an example of a company that has made an acquisition that apparently failed to create any value. Identify and critically evaluate the rationale used by top management to justify the acquisition at the time it was made. Explain why the acquisition subsequently failed.

• •

STRATEGIC MANAGEMENT PROJECT
Module 10

This module requires you to assess your company's use of acquisitions, internal new ventures, and joint ventures as strategies for entering a new business area and/or as attempts to restructure its portfolio of businesses.

If Your Company Has Entered a New Business Area During the Last Decade

1. Pick one new business area that your company has entered into during the last ten years.

2. Identify the rationale for entering this business area.

3. Identify the strategy used to enter this business area.

4. Evaluate the rationale for using this particular entry strategy. Do you think that this was the best entry strategy to use? Justify your answer.

5. Do you think that the addition of this business area to the company has added or dissipated value? Justify your answer.

If Your Company Has Restructured its Business During the Last Decade

1. Identify the rationale for pursuing a restructuring strategy.

2. Pick one business area that your company has exited during the last ten years.

3. Identify the strategy used to exit this particular business area. Do you think that this was the best exit strategy to use? Justify your answer.

4. In general, do you think that exiting from this business area has been in the company's best interest?

CLOSING CASE

Restructuring Xerox

In the early 1980s, with its core photocopier business under attack from Japanese companies such as Canon and Ricoh, Xerox's top management took the decision to diversify into the financial service industry. The move was an attempt to counterbalance its troubled copier business and protect Xerox's income stream. The Wall Street investment community reacted with disapproval, arguing that Xerox was running away from problems in its core business. It also noted that the expansion of Xerox's portfolio would make it more difficult for the investment community to make sense of the company. Despite these criticisms, Xerox went ahead. In order to enter the financial services industry, an area in which it had no prior experience, Xerox decided to acquire established enterprises with sound management and a good track record. Over the course of several years, Xerox acquired several companies, including Crum and Forster, an insurance company; Furman Selz, an investment banking concern; and Van Kampen Merritt, a mutual fund business.

By the mid 1980s this strategy seemed to be paying off. At that time the financial services arm was contributing almost half of Xerox's profits. However, this was also a boom period for the financial services industry in general. By the late 1980s the picture began to change. Strong management had revolutionized the performance of Xerox's photocopier business by focusing on superior product quality and tight cost controls. This enabled the company to recapture market share from Japanese competitors. At the same time the performance of the financial service businesses began to deteriorate rapidly. Indeed, although Xerox's financial services operations contributed one-third of Xerox's 1991 revenues of $13.8 billion, they accounted for only 3 percent of profits. The root of the problem was that Xerox's financial services businesses had turned out to be high-cost providers in an industry that was becoming increasingly competitive. While they could make good returns in the easy years of the mid 1980s, they were struggling in the lean years at the end of the decade. To make matters worse, in 1992 the balance sheet of the Crum and Forster insurance business was hard hit by massive insurance losses from Hurricanes Andrew and Iniki, an event that led Moody's Investors Service to downgrade the bond rating of Crum and Forster and placed some $6 billion of Xerox debt under review.

Xerox had already begun to reconsider the logic underlying its diversification strategy in May 1991, when Paul Allaire became chairman of the company. Allaire had been the major architect of the company's comeback in copiers. He had no tie to the diversification strategy, which was the brainchild of the former CEO, David Kearns. Under Allaire's leadership Xerox quickly fenced off financial services from the rest of the company, declining to prop up these faltering businesses with profits from copiers. After reviewing the company's diversification strategy, Allaire decided that Xerox's shareholders would be best served by a complete disengagement of the financial services operations from the rest of the company. Wall Street reacted positively to the news, but at the same time securities analysts noted that the restructuring could not be achieved without some financial pain for Xerox and its shareholders.

The process of divestment began in October 1992, when Xerox sold its Van Kampen Merritt mutual fund business to Clayton Dubilier & Rice for $360 million. To make its troubled Crum and Forster insurance business marketable, Xerox took a $470 million charge in the fourth quarter of 1992, primarily to strengthen the balance sheet of Crum and Forster, thereby making it more attractive to potential buyers. Xerox sliced Crum and Forster into pieces, which the company then sold to various other insurance companies. As for the Furman Selz investment banking concern, this was spun off to the unit's managers by way of an MBO.

Having sold its financial services businesses, Xerox was able to remove about $2.6 billion worth of debt from its books. However, since that debt was originally serviced by the financial service businesses themselves, the sale did not free up any additional funds for the rest of Xerox's business. In a move to strengthen the company's equity base, Xerox issued $500 million of new equity, which diluted the earnings value of Xerox shares. Most securities analysts see this dilution as an inevitable result of a series of bad investment decisions made in the early 1980s. It is part of the price Xerox shareholders had to pay for management's unsuccessful attempt to diversify into financial services.[34]

Case Discussion Questions

1. Is there any way in which Xerox might have been able to add value to the financial services operations it acquired in the early 1980s? If not, why do you think that the company pursued this strategy?

2. Do you think that the interests of Xerox's shareholders were best served by the divestment of Xerox's financial services businesses?

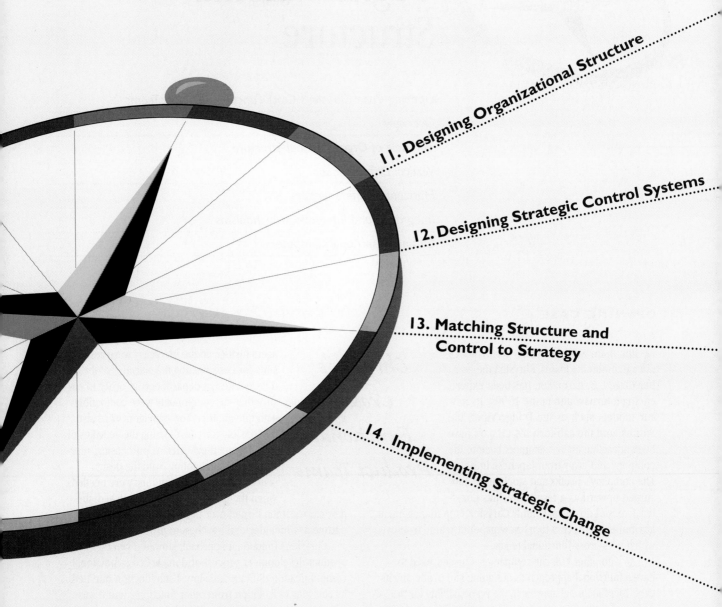

PART FOUR

Implementing Strategy

11. Designing Organizational Structure

12. Designing Strategic Control Systems

13. Matching Structure and Control to Strategy

14. Implementing Strategic Change

CHAPTER 11

Designing Organizational Structure

Opening Case: Chrysler's Cross-Functional Product Teams

Overview

The Role of Organizational Structure

Vertical Differentiation

Horizontal Differentiation

Integration and Integrating Mechanisms

Closing Case: Apple Computer

OPENING CASE

Chrysler's Cross-Functional Product Teams

After many years of poor performance and mounting losses, Chrysler, the number three U.S. carmaker, has been experiencing a turnaround in the 1990s. Its new car models such as the Dodge Viper, the Stratus, and the cab-forward LH cars have been attracting many customers back to the company and away from Japanese imports. The company's profits and stock price have surged upward as a result. How has Chrysler achieved this turnaround? Chrysler's top management attributes its success to its new product-team structure, which uses cross-functional teams.

As with other U.S. car companies, Chrysler used to have a functional approach to designing and producing its cars. In a functional approach, the responsibility for the design of a new car was allocated to many different design departments, each of which was responsible for the design of one component, such as the engine or the body. Man-

agers further up the hierarchy were responsible for coordinating the activities of the different design departments in order to ensure that the components were compatible with one another. Top managers were also responsible for coordinating the activities of support functions, such as purchasing, marketing, and accounting, with the design process as their contributions were needed. When the design process was finished, the new car was then turned over to the manufacturing department, which decided how best to produce it.

Chrysler's functional approach slowed down the product-development process and made cross-functional communication difficult and slow. Each function pursued its activities in isolation from other functions, and it was left to top management to provide the integration necessary to coordinate functional activities. As a result, it took Chrysler an average of five years to bring a new car to market, a figure that was well behind the record of the Japanese, who took two to three years. Chrysler's structure was raising its costs, slowing innovation, and making the company less responsive to the needs of its customers. The company's top managers began to search for a new way of organizing its value creation activities to turn the company around. To begin this process, top management looked at the way Japanese companies were organized, particularly at the way Honda structured its value creation activities. Chrysler sent fourteen of its managers to study Honda's system and report back on its operation.[1]

Honda had pioneered the Honda Way concept of organizing its activities. It created small teams, comprising members from various functions, and gave them the responsibility and authority to manage a project from its conception through all design activities to final manufacture and sale. Honda had found that when it used these cross-functional teams, product development time dropped dramatically because functional communication and coordination were much easier in teams. Moreover, design costs were much lower when different functions worked together to solve problems as they emerged, because to change a design later (for example, to add a second air bag) could cost millions of dollars. Honda had also found that its policy of decentralizing authority to the team kept the organization flexible, innovative, and able to take advantage of emerging technical opportunities.

Chrysler decided to imitate Honda's structure and took the opportunity to do so when it chose to build an expensive luxury car called the Viper. To manage the development of this new car, Chrysler created a cross-functional product team consisting of eighty-five people.[2] It established the team in a huge new research and development center it had built in Auburn Hills, Michigan, and gave it the authority and responsibility to bring the car to market. The outcome was dramatic. Within one year top management could see that the team had achieved what would have taken three years under Chrysler's old system. In fact, the team brought the car to market in just thirty-six months at a development cost of $75 million, results that compared favorably with those obtained by Japanese companies.

With this success in hand, Chrysler's top management moved to restructure the whole company according to the product-team concept. Top management divided up functional personnel and assigned them to work in product teams charged with developing new cars, such as those with the cab-forward design. The number of levels in Chrysler's hierarchy decreased since authority was decentralized to managers in the product teams, who were responsible for all aspects of new-car development. Instead of having to integrate the activities of different functions, top managers could concentrate on allocating resources among projects, deciding future product developments, and continually challenging the teams to improve their efforts. Chrysler's efforts brought the reward of a dramatic drop in costs and an increase in quality and customer responsiveness. Stock price for the firm's shares doubled in 1993 and 1995 as customers rushed to buy its cars.

OVERVIEW

As the story of Chrysler's turnaround suggests, in this chapter we examine how a company should organize its activities to create the most value. In Chapter 1, we define *strategy implementation* as the way in which a company creates the organizational arrangements that allow it to pursue its strategy most effectively. Strategy is implemented through organizational design. **Organizational design** means selecting the combination of organizational structure and control systems that lets a company pursue its strategy most effectively—that lets it *create and sustain a competitive advantage.*

The primary role of organizational structure and control is twofold: (1) to *coordinate* the activities of employees so that they work together most effectively to implement a strategy that increases competitive advantage and (2) to *motivate* employees and provide them with the incentives to achieve superior efficiency, quality, innovation, or customer responsiveness. Chrysler's strategy, for example, was to increase efficiency and quality by implementing a new product-development process. This strategy required managers to adopt a structure allowing increased cross-functional coordination, so that people in different functions such as manufacturing, materials management, and research and development could learn new ways of cooperating to reduce costs and improve quality. Manufacturing, for instance, had to adapt to a just-in-time inventory system to reduce inventory costs, and R&D had to learn how to work with manufacturing to design new products that could be produced reliably and inexpensively. However, top management had to provide the incentives for employees to learn new work methods. Chrysler's manufacturing employees received bonuses for learning to operate under the increased pressures that a just-in-time inventory system puts on the production process, and engineers were rewarded with promotions and bonuses for coming up with innovative product designs.

Organizational structure and control shape the way people behave and determine how they will act in the organizational setting. If a new CEO wants to know why it takes a long time for people to make decisions in a company, why there is a lack of cooperation between sales and manufacturing, or why product innovations are few and far between, he or she needs to look at the design of the organizational structure and control system and analyze how it coordinates and motivates employees' behavior. An analysis of how structure and control work makes it possible to change them to improve both coordination and motivation. Good organizational design allows an organization to improve its ability to create value and obtain a competitive advantage.

In this chapter we examine the organizational structures available to strategic managers to coordinate and motivate employees. In Chapter 12, we consider the strategic control systems that managers use in conjunction with their organizational structures to monitor, motivate, and reward corporate, divisional, and functional performance. In Chapter 13 we trace the ways in which different strategy choices lead to the use of different kinds of structure and control systems. After reading these three chapters, you will be able to understand the principles behind Chrysler's redesign of its organizational structure and control system and you will be able to choose the right organizational design for implementing a company's strategy.

THE ROLE OF ORGANIZATIONAL STRUCTURE

After formulating a company's strategy, management must make designing organizational structure its next priority, for strategy is implemented through organizational structure. The value creation activities of organizational members are meaningless unless some type of structure is used to assign people to tasks and connect the activities of different people and functions.[3] As we discuss in Chapter 4, each organizational function needs to develop a distinctive competency in a value creation activity in order to increase efficiency, quality, innovation, or customer responsiveness. Thus, each function needs a structure designed to allow it to develop its skills and become more specialized and productive. As functions become increasingly specialized, however, they often begin to pursue their own goals exclusively and lose sight of the need to communicate and coordinate with other functions. The goals of R&D, for example, center on innovation and product design, whereas the goals of manufacturing often revolve around increasing efficiency. Left to themselves, the functions may have little to say to one another, and value creation opportunities will be lost.

The role of organizational structure is to provide the vehicle through which managers can coordinate the activities of the various functions or divisions to exploit fully their skills and capabilities. To pursue a cost-leadership strategy, for example, a company must design a structure that facilitates close coordination between the activities of manufacturing and R&D to ensure that innovative products can be produced both reliably and cost effectively. To achieve gains from synergy between divisions, managers must design mechanisms that allow divisions to communicate and share their skills and knowledge. In pursuing a global or multidomestic strategy, managers must create the right kind of organizational structure for managing the flow of resources and capabilities between domestic and foreign divisions. In Chapter 13, we examine in detail how managers match their strategies to different kinds of structure and control systems. Our goal now is to examine the basic building blocks of organizational structure to understand how it shapes the behavior of people, functions, and divisions.

Building Blocks of Organizational Structure

The basic building blocks of organizational structure are differentiation and integration. **Differentiation** is the way in which a company allocates people and resources to organizational tasks in order to create value.[4] Generally, the greater the number of different functions or divisions in an organization and the more skilled and specialized they are, the higher is the level of differentiation. For example, a company such as General Motors, with more than 300 different divisions and a multitude of different sales, research and development, and design departments, has a much greater level of differentiation than a local manufacturing company or restaurant. In deciding how to differentiate the organization to create value, strategic managers face two choices.

First, strategic managers must choose how to distribute *decision-making authority* in the organization to control value creation activities best; these are **vertical differentiation** choices.[5] For example, corporate managers must decide how much authority to delegate to managers at the divisional or functional level. Second, corporate managers must choose how to divide people and tasks into functions and divisions to increase their ability to create value; these are **horizontal differentiation** choices. Should there be separate sales and marketing departments, for example, or should the two be combined? What is the best way to divide the sales force to maximize its ability to serve customers' needs—by type of customer or by region in which customers are located?

Integration is the means by which a company seeks to coordinate people and functions to accomplish organizational tasks.[6] As just noted, when separate and distinct value creation functions exist, they tend to pursue their own goals and objectives. An organization has to create an organizational structure that lets the different functions and divisions coordinate their activities to pursue a strategy effectively. An organization uses integrating mechanisms, as well as the various types of control systems discussed in the next chapter, to promote coordination and cooperation between functions and divisions. In the case of Chrysler, for instance, to speed innovation and product development, the company established cross-functional teams so that employees from different functions could work together to exchange information and ideas. Similarly, establishing organizational norms, values, and a common culture that supports innovation promotes integration.

In short, differentiation refers to the way in which a company divides itself into parts (functions and divisions), and integration refers to the way in which the parts are then combined. Together, the two processes determine how an organizational structure will operate and how successfully strategic managers will be able to create value through their chosen strategies.

Differentiation, Integration, and Bureaucratic Costs

Implementing a structure to coordinate and motivate task activities is very expensive. The costs of operating an organizational structure and control system are called **bureaucratic costs.** The more complex the structure—that is, the higher the level of differentiation and integration—the higher are the bureaucratic costs of managing it. The more differentiated the company, for example, the more managers there are in specialized roles and the more resources each manager requires to perform that role effectively. Managers are expensive, and the more managers a company employs the higher are its bureaucratic costs.

Similarly, the more integrated the company, the more managerial time is spent in face-to-face meetings to coordinate task activities. Managerial time also costs money, and thus the higher the level of integration, the more costly it is to operate the structure. A large company such as IBM or GM spends billions of dollars a year to operate its structures, that is, to pay its managers and employees and to provide them with the resources—offices, computers, equipment, laboratories, and so forth—they need to create value.

The high bureaucratic costs associated with strategy implementation can reduce a company's profits as fast or faster than poor strategy formulation, and thus they directly affect bottom-line organizational performance. This is why good organizational design is so important. You will recall from Chapter 4 that profit is the difference between revenues and costs. Bureaucratic costs are a large component of the cost side of the equation. Thus, a poor organizational design (for instance, one that has too many levels in the hierarchy or a badly thought-out pattern of work relationships) results in high costs that reduce profits. By contrast, good organizational design, which economizes on bureaucratic costs, can give a company a low-cost advantage that raises profits.

Organizational design also affects the revenue side of the equation. If strategic managers choose the right structure to coordinate value creation activities, they enhance the company's ability to create value, charge a premium price, and thus increase revenues. Chrysler's new structure increased its ability to create value and reduce its costs. Thus, good design affects both the revenue and the cost side of the profit equation, as Figure 11.1 illustrates. This is why strategy implementation is such a vital issue. In today's competitive environment, more and more companies are restructuring or reengineering their organizations to improve bottom-line performance through good organizational design. Consequently, it is necessary to understand the principles behind organizational design. We start by looking at differentiation.

FIGURE 11.1
• • • • • • • • • • • •
How Organizational
Design Increases
Profitability

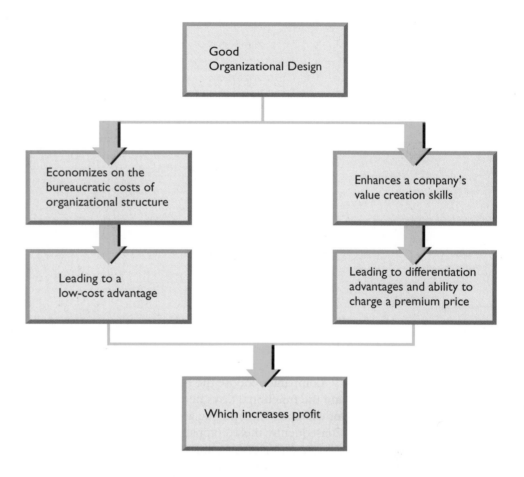

FIGURE 11.1
• • • • • • • • • • • •
How Organizational
Design Increases
Profitability

VERTICAL DIFFERENTIATION
• •

The aim of vertical differentiation is to specify the reporting relationships that link people, tasks, and functions at all levels of a company. Fundamentally, this means that management chooses the appropriate number of hierarchical levels and the correct span of control for implementing a company's strategy most effectively.

The organizational hierarchy establishes the authority structure from the top to the bottom of the organization. The **span of control** is defined as the number of subordinates a manager directly manages.[7] The basic choice is whether to aim for a **flat structure,** with few hierarchical levels and thus a relatively wide span of control, or a **tall structure,** with many levels and thus a relatively narrow span of control (see Figure 11.2). Tall structures have many hierarchical levels relative to size; flat structures have few levels relative to size.[8] For example, research suggests that the average number of hierarchical levels for a company employing 3,000 persons is seven. Thus, an organization having nine levels would be called tall, and one having four would be called flat. With its 4,000 employees and four hierarchical levels, Liz Claiborne, for instance, has a relatively flat structure. On the other hand, before reorganization, Westinghouse, with its ten hierarchical levels, had a relatively tall structure. Now it has seven levels, the average for a large organization.

FIGURE 11.2

Tall and Flat Surfaces

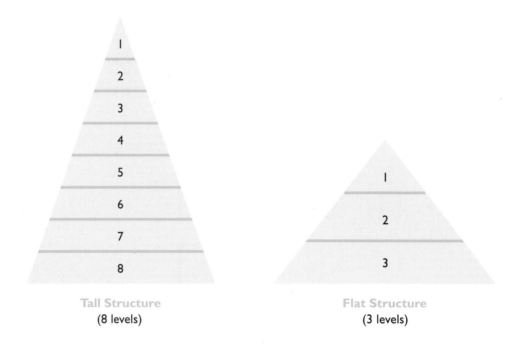

Tall Structure
(8 levels)

Flat Structure
(3 levels)

Companies choose the number of levels they need on the basis of their strategy and the functional tasks necessary to achieve this strategy.[9] High-tech companies, for example, often pursue a strategy of differentiation based on service and quality. Consequently, these companies usually have flat structures, giving employees wide discretion to meet customers' demands without having to refer constantly to supervisors.[10] (We discuss this subject further in Chapter 12.) The crux of the matter is that the allocation of authority and responsibility in the organization must match the needs of corporate-, business-, and functional-level strategies.[11]

Problems with Tall Structures

As a company grows and diversifies, the number of levels in its hierarchy of authority increases to allow it to efficiently monitor and coordinate employee activities. Research shows that the number of hierarchical levels relative to company size is predictable as the size increases (see Figure 11.3).[12]

Companies with approximately 1,000 employees usually have four levels in the hierarchy: chief executive officer, departmental vice presidents, first-line supervisors, and workers. Those with 3,000 employees have increased their level of vertical differentiation by raising the number of levels to eight. Something interesting happens to those with more than 3,000 employees, however. Even when companies grow to 10,000 employees or more, the number of hierarchical levels rarely increases beyond nine or ten. As organizations grow, managers apparently try to limit the number of hierarchical levels.

Managers try to keep the organization as flat as possible and follow what is known as the **principle of the minimum chain of command,** which states that an organization should choose a hierarchy with the minimum number of levels of authority necessary to achieve its strategy. Managers try to keep the hierarchy as flat as possible because when companies become too tall, problems occur, making

FIGURE 11.3

FIGURE 11.3
•••••••••••••

Relationship Between
Company Size and
Number of Hierarchical
Levels

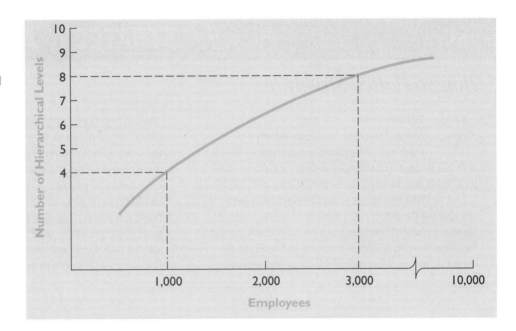

strategy more difficult to implement and raising the level of bureaucratic costs.[13]
Several factors that raise bureaucratic costs are illustrated in Figure 11.4 and discussed in the following paragraphs.

Coordination Problems   Too many hierarchical levels impede communication
and coordination between employees and functions and raise bureaucratic costs.
Communication between the top and the bottom of the hierarchy takes much
longer as the chain of command lengthens. This leads to inflexibility, and valuable
time is lost in bringing a new product to market or in keeping up with technological developments.[14] For Federal Express, communication and coordination are vital.
Therefore, to avoid problems with them, the company allows a maximum of only
five layers of management between the employee and the CEO.[15] In contrast, Procter & Gamble had a tall hierarchy, with the result that the company needed twice as

FIGURE 11.4
•••••••••••••

Sources of
Bureaucratic Costs

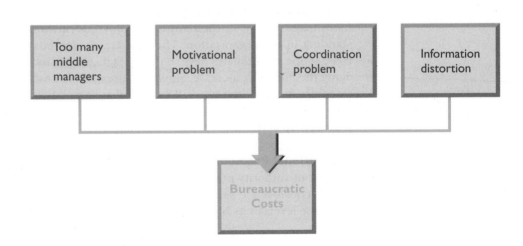

STRATEGY *in* ACTION

How to Flatten Structure

Tall hierarchies cause such severe coordination and communications problems that many companies have been striving to shrink their hierarchies. For example, at General Electric, CEO Jack Welch has flattened the hierarchy from nine levels to four to bring him closer to his divisional managers and shorten the time it takes them to make decisions. At Alcoa International, planning and decision making at the divisional level once were scrutinized by five levels of corporate management before divisional managers were

allowed to proceed with their plans. Chairman Paul O'Neill wiped out these layers so that divisional managers would report directly to him. At both companies, these changes have brought top management closer to customers and provided divisional managers with the autonomy to be innovative and responsive to customers' needs. Moreover, flattening the hierarchy has saved these companies billions of dollars in managerial salaries and significantly reduced bureaucratic costs. Flattening their structures has clearly paid off for them.

---

much time as its competitors to introduce new products. To improve coordination and reduce costs, the company moved to streamline its structure and reduce its number of hierarchical levels.[16] Other companies have also taken measures to flatten their structures in order to speed communication and decision making. Strategy in Action 11.1 describes the changes made at General Electric and Alcoa.

Information Distortion   More subtle, but just as important, are the problems of information distortion that occur as the hierarchy of authority lengthens. Going down the hierarchy, managers at different levels (for example, divisional or corporate managers) may misinterpret information, either through accidental garbling of messages or on purpose to suit their own interests. In either case, information from the top may not reach its destination intact. For instance, a request to share divisional knowledge to achieve gains from synergy may be overlooked or ignored by divisional managers who perceive it as a threat to their autonomy and power. This attitude among managers was one of the problems that led Lee Iacocca to reorganize Chrysler so that cost-cutting measures could be coordinated across divisions.

Information transmitted upward in the hierarchy may also be distorted. Subordinates may transmit to their superiors only information that improves their own standing in the organization. The greater the number of hierarchical levels, the more scope subordinates have to distort facts, so that the bureaucratic costs of managing the hierarchy increase. Similarly, bureaucratic costs increase if managers start to compete with each other. When they are free of close corporate supervision, they may hoard information to promote their own interests at the expense of the organization's. This also reduces coordination.

Motivational Problems   As the number of levels in the hierarchy increases, the amount of authority possessed by managers at each hierarchical level falls. For example, consider the situation of two identically sized organizations, one of which has three levels in its hierarchy and the other seven. Managers in the flat structure have much more authority, and greater authority increases their motivation to perform effectively and take responsibility for the organization's performance. Besides, when there are fewer managers, their performance is more visible and, therefore, they can expect greater rewards when the business does well.

By contrast, the ability of managers in a tall structure to exercise authority is limited, and their decisions are constantly scrutinized by their superiors. As a result, managers tend to pass the buck and refuse to take the risks that are often necessary when new strategies are pursued. This increases the bureaucratic costs of managing the organization because more managerial time is spent coordinating task activities. Thus, the shape of the organization's structure strongly affects the motivation of people within it and the way in which strategy is implemented.[17]

Too Many Middle Managers   Another drawback of tall structures is that having many hierarchical levels implies having many middle managers, and employing managers is expensive. As noted earlier, managerial salaries, benefits, offices, and secretaries are a huge expense for an organization. If the average middle manager costs a company a total of $200,000 a year, then employing 100 surplus managers costs $20 million a year. Most large U.S. companies have recognized this fact, and in the 1990s companies such as IBM, GM, Compaq, and Procter & Gamble have moved to downsize their hierarchies, terminating thousands of managers. When these companies made billions of dollars in profits, they had little incentive to control the number of levels in the hierarchy and the number of managers. Once they grew aware of the cost of these managers, however, the companies ruthlessly purged the hierarchy, reducing the number of levels and thus the number of managers in order to lower bureaucratic costs and restore profitability.

To offer another example, when companies grow and are successful, they often hire personnel and create new positions without much regard for the effect of these actions on the organizational hierarchy. Later, when managers review that structure, it is quite common to see the number of levels reduced because of the disadvantages just discussed. Deregulation, too, prompts a reduction in levels and personnel. In a deregulated environment, companies must respond to increased competition. After deregulation, AT&T and the "Baby Bell" telephone companies, as well as most airline companies, reduced costs and streamlined their structures so that they could respond more rapidly to opportunities and threats brought about by increased competition. For example, Delta Air Lines announced in 1993 that it would lay off more than 600 pilots, or 7 percent of its work force, and retire fifteen jets for an annual saving of more than $100 million, and its work force has continued to shrink ever since.

In sum, many problems arise when companies become too tall and the chain of command becomes too long. Strategic managers tend to lose control over the hierarchy, which means that they lose control over their strategies. Disaster often follows because a tall organizational structure decreases, rather than promotes, motivation and coordination between employees and functions and, as a result, bureaucratic costs escalate. One way to overcome such problems, at least partially, and to lessen bureaucratic costs is to decentralize authority—that is, vest authority in the hierarchy's lower levels as well as at the top. Because this is one of the most important implementation decisions a company can make, we discuss it next in more detail.

Centralization or Decentralization?

Authority is centralized when managers at the upper levels of the organizational hierarchy retain the authority to make the most important decisions. When authority is decentralized, it is delegated to divisions, functions, and managers and workers at lower levels in the organization. By delegating authority in this fashion, managers can economize on bureaucratic costs and avoid communication and co-ordination problems because information does not have to be constantly sent to the top of the organization for decisions to be made. There are three advantages to decentralization.

First, when strategic managers delegate operational decision-making responsibility to middle and first-level managers, they reduce information overload, enabling strategic managers to spend more time on strategic decision making. Consequently, they can make more effective decisions.

Second, when managers in the bottom layers of the organization become responsible for adapting the organization to suit local conditions, their motivation and accountability increase. The result is that decentralization promotes organizational flexibility and reduces bureaucratic costs because lower-level managers are authorized to make on-the-spot decisions. As AT&T has demonstrated, this can be an enormous advantage for business strategy. AT&T has a tall structure, but it is well known for the amount of authority it delegates to lower-level employees. Operational personnel can respond quickly to customers' needs and so ensure superior service, which is a major source of AT&T's competitive advantage. Similarly, to revitalize its product strategy, Westinghouse has massively decentralized its operations to give divisions more autonomy and encourage risk taking and quick response to customers' needs.[18]

The third advantage of decentralization is that when lower-level employees are given the right to make important decisions, fewer managers are needed to oversee their activities and tell them what to do. Fewer managers mean lower bureaucratic costs.

If decentralization is so effective, why do not all companies decentralize decision making and avoid the problems of tall hierarchies? The answer is that centralization has its advantages, too. Centralized decision making allows easier coordination of the organizational activities needed to pursue a company's strategy. If managers at all levels can make their own decisions, overall planning becomes extremely difficult, and the company may lose control of its decision making.

Centralization also means that decisions fit broad organization objectives. When its branch operations were getting out of hand, for example, Merrill Lynch increased centralization by installing more information systems to give corporate managers greater control over branch activities. Similarly, Hewlett Packard centralized research and development responsibility at the corporate level to provide a more directed corporate strategy. Furthermore, in times of crisis, centralization of authority permits strong leadership because authority is focused on one person or group. This focus allows for speedy decision making and a concerted response by the whole organization.

Perhaps Lee Iacocca personifies the meaning of centralization in times of crisis. Iacocca provided the centralized control and vision needed for Chrysler's managers to respond creatively to the company's problems and move to the product-team

11.2 — STRATEGY *in* ACTION

Honda's Change of Heart

In 1992 Honda, like many other Japanese firms, found itself facing increased competition in a depressed global marketplace. It realized that its strategy of relying on product innovation to increase its sales growth had caused it to neglect the cost and efficiency side of the equation. As a result, its profit margins were eroding. Under its founder, Shoichiro Honda, the company had pioneered the concept of the Honda Way, based on a decentralized, participative, consensus approach to management. Teams led the decision-making process, and authority was decentralized throughout the company.

However, Honda's new president, Nobuhiko Kawamoto, concluded that this process had gone too far. He decided to recentralize authority in order to provide the control and direction needed to slash costs and increase efficiency. He began to give Honda's top managers more and more authority for corporatewide strategy and made them responsible for overseeing both the company's domestic and global strategy. The effect of this move was unexpected: Many of his top executives found it physically impossible to assume the extra responsibility that this new policy of centralization re-

quired. One key executive, Shoichiro Irimajiri, who was assigned responsibility for overseeing both Honda's global R&D *and* manufacturing operations, was forced to resign abruptly after his doctors told him that his extra workload had pushed him to the brink of a heart attack. As Kawamoto commented, maybe he had given Irimajiri too much responsibility.[19]

Since the new policy of centralization was not working, Kawamoto had to find another solution to the centralization/decentralization dilemma. He decided to delegate more authority down the hierarchy on a global basis. Managers in Honda's North American, European, and Japanese divisions would take over responsibility for managing strategy for their divisions. The role of Honda's corporate executives in Japan would be to provide coordination among divisions and facilitate the sharing of skills and resources to reduce costs. In this way, Honda hopes to strike a new balance between centralization and decentralization, so that the company can remain innovative and responsive to customers' needs in order to encourage sales growth but, at the same time, become more efficient to reduce costs. The company has returned to the Honda Way it pioneered.

structure, which has helped restore the company's profitability. On the other hand, Honda's experience with recentralizing authority, detailed in Strategy in Action 11.2, warns against going too far.

Summary

Managing the strategy/structure relationship when the number of hierarchical levels becomes too great is difficult and expensive. Depending on a company's situation, the bureaucratic costs of tall hierarchies can be reduced by decentralization. As company size increases, however, decentralization may become less effective. How then, as firms grow and diversify, can they economize on bureaucratic costs without becoming too tall or too decentralized? How can a firm such as Exxon control 300,000 employees without becoming too bureaucratic and inflexible? There must be alternative ways of creating organizational arrangements to achieve corporate objectives. The first of these ways is to choose the appropriate form of horizontal differentiation, that is, to decide how best to group organizational activities and tasks in order to create value.

HORIZONTAL DIFFERENTIATION

Whereas vertical differentiation concerns the division of authority, horizontal differentiation focuses on the division and grouping of tasks to meet the objectives of the business.[20] Because, to a large degree, an organization's tasks are a function of its strategy, the dominant view is that companies choose a form of horizontal differentiation or structure to match their organizational strategy. Perhaps the first person to address this issue formally was the Harvard business historian Alfred D. Chandler.[21] After studying the organizational problems experienced in large U.S. corporations such as Du Pont and General Motors as they grew and diversified in the early decades of this century, Chandler reached two conclusions: (1) that in principle organizational structure follows the growth strategy of a company, or, in other words, the range and variety of tasks it chooses to pursue and (2) that U.S. companies' structures change as their strategy changes in a predictable way over time.[22] The kinds of structure that companies adopt are discussed in this section.

Simple Structure

The simple structure is normally used by the small, entrepreneurial company producing one or a few related products for a specific market segment. Often in this situation, one person, the entrepreneur, takes on most of the managerial tasks. No formal arrangements regarding organization exist, and horizontal differentiation is low because employees perform multiple duties.

A classic example of this structure is Apple Computer in its earliest stage, as a venture between two persons. Steven Jobs and Steven Wozniak worked together in a garage to perform all the necessary tasks to market their personal computer. They bought the component parts, assembled the first machines, and shipped them to customers. The success of their product, however, made this simple structure outdated almost as soon as it was adopted. To grow and perform all the tasks required by a rapidly expanding company, Apple needed a more complex form of horizontal differentiation. It needed to invest resources in creating an infrastructure to develop and enhance its distinctive competencies. Although developing a more complex structure raises bureaucratic costs, this is acceptable as long as the structure increases the amount of value a company can create.

Functional Structure

As companies grow, two things happen. First, the range of tasks that must be performed expands. For example, it suddenly becomes apparent that the services of a professional accountant or a production manager or a marketing expert are needed to take control of specialized tasks. Second, no one person can successfully perform more than one organizational task without becoming overloaded. The founder, for instance, can no longer simultaneously make and sell the product. The question that arises is what grouping of activities, or what form of horizontal differentiation, can most efficiently handle the needs of the growing company at least cost? The answer for most companies is a functional structure.

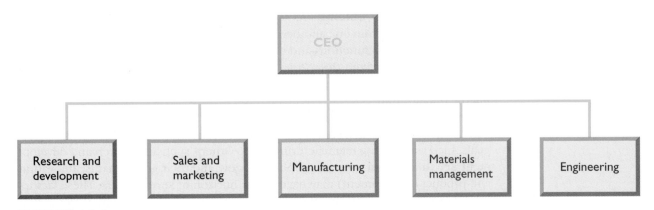

FIGURE 11.5

Functional Structure

Functional structures group people on the basis of their common expertise and experience or because they use the same resources.[23] For example, engineers are grouped in a function because they perform the same tasks and use the same skills or equipment. Figure 11.5 shows a typical functional structure. Each of the rectangles represents a different functional specialization—research and development, sales and marketing, manufacturing, and so on—and each function concentrates on its own specialized task.

Advantages of a Functional Structure

Functional structures have several advantages. First, if people who perform similar tasks are grouped together, they can learn from one another and become better—more specialized and productive—at what they do.

Second, they can monitor each other to make sure that all are performing their tasks effectively and not shirking their responsibilities. As a result, the work process becomes more efficient, reducing manufacturing costs and increasing operational flexibility.

A third important advantage of functional structures is that they give managers greater control of organizational activities. As already noted, many difficulties arise when the number of levels in the hierarchy increases. If people are grouped into different functions, however, each with their own managers, then *several different hierarchies are created,* and the company can avoid becoming too tall. There will be one hierarchy in manufacturing, for example, and another in accounting and finance. Managing the business is much easier when different groups specialize in different organizational tasks and are managed separately.

Disadvantages of a Functional Structure

In adopting a functional structure, a company increases its level of horizontal differentiation to handle more complex tasks. The structure allows it to keep control of its activities as it grows. This structure serves the company well until it starts to grow and diversify. If the company becomes geographically diverse and begins operating in many locations or if it starts producing a wide range of products, control and coordination problems arise that lower a company's ability to coordinate its activities and increase bureaucratic costs.[24]

Communications Problems   As separate functional hierarchies evolve, functions grow more remote from one another. As a result, it becomes increasingly difficult to communicate across functions and to coordinate their activities. This communication problem stems from *functional orientations*.[25] With greater differentiation, the various functions develop different orientations to the problems and issues facing the organization.

Different functions have different time or goal orientations. Some, such as manufacturing, see things in a short time frame and concentrate on achieving short-run goals, such as reducing manufacturing costs. Others, such as research and development, see things from a long-term point of view, and their goals (that is, innovation and product development) may have a time horizon of several years. These factors may cause each function to develop a different view of the strategic issues facing the company. Manufacturing, for example, may see the strategic issue as the need to reduce costs, sales may see it as the need to increase customer responsiveness, and research and development may see it as the need to create new products. In such cases, the functions have trouble communicating and coordinating with one another, and bureaucratic costs increase.

Measurement Problems   As the number of its products proliferates, a company may find it difficult to gauge the contribution of a product or a group of products to its overall profitability. Consequently, the company may turn out some unprofitable products without realizing it and may also make poor decisions about resource allocation. This means that the company's measurement systems are not complex enough to serve its needs. Dell Computer's explosive growth, for example, caused it to lose control of its inventory management systems; hence, it could not accurately project supply and demand for the components that go into its personal computers. Problems with its organizational structure have plagued Dell, reducing efficiency and quality. As one manager commented, designing its structure to keep pace with its growth has been like "building a high performance car while going around the race track."[26]

Location Problems   Location factors may also hamper coordination and control. If a company is producing or selling in many different regional areas, then the centralized system of control provided by the functional structure no longer suits it because managers in the various regions must be flexible enough to respond to the needs of these regions. Thus, the functional structure is not complex enough to handle regional diversity.

Strategic Problems   Sometimes the combined effect of all these factors is that long-term strategic considerations are ignored because management is preoccupied with solving communication and coordination problems. As a result, a company may lose direction and fail to take advantage of new opportunities while bureaucratic costs escalate.

Experiencing these problems is a sign that the company does not have an appropriate level of differentiation to achieve its objectives. A company must change its mix of vertical and horizontal differentiation if it is to perform effectively the organizational tasks that will enhance its competitive advantage. Essentially, these problems indicate that the company has outgrown its structure. It needs to invest more resources in developing a more complex structure, one that can meet the needs of its competitive strategy. Once again, this is expensive, but as long as the value a company can create is greater than the bureaucratic costs of operating the structure, it makes sense to adopt a more complex structure. Many companies choose a multidivisional structure.

Multidivisional Structure

The multidivisional structure possesses two main innovations over a functional structure, innovations that let a company grow and diversify yet overcome problems that stem from loss of control. First, each distinct product line or business unit is placed in its own *self-contained unit or division,* with all support functions. For example, PepsiCo has three major divisions—soft drinks, snack foods, and restaurants—and each has its own functions, such as marketing and research and development. The result is a higher level of horizontal differentiation.

Second, the office of *corporate headquarters staff* is created to monitor divisional activities and to exercise financial control over each of the divisions.[27] This staff contains corporate managers who oversee the activities of divisional and functional managers, and it constitutes an additional level in the organizational hierarchy. Hence, there is a higher level of vertical differentiation in a multidivisional structure than in a functional structure.

Figure 11.6 presents a typical multidivisional structure found in a large chemical company such as Du Pont. Although this company might easily have seventy operating divisions, only three—the oil, pharmaceuticals, and plastics divisions—are represented here. As a self-contained business unit, each division possesses a full array of support services. For example, each has self-contained accounting, sales, and personnel departments. Each division functions as a profit center, making it much easier for corporate headquarters staff to monitor and evaluate each division's activities.[28]

FIGURE 11.6

Multidivisional Structure

Typical Chemical Company

CEO

Corporate headquarters staff

Oil division
(functional structure)

Pharmaceuticals division
(product-team structure)

Plastics division
(matrix structure)

The bureaucratic costs of operating a multidivisional structure are very high compared with a functional structure. The size of the corporate staff is a major expense, and companies such as GM and IBM have thousands of managers on their corporate staffs even after their massive downsizing. Similarly, the use of product divisions, each with its own specialist support functions such as research and development and marketing, is a major expense. However, once again, if higher bureaucratic costs are offset by a higher level of value creation, it makes sense to move to a more complex structure.

Each division is also able to adopt the structure that best suits its needs. Figure 11.6 shows that the oil division has a functional structure because its activities are standardized; the pharmaceuticals division has a product-team structure; and the plastics division has a matrix structure. (The latter two structures are discussed in detail later in this chapter.) Similarly, General Motors operates the whole corporation through a multidivisional structure, but each auto division organizes itself into different product groups, based on the type of auto made.

In the multidivisional structure, day-to-day operations of a division are the responsibility of divisional management; that is, divisional management has **operating responsibility.** Corporate headquarters staff, however, which includes members of the board of directors as well as top executives, is responsible for overseeing long-term plans and providing the guidance for interdivisional projects. This staff has **strategic responsibility.** Such a combination of self-contained divisions with a centralized corporate management represents a higher level of both vertical and horizontal differentiation, as noted earlier. These two innovations provide the extra control necessary to coordinate growth and diversification. Because this structure, despite its high bureaucratic costs, has now been adopted by more than 90 percent of all large U.S. corporations, we need to consider its advantages and disadvantages in more detail.

Advantages of a Multidivisional Structure

When managed effectively at both the corporate and the divisional levels, a multidivisional structure offers several advantages. Together, they can raise corporate profitability to a new peak because they allow the organization to operate more complex kinds of corporate-level strategy.

Enhanced Corporate Financial Control   The profitability of different business divisions is clearly visible in the multidivisional structure.[29] Because each division is its own profit center, financial controls can be applied to each business on the basis of profit criteria. Typically, these controls cover establishing targets, monitoring performance on a regular basis, and selectively intervening when problems arise. Corporate headquarters is also in a better position to allocate corporate financial resources among competing divisions. The visibility of divisional performance means that corporate headquarters can identify the divisions in which investment of funds will yield the greatest long-term returns. In a sense, the corporate office is in a position to act as the investor or banker in an internal capital market, channeling funds to high-yield uses.

Enhanced Strategic Control   The multidivisional structure frees corporate staff from operating responsibilities. The staff thus gains time for contemplating wider strategic issues and for developing responses to environmental changes. The multidivisional structure also enables corporate headquarters to obtain the proper information to perform strategic planning functions. For example, separating individual businesses is a necessary prerequisite for portfolio planning.

Growth The multidivisional structure lets the company overcome an organizational limit to its growth. By reducing information overload at the center, corporate managers can handle a greater number of businesses. They can consider opportunities for further growth and diversification. Communication problems are reduced because the same set of standardized accounting and financial control techniques can be used for all divisions. Also, corporate managers are able to implement a policy of management by exception, which means that they intervene only when problems arise.

Stronger Pursuit of Internal Efficiency Within a functional structure, the interdependence of functional departments means that the *individual* performance of each function inside a company cannot be measured by objective criteria. For example, the profitability of the finance function, marketing function, or manufacturing function cannot be assessed in isolation, because they are only part of the whole. This often means that within the functional structure considerable degrees of organizational slack, that is, functional resources that are used unproductively, can go undetected. For example, the head of the finance function might employ a larger staff than required for efficiency to reduce work pressures inside the department and to bring the manager higher status.

In a multidivisional structure, however, the individual efficiency of each autonomous division can be directly observed and measured in terms of the profit it generates. Thus, autonomy makes divisional managers accountable for their own performance; they can have no alibis for poor performance. The corporate office is thus in a better position to identify inefficiencies.

Disadvantages of a Multidivisional Structure

Because a multidivisional structure has a number of powerful advantages, that is why, no doubt, it seems to be the preferred choice of most large diversified enterprises today. Indeed, research suggests that large companies that adopt this structure outperform those that retain the functional structure.[30] A multidivisional structure has its disadvantages as well, however. Good management can eliminate some of them, but others are inherent in the way the structure operates and require constant managerial attention. These disadvantages are discussed next.

Establishing the Divisional-Corporate Authority Relationship The authority relationship between corporate headquarters and the divisions must be correctly established. The multidivisional structure introduces a new level in the hierarchy—the corporate level. The problem lies in deciding how much authority and control to assign to the operating divisions and how much authority to retain at corporate headquarters.

This problem was first noted by Alfred Sloan, the founder of General Motors. He introduced the multidivisional structure at General Motors, which became the first company to adopt it, and created General Motors' familiar five-automobile divisions: Chevrolet, Pontiac, Oldsmobile, Buick, and Cadillac.[31] What Sloan found, however, was that when headquarters retained too much power and authority, the operating divisions lacked sufficient autonomy to develop the business strategy that might best meet the needs of the division. On the other hand, when too much power was delegated to the divisions, they pursued divisional objectives, with little heed to the needs of the whole corporation. As a result, for example, not all of the potential gains from synergy discussed earlier could be achieved.

Thus, the central issue in managing the multidivisional structure is how much authority should be *centralized* at corporate headquarters and how much should be *decentralized* to the divisions. This issue must be decided by each company in reference to the nature of its business- and its corporate-level strategies. There are no easy answers, and over time, as the environment changes or the company alters its strategies, the balance between corporate and divisional control will also change. Strategy in Action 11.3 illustrates this problem. It highlights the changes that Amoco, one of the largest U.S. oil companies, has made to its divisional structure.

Distortion of Information   If corporate headquarters puts too much emphasis on divisional return on investment—for instance, by setting very high and stringent return-on-investment targets—divisional managers may choose to distort the information they supply top management and paint a rosy picture of the present situation at the expense of future profits. That is, divisions may maximize short-run profits, perhaps by cutting product development or new investments or marketing expenditures. This may cost the company dearly in the future. The problem stems from too tight financial control. General Motors has suffered from this problem in recent years, as declining performance has prompted divisional managers to try to make their divisions look good to corporate headquarters. Managing the corporate-divisional interface requires coping with subtle power issues.

Competition for Resources   The third problem of managing a multidivisional structure is that the divisions themselves may compete for resources, and this rivalry prevents synergy gains from emerging. For example, the amount of money that corporate personnel has to distribute to the divisions is fixed. Generally, the divisions that can demonstrate the highest return on investment will get the lion's share of the money. Because that large share strengthens them in the next time period, the strong divisions grow stronger. Consequently, divisions may actively compete for resources and, by doing so, reduce interdivisional coordination.

Transfer Pricing   Divisional competition may also lead to battles over **transfer pricing**. As we discuss in Chapter 9, one of the problems with vertical integration or related diversification is setting transfer prices between divisions. Rivalry among divisions increases the problem of setting fair prices. Each supplying division tries to set the highest price for its outputs to maximize its own return on investment. Such competition can completely undermine the corporate culture and make a company a battleground. Many companies have a history of competition among divisions. Some, of course, may encourage competition, if managers believe that it leads to maximum performance.

Short-Term Research and Development Focus   If extremely high ROI targets are set by corporate headquarters, there is a danger that the divisions will cut back on research and development expenditures to improve the financial performance of the division. Although this inflates divisional performance in the short term, it re-

Amoco's New Approach

As with most other global oil companies, Amoco is engaged in three major activities: oil exploration, refining, and chemicals manufacturing. To manage these activities, Amoco used a three-legged structure and created three independent operating subsidiaries to manage each of its three main activities. Each subsidiary had its own set of managers who were responsible for overseeing all the many different business divisions inside each subsidiary. The managers of all three subsidiaries then reported to Amoco's corporate-level managers who oversaw their activities and made the final decision on what each subsidiary should be doing. Thus, all important decision making at Amoco took place at the top of the organization. As a result, it often took a long time to make decisions because of the many managerial layers between Amoco's corporate managers and its divisional managers. Since divisional managers were responsible for developing an effective business-level strategy, the slow decision-making process hampered their attempts to build a competitive advantage.[32]

In the early 1990s, however, Amoco, like other global oil companies such as Exxon, British Petroleum, and Mobil, experienced intense pressure to reduce costs because of flat gas prices. To try to boost profits, Amoco laid off more than one-quarter of its work force, but this did not work. So, in 1995, Amoco's managers took a close look at its structure to see whether there was a way to increase its performance.

Amoco's chairman and CEO, H. Laurance Fuller, decided that a massive reorganization of Amoco's structure was necessary. Fuller decided to eliminate Amoco's three-legged structure completely and to remove all the managers at the subsidiary level. The three subsidiaries were divided into seventeen independent business divisions, and Amoco changed to a multidivisional structure. Henceforth, decision-making authority was decentralized to the managers of each division, who are free to choose their own strategy for the division. Each division is evaluated on the basis of its ability to reach certain growth targets set by corporate managers, but the way they achieve those targets is determined by their own managers.

Fuller hopes that this new flatter, decentralized product-division structure will lead managers to be more entrepreneurial and more motivated both to increase efficiency and to develop new, high-quality products. Fuller also hopes that because the seventeen new product divisions are closer to their customers, each will be more responsive to customers' needs. Thus, Fuller hopes that changing the way it organizes its people and resources will allow Amoco to build new sources of competitive advantage that, in turn, will lead to the boost in profitability the company so badly needs. So far, the new structure seems to be working. Amoco's ROI has been on an upward path.

---

duces a division's ability to develop new products and leads to a fall in the stream of long-term profits. Hence, corporate headquarters personnel must carefully control their interactions with the divisions to ensure that both the short- and long-term goals of the business are being achieved.

Bureaucratic Costs As noted earlier, because each division possesses its own specialized functions, such as finance or research and development, multidivisional structures are expensive to run and manage. Research and development is especially costly, and so some companies centralize such functions at the corporate level to serve all divisions. The duplication of specialist services is not a problem if the gains from having separate specialist functions outweigh the costs. Again, strategic managers must decide whether duplication is financially justified. Activities are often centralized in times of downturn or recession, particularly advisory services and planning functions; divisions, however, are retained as profit centers.

The advantages of divisional structures must be balanced against their disadvantages, but, as we already noted, the disadvantages can be managed by an observant, professional management team that is aware of the issues involved. The multidivisional structure is the dominant one today, which clearly suggests its usefulness as the means of managing the multibusiness corporation.

Matrix Structure

A matrix structure differs from the structures discussed so far in that it is based on two forms of horizontal differentiation rather than on one, as in the functional structure.[33] In the matrix design, activities on the vertical axis are grouped by *function,* so that there is a familiar differentiation of tasks into functions such as engineering, sales and marketing, and research and development. In addition, superimposed on this vertical pattern is a horizontal pattern based on differentiation by *product or project.* The result is a complex network of reporting relationships among projects and functions, as depicted in Figure 11.7.

This structure also employs an unusual kind of vertical differentiation. Although matrix structures are flat, with few hierarchical levels, employees inside the matrix have two bosses: a **functional boss,** who is the head of a function, and a **project boss,** who is responsible for managing the individual projects. Employees work on a project team with specialists from other functions and report to the project boss on project matters and the functional boss on matters relating to functional issues. All employees who work in a project team are called **two-boss employees** and are responsible for managing coordination and communication among the functions and projects.

Matrix structures were first developed by companies such as TRW and Hughes Aircraft that are in high-technology industries such as aerospace and electronics. These companies were developing radically new products in uncertain, competitive environments, and speed of product development was the crucial consideration. They needed a structure that could respond to this need, but the functional structure was too inflexible to allow the complex role and task interactions necessary to meet new-product development requirements. Moreover, employees in these companies tend to be highly qualified and professional and perform best in autonomous, flexible working conditions. The matrix structure provides such conditions.

For example, this structure requires a minimum of direct hierarchical control by supervisors. Team members control their own behavior, and participation in project teams allows them to monitor other team members and learn from each other. Furthermore, as the project goes through its different phases, different specialists from various functions are required. Thus, for example, at the first stage the services of research and development specialists may be called for, and then at the next stage engineers and marketing specialists may be needed to make cost and marketing projections. As the demand for the type of specialist changes, team members can be moved to other projects that require their services. Thus, the matrix structure can make maximum use of employees' skills as existing projects are completed and new ones come into existence.

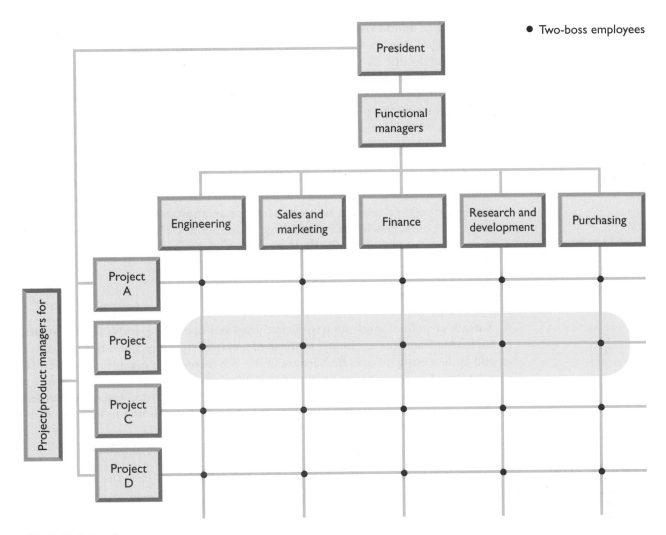

FIGURE 11.7

Matrix Structure

Finally, the freedom given by the matrix not only provides the autonomy to motivate employees but also leaves top management free to concentrate on strategic issues, since they do not have to become involved in operating matters. On all these counts, the matrix is an excellent tool for creating the flexibility necessary for quick reactions to competitive conditions.

There are disadvantages to the matrix structure, however.[34] First, the bureaucratic costs of operating this structure are very high compared with those of operating a functional structure. Because employees tend to be highly skilled, both salaries and overhead are high. Second, the constant movement of employees around the matrix means that time and money are spent establishing new team relationships and getting the project off the ground. Third, the two-boss employee's role, balancing as it does the interests of the project with the function, is difficult to manage, and care must be taken to avoid conflict between functions and projects over resources. Over time, it is possible that project managers will take the leading role in planning and goal setting, in which case the structure would work more like a product or multidivisional structure. If function and project relationships are left uncontrolled, they can lead to power struggles among managers, resulting in stagnation and decline rather than increased flexibility. Finally, the larger the organization, the more difficult it is to operate a matrix structure, because task and role relationships become complex. In such situations, the only option may be to change to a multidivisional structure.

Given these advantages and disadvantages, the matrix is generally used only when a company's strategy warrants it. There is no point in using a more complex structure than necessary because it will only cost more to manage. In dynamic product/market environments, such as biotechnology and computers, the benefits of the matrix in terms of flexibility and innovation are likely to exceed the high bureaucratic costs of using it, and so it becomes an appropriate choice of structure. However, companies in the mature stage of an industry's life cycle or those pursuing a low-cost strategy would rarely choose this structure because it is expensive to operate. We discuss matrix structure further in Chapter 13.

Product-Team Structure

A major structural innovation in recent years has been the **product-team structure.** Its advantages are similar to those of a matrix structure, but it is much easier and far less costly to operate because of the way people are organized into permanent cross-functional teams, as Figure 11.8 illustrates.

In the product-team structure, as in the matrix structure, tasks are divided along product or project lines to reduce bureaucratic costs and to increase man-

FIGURE 11.8

Product-Team Structure

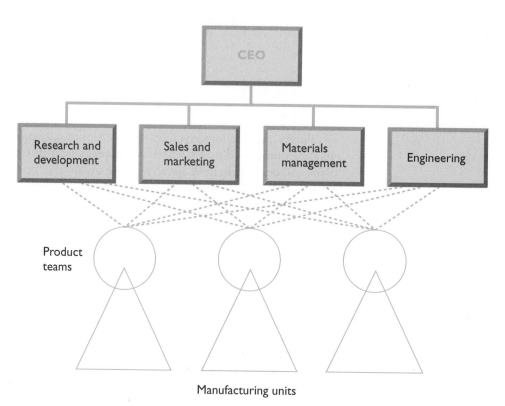

11.4 STRATEGY in ACTION

Restructuring at Lexmark

Lexmark, a printer and typewriter manufacturer, was a division of IBM until it was sold to a New York investment firm in 1992. As an IBM division it had performed badly, and IBM sold it after years of losses brought on by high operating costs and an inability to produce new products that could compete with Hewlett Packard and Japanese printer makers such as Epson. Its new top-management team, led by Marvin Mann, an ex-IBM executive, had the task of reengineering its structure to turn the company around.

Mann first destroyed the organizational structure that the company had developed under its former IBM management. Like the rest of IBM, the division had a tall, centralized structure, where all important decisions were made high in the organization by top managers. This slowed decision making and made it very difficult to communicate across functions because so many managers at different levels and in different functions had to approve new plans.

Moving quickly to change this system, Mann streamlined the company's hierarchy, which meant terminating 50 percent of its managers and eliminating all staff managers—that is, those with no direct-line responsibility. This action cut out three levels in the hierarchy. He then decentralized authority to the product managers of the company's four product groups and told them to develop their own plans and goals. In addition, to continue the process of decentralization, product managers were instructed to develop cross-functional teams comprising employees from all functions, with the goal of finding new and improved ways of organizing task activities to reduce costs. The teams were to use competitive benchmarking and evaluate their competitors' products in order to establish new performance standards to guide their activities. Finally, as an incentive for employees to work hard at increasing efficiency, innovation, and quality, Mann established a company stock ownership scheme to reward employees for their efforts.

The reengineering of the organizational structure to a product-team structure has been very successful for Lexmark. By the end of 1993, the company had made a profit of more than $100 million on sales of $2 billion, and its rate of product development and profitability has continued to increase ever since. Lexmark's new structure is viewed by many as a benchmark that IBM's CEO Lou Gerstner has used as he has continued IBM's restructuring efforts.

agement's ability to monitor and control the manufacturing process. However, instead of being assigned only *temporarily* to different projects, as in the matrix structure, functional specialists are placed in *permanent* cross-functional teams. As a result, the costs associated with coordinating their activities are much lower than in a matrix structure, in which tasks and reporting relationships change rapidly.

Cross-functional teams are formed right at the beginning of the product-development process so that any difficulties that arise can be ironed out early, before they lead to major redesign problems. When all functions have direct input from the beginning, design costs and subsequent manufacturing costs can be kept low. Moreover, the use of cross-functional teams speeds innovation and customer responsiveness because when authority is decentralized to the team, decisions can be made more quickly. The Opening Case focuses on how Chrysler moved to a product-team structure. Strategy in Action 11.4 offers another example, that of Lexmark, which shifted to a product-team structure to reduce costs and speed product development.

Geographic Structure

When a company operates as a geographic structure, geographic regions become the basis for the grouping of organizational activities. A company may divide its manufacturing operations and establish manufacturing plants in different regions of the country, for example. This allows it to be responsive to the needs of regional customers and reduces transportation costs. Similarly, service organizations such as store chains or banks may organize their sales and marketing activities on a regional, rather than on a national, level to get closer to their customers.

A geographic structure provides more control than a functional structure because there are several regional hierarchies carrying out the work previously performed by a single centralized hierarchy. A company such as Federal Express clearly needs to operate a geographic structure to fulfill its corporate goal: next-day delivery. Large merchandising organizations, such as Neiman Marcus, Dillard Department Stores, and Wal-Mart, also moved to a geographic structure soon after they started building stores across the country. With this type of structure, different regional clothing needs (for example, sun wear in the Southwest, down coats in the East) can be handled as required. At the same time, because the purchasing function remains centralized, one central organization can buy for all regions. Thus, in using a geographic structure a company can both achieve economies of scale in buying and distribution and reduce coordination and communication problems.

Neiman Marcus developed a geographic structure similar to the one shown in Figure 11.9 to manage its nationwide chain of stores. In each region, it established a team of regional buyers to respond to the needs of customers in each geographic area, for example, the western, central, eastern, and southern regions. The regional buyers then fed their information to the central buyers at corporate headquarters,

FIGURE 11.9

Geographic Structure

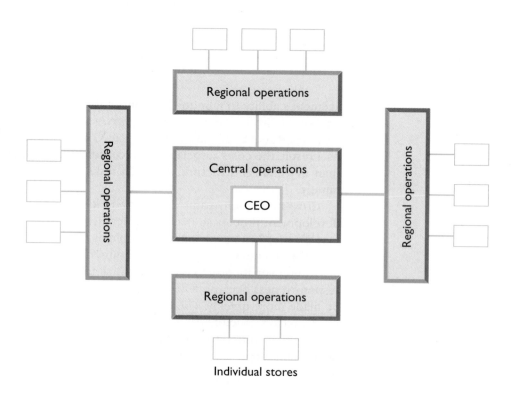

Individual stores

who coordinated their demands to obtain purchasing economies and to ensure that Neiman Marcus's high quality standards, on which its differentiation advantage depends, were maintained nationally.

The usefulness of the matrix, product-team, or geographic structure depends, however, on the size of the company and its range of products and regions. If a company starts to diversify into unrelated products or to integrate vertically into new industries, these structures cannot handle the increased diversity, and a company must move to a multidivisional structure. Only the multidivisional structure is complex enough to deal with the needs of the large, multibusiness company.

INTEGRATION AND INTEGRATING MECHANISMS

As just discussed, an organization must choose the appropriate form of differentiation to match its strategy. Greater diversification, for example, requires that a company move from a functional structure to a multidivisional structure. Differentiation, however, is only the first organizational design decision to be made. The second decision concerns the level of integration necessary to make an organizational structure work effectively. As noted earlier, *integration* refers to the extent to which an organization seeks to coordinate its value creation activities and make them interdependent. The design issue can be summed up simply: the higher a company's level of differentiation, the higher is the level of integration needed to make organizational structure work effectively.[35] Thus, if a company adopts a more complex form of differentiation, it requires a more complex form of integration to accomplish its goals. Federal Express, for example, needs an enormous amount of integration and coordination to allow it to fulfill its promise of next-day package delivery. It is renowned for its innovative use of integrating mechanisms, such as customer-liaison personnel, to manage its transactions quickly and efficiently.

Forms of Integrating Mechanisms

There is a series of integrating mechanisms a company can use to increase its level of integration as its level of differentiation increases.[36] These mechanisms—on a continuum from simple to complex—are listed in Table 11.1, together with examples of the individuals or groups that might perform these integrating roles. As is the case when increasing the level of differentiation, however, increasing the level of integration is expensive. There are high bureaucratic costs associated with using managers to coordinate value creation activities. Hence, a company only uses more complex integrating mechanisms to coordinate its activities to the extent necessary to implement its strategy effectively.

Direct Contact   The aim behind establishing direct contact among managers is to set up a context within which managers from different divisions or functions can work together to solve mutual problems. Managers from different functions have different goals and interests but equal authority, and so they may tend to compete rather than cooperate when conflicts arise. In a typical functional structure, for example, the heads of each of the functions have equal authority; the nearest common point of authority is the CEO. Consequently, if disputes arise, no mechanism exists to resolve the conflicts apart from the authority of the boss.

TABLE 11.1
• • • • • • • • • • •
Types and Examples of Integrating Mechanisms

Direct contact	Sales and production managers
Liaison roles	Assistant sales and plant managers
Task forces	Representatives from sales, production, and research and development
Teams	Organizational executive committee
Integrating roles	Assistant vice president for strategic planning or vice president without portfolio
Integrating departments	Corporate headquarters staff
Matrix	All roles are integrating roles

In fact, one sign of conflict in organizations is the number of problems sent up the hierarchy for upper-level managers to solve. This wastes management time and effort, slows down strategic decision making, and makes it difficult to create a cooperative culture in the company. For this reason, companies generally choose more complex integrating mechanisms to coordinate interfunctional and divisional activities.

Interdepartmental Liaison Roles   A company can improve its interfunctional coordination through the interdepartmental liaison role. When the volume of contacts between two departments or functions increases, one of the ways of improving coordination is to give one manager in *each* division or function the responsibility for coordinating with the other. These managers may meet daily, weekly, monthly, or as needed. Figure 11.10a depicts the nature of the liaison role, the small dot representing the manager inside the functional department who has responsibility for coordinating with the other function. The responsibility for coordination is part of a manager's full-time job, but through these roles a permanent relationship forms between the managers involved, greatly easing strains between departments. Furthermore, liaison roles offer a way of transferring information across the organization, which is important in large, anonymous organizations whose employees may know no one outside their immediate department.

Temporary Task Forces   When more than two functions or divisions share common problems, direct contact and liaison roles are of limited value because they do not provide enough coordination. The solution is to adopt a more complex form of integrating mechanism called a task force. The nature of the task force is represented diagrammatically in Figure 11.10b. One member of each function or division is assigned to a task force created to solve a specific problem. Essentially, task forces are *ad hoc committees,* and members are responsible for reporting back to their departments on the issues addressed and solutions recommended. Task forces are temporary because, once the problem has been solved, members return to their normal roles in their own departments or are assigned to other task forces. Task force members also perform many of their normal duties while serving on the task force.

FIGURE 11.10

Forms of Integrating
Mechanisms

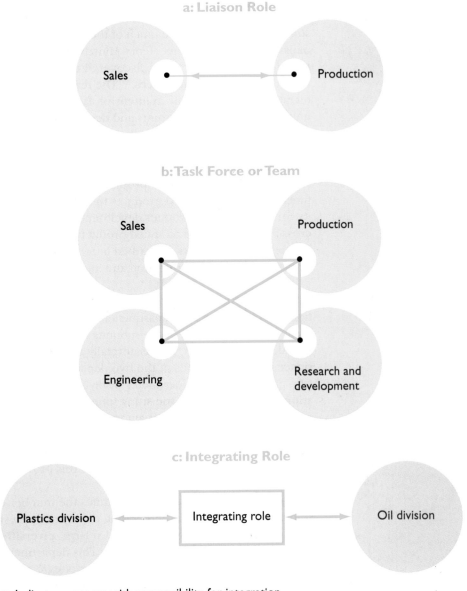

a: Liaison Role

b: Task Force or Team

c: Integrating Role

● Indicates manager with responsibility for integration

Permanent Teams   In many cases, the issues addressed by a task force recur. To deal with these issues effectively, an organization must establish a permanent integrating mechanism, such as a permanent team. An example of a permanent team is a new-product development committee, which is responsible for the choice, design, and marketing of new products. Such an activity obviously requires a great deal of integration among functions if new products are to be successfully introduced, and establishing a permanent integrating mechanism accomplishes this. Intel, for instance, emphasizes teamwork. It formed a council system based on approximately ninety cross-functional groups, which meet regularly to set functional strategy in areas such as engineering and marketing and to develop business-level strategy.

The importance of teams in the management of the organizational structure cannot be overemphasized. Essentially, permanent teams are the organization's *standing committees,* and much of the strategic direction of the organization is formulated in their meetings. Henry Mintzberg, in a study of how the managers of corporations spend their time, discovered that they spend more than 60 percent of their time in these committees.[37] The reason is not bureaucracy but rather that integration is possible only in intensive, face-to-face sessions, in which managers can understand others' viewpoints and develop a cohesive organizational strategy. The more complex the company, the more important these teams become. Westinghouse, for example, has established a whole new task force and team system to promote integration among divisions and improve corporate performance.

As discussed earlier, the product-team structure is based on the use of cross-functional teams to speed products to market. These teams assume the responsibility for all aspects of product development. The way in which AT&T made use of cross-functional teams to speed product development in its race to compete with Japanese manufacturers (described in Strategy in Action 11.5) illustrates how these teams can increase coordination and integration among functions.

Integrating Roles   The only function of the integrating role is to prompt integration among divisions or departments; it is a full-time job. As Figure 11.10c indicates, the role is independent of the subunits or divisions being integrated. It is staffed by an independent expert, who is normally a senior manager with a great deal of experience in the joint needs of the two departments. The job is to coordinate the decision process among departments or divisions so that synergetic gains from cooperation can be obtained. One study found that Du Pont had created 160 integrating roles to provide coordination among the different divisions of the company and improve corporate performance.[38] Once again, the more differentiated the company, the more common are these roles. Often people in these roles take the responsibility for chairing task forces and teams, and this provides additional integration.

Integrating Departments   Sometimes the number of integrating roles becomes so high that a permanent integrating department is established at corporate headquarters. Normally, this occurs only in large, diversified corporations that see the need for integration among divisions. This department consists mainly of strategic planners and may indeed be called the strategic planning department. Corporate headquarters staff in a divisional structure can also be viewed as an integrating department from the divisional perspective.

Matrix Structure   Finally, when differentiation is very high and the company must be able to respond quickly to the environment, a matrix structure becomes the appropriate integrating device. The matrix contains many of the integrating mechanisms already discussed. The subproject managers integrate among functions and projects, and the matrix is built on the basis of temporary task forces.

Integration and Control

Clearly, firms have a large number of options open to them when they increase their level of differentiation as a result of increased growth or diversification. The implementation issue is for managers to match differentiation with the level of integra-

11.5	STRATEGY *in* ACTION

Teamwork at AT&T

As with other large companies, AT&T had developed a very tall, centralized structure to manage its activities. While the telephone industry was regulated, AT&T cared little about the way its massive bureaucracy slowed down decision making. However, after deregulation a major problem facing the company was how to speed the development of new telephones and answering machines that could compete with those of Japanese companies such as Panasonic and Sony. These companies led the market in terms of both the features and the low price of telephone products, and AT&T was a poor third in the competitive marketplace.

AT&T's answer was to bypass the bureaucracy by creating cross-functional teams. Previously, AT&T had employed the usual functional approach to managing product development. The product started in engineering and then went to manufacturing, which in turn handed the product over to marketing. This was a slow and time-consuming process. In the new approach, John Hanley, the AT&T vice president of product development, decided to form teams of six to twelve people from all these functions to handle all aspects of the development process. Each team was given a deadline for the various project phases and then left to get on with the job. The results were astonishing. Product development time was reduced by 50 percent (for example, AT&T's new 4200 phone was produced in one year, not the usual two), costs went down, and quality went up. Today AT&T's answering machines and cordless phones are the market leaders, and AT&T has extended the use of cross-functional teams throughout its business.

tion to meet organizational objectives. Note that while too much differentiation and not enough integration leads to a failure of implementation, the converse is also true. That is, the combination of low differentiation and high integration leads to an overcontrolled, bureaucratized organization, in which flexibility and speed of response are reduced rather than enhanced by the level of integration. Besides, too much integration is expensive for the company because it raises bureaucratic costs. For these reasons the goal is to decide on the optimum amount of integration necessary for meeting organizational goals and objectives. A company needs to operate the simplest structure consistent with implementing its strategy effectively.

In practice, integrating mechanisms are only the first means through which a company seeks to increase its ability to control and coordinate its activities. To facilitate the use of integrating mechanisms and to make organizational structure work, a company must create a control and incentive structure to motivate people and subunits to cooperate and raise organizational performance. In the next chapter, we discuss the various kinds of strategic control systems that organizations can use to make their organizational structures work effectively.

SUMMARY OF CHAPTER

This chapter discusses the issues involved in designing a structure to meet the needs of a company's strategy. Companies can adopt a large number of structures to match changes in their size and strategy over time. The structure a company selects is the one whose logic of grouping activities (that is, whose form of horizontal differentiation) best meets the needs of its business or businesses. The company must match its form of horizontal differentiation to vertical differentiation. That is, it must choose a structure and then make choices about levels in the hierarchy and the degree of centralization or decentralization. It is the combination of both kinds of differentiation that produces internal organizational arrangements.

Once a company has divided itself into parts, however, it then must integrate itself. A company must choose the appropriate level of integration to match its level of differentiation if it is to coordinate its value creation activities successfully. Since differentiation and integration are expensive, a company's goal is to economize on bureaucratic costs by adopting the simplest structure consistent with achieving its strategy. We stress the following points:

✔ Implementing a strategy successfully depends on selecting the right organizational structure and control system to match a company's strategy.

✔ The basic tool of strategy implementation is organizational design. Good organizational design increases profits in two ways. First, it economizes on bureaucratic costs and lowers the costs of value creation activities. Second, it enhances the ability of a company's value creation functions to achieve superior efficiency, quality, innovativeness, and customer responsiveness and to obtain a differentiation advantage.

✔ Differentiation and integration are the two design concepts that govern how a structure will work. The higher the level of differentiation and integration, the higher are bureaucratic costs.

✔ Differentiation has two aspects: (a) vertical differentiation, which refers to how a company chooses to allocate its decision-making authority, and (b) horizontal differentiation, which refers to the way a company groups organizational activities into functions, departments, or divisions.

✔ The basic choice in vertical differentiation is whether to have a flat or a tall structure. Tall hierarchies have a number of disadvantages, such as problems with communication and information transfer, motivation, and cost. Decentralization, or delegation of authority, however, can solve some of these problems.

✔ As a company grows and diversifies, it adopts a multidivisional structure. Although a multidivisional structure has higher bureaucratic costs than a functional structure, it overcomes the control problems associated with a functional structure and gives a company the capability to handle its value creation activities effectively.

✔ Other specialized kinds of structures include the matrix, product-team, and geographic structures. Each has a specialized use and, to be chosen, must match the needs of the organization.

✔ The more complex the company and the higher its level of differentiation, the higher the level of integration that the company needs to manage its structure.

✔ The kinds of integrating mechanisms available to a company range from direct contact to matrix structure. The more complex the mechanism, the greater are the costs of using it. A company should take care to match these mechanisms to its strategic needs.

DISCUSSION QUESTIONS

1. What is the difference between vertical and horizontal differentiation? Rank the various structures discussed in this chapter along these two dimensions.

2. What kind of structure best describes the way your (a) business school and (b) university operate? Why is the structure appropriate? Would another structure fit better?

3. When would a company decide to change from a functional to a multidivisional structure?

4. When would a company choose a matrix structure? What are the problems associated with managing this structure, and why might a product-team structure be preferable?

Practicing Strategic Management

SMALL-GROUP EXERCISE
Speeding Up Product Development

Break up into groups of three to five people, and discuss the following scenario:

You are the top functional managers of a small greeting card company whose new lines of humorous cards for every occasion are selling out as fast as they are reaching the stores. Currently, your employees are organized into different functions such as card designers, artists, and joke writers, as well as functions such as marketing and manufacturing. Each function works on a wide range of different kinds of cards such as birthday, Christmas, Hanukkah, Thanksgiving, and so on. Sometimes, the design department comes up with the initial idea for a new card and sends the idea to the artists, who draw and color the picture. Then, the card is sent to the joke writers who write the joke to suit the card. At other times the process starts with writing the joke, which is sent to the design department to find the best use for the idea.

The problem you are experiencing is that your current functional structure does not allow you to produce new cards fast enough to satisfy customers' demands. It typically takes a new card one year to reach the market, and you want to shorten this time by half to protect and expand your market niche.

1. Discuss ways in which you can improve the way your current functional structure operates to speed the product-development process.

2. Discuss the pros and cons of moving to a (a) multidivisional, (b) matrix, and (c) product-team structure to reduce card development time.

3. Which of these structures do you think is most appropriate and why?

EXPLORING THE WEB
What Kind of Organizational Structure?

Enter the Web site of the German publishing company, Bertelsmann (www.bertelsmann.de/). Click on the English language version. Click on "A Portrait of Bertelsmann." Click on "Scope of Activities" to examine organizational structure. Click on "Corporate Con-

cept," and particularly examine the section on "Entrepreneurial Leadership and Organization."

1. What is Bertelsmann's mission and corporate goals?

2. What kind of organizational structure does Bertelsmann have?

3. What is Bertelsmann's approach to managing its structure (its approach to decentralization, delegation, and so forth)?

Explore the Web to find a Web site that displays a company's organizational chart or that talks about a company's method of managing its structure. (For example, does it use a centralized or decentralized approach?) What kind of structure does the company use to manage its activities?

ARTICLE FILE 11

Find an example(s) of a company that has recently changed its organizational structure. What changes did it make? Why did it make these changes? What effect did these changes have on the behavior of people and subunits?

STRATEGIC MANAGEMENT PROJECT
Module 11

This module asks you to identify the type of organizational structure used by your organization and to explain why your company has selected this form of differentiation and integration. If you are studying a company in your area, you will probably have more information about the company's structure than if you are studying a company using published sources. However, you can make many inferences about the company's structure from the nature of its activities, and if you write to the company, it may provide you with an organizational chart and other information.

1. How large is the company as measured by the number of its employees? How many levels in the hierarchy does it have from the top to the bottom?

2. Based on these two measures and any other information you may have, would you say your company operates with a relatively tall or flat

structure? What effect does this have on people's behavior?

3. Does your company have a centralized or a decentralized approach to decision making? How do you know?

4. In what ways do the company's vertical differentiation choices affect the behavior of people and subunits? Do you think the company's choice of vertical differentiation is appropriate for its activities? Why or why not?

5. What changes (if any) would you make to the way the company operates in a vertical direction?

6. Draw an organizational chart showing the main way in which your company groups its activities. Based on this chart, what kind of structure (functional or divisional) does your company operate with?

7. Why did your company choose this structure? In what ways is it appropriate for its business? In what ways is it not?

8. What changes (if any) would you make to the way your company operates in a horizontal direction?

9. Given this analysis, does your company have a low or a high level of differentiation?

10. What kind of integration or integration mechanisms does your company use? Why? Does its level of integration match its level of differentiation?

11. Based on the analysis of your company's level of differentiation and integration, would you say your company is coordinating and motivating its people and subunits effectively? Why or why not?

12. What changes would you make to the company's structure to increase the firm's effectiveness? What changes has the company itself made to improve effectiveness? Why?

CLOSING CASE

Apple Computer

Incorporated in 1977, Apple Computer designs, manufactures, and markets personal computers for use in business, education, and the home. Apple Computer was created in 1976, when two engineers, Steven Jobs and Steven Wozniak, collaborated to produce a computer designed for personal use.[39] As early orders for their computer increased, Jobs and Wozniak soon realized that they could not do everything themselves. They needed to employ more people to produce Apple's goods and services. To produce more effectively, Jobs and Wozniak structured their company so that different people were grouped together to perform specific business functions such as sales and marketing, purchasing, engineering, and manufacturing, thus creating a functional structure. Jobs and Wozniak also kept their organization flat so that it had few levels of managers, and employees were encouraged to be creative, flexible, and responsive to the uncertainty that characterized the new personal computer industry. With few rules and few managers, Apple operated on the basis of personal contact between people in different functions who were members of teams and task forces.

By 1982 Apple's structure had become taller, with more levels of management. A new chief executive, John Sculley, had been hired to take control of the management side of the business. Fast growth and the introduction of a wider range of products, including the Macintosh computer, had led to many communication and coordination problems among the different functions. Sculley decided that Apple would change from a structure based on functions to one based on products—a multidivisional structure—so that each product would be manufactured by a separate division, each of which would have its own set of functions such as marketing, research and development, and product engineering.

Problems arose with this multidivisional structure. Jobs, by this time the head of the Macintosh division, began to champion the development of his project, the Macintosh computer, over other types of computers, which triggered hostile competition for resources among Apple's divisions. The organization's values began to change as cooperation fell and people began to become more loyal to their division than to the organization as a whole. Moreover, the costs of running the company rose dramatically because functions were duplicated in each division.

By 1985 recession in the computer industry had exacerbated these problems and made reorganization imperative. Jobs was ousted from the company, and Sculley took total control. Faced with increasing competition from computer clone makers, Sculley searched for new ways to change Apple's structure to reduce costs.[40] Apple moved back to a functional structure in which, once again, one set of functions served the needs of all the different kinds of computers Apple produced. For example, all computers were now manufactured in one central production function over which one management team had overall control, rather than in separate divisions by different teams of managers. In 1996 Apple's managers continued to look for new ways to organize Apple's activities to cut costs and maintain its technological edge in its fierce battle with companies such as Compaq, Dell, IBM, and AST.

Case Discussion Questions

1. Why did Apple move from a functional to a multidivisional structure and back again?

2. Does Apple have the right structure now?

CHAPTER 12

Designing Strategic Control Systems

Opening Case: Sam Walton's Approach to Control

Overview

What Is Strategic Control?

Strategic Control Systems

Organizational Culture

Strategic Reward Systems

Closing Case: Getting It Right at McDonald's

OPENING CASE

Wal-Mart, headquartered in Bentonville, Arkansas, is the largest retailer in the world, with sales of almost $100 billion in 1996. Its success rests on the nature of the strategic control systems that its founder, the late Sam Walton, established for the company. Walton wanted all his managers and workers to have a hands-on approach to their jobs and to be totally committed to Wal-Mart's main goal, which he defined as total customer satisfaction. To motivate his employees, Walton created a strategic control system that gave employees at all levels continuous feedback about their and the company's performance.

First, Walton developed a financial control system that provided managers with day-to-day feedback about the performance of all aspects of the business. Through a sophisticated companywide satellite system, corporate managers at its Bentonville headquarters can evaluate the performance of each store, and even of each department in each store. Information about store profits and the rate of turnover of goods is provided to store managers on a

Sam Walton's Approach to Control

daily basis, and store managers in turn communicate this information to Wal-Mart's 625,000 employees (who are called associates). By sharing such information, Walton's method encourages all associates to learn the fundamentals of the retailing business so they can work to improve it.[1]

If any store seems to be underperforming, managers and associates meet to probe the reasons and to find solutions to help raise performance. Wal-Mart's top managers routinely visit stores having problems to lend their expertise, and each month top managers use the company's aircraft to fly to various Wal-Mart's stores so they can keep their fingers on the pulse of the business. It is also customary for Wal-Mart's top managers to spend their Saturdays meeting together to discuss the week's financial results and their implications for the future.[2]

Walton also insisted on linking performance to rewards. Each manager's individual performance, measured by his or her ability to meet specific goals or output targets, is reflected in pay raises and chances for promotion

(promotion both to bigger stores in the company's 2,000-store empire and even to corporate headquarters, since Wal-Mart routinely promotes from within the company rather than hiring managers from other companies). While top managers receive large stock options linked to the company's performance targets and stock price, even ordinary associates receive stock in the company. An associate who started with Walton in the 1970s would by now have accumulated more than $250,000 in stock because of the appreciation of Wal-Mart's stock over time.

Walton also instituted an elaborate system of controls, such as rules and budgets, to shape employees' behavior. Each store performs the same activities in the same way, and all employees receive the same kind of training so they know how to behave toward customers. In this way Wal-Mart is able to standardize its operations, which leads to major cost savings and allows managers to make storewide changes easily when they need to.

Finally, Walton was not content just to use output and behavior controls and monetary rewards to motivate his associates. To involve his associates in the business and encourage them to develop work behaviors focused on providing quality customer service, he established strong cultural values and norms for his company. Some norms

that associates are expected to follow include the *ten-foot attitude* that developed when Walton, during his visits to the stores, encouraged associates to "promise that whenever you come within 10 feet of a customer you will look him in the eye, greet him, and ask him if you can help him"; the *sundown rule,* which states that employees should strive to answer customers' requests by sundown on the day they receive them; and the *Wal-Mart cheer* ("Give me a *W,* give me an *A,*" and so on), which is used in all its stores.

The strong customer-oriented values that Walton created are exemplified in the stories its members tell one another about the company's concern for its customers. They include stories such as the one about Sheila, who risked her own safety when she jumped in front of a car to prevent a little boy from being struck; about Phyllis, who administered CPR to a customer who had suffered a heart attack in her store; and about Annette, who gave up the Power Ranger she had on layaway for her own son so a customer's son could have his birthday wish.[3] The strong Wal-Mart culture also helps to control and motivate its employees and helps associates to achieve the stringent output and financial targets the company has set for itself.

OVERVIEW

As we note in Chapter 11, strategy implementation requires selecting the right combination of structure and control for achieving a company's strategy. An organizational structure assigns people to tasks and roles (differentiation) and specifies how these are to be coordinated (integration). Nevertheless, organizational structure does not of itself provide or contain the mechanism through which people can be *motivated* to make it work. Hence the need for control. The purpose of strategic control is to provide managers with (1) a means of motivating employees to work toward organizational goals and (2) specific feedback on how well an organization and its members are performing. Structure provides an organization with a skeleton, but control gives it the muscles, sinews, nerves, and sensations that allow managers to regulate and govern its activities.

In this chapter we first look in detail at the nature of strategic control and describe the main steps in the control process. We then discuss the main types of strategic control systems available to managers to shape and influence employees—financial controls, output controls, behavior controls, and control through the values and norms of an organization's culture. Finally, we discuss how the design of reward systems becomes an important part of the strategic control process. By the end of this chapter, you will appreciate the rich variety of different control systems available to managers and understand why developing an appropriate control system is vital to maximizing the performance of an organization and its members.

WHAT IS STRATEGIC CONTROL?

Strategic control is the process by which managers monitor the ongoing activities of an organization and its members to evaluate whether activities are being performed efficiently and effectively and to take corrective action to improve performance if they are not. First, strategic managers choose the organizational strategy and structure they hope will allow the organization to use its resources most effectively to create value for its customers. Second, strategic managers create control systems to monitor and evaluate whether, in fact, their organization's strategy and structure are working as managers intended, how they could be improved, and how they should be changed if they are not working.

Strategic control does not just mean reacting to events *after* they have occurred; it also means keeping an organization on track, anticipating events that might occur, and responding swiftly to new opportunities that present themselves. You'll recall from Chapter 1 that *strategic intent* refers to the obsession strategic managers have for building organizational resources and capabilities in order to dominate their environments and that it means managers' "focusing the organization's attention on the essence of winning, motivating people by communicating the value of the target, leaving room for individual and team contributions, sustaining enthusiasm . . . and using intent consistently to guide resource allocation."[4] Behind the concept of strategic intent is a vision of strategic control as a system that sets ambitious goals and targets for all managers and employees and then develops performance measures that stretch and encourage the managers and employees to excel in their quest to raise performance.

Thus, strategic control is not just about monitoring how well an organization and its members are achieving current goals or about how well the firm is utilizing its existing resources. It is also about keeping employees motivated, focused on the important problems confronting an organization now and in the future, and working together to find solutions that can help an organization perform better over time.[5]

The Importance of Strategic Control

To understand the vital importance of strategic control, consider how it helps managers to obtain superior efficiency, quality, innovation, and responsiveness to customers, the four basic building blocks of competitive advantage.

Control and Efficiency   To determine how *efficiently* they are using organizational resources, managers must be able to measure accurately how many units of inputs (raw materials, human resources, and so on) are being used to produce a unit of output. They must also be able to measure the number of units of outputs (goods and services) they produce. A control system contains the measures or yardsticks that allow managers to assess how efficiently they are producing goods and services. Moreover, if managers experiment with changing the way they produce goods and services to find a more efficient way of producing them, these measures tell managers how successful they have been.

Thus, for example, when managers at Chrysler decided to change to a product-team structure to design, engineer, and manufacture their new cars, they used such measures as time taken to design a new car and cost savings per car produced to evaluate how well this new structure worked. When they used these measures to compare the performance of the new structure with that of the old structure, they found that the new structure performed better. Without a control system in place, managers have no idea how well their organizations are performing and how they can make it perform better, something that is becoming increasingly important in today's highly competitive environment.[6]

Control and Quality   Today, much of the competition between organizations revolves around increasing the *quality* of goods and services. In the car industry, for example, within each price range, cars compete against one another in terms of their features, design, and reliability over time. So, whether a customer buys a Ford Taurus, a GM Cavalier, a Chrysler Intrepid, a Toyota Camry, or a Honda Accord depends significantly on the quality of each company's product. Organizational control is important in determining the quality of goods and services because it gives managers feedback on product quality. If managers of an organization such as Chrysler consistently measure the number of customers' complaints and the amount of new cars returned for repairs, they have a good indication of how much quality they have built into their product. That is, do they have a car that does not break down?

Strategic managers create a control system that consistently monitors the quality of goods and services so that they can make continuous improvements to quality over time, which gives them a competitive advantage. Total quality management, an organizationwide control system that focuses on improving quality and reducing costs, is discussed at length in Chapter 5.

Control and Innovation   Strategic control can also help to raise the level of *innovation* in an organization. Successful innovation takes place when managers create an organizational setting in which employees feel empowered to be creative and in which authority is decentralized to employees so that they feel free to experiment and take risks. Deciding on the appropriate control systems to encourage risk taking is an important management challenge, and, as discussed later in the chapter, an organization's culture becomes important in this regard. At Chrysler, for example, to encourage each product team to perform, top managers monitored the performance of each team separately (by examining how each team reduced costs or increased quality, for example) and then paid each team on a bonus system related to its performance. The product-team manager then evaluated each team member's individual performance, and the most innovative employees received promotions and rewards based on that performance level.

Control and Responsiveness to Customers   Finally, strategic managers can help make their organizations more *responsive to customers* if they develop a control system that allows them to evaluate how well employees with customer contact are performing their jobs. Monitoring employees' behavior can help managers find ways to help increase employees' performance level, perhaps by revealing areas in which skill training can help employees or by finding new procedures that allow employees to perform their jobs better. When employees know their behaviors are being monitored, they may have more incentive to be helpful and consistent in the way they act toward customers. To help improve customer service, for example, Chrysler regularly surveys customers about their experiences with particular Chrysler dealers. If a dealership receives too many complaints from customers, Chrysler's managers investigate the dealership to uncover the sources of the problems and suggest solutions. If necessary, they can threaten to reduce the number of cars a dealership receives to force it to improve the quality of customer service.

A Balanced Scorecard Approach to Strategic Control

As just discussed, strategic control entails developing performance measures that allow managers both to evaluate how well they have utilized organizational resources to create value *and* to sense new opportunities for creating value in the future. One increasingly influential model that guides managers through the process of creating the right kind of strategic control systems to enhance organizational performance is the balanced scorecard model.[7]

According to the **balanced scorecard model,** traditionally strategic managers have primarily used financial measures of performance such as profit and return on investment to measure and evaluate organizational performance. While financial information is important, it is not enough by itself. If strategic managers are to obtain a true picture of organizational performance, financial information must be supplemented with performance measures that indicate how well an organization has been achieving the four building blocks of competitive advantage—efficiency, quality, innovation, and responsiveness to customers. This is so because financial results simply inform strategic managers about the results of decisions they have *already taken*; the other measures balance this picture of performance by informing managers about how accurately the organization has in place the building blocks that drive *future performance*.[8]

One version of the way the balanced scorecard operates is presented in Figure 12.1. Based on an organization's mission and goals, strategic managers develop a set of strategies to build competitive advantage to achieve these goals. They then establish an organizational structure to use resources to obtain a competitive advantage.[9] To evaluate how well the strategy and structure are working, managers develop specific performance measures that assess how well the four building blocks of competitive advantage are being achieved:

- *Efficiency* can be measured by the level of production costs, the number of hours needed to produce a product, and the cost of raw materials.

- *Quality* can be measured by the number of rejects, the number of defective products returned from customers, and the level of product reliability over time.

- *Innovation* can be measured by the number of new products introduced, the time taken to develop the next generation of new products versus the competition, and the cost of product development.

- *Responsiveness to customers* can be measured by the number of repeat customers, the level of on-time delivery to customers, and the level of customer service.

As Kaplan and Norton, the developers of this approach, suggest:

Think of the balanced scorecard as the dials and indicators in an airplane cockpit. For the complex task of navigating and flying an airplane, pilots need detailed

FIGURE 12.1
· · · · · · · · · · · · · · · ·
A Balance Scorecard
Approach

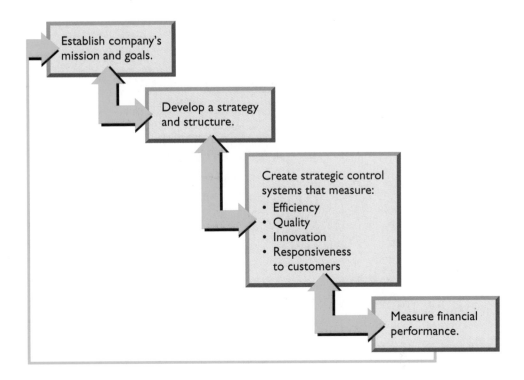

information about many aspects of the flight. They need information on fuel, air speed, altitude, learning, destination, and other indicators that summarize the current and predicted environment. Reliance on one instrument can be fatal. Similarly, the complexity of managing an organization today requires that managers be able to view performance in several areas simultaneously.[10]

The way in which strategic managers' ability to build a competitive advantage translates into organizational performance is then measured using financial measures such as cash flow, quarterly sales growth, increase in market share, and return on investment or equity. Based on an evaluation of the complete set of measures in the balanced scorecard, strategic managers are in a good position to reevaluate the company's mission and goals and to take corrective action to rectify problems or to exploit new opportunities by changing the organization's strategy and structure, which is the purpose of strategic control.

STRATEGIC CONTROL SYSTEMS

· ·

Strategic control systems are the formal target-setting, measurement, and feedback systems that allow strategic managers to evaluate whether a company is achieving superior efficiency, quality, innovation, and customer responsiveness and implementing its strategy successfully. An effective control system should have three characteristics. It should be *flexible* enough to allow managers to respond as necessary to unexpected events; it should provide *accurate information*, giving a true picture of organizational performance; and it should supply managers with the information in a *timely manner* because making decisions on the basis of outdated

FIGURE 12.2
· · · · · · · · · · · · ·

Steps in Designing an
Effective Control System

information is a recipe for failure.[11] As Figure 12.2 shows, designing an effective strategic control system requires four steps.

1. *Establish the standards and targets against which performance is to be evaluated.* The standards and targets managers select are the ways in which a company chooses to evaluate its performance. General performance standards often derive from the goal of achieving superior efficiency, quality, innovation, or customer responsiveness. Specific performance targets are derived from the strategy pursued by the company. For example, if a company is pursuing a low-cost strategy, then reducing costs by 7 percent a year might be a target. If the company is a service organization such as Wal-Mart or McDonald's, its standards might include time targets for serving customers or guidelines for food quality.

2. *Create the measuring and monitoring systems that indicate whether the standards and targets are being reached.* The company establishes procedures for assessing whether work goals at all levels in the organization are being achieved. In some cases measuring performance is fairly straightforward. For example, managers can measure quite easily how many customers their employees serve by counting the number of receipts from the cash register. In many cases, however, measuring performance is a difficult task because the organization is engaged in many complex activities. How can managers judge how well their research and development department is doing, when it may take five years for products to be developed? How can they measure the company's performance when the company is entering new markets and serving new customers? How can they evaluate how well divisions are integrating? The answer is that managers need to use various types of control systems, which we discuss later in this chapter.

3. *Compare actual performance against the established targets.* Managers evaluate whether and to what extent performance deviates from the standards and targets developed in step 1. If performance is higher, management may decide that it has set the standards too low and may raise them for the next time period. The Japanese are renowned for the way they use targets on the production line to control costs. They are constantly trying to raise performance, and they raise the standards to provide a goal for managers to work toward. On the other hand, if performance is too low, managers must decide whether to take remedial action. This decision is easy when the reasons for poor performance can be identified, for instance, high labor costs. More often, however, the reasons for poor performance are hard to uncover. They may stem from involved external factors, such as a recession. Alternatively, the cause may be internal. For instance, the research and development laboratory may have underestimated the problems it would encounter or the extra costs of doing unforeseen research. For any form of action, however, step 4 is necessary.

4. *Initiate corrective action when it is decided that the standards and targets are not being achieved.* The final stage in the control process is to take the corrective action that will allow the organization to meet its goals. Such corrective action may mean changing any aspect of strategy or structure discussed in this book. For example, managers may invest more resources in improving R&D, or diversify, or even decide to change their organizational structure. The goal is to enhance continually an organization's competitive advantage.

Levels of Strategic Control

Strategic control systems are developed to measure performance at four levels in an organization: the corporate, divisional, functional, and individual levels. Managers at all levels must develop the most appropriate set of measures to evaluate corporate-, business-, and functional-level performance. As the balanced scorecard approach suggests, these measures should be tied as closely as possibly to the goals of achieving superior efficiency, quality, innovativeness, and responsiveness to customers. Care must be taken, however, to ensure that the standards used at each level do not cause problems at the other levels, for example, that divisions' attempts to improve their performance do not conflict with corporate performance. Furthermore, controls at each level should provide the basis on which managers at the levels below can select their control systems. Figure 12.3 illustrates these links.

Table 12.1 shows the various types of strategic control systems managers can use to monitor and coordinate organizational activities. Each of these types of control and its use at various organizational levels—corporate, divisional, functional, and individual—is discussed in the text that follows.

Financial Controls

As noted earlier, the most common measures managers and other stakeholders use to monitor and evaluate a company's performance are financial controls. Typically, strategic managers select financial goals they wish their company to achieve, such as growth, profitability, and return to shareholder goals, and then they measure whether or not these goals have been achieved. One reason for the popularity of

FIGURE 12.3
● ● ● ● ● ● ● ● ● ●
Levels of Organizational
Control

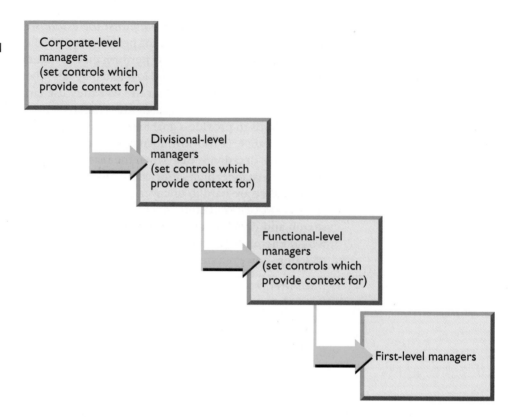

financial performance measures is that they are objective. The performance of one company can be compared with that of another in terms of its stock market price, return on investment, market share, or even cash flow so that strategic managers and other stakeholders, particularly shareholders, have some way of judging their company's performance relative to that of other companies.

Stock price, for example, is a useful measure of a company's performance, primarily because the price of the stock is determined competitively by the number of buyers and sellers in the market. The stock's value is a indication of the market's *expectations* for the firm's future performance. Thus, movements in the price of a stock provide shareholders with feedback on a company's and its manager's performance. Stock market price acts as an important measure of performance be-

TABLE 12.1
● ● ● ● ● ● ● ● ● ●
Types of Control Systems

Financial Controls	Output Controls	Behavior Controls	Organizational Culture
Stock price	Divisional goals	Budgets	Values
ROI	Functional goals	Standardization	Norms
	Individual goals	Rules and procedures	Socialization

cause top managers watch it closely and are sensitive to its rise and fall, particularly its fall. When Ford Motor's stock price failed to increase in 1996, for example, CEO Alex Trotman took heed of the shareholders' complaint that Ford's product development costs and cars prices were too high. In response, he took steps to reduce costs and boost the company's ROI and stock price. Finally, because stock price reflects the long-term future return from the stock, it can be regarded as an indicator of the company's long-run potential.

Return on investment (ROI), determined by dividing net income by invested capital, is another popular kind of financial control. At the corporate level, the performance of the whole company can be evaluated *against* that of other companies to assess its relative performance. Top managers, for example, can assess how well their strategies have worked by comparing their company's performance against that of similar companies. In the personal computer industry, companies such as Dell, Compaq, and Apple use ROI to gauge their performance relative to that of their competitors. A declining ROI signals a potential problem with a company's strategy or structure. Apple's ROI, for example, has been falling in relation to Dell's and Compaq's. The reason, according to analysts, is that Apple has been rather slow both in product innovation and in reacting to the price-cutting moves of its rivals.

ROI can also be used inside the company at the divisional level to judge the performance of an operating division by comparing it to that of a similar freestanding business or other internal division. Indeed, one reason for selecting a multidivisional structure is that each division can be evaluated as a self-contained profit center. Consequently, management can directly measure the performance of one division against another. General Motors moved to a divisional structure partly because it could use this standard. It gave GM's corporate managers information about the relative costs of the various divisions, allowing them to base capital allocations on relative performance.

Similarly, manufacturing companies often establish production facilities at different locations, domestically and globally, so that they can measure the relative performance of one against the other. For example, Xerox was able to identify the relative inefficiency of its U.S. division by comparing its profitability with that of its Japanese counterpart. ROI is a powerful form of control at the divisional level, especially if divisional managers are rewarded on the basis of their performance vis-à-vis other divisions. The most successful divisional managers are promoted to become the next generation of corporate executives.

Failure to meet stock price or ROI targets also indicates that corrective action is necessary. It signals the need for corporate reorganization in order to meet corporate objectives, and such reorganization can involve a change in structure or even liquidation and divestiture of businesses. It can also indicate the need for new strategic leadership. In recent years, the CEOs of American Express, Digital Equipment, Westinghouse, and GM have all been ousted by disgruntled boards of directors, dismayed at the declining performance of their companies relative to that of the competition.

Output Controls

While financial goals and controls are an important part of the balanced scorecard approach, it is also necessary to develop goals and controls that tell managers how well their strategies are creating a competitive advantage and building distinctive competencies and capabilities that will lead to future success. When strategic managers implement the balanced scorecard approach and establish goals and measures to evaluate efficiency, quality, innovation, and responsiveness to customers, they are using output control. **Output control** is a system of control in which strategic managers estimate or forecast appropriate performance goals for each division, department, and employee and then measure actual performance relative to these goals. Often a company's reward system is linked to performance on these goals, so that output control also provides an incentive structure for motivating employees at all levels in the organization.

Divisional Goals   Divisional goals state corporate managers' expectations for each division concerning performance on such dimensions as efficiency, quality, innovation, and responsiveness to customers. Generally, corporate managers set challenging divisional goals to encourage divisional managers to create more effective strategies and structures in the future. At General Electric, for example, CEO Jack Welch has set clear performance goals for GE's more than 150 divisions. He expects each division to be number one or two in its industry in terms of market share. Divisional managers are given considerable autonomy to formulate a strategy to meet this goal (to find ways to increase efficiency, innovation, and so on), and the divisions that fail are divested.

Functional and Individual Goals   Output control at the functional and individual levels is a continuation of control at the divisional level. Divisional managers set goals for functional managers that will allow the division to achieve its goals. As at the divisional level, functional goals are established to encourage development of competencies that provide the company with a competitive advantage. The same four building blocks of competitive advantage (efficiency, quality, innovation, and customer responsiveness) act as the goals against which functional performance is evaluated. In the sales function, for example, goals related to efficiency (such as cost of sales), quality (such as number of returns), and customer responsiveness (such as the time needed to respond to customer needs) can be established for the whole function.

Finally, functional managers establish goals that individual employees are expected to achieve to allow the function to achieve its goals. Sales personnel, for example, can be given specific goals (related to functional goals), which they in turn are required to achieve. Functions and individuals are then evaluated on the basis of achieving or not achieving their goals, and in sales compensation is commonly pegged to achievement. The achievement of these goals is a sign that the company's strategy is working and it is meeting organizational objectives. The way in which Informix used output controls to make its structure work after an acquisition illustrates many of the advantages of output control. Informix's approach is highlighted in Strategy in Action 12.1.

Management by Objectives

To use output control most effectively, many organizations implement management by objectives. **Management by objectives (MBO)** is a system of evaluating managers by their ability to achieve specific organizational goals or performance

12.1   STRATEGY *in* ACTION

Output Control and Acquisitions

Informix, based in Menlo Park, California, specializes in producing software that links networks of UNIX-based PCs and workstations. To expand its product range and give it a fully developed distribution system, which would make it the leading competitor in its market niche, Informix purchased Innovative Software of Kansas City. The acquisition was a disaster. Instead of an improvement in its value creation capabilities, Informix saw a dramatic increase in its operating costs. Its work force swelled from 350 to 1,200 people, and it had to manage two sets of sales forces, manufacturing operations, and all the other value creation functions. In 1990 the company registered a $46.3 million loss, and its future was in jeopardy.

Informix's CEO, Philip White, realized that he had to regain control of the company's structure if he were to get costs back under control. He established a series of strict output controls for the various functions and

forced managers to carefully monitor and evaluate their activities in order to find new ways of organizing to reduce costs. For example, he established efficiency goals for cutting costs in manufacturing that forced managers to streamline and combine the two manufacturing operations. Within four years, manufacturing costs dropped from 13 percent of revenue to 5 percent. In product development, he established stringent targets for profit returns from new products, which forced managers to carefully screen potential new products. The result was the launch of a large number of highly successful products that have greatly boosted revenues. Indeed, White's program of developing a set of output controls to measure performance and to motivate and challenge his managers has been so successful that the company's stock, which was trading at $1.31 in January 1992, was at more than $65 by 1996, and the company has a commanding lead over its competitors.

---

standards and to meet their operating budgets.[12] A management by objectives system follows a series of specific steps:

1. *Specific goals and objectives are established at each level of the organization.* Management by objectives starts when corporate managers establish overall organizational objectives, such as specific financial performance goals already discussed. Then the objective setting cascades down the organization as managers at the divisional and functional levels set their objectives so as to achieve corporate objectives.[13]

2. *Goal setting is a participatory process.* An important part of a management by objectives system is that, at every level, managers sit down with their subordinate managers to determine jointly appropriate and feasible objectives and to decide on the budget that will be needed to achieve them. Thus, subordinates participate in the objective-setting process, which is a way of getting their commitment to achieve those goals and meet their budgets.[14]

3. *Periodic review of progress toward meeting goals.* Once specific objectives have been agreed upon for managers at each level, managers become accountable for meeting them. Periodically, they sit down with their subordinates and evaluate their progress. Normally, salary raises and promotions are linked to the goal-setting process, and managers who have achieved their goals receive the most rewards. The issue of how to design reward systems to motivate managers and other organizational employees is detailed later in the chapter.

One company that has spent considerable time developing an effective MBO system is Zytec, a leading manufacturer of power supplies for computers and other electronic equipment. All Zytec's managers and workers are involved in its goal-setting process. Top managers first set up six cross-functional teams to create a five-year plan for the company and set broad goals for each function.[15] This plan is then reviewed by employees from all areas of the company, who evaluate its feasibility and make suggestions as to how it could be modified or improved. Each function then uses the broad goals in the plan to set more specific goals for each manager within each function, which are reviewed with top managers. At Zytec the MBO system is organizationwide and fully participatory, and performance is reviewed both from an annual and a five-year perspective in keeping with the company's five-year plan. So successful has Zytec's MBO system been that not only have its costs dropped dramatically but it also won the Baldrige Award for quality.

While Zytec illustrates the advantages of MBO, the story of Giddings and Lewis, highlighted in Strategy in Action 12.2, illustrates some of the problems that can arise if it is used inappropriately.

The inappropriate use of output control can also promote conflict among divisions. In general, setting across-the-board output targets, such as ROI targets, for divisions can lead to destructive results if divisions single-mindedly try to maximize divisional profits at the expense of corporate objectives. Moreover, to reach output targets, divisions may start to distort the numbers and engage in strategic manipulation of the figures to make their divisions look good.[16]

In sum, strategic managers need to use the balanced scorecard approach to design the set of output controls that will best promote long-run profitability. In practice, output controls must be used in conjunction with behavior controls and organizational culture if the right strategic behaviors are to be encouraged.

Behavior Controls

The first step in strategy implementation is for managers to design the right kind of organizational structure. To make the structure work, however, employees must learn the kinds of behaviors they are expected to perform. Using managers to tell employees what to do lengthens the organizational hierarchy, is expensive, and raises bureaucratic costs; consequently, strategic managers rely on behavior controls. **Behavior control** is control through the establishment of a comprehensive system of rules and procedures to direct the actions or behavior of divisions, functions, and individuals.[17]

In using behavior controls, the intention is not to specify the goals, but to standardize the way of reaching them. Rules standardize behavior and make outcomes predictable. If employees follow the rules, then actions are performed and decisions handled the same way time and time again. The result is predictability and accuracy, the aim of all control systems. The main kinds of behavior controls are operating budgets and standardization.

Operating Budgets   Once managers at each level have been given a goal to achieve, operating budgets that regulate how managers and workers are to attain those goals are established. An **operating budget** is a blueprint that states how managers intend to use organizational resources to achieve organizational goals

STRATEGY *in* ACTION

12.2

How Not to Use Output Control to Get Ahead

William J. Fife masterminded the turnaround of Giddings and Lewis, a manufacturer of automated factory equipment for companies such as GM, Boeing, AMR, and Ford. In 1988 the company was losing money and had a declining customer base. By 1993 Fife had made it the largest company in the industry, with sales that for every quarter exceeded year-earlier results and a stock price that had quadrupled since Fife sold its stock on the open market in 1989. Nevertheless, in April 1993 the board of directors decided that Fife was no longer a suitable leader and asked him to resign because, as the board saw it, his use of output controls was damaging the future of the company.

Fife's turnaround strategy relied on broadening the company's product base by innovating products to suit new kinds of customers, for example, airlines and consumer manufacturing companies. Then his goal was to increase sales by promoting customer responsiveness. As an example to his managers and employees, Fife would fly anywhere in the United States to solve customer problems personally. To promote his strategy of increasing sales through innovation and customer responsiveness, Fife made extensive use of output controls as the main way of evaluating the performance of his product and financial managers. Periodically, he would sit down with his executives to review the financial, sales, and cost figures for a product or product range.

However, when the figures failed to please him, he would verbally attack and abuse the executive concerned in front of his or her peers, who sat through the assault in embarrassed silence. Any attempts to fight back would merely prolong the attack, and top managers began to complain to board members that Fife was destroying working relationships. Moreover, top managers claimed that Fife's preoccupation with the short-term bottom line was causing problems for the organization because his focus on sales and cost targets was forcing them to cut back on research and development or customer service to meet the stringent targets that he set. Eventually, they pointed out, this practice would hurt customer relations. Thus, Fife's managers claimed that his exclusive focus on output control goal setting was reducing flexibility and integration and threatening the company's future performance.

Whatever the truth in these claims, the board of directors (which Fife had appointed) listened to the disgruntled managers and decided that for the good of the organization they should ask Fife to resign. As Clyde Folley, the acting chairman, put it, the board wanted "nice quiet, level leadership" and the reestablishment of good working relationships between managers at all levels. However, the stock market reacted differently to the news of Fife's departure, and the company's stock price plunged by more than 20 percent on the announcement. Clearly, shareholders liked the effect of Fife's output controls on the company's performance, even if his managers did not.

---

most efficiently. Most commonly, managers at one level allocate to managers at a lower level a specific amount of resources to use to produce goods and services.

Once they have been given a budget, managers must decide how they will allocate certain amounts of money for different organizational activities. These lower-level managers are then evaluated on the basis of their ability to stay inside the budget and make the best use of it. Thus, for example, managers at GE's washing machine division might have a budget of $50 million to develop and sell a new line of washing machines, and they have to decide how much money to allocate to R&D, engineering, sales, and so on so that the division generates the most revenue and hence makes the biggest profit.

Most commonly, large organizations treat each division as a stand-alone profit center, and corporate managers evaluate each division's performance by its relative

Japan Focuses on Budgets

In the 1990s, Japanese companies have been facing increasing problems competing in the global marketplace because the rising value of the yen has made their products so expensive abroad. In addition, the Japanese have experienced problems because their global competitors have lowered their costs by imitating many of the cost-saving innovations in manufacturing that Japanese companies pioneered, such as total quality management. With their competitive advantage eroding because their foreign competitors' costs are as low or lower than theirs, Japanese companies have been seeking new ways to cut costs to increase their efficiency.

At the top of their list of ways to reduce costs is making ingenious use of budgets to increase efficiency but to do so in a way that does not destroy innovation. One of the techniques is to decentralize the responsibility for meeting budgets targets right down to the level of the first-line supervisor and worker. At Kirin's brewery in Kyoto, for example, managers at all levels compete against one another to report the biggest profits, and information about costs is posted on the wall for all em-

ployees to see how their day-to-day performance affects progress toward meeting goals and budget targets.[18] Some companies have divided up their work force into small teams and even split into many divisions so that employees are more aware of how the level of their performance affects costs and profits. The high-tech Kyocera company, for example, divided itself up into more than 800 small units (nicknamed amoebas) that trade among each other and try to get the most value for what they do.

In addition, recognizing that a large proportion of their costs are those they pay for inputs such as component parts, Japanese companies work with their suppliers to help them reduce their costs and raise product quality. Members of their research and development, engineering, and manufacturing functions become part of cross-company teams established to find new ways to reduce costs, not the least of which is to teach their suppliers how to use budgets and goals to reduce their costs. This new focus on budgets as a control system has paid off, and companies such as Toyota and Honda claim that by the year 2000 they will be competitive in world markets no matter how high the value of the yen.

contribution to corporate profitability. The way in which Japanese companies have been using operating budgets and setting challenging goals to increase efficiency is very instructive in this context, as Strategy in Action 12.3 shows.

Standardization

Standardization refers to the degree to which a company specifies how decisions are to be made so that employees' behavior becomes predictable.[19] In practice, there are three things an organization can standardize: *inputs, conversion activities,* and *outputs.*

1. *Standardization of inputs.* One way in which an organization can control the behavior of both people and resources is to standardize the inputs into the organization. This means that managers screen inputs according to preestablished criteria or standards and then decide which inputs to allow into the organization. If employees are the input in question, for example, then one way of standardizing them is to specify which qualities and skills they must possess and then to select only those applicants who possess them. Arthur Andersen, the accounting firm, is a very selective recruiter, as are most prestigious organizations.

If the inputs in question are raw materials or component parts, then the same considerations apply. The Japanese are renowned for the high quality and precise tolerances they demand from component parts to minimize problems with the product at the manufacturing stage. Just-in-time inventory systems also help standardize the flow of inputs.

2. *Standardization of conversion activities.* The aim of standardizing conversion activities is to program work activities so that they are done the same way time and time again. The goal is predictability. Behavior controls, such as rules and procedures, are among the chief means by which companies can standardize throughputs. Fast-food restaurants such as McDonald's and Burger King, for example, standardize all aspects of their restaurant operations; the result is standardized fast food.

3. *Standardization of outputs.* The goal of standardizing outputs is to specify what the performance characteristics of the final product or service should be—what the dimensions or tolerances the product should conform to, for example. To ensure that their products are standardized, companies apply quality control and use various criteria to measure this standardization. One criterion might be the number of goods returned from customers or the number of customers' complaints. On production lines, periodic sampling of products can indicate whether they are meeting performance characteristics.

    Given the intensity of foreign competition, companies are devoting extra resources to standardizing outputs, not just to reduce costs but to retain customers. If the product's performance satisfies customers, they will continue buying from that company. For example, if a consumer purchases a Japanese car and has no problems with its performance, which car is he or she most likely to buy next time? That is why companies such as U.S. carmakers have been emphasizing the quality dimension of their products. They know how important standardizing outputs is in a competitive market.

As with other kinds of controls, the use of behavior control is accompanied by potential pitfalls that must be managed if the organization is to avoid strategic problems. Top management must be careful to monitor and evaluate the usefulness of behavior controls over time. Rules constrain people and lead to standardized, predictable behavior. However, rules are always easier to establish than to get rid of, and over time the number of rules an organization uses tends to increase. As new developments lead to additional rules, often the old rules are not discarded, and the company becomes overly bureaucratized. Consequently, the organization and the people in it become inflexible and are slow to react to changing or unusual circumstances. Such inflexibility can reduce a company's competitive advantage by lowering the pace of innovation and by reducing customer responsiveness.

Similarly, inside the organization integration and coordination may fall apart as rules impede communication between functions. Managers must therefore be continually on the alert for opportunities to reduce the number of rules and procedures necessary to manage the business and should always prefer to discard a rule rather than add a new one. Hence, reducing the number of rules and procedures to the essential minimum is important. Strategic managers frequently neglect this task, however, and often only a change in strategic leadership brings the company back on course.

ORGANIZATIONAL CULTURE

The first function of strategic control is to shape the behavior of organizational members to ensure they are working toward organizational goals and to take corrective action if those goals are not being met. The second function of strategic control, however, is to keep organizational members focused on thinking about what is best for their organization in the future and to keep them looking for new opportunities to use organizational resources and competencies to create value. One important kind of strategic control system that serves this dual function of keeping organizational members goal-directed while open to new opportunities to use their skills to create value is organizational culture.

What Is Organizational Culture?

Organizational culture is the specific collection of values and norms that are shared by people and groups in an organization and that control the way they interact with each other and with stakeholders outside the organization.[20] *Organizational values* are beliefs and ideas about what kinds of goals members of an organization *should* pursue and about the appropriate kinds or standards of behavior organizational members *should* use to achieve these goals. The Opening Case recounts how Sam Walton succeeded in creating a strong culture at Wal-Mart. Jack Welch of General Electric is another CEO who is famous for the set of organizational values that he emphasizes, which include entrepreneurship, ownership, honesty, frankness, and open communication. By stressing entrepreneurship and ownership, Welch has been trying to get GE to behave less like a big bureaucracy and more like a collection of smaller and very adaptive companies. Welch has emphasized giving lower-level managers considerable decision-making autonomy and encouraged them to take risks—that is, to be more like entrepreneurs and less like corporate bureaucrats. The stress Welch places on values such as honesty, frankness, and open communication is a reflection of his belief that an open internal dialogue is necessary for successful operations at General Electric.[21]

From organizational values develop *organizational norms,* guidelines or expectations that *prescribe* appropriate kinds of behavior by employees in particular situations and control the behavior of organizational members toward one another. The norms of behavior for software programmers at Microsoft, the world's largest manufacturer of computer software, include working long hours and weekends, wearing whatever clothing is comfortable (but never a suit and tie), consuming junk food, and communicating with other employees via electronic mail.

Organizational culture functions as a kind of control in that strategic managers can influence the kind of values and norms that develop in an organization—values and norms that specify appropriate and inappropriate behaviors and that shape and influence the way its members behave.[22] Strategic managers such as Sam Walton and Jack Welch, for example, deliberately cultivate values that tell their subordinates they should perform their roles in innovative, creative ways. They establish and support norms dictating that, to be innovative and entrepreneurial, employees should feel free to experiment and go out on a limb even if there is a significant chance of failure. Top managers at organizations such as Intel, Microsoft, and Sun Microsystems also encourage their employees to adopt such values to support their commitment to innovation as a source of their competitive advantage.

Other managers, however, might cultivate values that say employees should always be conservative and cautious in their dealings with others, consult with their superiors before they make important decisions, and record their actions in writing so they can be held accountable for what happens. Managers of organizations such as chemical and oil companies, financial institutions, and insurance companies—any organization in which caution is needed—may encourage a conservative, cautious approach to making decisions.[23] In a bank or mutual fund, for example, the risk of losing all your investors' money makes a cautious approach to investing highly appropriate. Thus, we might expect that managers of different kinds of organizations will deliberately try to cultivate and develop the organizational values and norms that are best suited to their strategy and structure.

Organizational socialization is the term used to describe how people learn organizational culture. Through socialization, people internalize and learn the norms and values of the culture so that they *become* organizational members.[24] Control through culture is so powerful because, once these values have been internalized, they become a part of the individual's values, and the individual follows organizational values without thinking about them.[25] Very often the values and norms of an organization's culture are transmitted to its members through the stories, myths, and language that people in the organization use, as well as by other means (see Figure 12.4). The Opening Case, for example, discusses many of the stories that Wal-Mart's associates use to remind themselves about the values of the company. In addition, there are many myths about Sam Walton and about how frugal he was (he used to drive a thirty-year-old pickup truck, for example, and lived in a very modest home) to reinforce Wal-Mart's low-cost strategy and frugal approach. Some of the rites and ceremonies that Wal-Mart uses are a huge extravaganza every year at its headquarters to which all high-performing associates are invited and the Wal-Mart cheer that happens every morning at the store. The way in which culture developed in an IBM-Apple joint venture, described in Strategy in Action 12.4, also illustrates how organizational culture affects organizational members' behavior.

FIGURE 12.4
● ● ● ● ● ● ● ● ● ● ● ●

Ways of Transmitting
Organizational Culture

Taligent's New Culture

Taligent was created through a joint venture by IBM and Apple to explore ways of developing a new operating system that would compete with Microsoft's Windows. Taligent's CEO, Joe Guglielmi, was charged with creating a corporate culture for Taligent that would enable it to blend the human and technological resources of both IBM and Apple to produce innovative products. Because the cultures of IBM and Apple are so different, Guglielmi faced a considerable challenge in creating a culture for the new company.

Apple has a freewheeling culture that encourages the company's scientists and programmers to experiment and to form informal task forces and teams to solve problems. To encourage creativity and quick decision making, norms and values emphasize employees' empowerment and their freedom to find their own solutions to problems. A manager's role is not to monitor or oversee employee activities but to act as a facilitator and to provide employees with the resources they need in order to solve problems. The use of formal decision-making procedures is kept to a minimum, and face-to-face contact is the norm.

By contrast, IBM has a very conservative, hierarchical culture, and decision making is a formal, centralized process. Both this process and the approach to problem solving are highly structured; managers at all levels of the hierarchy have to follow set procedures for approving a project. Norms and values emphasize the importance of consensus, and the company has specified procedures for monitoring and evaluating performance on an ongoing basis. As a result, decision making at IBM tends to be slow because employees are used to following rules closely.

Guglielmi, brought up in the IBM culture, had to tackle the problem of managing people who, accustomed to Apple's much looser culture, resented having to report to IBM managers, who constantly wanted to know what was going on. For his part, Guglielmi disliked not knowing what his Apple employees were doing and missed the security that IBM's hierarchical culture provided. To develop a culture at Taligent that both Apple and IBM people could live with, Guglielmi accepted the informal Apple style, right down to the informal dress, to speed decision making and enhance creativity. However, he also created a system of output controls to measure team performance periodically because he believes that no control means no direction and less creativity. In the end, however, the task of merging such different cultures was too much for him, and as Taligent continued to perform poorly, in 1995 the venture was dissolved.

Culture and Strategic Leadership

Since both an organization's structure (the design of its task and reporting relationships) and its culture shape employees' behavior, it is crucial to match organizational structure and culture to implement strategy successfully. The ways that organizations design and create their structures are discussed in Chapter 11. The question that remains is, how do they design and create their cultures? In general, organizational culture is the product of strategic leadership.

The Influence of the Founder   First, organizational culture is created by the strategic leadership provided by an organization's founder and top managers. The organization's founder is particularly important in determining culture because the founder imprints his or her values and management style on the organization. Walt Disney's conservative influence on the company he established continued until well after his death, for example. Managers were afraid to experiment with new forms of entertainment because they were afraid Walt Disney wouldn't like it. It took the installation of a new management team under Michael Eisner to turn around the company's fortunes and allow it to deal with the realities of the new entertainment industry.

As another example, consider Hewlett Packard (HP), a recognized leader in the electronic instrumentation industry. Established in the 1940s, HP's culture is an outgrowth of the strong personal beliefs of the company's founders, Bill Hewlett and Dave Packard. Bill and Dave, as they were known within the company, created HP's culture in a formal statement of HP's basic values to serve everyone who had a stake in the company with integrity and fairness, including customers, suppliers, employees, stockholders, and society in general. Bill and Dave helped establish these values and build HP's culture by hiring like-minded people and by letting these values guide their own actions as managers. One outgrowth of their commitment to employees was a policy that HP would not be a "hire and fire company." This principle was severely tested on a couple of occasions in the 1970s, when declines in business forced the company to adopt the policy of a nine-day fortnight, under which all staff took a 10 percent pay cut and worked 10 percent fewer hours. While other companies took layoffs, HP kept its full complement of staff, thereby emphasizing the company's commitment to its employees.[26]

Thus, the values developed by HP's founders helped guide managerial action at HP and led directly to the policy of no layoffs. In turn, the commitment to employees that this action signaled has helped foster a productive work force at HP that is willing to go to great lengths to help the company succeed. The result has been superior company performance over time.

The leadership style established by the founder is transmitted to the company's managers, and as the company grows, it typically attracts new managers and employees who share the same values. Moreover, members of the organization typically recruit and select only those who do share their values. Thus, a company's culture becomes more and more distinct as its members become more similar. The virtue of these shared values and common culture is that it *increases integration and improves coordination among organizational members.* For example, the common language that typically emerges in an organization because people share the same beliefs and values facilitates cooperation among managers. Similarly, rules and procedures and direct supervision are less important when shared norms and values control behavior and motivate employees. When organizational members buy into cultural norms and values, this bonds them to the organization and increases their commitment to find new ways to help it succeed. That is, employees are more likely to commit themselves to organizational goals and work actively to develop new skills and competencies to help achieve those goals.

Organizational Structure Strategic leadership also affects organizational culture through the way managers design organizational structure, that is, the way managers delegate authority and divide up task relationships. Microsoft's chairman Bill Gates, for example, has always tried to keep his company as flat as possible and has decentralized authority to teams that are given control of all the resources they need to complete a project. As a result, he has created an entrepreneurial culture at Microsoft in which managers experiment and take risks. By contrast, Henry Ford I designed his company to give him absolute control over decision making. He even scrutinized the actions of his top management team, and his successor, Henry Ford II, continued to manage the company in a highly centralized way. The result for Ford Motor Car Company was an organizational culture in which managers became conservative and afraid to take risks, and the company was known for its slow pace of change and innovation. Thus, the way an organization designs its structure affects the cultural norms and values that develop within the organization. Managers need to be aware of this fact when implementing their strategies.

Adaptive and Inert Cultures

Few environments are stable for any prolonged period of time. Thus, if an organization is to survive, managers must take actions that enable an organization to adapt to environmental changes. If they do not take such action, they may find themselves faced with declining demand for their products. In the last section we suggested that strategic managers can build an organizational culture that encourages employees to find new opportunities to develop organizational competencies to exploit new opportunities in the environment. Recent research evidence has largely confirmed this. In a study of 207 companies, John Kotter and James Heskett distinguished between adaptive cultures and inert cultures.[27] **Adaptive cultures** are those that are innovative and encourage and reward initiative taking by middle- and lower-level managers. **Inert cultures** are those that are cautious and conservative, do not value middle- and lower-level managers' taking such action, and, indeed, may actively discourage such behavior.

According to Kotter and Heskett, managers in organizations with adaptive cultures are able to introduce changes in the way the organization operates, including changes in its strategy and structure, that allow the organization to adapt to changes occurring in the external environment. This does not occur at organizations with inert cultures. As a result, organizations with adaptive cultures are more likely to survive in a changing environment and indeed should have higher performance than organizations with inert cultures. This, in fact, is exactly what Kotter and Heskett found among the 207 companies they examined.

When an inert culture exists in an organization, strategic problems can result. If, for example, top managers all accept the same set of norms and values, the danger arises that they will be unable to steer the organization in a new strategic direction should the environment change and new competitors or technology demand such a change. Furthermore, having designed their structures, managers become used to the way they operate, and they rarely recognize the important effect structure has on cultural norms and values. Thus, organizational culture can promote inertia. At IBM, for instance, managers were unable to see—until it was too late—that the development of powerful personal computers and interactive, networking software would have long-term implications for IBM's cash cow, mainframe computers. Their blindness resulted from the tenets of IBM's culture that mainframes would always be the dominant product design and personal computers would only be appendages to mainframes. Moreover, IBM's tall, centralized structure slowed decision making and encouraged the development of conservative norms and values, making managers averse to risk and reluctant to challenge the status quo.

As Chapter 1 points out, cognitive biases can distort the decision-making process. Over time the norms and values of an organization's culture can bias decision making and cause managers to misperceive the reality of the situation facing their company. To prevent these strategic leadership problems from arising, great care needs to be taken in composing the top management team.

The Composition of the Top Management Team

The composition of the top management team helps determine the company's strategic direction, and the personalities and vision of the team's members establish the values and norms that lower-level managers will follow. Researchers have found that when a company has a diverse top management team, with managers drawn from different functional backgrounds or from different organizations or national cultures, the threat of inertia and of faulty decision making is reduced and the culture becomes adaptive. One of the reasons for IBM's failure to change was that almost all its top managers came from inside IBM and from the mainframe computer division. They had all been exposed to the same set of learning experiences and had developed similar norms and values. When Coca-Cola concluded that its top management team was becoming too inbred and homogeneous, it deliberately recruited a new top management team, including the CEO, composed of several foreign nationals, to manage its global strategy. Like Coca-Cola, many organizations are paying increasing attention to planning for executive succession in the top management team so they can manage their cultures over time.

Traits of Strong and Adaptive Corporate Cultures

Several scholars in the field have tried to uncover the common traits that strong and adaptive corporate cultures share and to find out whether there is a particular set of values that dominates adaptive cultures that is missing from weak or inert ones. An early but still influential attempt is T. J. Peters and R. H. Waterman's account of the values and norms characteristic of successful organizations and their cultures.[28] They argue that adaptive organizations show three common value sets. First, successful companies have values promoting a *bias for action*. The emphasis is on autonomy and entrepreneurship, and employees are encouraged to take risks, for example, to create new products, even though there is no assurance that these products will be winners. Managers are closely involved in the day-to-day operations of the company and do not simply make strategic decisions isolated in some ivory tower, and employees have a "hands-on, value-driven approach."

The second set of values stems from the *nature of the organization's mission*. The company must stick with what it does best and maintain control over its core activities. A company can easily get sidetracked into pursuing activities outside its area of expertise just because they seem to promise a quick return. Management should cultivate values so that a company sticks to its knitting, which means staying with the businesses it knows best. A company must also establish close relationships with customers as a way of improving its competitive position. After all, who knows more about a company's performance than those who use its products or services? By emphasizing customer-oriented values, organizations are able to learn customers' needs and improve their ability to develop products and services customers desire. All these management values are strongly represented in companies such as IBM, Hewlett Packard, and Toyota, which are sure of their mission and take constant steps to maintain it.

The third set of values bears on *how to operate the organization*. A company should try to establish an organizational design that will motivate employees to do their best. Inherent in this set of values is the belief that productivity is obtained through people and that respect for the individual is the primary means by which a company can create the right atmosphere for productive behavior. As William

Ouchi has noted, a similar philosophy pervades the culture of Japanese companies.[29] Many U.S. companies, for instance, Eastman Kodak, Procter & Gamble, and Levi Strauss, pay this kind of attention to their employees. An emphasis on entrepreneurship and respect for the employee leads to the establishment of a structure that gives employees the latitude to make decisions and motivates them to succeed. Because a simple structure and a lean staff best fit this situation, the organization should be designed with only the number of managers and hierarchical levels that are necessary to get the job done. The organization should also be sufficiently decentralized to permit employees' participation but centralized enough for management to make sure that the company pursues its strategic mission and that cultural values are followed.

These three main sets of values are at the heart of an organization's culture, and management transmits and maintains them through strategic leadership. Strategic managers need to establish the values and norms that will help them bring their organizations into the future. When this is accomplished, only those people who fit the values are recruited into the organization, and, through training, they become a part of the organization's culture. Thus, the types of control systems chosen should reinforce and build on one another in a cohesive way. Organizational culture cannot by itself make structure work. It must be backed by output and behavior controls and matched to a reward system so that employees will in fact cultivate organizational norms and values and pursue organizational goals.

STRATEGIC REWARD SYSTEMS

Organizations also strive to control employees' behavior by linking reward systems to their control systems.[30] Based on its strategy (low cost or differentiation, for example), strategic managers must decide which behaviors to reward. They then create a control system to measure these behaviors and link the reward structure to them. Determining how to relate rewards to performance is a crucial strategic decision because it determines the incentive structure that affects the way managers and employees at all levels in the organization behave. You learned earlier how structure and control shape employees' behavior. The design of the organization's incentive system is a vital element in the control process because it motivates and reinforces desired behaviors.

As Chapter 2 points out, top managers can be encouraged to work in the shareholders' interests by being rewarded with stock options linked to the company's long-term performance. Furthermore, companies such as Kodak and GM require managers to buy company stock. When managers are made shareholders, they are more motivated to pursue long-term rather than short-term goals. Similarly, in designing a pay system for salespeople, the choice is whether to motivate salespeople through straight salary or salary plus a bonus based on how much is sold. Neiman Marcus, the luxury retailer, pays employees a straight salary because it wants to encourage high-quality service but to discourage a hard-sell approach. Thus, there are no incentives based on quantity sold. On the other hand, the pay system for rewarding car salespeople encourages high-pressure selling; it typically contains a large bonus for the number and price of cars sold.

Since the design of a company's reward system affects the way managers and employees behave, the reward system also affects the *kinds of norms, values, and culture that develop in an organization.* Thus, top management teams rewarded solely by salary and those rewarded by stock options linked to performance are likely to have different norms and values. Specifically, top management teams rewarded with stock options may be more entrepreneurial and more concerned with increasing quality and innovation than those that lack this reward. Companies such as Sears, GM, Kodak, and Westinghouse, which previously made little attempt to link performance to rewards, had slow-moving, bureaucratic cultures. All these companies now require managers to own company stock.

We now take a closer look at the types of reward systems available to strategic managers.[31] Generally, reward systems are found at the individual and group or total organizational levels. Often these systems are used in combination; for example, merit raises at the individual level may be accompanied by a bonus based on divisional or corporate performance. Within each type, several forms of reward systems are available.

Individual Reward Systems

Piecework Plans Piecework plans are used when outputs can be objectively measured. Essentially, employees are paid on the basis of some set amount for each unit of output produced. Piecework plans are most commonly used for employees on production lines, where individuals work alone and their performance can be directly measured. Because this system encourages quantity rather than quality, the company normally applies stringent quality controls to ensure that the quality is acceptable.

Commission Systems Commission systems resemble piecework systems, except that they are normally tied not to what is produced, but to how much is sold. Thus, they are most commonly found in sales situations. Often the salaries of salespeople are based principally on commission to encourage superior performance. First-rate salespeople can earn more than $1 million per year in many industries.

Bonus Plans Bonus plans at the individual level generally reward the performance of a company's key individuals, such as the CEO and senior vice presidents.[32] The performance of these people is visible to the organization as a whole and to stakeholders such as shareholders. Consequently, there is a strong rationale for paying these individuals according to some measure of functional or divisional performance. A company must proceed carefully, however, if it is to avoid problems such as emphasis on short-run rather than long-term objectives. For example, paying bonuses based on quarterly or yearly ROI rather than on five-year growth can have a markedly different effect on the way strategic managers behave. Insisting that members of a top management team own stock in the company motivates managers and ties their interests to those of the shareholders. As Strategy in Action 12.5 details, Campbell Soup was one of the first companies to take this approach.

Promotion Last, but not least, promotion is an important source of reward for individuals at all organizational levels. Managers compete for promotion to the next level in the hierarchy; the highest-performing functional managers become the next

How to Motivate a Top Manager

For years Campbell Soup, based in Camden, New Jersey, had experienced deteriorating performance. Its operating costs were well above its archrival, H. J. Heinz, which under the leadership of its CEO, Anthony J. F. O'Reilly, had been achieving record sales and profits. O'Reilly is paid a very high salary and bonus; in fact in 1992 he earned almost $37 million in salary and stock options. Heinz's other top managers are also given stock options. It was no surprise, therefore, when in 1993 Campbell Soup's board of directors, attributing Heinz's superior performance to its stock option plan for top managers, announced that it, too, was establishing a stock option plan for its CEO, David Johnson, and more than seventy other managers.

Under the terms of the plan, the CEO was required to hold Campbell's shares worth three times his 1992 salary of $757,000 by the end of 1994. Senior vice presidents were expected to hold shares worth one year's salary; and senior executives, shares worth one-half their annual salaries. Top managers would have to hold these shares for as long as they worked for the company. Clearly, Campbell's goal was to tie the fortunes of its managers to the fortunes of the company, and the new reward structure has worked. With their new incentives, managers found many ways to reduce costs and by 1996 top managers earned millions of dollars in capital appreciation on their stock as the price of Campbell's stock soared.

generation of divisional managers, and the highest-performing divisional managers become the next generation of corporate managers. Promotion is so important because salary and bonuses rise sharply as managers ascend the hierarchy. The CEO often earns in salary alone 50 percent more than the person next in the chain of command. In 1996, for example, the average CEO in the top *Fortune* 200 companies earned nearly $4.7 million dollars, almost double the $2.4 million earned by the next highest-ranking executive.[33] The rewards from promotion are enormous, and this is why organizational career ladders are closely watched by aspiring managers. Some organizations deliberately encourage promotion tournaments, contests between managers for promotion, to motivate high performance.

Group and Organizational Reward Systems

Group and organizational reward systems provide additional ways in which companies can relate pay to performance. The increasing use of product-team structures and cross-functional teams has led many organizations to develop some form of group-based rewards system to encourage high team performance. The most common reward systems at these levels are group bonuses, profit sharing, employee stock options, and organization bonuses.

Group-Based Bonus Systems   Sometimes a company can establish project teams, or work groups, that perform all the operations needed to turn out a product or provide a service. This arrangement makes it possible to measure group performance and offer rewards on the basis of group productivity. The system can be highly motivating because employees are allowed to develop the best work procedures for doing the job and are responsible for improving their own productivity. For example, Wal-Mart supports a group bonus plan based on controlling shrinkage (that is, employee theft).

Profit Sharing Systems   Profit sharing plans are designed to reward employees on the basis of the profit a company earns in any one time period. Such plans encourage employees to take a broad view of their activities and feel connected with the company as a whole. Wal-Mart uses this method as well to develop its organizational culture.

Employee Stock Option Plans   Rather than reward employees on the basis of short-term profits, a company sometimes establishes an employee stock ownership plan (ESOP) and allows employees to buy its shares at below-market prices, heightening employees' motivation. As shareholders, the employees focus not only on short-term profits but also on long-term capital appreciation, for they are now the company's owners. Over time, if enough employees participate, they can control a substantial stock holding, as do the employees of United Airlines, and thus become vitally interested in the company's performance. ESOPs can be very important in developing an adaptive corporate culture because employees share in the profits that result.

Organization Bonus Systems   Profit is not the only basis on which a company can reward organizationwide performance. Rewards are also commonly based on cost savings, quality increases, and production increases obtained in the most recent time period. Because these systems usually require that outputs be measured accurately, they are most common in assembly-line organizations or in service companies, where it is possible to cost out the price of the services of personnel. The systems are mainly a backup to other forms of pay systems. In rare situations, however, they become the principal means of control. That is the case at Lincoln Electric, a company renowned for the success of its cost-savings group plan.

Control through organizational reward systems complements all the other forms of control we discuss in this chapter. Rewards act as the oil that makes a control system function effectively. To ensure that the right strategic behaviors are being rewarded, rewards should be closely linked to an organization's strategy. Moreover, they should be so designed that they do not lead to conflicts among divisions, functions, or individuals. Since organizational structure and organizational control and reward systems are not independent dimensions of organizational design but are highly interrelated, they must be compatible if an organization is to implement its strategy successfully. Matching structure and control to strategy is the issue we focus on in Chapter 13.

SUMMARY OF CHAPTER
• • • • • • • • • • • • • • • • • •

Choosing a control system to match the firm's strategy and structure offers management a number of important challenges. Management must select controls that provide a framework to monitor, measure, and evaluate accurately whether or not it has achieved its goals and strategic objectives. Financial and output controls must be backed up with behavior controls and organi-zational culture to ensure that the firm is achieving its goals in the most efficient way possible. In general, these controls should reinforce one another, and care must be taken to ensure that they do not result in unforeseen consequences, such as competition among functions, divisions, and individuals. It is the difficulty of changing organizational culture that many top managers point to when they talk about reengineering their organization so that it can pursue new strategic goals. This is because culture is the product of the complex interaction of many factors such as top management, organizational structure, and the organization's reward and incentive systems. This chapter makes the following main points:

✔ Organizational structure does not operate effectively unless the appropriate control and incentive systems are in place to shape and motivate employees' behavior.

✔ Strategic control is the process of setting targets, monitoring, evaluating, and rewarding organizational performance. The balanced scorecard approach to strategic control suggests that managers should develop strategic control systems that measure all important aspects of their organization's performance.

✔ Control takes place at all levels in the organization: corporate, divisional, functional, and individual.

✔ Effective control systems are flexible, accurate, and able to provide quick feedback to strategic planners.

✔ Many kinds of performance standards are available to implement a company's strategy. The kinds of measures managers choose affect the way a company operates.

✔ Control systems range from those directed at measuring outputs to those measuring behaviors or actions.

✔ The two main forms of financial control are stock market price and return on investment (ROI).

✔ Output controls establish goals for divisions, functions, and individuals. They can be used only when outputs can be objectively measured and are often linked to a management by objectives system.

✔ Behavior controls are achieved through budgets, standardization, and rules and procedures.

✔ Organizational culture is the collection of norms and values that govern the way in which people act and behave inside the organization.

✔ An organization's culture is the product of a founder's or top management team's values and attitudes, of the way managers choose to design the organization's structure, and of the strategic reward systems managers use to shape and motivate employees' behavior.

✔ An organization's reward systems constitute the final form of control. A company designs its reward systems to provide employees with the incentives to make its structure work effectively and to align their interests with organizational goals and objectives.

✔ Organizations use all these forms of control simultaneously. Management must select and combine those that are consistent with each other and with the strategy and structure of the organization.

DISCUSSION QUESTIONS

1. What are the relationships among differentiation, integration, and strategic control systems? Why are these relationships important?

2. For each of the structures we discuss in Chapter 11, outline the most suitable control systems.

3. What kind of control and reward systems would you be likely to find in (a) a small manufacturing company, (b) a chain store, (c) a high-tech company, and (d) a Big Five accounting firm?

Practicing Strategic Management

SMALL-GROUP EXERCISE
Creating a Strategic Control System

Break up into groups of three to five people, and discuss the following scenario:

You are managers in charge of project teams of design engineers, each of which is working on a different aspect of the design for a new generation of luxury sports sedans. You are meeting to design a control system that will be used to motivate and reward all the teams. Your objective is to create a control system that will help to increase the performance of each team separately and facilitate cooperation between the teams, something that is necessary since the various projects are interlinked and affect one another (the different parts of the car must fit together). Since competition in the luxury-car market is intense, it is imperative that the car be of the highest quality possible and incorporate all state-of-the-art technology.

1. Using the balanced scorecard approach, discuss what kind of output controls are most important for measuring the teams' performance.

2. Discuss what kinds of behavior controls you should establish to facilitate interactions both within the teams and between the teams.

3. Discuss how you might go about developing a culture to help promote high team performance.

EXPLORING THE WEB
What Kind of Control?

Enter Hewlett Packard's Web site and, in particular, the location on the "HP Way" (www.jobs.hp.com/why HP/HP way/hp.com/). Click on the various subheadings in this location and, in particular, the section on operating philosophy and corporate objectives.

1. What are the main elements of the HP Way?

2. How does the HP Way lead to an organizational culture that helps Hewlett Packard achieve its strategies?

3. How easy would it be to implement the HP Way and culture in other companies?

Search the Web for an example of a company that uses one or more of the types of control systems discussed in the chapter. What control system is it? Why does the company use it?

ARTICLE FILE 12

Find an example of a company that has recently changed one or more of its control and incentive systems. Which of its control systems did it change (for instance, output control or culture)? Why did it make the change? What does it hope to achieve by the change? How will changing the control system affect the way its structure operates?

STRATEGIC MANAGEMENT PROJECT
Module 12

For this part of your project, you need to obtain information about your company's control and incentive systems. This information may be hard to obtain unless you are doing your project on a real company and can interview managers directly. However, some forms of information, such as compensation for top management, are available in the company's annual reports or 10-K. If your company is well known, magazines such as *Fortune* or *Business Week* frequently report on corporate culture or control issues. Nevertheless, you may be forced to make some bold assumptions to complete this part of the project.

1. What are the major kinds of control problems facing your company? How do these control problems relate to your organization's structure, which you identified in the last chapter?

2. With the information at your disposal, list the main kinds of control systems used by your organization to solve these problems. Specifically, what use does your company make of (a) financial controls, (b) output controls, (c) behavior controls, and (d) organizational culture?

3. What kinds of behaviors is the organization trying to (a) shape and (b) motivate through the use of these control systems?

4. What role does the top management team play in creating the culture of your organization? Can you identify the characteristic norms and values that describe the way people behave in your organization? How does the design of the organization's structure affect its culture?

5. Collect the salary and compensation data for your company's top management from its annual reports. How does the organization use rewards to shape and motivate its managers? For example, how much of top managers' total compensation is based on bonuses and stock options, and how much is based on straight salary?

6. Does the organization offer other kinds of employees any incentives based on performance? What kinds of incentives? For example, is there an employee stock ownership plan in operation?

7. Based on this analysis, do you think that your organization's control system is functioning effectively? For example, is your organization collecting the right kinds of information? Is it measuring the right kinds of behavior? How could the control system be improved?

8. To what degree is there a match between your company's structure and its control and incentive systems? That is, are its control systems allowing it to operate its structure effectively? How could they be improved?

CLOSING CASE

Getting It Right at McDonald's

In the restaurant business, maintaining product quality is a major problem because the quality of the food, the service, and the restaurant premises varies with the chefs and waiters as they come and go. If a customer gets a bad meal, poor service, or dirty silverware, not only may that customer be lost, but other potential customers, too, as negative comments travel by word of mouth.

In this context consider the problem Ray Kroc, the man who pioneered McDonald's growth, faced when McDonald's franchises began to open by the thousands throughout the United States. How could he maintain product quality to protect the company's reputation as it grew? Moreover, how could he try to increase efficiency and make the organization responsive to the needs of customers to promote its competitive advantage? Kroc's answer was to develop a sophisticated control system, which specified every detail of how each McDonald's restaurant was to be operated and managed.

Kroc's control system was based on several components. First, he developed a comprehensive system of rules and procedures for both franchise owners and employees to follow in running each restaurant. The most effective way to perform such tasks as cooking burgers, making fries, greeting customers, and cleaning tables was worked out in advance, written down in rule books, and then taught to each McDonald's manager and employee through a formal training process. For example, prospective franchise owners had to attend "Hamburger University," the company's training center in Chicago, where in an intensive, month-long program they learnt all aspects of a McDonald's operation. In turn, they were expected to train their work force and make sure that employees understood operating procedures thoroughly. Kroc's goal in establishing this system of rules and procedures was to standardize McDonald's activities so that whatever franchise customers walked into they would always find the same level of quality in food and service. If customers always get what they expect from a restaurant, the restaurant has developed superior customer responsiveness.

However, Kroc's attempt to control quality went well beyond written rules and procedures specifying the performance of various tasks. He also developed McDonald's franchise system to help the company control its structure as it grew. Kroc believed that a manager who is also a franchise owner (and who receives a large share of the profits) is more motivated to maintain higher efficiency and quality than a manager paid on a straight salary. Thus, McDonald's reward and incentive system allowed it to keep control over its operating structure as it expanded. Moreover, McDonald's was very selective in selling its franchises; the franchisees had to be people with the skills and capabilities to manage the business, and a franchise could be revoked if the holder did not maintain quality standards.

McDonald's managers frequently visited restaurants to monitor franchisees, and franchisees were allowed to operate their restaurant only according to McDonald's rules. For instance, they could not put in a television or otherwise modify the restaurant. McDonald's was also able to monitor and control the performance of its franchisees through output control. Each franchisee provided McDonald's with information about how many meals were sold, what operating costs were, and so forth. So, using this mix of personal supervision and output control, managers at McDonald's corporate headquarters could quickly learn whether sales in a franchise declined suddenly, and thus they could take corrective action.

Within each restaurant, franchise owners also paid particular attention to training their employees and instilling in them the norms and values of quality service. Having learned about McDonald's core cultural values at their training sessions, franchise owners were expected to transmit McDonald's concepts of efficiency, quality, and customer service to their employees. The development of shared norms, values, and an organizational culture also helped McDonald's standardize employees' behavior so that customers would know how they would be treated in a McDonald's restaurant. Moreover, McDonald's tried to

include customers in its culture. It had customers bus their own tables, but it also showed concern for customers' needs by building playgrounds, offering Happy Meals, and organizing birthday parties for customers' children. In creating its family-oriented culture, McDonald's was ensuring future customer loyalty because satisfied children are likely to remain loyal customers as adults.

Through all these means, McDonald's developed a control system that allowed it to expand its organization successfully and create an organizational structure that has led to superior efficiency, quality, and customer responsiveness. Its control system has played an important role in McDonald's becoming the largest and most successful fast-food company in the world, and many other fast-food companies have imitated it.

Case Discussion Questions

1. What were the main elements of the control system created by Ray Kroc?

2. In what ways would this control system facilitate McDonald's strategy of global expansion?

CHAPTER 13

Matching Structure and Control to Strategy

Opening Case: A Turnaround at Digital Equipment

Overview

Structure and Control at the Functional Level

Structure and Control at the Business Level

Designing a Global Structure

Structure and Control at the Corporate Level

Special Issues in Strategy/Structure Choice

Closing Case: Hughes' Aircraft Reengineers Its Structure

OPENING CASE

A Turnaround at Digital Equipment

By 1992 Digital Equipment, the computer maker, had lost more than $4 billion. It was losing $3 million every 24 hours, and many analysts thought that the company was near bankruptcy. Digital's problems had arisen because the growing popularity of the personal computer had eroded demand for its main product, minicomputers, which operated on Digital's proprietary technology. In an attempt to save the company, the board of directors ousted Digital's CEO and founder, Pat Olsen, and replaced him with Robert Palmer, a successful manager who had been head of Digital's semiconductor division and its manufacturing operations.

Palmer, trying to reverse Digital's desperate situation, decided to make major changes to its strategy and develop a new structure to implement the strategy. He wanted Digital to build sales of its new line of minicomputers that used its brand-new, high-speed Alpha chip. He decided to focus the company's efforts on selling these new minicomputers to companies in nine major indus-

tries that included banking, retailing, and manufacturing. To implement this strategy, Palmer introduced a multidivisional structure based on nine self-contained customer-focused units that operated separately and that specialized in providing a complete line of hardware and software products to one particular type of industry customer. At the same time, he began downsizing the organization, reducing Digital's work force by more than 30,000 employees, partly through layoffs in its corporate staff and engineering and manufacturing managers and partly by selling off noncore divisions.

Although Palmer had engineered a match between Digital's new strategy and its new structure, it did not solve the company's problems. Despite the promise of better customer service, Digital's 450,000 existing customers were wary of buying a new generation of hardware and software products from a company that still seemed to have a bleak future in the computer industry. Moreover, the new structure was causing its own problems, because each self-contained customer division was essentially doing the same thing, and the duplication of activities was leading to increased costs. Essentially, bureaucratic costs were still too high, and the structure was not helping to promote Digital's strategy.

Realizing these problems, Palmer once again moved quickly to find a new strategy/structure fit to turn the company around. Realizing that Digital's customers were worried about having to use the company's proprietary software, Palmer engineered a deal with Bill Gates, CEO of the leading software company Microsoft. Digital and Microsoft formed a strategic alliance whereby Microsoft would modify its state-of-the-art new networking software, Windows NT, to work on Digital's new high-speed Alpha-chip minicomputers. Palmer also made a deal with Oracle, the leading database software company, that Digital would sell its own database business to Oracle if Oracle would develop software to take advantage of Digital's Alpha chip.[1] Once again, customers would have the assurance they were buying state-of-the-art software matched to state-of-the-art hardware.

To implement this new strategy of focusing on the hardware side of the computer business, Palmer once again reorganized Digital's structure. He dissolved the customer-based divisions and in their place created five self-contained divisions based on the major products they sold (minicomputers, PCs, and so on). He also reduced levels in the hierarchy, cutting the work force by another 20,000 employees, and then he instituted strict financial controls and a management by objectives system that focused on the bottom line. Top managers who failed to meet their goals were replaced by those who could, and Digital's structure began to run mean and lean.

Palmer's new strategy/structure fit has succeeded dramatically. Sales of Digital's flagship minicomputers have soared as its existing customers have upgraded to its new machines, and many new customers, confident that they will be able to use leading software from Oracle and Microsoft on state-of-the-art machines, have placed large orders for its high-end minicomputers and data servers. Analysts expected Digital to earn more than $600 million profit on sales of more than $15.3 billion in 1996 and project that profits will increase dramatically throughout the 1990s as Digital exploits the potential of its new strategy and structure.

OVERVIEW

At Digital Equipment, Robert Palmer and his top management team moved to implement the right mix of structure and control systems so that the company could pursue a new strategy to manage the competitive environment. In this chapter we discuss how the nature of a company's corporate-, business-, and functional-level strategy affects the choice of structure and control systems—in other words, how strategic managers should match different forms of structure and control to strategy. As we emphasize in Chapter 1, the issue facing strategic managers is to match strategy formulation with strategy implementation. All the tools of strategy formulation and implementation are discussed in previous chapters. In this chapter we put the two sides of the equation together and examine how strategic managers match strategy and structure to build competitive advantage.

First, we consider how functional-level strategy and the attempt to achieve superior efficiency, quality, innovation, and customer responsiveness affect structure and control. Second, we examine how a company's choice of generic business-level strategy influences the choice of structure and control for implementing the strategy. Third, we focus on the implementation of a global strategy and discuss how to match different global strategies with different global structures. Finally, we take up the special problems that different kinds of corporate-level strategy pose for strategic managers in designing a structure and note how changes in corporate-level strategy over time affect the form of structure and control systems adopted by a company. By the end of this chapter, you will understand how to match strategy to structure to create a high-performing organization.

STRUCTURE AND CONTROL AT THE FUNCTIONAL LEVEL

Chapter 5, on functional-level strategy, discusses how a company's functions can help it achieve superior efficiency, quality, innovation, and customer responsiveness—the four building blocks of competitive advantage. Chapter 5 also discusses how strategic managers can help each function to develop a distinctive competency. We now examine the way strategic managers can create a structure and control system to encourage the development of various distinctive functional competencies, or skills.

Decisions at the functional level fall into two categories: choices about the level of vertical differentiation and choices about monitoring and evaluation systems. (Choices about horizontal differentiation are *not* relevant here because we are considering each function individually.) The choices depend on the distinctive competency a company is pursuing.

Manufacturing

In manufacturing, functional strategy usually centers on improving efficiency, quality, and responsiveness to customers. A company must create an organizational setting in which managers can learn from experience-curve effects how to economize on costs. Traditionally, to move down the experience curve quickly, companies have exercised tight control over work activities and employees and developed tall, centralized hierarchies to squeeze out costs wherever possible. As part of their attempt to increase efficiency, companies have also made great use of behavior and output controls to reduce costs. Activities are standardized. For example, human inputs are standardized through the recruitment and training of skilled personnel, the work process is standardized or programmed to reduce costs, and quality control is used to make sure that outputs are being produced correctly. In addition, managers use output controls such as operating budgets to monitor and contain costs continuously.

Recently, however, following the lead of Japanese companies such as Toyota and Sony, which operate total quality management (TQM) and flexible manufacturing systems, many U.S. companies have been moving to change the way they design the manufacturing setting. As Chapter 5 discusses, successful TQM requires a different approach to organizational design. With TQM, the inputs and involvement of all employees in the decision-making process are necessary to improve production efficiency and quality. Thus, it becomes necessary to decentralize authority to motivate employees to improve the production process. In TQM, work teams are created and workers are given the responsibility and authority to discover and implement improved work procedures. Quality control circles are created to exchange information and suggestions about problems and work procedures. A bonus system or employee stock ownership plan (ESOP) is frequently established to motivate workers and to allow them to share in the increased value that TQM often produces.

No longer are managers employed purely to supervise workers and make sure they are doing the job. Managers assume the role of coach and facilitator, and team members jointly take on the supervisory burden, reducing bureaucratic costs. Work teams are often given the responsibility to control and discipline their own members and even to decide who should work in their team. Frequently, work teams develop strong norms and values and work-group culture becomes an important means of control; this type of control matches the new decentralized team approach.

Although workers are given more freedom to control their activities, the extensive use of output controls and the continuous measurement of efficiency and quality ensure that the work team's activities meet the goals set for the function by management. Efficiency and quality increase as new and improved work rules and procedures are developed to raise the level of standardization. The aim is to find the match between structure and control and a TQM approach, so that manufacturing develops the distinctive competency that leads to superior efficiency and quality.

Research and Development

The functional strategy for a research and development department is to develop a distinctive competency in innovation and to develop technology that results in products that fit customers' needs. Consequently, the R&D department's structure and control systems should be designed to provide the coordination necessary for scientists and engineers to bring products quickly to market. Moreover, these systems should motivate R&D scientists to develop innovative products or processes.

In practice, R&D departments typically have flat, decentralized structures that group scientists into teams. Flat structures give research and development personnel the freedom and autonomy to be innovative. Furthermore, because the performance of scientists and engineers can typically be judged only over the long term (because it may take several years for a project to be completed), adding layers of hierarchy would simply raise bureaucratic costs and waste resources.[2]

By using teams, strategic managers can take advantage of scientists' ability to work jointly in solving problems and to enhance each other's performance. In small teams, too, the professional values and norms that highly trained employees bring to the situation promote coordination. A culture for innovation frequently emerges to control employees' behavior, as has occurred at Motorola and Intel, where the race to be first energizes the R&D teams. Strategy in Action 13.1 describes Intel's use of R&D teams to innovate and improve computer chips.

To spur teams to work effectively, the reward system should be linked to the performance of the team. If scientists, individually or in a team, do not share in the profits a company obtains from its new products or processes, they may have little motivation to contribute wholeheartedly to the team. To prevent the departure of their key employees and to encourage high motivation, companies such as Merck, Intel, and Microsoft give their researchers stock options and rewards tied to their individual performance, their team's performance, and the company's performance. As a result many of these scientists and engineers have become multimillionaires.

Sales

As with research and development, the sales function usually has a flat structure. Most commonly, three hierarchical levels—sales director, regional or product sales managers, and individual salespeople—can accommodate even large sales forces. Flat structures are possible because the organization does not depend on direct supervision for control. Salespeople's activities are often complex; moreover, because they are

Intel's R&D Department

Intel is the world leader in the development of chips, the microprocessors that are the heart of all computers. Intel is very profitable, and in 1995 it earned record profits because it had a monopoly on the production of the Pentium chip, which is still the industry standard. In the race to produce new and improved chips, Intel is constantly under attack from companies such as Motorola, Digital Equipment, and Japan's NEC and has to protect its competitive advantage. Consequently, the need to develop new chips or improved versions of existing ones (such as the Pentium Pro) forms the basis of Intel's differentiation strategy.

To speed product development, Intel has developed a team structure in its R&D department. To try to ensure that it will always have the leading-edge technology, the company has six different teams working on the next generation of chips so that each team's innovations can be put together to make the final product, as was done to make the Pentium chip that Intel unveiled in 1993. However, it also has six teams working simultaneously on the subsequent generation of chips, and six teams working on the generation of chips to follow that one. In other words, to sustain its leading-edge technology and maintain its monopoly, the company has created a team structure in which its scientists and engineers work on the frontiers of chip research so they can control the technology of tomorrow. This approach has certainly paid off for Intel. The company's stock price has more than quadrupled in the 1990s. Indeed, Intel is expected to outperform the market for as long as its teams succeed in making the company the innovation leader in the chip industry.

dispersed in the field, these employees are difficult to monitor. Rather than depend on the hierarchy, the sales function usually employs output and behavior controls.

Output controls, such as specific sales goals or goals for increasing responsiveness to customers, can be easily established and monitored by supervisors. Then output controls can be linked to a bonus reward system to motivate salespeople. Behavior controls, for instance, detailed reports that salespeople file describing their interactions with customers, can also be used to standardize salespeople's behavior and make it easier for supervisors to review their performance.[3]

Similar design considerations apply to the other functions, such as accounting, finance, engineering, and human resource management. Managers must select the right combination of structure and control mechanisms to allow each function to contribute to achieving superior efficiency, quality, innovation, and responsiveness to customers. When, as now, reducing costs is often required for survival, more and more companies are flattening their functional hierarchies and decentralizing control to reduce bureaucratic costs. Strategic managers must develop control and incentive systems that align employees' interests with those of the organization and that motivate employees.

STRUCTURE AND CONTROL AT THE BUSINESS LEVEL

Building competitive advantage through organizational design starts at the functional level. However, the key to successful strategy implementation is a structure that *links and combines* the skills and competencies of a company's value creation functions, allowing it to pursue a business-level strategy successfully. In this section we consider the organizational design issues for a company seeking to implement one of the generic competitive business-level strategies to build and sustain its competitive advantage.

Generic Business-Level Strategies

Designing the right mix of structure and control at the business level is a continuation of designing a company's functions. Having implemented the right structure and control system for each individual function, the company must then implement the organizational arrangements so that all the functions can be managed together to achieve business-level strategy objectives. Because the focus is on managing *cross-functional relationships*, the choice of horizontal differentiation (the grouping of organizational activities) and integration for achieving business-level strategies becomes very important.[4] Control systems must also be selected with the monitoring and evaluating of cross-functional activities in mind. Table 13.1 summarizes the appropriate organizational structure and control systems that companies can use when following a low-cost, differentiation, or focus strategy.

Cost-Leadership Strategy and Structure

The aim of the cost-leadership strategy is to make the company pursuing it the lowest-cost producer in the market.[5] At the business level, this means reducing costs not just in production, but across *all* functions in the organization, including research and development, and sales and marketing.

If a company is pursuing a cost-leadership strategy, its research and development efforts probably focus on product and process development rather than on the more expensive product innovation, which carries no guarantee of success. In

TABLE 13.1

Generic Strategy, Structure, and Control

	Strategy		
	Cost Leadership	**Differentiation**	**Focus**
Appropriate structure	Functional	Product team or matrix	Functional
Integrating mechanisms	Center on manufacturing	Center on R&D or marketing	Center on product or customer
Output controls	Great use (e.g., cost control)	Some use (e.g., quality goals)	Some use (e.g., cost and quality)
Behavior controls	Some use (e.g., budgets, standardization)	Great use (e.g., rules, budgets)	Some use (e.g., budgets)
Organizational culture	Little use (e.g., quality control circles)	Great use (e.g., norms and values)	Great use (e.g., norms and values)

other words, the company stresses research that improves product characteristics or lowers the cost of making existing products. Similarly, a company tries to decrease the cost of sales and marketing by offering a standard product to a mass market rather than by offering different products aimed at different market segments, which is also more expensive.[6]

To implement a cost-leadership strategy, the company chooses a structure and control system that has a low level of bureaucratic costs. As we discuss in earlier chapters, bureaucratic costs are those of managing a company's strategy through structure and control. Structure and control are expensive, and the more complex the structure, that is, the higher its level of differentiation and integration, the higher are bureaucratic costs. To economize on bureaucratic costs, a cost leader will, therefore, choose the simplest or least expensive structure compatible with the needs of the low-cost strategy.

In practice, the structure chosen is normally a functional structure. This structure is relatively inexpensive to operate because it is based on a low level of differentiation and integration. Even in a functional structure, cross-functional teams can be organized around the manufacturing function. For example, a TQM program implemented through task forces and teams can be developed to integrate the activities of manufacturing and the other functions. This allows for continuous improvements in the rules and procedures for standardizing task activities, which is a major source of cost saving.[7]

A cost-leadership company also tries to keep its structure as flat as possible to reduce bureaucratic costs, and functional structures have relatively flat structures. The cost leader continuously evaluates whether or not it needs that extra level in the hierarchy and whether or not it can decentralize authority (perhaps to the work group) to keep costs low. Seagate Technology, a producer of hard disks, is an example of a cost leader that continually streamlines its structure to maintain a competitive advantage. It periodically reduces levels in the hierarchy and institutes strict production controls to minimize costs. This process has kept it ahead of its Japanese competitors. Similarly, John Reed, the chairman of Citicorp, recently flattened his organization's structure, wiping out two levels of management and terminating dozens of executives to reduce costs. His cost-cutting efforts helped turn a loss of $457 million in 1991 into record profits throughout the 1990s, and Citicorp's share price has soared as a result.[8]

To further reduce costs, cost-leadership companies try to use the cheapest and easiest forms of control available—output controls. For each function, a company adopts output controls that allow it to monitor and evaluate functional performance closely. In the manufacturing function, for example, the company imposes tight controls and stresses meeting budgets based on production, cost, or quality targets.[9] In research and development, too, the emphasis falls on the bottom line. R&D personnel, eager to demonstrate their contribution to cost savings, may focus their efforts on improving process technology, where actual savings are calculable.

H. J. Heinz clearly illustrates such efforts. In following a cost-leadership strategy, it places enormous emphasis on production improvements that can reduce the cost of a can of beans. As with manufacturing and research and development, the sales function is closely monitored, and sales targets are usually challenging. Cost-leadership companies, however, are likely to reward employees through generous incentive and bonus plans to encourage high performance. Often their culture is based on values that emphasize the bottom line. Lincoln Electric and PepsiCo are other examples of such companies.

In short, pursuing a successful cost-leadership strategy requires close attention to the design of structure and control to limit bureaucratic costs. Managers, rules, and organizational control mechanisms cost money, and low-cost companies must try to economize when implementing their structures. When a company's competitive advantage depends on building and sustaining a low-cost advantage, adopting the right organizational arrangements is vital.

Differentiation Strategy and Structure

To pursue a differentiation strategy, a company must develop a distinctive competency in a function such as research and development or marketing and sales. As we have already discussed, doing so usually means that a company produces a wider range of products, serves more market niches, and generally has to customize its products to the needs of different customers. These factors make it difficult to standardize activities; they also increase the demands made on functional managers. Hence, the differentiated company usually employs a more complex structure—that is, a structure with a higher level of differentiation and integration—than the cost leader. The bureaucratic costs of a differentiator are higher than those of a cost leader, but these costs are recouped through the higher value it adds to its differentiated products.

To make its product unique in the eyes of the customer, for example, a differentiated company must design its structure and control system around the *particular source* of its competitive advantage.[10] Suppose that the differentiator's strength lies in technological competency; the company has the cutting-edge technology. In this case, the company's structure and control systems should be designed around the research and development function. Implementing a *matrix structure*, as Texas Instruments and TRW Systems have done, promotes innovation and speeds product development, for this type of structure permits intensive cross-functional integration. Integrating mechanisms, such as task forces and teams, help transfer knowledge among functions and are designed around the research and development function. Sales, marketing, and production targets are geared to research and development goals; marketing devises advertising programs that focus on technological possibilities, and salespeople are evaluated on their understanding of new-product characteristics and their ability to inform potential customers about them. Stringent sales targets are unlikely to be set in this situation because the goal is quality of service.

As is discussed in Chapter 11, however, there are many problems associated with a matrix structure. The changing composition of product teams, the ambiguity arising from having two bosses, the use of more complex integration mechanisms, and the greater difficulty of monitoring and evaluating the work of teams greatly increase the bureaucratic costs necessary to coordinate and control task activities. Nevertheless, companies are willing to incur the higher bureaucratic costs of a matrix structure when it allows them to create more value from their differentiation strategy.

Sometimes the advantages of a differentiation strategy can be obtained from a less expensive structure. For example, when the source of the differentiator's competitive advantage is superior quality or responsiveness to customers, companies design a structure around their products, and a *product-team* or *geographic* structure may fit best. In a product-team structure, each product group can focus on the needs of a particular product market. Support functions such as research and development or sales are organized by product, and task forces and teams have a product, not a research, orientation.

If a company's differentiation strategy is based on serving the needs of a number of different market segments, a geographic structure becomes appropriate. Thus, if it focuses on types of customers, a differentiated company may use a geographic structure designed according to a regional logic or even according to different types of customers, such as businesses, individual consumers, or the government. Both Compaq and Rockwell International have recently reorganized their structures to concentrate on the needs of specific customers or regions. The new geographic structure allows them to become more responsive to the needs of specific groups of customers and to serve those needs better. For example, information about changes in customers' preferences can be quickly fed back to R&D and product design so that a company can protect its competitive advantage.

The control systems used to match the structure can also be geared to the company's distinctive competency. For the differentiator it is important that the various functions do not pull in different directions; indeed, cooperation among the functions is vital for cross-functional integration. However, when functions work together, output controls become much harder to use. In general, it is much more difficult to measure the performance of people in different functions when they are engaged in cooperative efforts. Consequently, a company must rely more on behavior controls and shared norms and values when pursuing a strategy of differentiation.

That is why companies pursuing a differentiation strategy often have a markedly different kind of culture from those pursuing a low-cost strategy. Because human resources—good scientists, designers, or marketing people—are often the source of differentiation, these organizations have a culture based on professionalism or collegiality, a culture that emphasizes the distinctiveness of the human resource rather than the high pressure of the bottom line.[11] Hewlett Packard, Motorola, and Coca-Cola, all of which emphasize some kind of distinctive competency, exemplify companies with professional cultures.

The bureaucratic costs of operating the structure and control system of the differentiator are higher than the cost leader's, but the benefits are also greater if companies can reap the rewards of a premium price. Companies are willing to accept a higher level of bureaucratic costs provided their structure and control systems lead to superior efficiency, quality, innovation, or responsiveness to customers.

Implementing a Combined Differentiation and Cost-Leadership Strategy

As we discuss in Chapter 6, pursuing a combined differentiation and low-cost strategy is the most difficult challenge facing a company at the business level. On the one hand, the company has to coordinate its activities around manufacturing and materials management to implement a cost-reduction strategy. On the other hand, it must also coordinate its activities around the source of its differentiation advantage, such as R&D or marketing, to protect its competency in innovation or responsiveness to customers. For many companies in this situation, the answer has been the product-team structure, discussed in Chapter 11. It is far less costly to operate than a matrix structure but provides a much higher level of cross-functional integration than the functional structure.

As you recall from Chapter 11, a product-team structure groups tasks by product, and each product line is managed by a cross-functional team, which provides all the support services necessary to bring the product to market. The role of the

How 3M Uses Teams to Build Culture

A company well known for product innovation, 3M aims to achieve at least 25 percent of its growth each year through new products developed within the last five years. To promote product development, 3M has always taken care to design its structure and culture so that employees are provided with the freedom and motivation to experiment and take risks. For example, 3M has an informal norm that researchers should use 15 percent of their time to develop projects of their own choosing. It was this norm that brought about the development of new products such as Post-it Notes. In addition, 3M has been careful to establish career ladders for its scientists in order to gain their long-term commitment, and it rewards successful product innovators with substantial bonuses. All these practices have gained the loyalty and support of its scientists and helped create a culture of innovation.

The company has also recognized the increasing importance of linking and coordinating the efforts of people in different functions to speed product development. As we have noted, people in different functions tend to develop different subunit orientations and to focus their efforts on their own tasks to the exclusion of the needs of other functions. The danger of such tendencies is that each function will develop norms and values that suit its own needs but do little to promote organizational coordination and integration.

To avoid this problem, 3M has established a system of cross-functional teams composed of members of product development, process development, marketing, manufacturing, packaging, and other functions to create organizationwide norms and values of innovation. So that all groups have a common focus, the teams work closely with customers; customers' needs become the platform on which the different functions can then apply their skills and capabilities. For example, one of 3M's cross-functional teams worked closely with disposable diaper manufacturers to develop the right kind of sticky tape for their needs.

To promote integration in the team and foster cooperative norms and values, each team is headed by a "product champion," who takes the responsibility for building cohesive team relationships and developing a team culture. In addition, one of 3M's top managers becomes a "management sponsor," whose job is to help the team get resources and to provide support when the going gets tough. After all, product development is a very risky process, and many projects do not succeed. Finally, 3M established the Golden Step Program, which gives employees substantial monetary bonuses to honor and reward cross-functional teams, to create a culture in which innovation is a valued activity, and to develop norms and values that support and reward the sharing of information among scientists and among people in different functions. Clearly, all this attention to creating a culture of innovation has paid off for 3M.

product team is to protect and enhance a company's differentiation advantage and at the same time coordinate with manufacturing to lower costs. Chrysler, Hallmark Cards, and Xerox are among the companies that have recently reorganized from a functional to a product-team structure so that they can simultaneously speed product development and control their operating costs.

John Fluke Manufacturing, a leader in electronic testing tools, is a good example of a company that has made use of product teams to speed product development. The company assembles "Phoenix teams," which are cross-functional groups that are given 100 days and $100,000 to identify a market need and a new product to fill it.[12] So far, these teams have led to the development of two successful new products. Strategy in Action 13.2 describes how 3M uses cross-functional teams to promote a culture of innovation.

Focus Strategy and Structure

In Chapter 6 we define *focus strategy* as a strategy directed at a particular market or customer segment. A company focuses on a product or range of products aimed at one sort of customer or region. This strategy tends to have higher production costs than the other two strategies because output levels are lower, making it harder to obtain substantial economies of scale. As a result, a company using a focus strategy must exercise cost control. On the other hand, because some attribute of its product usually gives such a company its unique advantage—possibly its ability to provide customers with high-quality, personalized service—a company using a focus strategy has to develop a unique competency. For both these reasons, the structure and control system adopted by a company following a focus strategy has to be inexpensive to operate but flexible enough to allow a distinctive competency to emerge.

A company using a focus strategy normally adopts a functional structure to meet these needs. This structure is appropriate because it is complex enough to manage the activities necessary to service the needs of the market segment or produce a narrow range of products. At the same time, the bureaucratic costs of operating a functional structure are relatively low, and there is less need for complex, expensive integrating mechanisms. This structure permits more personal control and flexibility than the other two, and so it reduces bureaucratic costs while fostering the development of a distinctive competency.[13] Given its small size, a company using a focus strategy can rely less on output and behavior controls and more on culture, which is vital to the development of a service competency. Although output controls need to be used in production and sales, this form of control is inexpensive in a small organization.

The combination of functional structure and low cost of control helps offset the higher costs of production and at the same time allows the firm to develop unique strengths. It is little wonder, therefore, that there are so many companies using a focus strategy. Additionally, because such a company's competitive advantage is often based on personalized service, the flexibility of this kind of structure lets the company respond quickly to customers' needs and change its products in response to customers' requests. The structure then backs up the strategy and helps the firm develop and maintain its distinctive competency.

Au Bon Pain, a fast-food chain specializing in fancy coffees and baked goods such as croissants, is a good example of a company that has recognized the need to design a structure and control system to match a focus strategy aimed at an upscale customer group. To encourage franchises to perform at a high level and satisfy customers' needs, the company decentralized control to each franchise, making each a self-contained functional unit. Then, through a profit sharing plan that rewarded cost cutting and quality, it gave each franchise manager the incentive to create a set of control arrangements that minimized costs but maximized quality of service. The result was a strategy/structure fit that led to a massive increase in franchise profits.

Summary

Companies pursuing a generic business-level strategy must adopt the appropriate form of structure and control if they are to use their resources effectively to develop superior efficiency, quality, innovation, and responsiveness to customers.

Companies are willing to bear the bureaucratic costs of operating organizational structure and control systems if these systems increase their ability to create value from lowering their costs or charging a premium price for their products. Hence, over time, companies must manage and change their structures to allow them to create value. However, many companies do *not* use the right forms of structure over time and fail to manage their strategies. These companies are not as successful and do not survive as long as those that do match their strategy, structure, and control systems.[14]

DESIGNING A GLOBAL STRUCTURE

In Chapter 8 we note that the strategies of most large companies have a global dimension if the firms produce and sell their products in international markets. Procter & Gamble and food companies such as H. J. Heinz, Kellogg, and Nestlé Enterprises, for example, have production operations throughout the world, as do the large automakers and computer makers. In this section we examine how each of the four principal global strategies affects a company's choice of structure and control.

You'll recall from Chapter 8 that (1) a *multidomestic strategy* is oriented toward local responsiveness, and a company establishes semiautonomous national units in each country in which it operates to produce and customize products to local markets; (2) an *international strategy* is based on R&D and marketing being centralized at home and all the other value creation functions being decentralized to national units; (3) a *global strategy* is oriented toward cost reduction, with all the principal value creation functions centralized at the optimal global location; and (4) a *transnational strategy* is focused so that it can achieve both local responsiveness and global integration so that some functions are centralized at the optimal global location while others are decentralized, both to achieve local responsiveness and to facilitate global learning.

If a company is to operate each strategy successfully, the need to coordinate and integrate global tasks increases as the company moves from a multidomestic to an international to a global and then to a transnational strategy. The bureaucratic costs of managing a transnational strategy are much higher than those of managing a multidomestic strategy, for example. To achieve a transnational strategy, a company transfers its distinctive competencies to the global location where they can create the most value and then it establishes a global network to coordinate its foreign and domestic divisions. This coordination involves managing global resource transfers to facilitate global learning. Compared with the other strategies, more managerial time has to be spent coordinating organizational resources and capabilities to achieve the global synergies that justify pursuing a transnational strategy.

By contrast, pursuing a multidomestic strategy does not require coordination of activities on a global level because value creation activities are handled locally, by country or world region. The international and global strategies fit between the other two strategies; although products have to be sold and marketed globally, and hence global product transfers must be managed, there is less need to coordinate resource transfers than for a transnational strategy.

TABLE 13.2
. . . .

Global Strategy/Structure Relationships

	Multidomestic Strategy	International Strategy	Global Strategy	Transnational Strategy
	Low ◄——————— Need for Coordination ———————► High			
	Low ◄——————— Bureaucratic Costs ———————► High			
Centralization of Authority	Decentralized to national unit	Core competencies centralized, others decentralized to national units	Centralized at optimal global location	Simultaneously centralized and decentralized
Horizontal Differentiation	Global-area structure	International-division structure	Global product-group structure	Global-matrix structure, matrix in the mind
Need for Complex Integrating Mechanisms	Low	Medium	High	Very high
Organizational Culture	Not important	Quite important	Important	Very important

The implication is that as companies change from a multidomestic to an international, global, or transnational strategy, they require a more complex structure and control system to coordinate the value creation activities associated with that strategy. Therefore, the bureaucratic costs increase at each stage. For a multidomestic strategy they are low; for an international strategy, medium; for a global strategy, high; and for a transnational strategy, very high (see Table 13.2). In general, the choice of structure and control systems for managing a global business is a function of three factors:

1. The decision how to distribute and allocate responsibility and authority between domestic and foreign managers so that effective control over a company's foreign operations is maintained

2. The selection of a level of horizontal differentiation that groups foreign operations with domestic operations in a way that allows the best use of resources and serves the needs of foreign customers most effectively

3. The selection of the right kinds of integration mechanism and organizational culture to make the structure function effectively

Table 13.2 summarizes the appropriate design choices for companies pursuing each of these strategies.

Multidomestic Strategy and Structure
. . . .

When a company pursues a multidomestic strategy, it generally operates with a global-area structure (see Figure 13.1). When using this structure, a company duplicates all value creation activities and establishes a foreign division in every country

FIGURE 13.1
· · · · · · · · · ·
Global-Area Structure

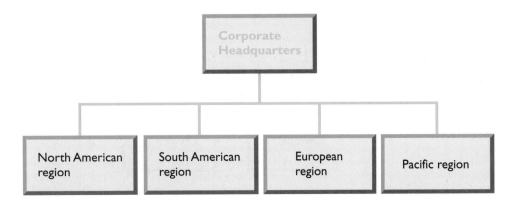

FIGURE 13.1
· · · · · · · · · ·
Global-Area Structure

or world area in which it operates. Authority is then decentralized to managers in each foreign division, and they devise the appropriate strategy for responding to the needs of the local environment. Because corporate headquarters managers are so far away from the scene of operations, it makes sense to decentralize control and grant decision-making authority to managers in the foreign operations. Managers at global headquarters use market and output controls, such as rate of return, growth in market share, and operation costs, to evaluate the performance of foreign divisions. On the basis of such global comparisons, they can make decisions about capital allocation and orchestrate the transfer of new knowledge among divisions.

A company that makes and sells the same products in many different markets often groups its foreign subsidiaries into world regions to simplify the coordination of products across countries. Europe might be one region, the Pacific Rim another, and the Middle East a third. Such grouping allows the same set of market and behavior controls to be applied across all divisions inside a region. Thus, companies can obtain synergies from dealing with broadly similar cultures because information can be transmitted more easily. For example, consumers' preferences regarding product design and marketing are likely to be more similar among countries in one world region than among countries in different world regions.

Because the foreign divisions themselves have little or no contact with each other, no integrating mechanisms are needed. Nor does a global organizational culture develop, since there are no transfers of personnel or informal contacts among managers from the various world regions. Car companies such as Chrysler, General Motors, and Ford all used to employ global-area structures to manage their foreign operations. Ford of Europe, for example, had little or no contact with its U.S. parent, and capital was the principal resource exchanged.

One problem with a global-area structure and a multidomestic strategy is that the duplication of specialist activities raises costs. Moreover, the company is not taking advantage of opportunities to trade information and knowledge on a global basis or of low-cost manufacturing opportunities. Multidomestic companies have chosen to keep behavior costs low; however, they lose the many benefits of operating globally.

International Strategy and Structure
· ·

A company pursuing an international strategy adopts a different route to global expansion. Normally, the company shifts to this strategy when it begins selling its domestically made products in foreign markets. Until recently, companies such as

FIGURE 13.2
·············
International-Division
Structure

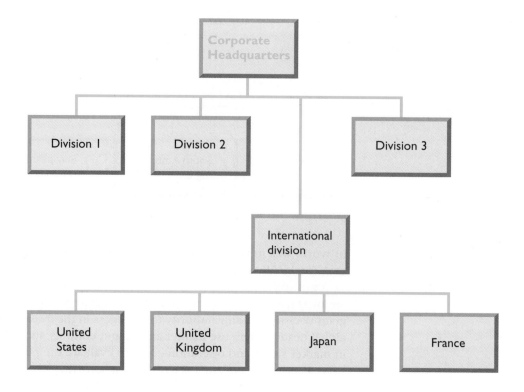

Mercedes-Benz and Jaguar made no attempt to produce in a foreign market; instead, they distributed and sold their domestically produced cars internationally. Such companies usually just add a **foreign operations department** to their existing structure and continue to use the same control system. If a company is using a functional structure, this department has to coordinate manufacturing, sales, and research and development activities with the needs of the foreign market. Efforts at customization are minimal, however.

In the foreign country, the company usually establishes a subsidiary to handle sales and distribution. For example, the Mercedes-Benz foreign subsidiaries allocate dealerships, organize supplies of spare parts, and, of course, sell cars. A system of behavior controls is then established to keep the home office informed of changes in sales, spare parts requirements, and so on.

A company with many different products or businesses operating from a multi-divisional structure has the challenging problem of coordinating the flow of different products across different countries. To manage these transfers, many companies create an international division, which they add to their existing divisional structure[15] (see Figure 13.2). International operations are managed as a separate divisional business, whose managers are given the authority and responsibility for coordinating domestic product divisions and foreign markets. The international division also controls the foreign subsidiaries that market the products and decides how much authority to delegate to foreign management. This arrangement permits the company to engage in more complex foreign operations at relatively low bureaucratic costs. However, managers in the foreign countries are essentially under the control of managers in the international division, and if the domestic and for-

FIGURE 13.3
• • • • • • • • • • • •
Global Product-
Group Structure

eign managers compete for control of operations in the foreign country, conflict and lack of cooperation can result.

Global Strategy and Structure

A company embarks on a global strategy when it starts to locate manufacturing and all the other value creation activities in the lowest-cost global location to increase efficiency, quality, and innovation. In seeking to obtain the gains from global learning, a company must cope with greater coordination and integration problems. It has to find a structure that can coordinate resource transfers between corporate headquarters and foreign divisions and at the same time provide the centralized control that a global strategy requires. The answer for many companies is a **global product-group structure** (see Figure 13.3).

In this structure, a product-group headquarters (similar to an SBU headquarters) is created to coordinate the activities of the domestic and foreign divisions within the product group. Product-group managers in the home country are responsible for organizing all aspects of value creation on a global basis. The product-group structure allows managers to decide how best to pursue a global strategy, for example, to decide which value creation activities, such as manufacturing or product design, should be performed in which country to increase efficiency. Increasingly, U.S. and Japanese companies are moving manufacturing to low-cost countries such as China but establishing product-design centers in Europe or the United States to take advantage of foreign skills and capabilities.

Transnational Strategy and Structure

The main failing of the global product-group structure is that while it allows a company to achieve superior efficiency and quality, it is weak when it comes to responsiveness to customers because the focus is still on centralized control to reduce

FIGURE 13.4
• • • • • • • • • • • •
Global-Matrix Structure

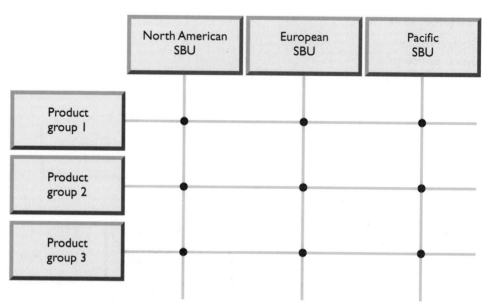

● Individual operating companies

costs. Moreover, this structure makes it difficult for the different product groups to trade information and knowledge and to obtain the benefits of cooperation. Sometimes the potential gains from sharing product, marketing, or research and development knowledge between product groups are very high, but because a company lacks a structure that can coordinate the groups' activities, these gains cannot be achieved.

More and more, companies are adopting **global-matrix structures**, which let them simultaneously reduce costs by increasing efficiency *and* differentiate their activities through superior innovation and responsiveness to customers. Figure 13.4 shows such a structure, adopted by a large chemical company such as Du Pont or Amoco.

On the vertical axis, instead of functions, there are the company's *product groups,* which provide specialist services such as R&D, product design, and marketing information to the foreign divisions, or SBUs. For example, these might be the petroleum, plastics, pharmaceuticals, or fertilizer product groups. On the horizontal axis are the company's *foreign divisions,* or *SBUs,* in the various countries or world regions in which it operates. Managers in the foreign subsidiary control foreign operations and through a system of behavior controls report to divisional personnel back in the United States. They are also responsible, together with U.S. divisional personnel, for developing control and reward systems that promote the sharing of marketing or research and development information to achieve gains from synergies.

This structure both provides a great deal of local flexibility and gives divisional personnel in the United States considerable access to information about local affairs. The matrix structure also allows knowledge and experience to be transferred among geographic regions and among divisions and regions. Since it offers many opportunities for face-to-face contact between domestic and foreign managers, the matrix facilitates the transmission of a company's norms and values and, hence, the development of a global corporate culture. This is especially important for an international company, for which lines of communication are longer and information is subject to distortion. Club Med, for instance, fully exploits these synergies in the way it manages its holiday resorts.

The matrix also lets each home division balance production so that, for example, a lack of demand in one region of the world can be compensated by increased demand in another. For example, Philip Morris balances cigarette production so that slumping demand in the United States is countered by expanding demand in other regions of the world. Similarly, Japanese car manufacturers plan their international strategy to compensate for import restrictions or currency changes in the world market.

To make these matrix structures work, many companies strive to develop a strong international organizational culture to facilitate communication and coordination among managers. For example, companies are increasingly transferring managers between foreign and domestic operations so they can develop a global view. Furthermore, to improve integration, companies are trying to form global networks of managers so they can turn to each other for help. The idea is to create a **matrix in the mind**, that is, an information network that lets a company capitalize globally on the skills and capabilities of its personnel.[16]

To foster the development of the matrix-in-the-mind concept and promote cooperation, companies are also using electronic integrating devices such as on-line teleconferencing, E-mail, and global intranets between different parts of their operations, both globally and domestically. For example, Hitachi coordinates its nineteen Japanese laboratories by means of an on-line teleconferencing system, and both Microsoft and Hewlett Packard make extensive use of electronic computer systems to integrate their activities.

These integration mechanisms provide the extra coordination that helps the global-matrix structure work effectively. It is a very complex structure to operate and carries a high level of bureaucratic costs. However, the potential gains for a company in terms of superior efficiency, quality, innovation, and responsiveness to customers make these costs worthwhile. In the complicated game of international competition, companies must increasingly adopt many of these elements of a global matrix to survive. Nestlé found itself in this situation, as Strategy in Action 13.3 details.

Summary

Most large companies have an international component in their organizational structures. The issue for international companies, as for all others, is to adopt the structure and control system that best fits their strategy. The need to implement international strategy successfully has put increasing pressures on corporate managers to design the company's structure and controls so that the firm can respond to the challenges of the world market.

STRUCTURE AND CONTROL AT THE CORPORATE LEVEL

At the corporate level, strategic managers need to choose the organizational structure that will allow them to operate a number of different businesses efficiently. The structure normally chosen at the corporate level is the multidivisional structure. The larger and more diverse the businesses in the corporate portfolio, the

Reengineering Nestlé's Global Structure

 Nestlé, based in Vevey, Switzerland, is the world's biggest food company. In 1996 its global sales passed $50 billion a year, a figure it wants to double by the year 2001. To achieve this goal, the company has been pursuing an ambitious program of global expansion by acquiring many famous companies—for instance, Perrier, the French mineral water producer, and Rowntree Mackintosh, the British candy maker. In the United States, Nestlé bought the giant Carnation Company in 1985, and it also purchased Stouffer Foods and Contadina, among other large food companies.

Traditionally, Nestlé pursued a multidomestic strategy and managed its operating companies through a global-area structure. In each country, each individual company (such as Carnation) was responsible for managing all aspects of its business-level strategy; in other words, companies were free to control their own product development and marketing and to manage all local operations. Acquisitions, expansions, and corporate resource decisions such as capital investment were decided at the Vevey headquarters by Nestlé's corporate executives. Because all important decisions were made centrally, the size of the corporate staff increased dramatically. In the early 1990s Nestlé's chairman, Helmut Maucher, realized that the company had major problems.

Corporate managers had become very remote from the difficulties experienced by the operating companies, and the centralized operating structure slowed down decision making. Nestlé had trouble responding quickly to the changing environment. Moreover, the company was forfeiting all the gains from global learning and possible synergies from resource sharing between operating companies and world regions, because each company was operated separately and corporate executives made no attempt to integrate across companies around the world. Maucher realized that the company could not increase its sales and profits through its existing operating structure. To create more value, it had to find a new way of organizing its activities

Maucher started the reengineering of Nestlé's structure from the top down. He massively reduced the power of corporate management by decentralizing authority to the managers of seven product groups, which he created to oversee the company's major product lines (for example, coffee, milk, and candy) on a global level. The role of each product group was to integrate the activities of operating companies in its area in order to obtain synergies and the gains from global learning. After the change, managers in the candy product group, for instance, began orchestrating the marketing and sale of Rowntree candy products, such as After Eight Mints and Smarties, throughout Europe, and sales climbed by 60 percent.

Maucher then turned his attention to the way the operating companies worked in each country or world region. He grouped all the operating companies within a country or region into one SBU and then created a team of SBU managers to link and coordinate the activities of the various companies in that country. When the different companies or divisions started to share joint purchasing, marketing, and sales activities, major cost savings resulted. In the United States, the SBU management team, headed by Timm Krull, reduced the number of sales offices nationwide from 115 to 22 and decreased the number of suppliers of packaging from 43 to 3.

Finally, Maucher decided to use a matrix structure to integrate the activities of the seven global product groups with the operations of Nestlé's country- or region-based SBUs. The goal of this matrix structure is to have the company pursue a transnational strategy, allowing it to obtain the gains from global learning and cost reduction. For example, Timm Krull now spends one week every month in Vevey with product-group executives, discussing ways of exploiting and sharing the resources of the company on a global basis. So far, this new decentralized matrix structure has speeded decision making and product development and has enabled the company to integrate the activities of its many new acquisitions. Maucher hopes it will help Nestlé reach its ambitious sales goal by the year 2001.

more likely the company is to have a multidivisional structure. The reason is that each division requires its own set of specialist support functions to operate efficiently, and a headquarters corporate staff is needed to oversee and evaluate divisional operations to ensure that corporate goals are being achieved. Once strategic managers select a multidivisional structure, they must then make choices about what kind of integrating mechanisms and control systems to use to make the structure work efficiently. Later in this chapter, we discuss how the corporate-level strategies of unrelated diversification, vertical integration, and related diversification affect the choice of structure and control systems.

As discussed in Chapter 9, the main reason a company pursues vertical integration is to achieve *economies of integration* among divisions.[17] For example, a company can coordinate resource-scheduling decisions among divisions to reduce costs and improve quality. This might mean locating a rolling mill next to a steel furnace to save the costs of reheating steel ingots and make it easier to control the quality of the final product. Similarly, the chief gains from related diversification come from obtaining synergies or *economies of scope* among divisions. Divisions benefit by transferring core competencies such as R&D or by sharing distribution and sales networks. With both these strategies, the benefits to the company come from some *transfer of resources* among divisions. To secure these benefits, the company must coordinate activities among divisions. Consequently, structure and control must be designed to handle the transfer of resources among divisions.

In the case of unrelated diversification, however, the benefits to the company come from restructuring and establishing of an *internal capital market,* which allows corporate personnel to make better allocations of capital than would be possible in an external capital market. With this strategy, there are no transactions or exchanges among divisions; each operates separately. Structure and control must therefore be designed to allow each division to operate independently.

A company's choice of structure and control mechanisms depends on the degree to which a company must control the interactions among divisions. The more interdependent the divisions—that is, the more they depend on each other for resources—the more complex are the control and integration mechanisms required to integrate their activities and make the strategy work.[18] Consequently, as the need for integration increases, so, too, does the level of bureaucratic costs. Once again, however, a company is willing to bear the increased bureaucratic costs associated with operating a more complex strategy if the strategy creates more value.[19] This is illustrated in Table 13.3, which also indicates what forms of structure and control companies should adopt to manage the three corporate strategies. We examine them in detail in the next sections.

Unrelated Diversification
· ·

Because there are *no linkages* among divisions, unrelated diversification is the easiest and cheapest strategy to manage; it is associated with the lowest level of bureaucratic costs. The main requirement of the structure and control system is that it allow corporate managers to evaluate divisional performance easily and accurately. Thus, companies use a multidivisional structure, and each division is evaluated by financial controls such as return on investment. A company also applies sophisticated accounting controls to obtain information quickly from the divisions so that corporate managers can readily compare divisions on several dimensions.

TABLE 13.3
. . . .

Corporate Strategy and Structure and Control

Corporate Strategy	Appropriate Structure	Need for Integration	Type of Control		
			Financial Control	Behavior Control	Organizational Culture
Unrelated diversification	Multidivisional	Low (no exchanges between divisions)	Great use (e.g., ROI)	Some use (e.g., budgets)	Little use
Vertical integration	Multidivisional	Medium (scheduling resource transfers)	Great use (e.g., ROI, transfer pricing)	Great use (e.g., standardization, budgets)	Some use (e.g., shared norms and values)
Related diversification	Multidivisional	High (achieving synergies between divisions by integrating roles)	Little use	Great use (e.g., rules, budgets)	Great use (e.g., norms, values, common language)

Textron and Dover are good examples of companies that use sophisticated computer networks and accounting controls to manage their structures, which allow them almost daily access to divisional performance.

Divisions usually have considerable autonomy, unless they fail to reach their ROI objectives. Generally, corporate headquarters is not interested in the types of business-level strategy pursued by each division unless there are problems. If problems arise, corporate headquarters may step in to take corrective action, perhaps replacing managers or providing additional financial resources, depending on the reason for the problem. If they see no possibility of a turnaround, however, corporate personnel may just as easily decide to divest the division. The multidivisional structure allows the unrelated company to operate its businesses as a portfolio of investments, which can be bought and sold as business conditions change. Usually, managers in the various divisions do not know one another, and they may not know what companies are in the corporate portfolio.

The use of financial controls to manage a company means that no integration among divisions is necessary. This is why the bureaucratic costs of managing an unrelated company are low. The biggest problem facing corporate personnel is determining capital allocations to the various divisions so that the overall profitability of the portfolio is maximized. They also have to oversee divisional managers and make sure that divisions are achieving ROI targets. Alco Standard's way of managing its businesses, described in Strategy in Action 13.4, demonstrates how to operate a strategy of unrelated diversification.

Vertical Integration
. . . .

Vertical integration is a more expensive strategy to manage than unrelated diversification because *sequential resource flows* from one division to the next must be coordinated. The multidivisional structure effects such coordination. This structure

Alco Standard Gets It Right

Alco Standard, based in Valley Forge, Pennsylvania, is one of the largest office supply companies in the United States, distributing office and paper supplies and materials through a nationwide network of wholly owned distribution companies. It pursues a highly successful strategy of unrelated diversification. Since 1965 the company has bought and sold more than 300 different companies. It used to be involved in more than 50 different industries, but now it operates 50 businesses in only two main areas: office products and paper distribution. However, the corporate office makes no attempt to intervene in the activities of the different divisions.

The policy of Alco's top management is that authority and control should be completely decentralized to the managers in each of the company's businesses. Each business is left alone to make its own manufacturing or purchasing decisions even though some potential synergies, in the form of corporationwide purchasing or marketing, are being lost. Top management pursues this nonintervention policy because it believes that the gains from allowing its managers to act as independent entre-

preneurs exceed any potential economies of scope that might result from coordinating interdivisional activities. It believes that a decentralized operating system allows a big company to act in a way that is similar to a small company, avoiding the problem of growing bureaucracy and organizational inertia.

At Alco, top management interprets its role as relieving the divisions of administrative chores, such as bookkeeping and accounting, and collecting market information on competitive pricing and products, which allows divisional managers to improve their business-level strategy. Centralizing these information activities reduces each division's bureaucratic costs and provides the standardization that lets top management make better decisions about resource allocation. Alco's division heads are regarded as partners in the corporate enterprise and are rewarded through stock options linked to the performance of their divisions. So far, Alco has been very successful with its decentralized operating structure and has achieved a compound growth rate of 19 percent a year.

provides the centralized control necessary for the vertically integrated company to achieve benefits from the control of resource transfers. Corporate personnel assume the responsibility for devising financial and behavior controls to promote the efficient transfer of resources among divisions. Complex rules and procedures are instituted to manage interdivisional relationships and specify how exchanges are to be made; consequently, bureaucratic costs rise. As previously noted, complex resource exchanges can lead to conflict among divisions, and corporate managers must try to minimize divisional conflicts.

Centralizing authority at corporate headquarters must be done with care in vertically related companies. It carries the risk of involving corporate managers in operating issues at the business level to the point at which the divisions lose their autonomy and motivation. As we point out in Chapter 11, the company must strike the right balance of centralized control at corporate headquarters and decentralized control at the divisional level if it is to implement this strategy successfully.

Because their interests are at stake, divisions need to have input into scheduling and decisions regarding resource transfer. For example, the plastics division in a chemical company has a vital interest in the activities of the oil division, for the quality of the products it gets from the oil division determines the quality of its own products. Divisional integrating mechanisms can bring about direct coordination and information transfers among divisions.[20] To handle communication among divisions, a company sets up task forces or teams for the purpose; it can also establish liaison roles. In high-tech and chemical companies, for example, integrating roles among divisions is common. These integrating mechanisms also increase bureaucratic costs.

Thus, a strategy of vertical integration is managed through a combination of corporate and divisional controls. Although the organizational structure and control systems used for managing this strategy have higher bureaucratic costs than those used for unrelated diversification, the benefits derived from vertical integration often outweigh its extra costs.

Related Diversification

In the case of related diversification, divisions share research and development knowledge, information, customer bases, and goodwill to obtain gains from synergies. The process is difficult to manage, and so a multidivisional structure is used to facilitate the transfer of resources to obtain synergies. Even with this structure, however, high levels of resource sharing and joint production by divisions make it hard for corporate managers to measure the performance of each individual division.[21] If a related company is to obtain gains from synergy, it has to adopt more complicated forms of integration and control at the divisional level to make the structure work efficiently.

First, financial control is difficult to use because divisions share resources, so it is not easy to measure the performance of an individual division. Therefore, a company needs to develop a corporate culture that stresses cooperation among divisions and corporate, rather than purely divisional, goals. Second, corporate managers must establish sophisticated integrating devices to ensure coordination among divisions. Integrating roles and teams are crucial because they provide the context in which managers from different divisions can meet and develop a common vision of corporate goals. Hewlett Packard, for instance, created three new high-level integrating teams to make certain that the new products developed by its technology group made their way quickly to its product divisions. All this extra integration is very expensive, however, and must be carefully managed.

An organization with a multidivisional structure must have the right mix of incentives and rewards for cooperation if it is to achieve gains from sharing skills and resources among divisions.[22] With unrelated diversification, divisions operate autonomously, and the company can quite easily reward managers on their division's individual performance. With related diversification, however, rewarding divisions is more difficult because they are engaged in joint production, and strategic managers must be sensitive and alert to achieve equity in rewards among divisions. The aim always is to design the structure so that it can maximize the benefits from the strategy at the lowest bureaucratic cost.

Managing a strategy of related diversification also raises the issue of how much authority to centralize and how much to decentralize. Corporate managers need to take a close look at how their controls affect divisional performance and autonomy. If corporate managers get too involved in the day-to-day operations of the divisions, they can endanger divisional autonomy and undercut divisional managers' decision making.[23] Corporate managers, after all, see everything from a corporate, rather than a divisional, perspective. For instance, in the Heinz example mentioned earlier, management tried to develop one form of competitive advantage, a low-cost advantage, in every division.[24] Although this approach may work well for Heinz, it may be markedly inappropriate for a company that is operating a totally diverse set of businesses, each of which needs to develop its own unique competency. Too much corporate control can put divisional managers in a straitjacket. When too many managers become involved in managing the business, performance suffers and bureaucratic costs escalate. Companies such as IBM and General Motors experienced this problem; their corporate staffs became top-heavy, slowing decision making and draining the company's profits.

SPECIAL ISSUES IN STRATEGY/STRUCTURE CHOICE

As we noted in Chapter 10, today many organizations are changing their corporate-level strategies and restructuring their organizations to find new ways to use their resources and capabilities to create value. In this section we focus on three strategy/structure issues that arise during the rebuilding or restructuring process: the management of mergers and acquisitions, the management of new ventures, and the management of outsourcing through the development of a network structure.

Mergers, Acquisitions, and Structure

In Chapter 10, we note that mergers and acquisitions are the principal vehicles by which companies enter new product markets and expand the size of their operations.[25] Earlier we discuss the strategic advantages and disadvantages of mergers. We now consider how to design structure and control systems to manage new acquisitions. This issue is important because many acquisitions are unsuccessful, and one of the main reasons is that many companies do a very poor job of integrating the new divisions into their corporate structure.[26]

The first factor that makes managing new acquisitions difficult is the nature of the businesses a company acquires. If a company acquires businesses related to its existing businesses, it should find it fairly easy to integrate them into its corporate structure. The controls already being used in the related company can be adapted to the new divisions. To achieve gains from synergies, the company can expand its task forces or increase the number of integrating roles, so that the new divisions are drawn into the existing divisional structure.

If managers do not understand how to develop connections among divisions to permit gains from economies of scope, the new businesses will perform poorly.[27] Some authors have argued that this is why the quality of management is so important. A company must employ managers who have the ability to recognize synergies among apparently different businesses and so derive benefits from acquisitions and mergers.[28] For instance, Porter cites the example of Philip Morris, the cigarette producer, which took over Miller Brewing.[29] On the surface these seem to be very different businesses. However, when their products are viewed as consumer products that are often bought and consumed together, the possibility of sales, distribution, and marketing synergies becomes clearer, and this merger was a great success.

However, if companies acquire unrelated businesses only to operate them as a portfolio of investments, they should have no trouble managing the acquisitions.

No Problems for ABP

One of the largest manufacturers of business forms in the United States, American Business Products (ABP) developed a multi-divisional structure to manage its strategy of related diversification. The Atlanta-based company created three separate divisions to manufacture invoices, customized envelopes, and continuous forms for computer printers. However, in 1990, with the market for business products slowing down and profit margins shrinking, ABP decided to break with the past and search for new business opportunities. It embarked on a strategy of unrelated diversification and bought Jen-Coat, a maker of plastic packaging for food and health care products, as well as Bookcrafters, a specialty printing company. Because top management established distinct roles for corporate headquarters and for the operating divisions, ABP experienced no problems in managing the new businesses through its multidivisional structure. The role of the corporate center was to control finances, establish budgets, and manage executive compensation for the five divisions—that is, to focus on corporate-level strategy. The role of the division heads was to handle sales, marketing, and manufacturing—that is, to manage business-level strategy. This clear apportioning of responsibility has been good for the company, which has encountered no difficulties in managing both strategies simultaneously and is currently on the lookout for more acquisitions.

For example, consider the acquisition strategy of American Business Products, highlighted in Strategy in Action 13.5.

Implementation problems are likely to arise only when corporate managers try to interfere in businesses they know little about or when they use inappropriate structure and controls to manage the new business and attempt to achieve the wrong kind of benefits from the acquisition. For example, if managers try to integrate unrelated companies with related ones, apply the wrong kinds of controls at the divisional level, or interfere in business-level strategy, corporate performance suffers as bureaucratic costs skyrocket. These mistakes explain why related acquisitions are sometimes more successful than unrelated ones.[30]

Therefore, strategic managers need to be very sensitive to the problems involved in taking over new businesses through mergers and acquisitions. As with other managers, they rarely appreciate the real issues inherent in managing the new business and the level of bureaucratic costs involved in managing a strategy until they have to deal with these issues personally. Even when acquiring closely related businesses, new managers must realize that each business has a unique culture, or way of doing things. Such idiosyncrasies must be understood in order to manage the new organization properly. Over time new management can change the culture and alter the internal workings of the company, but this is a difficult implementation task. Besides, the bureaucratic costs of changing a culture are often enormous because the top management team and the organizational structure have to be changed in order to change the way people behave. We discuss this in detail in Chapter 14, where organizational politics and strategic change are considered.

Internal New Ventures and Structure

The main alternative to growth through acquisition and merger is for a company to develop new businesses internally. In Chapter 10 we call this strategy *internal new venturing* and discuss its advantages for growth and diversification. Now we consider the design of the appropriate internal arrangements for encouraging the development of new ventures.

At the heart of new-venture design must be the realization by corporate managers that internal new venturing is a form of entrepreneurship. The design should encourage creativity and give new-venture managers the opportunity and resources to develop new products or markets. Hewlett Packard, for example, gives managers a great deal of latitude in this respect. To encourage innovation, it allows them to work on informal projects while they carry out their assigned tasks.[31] More generally, management must choose the appropriate structure and controls for operating new ventures.[32]

One of the main design choices is the creation of **new-venture divisions**. To provide new-venture managers with the autonomy to experiment and take risks, the company sets up a new-venture division separate from other divisions and makes it a center for new product or project development. Away from the day-to-day scrutiny of top management, divisional personnel pursue the creation of new business as though they were external entrepreneurs. The division is operated by controls that reinforce the entrepreneurial spirit. Thus, market and output controls are inappropriate because they can inhibit risk taking. Instead, the company develops a culture for entrepreneurship in this division to provide a climate for innovation. Care must be taken, however, to institute bureaucratic controls that put some limits on freedom of action. Otherwise, costly mistakes may be made, and resources wasted on frivolous ideas.

In managing the new-venture division, it is important to use integrating mechanisms such as task forces and teams to screen new ideas. Managers from research and development, sales and marketing, and product development are heavily involved in this screening process. Generally, the champions of new products must defend their projects before a formal evaluation committee, consisting of proven entrepreneurs and experienced managers from the other divisions, to secure the resources for developing them. Companies such as 3M, IBM, and Texas Instruments are examples of successful companies that use this method for creating opportunities internally.

Care must be taken to preserve the autonomy of the new-venture division. As mentioned earlier, the costs of research and development are high, and the rewards uncertain. After spending millions of dollars, corporate managers often become concerned about the division's performance and introduce tight output controls or strong budgets to increase accountability. These measures hurt the entrepreneurial culture.

Sometimes, however, after creating a new invention, the new-venture division wants to reap the benefits by producing and marketing it. If this happens, the division becomes an ordinary operating division and entrepreneurship declines.[33] Strategic managers must take steps to provide a structure that can sustain the entrepreneurial spirit.[34]

Hewlett Packard has a novel way of dealing with new venturing. In the operating divisions, as soon as a new, self-supporting product is developed, a new division is formed to produce and market the product. By spinning off the product in this fashion, the company keeps all its divisions small and entrepreneurial. The arrangement also provides a good climate for innovation. In the last several years, however, Hewlett Packard found that having many new venture divisions was too expensive and so has merged some of them. The company appears to be moving toward the creation of a single new-venture division.

Internal new venturing is an important means by which large, established companies can maintain their momentum and grow from within.[35] The alternative is to acquire small businesses that have already developed some technological competency and to pump resources into them. This approach can also succeed, and it obviously lessens management's burden if the company operates the new business as an independent entity. In recent years Eastman Kodak has taken this path to diversification, buying a share in many small companies. By and large, companies are likely to operate in both ways, acquiring some new businesses and developing others internally. As increasing competition from abroad has threatened their dominance in existing businesses, companies have been forced to evaluate opportunities for maximizing long-term growth in new businesses, and many of them have made acquisitions.

Network Structure and the Virtual Organization

As we discuss in Chapters 9 and 10, the use of outsourcing is increasing rapidly as organizations recognize the many opportunities it offers to reduce costs and increase their flexibility. U.S. companies will spend $100 billion on outsourcing in 1997, and companies such as EDS, which manages the information systems of large organizations such as Xerox and Kodak, are major beneficiaries of this new organizing approach. Similarly, on a global level, the development of a global network of strategic alliances between companies is an alternative to the use of the complex global-matrix structure.[36]

In order to implement outsourcing effectively, strategic managers must decide what organizational arrangements to adopt. Increasingly, a **network structure**, the set of strategic alliances that an organization creates with suppliers, manufacturers, and distributors to produce and market a product, is becoming the structure of choice to implement outsourcing. An example of a network structure is the series of strategic alliances that Japanese car companies such as Toyota and Honda formed with their suppliers of inputs such as car axles, gearboxes, and air conditioning systems. Members of the network work together on a long-term basis to find new ways to reduce costs and increase the quality of their products. Moreover, developing a network structure allows an organization to avoid the high costs of operating a complex organizational structure (the costs of employing many managers, for example).

Finally, a network structure allows a company to form strategic alliances with foreign suppliers, which gives managers access to low-cost foreign sources of inputs, keeping costs low. Strategy in Action 13.6 describes the network structure that NIKE uses to produce and market its sports shoes.

Some small companies that use a focus strategy go even further than NIKE and create a network structure to perform almost all their functional activities. Topsy Tail, a small Texas company that sells hair-styling gadgets such as false ponytails, has created strategic alliances with other companies that not only manufacture and distribute its products but also design, market, and package them. Apart from its CEO Tomima Edmark, who orchestrates these alliances and is at the hub of the network, the company has almost no permanent employees—only outside companies and people who contract with Edmark to perform certain services in return for which they receive a set fee![37]

The ability of managers to develop a network structure to produce or provide the goods and services their customers want, rather than create a complex organizational structure to do so, has led many researchers and consultants to popularize

13.6

STRATEGY *in* ACTION

NIKE's Network Structure

NIKE, located in Beaverton, Oregon, is the largest and most profitable sports shoe manufacturer in the world. The key to NIKE's success is the network structure that Philip Knight, NIKE's founder and CEO, created to allow his company to produce and market shoes. As discussed earlier, the most successful companies today simultaneously pursue a low-cost and a differentiation strategy. Knight realized this early on, and he created an organizational structure to allow his company to achieve this goal.

By far the largest function at NIKE's headquarters in Beaverton is the design function, staffed by talented designers who pioneer innovations in sports shoe design such as the air pump and Air Jordans that NIKE introduced so successfully. Designers use computer-aided design (CAD) to design their shoes, and all new-product information including manufacturing instructions is stored electronically. When the designers have done their work, they relay all the blueprints for the new products electronically to a network of suppliers and manufacturers throughout Southeast Asia with whom NIKE has formed strategic alliances.[38] Instructions for the design of a new sole, for example, may be sent to a supplier in Taiwan, and instructions for the leather uppers to a supplier in Malaysia. These suppliers produce the shoe parts, which are then sent for final assembly to a manufacturer in China with whom NIKE

has established an alliance. From China these shoes are shipped to distributors throughout the world. Of the 99 million pairs of shoes NIKE makes each year, 99 percent are made in Southeast Asia.

There are two main advantages to this network structure for NIKE. First, NIKE's costs are very low because wages in Southeast Asia are a fraction of what they are in the United States and this gives NIKE a low-cost advantage. Second, NIKE is able to respond to changes in sports shoe fashion very quickly. Using its global computer system, NIKE can, literally overnight, change the instructions it gives to each of its suppliers so that within a few weeks new kinds of shoes are being produced by its foreign manufacturers.[39] If any of its alliance partners fails to perform up to NIKE's standards, they are simply replaced with new partners, so NIKE has great control over its network structure. In fact, the company works closely with its suppliers to take advantage of any new developments in technology that can help it reduce costs and increase quality.

The ability of NIKE to outsource all its manufacturing abroad allows Knight to keep NIKE's U.S. structure small and flexible. NIKE is able to use a functional structure to organize its activities, and Knight decentralizes control of the design process to teams that are assigned to develop each of the new kinds of sports shoes for which NIKE is known.

---

the idea of the "virtual organization." The virtual organization is composed of people who are linked by computers, faxes, computer-aided design systems, and video teleconferencing and who may rarely if ever see one another face to face. People come and go as and when their services are needed, much as in a matrix structure, but they are not formal members of an organization, just functional experts who form an alliance with an organization, fulfill their contractual obligations, and then move on to the next project.

Andersen Consulting, the global management consulting company, is becoming just such a virtual organization. CEO George Shaheen says the company's headquarters are wherever he happens to be at the time. (He spends 80 percent of his time traveling.)[40] The company's 40,000 consultants often work from their homes, traveling to meet the company's clients throughout the world and only rarely stopping in at one of Andersen's branch offices to meet their superiors and colleagues. The consultants all pool their knowledge in a massive internal database they can easily access through computer and the company's intranet.

SUMMARY OF CHAPTER

This chapter brings together strategy formulation and strategy implementation and examines how a company's choice of strategy affects the form of its structure and control systems. The reason that many companies such as IBM and General Motors experience problems with their structure should now be clear: they have lost control over their structure, and their bureaucratic costs are escalating. The challenge for a company is to manage its structure and control systems so that it can economize on bureaucratic costs and ensure that they match the potential gains from its strategy. The following are the main points of the chapter:

✔ Implementing strategy through organizational structure and control is expensive, and companies need to monitor and oversee their structures constantly in order to economize on bureaucratic costs.

✔ At the functional level, each function requires a different kind of structure and control system to achieve its functional objectives.

✔ At the business level, the structure and control system must be designed to achieve business-level objectives, which means managing the relationships among all the functions to permit the company to develop a distinctive competency.

✔ Cost-leadership and differentiation strategies each requires a structure and control system that matches the source of their competitive advantage. Implementing a simultaneous cost-leadership and differentiation strategy is the problem facing many companies today.

✔ As a company moves from a multidomestic to an international, global, and transnational strategy, it needs to switch to a more complex structure that allows it to coordinate increasingly complex resource transfers. Similarly, it needs to adopt a more complex integration and control system that facilitates global learning. When there are gains to be derived from synergy, companies frequently adopt a global-matrix structure to share knowledge and expertise.

✔ At the corporate level, a company must choose the structure and control system that will allow it to operate a collection of businesses efficiently.

✔ Unrelated diversification, vertical integration, and related diversification require different forms of structure and control if the benefits of pursuing the strategy are to be realized.

✔ As companies change their corporate strategies over time, they must change their structure because different strategies are managed in different ways.

✔ The profitability of mergers and acquisitions depends on the structure and control systems that companies adopt to manage them and the way a company integrates them into its existing businesses.

✔ To encourage internal new venturing, companies must design a structure that gives the new-venture division the autonomy it needs in order to develop new products and protect it from excessive interference by corporate managers.

✔ Increasingly, the growth of outsourcing has led companies to develop network structures. The virtual corporation is becoming a reality as computer information systems become more sophisticated.

DISCUSSION QUESTIONS

1. How should (a) a high-tech company, (b) a fast-food franchise, and (c) a small manufacturing company design their functional structures and control systems to implement a generic strategy?

2. If a related company begins to buy unrelated businesses, in what ways should it change its structure or control mechanisms to manage the acquisitions?

3. How would you design a structure and control system to encourage entrepreneurship in a large, established corporation?

Practicing Strategic Management

SMALL-GROUP EXERCISE
Deciding on an Organizational Structure

Break up into groups of three to five people, and discuss the following scenario:

You are a group of managers of a major soft drinks company that is going head-to-head with Coca-Cola to increase market share. Your strategy is to increase your product range to offer a soft drink in every segment of the market to attract customers. Currently you have a functional structure. What you are trying to work out now is how best to implement your strategy in order to launch your new products. Should you move to a more complex kind of product structure, and, if so, which one? Alternatively, should you establish new-venture divisions and spin off each kind of new soft drink into its own company so that it can focus its resources on its market niche? There is also a global dimension to your strategy, because it is your intention to compete with Coca-Cola for market share worldwide, and you must consider what is the best structure globally as well as domestically.

1. Debate the pros and cons of the different possible organizational structures, and decide which structure you are going to implement.

2. Debate the pros and cons of the different types of global structures, and decide which is most appropriate and which will best fit with your domestic structure.

EXPLORING THE WEB
Matching Strategy and Structure

Enter Total's, the French oil company's, Web site (www. webnet.fr/total/english/enbref.htm). Click on (and print if desired) "Corporate Profile," "Strategy," and "Corporate Structure," and answer the following questions:

1. What are Total's corporate-level strategies?

2. What kind of structure does Total use to operate its corporate strategy? Is the structure appropriate?

Search the Web for a company that is in the process of modifying or changing its organizational

structure (domestic or global) to manage its new strategy. What structure is it moving toward? Why is this structure more appropriate than the old one?

ARTICLE FILE 13

Find an example(s) of a company that has changed its structure and control systems to manage its strategy better. What were the problems with its old structure? What changes did it make to its structure and control systems? What effects does it expect these changes to have on performance?

STRATEGIC MANAGEMENT PROJECT
Module 13

This part of the Strategic Management Project requires you to take the information you have collected in the last two chapters on organizational structure and controls and link it to the strategy pursued by your company, which you identified in earlier chapters.

1. What are the sources of your company's distinctive competencies? Which functions are most important to it? How does your company design its structure at the *functional level* to enhance its (a) efficiency, (b) quality, (c) innovativeness, and (d) responsiveness to customers?

2. What is your company's business-level strategy? How does it design its structure and control systems to enhance and support its business-level strategy? For example, what steps does it take to further cross-functional integration? Does it have a functional, product, or matrix structure?

3. How does your company's culture support its strategy? Can you determine any ways in which its top management team influences its culture?

4. What kind of international strategy does your company pursue? How does it control its global activities? What kind of structure does it use? Why?

5. At the corporate level, does your company use a multidivisional structure? Why or why not? What crucial implementation problems must your company manage to implement its strategy effectively?

For example, what kind of integration mechanisms does it employ?

6. Based on this analysis, does your company have high or low bureaucratic costs? Is this level of bureaucratic costs justified by the value it can create through its strategy?

7. Can you suggest ways of altering the company's structure to reduce the level of bureaucratic costs?

8. Can you suggest ways of altering the company's structure or control systems to allow it to create more value? Would this change increase or decrease bureaucratic costs?

9. In sum, do you think your company has achieved a good fit between its strategy and structure?

CLOSING CASE

Hughes Aircraft Reengineers Its Structure

Hughes Aircraft is one of the large U.S. defense companies that has been battered by the end of the cold war and the decline in the defense budget. Hughes had been accustomed to a protected environment in which lavish government revenues allowed it to develop advanced technology for military uses, such as missiles, satellites, and radar systems. However, by 1990 Hughes was confronted with a major strategic problem. How could it compete in a new environment in which government revenues were scarce? To survive, Hughes had to find a new strategy based on the development of new technology for nonmilitary uses—and find it fast.

As a first step in changing Hughes's direction, C. Michael Armstrong, an ex-IBM top manager, was appointed as CEO of Hughes in 1991. In IBM's European division, Armstrong had developed a reputation as someone who could turn around a company and redeploy its resources quickly and effectively; investors hoped he could do so at Hughes.

Armstrong began his task by analyzing the company's strategy and structure. What he found was a firm pursuing a differentiated strategy based on developing advanced technological products. To pursue its differentiated strategy, Hughes had developed a divisional structure to lead its development efforts. It had created seven separate technology divisions, each responsible for a different kind of product—missiles, radar, and so forth. Over time, the organization had become very tall and centralized, as each technology division developed its own empire to support its efforts. The primary coordination between divisions took place at the top of the organization, where top divisional managers met regularly with corporate managers to report on and plan future product developments.

Armstrong recognized that this fit between strategy and structure might be appropriate for a company operating in a protected environment, in which money was not a problem. However, it was not appropriate for a company facing intense pressure to lower costs and develop products for nonmilitary applications, such as consumer electronics and home satellites. The divisional structure duplicated expensive R&D activities, and no mechanism was in place to promote the sharing of knowledge and expertise among the different divisions. Moreover, there were few incentives for managers to cut costs because scarce resources had not been a problem, and managers had been rewarded mainly for the success of their product development efforts. Armstrong realized that to make the company more competitive and improve the way it utilized its skills and resources, he had to find a new operating strategy and structure.

Armstrong began the process of change by focusing the company's strategy on customers and markets, not on technology and products. Henceforth, the needs of customers, not the needs of technology, would be the logic behind the organization of the company's activities. He changed the structure from a divisional one based on technology to one based on the needs of customers. The seven technology divisions were reengineered into five market groups according to the kinds of customers' needs they satisfied. Thus, consumer electronics became one market group, and industrial and commercial applications became another. Then technological expertise was reorganized to serve the needs of each kind of customer.

Continuing his reengineering program, Armstrong slashed the number of levels in the managerial hierarchy, eliminating two levels in order to bring managers closer to the customer. He continued this reengineering effort by decentralizing authority and pushing decision making down into the divisions, so that lower-level managers could better respond to customers' needs. In addition, he reorganized the company's international operations by transferring managers from the United States to foreign countries so that they would be closer to their customers.

To make this new customer-oriented structure work effectively, Armstrong also changed the organization's control systems. He created a system of output controls based on benchmarking competitors' costs to provide managers with standards against which to evaluate their performance and to force them to pay attention to costs and quality. He then set up new incentive programs for managers and workers at all levels, linking the programs to achievement of the new targets for efficiency, quality, and responsiveness to customers. Finally, he worked hard with his top management team to establish and promote the norms and values of a customer-oriented organizational culture across the new market divisions. Henceforth, at Hughes technology would be made to fit the customer, not vice versa.

Armstrong's efforts to engineer a new fit between strategy and structure at Hughes have been spectacularly successful. His top management team has fully bought into the new corporate culture, and divisional managers are adopting new entrepreneurial values based on meeting customers' needs. Some of the company's successes include the launch of its RCA minidish satellite television system and the development of one of the largest private space-based satellite systems in the world.[41] Its stock price has soared as Hughes uses its leading-edge technology to provide customers with quality products at competitive prices. With its new simultaneous differentiation/low-cost strategy, Hughes is performing well in the new competitive environment.

Case Discussion Questions

1. What problems did Armstrong discover with Hughes's strategy and structure?

2. What steps did he take to reengineer the company?

CHAPTER 14

Implementing Strategic Change

Opening Case: Raising Quality at Eastman Chemicals

Overview

Strategic Change

Determining the Need for Change

Determining the Obstacles to Change

Implementing Strategic Change and the Role of Organizational Politics

Managing and Evaluating Change

Closing Case: Which Way for Merck?

Raising Quality at Eastman Chemicals

Eastman Chemicals, a former division of Eastman Kodak, is one of the success stories of the 1990s. Since 1991 it has totally restructured and reengineered its operations to make product quality and responsiveness to customers its major goals. So successful has it been in its quest to increase quality that in 1993 it won the prestigious Malcolm Baldridge National Quality Award.[1] How did Eastman's managers bring about this change?

First, top management decided to change from its old, centralized, product-oriented divisional structure to one that was based more on the needs of its customers. Prior to the restructuring, the managers at Eastman Chemicals viewed their job as creating new kinds of chemicals and worrying about who to sell them to later. After the change, the needs of customers became their paramount concern, and they saw their business as discovering what customers wanted and then marshaling organizational resources to create new products that satisfied those wants.

Second, with their new customer-oriented structure in place, top management sat down to reengineer the product-innovation process. Under Eastman's old product-oriented division structure, all divisions operated separately and there was little communication between them. Moreover, each division was organized on functional lines and made a separate and distinct contribution to product development. The result was that product development typically took a long time, and, as mentioned earlier, the product, not the customer, was the focus. Top managers decided to change totally the way their organization worked. Cooperation between divisions and functions to speed product development and to raise product quality and customer responsiveness became the goal. Therefore, management reengineered the organization on horizontal, not vertical, lines.

Third, inside each division the old functional structure was scrapped and new cross-functional product teams, composed of people from all relevant functions, were charged with the responsibility for bringing a new product to market. To understand customers' needs better, Eastman Chemicals contacted its major customers and asked them to appoint one of their managers to work with each team. Essentially, each team was empowered to take responsibility for all aspects of the management of the project, and decision-making responsibility in the company was forced down to the team level.

Fourth, top managers decided to change the reward system and introduce an employee stock ownership plan. The result of these changes, Eastman Chemicals top managers found, was an increase in motivation; faster communication and coordination; and, what they wanted most, an increase in quality and the rate of new-product innovation.

Fifth, top managers also reengineered the relationships between divisions to promote innovation, and new interdivisional teams composed of managers from each division were created. The level of cooperation and the number of new interdivisional projects started between divisions are now monitored closely by top managers, who measure performance on both a divisional and an interdivisional level. Indeed, with the new decentralized approach to decision making, corporate managers see one of their major roles as fostering integration between divisions, just as divisional managers see one of their major roles as acting as facilitators between the cross-functional teams in their respective divisions.

This dramatic change in strategy and structure at Eastman Chemicals has not been easily achieved. Many divisional managers were very skeptical of top management's efforts at change, as were managers inside each division. There was considerable resistance at all levels; managers who saw their jobs and their responsibilities shifting were afraid of the effects the changes might have on them. Nevertheless, top managers forced through the changes, and over time, as the positive effects were seen—in an increase in the number of satisfied customers, in higher profits, and in increased salaries and stock appreciation—the whole organization bought into the new philosophy. The performance of Eastman Chemicals has soared throughout the 1990s.

OVERVIEW

In today's global environment, change rather than stability is the order of the day. Rapid changes in technology, competition, and customers' demands have increased the rate at which companies need to alter their strategies and structures to survive in the marketplace. As we discuss in Chapter 4, however, one of the principal reasons companies fail is their inability to change themselves and adapt to a new competitive environment because of *organizational inertia*.[2] Once an organization has been created and task and role relationships are defined, a set of forces is put into operation that makes an organization resistant to change. In considering *The Icarus Paradox* in Chapter 4, for example, we note the tendency of organizations to continue to rely on the skills and capabilities that made them successful even when those capabilities do not match the new competitive environment.[3] We also point out that there is another cause of organizational inertia: the conflict and power struggles that occur at the top of an organization as managers strive to influence decision making to protect and enhance their own positions.

In this chapter we look at the issues strategic managers must deal with as they seek to overcome organizational inertia and change an organization's strategy and structure—in short, the issue of how to implement strategic change. Until now in our study of strategic management, we have treated strategy formulation and implementation from an impersonal, rational perspective, one from which decisions are made coldly and logically. In reality, this picture of how strategic managers decide on and change strategy and structure is incomplete; it ignores the way power and political processes influence the decision-making process and the selection of organizational objectives.

This chapter discusses why it is difficult to change organizations and outlines the issues and problems that managers must address and solve if they are successfully to change a company's strategy and structure so that it matches new competitive environments. By the end of this chapter, you will understand the forces at play when strategic managers try to change their organizations and the role of power and politics in helping to implement change successfully.

STRATEGIC CHANGE

Strategic change is the movement of a company away from its present state toward some desired future state to increase its competitive advantage. In the last decade, most large *Fortune* 500 companies have gone through some kind of strategic change as their managers have tried to strengthen their existing core competences and build new ones to compete more effectively.[4] Most of these companies have been pursuing one of three major kinds of strategic change—reengineering, restructuring, and innovation (see Figure 14.1).

Reengineering

Often, because of drastic unexpected changes in the environment, such as the emergence of aggressive new competitors or technological breakthroughs, strategic managers need to develop a new strategy and structure to raise the level of their businesss's performance. One way of changing a company to allow it to operate more effectively is by using reengineering. **Reengineering** is the "fundamental rethinking and radical redesign of business processes to achieve dramatic improvements in critical, contemporary measures of performance such as cost, quality, service, and speed."[5] As this definition suggests, strategic managers who use reengineering must completely rethink how their organization goes about its business. Instead of focus-

FIGURE 14.1

Three Major Types of Strategic Change

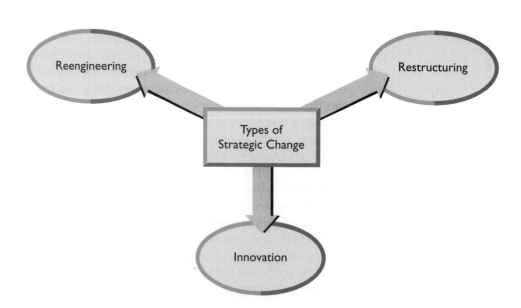

ing on a company's *functions,* strategic managers make *business processes* the focus of attention.

A **business process** is any activity (such as order processing, inventory control, or product design) that is vital to delivering goods and services to customers quickly or that promotes high quality or low costs. Business processes are not the responsibility of any one function but *cut across functions.* Hallmark Cards, for example, reengineered its card-design process with great success. Before the reengineering effort, artists, writers, and editors worked in different functions to produce all kinds of cards. After reengineering, these same artists, writers, and editors were put in cross-functional teams, each of which now works on a specific type of card such as birthday, Christmas, or Mother's Day. The result was that the time it took to bring a new card to market dropped from years to months, and Hallmark's performance increased dramatically.

Because reengineering focuses on business processes and not on functions, an organization that reengineers always has to adopt a different approach to organizing its activities. Organizations that take up reengineering deliberately ignore the existing arrangement of tasks, roles, and work activities. They start the reengineering process with the customer (not the product or service) and ask, How can we reorganize the way we do our work, our business processes, to provide the best quality and the lowest-cost goods and services to the customer?

Frequently, when companies ask this question, they realize that there are more effective ways to organize their activities. For example, a business process that currently involves members of ten different functions working sequentially to provide goods and services might be performed by one person or a few people at a fraction of the cost after reengineering. Often, individual jobs become increasingly complex, and people are grouped into cross-functional teams as business processes are reengineered to reduce costs and increase quality. This occurred at Eastman Chemicals as it reengineered itself to raise quality and responsiveness to customers.

Reengineering and total quality management (TQM), discussed in Chapter 5, are highly interrelated and complementary. After reengineering has taken place and the question, What is the best way to provide customers with the goods or service they require? has been answered, TQM takes over, with its focus on, How can we now continue to improve and refine the new process and find better ways of managing task and role relationships? Successful organizations examine both questions simultaneously and continuously attempt to identify new and better processes for meeting the goals of increased efficiency, quality, and customer responsiveness. Thus, they are always seeking to improve their visions of their desired future state. Another example of reengineering is the change program that took place at IBM Credit, which is described in Strategy in Action 14.1.

Restructuring

Restructuring is a second form of change that strategic managers choose to implement strategic change to improve performance. There are two basic steps to **restructuring**. First, an organization reduces its level of differentiation and integration by eliminating divisions, departments, or levels in the hierarchy. Second, an organization *downsizes* by reducing the number of its employees to reduce operating costs. When Jack Smith took over as the head of General Motors in 1992, for example, GM had more than twenty-two levels in the hierarchy and more than 20,000

14.1   STRATEGY*in* ACTION

A New Approach at IBM Credit

 IBM Credit, a wholly owned division of IBM, manages the financing and leasing of IBM computers, particularly mainframes, to IBM's customers. Before reengineering took place, when a financing request arrived at the division's headquarters in Old Greenwich, Connecticut, it went through a five-step approval process that involved the activities of five different functions. First, the IBM salesperson called up the credit department, which logged the request and took details about the potential customer. Second, this information was taken to the credit-checking department, where a credit check on the potential customer was made. Third, when the credit check was complete, the request was taken to the contracts department, which wrote the contract. Fourth, from there it went to the pricing department, which determined the actual financial details of the loan, such as the interest rate and the term of the loan. Finally, the whole package of information was assembled by the dispatching department and was delivered to the sales representative, who gave it to the customer.

This series of cross-functional activities took an average of seven days to complete, and sales representatives constantly complained that this delay resulted in a low level of customer responsiveness that reduced customer satisfaction. Also, potential customers were tempted to shop around for financing and even to look at competitors' machines. The delay in closing the deal caused uncertainty for all concerned.

The change process began when two senior IBM credit managers reviewed the whole finance-approval process. They found that the actual time spent by different specialists in the different functions actually processing a loan application was only ninety minutes. The seven-day approval process was caused because of the delay in transmitting information and requests between departments. The managers also came to understand that the activities taking place in each department were not complex; each department had its own computer system containing its own work procedures, but the work done in each department was pretty routine.

Armed with this information, IBM managers realized that the approval process could, in fact, be reengineered into one overarching process handled by one person with a computer system containing all the necessary information and work procedures to perform the five loan-processing activities. If the application were very complex, a team of experts stood ready to help process it, but IBM found that after the reengineering effort a typical application could be done in four hours rather than the previous seven days. A sales representative could go back to the customer the same day to close the deal, and all the uncertainty surrounding the transaction was removed. As reengineering consultants Hammer and Champy note, this *dramatic* performance increase was brought about by a *radical* change to the *process* as a whole.[6] Change through reengineering requires managers to go back to the basics and pull apart each step in the work process to identify a better way to coordinate and integrate the activities necessary to provide customers with goods and services.

corporate managers. Describing his organization as a top-heavy bureaucracy, Smith quickly moved to slash costs and restructure the company. Today, while still tall, GM has only twelve levels in the hierarchy and half as many corporate managers.

Changes in the relationships between divisions or functions are common in restructuring programs. IBM, in an effort to cut development costs and speed cooperation among engineers, created a new division in 1994 to take control of the production of microprocessors and memory systems. This restructuring move took engineers from IBM's thirteen divisions and grouped them together in a brand-new headquarters in Austin, Texas, to increase their effectiveness.

There are many reasons why restructuring becomes necessary and why an organization may need to downsize its operations.[7] Sometimes a change in the business environment occurs that could not have been foreseen; perhaps a shift in technology made the company's products obsolete, or a worldwide recession has reduced the demand for its products. Sometimes an organization has excess capacity because customers no longer want the goods and services it provides, perhaps because they are outdated or offer poor value for the money. Sometimes organizations downsize because over time they have grown too tall and bureaucratic and operating costs have become much too high. Sometimes, as with Hallmark Cards and Eastman Chemicals, they restructure even when they are in a strong position simply to build and improve their competitive advantage and stay on top.

All too often, however, companies are forced to downsize and lay off employees because they have not continually monitored the way they operate their basic business processes and have not made the incremental changes to their strategies and structures that would allow them to contain costs and adjust to changing conditions. Paradoxically, because they have not paid attention to the need to reengineer themselves, they are forced into a position in which restructuring becomes the only way they can survive and compete in an increasingly competitive environment. The story of Sunbeam-Oster, outlined in Strategy in Action 14.2, illustrates this well.

Innovation

Restructuring is often necessary because changes in technology make the technology an organization uses to produce goods and services, or the goods and services themselves, obsolete. For example, changes in technology have made computers much cheaper to manufacture and more powerful and have changed what customers want. If organizations are to avoid being left behind in the competitive race to produce new goods and services, they must take steps to introduce new products or develop new technologies to produce those products reliably and at low cost.

As discussed elsewhere, **innovation** is the process by which organizations use their skills and resources to create new technologies or goods and services so that they can change and better respond to the needs of their customers.[8] Innovation can result in spectacular success for an organization. For example, Apple Computer changed the face of the computer industry when it introduced its personal computer, Honda changed the face of the small motorbike market when it introduced 50-cc motorcycles, and Mary Kay Cosmetics changed the way cosmetics were sold to customers when it introduced its at-home cosmetics parties and its personalized style of selling.

While innovation brings about change, it also is associated with a high level of risk because the outcomes of research and development activities are often uncertain.[9] Thus, while innovation can lead to change of the sort organizations want—the introduction of profitable new technologies and products—it can also lead to the kind of change they want to avoid—technologies that are inefficient and products customers don't want. In 1993, for example, Synergen, the biotechnology company, was riding high on the promise of its new drug Antril as an effective treatment for severe blood infections. By 1994 tests of the drug had revealed that it had no promise, and Synergen announced that it was laying off 375 people, or about 60 percent of its Boulder, Colorado, work force, and looking for a prospective buyer.[10]

Innovation is one of the most difficult change processes to manage. As we discuss in previous chapters, when organizations rely on innovation as the source of their competitive advantage, they need to adopt flexible structures such as matrix

STRATEGY *in* ACTION

14.2

Turnaround at Sunbeam-Oster

In 1990 Sunbeam-Oster Company, the well-known small-appliance maker, had a $40 million loss; in 1991 it made a $47 million profit. This turnaround in the company's fortunes was achieved by the actions of one man, Paul Kazarian, a former investment banker who identified the cause of Sunbeam's problems and knew how to restructure the company to solve them.

In 1990 Kazarian led a group of investors in a hostile takeover of Sunbeam and paid $660 million for the company. He had convinced these investors that Sunbeam's recent poor showing was due to a mismanagement of its resources and capabilities, and he laid out a plan for restructuring the company if they were successful in taking over the company. Kazarian had identified three main problems at the company. It was in far too many different businesses and business segments, many of which were losing money; its structure was inefficient and leading to high costs; and it was not investing its money in the businesses with the biggest payoff.

In a presentation to investors, Kazarian outlined the way to restructure the company and offered his vision of the Sunbeam of the future. His first proposed change was to sell off Sunbeam's money-losing businesses and invest the proceeds in the company's core businesses to build their competitive advantage. For example, he outlined a plan for investing capital to develop new products in the company's core small-appliance businesses. Second, he proposed to streamline the company's remaining businesses and to rationalize their operating structures, reducing the levels in the hierarchy and downsizing the corporate staff to decrease costs.

After the takeover, he began the restructuring process, implemented his new strategy and structure, and transformed the company. By 1992 Sunbeam-Oster was worth more than $1.5 billion, and Kazarian had created more than $1 billion of value. However, his success in identifying the company's problems and devising a new strategy was not matched by his skill in managing the restructured organization. Despite the amazing operating results, in January 1993 Kazarian was informed that Sunbeam-Oster's board of directors had voted him out of office. Although no one doubted his strategy-making skills, apparently Kazarian lacked interpersonal management skills, and it was claimed that he went out of his way to abuse and humiliate managers, employees, and suppliers. His confrontational management style was impeding the top management team's ability to restructure the company and to prepare it for future growth.

---

or cross-functional team structures that give people the freedom to experiment and be creative.[11] Functions need to coordinate their activities and work together if innovation is to be successful, and companies that rely on innovation have to facilitate the change effort and support the efforts of their members to be creative. For example, the term *skunk works* was coined at Lockheed when that company set up a specialized unit, separate from its regular functional organization, to pioneer the development of a new spy plane, the U2. Creating a separate unit allowed managers to act more flexibly and autonomously. To try to increase the success rate of innovation and new product development, many high-tech organizations have developed the role of "product champion" and appointed an expert manager to head a new team and lead a new project from its beginning to commercialization.[12] Of all the kinds of change programs that strategic managers can implement, innovation has the prospects for the greatest long-term success but also the greatest risks.

In order to understand the issues involved in implementing these kinds of strategic change, it is useful to focus on the series of distinct steps that strategic managers

FIGURE 14.2

Stages in the
Change Process

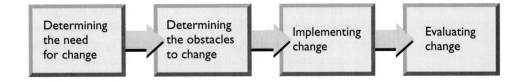

must follow if the change process is to succeed.[13] These steps are listed in Figure 14.2 and discussed in the rest of this chapter.

DETERMINING THE NEED FOR CHANGE

The first step in the change process is for strategic managers to recognize the need for change. Sometimes this need is obvious, as when divisions are fighting or when competitors introduce a product that is clearly superior to anything that the company has in production. More often, however, managers have trouble determining that something is going wrong in the organization. Problems may develop gradually, and organizational performance may slip for a number of years before it becomes obvious. At GM and IBM, for example, profitability fell, but because these were reputable companies, the fall caused little stir. After a lapse of time, however, investors realized that these companies' stock was overvalued, and their prices plunged when investors saw that managers were not taking the steps necessary to restructure the companies and turn around their performance quickly.

Thus, the first step in the change process occurs when a company's strategic managers or others in a position to take action recognize that there is a *gap between desired company performance and actual performance.*[14] Using measures such as a decline in profitability, ROI, stock price, or market share as indicators that change is needed, managers can start looking for the source of the problem. To discover it, they conduct a SWOT analysis.

Strategic managers examine the company's *strengths* and *weaknesses.* For example, management conducts a strategic audit of all functions and divisions and looks at their contribution to profitability over time. Perhaps some divisions have become relatively unprofitable as innovation has slowed without management's realizing it. Perhaps sales and marketing have failed to keep pace with changes occurring in the competitive environment. Perhaps the company's product is simply outdated. Strategic managers also analyze the company's level of differentiation and integration to make sure that it is appropriate for its strategy. Perhaps a company does not have the integrating mechanisms in place to achieve gains from synergy, or perhaps the structure has become tall and inflexible so that bureaucratic costs have escalated. Perhaps it is necessary to quickly implement a product-team structure to speed the process of product development.

Strategic managers then examine environmental *opportunities* and *threats* that might explain the problem, using all the concepts developed in Chapter 3 of this book. For instance, intense competition may have arisen unexpectedly from substitute products, or a shift in consumers' tastes or technology may have caught the company unawares. Perhaps the strategic group structure in the industry has changed and new kinds of competitors have emerged, such as one or more companies pursuing a simultaneous low-cost/differentiation strategy.

Once the source of the problem has been identified using SWOT analysis, strategic managers must determine the desired future state of the company—that is, how it should change its strategy and structure to achieve the new goals they have set for it. As occurred at IBM and Westinghouse, managers may decide to lower costs by restructuring operations. Alternatively, as happened at Merck and General Motors, the company may increase its research and development budget or diversify into new products to increase the rate of product innovation. Essentially, strategic managers apply the conceptual tools this book has described to work out the best strategy and structure for maximizing profitability. The choices they make are specific to each individual company, and, as noted earlier, there is no way that managers can determine their correctness in advance.

In sum, the first step in the change process involves determining the need for change, analyzing the organization's current position, and determining how to achieve the desired future state that strategic managers would like it to attain—by implementing a reengineering, restructuring, or innovation program, for example.

DETERMINING THE OBSTACLES TO CHANGE

Restructuring, reengineering, innovation, and other forms of strategic change are often resisted by people and groups inside an organization. Often, for example, the decision to restructure and downsize an organization requires the establishment of a new set of task and role relationships among organizational employees. Because this change may threaten the jobs of some employees, they resist the changes taking place, as happened at Eastman Chemicals profiled in the Opening Case. Many efforts at change, restructuring included, take a long time and often fail because of the high level of resistance to change at all levels in the organization. Thus, the second step in implementing strategic change is to determine the obstacles or resistance to change that exists in a company.[15]

Types of Obstacles to Change

Strategic managers must analyze the factors that are causing organizational inertia and preventing the company from reaching its ideal future state. Obstacles to change can be found at four levels in the organization: corporate, divisional, functional, and individual.

Corporate Obstacles   At the corporate level, several potential obstacles must be considered. Changing strategy or structure, even in seemingly trivial ways, may significantly affect a company's behavior. For example, suppose that to reduce costs, a company decides to centralize all divisional purchasing and sales activities at the corporate level. Such consolidation could severely damage each division's ability to develop a unique strategy for its own individual markets. Alternatively, suppose that in response to low-cost foreign competition, a company decides to pursue a policy of differentiation. This action would change the balance of power among functions and lead to problems as functions start fighting to retain their status in the organization. A *company's present structure and strategy* may constitute powerful obstacles to change. They produce a massive amount of inertia, which has to be overcome before change can take place. This is why strategic change is usually a slow process.[16]

The *type of structure* a company uses can be a second impediment to change. For example, it is much easier to change strategy if a company is using a matrix rather than a functional structure, or if it is decentralized rather than centralized, or if it has a high rather than a low level of integration. Decentralized, matrix structures are more flexible than highly controlled functional structures, and thus there is less potential for conflict between functions or divisions because people are used to cooperative cross-functional relationships.

Although some are easier to change than others, *corporate culture* can provide a third obstacle to change. For example, change is notoriously difficult in the military because everything is sacred to obedience and the following of orders. Some cultures, however, such as Hewlett Packard's, are based on values that emphasize flexibility or change itself; they are much easier to change when change becomes necessary.

Divisional Obstacles   Similar factors operate at the divisional level. Change is difficult at the divisional level if divisions are *highly interrelated and trade resources,* because a shift in one division's operations affects other divisions. Consequently, it is more difficult to manage change if a company is pursuing a strategy of related, rather than unrelated, diversification. Furthermore, changes in strategy affect different divisions in different ways, because change generally favors the interests of some divisions over those of others. Managers in the different divisions may thus have *different attitudes to change,* and some will be less supportive than others. Existing divisions may resist establishing new product divisions, for example, because they will lose resources and their status in the organization will diminish.

Functional Obstacles   The same obstacles to change exist at the functional level. As with divisions, different functions have *different strategic orientations and goals* and react differently to the changes management proposes. For example, manufacturing generally has a short-term, cost-directed efficiency orientation; research and development is oriented toward long-term, technical goals; and sales is oriented toward satisfying customers' needs. Thus, production may see the solution to a problem as one of reducing costs, sales as one of increasing demand, and research and development as product innovation. Differences in functional orientation make it hard to formulate and implement a new strategy and slow a company's response to changes in the competitive environment.

Individual Obstacles   At the individual level, too, people are notoriously *resistant to change* because change implies uncertainty, which breeds insecurity and fear of the unknown.[17] Because managers are people, this individual resistance reinforces the tendency of each function and division to oppose changes that may have uncertain effects on them. Restructuring and reengineering efforts can be particularly stressful for managers at all levels of the organization. During the 1990s, for example, AT&T announced the layoff of thousands of its managers every few years.

The Shakeout at Tenneco

A sprawling conglomerate, Tenneco operates in such businesses as natural gas, shipbuilding, auto parts, chemicals, and farm equipment. In 1991 the company, which is based in Houston, Texas, was ranked twenty-seventh in the *Fortune* 500, with sales at more than $14 billion. Nevertheless, when Michael H. Walsh became president of Tenneco in 1991, he entered a company that had experienced falling earnings for years and was expected to post a net loss of $732 million in 1991. His mission was to turn Tenneco around and restructure its assets.

Walsh was used to the challenge of changing a large company. He had successfully turned around Union Pacific, a large railroad company, and it was on the basis of his reputation as a change agent that Tenneco's board of directors had hired him. On taking over the restructuring effort, Walsh's first step was to analyze Tenneco's problems in order to see why it was having them. What he found were serious flaws in the company's structure and culture, which led to poor performance in the various operating divisions. For example, Case, the company's agricultural equipment maker, was in very poor

financial shape and was a major contributor to poor corporate performance. To keep Case afloat, top management had continually siphoned off the profits of the chemicals and auto parts divisions, which were doing well. As a result, managers in these divisions had little incentive to improve divisional performance or to cooperate with one another and share resources or capabilities.

Over the years top management had failed to institute a rigorous system of financial and output controls to monitor and control divisional performance. Divisional managers had been allowed to run their operations with little corporate oversight. Consequently, they had made investments that supported their own interests, not those of the corporation. With few checks on their activities, the divisions had become top heavy and noncompetitive. Furthermore, as mentioned, they lacked any incentive to cooperate and improve corporate performance together.

Walsh recognized that the way Tenneco's structure and culture were working had become a powerful obstacle to change. He realized that to change divisional managers' behavior and overcome the inertia that had brought the company continual losses, he would have to

Successive waves of layoffs breed fear and insecurity among employees, lessening their commitment to the organization and lowering their morale.

All these obstacles make it difficult to change organizational strategy or structure quickly. That is why U.S. car manufacturers took so long to respond to the Japanese challenge and why companies such as IBM and Digital Equipment were so slow to respond to the threat of powerful workstations and personal computers from companies such as Sun Microsystems and Dell Computer. These companies were accustomed to a situation of complete dominance in their industries and had developed inflexible, centralized structures that inhibited risk taking and quick reaction to change.

Paradoxically, companies that experience the greatest uncertainty may become best able to respond to it. When companies have been forced to change frequently, strategic managers often develop the ability to handle change easily.[18] Strategic managers must understand potential obstacles to change as they design a new strategy and structure. Obstacles must be recognized, and the strategic plan must take them into account. The larger and more complex the organization, the harder it is to implement change because inertia is likely to be more pervasive. Strategy in Action 14.3, which tells how Michael Walsh overcame inertia at Tenneco, illustrates a way of overcoming obstacles to change in a large, complex organization.

restructure the corporate-divisional relationship. He started from the top by changing managers' attitudes and behavior. First, he instituted a set of output controls and made it clear that these goals would be monitored and enforced. Second, he created a system of teams in which the managers from the different divisions met together to critique each other's performance. Third, he flattened the corporate hierarchy, wiping out three layers of corporate managers to bring him closer to the divisions and to let the heads of the divisions function as the company's top management team. (Previously, divisional managers had met one-on-one with the CEO; now they operated as a corporate team.)

After this restructuring, Walsh decentralized more control to divisional managers. At the same time, he made them more accountable for their actions, since each manager's performance was now more visible to the CEO and to other top managers. As a result, divisional managers had more incentive to improve corporate performance. These changes effectively destroyed the inertia permeating Tenneco's old organizational structure and led to the evolution of a new culture, in which corporate, not divisional, goals and values guided divisional behavior.

Walsh continued these change efforts at all levels of the company. To change attitudes and behavior at the functional level, he instituted a system of quality teams in every division in the company. In these cross-functional teams, employees are expected to search for solutions to improve quality and reduce costs, and Walsh regularly videotapes messages to Tenneco's employees to exhort them to find new ways of improving performance. He also set an example by wiping out top management's perks such as private dining rooms, luxury yachts, jets, and cars.

Throughout the company, Walsh has tried to destroy the old culture of apathy, under which managers and employees were content to maintain the status quo and avoid confronting the company's problems. So far, Walsh's efforts to change the company have been spectacularly successful. Tenneco has been making record profits in the 1990s, and analysts forecast steadily increasing gains over the years from his restructuring efforts. Overcoming obstacles to change in a company may be a very difficult process, but as Tenneco's experience suggests, managers, employees, and shareholders can reap big dividends from it.

Organizational Conflict: An Important Obstacle to Change

The obstacles to change just discussed can also dramatically reduce a company's ability to change when they spawn organizational conflict between functions and between divisions. **Organizational conflict** is the struggle that arises when the goal-directed behavior of one organizational group blocks the goal-directed behavior of another.[19] Different functions and divisions have different orientations, so if organizational change favors one division over another, for example, this can lead to high levels of organizational conflict and a failure to move quickly to exploit new strategic opportunities. A model developed by Lou R. Pondy helps show how conflict emerges in organizations and how it can become a powerful obstacle to change in its own right.[20]

The five stages in the conflict process are summarized in Figure 14.3. The first stage in the conflict process is *latent conflict,* potential conflict that can flare up when the right conditions arise. All the obstacles to change just discussed are potential sources of conflict. For example, latent conflicts are frequently activated by changes in an organization's strategy or structure that affect the relationship among functions or divisions. Suppose a company has been producing one major product type but then decides to diversify and produce different kinds of products. To

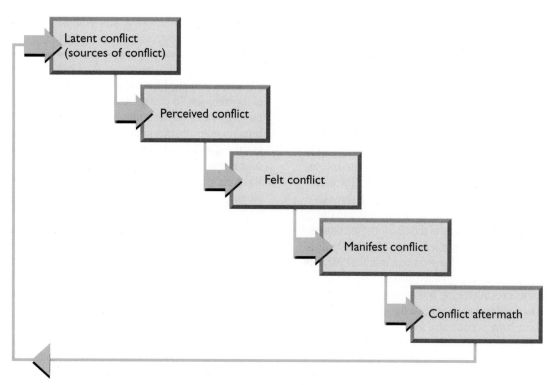

FIGURE 14.3
· · · · · · · · · · · ·
Stages in the
Conflict Process

overcome problems of coordinating a range of specialist services over many products, the company moves from a functional to a divisional structure. The new structure changes task relationships among divisional managers, and this in turn changes the relative status and areas of authority of the different functional and product managers. Conflict between functional and product managers or among product managers is likely to ensue.

Because every change in a company's strategy and structure alters the organizational context, conflict can easily arise unless the situation is carefully managed to avoid it. Good strategic planning allows managers to anticipate problems that may arise later so they can move early to prevent them.[21] For example, when managers change a company's strategy, they should also consider the effect of these changes on future group relationships. Similarly, when changing organizational structure, strategic managers should anticipate the effects of the changes on functional and divisional relationships. However, because avoidance is not always possible, latent conflict may quickly lead to *perceived conflict,* the second stage.

Perceived conflict occurs when managers become aware of the clashes. After a change in strategy and structure, managers discover that the actions of another function or group obstruct the operations of their group. Managers start to react to the situation, and from the perceived stage they go quickly to the third stage, *felt conflict.* It is at this point that managers start to personalize the conflict. Opinions polarize as one function or division starts to blame the others for causing the conflict. Production might blame the inefficiency of sales for a fall in orders, while sales might blame production for a fall in product quality. Typically, there is a marked lack of cooperation at this stage, and integration among functions or divisions breaks down as the groups start to develop an us-versus-them mentality. If not managed, this stage in the conflict process leads quickly to the fourth stage, *manifest conflict.*

At this point, the conflict among functions or divisions comes into the open, and each group strives to thwart the goals of the other. Groups compete to protect their own interests and block the interests of other groups. Naturally, this blocks change and prevents an organization from adapting to its environment. Manifest conflict can take many forms. The most obvious is fighting or a lack of cooperation among top managers as they start to blame the managers of other functions or divisions for causing the problem. Other forms of manifest conflict are transfer pricing battles between divisions and knowledge hoarding. If divisional managers refuse to share resources or information, a company cannot develop synergy between divisions, and all the benefits of changing to a strategy of related diversification will be lost.

At the functional level, the effects of conflict can be equally devastating. A company in trouble cannot change and pursue a low-cost strategy if its functions are competing. For example, if sales makes no attempt to keep manufacturing informed about customers' demands, manufacturing cannot maximize the length of production runs. Similarly, a struggling company trying to change and regain its differentiated appeal cannot do so if marketing does not inform research and development about changes in consumers' preferences or if product engineering and research and development are competing over product specifications. Most companies have experienced each of these conflicts at one time or another and suffered a loss in performance and competitive advantage when conflict blocks the companies' ability to change and adapt quickly to a changing environment.

Manifest conflict is also common in top management circles, in which managers are fighting for promotion to high office or for resources to enhance their status and prestige in the organization. If top managers are all fighting, how can a company reengineer or restructure itself successfully? Manifest conflict is also common when a family controls a corporation, as a fight in the Dart Group, described in Strategy in Action 14.4, illustrates.

The long-term effects of manifest conflict emerge in the last stage of the conflict process, the *conflict aftermath.* Suppose that in one company a change in strategy led to conflict among division managers over transfer prices. Then divisional managers, with the help of corporate personnel, resolved the problem to everyone's satisfaction and reestablished good working relationships. In another company, however, the conflict between divisions over transfer prices was settled only by the intervention of corporate managers, who *imposed* a solution on divisional managers. A year later, a change in the environment occurred that made the transfer pricing system in both companies inequitable, and prices had to be renegotiated. How would the two companies react to the need to change again? The managers in the company in which the conflict was settled amicably would likely approach this new round of negotiations with a cooperative, not an adversarial, attitude, and necessary changes could be achieved rapidly. However, in the company in which divisions never really established an agreement, a new round of intense clashes would be likely and change would be difficult to achieve.

Conflict aftermath sets the scene for the next round of conflict or conflict episode, which will certainly occur because the environment is constantly changing and so must companies. The reason some companies have a long history of bad relationships among functions or divisions is that their conflict has never been

Father and Son Go Head-to-Head

The $1.3 billion Dart Group, which owns large stakes in Crown, the nation's third largest book merchant, and Track Auto, a discount auto parts chain, is headed by Herbert Haft, now in his seventies. As chairman, Haft, who earned a reputation as a corporate raider from his attempts to take over Safeway and Eckerd, keeps close control over his company and is known for his centralized management style. In 1977 his son Robert Haft joined him as a manager in the Dart Group after leaving Harvard Business School; he became chairman of Crown Books, a Dart division, and the heir apparent of Dart Group.

By 1993, however, tired of waiting for his father to retire as chairman and pass the reins of power to him, Robert Haft attempted a coup to oust his father as head of Dart. With the support of his mother and sister, he formed a plan to succeed his father. When his father discovered it, he took immediate steps to try to reduce the power his son had developed in the corporation and to consolidate his own position. He started by relieving Robert Haft of his duties as chairman of Crown Books and subsequently fired him after the details of his plot and the extent of the involvement of other family members became apparent.

By 1995 the situation had further deteriorated as Haft and his wife divorced over her support for their son. Under pressure from other stockholders, the elder Haft was forced to retire, and the company was split up, with Robert Haft taking control of the auto parts division.

managed successfully. In companies in which strategic managers have resolved the conflict, a cohesive organizational culture develops. In these companies, managers adopt a cooperative, not a competitive, attitude when conflict occurs because of change. The question that needs to be tackled, then, is how best to manage conflict strategically to avoid its bad effects and to make changes in strategy and structure as smooth as possible. There are several tactics and techniques that strategic managers can use to overcome conflict and implement strategic change effectively. Perhaps the most important of these is the way they use power and political tactics to manage strategic change.

IMPLEMENTING STRATEGIC CHANGE AND THE ROLE OF ORGANIZATIONAL POLITICS

Decisions about strategy and structure and how to change strategy and structure are not made just by following a calculated, rational plan in which only shareholders' interests are considered. In reality, strategic decision making is quite different. When evaluating alternative courses of action and choosing a new strategic direction, managers often make decisions that will further their personal, functional, or divisional interests. **Organizational politics** are tactics that strategic managers engage in to obtain and use power to influence organizational goals and change strategy and structure to further their own interests.[22] Top-level managers constantly come into conflict over what the correct policy decisions should be, and power struggles and coalition building are a major part of strategic decision making. In this political view of decision making, obstacles to change are over-

come and conflicts over goals are settled by compromise, bargaining, and nego-
tiation between managers and coalitions of managers and by the outright use
of power.[23]

In this section we examine the relationship between strategic change and organizational politics and the process of political decision making. First, we consider the
sources of politics and why politics is a necessary part of managing the strategic
change process. Second, we look at how managers or divisions can increase their
power so they can influence the company's strategic direction. Third, we explore
the ways in which a company can manage politics to overcome inertia and implement strategic change.

Sources of Organizational Politics

To understand why politics is an integral part of strategic change, it is useful to contrast the rational view of organizational decision making with the political view of
how strategic decisions get made (see Figure 14.4). The rational view assumes that
complete *information* is available and no uncertainty exists about outcomes, but
the political view suggests that strategic managers can never be sure that they are
making the best decisions. From a political perspective, decision making always
takes place in uncertainty, in which the outcomes of strategic change are difficult
to predict. According to the rational view, moreover, managers always agree about
appropriate organizational *goals* and the appropriate *means,* or strategies, for

FIGURE 14.4

Rational and
Political Views of
Decision Making

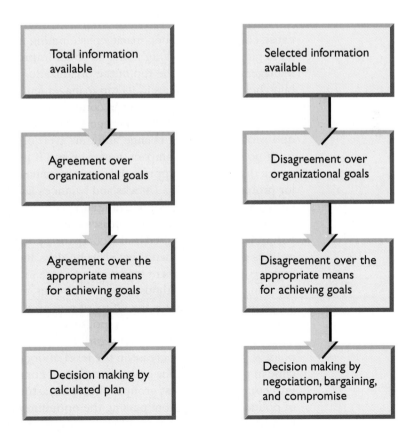

achieving these goals. According to the political view, on the other hand, the choice of goals and means is linked to each individual's, function's, or division's pursuit of self-interest. Disagreement over the best course of action is inevitable in the political view, because strategic change necessarily favors some individuals or divisions over others. For example, if managers decide to invest in resources to promote and develop one product, other products will not be created. Some managers win; others lose.

Given the political point of view, strategy choices are never right or wrong; they are simply better or worse. As a result, managers have to promote their ideas and lobby for support from other managers so that they can build up backing for a course of future action. Thus, coalition building is a vital part of managing strategic change.[24] Managers join coalitions to lobby for their interests, because in doing so they increase their political muscle in relation to their organizational opponents.

Managers also engage in politics for personal reasons. Because organizations are shaped like pyramids, individual managers realize that the higher they rise, the more difficult it is to climb to the next position.[25] If their views prevail and the organization follows their lead, however, *and* if their decisions bear results, they reap rewards and promotions. Thus, by being successful at politics and claiming responsibility for successful change, they increase their visibility in the organization and make themselves contenders for higher organizational office.

The assumption that personal, rather than shareholder or organizational, interest governs strategic choice is what gives the word *politics* bad connotations in many people's minds. However, because no one knows for certain what will happen as a result of strategic change, letting people pursue their own interest may in the long run mean that the organization's interests are being followed. This is because competition among managers stemming from self-interest may lead to better strategic decision making and lead to an improved change plan, with successful managers moving to the top of the organization over time. If a company can maintain checks and balances in its top management circles (by preventing any particular manager or coalition from becoming too powerful), politics can be a healthy influence, for it can prevent managers from becoming complacent about the status quo, promote strategic change, and thus avert organizational decline.

If politics grows rampant, however, and if powerful managers gain such dominance that they can suppress the views of managers who oppose their interests, major problems may arise. Checks and balances fade, organizational inertia increases, and performance suffers. For example, at Gulf & Western, as soon as its founder died, the company sold off fifty businesses that the new top management considered his pet projects and not suited to the company's portfolio. Ultimately, companies that let politics get so out of hand that shareholders' interests suffer are taken over by aggressive new management teams who engage in major restructuring activities, often involving the layoff of thousands of employees, to turn around a company.

Figure 14.5 illustrates the effect of organizational politics on performance. The figure shows that up to point A, politics can increase organizational performance because it can *overcome inertia and induce needed organizational change.* After point A, however, an increase in the level of organizational politics can lead to a decline in performance, for politics gets out of control and the organization fragments into competing interest groups. Therefore, astute managers seek to keep the level of political behavior from passing the optimum point. If kept in check, politics can be a useful management tool for overcoming inertia and bringing about strategic

FIGURE 14.5

Effect of Organizational
Politics on Performance

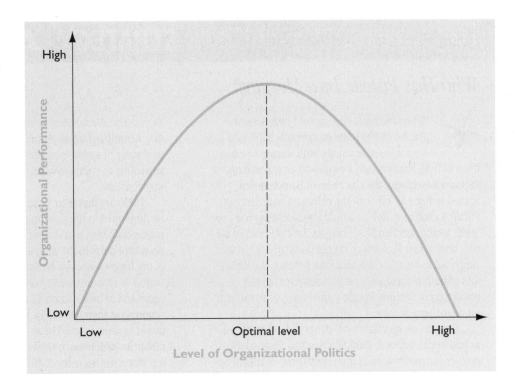

change. The best CEOs recognize this fact and create a strategic context in which managers can fight for their ideas and reap the rewards from successfully promoting change in organizational strategy and structure. For example, 3M is well known for its top management committee structure, in which divisional managers who request new funds and new-venture managers who champion new products must present their projects to the entire top management team and lobby for support for their ideas. All top managers in 3M experienced this learning process, and presumably the ones in the top management team are those who succeeded best at mobilizing support and commitment for their concepts.

Legitimate Power and Politics

To play politics and bring about the strategic change that they support, managers must have power. *Power* can be defined as the ability of one individual, function, or division to cause another individual, function, or division to do something that it would not otherwise have done.[26] Perhaps the simplest way to understand power is to look at its sources: legitimate power and informal power.

Legitimate power is the authority a manager possesses by virtue of holding a formal position in the hierarchy. This is why the CEO is so powerful. As the top manager of a company, he or she decides whom to delegate power to and how much to give. Authority also gives a manager the power to resolve conflicts and decide what needs to be done. This is the power that *gives a manager the ability to overcome obstacles to change.* As discussed earlier, for example, conflict often occurs between functions and divisions because they have different goals and interests. Because functional managers have equal authority, they cannot control each other,

Who Has Power in a Merger?

When BankAmerica merged with Security Pacific in 1991, the merger was supposed to be a merger of equals, with the top management of both banks jointly running the new company. Richard Rosenberg, the chairman of BankAmerica, agreed to form an office of the chairman with Security Pacific's chairman Robert Smith; it was also agreed that Smith would succeed Rosenberg as the chairman of the new bank when Rosenberg retired. Similarly, there was supposed to be a 50/50 board split between the directors of both companies, and BankAmerica agreed to name four of Security Pacific's top managers to the new top management team.

After the merger, however, things did not work out as had been expected. BankAmerica had planned the merger hurriedly, without investigating the details of Security Pacific's financial condition thoroughly. After the merger, BankAmerica's managers began to find major flaws in the way Security Pacific's managers made loans, which had resulted in more than $300 million of write-offs for the company, with equally large sums to follow. BankAmerica's top management team came to despise and ridicule the way Security Pacific's managers did business. They blamed a large part of the problem on Security Pacific's culture, which was decentralized and freewheeling and allowed top managers to loan large sums of money to clients on the basis of personal ties.

By contrast, BankAmerica had developed a conservative, centralized decision-making style and curbed the autonomy of lower-level managers; loans were made according to companywide criteria scrutinized by top management.

Believing that their culture was the one that had to be developed in the new organization, BankAmerica's managers began to use their legitimate power as the dominant party in the merger (Rosenberg as chairman of the bigger company had more legitimate power than Smith) to strip authority from Security Pacific's managers and to take control of the reins of the new organization. Less than two weeks after the merger, Smith found himself relieved of all important decision-making authority, which was transferred to Rosenberg and his top management team. Similarly, whenever BankAmerica's top managers were negotiating with Security Pacific's managers over future task and authority relationships, they used their power to cut the authority of Security Pacific's managers and to drive them from the organization. After a few months almost all of Security Pacific's top managers had left the new organization, followed by thousands of middle-level managers, who, BankAmerica managers felt, could not be trusted to maintain the company's new cultural standards and way of doing business.

so when functional managers cannot solve their problems, these problems are often passed on to corporate managers or the CEO, who has the authority to impose a solution on parties. The story of the way managers at BankAmerica took full control over another bank after a merger demonstrates the potency of legitimate power in bringing about strategic change. Details are given in Strategy in Action 14.5.

Informal Sources of Power and Politics

While a considerable amount of a strategic manager's power derives from his or her level in the hierarchy, many other informal sources of power are crucial in determining what kinds of changes will be made to strategy and structure and thus to a company's future direction. To a large degree, how much informal power the managers of the different functions and divisions possess derives from a company's corporate- and business-level strategies. Different strategies make some functions

FIGURE 14.6

Informal Sources of Power

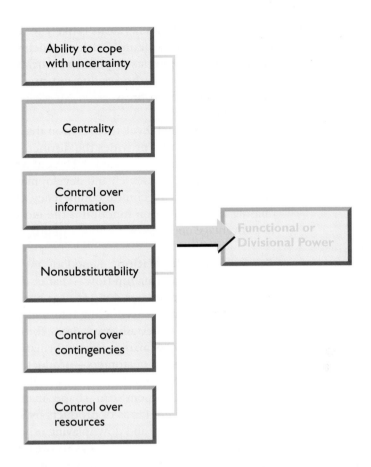

or divisions, *and thus their managers,* more important than others in achieving the corporate mission and thus confer a greater ability to implement strategic change. Figure 14.6 lists the informal sources of power that we discuss next.

Ability to Cope with Uncertainty   A function or division gains power if it can reduce uncertainty for another function or division.[27] Suppose that a company is pursuing a strategy of vertical integration. A division that controls the supply and quality of inputs to another division has power over it because it controls the uncertainty facing the second division. At the business level, in a company pursuing a low-cost strategy, sales has power over production because sales provide information about customers' needs necessary to minimize production costs. In a company pursuing a differentiation strategy, research and development has power over marketing at the early stages in a product's life cycle because it controls product innovations. However, once innovation problems have been solved, marketing is likely to be the most powerful function because it supplies research and development with information on customers' needs. Thus, a function's power depends on the degree to which other functions rely on it.

Centrality   Power also derives from the centrality of a division or function.[28] *Centrality* refers to the extent to which a division or function is at the center of resource transfers among divisions. For example, in a chemical company, the division supplying specialized chemicals is likely to be central because its activities are critical to both the petroleum division, which supplies its inputs, and the end-using divisions such as plastics or pharmaceuticals, which depend on its outputs. Its activities are central to the production process of all the company's businesses. Therefore, it can exert pressure on corporate headquarters to pursue policies in its own interest.

At the functional level, the function that has the most centrality and therefore power is the one that provides the distinctive competency on which a company's business-level strategy is based.[29] Thus, at Apple Computer the function with the greatest centrality is research and development because the company's competitive advantage rests on a technical competency. On the other hand, at Wal-Mart the purchasing and distribution function is the most central because Wal-Mart's competitive advantage depends on its ability to provide a low-cost product.

Control over Information   Functions and divisions are also central if they are at the heart of the information flow—that is, if they can control the flow of information to other functions or divisions (or both).[30] Information is a power resource because, by giving or withholding information, one function or division can cause others to behave in certain ways. Sales, for instance, can control the way production operates. If sales manipulates information to satisfy its own goals—for example, responsiveness to customers—production costs will rise, but production may be unaware that costs could be lowered with a different sales strategy. Similarly, research and development can shape managers' attitudes to the competitive prospects of different kinds of products by supplying favorable information about the products it prefers and downplaying others.

In a very real sense, managers in organizations are engaging in a subtle information game when they form policies, set objectives, and influence the change process. We discuss in Chapter 11 how divisions can disguise their performance by providing only positive information to corporate managers. The more powerful a division, the more easily it can do this. In both strategy formulation and implementation, by using information to develop a power base, divisions and functions can strongly influence policy changes that favor their own interests.

Nonsubstitutability   A function or division can accrue power proportionately to the degree to which its activities are nonsubstitutable—that is, cannot be duplicated. For example, if a company is vertically integrated, supplying divisions are nonsubstitutable to the extent that the company cannot buy in the marketplace what they produce. Thus, the petroleum products division is not very powerful if large quantities of oil are available from other suppliers. In an oil crisis, the opposite is true. On the other hand, the activities of a new-venture division—a division in which new products are developed—are nonsubstitutable to the extent that a company cannot buy another company that possesses similar knowledge or expertise. If knowledge or information can be bought, the division is substitutable.

The same holds true at the functional level. A function and the managers within it are powerful to the extent that no other function can perform their task. As in the case of centrality, which function is nonsubstitutable depends on the nature of a company's business-level strategy. If the company is pursuing a low-cost strategy, then production is likely to be the key function, and research and development or marketing has less power. However, if the company is pursuing a strategy of differentiation, then the opposite is likely to be the case.

Thus, the power that a function or division gains by virtue of its centrality or nonsubstitutability derives from the company's strategy. Eventually, as a company's strategy changes, the relative power of the functions and divisions also changes. This is the next informal source of power that we discuss.

Control over Contingencies   Over time, the contingencies—that is, the opportunities and threats—facing a company from the competitive environment change as the environment changes.[31] The functions or divisions that can deal with the problems confronting the company and allow it to achieve its objectives gain power. Conversely, the functions that can no longer manage the contingency lose power. For example, consider which functional executives rose to top management positions during the last fifty years. Generally, the executives who reached the highest posts did so from functions or divisions that were able to deal with the opportunities and threats facing the company.[32]

In the 1950s, for instance, the main contingency problem a company had to cope with was to produce goods and services. Pent-up demand from the years of World War II led to a huge increase in consumer spending for automobiles, homes, and durable goods. Goods needed to be produced quickly and cheaply to meet demand, and during this period the managers who rose to the top were from the *manufacturing* function or *consumer products* divisions.

In the 1960s the problem changed. Most companies had increased their productive capacity, and the market was saturated. Producing goods was not as difficult as selling them. Hence, *marketing and sales* functions rose to prominence. The rise of executives in companies reflected this critical contingency, for greater numbers of them emerged from the sales function and from *marketing-oriented* divisions than from any other groups.

In the 1970s companies began to realize that competitive conditions were permanent. They had to streamline their strategies and structures to survive in an increasingly hostile environment. As a result, *accounting and finance* became the function that supplied most of the additions to the top management team. Today, a company's business- and corporate-level strategy determines which group gains preeminence.

Control over Resources   The final informal source of power examined here is the ability to control and allocate scarce resources.[33] This source gives corporate-level managers their clout. Obviously, the power of corporate managers depends to a large extent on their ability to allocate capital to the operating divisions and to allot cash to or take it from a division on the basis of their expectations of its future success.

However, the power of resources is not a function merely of the ability to allocate resources immediately; it also comes from the ability to *generate resources in the future*. Thus, individual divisions that can generate resources will have power in the corporation. For example, divisions that can generate high revenues from sales to consumers have great power. At the functional level, the same kinds of considerations apply. The ability of sales and marketing to increase customers' demand and generate revenues explains their power in the organization. In general, the function that can generate the most resources has the most power.

Summary

The most powerful division or function in a company, then, is the one that can reduce uncertainty for others, is most central and nonsubstitutable, has control over resources and can generate them, and is able to deal with the critical external strategic contingency facing the company. In practice, each function or division in a company has power from one or more of these sources, and so there is a distribution of power among functions and divisions.

At the level of individual managers, too, there are various informal ways to increase personal power. First, managers can try to make themselves *irreplaceable*.[34] For example, they may develop specialized skills, such as a knowledge of computers or special relationships with key customers, that allow them to solve problems or limit uncertainty for others managers in the organization. Second, they may specialize in an area of increasing concern to the organization so that they eventually control a crucial *contingency* facing the organization. Third, managers can also try to make themselves more *central* in an organization by deliberately accepting responsibilities that bring them into contact with many functions or managers. Finally, another tactic to obtain power is to be associated with powerful managers who are clearly on their way to the top. By supporting a powerful manager and being indispensable to him or her, it is possible to rise up the organizational ladder with that manager. Political managers cultivate both people and information, and they are able to build up a personal network of contacts in the organization they can then use to pursue personal goals such as promotion.

Effects of Power and Politics on Strategic Change

Power and politics strongly influence a company's choice of strategy and structure, for a company has to maintain an organizational context that is responsive both to the aspirations of the various divisions, functions, and managers and to changes in the external environment.[35] The problem companies face is that the internal structure of power always lags behind changes in the environment because, in general, the environment changes faster than companies can respond. Those in power never voluntarily give up engaging in politics, but excessive politicking and power struggles reduce a company's flexibility, cause inertia, and erode competitive advantage.

To use politics to promote effective change, a company must devise organizational arrangements that create a **power balance** among the various divisions or functions so that no single one dominates the whole enterprise. If no power balance exists, power struggles proceed unchecked and change becomes impossible as divisions start to compete and to hoard information or knowledge to maximize their own returns. As we noted in Chapter 13, this condition prevailed at Digital Equipment when its industry-focused divisions became self-contained units that cared more about protecting their interests than about changing corporate strategy to survive in an increasingly hostile environment. In such situations, exchanging resources among divisions becomes expensive, and gains from synergy are difficult to obtain. These factors in turn lower a company's profitability and reduce organizational growth.

In the divisional structure, the corporate headquarters staff plays the balancing role because they can exert power even over strong divisions and force them to share resources for the good of the whole corporation. In a single-business company, a strong chief executive officer is important because he or she must replace the corporate center and balance the power of the strong functions against the weak. The forceful CEO takes the responsibility for giving weak functions an opportunity to air their concerns and interests and tries to avoid being railroaded into decisions by the strong function pursuing its own interests. Thus, the CEO of a large corporation has great potential for exercising power to bring about change. The CEO also plays another important role, however, that of arbiter of acceptable political decision making.

Politics pervades all companies, but the CEO and top-level managers can shape its character. In some organizations, power plays are the norm because the CEOs themselves garnered power in that way. However, other companies—especially those founded by entrepreneurs who believe in democracy or in decentralized decision making—may not tolerate power struggles, and a different kind of political behavior becomes acceptable. It is based on a function or division manager's competency or expertise rather than on her or his ability to form powerful coalitions.

At PepsiCo, politics is of the cutthroat power play variety, and there is a rapid turnover of managers who fail to meet organizational aspirations. At Coca-Cola, however, ideas and expertise are much more important in politics than power plays directed at maximizing functional or divisional self-interest. Similarly, Intel does not tolerate politicking or lobbying for personal gain; instead, it rewards risk taking and makes promotion contingent on performance, not seniority.

To design an organizational structure to create a power balance that facilitates change, strategic managers can use the tools of implementation that we discuss in Chapters 11 and 12. First, they must create the right mix of integrating mechanisms so that functions or divisions can share information and ideas. A multidivisional structure offers one means of balancing power among divisions, and the matrix or product-team structure offers another among functions. A company can then develop norms, values, and a common culture that emphasize corporate, rather than divisional, interests and that stress the company's mission. In companies such as Microsoft or 3M, for instance, culture serves to harmonize divisional interests with the achievement of corporate goals.

Finally, as we note earlier, strong hierarchical control by a gifted chief executive officer can also create the organizational context in which politics can facilitate the change process. When CEOs use their expert knowledge as their power, they provide the strategic leadership that allows a company to overcome inertia and change its strategy and structure. Indeed, it should be part of the strategic manager's job to learn how to manage politics and power to further corporate interests, because politics is an essential part of the process of strategic change.

MANAGING AND EVALUATING CHANGE

Even with the political situation under control, implementing change—that is, managing and evaluating change—raises several questions. For instance, who should actually carry out the change: internal managers or external consultants? Although internal managers may have the most experience or knowledge about a company's operations, they may lack perspective because they are too much a part of the organization's culture. They also run the risk of appearing to be politically motivated and of having a personal stake in the changes they recommend. Companies, therefore, often turn to external consultants, who can view a situation more objectively. Outside consultants, however, must spend a lot of time learning about the company and its problems before they can propose a plan of action. It is for both these reasons that many companies such as Tenneco and IBM have brought in new CEOs from outside the company to spearhead their change efforts. In this way, companies can get the benefits of both inside information and external perspective.

Generally, a company can take two main approaches to managing change: top-down change or bottom-up change. With **top-down change,** a strong CEO such as Walsh or a top management team analyzes how to alter strategy and structure, recommends a course of action, and then moves quickly to restructure and implement change in the organization. The emphasis is on speed of response and management of problems as they occur. **Bottom-up change** is much more gradual. Top management consults with managers at all levels in the organization. Then, over time, it develops a detailed plan for change, with a timetable of events and stages that the company will go through. The emphasis in bottom-up change is on participation and on keeping people informed about the situation, so that uncertainty is minimized.

The advantage of bottom-up change is that it removes some of the obstacles to change by including them in the strategic plan. Furthermore, the purpose of consulting with managers at all levels is to reveal potential problems. The disadvantage of bottom-up change is its slowness.

On the other hand, in the case of the much speedier top-down change, the problems may emerge later and may be difficult to resolve. Lumbering giants such as Tenneco and IBM often need top-down change because managers are so unaccustomed to and threatened by change that only a radical restructuring effort provides the momentum to overcome organizational inertia.

Managers at McDonnell Douglas learned this lesson when they sought ways to turn around their company's performance in the 1990s after the huge cutbacks in defense spending brought about by the end of the cold war. To improve performance, managers started a program of bottom-up change and tried to involve employees in finding ways to cut costs and raise the level of innovation. After several months they realized that nothing was changing, and so on a day that has gone down in McDonnell Douglas history as "The Monday Massacre" top managers instituted a radical program of top-down change.

They eliminated the positions of all 5,000 of McDonnell Douglas's managers and supervisors and restructured the company from seven layers in the hierarchy to five, so that in the future only 2,800 managers would be required. They then let the 5,000 managers and supervisors compete for the 2,800 new positions.[36] The placing of new managers in all-new positions totally destroyed McDonnell Douglas's old culture and ways of operating and allowed top management to bring about needed changes to the organization quickly. The result for McDonnell Douglas was a complete turnaround of its business and, eventually, a higher rate of new-product innovation. However, for about a year after the change, the company was in upheaval as managers essentially had to create a new organizational structure to operate their business. The moral of the story is that organizations that change the most find change easiest because inertia has not yet built up and those such as McDonnell Douglas that do not change find change the most difficult.

The last step in the change process is to evaluate the effects of the changes in strategy and structure on organizational performance. A company must compare the way it operates after implementing change with the way it operated before. Managers use indexes such as changes in stock market price or market share to assess the effects of change in strategy. It is much more difficult, however, to assess the effects of changes in structure on a company's performance because they are so much harder to measure. Whereas companies can easily measure the increased revenue from increased product differentiation, they do not have any sure means of evaluating how a shift from a product to a divisional structure has affected performance. Managers can be surveyed, however, and over time it may become obvious that organizational flexibility and the company's ability to manage its strategy have increased. Managers can also assess whether the change has decreased the level of politicking and conflict and strengthened cooperation among the divisions and functions.

SUMMARY OF THE CHAPTER
. . . .

Organizational change is a complex and difficult process for companies to manage successfully. The first hurdle is getting managers to realize that change is necessary and to admit that there is a problem. Once the need for change has been recognized, managers can go about the process of recommending a course of action and analyze potential obstacles to change. Strategic managers need to appreciate, however, that companies are not just rational decision-making systems in which managers coldly calculate the potential returns from their investments. Organizations are arenas of power, in which individuals and groups fight for prestige and possession of scarce resources. In the pursuit of their interests, managers compete and come into conflict. The very nature of the organization makes this inevitable. Managers have to deal with politics and conflict creatively to implement strategic change successfully and enhance or restore a company's competitive advantage. The most successful companies are those in which change is regarded as the norm and managers are constantly seeking to improve organizational strengths and eliminate weaknesses so that they can maximize future profitability. This chapter makes the following main points:

✔ Strategic change is the movement of a company away from its present state to some desired future state to increase its competitive advantage. Three main types of strategic change are reengineering, restructuring, and innovation.

✔ Strategic change is implemented through a series of steps that strategic managers must follow if the change process is to succeed.

✔ The first step in the change process is determining the need for change. Strategic managers must recognize a gap between actual performance and desired performance, use a SWOT analysis to define the company's present state, and then determine its desired future state.

✔ The second step in the change process is identifying the obstacles to change that may prevent a company from reaching its desired future state. Obstacles to change are found at the corporate, divisional, functional, and individual levels. Important obstacles include the inertia produced by an organization's present strategy, structure, and culture and differences in divisional and functional goals and interests.

✔ Organizational conflict results from fights between divisions, functions, and individual managers pursuing different goals and interests. Conflict is also a major obstacle to change, and managers must seek ways to resolve conflict to implement strategic change successfully.

✔ Strategic managers play organizational politics to overcome obstacles to change, resolve conflicts, and bring about strategic change. Organizational politics are the tactics that strategic managers engage in to use power and to influence goals and change strategy and structure to further their own interests.

✔ To play politics, managers must have power. Power is the ability of one party to cause another party to act in a way that it would not otherwise have done.

✔ Power available to strategic managers includes legitimate power and power from informal sources, such as coping with uncertainty, centrality, control over information, nonsubstitutability, and control over contingencies and resources.

✔ Power and politics influence a company's choice of strategy and structure and the nature of the strategic changes that are implemented.

✔ Strategic managers need to evaluate the results of each change process and use this analysis to define the organization's present condition so that they can start the next change process. Well-run companies are constantly aware of the need to monitor their performance, and strategic managers institutionalize change so that they can continually realign their strategy and structure to suit the competitive environment.

DISCUSSION QUESTIONS

1. What is the difference between reengineering and restructuring?

2. What are the main obstacles to change that a company pursuing a differentiation strategy faces if forced to pursue a cost-leadership strategy?

3. Discuss how you would set up a plan for change for an unrelated company that is starting to pursue a strategy of related diversification. What problems will the company encounter? How should it deal with them?

4. How can using politics to overcome obstacles to change and to resolve conflict help to implement strategic change?

Practicing Strategic Management

SMALL-GROUP EXERCISE
Handling Change

Break up into groups of three to five people, and discuss the following scenario:

You are a group of top-level strategic managers of a large well-established computer company that has traditionally pursued a strategy of differentiation based on research and development. Now, because of intense competition, your company is being forced to pursue a combined low-cost/differentiation strategy. You have been charged with preparing a plan to change the company's structure and strategy, and you have decided on two main changes. First, you plan to reengineer the company and move from a multidivisional structure to one in which cross-functional product teams become responsible for developing each new computer model. Second, to decentralize decision making and reduce costs, you propose to restructure the company and severely cut the number of corporate and top divisional managers.

1. Discuss the nature of the obstacles to change at the organizational, functional, and individual level that you, as internal change agents, will encounter in implementing this new strategy and structure. Which do you think will be the most important obstacles to change?

2. Discuss some ways you can overcome obstacles to change to help your organization move to its desired future state.

EXPLORING THE WEB
Managing Change

Enter the Web site of Sybase (www.Sybase.com), and click on "Corporate Information." Analyze the nature of the company and its business. Then click on "Press Releases," and click on the press release dated April 2, 1996, which outlines Sybase's recent change in structure (www.Sybase.com/inc/corpinfo/press/960402a.html).

1. What changes has Sybase made to its structure?

2. Why did Sybase make these changes? Do you think they are appropriate?

Search the Web to find a company that has recently been involved in some major kind of change process. What was the nature of the change? Why did the change take place? What problems did the company experience during the change process?

ARTICLE FILE 14

Find an example of a company that has been implementing a major change in its strategy and/or structure. Why did managers think that change was necessary? What kind of change was implemented, and what were its effects?

STRATEGIC MANAGEMENT PROJECT
Module 14

For the final part of the Strategic Management Project, your task is to examine how your organization has managed the process of strategic change.

1. Find some examples of recent changes in your company's strategy or structure. What kinds of change did your company implement? Why did your company make these changes?

2. What do you think are the major obstacles to change in your organization?

3. Given the nature of your organization's strategy and structure, is conflict a likely obstacle to change in your organization? Can you find any examples of conflicts that have occurred in your organization?

4. Is there any evidence of political contests or struggles between top managers or between divisions or functions in your organization? What can you find about the power of the CEO and the top management team?

5. Using the informal sources of power discussed in the chapter (e.g., centrality, control over resources), draw a map of the power relationships between the various managers, divisions, or functions inside

your organization. On the basis of this analysis, which are the most powerful managers or sub-units? Why? How do managers in the powerful sub-units use power to influence decision making?

6. How well do you think strategic managers have managed the change process? What other changes do you think your company should make to its strategy or structure?

Which Way for Merck?

Merck, the giant pharmaceutical company based in Whitehouse Station, New Jersey, is regarded as one of the best-managed companies in the United States. Over the years the company's innovative research and development has created many blockbuster drugs, such as Mevacor, its new cholesterol-lowering drug, which is earning billions in revenues. Since 1986 Merck has been headed by Dr. P. Roy Vagelos, a famous researcher who pioneered the development of many of its new drugs, and the company has had dramatic success under his leadership.

As with all the major pharmaceutical companies, however, Merck has been experiencing major problems in the 1990s. The increasing R&D costs of developing new drugs and the pressures from consumers and health maintenance organizations (HMOs) to reduce the price of drugs have reduced the profits of the large pharmaceutical companies, and Merck has been searching for a new strategy to prosper in this competitive environment.[37]

As part of his plan to develop a new strategy for the company, Vagelos decided to appoint Richard J. Markham as his successor as CEO, and Markham was named president of Merck. Vagelos saw marketing as the key to future profitability in the industry. Therefore, he promoted Markham over four other top managers who were senior to Markham at Merck and who had been leading candidates to succeed Vagelos on his retirement.

Vagelos believed that Markham, a brilliant marketing expert, not an R&D scientist, was best suited to tailor the company's strategy to its new competitive environment. Markham had risen quickly through the ranks of the company based on his success at promoting Merck's products and convincing powerful customers such as HMOs to continue to prescribe Merck's expensive drugs. Describing him as an "agent of change," Vagelos believed that Markham could alter the company's focus and give it a new way to compete in the 1990s and beyond.[38] Imagine the surprise when less than one year later Merck suddenly announced that Markham had resigned. What had happened?

In general, Markham's new strategy, with its emphasis on marketing rather than research, had caused conflict in Merck's top management team on two levels. First, Merck's success had been built on its R&D skills, and its scientists had been the acknowledged heroes of the corporation. Merck's scientists, and particularly the top managers in charge of research and development, resented Markham's new marketing-based strategy, which took both resources and prestige away from their activities.

For example, Markham had decided that Merck would produce its own line of generic drugs, which it would sell side by side with its branded drugs. In this way Merck would be able to offer lower drug prices to HMOs and still keep its share of the more expensive brand-name market. However, many top managers thought that producing generic drugs cheapened the image of the company and was not in keeping with Merck's high-price differentiated image. They thought it might backfire and hurt their R&D reputation.

Second, Markham had come into conflict with Merck's top managers over his proposed $5 billion purchase of Medco, a company that specialized in supplying generic drugs through mail order to the customers of HMOs. In purchasing Medco, Merck would control a significant part of the distribution of generic drugs and have avenues for selling its own generic drugs. Markham's new marketing strategy was based on Merck's taking control of both the production and the distribution of generic drugs. In the future Merck would be both a differentiator, still involved in the discovery of new drugs, and a cost leader in the production and distribution of generics. Markham believed that this dual strategy would pay rich rewards.

However, such a radical change in strategy was apparently too much for Merck's top management team and even for his mentor, Vagelos, to take. It called for a new vision of the company, one that would require new leadership from cost-conscious marketing- and production-oriented managers, who would directly threaten the power and status of Merck's R&D-oriented top management team. These top managers had already lost out when Vagelos had made Markham his successor, and they resented Markham's quick rise to power in the company. They would lose further if Markham began to hire more production- and marketing-oriented managers, who would manage Merck's transition to a generic drug producer.

Top managers began to resist the changes Markham was introducing and to lobby against his new strategy. They formed a coalition to convince Vagelos that Merck would only suffer from the changes Markham was proposing and that the company should retain its R&D focus. Using their power as the leaders of the function that gave Merck its chief distinctive competency—R&D—managers began to lobby for a change in strategic leadership. Facing dissent in its top management team and criticism from the board of directors, the company decided to end its experiment. Markham resigned, and the fight was on for the top job at Merck.

Case Discussion Questions

1. What was the source of the conflict in Merck?

2. Why is the new head of Merck likely to come from R&D?

Analyzing a Case Study and Writing a Case Study Analysis

WHAT IS CASE STUDY ANALYSIS?

Case study analysis is an integral part of a course in strategic management. The purpose of a case study is to provide students with experience of the strategic management problems faced by actual organizations. A case study presents an account of what happened to a business or industry over a number of years. It chronicles the events that managers had to deal with, such as changes in the competitive environment, and charts the managers' response, which usually involved changing the business- or corporate-level strategy. The cases in Part V of this book cover a wide range of issues and problems that managers have had to confront. Some cases are about finding the right business-level strategy to compete in changing conditions. Some are about companies that grew by acquisition, with little concern for the rationale behind their growth, and how growth by acquisition affected their future profitability. Each case is different because each organization is different. The underlying thread in all the cases, however, is the use of strategic management techniques to solve business problems.

Cases prove valuable in a strategic management course for several reasons. First, cases provide you, the student, with experience of organizational problems that you probably have not had the opportunity to experience firsthand. In a relatively short period of time, you will have the chance to appreciate and analyze the problems faced by many different companies and to understand how managers tried to deal with them.

Second, cases illustrate the theory and content of strategic management—that is, all the information presented to you in the previous chapters of this book. This information has been collected, discovered, and distilled from the observations, research, and experience of managers and academicians. The meaning and implication of this information are made clearer when they are applied to case studies. The theory and concepts help reveal what is going on in the companies studied and allow you to evaluate the solutions that specific companies adopted to deal with their problems. Consequently, when you analyze cases, you will be like a detective who, with a set of conceptual tools, probes what happened and what or who was responsible and then marshals the evidence that provides the solution. Top managers enjoy the thrill of testing their problem-solving abilities in the real world. It is important to remember, after all, that no one knows what the right answer is. All that managers can do is to make the best guess. In fact, managers say repeatedly that they are happy if they are right only half the time in solving strategic problems. Strategic management is an uncertain game, and using cases to see how theory can be put into practice is one way of improving your skills of diagnostic investigation.

Third, case studies provide you with the opportunity to participate in class and to gain experience in presenting your ideas to others. Instructors may sometimes call on students as a group to identify what is going on in a case, and through class-room discussion the issues in and solutions to the case problem will reveal them-selves. In such a situation, you will have to organize your views and conclusions so that you can present them to the class. Your classmates may have analyzed the is-sues differently from you, and they will want you to argue your points before they will accept your conclusions; so be prepared for debate. This mode of discussion is an example of the dialectical approach to decision making that you may recall from Chapter 1. This is how decisions are made in the actual business world.

Instructors also may assign an individual, but more commonly a group, to ana-lyze the case before the whole class. The individual or group probably will be re-sponsible for a thirty- to forty-minute presentation of the case to the class. That pre-sentation must cover the issues involved, the problems facing the company, and a series of recommendations for resolving the problems. The discussion then will be thrown open to the class, and you will have to defend your ideas. Through such dis-cussions and presentations, you will experience how to convey your ideas effec-tively to others. Remember that a great deal of managers' time is spent in these kinds of situations, presenting their ideas and engaging in discussion with other managers, who have their own views about what is going on. Thus, you will experi-ence in the classroom the actual process of strategic management, and this will serve you well in your future career.

If you work in groups to analyze case studies, you also will learn about the group process involved in working as a team. When people work in groups, it is often dif-ficult to schedule time and allocate responsibility for the case analysis. There are al-ways group members who shirk their responsibilities and group members who are so sure of their own ideas that they try to dominate the group's analysis. Most of the strategic management takes place in groups, however, and it is best if you learn about these problems now.

ANALYZING A CASE STUDY

As just mentioned, the purpose of the case study is to let you apply the concepts of strategic management when you analyze the issues facing a specific company. To analyze a case study, therefore, you must examine closely the issues with which the company is confronted. Most often you will need to read the case several times— once to grasp the overall picture of what is happening to the company and then several times more to discover and grasp the specific problems.

Generally, detailed analysis of a case study should include eight areas:

1. The history, development, and growth of the company over time

2. The identification of the company's internal strengths and weaknesses

3. The nature of the external environment surrounding the company

4. A SWOT analysis

5. The kind of corporate-level strategy pursued by the company

6. The nature of the company's business-level strategy

7. The company's structure and control systems and how they match its strategy

8. Recommendations

To analyze a case, you need to apply the concepts taught in this course to each of these areas. Where to look for a review of the concepts you need to use is obvious from the chapter titles. For example, to analyze the company's environment, you would use Chapter 3, on environmental analysis.

To help you further, we next offer a summary of some of the steps you can take to analyze the case material for each of the eight points we have just noted.

1. *Analyze the company's history, development, and growth.* A convenient way to investigate how a company's past strategy and structure affect it in the present is to chart the critical incidents in its history—that is, the events that were the most unusual or the most essential for its development into the company it is today. Some of the events have to do with its founding, its initial products, how it made new-product market decisions, and how it developed and chose functional competencies to pursue. Its entry into new businesses and shifts in its main lines of business are also important milestones to consider.

2. *Identify the company's internal strengths and weaknesses.* Once the historical profile is completed, you can begin the SWOT analysis. Use all the incidents you have charted to develop an account of the company's strengths and weaknesses as they have emerged historically. Examine each of the value creation functions of the company, and identify the functions in which the company is currently strong and currently weak. Some companies might be weak in marketing; some might be strong in research and development. Make lists of these strengths and weaknesses. The table on page C14 gives examples of what might go in these lists.

3. *Analyze the external environment.* The next step is to identify environmental opportunities and threats. Here you should apply all the concepts from Chapter 3, on industry and macroenvironments, to analyze the environment the company is confronting. Of particular importance at the industry level is Porter's five forces model and the stage of the life cycle model. Which factors in the macroenvironment will appear salient depends on the specific company being analyzed. However, use each concept in turn (for instance, demographic factors) to see whether it is relevant for the company in question.

Having done this analysis, you will have generated both an analysis of the company's environment and a list of opportunities and threats. The table on page C14 also lists some common environmental opportunities and threats that you might look for, but the list you generate will be specific to your company.

4. *Evaluate the SWOT analysis.* Having identified the company's external opportunities and threats as well as its internal strengths and weaknesses, you need to

consider what your findings mean. That is, you need to balance strengths and weaknesses against opportunities and threats. Is the company in an overall strong competitive position? Can it continue to pursue its current business- or corporate-level strategy profitably? What can the company do to turn weaknesses into strengths and threats into opportunities? Can it develop new functional, business, or corporate strategies to accomplish this change? *Never merely generate the SWOT analysis and then put it aside*. Because it provides a succinct summary of the company's condition, a good SWOT analysis is the key to all the analyses that follow.

5. *Analyze corporate-level strategy.* To analyze a company's corporate-level strategy, you first need to define the company's mission and goals. Sometimes the mission and goals are stated explicitly in the case; at other times you will have to infer them from available information. The information you need to collect to find out the company's corporate strategy includes such factors as its line(s) of business and the nature of its subsidiaries and acquisitions. It is important to analyze the relationship among the company's businesses. Do they trade or exchange resources? Are there gains to be achieved from synergy? Alternatively, is the company just running a portfolio of investments? This analysis should enable you to define the corporate strategy that the company is pursuing (for example, related or unrelated diversification, or a combination of both) and to conclude whether the company operates in just one core business. Then, using your SWOT analysis, debate the merits of this strategy. Is it appropriate, given the environment the company is in? Could a change in corporate strategy provide the company with new opportunities or transform a weakness into a strength? For example, should the company diversify from its core business into new businesses?

Other issues should be considered as well. How and why has the company's strategy changed over time? What is the claimed rationale for any changes? Often it is a good idea to analyze the company's businesses or products to assess its situation and identify which divisions contribute the most to or detract from its competitive advantage. It is also useful to explore how the company has built its portfolio over time. Did it acquire new businesses, or did it internally venture its own? All these factors provide clues about the company and indicate ways of improving its future performance.

6. *Analyze business-level strategy.* Once you know the company's corporate-level strategy and have done the SWOT analysis, the next step is to identify the company's business-level strategy. If the company is a single-business company, its business-level strategy is identical to its corporate-level strategy. If the company is in many businesses, each business will have its own business-level strategy. You will need to identify the company's generic competitive strategy—differentiation, low cost, or focus—and its investment strategy, given the company's relative competitive position and the stage of the life cycle. The company also may market different products using different business-level strategies. For example, it may offer a low-cost product range and a line of differentiated products. Be sure to give a full account of a company's business-level strategy to show how it competes.

Identifying the functional strategies that a company pursues to build competitive advantage through superior efficiency, quality, innovation, and customer responsiveness and to achieve its business-level strategy is very important. The SWOT analysis will have provided you with information on the company's functional competencies. You should further investigate its production, marketing, or research and development strategy to gain a picture of where the company is going. For example, pursuing a low-cost or a differentiation strategy successfully requires a very different set of competencies. Has the company developed the right ones? If it has, how can it exploit them further? Can it pursue both a low-cost and a differentiation strategy simultaneously?

The SWOT analysis is especially important at this point if the industry analysis, particularly Porter's model, has revealed the threats to the company from the environment. Can the company deal with these threats? How should it change its business-level strategy to counter them? To evaluate the potential of a company's business-level strategy, you must first perform a thorough SWOT analysis that captures the essence of its problems.

Once you complete this analysis, you will have a full picture of the way the company is operating and be in a position to evaluate the potential of its strategy. Thus, you will be able to make recommendations concerning the pattern of its future actions. However, first you need to consider strategy implementation, or the way the company tries to achieve its strategy.

7. *Analyze structure and control systems.* The aim of this analysis is to identify what structure and control systems the company is using to implement its strategy and to evaluate whether that structure is the appropriate one for the company. As we discuss in Chapter 13, different corporate and business strategies require different structures. Chapter 13 provides you with the conceptual tools to determine *the degree of fit between the company's strategy and structure.* For example, does the company have the right level of vertical differentiation (for instance, does it have the appropriate number of levels in the hierarchy or decentralized control?) or horizontal differentiation (does it use a functional structure when it should be using a product structure?)? Similarly, is the company using the right integration or control systems to manage its operations? Are managers being appropriately rewarded? Are the right rewards in place for encouraging cooperation among divisions? These are all issues that should be considered.

In some cases there will be little information on these issues, whereas in others there will be a lot. Obviously, in writing each case you should gear the analysis toward its most salient issues. For example, organizational conflict, power, and politics will be important issues for some companies. Try to analyze why problems in these areas are occurring. Do they occur because of bad strategy formulation or because of bad strategy implementation?

Organizational change is an issue in most of the cases because the companies are attempting to alter their strategies or structures to solve strategic problems. Thus, as a part of the analysis, you might suggest an action plan that the company in question could use to achieve its goals. For example, you might list in a logical sequence the steps the company would need to follow to alter its business-level strategy from differentiation to focus.

8. *Make recommendations.* The last part of the case analysis process involves making recommendations based on your analysis. Obviously, the quality of your recommendations is a direct result of the thoroughness with which you prepared the case analysis. The work you put into the case analysis will be obvious to the

professor from the nature of your recommendations. Recommendations are directed at solving whatever strategic problem the company is facing and at increasing its future profitability. Your recommendations should be in line with your analysis; that is, they should follow logically from the previous discussion. For example, your recommendations generally will center on the specific ways of changing functional, business, and corporate strategy and organizational structure and control to improve business performance. The set of recommendations will be specific to each case, and so it is difficult to discuss these recommendations here. Such recommendations might include an increase in spending on specific research and development projects, the divesting of certain businesses, a change from a strategy of unrelated to related diversification, an increase in the level of integration among divisions by using task forces and teams, or a move to a different kind of structure to implement a new business-level strategy. Again, make sure your recommendations are mutually consistent and are written in the form of an action plan. The plan might contain a timetable that sequences the actions for changing the company's strategy and a description of how changes at the corporate level will necessitate changes at the business level and subsequently at the functional level.

After following all these stages, you will have performed a thorough analysis of the case and will be in a position to join in class discussion or present your ideas to the class, depending on the format used by your professor. Remember that you must tailor your analysis to suit the specific issue discussed in your case. In some cases, you might completely omit one of the steps in the analysis because it is not relevant to the situation you are considering. You must be sensitive to the needs of the case and not apply the framework we have discussed in this section blindly. The framework is meant only as a guide and not as an outline that you must use to do a successful analysis.

WRITING A
CASE STUDY ANALYSIS

Often, as part of your course requirements, you will need to present your instructor with a written case analysis. This may be an individual or a group report. Whatever the situation, there are certain guidelines to follow in writing a case analysis that will improve the evaluation your work will receive from your instructor. Before we discuss these guidelines and before you use them, make sure that they do not conflict with any directions your instructor has given you.

The structure of your written report is critical. Generally, if you follow the steps for analysis discussed in the previous section, *you already will have a good structure for your written discussion*. All reports begin with an *introduction* to the case. In it you outline briefly what the company does, how it developed historically, what problems it is experiencing, and how you are going to approach the issues in the case write-up. Do this sequentially by writing, for example, "First, we discuss the environment of Company X. . . . Third, we discuss Company X's business-level strategy. . . . Last, we provide recommendations for turning around Company X's business."

In the second part of the case write-up, the strategic-analysis section, do the SWOT analysis, analyze and discuss the nature and problems of the company's business-level and corporate strategy, and then analyze its structure and control systems. Make sure you use plenty of headings and subheadings to structure your analysis. For example, have separate sections on any important conceptual tool you use. Thus, you might have a section on Porter's five forces model as part of your analysis of the environment. You might offer a separate section on portfolio techniques when analyzing a company's corporate strategy. Tailor the sections and subsections to the specific issues of importance in the case.

In the third part of the case write-up, present your solutions and recommendations. Be comprehensive, and make sure they are in line with the previous analysis so that the recommendations fit together and move logically from one to the next. The recommendations section is very revealing because, as mentioned earlier, your instructor will have a good idea of how much work you put into the case from the quality of your recommendations.

Following this framework will provide a good structure for most written reports, though obviously it must be shaped to fit the individual case being considered. Some cases are about excellent companies experiencing no problems. In such instances, it is hard to write recommendations. Instead, you can focus on analyzing why the company is doing so well, using that analysis to structure the discussion. Following are some minor suggestions that can help make a good analysis even better.

1. Do not repeat in summary form large pieces of factual information from the case. The instructor has read the case and knows what is going on. Rather, use the information in the case to illustrate your statements, to defend your arguments, or to make salient points. Beyond the brief introduction to the company, you must avoid being *descriptive;* instead, you must be *analytical.*

2. Make sure the sections and subsections of your discussion flow logically and smoothly from one to the next. That is, try to build on what has gone before so that the analysis of the case study moves toward a climax. This is particularly important for group analysis, because there is a tendency for people in a group to split up the work and say, "I'll do the beginning, you take the middle, and I'll do the end." The result is a choppy, stilted analysis because the parts do not flow from one to the next, and it is obvious to the instructor that no real group work has been done.

3. Avoid grammatical and spelling errors. They make the paper sloppy.

4. Some cases dealing with well-known companies end in 1993 or 1994 because no later information was available when the case was written. If possible, do a library search for more information on what has happened to the company in subsequent years. Following are sources of information for performing this search:

   The Internet with its World Wide Web is the place to start your research. Very often you can download copies of a company's annual report from its Web site, and many companies also keep lists of press releases and articles that have been written about them. Thoroughly search the company's Web site for information such as the company's history and performance, and download all relevant information at the beginning of your project. Yahoo is a particularly good search engine to use to discover the address of your company's Web site, although others work as well.

   Compact disk sources such as Lotus One Source and InfoTrac provide an amazing amount of good information, including summaries of recent articles written on specific companies that you can then access in the library.

F&S Predicasts provide a listing on a yearly basis of all the articles written about a particular company. Simply reading the titles gives an indication of what has been happening in the company.

Annual reports on a Form 10-K often provide an organization chart.

Companies themselves provide information if you write and ask for it.

Fortune, *BusinessWeek*, and *Forbes* have many articles on companies featured in the cases in this book.

Standard & Poor's industry reports provide detailed information about the competitive conditions facing the company's industry. Be sure to look at this journal.

5. Sometimes instructors hand out questions for each case to help you in your analysis. Use these as a guide for writing the case analysis. They often illuminate the important issues that have to be covered in the discussion.

If you follow the guidelines in this section, you should be able to write a thorough and effective evaluation.

GUIDELINES FOR THE
STRATEGIC MANAGEMENT PROJECT

The case study guidelines just discussed also can be followed to help you conduct research for the Strategic Management Project Modules that are at the end of every chapter in this book. In order to answer the questions contained in each module, for example, it is necessary to locate and access articles on your chosen company in the same way that you will update the information on companies highlighted in the case studies. Obviously, however, you need to collect more information on your chosen company because it is *your case*.

The guidelines also can be used to help you to write your Strategic Management Project. The experience you develop from analyzing one or more of the companies in the case studies and writing the resulting report should help you improve the analytical skills needed for the Strategic Management Project. Essentially, in your Strategic Management Project, you are writing about and analyzing a company at the same time to show how that company creates value through its strategy and structure.

THE ROLE OF FINANCIAL ANALYSIS
IN CASE STUDY ANALYSIS

Another important aspect of analyzing a case study and writing a case study analysis is the role and use of financial information. A careful analysis of the company's financial condition immensely improves a case write-up. After all, financial data represent the concrete results of the company's strategy and structure. Although analyzing financial statements can be quite complex, a general idea of a company's financial position can be determined through the use of ratio analysis. Financial performance ratios can be calculated from the balance sheet and income statement. These ratios can be classified into five different subgroups: profit ratios, liquidity ratios, activity ratios, leverage ratios, and shareholder-return ratios. These ratios should be compared with the industry average or the company's prior years of performance. It should be noted, however, that deviation from the average is not necessarily bad; it simply warrants further investigation. For example, young companies will have purchased assets at a different price and will likely have a different capital structure than older companies. In addition to ratio analysis, a company's cash flow position is of critical importance and should be assessed. Cash flow shows how much actual cash a company possesses.

Profit Ratios

Profit ratios measure the efficiency with which the company uses its resources. The more efficient the company, the greater is its profitability. It is useful to compare a company's profitability against that of its major competitors in its industry. Such a comparison tells whether the company is operating more or less efficiently than its rivals. In addition, the change in a company's profit ratios over time tells whether its performance is improving or declining.

A number of different profit ratios can be used, and each of them measures a different aspect of a company's performance. The most commonly used profit ratios are as follows:

1. *Gross profit margin.* The gross profit margin simply gives the percentage of sales available to cover general and administrative expenses and other operating costs. It is defined as follows:

$$\text{Gross Profit Margin} = \frac{\text{Sales Revenue} - \text{Cost of Goods Sold}}{\text{Sales Revenue}}$$

2. *Net profit margin.* Net profit margin is the percentage of profit earned on sales. This ratio is important because businesses need to make a profit to survive in the long run. It is defined as follows:

$$\text{Net Profit Margin} = \frac{\text{Net Income}}{\text{Sales Revenue}}$$

3. *Return on total assets.* This ratio measures the profit earned on the employment of assets. It is defined as follows:

$$\text{Return on Total Assets} = \frac{\text{Net Income Available to Common Stockholders}}{\text{Total Assets}}$$

Net income is the profit after preferred dividends (those set by contract) have been paid. Total assets include both current and noncurrent assets.

4. *Return on stockholders' equity.* This ratio measures the percentage of profit earned on common stockholders' investment in the company. In theory, a company attempting to maximize the wealth of it stockholders should be trying to maximize this ratio. It is defined as follows:

$$\text{Return on Stockholders' Equity} = \frac{\text{Net Income Available to Common Stockholders}}{\text{Stockholders' Equity}}$$

Liquidity Ratios

A company's liquidity is a measure of its ability to meet short-term obligations. An asset is deemed liquid if it can be readily converted into cash. Liquid assets are current assets such as cash, marketable securities, accounts receivable, and so on. Two commonly used liquidity ratios are as follows:

1. *Current ratio.* The current ratio measures the extent to which the claims of short-term creditors are covered by assets that can be quickly converted into cash. Most companies should have a ratio of at least 1, because failure to meet these commitments can lead to bankruptcy. The ratio is defined as follows:

$$\text{Current Ratio} = \frac{\text{Current Assets}}{\text{Current Liabilities}}$$

2. *Quick ratio.* The quick ratio measures a company's ability to pay off the claims of short-term creditors without relying on the sale of its inventories. This is a valuable measure since in practice the sale of inventories is often difficult. It is defined as follows:

$$\text{Quick Ratio} = \frac{\text{Current Assets} - \text{Inventory}}{\text{Current Liabilities}}$$

Activity Ratios

Activity ratios indicate how effectively a company is managing its assets. The following two ratios are particularly useful:

1. *Inventory turnover.* This measures the number of times inventory is turned over. It is useful in determining whether a firm is carrying excess stock in inventory. It is defined as follows:

$$\text{Inventory Turnover} = \frac{\text{Cost of Goods Sold}}{\text{Inventory}}$$

Cost of goods sold is a better measure of turnover than sales, since it is the cost of the inventory items. Inventory is taken at the balance sheet date. Some companies choose to compute an average inventory, beginning inventory, plus ending inventory, but for simplicity use the inventory at the balance sheet date.

2. *Days sales outstanding (DSO), or average collection period.* This ratio is the average time a company has to wait to receive its cash after making a sale. It measures how effective the company's credit, billing, and collection procedures are. It is defined as follows:

$$\text{DSO} = \frac{\text{Accounts Receivable}}{\text{Total Sales}/360}$$

Accounts receivable is divided by average daily sales. The use of 360 is standard number of days for most financial analysis.

Leverage Ratios

A company is said to be highly leveraged if it uses more debt than equity, including stock and retained earnings. The balance between debt and equity is called the *capital structure.* The optimal capital structure is determined by the individual company. Debt has a lower cost because creditors take less risk; they know they will get their interest and principal. However, debt can be risky to the firm because if enough profit is not made to cover the interest and principal payments, bankruptcy can occur.

Three commonly used leverage ratios are as follows:

1. *Debt-to-assets ratio.* The debt-to-asset ratio is the most direct measure of the extent to which borrowed funds have been used to finance a company's investments. It is defined as follows:

$$\text{Debt-to-Assets Ratio} = \frac{\text{Total Debt}}{\text{Total Assets}}$$

Total debt is the sum of a company's current liabilities and its long-term debt, and total assets are the sum of fixed assets and current assets.

2. *Debt-to-equity ratio.* The debt-to-equity ratio indicates the balance between debt and equity in a company's capital structure. This is perhaps the most widely used measure of a company's leverage. It is defined as follows:

$$\text{Debt-to-Equity Ratio} = \frac{\text{Total Debt}}{\text{Total Equity}}$$

3. *Times-covered ratio.* The times-covered ratio measures the extent to which a company's gross profit covers its annual interest payments. If the times-covered ratio declines to less than 1, then the company is unable to meet its interest costs and is technically insolvent. The ratio is defined as follows:

$$\text{Times-Covered Ratio} = \frac{\text{Profit Before Interest and Tax}}{\text{Total Interest Charges}}$$

Shareholder-Return Ratios

Shareholder-return ratios measure the return earned by shareholders from holding stock in the company. Given the goal of maximizing stockholders' wealth, providing shareholders with an adequate rate of return is a primary objective of most companies. As with profit ratios, it can be helpful to compare a company's shareholder returns against those of similar companies. This provides a yardstick for determining how well the company is satisfying the demands of this particularly important group of organizational constituents. Four commonly used ratios are as follows:

1. *Total shareholder returns.* Total shareholder returns measure the returns earned by time $t + 1$ on an investment in a company's stock made at time t. (Time t is the time at which the initial investment is made.) Total shareholder returns include both dividend payments and appreciation in the value of the stock (adjusted for stock splits) and are defined as follows:

$$\text{Total Shareholder Returns} = \frac{\text{Stock Price } (t + 1) - \text{Stock Price } (t) + \text{Sum of Annual Dividends per Share}}{\text{Stock Price } (t)}$$

Thus, if a shareholder invests $2 at time t, and at time $t + 1$ the share is worth $3, while the sum of annual dividends for the period t to $t + 1$ has amounted to $0.2, total shareholder returns are equal to $(3 - 2 + 0.2)/2 = 0.6$, which is a 60 percent return on an initial investment of $2 made at time t.

2. *Price-earnings ratio.* The price-earnings ratio measures the amount investors are willing to pay per dollar of profit. It is defined as follows:

$$\text{Price-Earnings Ratio} = \frac{\text{Market Price per Share}}{\text{Earnings per Share}}$$

3. *Market to book value.* Another useful ratio is market to book value. This measures a company's expected future growth prospects. It is defined as follows:

$$\text{Market to Book Value} = \frac{\text{Market Price per Share}}{\text{Earnings per Share}}$$

4. *Dividend yield.* The dividend yield measures the return to shareholders received in the form of dividends. It is defined as follows:

$$\text{Dividend Yield} = \frac{\text{Dividend per Share}}{\text{Market Price per Share}}$$

Market price per share can be calculated for the first of the year, in which case the dividend yield refers to the return on an investment made at the beginning of the year. Alternatively, the average share price over the year may be used. A company must decide how much of its profits to pay to stockholders and how much to reinvest in the company. Companies with strong growth prospects should have a lower dividend payout ratio than mature companies. The rationale is that shareholders can invest the money elsewhere if the company is not growing. The optimal ratio depends on the individual firm, but the key decider is whether the company can produce better returns than the investor can earn elsewhere.

Cash Flow

Cash flow position is simply cash received minus cash distributed. The net cash flow can be taken from a company's statement of cash flows. Cash flow is important for what it tells us about a company's financing needs. A strong positive cash flow enables a company to fund future investments without having to borrow money from bankers or investors. This is desirable because the company avoids the need to pay out interest or dividends. A weak or negative cash flow means that a company has to turn to external sources to fund future investments. Generally, companies in strong-growth industries often find themselves in a poor cash flow position (because their investment needs are substantial), whereas successful companies based in mature industries generally find themselves in a strong cash flow position.

A company's internally generated cash flow is calculated by adding back its depreciation provision to profits after interest, taxes, and dividend payments. If this figure is insufficient to cover proposed new-investment expenditures, the company has little choice but to borrow funds to make up the shortfall or to curtail investments. If this figure exceeds proposed new investments, the company can use the excess to build up its liquidity (that is, through investments in financial assets) or to repay existing loans ahead of schedule.

CONCLUSION

When evaluating a case, it is important to be *systematic*. Analyze the case in a logical fashion, beginning with the identification of operating and financial strengths and weaknesses and environmental opportunities and threats. Move on to assess the value of a company's current strategies only when you are fully conversant with the SWOT analysis of the company. Ask yourself whether the company's current strategies make sense, given its SWOT analysis. If they do not, what changes need to be made? What are your recommendations? Above all, link any strategic recommendations you may make to the SWOT analysis. State explicitly how the strategies you identify take advantage of the company's strengths to exploit environmental opportunities, how they rectify the company's weaknesses, and how they counter environmental threats. Also, do not forget to outline what needs to be done to implement your recommendations.

TABLE 1

A SWOT Checklist

Potential internal strengths	Potential internal weaknesses
Many product lines?	Obsolete, narrow product lines?
Broad market coverage?	Rising manufacturing costs?
Manufacturing competence?	Decline in R&D innovations?
Good marketing skills?	Poor marketing plan?
Good materials management systems?	Poor materials management systems?
R&D skills and leadership?	Loss of customer good will?
Information system competencies?	Inadequate information systems?
Human resource competencies?	Inadequate human resources?
Brand name reputation?	Loss of brand name capital?
Portfolio management skills?	Growth without direction?
Cost of differentiation advantage?	Bad portfolio management?
New-venture management expertise?	Loss of corporate direction?
Appropriate management style?	Infighting among divisions?
Appropriate organizational structure?	Loss of corporate control?
Appropriate control systems?	Inappropriate organizational structure and control systems?
Ability to manage strategic change?	High conflict and politics?
Well-developed corporate strategy?	Poor financial management?
Good financial management?	Others?
Others?	
Potential environmental opportunities	**Potential environmental threats**
Expand core business(es)?	Attacks on core business(es)?
Exploit new market segments?	Increases in domestic competition?
Widen product range?	Increase in foreign competition?
Extend cost or differentiation advantage?	Change in consumer tastes?
Diversify into new growth businesses?	Fall in barriers to entry?
Expand into foreign markets?	Rise in new or substitute products?
Apply R&D skills in new areas?	Increase in industry rivalry?
Enter new related businesses?	New forms of industry competition?
Vertically integrate forward?	Potential for takeover?
Vertically integrate backward?	Existence of corporate raiders?
Enlarge corporate portfolio?	Increase in regional competition?
Overcome barriers to entry?	Changes in demographic factors?
Reduce rivalry among competitors?	Changes in economic factors?
Make profitable new acquisitions?	Downturn in economy?
Apply brand name capital in new areas?	Rising labor costs?
Seek fast market growth?	Slower market growth?
Others?	Others?

ENDNOTES

Chapter 1: The Strategic Management Process

1. Lisa Bannon, "Mattel Names Jill Barad Chief Executive," *Wall Street Journal*, August 23, 1996, p. B3; Linda Sandler, "Mattel's Marriage to Disney Falters," *Wall Street Journal*, August 16, 1996, p. C2; Staff reporter, "Mattel Growth Strategy to Pursue Acqusitions, Overseas Expansion," *Wall Street Journal*, June 15, 1996, p. B10; and Eric Schine, "Toys R Her," *Business Week*, September 2, 1996, p. 47.

2. K. R. Andrews, *The Concept of Corporate Strategy* (Homewood, Ill.: Dow Jones Irwin, 1971); H. I. Ansoff, *Corporate Strategy* (New York: McGraw-Hill, 1965); and C. W. Hofer and D. Schendel, *Strategy Formulation: Analytical Concepts* (St. Paul, Minn.: West, 1978).

3. Andrews, *The Concept of Corporate Strategy;* Ansoff, *Corporate Strategy;* Hofer and Schendel, *Strategy Formulation.*

4. S. Tully, "So Mr. Bossidy, We Know You Can Cut. Now Show Us How to Grow," *Fortune*, August 21, 1995, pp. 70-80; and E. G. Randall, "AlliedSignal," *Value Line*, February 9, 1996, p. 1353.

5. For a summary of recent research on strategic leadership, see D. C. Hambrick, "Putting Top Managers Back into the Picture," *Strategic Management Journal,* Special Issue, 10 (1989), 5-15.

6. N. M. Tichy and D. O. Ulrich, "The Leadership Challenge: A Call for the Transformational Leader," *Sloan Management Review* (Fall 1984), 59-68; F. Westley and H. Mintzberg, "Visionary Leadership and Strategic Management," *Strategic Management Journal,* Special Issue, 10 (1989), 17-32.

7. E. Wrapp, "Good Managers Don't Make Policy Decisions," *Harvard Business Review,* September-October 1967, pp. 91-99.

8. J. Pfeffer, *Managing with Power* (Boston: Harvard Business School Press, 1992).

9. For details see R. A. Burgelman, "Intraorganizational Ecology of Strategy Making and Organizational Adaptation: Theory and Field Research," *Organization Science*, 2 (1991), 239-262; H. Mintzberg, "Patterns in Strategy Formulation," *Management Science*, 24 (1978), 934-948; S. L. Hart, "An Integrative Framework for Strategy Making Processes," *Academy of Management Review*, 17, 327-351.

10. This is the premise of those who advocate that chaos theory should be applied to strategic management. See R. Stacey and D. Parker, *Chaos, Management and Economics.* (London: Institute for Economic Affairs, 1994).

11. C. von Clausewitz, *On War*, translated and edited by M. Howard and P. Paret (Princeton, 1976), pp. 134, 136.

12. S. L. Hart, "An Integrative Framework for Strategy Making Processes," *Academy of Management Review*, 17, 327-351.

13. See R. A. Burgelman, "Intraorganizational Ecology of Strategy Making and Organizational Adaptation: Theory and Field Research," *Organization Science*, 2 (1991), 239-262; H. Mintzberg, "Patterns in Strategy Formulation," *Management Science*, 24 (1978), 934-948.

14. R. A. Burgelman and A. S. Grove. "Strategic Dissonance," *California Management Review*, Winter 1996, pp. 8-28.

15. M. Dickson, "Back to the Future," *Financial Times*, May 30, 1994, p. 7.

16. Richard T. Pascale, "Perspectives on Strategy: The Real Story Behind Honda's Success," *California Management Review*, 26 (1984), 47-72.

17. Sources: "The Accidental Superhighway: A Survey of the Internet," *The Economist*, July 1, 1995; and G. Gilder, "The Coming Software Shift," *Forbes ASAP*, August 28, 1995, 147-162; R. D. Hof, K. Rebello, and P. Burrows, "Scott McNealy's Rising Sun," *Business Week*, January 22, 1996, pp. 66-73; and A. Cortese, J. Verity, K. Rebello, R. Hof, "The Software Revolution," *Business Week*, December 4, 1995, pp. 78-90.

18. This viewpoint is strongly emphasized by R. A. Burgelman and A. S. Grove, "Strategic Dissonance," *California Management Review*, Winter 1996, pp. 8-28.

19. Burgelman and Grove, "Strategic Dissonance," pp. 8-28.

20. C. C. Miller and L. B. Cardinal, "Strategic Planning and Firm Performance: A Synthesis of More than Two Decades of Research," *Academy of Management Journal*, 37, 1649-1665.

21. Thomas J. Peters and Robert H. Waterman, *In Search of Excellence* (New York: Harper & Row, 1982); Thomas J. Peters. *Liberation Management: Necessary Disorganization for the Nanosecond Nineties* (New York: A. A. Knopf, 1992).

22. Henry Mintzberg, "The Design School: Reconsidering the Basic Premises of Strategic Management," *Strategic Management Journal*, 11 (1990), 171-196; Henry Mintzberg, *The Rise and Fall of Strategic Planning* (New York: Free Press, 1994).

23. "According to Plan," *The Economist*, July 22, 1989, pp. 60-63; Arie P. de Geus, "Planning as Learning," *Harvard Business Review,* March-April 1988, pp. 70-74; Pierre Wack, "Scenarios: Uncharted Waters Ahead," *Harvard Business Review,* September-October 1985, pp. 73-89; Toni Mack, "It's Time to Take Risks," *Forbes,* October 6, 1986, pp. 125-133.

24. P. J. H. Schoemaker, "Multiple Scenario Development: Its Conceptual and Behavioral Foundation," *Strategic Management Journal*, 14 (1993), 193-213.

25. G. Hamel and C. K. Prahalad, *Competing for the Future* (Free Press: New York, 1994).

26. See G. Hamel and C. K. Prahalad, "Strategic Intent," *Harvard Business Review,* May-June 1989, p. 64.

27. For a review of the evidence, see C. R. Schwenk, "Cognitive Simplification Processes in Strategic Decision Making," *Strategic Management Journal*, 5 (1984), 111-128; and K. M. Eisenhardt and M. Zbaracki, "Strategic Decision Making," *Strategic Management Journal*, Special Issue, 13 (1992), 17-37.

28. H. Simon, *Administrative Behavior* (New York: McGraw-Hill, 1957).

29. The original statement of this phenomenon was made by A. Tversky and D. Kahneman, "Judgment Under Uncertainty: Heuristics and Biases," *Science,* 185 (1974), 1124-1131.

30. Schwenk, "Cognitive Simplification Processes," pp. 111-128.

31. B. M. Staw, "The Escalation of Commitment to a Course of Action," *Academy of Management Review*, 6 (1981), 577-587.

32. Ibid.

33. M. J. Tang, "An Economic Perspective on Escalating Commitment," *Strategic Management Journal,* 9 (1988), 79-92.

34. R. Roll, "The Hubris Hypotheses of Corporate Takeovers," *Journal of Business,* 59 (1986), 197-216.

35. Irvin L. Janis, *Victims of Groupthink,* 2nd ed. (Boston: Houghton Mifflin, 1982).

36. The story ran on an almost daily basis in the *Financial Times* of London during the autumn of 1979.

37. See R. O. Mason, "A Dialectic Approach to Strategic Planning," *Management Science,* 13 (1969), 403-414; R. A. Cosier and J. C. Aplin, "A Critical View of Dialectic Inquiry in Strategic Planning," *Strategic Management Journal,* 1 (1980), 343-356; and I. I. Mintroff and R. O. Mason, "Structuring III—Structured Policy Issues: Further Explorations in a Methodology for Messy Problems," *Strategic Management Journal,* 1 (1980), 331-342.

38. Mason, "A Dialectic Approach," pp. 403-414.

39. D. M. Schweiger and P. A. Finger, "The Comparative Effectiveness of Dialectic Inquiry and Devil's Advocacy," *Strategic Management Journal,* 5 (1984), 335-350.

40. B. O'Brian, "Flying on the Cheap," *Wall Street Journal,* October 26, 1992, p. A1; B. O'Reilly, "Where Service Flies Right," *Fortune,* August 24, 1992, pp. 116-117; A. Salpukas, "Hurt in Expansion, Airlines Cut Back and May Sell Hubs," *Wall Street Journal,* April 1, 1993, pp. A1, C8.

Chapter 2: Stakeholders and the Corporate Mission

1. J. E. Rigdon and J. S. Lubin, "Why Morrison Board Fired Agee," *Wall Street Journal,* February 13, 1995, p. B1; C. McCoy, "Worst 5 and 1 Year Performer: Morrison Knudsen," *Wall Street Journal,* February 29, 1996, p. R2; Staff Reporter, "Morrison Knudsen Settles Most Shareholder Lawsuits," *Wall Street Journal,* September 21, 1995, p. B8; and J. E. Rigdon, "William Agee to Leave Morrison Knudsen," *Wall Street Journal,* February 2, 1995, p. B1.

2. E. Freeman, *Strategic Management: A Stakeholder Approach* (Boston: Pitman Press, 1984).

3. C. W. L. Hill and T. M. Jones, "Stakeholder-Agency Theory," *Journal of Management Studies,* 29 (1992), 131-154; and J. G. March and H. A. Simon, *Organizations* (New York: Wiley, 1958).

4. Hill and Jones, "Stakeholder-Agency Theory."

5. I. C. Macmillan and P. E. Jones, *Strategy Formulation: Power and Politics* (St. Paul, Minn.: West, 1986).

6. Kenneth Labich, "How Dick Ferris Blew It," *Fortune,* July 6, 1987, pp. 42-46; Jodi Klein, "The Lack of Allegiance at Allegis," *Business & Society Review,* Spring 1988, pp. 30-33; and James Ellis, "The Unraveling of an Idea," *Business Week,* June 22, 1987, pp. 42-43.

7. Derek F. Abell, *Defining the Business: The Starting Point of Strategic Planning* (Englewood Cliffs, N.J.: Prentice-Hall, 1980); K. Andrews, *The Concept of Corporate Strategy* (Homewood, Ill.: Dow Jones Irwin, 1971); and John A. Pearce, "The Company Mission as a Strategic Tool," *Sloan Management Review* (Spring 1982), 15-24.

8. Source: Boeing's World Wide Web home page (http://www.boeing.com).

9. Source: Intel's World Wide Web home page (http://www.intel.com). This statement was given in the on-line version of Intel's 1995 Annual Report.

10. Source: Weyerhaeuser's 1996 Annual Report.

11. G. Hamel and C. K. Prahalad, *Competing for the Future* (Boston: Harvard Business School Press, 1994).

12. Quoted in S. Tully, "Why Go for Stretch Targets?" *Fortune,* November 14, 1995, pp. 145-158.

13. These three questions were first proposed by P. F. Drucker. See P. F. Drucker, *Management—Tasks, Responsibilities, Practices* (New York: Harper & Row, 1974), pp. 74-94.

14. Derek F. Abell, *Defining the Business: The Starting Point of Strategic Planning* (Englewood Cliffs, N.J.: Prentice-Hall, 1980).

15. Sources: Tully, "Why Go for Stretch Targets?"; 3M 1994 Annual Report.

16. Theodore Levitt, "Marketing Myopia," *Harvard Business Review* (July-August 1960), 45-56.

17. P. A. Kidwell and P. E. Ceruzzi, *Landmarks in Digital Computing* (Washington, D.C., Smithsonian Institute, 1994).

18. Source: Kodak's World Wide Web site. (http://www.kodak.com).

19. Source: J. Welsh, "To Our Share Owners," letter in GE's 1994 Annual Report.

20. Source: J. Welsh, "To Our Share Owners," letter in GE's 1994 Annual Report.

21. M. D. Richards, *Setting Strategic Goals and Objectives* (St. Paul, Minn.: West, 1986).

22. For details, see "Johnson & Johnson (A)," *Harvard Business School Case* No. 384-053.

23. J. P. Kotter and J. L. Heskett, *Corporate Culture and Performance* (New York: Free Press, 1992).

24. Richards, *Setting Strategic Goals and Objectives.*

25. E. A. Locke, G. P. Latham, and M. Erez, "The Determinants of Goal Commitment," *Academy of Management Review,* 13 (1988), 23-39.

26. M. Hammer and J. Champy, *Reengineering the Corporation* (New York: Harper Business, 1993).

27. R. E. Hoskisson, M. A. Hitt, and C. W. L. Hill, "Managerial Incentives and Investment in R&D in Large Multiproduct Firms," *Organization Science,* 3 (1993), 325-341.

28. Robert H. Hayes and William J. Abernathy, "Managing Our Way to Economic Decline," *Harvard Business Review* (July-August 1980), 67-77.

29. Lester C. Thurow, *The Zero Sum Solution* (New York: Simon and Schuster, 1985), pp. 69-89.

30. Michael L. Dertouzos, Richard K. Lester, and Robert M. Solow, *Made in America* (Cambridge, Mass.: MIT Press, 1989).

31. M. C. Jensen and W. H. Meckling, "Theory of the Firm: Managerial Behavior, Agency Costs and Ownership Structure," *Journal of Financial Economics,* 3 (1976), 305-360.

32. Sources: Anonymous, "Flat Out in Japan," *The Economist,* February 1, 1992, pp. 79-80; H. Nomura, "IBM, Apple Fight LCD Screen Tariffs: U.S. Decision Forcing Assembly Offshore," *The Nikkei Weekly,* October 26, 1992; A. Tanzer, "The New Improved Color Computer," *Forbes,* July 23, 1990, pp. 276-280.

33. For example, see R. Marris, *The Economic Theory of Managerial Capitalism* (London: Macmillan, 1964) and J. K. Galbraith, *The New Industrial State* (Boston: Houghton Mifflin, 1970).

34. E. F. Fama, "Agency Problems and the Theory of the Firm," *Journal of Political Economy,* 88 (1980), 375-390.

35. John A. Byrne and Chuck Hawkins, "Executive Pay: The Party Ain't Over Yet," *Business Week,* April 26, 1993, pp. 56–64.

36. George Will, "CEOs Aren't Paid for Performance," *Seattle Times,* September 1, 1991, p. 1.

37. For academic studies that look at the determinants of CEOs' pay, see M. C. Jensen and K. J. Murphy, "Performance Pay and Top Management Incentives," *Journal of Political Economy,* 98 (1990), 225–264; Charles W. L. Hill and Phillip Phan, "CEO Tenure as a Determinant of CEO Pay," *Academy of Management Journal,* 34 (1991), 707–717; and H. L. Tosi and L. R. Gomez-Mejia, "CEO Compensation Monitoring and Firm Performance," *Academy of Management Journal,* 37 (1994), 1002–1016.

38. Byrne and Hawkins, "Executive Pay: The Party Ain't Over Yet."

39. Carl Icahn, "What Ails Corporate America—And What Should Be Done?" *Business Week,* October 27, 1986, p. 101.

40. E. T. Penrose, *The Theory of the Growth of the Firm* (London: Macmillan, 1958).

41. O. E. Williamson, *The Economic Institutions of Capitalism* (New York: Free Press, 1985).

42. Fama, "Agency Problems and the Theory of the Firm."

43. S. Finkelstein and R. D'Aveni, "CEO Duality as a Double Edged Sword," *Academy of Management Journal,* 37 (1994), 1079–1108; B. Ram Baliga and R. C. Moyer, "CEO Duality and Firm Performance," *Strategic Management Journal,* 17 (1996), 41–53; M. L. Mace, *Directors: Myth and Reality* (Cambridge, Mass.: Harvard University Press, 1971); and S. C. Vance, *Corporate Leadership: Boards of Directors and Strategy* (New York: McGraw-Hill, 1983).

44. Michele Galen, "A Seat on the Board Is Getting Hotter," *Business Week,* July 3, 1989, pp. 72–73.

45. J. S. Lublin, "Irate Shareholders Target Ineffective Board Members," *Wall Street Journal,* November 6, 1995, p. B1.

46. Gilbert Fuchsberg, "Chief Executives See Their Power Shrink," *Wall Street Journal,* March 15, 1993, pp. B1, B3.

47. John Byrne, "If CEO Pay Makes You Sick, Don't Look at Stock Options," *Business Week,* April 13, 1992, pp. 34–35.

48. W. G. Lewellen, C. Eoderer, and A. Rosenfeld, "Merger Decisions and Executive Stock Ownership in Acquiring Firms," *Journal of Accounting and Economics,* 7 (1985), 209–231.

49. C. W. L. Hill and S. A. Snell, "External Control, Corporate Strategy, and Firm Performance," *Strategic Management Journal,* 9 (1988), 577–590.

50. J. P. Walsh and R. D. Kosnik, "Corporate Raiders and Their Disciplinary Role in the Market for Corporate Control," *Academy of Management Journal,* 36 (1993), 671–700.

51. See Michael C. Jensen, "Agency Costs of Free Cash Flow, Corporate Finance, and Takeovers," *American Economic Review* (1986), 323–329; and Michael C. Jensen, "The Eclipse of the Public Corporation," *Harvard Business Review,* 76 (September–October 1989), 61–74.

52. Robert B. Reich, "Leveraged Buyouts: America Pays the Price," *New York Times Magazine,* January 29, 1989, pp. 32–40.

53. P. H. Pan and C. W. L. Hill, "Organizational Restructuring and Economic Performance in Leverage Buyouts," *Academy of Management Journal,* 38 (1995), 704–739; M. F. Wiersema and J. P. Liebskind, "The Effects of Leverage Buy-

outs on Corporate Growth and Diversification in Large Firms," *Strategic Management Journal,* 16 (1995), 447–460; and J. P. Liebskind, M. F. Wiersema, and G. Hansen. "LBOs, Corporate Restructuring, and the Incentive Intensity Hypothesis," *Financial Management,* 21 (1992), 50–57.

54. R. Edward Freeman and Daniel Gilbert, *Corporate Strategy and the Search for Ethics* (Englewood Cliffs, N.J.: Prentice-Hall, 1988).

55. Robert C. Solomon, *Ethics and Excellence* (Oxford: Oxford University Press, 1992).

56. Saul W. Gellerman, "Why Good Managers Make Bad Ethical Choices," *Ethics in Practice: Managing the Moral Corporation,* ed. Kenneth R. Andrews (Boston: Harvard Business School Press, 1989).

57. Kirk O. Hanson and Manuel Velasquez, "Hewlett Packard Company: Managing Ethics and Values," in *Corporate Ethics: A Prime Business Asset,* The Business Roundtable, February 1988.

58. Sources: Benjamin Holden, "Foodmaker Delays Expansion Plans in Wake of Food-Poisoning Outbreak," *Wall Street Journal,* February 16, 1993, p. B10; and Benjamin Holden, "Foodmaker, Struggling after Poisonings, Breaks with Its Public Relations Firm," *Wall Street Journal,* February 12, 1993, p. A4.

59. For example, see Freeman and Gilbert, *Corporate Strategy and the Search for Ethics;* Thomas Jones, "Ethical Decision Making by Individuals in Organizations," *Academy of Management Review,* 16 (1991), 366–395; and J. R. Rest, *Moral Development: Advances in Research and Theory* (New York: Praeger, 1986).

60. Milton Friedman, "A Friedman Doctrine: The Social Responsibility of Business Is to Increase Its Profits," *New York Times Magazine,* September 13, 1970, p. 33.

61. Edward H. Bowman, "Corporate Social Responsibility and the Investor," *Journal of Contemporary Business* (Winter 1973), 49–58.

62. Tara Parker Poe, "Body Shop Comes Clean About Audit of Its Operation," *Wall Street Journal,* January 26, 1996, p. B12; Staff reporter, "Storm in a Bubble Bath," *Economist,* September 3, 1994, p. 56; and J. Entine, "Shattered Image," *Business Ethics* magazine, September/October 1994, pp. 23–28; and Gordon Roddick, letter to *Business Ethics* subscribers, September 22, 1994, Body Shop International.

Chapter 3: External Analysis: The Identification of Industry Opportunities and Threats

1. Sources: The World Wide Web page for Micron Technology (http://www.micron.com); Staff reporter, "When the Chips Are Down," *Economist,* March 23, 1996, pp. 19–21; L. Kehoe, "US Chip Makers Seek to Dispel the Gloom," *Financial Times,* June 17, 1996, p. 20; Staff reporter, "Remind Me How to Make Money," *Economist,* August 26, 1995, pp. 55–56; and Standard & Poor's, *Industry Surveys,* "Electronics." August 3, 1995.

2. M. E. Porter, *Competitive Strategy* (New York: Free Press, 1980).

3. J. E. Bain, *Barriers to New Competition* (Cambridge, Mass.: Harvard University Press, 1956). For a review of the modern literature on barriers to entry, see R. J. Gilbert, "Mobility Barriers and the Value of Incumbency," in R. Schmalensee and R.D. Willig, *Handbook*

of Industrial Organization, Vol. 1 (Amsterdam: North Holland, 1989).

4. Most of this information on barriers to entry can be found in the industrial organization economics literature. See especially the following works: Bain, *Barriers to New Competition;* M. Mann, "Seller Concentration, Barriers to Entry and Rates of Return in 30 Industries," *Review of Economics and Statistics,* 48 (1966), 296-307; W. S. Comanor and T. A. Wilson, "Advertising, Market Structure and Performance," *Review of Economics and Statistics,* 49 (1967), 423-440; and R. J. Gilbert, Mobility Barriers and the Value of Incumbency.

5. Staff reporter, "Only Here for the Biru," *Economist,* May 14, 1994, pp. 69-71; and T. Craig, "The Japanese Beer Industry," in. C. W. L. Hill and G. R. Jones, *Strategic Management: An Integrated Approach* (Boston: Houghton Mifflin, 1995).

6. For a discussion of tacit agreements, see T. C. Schelling, *The Strategy of Conflict* (Cambridge, Mass.: Harvard University Press, 1960).

7. R. Oram. "Washing Whiter Proves a Murky Business," *Financial Times,* December 21, 1994, p. 6.

8. P. Ghemawat, *Commitment: The Dynamics of Strategy* (Boston: Harvard Business School Press, 1991).

9. For details see D. F. Barnett and R. W. Crandall, *Up from the Ashes* (Washington, D.C.: Brookings Institute, 1986); and F. Koelbel, "Strategies for Restructuring the Steel Industry," *33 Metal Producing,* December 1986, pp. 28-33.

10. D. Kirkpatrick, "Why Compaq Is Mad at Intel," *Fortune,* October 31, 1994, pp. 171-178.

11. Sources: E. Tanouye, "Drug Prices Get a Dose of Market Pressure," *Wall Street Journal,* March 11, 1993, p. B1; and C. G. McLaughlin, "Market Responses to HMOs: Price Competition or Rivalry?" *Inquiry,* 25 (1988), 207-218.

12. See M. Gort and J. Klepper, "Time Paths in the Diffusion of Product Innovations," *Economic Journal* (September 1982), 630-653. Looking at the history of forty-six different products, Gort and Klepper found that the length of time before other companies entered the markets created by a few inventive companies declined from an average of 14.4 years for products introduced before 1930 to 4.9 years for those introduced after 1949.

13. The phrase was originally coined by J. Schumpeter, *Capitalism, Socialism and Democracy* (London: Macmillan, 1950), p. 68.

14. The development of strategic-group theory has been a strong theme in the strategy literature during recent years. Important contributions include the following: R. E. Caves and Michael E. Porter, "From Entry Barriers to Mobility Barriers," *Quarterly Journal of Economics* (May 1977), 241-262; K. R. Harrigan, "An Application of Clustering for Strategic Group Analysis," *Strategic Management Journal,* 6 (1985), 55-73; K. J. Hatten and D. E. Schendel, "Heterogeneity Within an Industry: Firm Conduct in the U.S. Brewing Industry, 1952-71," *Journal of Industrial Economics,* 26 (1977), 97-113; and Michael E. Porter, "The Structure Within Industries and Companies' Performance," *Review of Economics and Statistics,* 61 (1979), 214-227. For an example of more recent work, see K. Cool and D. Schendel, "Performance Differences Among Strategic Group Members," *Strategic Management Journal,* 9 (1988), 207-233; and C. S. Galbraith, G. B. Merrill, and G. Morgan, "Bilateral

15. Strategic Groups," *Strategic Management Journal,* 15 (1994), 613-626.

15. For details on the strategic-group structure in the pharmaceutical industry, see K. Cool and I. Dierickx, "Rivalry, Strategic Groups, and Firm Profitability," *Strategic Management Journal,* 14 (1993), 47-59.

16. This perspective is associated with the Austrian School Economics. The perspective goes back to Schumpeter. For a recent summary of this school and its implications for strategy, see R. Jacobson, "The Austrian School of Strategy," *Academy of Management Review,* 17 (1992), 782-807; and C. W. L. Hill and D. Deeds, "The Importance of Industry Structure for the Determination of Industry Profitability: A Neo-Austrian Approach," *Journal of Management Studies,* 33 (1996), 429-451.

17. D. F. Barnett, and R. W. Crandall, *Up from the Ashes* (Washington, D.C.: Brookings Institute, 1986).

18. M. E. Porter, *The Competitive Advantage of Nations* (New York: Free Press, 1990).

19. The term *punctuated equilibrium* is borrowed from evolutionary biology. For a detailed explanation of the concept, see M .L. Tushman, W. H. Newman, and E. Romanelli, "Convergence and Upheaval: Managing the Unsteady Pace of Organizational Evolution," *California Management Review,* 29, No. 1 (1985), 29-44; and C. J. G. Gersick, "Revolutionary Change Theories: A Multilevel Exploration of the Punctuated Equilibrium Paradigm," *Academy of Management Review,* 16 (1991), 10-36.

20. R. D'Avani, *Hypercompetition* (New York: Free Press, 1994).

21. C. W. L. Hill and D. Deeds, "The Importance of Industry Structure for the Determination of Industry Profitability: A Neo-Austrian Approach," *Journal of Management Studies,* 33 (1996), 429-451.

22. R. P. Rumelt, "How Much Does Industry Matter?" *Strategic Management Journal,* 12 (1991), 167-185.

23. See R. Schmalensee, "Inter-Industry Studies of Structure and Performance," in Schmalensee and Willig, *Handbook of Industrial Organization.*

24. For example, see K. Cool and D. Schendel, "Strategic Group Formation and Performance: The Case of the U.S. Pharmaceutical Industry 1932-1992," *Management Science* (September 1987), 1102-1124.

25. Charles W. Hofer has argued that life cycle considerations may be the most important contingency when formulating business strategy. See Charles W. Hofer, "Towards a Contingency Theory of Business Strategy," *Academy of Management Journal,* 18 (1975), 784-810. There is also empirical evidence to support this view. See C. R. Anderson and C. P. Zeithaml, "Stages of the Product Life Cycle, Business Strategy, and Business Performance," *Academy of Management Journal,* 27 (1984), 5-24; and D. C. Hambrick and D. Lei, "Towards an Empirical Prioritization of Contingency Variables for Business Strategy," *Academy of Management Journal,* 28 (1985), 763-788. Also see G. Miles, C. C. Snow, and M. P. Sharfman, "Industry Variety and Performance," *Strategic Management Journal,* 14 (1993), 163-177.

26. The characteristics of declining industries have been summarized by K. R. Harrigan, "Strategy Formulation in Declining Industries," *Academy of Management Review,* 5 (1980), 599-604.

27. P. Dicken, *Global Shift* (New York: Guilford Press, 1992).

28. I. Metthee, "Playing a Large Part," *Seattle-Post Intelligence*, April 9, 1994, p. 13.

29. T. Levitt, "The Globalization of Markets," *Harvard Business Review* (May–June 1983), 92–102.

30. M.E. Porter, *The Competitive Advantage of Nations* (New York: Free Press, 1990). See also R. Grant, "Porter's Competitive Advantage of Nations: An Assessment," *Strategic Management Journal*, 7 (1991), 535–548.

31. M. E. Porter, *The Competitive Advantage of Nations*, p. 121.

32. Staff reporter, "Lessons from the Frozen North," *Economist* October 8, 1994, pp. 76–77; and G. Edmondson, "Grabbing Markets from the Giants," *Business Week*, Special Issue: 21st Century Capitalism, 1995, pp. 156.

33. Sources: P. Andrews, "Wrong Turns on the Road to PCdom Come Back to Haunt Wang," *Seattle Times*, August 25, 1992, p. D3; B. Ziegler, "Once Booming Wang Laboratories Failed to Heed the Changing Market," *Seattle Times*, August 23, 1992, p. C6; and W. M. Bulkeley and J. R. Wilkes, "Steep Slide: Filing in Chapter 11, Wang Sends Warning to High Tech Circles," *Wall Street Journal*, August 19, 1992, p. A1.

Chapter 4: Internal Analysis: Resources, Capabilities, Competencies, and Competitive Advantage

1. Sources: R. D. Hof, "The Education of Andy Grove," *Business Week*, January 16, 1995, 60–62; B. Schlender, "Why Andy Grove Can't Stop," *Fortune*, July 10, 1995, 88–98; Staff reporter, "Intel's Chip of Worms," *Economist,* December 17, 1994, 65–66; and E. B. Swort, "Intel," *Value Line Investment Survey*, April 26, 1996, p. 1058.

2. The data are taken from the *Value Line Investment Survey*, 1996.

3. The concept of consumer surplus is an important one in economics. For a more detailed exposition, see D. Besanko, D. Dranove, and M. Shanley, *Economics of Strategy* (New York: John Wiley & Sons, 1996).

4. However, $P = V$ only applies in the special case in which the company has a perfect monopoly and in which it can charge each customer a unique price that reflects the value of the product to that customer (that is, in cases in which perfect price discrimination is possible). More generally, except in the limiting case of perfect price discrimination, even a monopolist will see most consumers capture some of the value of a product in the form of a consumer surplus.

5. This point is central to the work of Michael Porter. See M. E. Porter, *Competitive Advantage* (New York: Free Press, 1985). See also Chapter 4 in P. Ghemawat, *Commitment: The Dynamic of Strategy* (New York: Free Press, 1991).

6. M. E. Porter. *Competitive Strategy* (New York: Free Press, 1980).

7. Sources: D. Lavin, "Chrysler Is Now Low-Cost Producer in the Automobile Industry," *Wall Street Journal*, June 23, 1994, p. B5; N. Templin, "The Auto Trade Fight," *Wall Street Journal*, May 18, 1995, p. A6; W. M. Bulkeley, "Pushing the Pace," *Wall Street Journal*, December 23, 1994, p. A1; D. Levin, "GM Would Have to Cut 20,000 Workers to Match Ford," *Wall Street Journal*, June 24, 1994, p. C22.

8. See D. Garvin, "What Does Product Quality Really Mean?" *Sloan Management Review*, 26 (Fall 1984), 25–44; P. B. Crosby, *Quality Is Free* (New York: Mentor, 1980); and A. Gabor, *The Man Who Discovered Quality* (New York: Times Books, 1990).

9. G. Stalk and T. M. Hout, *Competing Against Time* (New York: Free Press, 1990).

10. Ibid.

11. R. Guenther, Citicorp Shakes Up the Mortgage Market, *Wall Street Journal*, November 13, 1988, p. B1; and Anonymous, Mortgage Lenders Lavish New Attention on Real Estate Agents, *Savings Institutions*, February 1988, p. 82.

12. Porter, *Competitive Advantage*.

13. R. Langreth, "High Anxiety: Rivals Threaten Prozac's Reign," *Wall Street Journal*, May 9, 1996, pp. B1–B2.

14. M. Cusumano, *The Japanese Automobile Industry* (Cambridge, Mass.: Harvard University Press, 1989).

15. The material in this section relies on the so-called resource-based view of the firm. For summaries of this perspective, see J. B. Barney, "Firm Resources and Sustained Competitive Advantage," *Journal of Management*, 17 (1991), 99–120; J. T. Mahoney and J. R. Pandian, "The Resource-Based View Within the Conversation of Strategic Management," *Strategic Management Journal*, 13 (1992), 63–380; R. Amit and P. J. H. Schoemaker, "Strategic Assets and Organizational Rent," *Strategic Management Journal*, 14 (1993), 33–46; M. A. Peteraf, "The Cornerstones of Competitive Advantage: A Resource-Based View," *Strategic Management Journal*, 14 (1993), 179–191; and B. Wernerfelt, "A Resource Based View of the Firm," *Strategic Management Journal*, 5 (1994), 171–180.

16. For a discussion of organizational capabilities, see R. R. Nelson and S. Winter, *An Evolutionary Theory of Economic Change* (Cambridge, Mass.: Belknap Press, 1982).

17. R. M. Grant, *Contemporary Strategic Analysis* (Cambridge, Mass.: Blackwell, 1991).

18. "Disney's Magic," *Business Week*, March 9, 1987. "Michael Eisner's Hit Parade," *Business Week*, February 1, 1988.

19. D. Kearns, "Leadership Through Quality," *Academy of Management Executive*, 4 (1990), 86–89; and J. Sheridan, "America's Best Plants," *Industry Week*, October 15, 1990, pp. 27–40.

20. The classic statement of this position was made by A. A. Alchain, "Uncertainty, Evolution, and Economic Theory," *Journal of Political Economy*, 84 (1950), 488–500.

21. Stephen Manes and Paul Andrews, *Gates* (New York: Simon & Schuster, 1993).

22. This is the nature of the competitive process. For more details, see C. W. L. Hill and D. Deeds, "The Importance of Industry Structure for the Determination of Firm Profitability: A Neo-Austrian Perspective," *Journal of Management Studies*, 33 (1996), 429–451.

23. As with resources and capabilities, the concept of barriers to imitation is also grounded in the resource-based view of the firm. For details, see R. Reed and R. J. DeFillippi, "Causal Ambiguity, Barriers to Imitation, and Sustainable Competitive Advantage," *Academy of Management Review*, 15 (1990), 88–102.

24. E. Mansfield, "How Economists See R&D," *Harvard Business Review* (November–December 1981), 98–106.

25. P. Ghemawat, *Commitment: The Dynamic of Strategy* (New York: Free Press, 1991).

26. M. T. Hannah and J. Freeman, "Structural Inertia and Organizational Change," *American Sociological Review*, 49 (1984), 149-164.

27. See IBM Corporation, *Harvard Business School Case* No. 180-034.

28. Ghemawat, *Commitment*.

29. D. Miller, *The Icarus Paradox* (New York: Harper Business, 1990).

30. D. Miller, *The Icarus Paradox* (New York: Harper Business, 1990); and P. D. Llosa, "We Must Know What We Are Doing," *Fortune*, November 14, 1994, p. 68.

31. P. M. Senge, *The Fifth Discipline: The Art and Practice of the Learning Organization* (New York: Doubleday, 1990).

32. D. Kearns, "Leadership Through Quality."

33. Sources: J. Thornhill, "A European Spark for Marks," *Financial Times*, July 13, 1992, p. 8.; Marks & Spencer, Ltd. (A), *Harvard Business School Case* No. 91-392-089; J. Marcom, "Blue Blazers and Guacamole," *Forbes*, November 25, 1991, pp. 64-68; and M. Evans, "Marks & Spencer Battles On," *Financial Post*, December 11, 1989, p. 32.

Chapter 5: Building Competitive Advantage Through Functional-Level Strategy

1. Sources: Staff reporter, "The Black Horse Goes to the Vet," *Economist*, July 22, 1995, pp. 71-72; J. Kelley, "London Calling," *Journal of Business Strategy* (March-April 1995), 22-26; K. Waterhouse and A. Morgan, "Using Research to Help Keep Good Customers," *Marketing and Research Today,* August 1994, pp. 181-194; and M. Hammer and J. Champy, *Reengineering the Corporation* (New York: Harper Business, 1993).

2. W. J. Abernathy and K. Wayne, "Limits of the Learning Curve," *Harvard Business Review* (September-October 1974), pp. 109-119.

3. For example, see F. M. Scherer, A. Beckenstein, E. Kaufer, and R. D. Murphy, *The Economies of Multiplant Operations* (Cambridge, Mass.: Harvard University Press, 1975).

4. Sources: Chase Press Release "Chase and Chemical Merger Creating Largest Banking Company in the United States," March 21, 1996, Chase at http://www.chase.com; S. Lipin, "Joining Fortunes," *Wall Street Journal,* August 28, 1995, p. 1; and G. B. Knecht, "Chemical Merger with Chase Echoes Earlier Alliance," *Wall Street Journal*, September 1, 1995, p. 4.

5. H. Luft, J. Bunker, and A. Enthoven, "Should Operations Be Regionalized?" *New England Journal of Medicine,* 301 (1979), 1364-1369.

6. G. Hall and S. Howell, "The Experience Curve from an Economist's Perspective," *Strategic Management Journal,* 6 (1985), 197-212; and M. Lieberman, "The Learning Curve and Pricing in the Chemical Processing Industries," *RAND Journal of Economics,* 15 (1984), 213-228.

7. Boston Consulting Group, *Perspectives on Experience* (Boston: Boston Consulting Group, 1972), Hall and Howell, "The Experience Curve"; and W. B. Hirschmann, "Profit from the Learning Curve," *Harvard Business Review* (January-February 1964), 125-139.

8. A. A. Alchian, "Reliability of Progress Curves in Airframe Production," *Econometrica,* 31 (1963), 679-693.

9. G. Stalk, and T. M. Hout, *Competing Against Time*. (New York: Free Press, 1990); and D. Miller, *The Icarus Paradox* (New York: Harper Business, 1990).

10. M. Borrus, L. A. Tyson and J. Zysman, "Creating Advantage: How Government Policies Create Trade in the Semi-Conductor Industry," *Strategic Trade Policy and the New International Economics*, ed. P. R. Krugman (Cambridge, Mass.: MIT Press, 1986); and S. Ghoshal and C. A. Bartlett, "Matsushita Electrical Industrial (MEI) in 1987," *Harvard Business School Case* No. 388-144, 1988.

11. Abernathy and Wayne, "Limits of the Learning Curve."

12. D. F. Barnett and R. W. Crandall, *Up from the Ashes: The Rise of the Steel Minimill in the United States* (Washington, D.C.: Brookings Institution, 1986).

13. See P. Nemetz and L. Fry, "Flexible Manufacturing Organizations: Implications for Strategy Formulation," *Academy of Management Review,* 13 (1988), 627-638; N. Greenwood, *Implementing Flexible Manufacturing Systems* (New York: Halstead Press, 1986); J. P. Womack, D. T. Jones, and D. Roos, *The Machine That Changed the World* (New York: Rawson Associates, 1990); and R. Parthasarthy and S. P. Seith, "The Impact of Flexible Automation on Business Strategy and Organizational Structure," *Academy of Management Review,* 17 (1992), 86-111.

14. B. J. Pine, *Mass Customization: The New Frontier in Business Competition* (Boston: Harvard Business School Press, 1993); and S. Kotha, "Mass Customization: Implementing the Emerging Paradigm for Competitive Advantage," *Strategic Management Journal,* 16 (1995), 21-42.

15. Staff reporter, "The Celling Out of America," *Economist,* December 17, 1994, pp. 63-64.

16. Sources: M. A. Cusumano, *The Japanese Automobile Industry* (Cambridge, Mass.: Harvard University Press, 1989); Ohno Taiichi, *Toyota Production System* (Cambridge, Mass.: Productivity Press, 1980); and Womack, Jones, and Roos, *The Machine that Changed the World.*

17. Staff reporter, "The Ceiling Out of America."

18. F. F. Reichheld and W. E. Sasser, "Zero Defections: Quality Comes to Service," *Harvard Business Review* (September-October 1990), 105-111.

19. The example comes from Reichheld and Sasser, "Zero Defections."

20. Ibid.

21. R. Narasimhan and J. R. Carter, "Organization, Communication and Coordination of International Sourcing," *International Marketing Review,* 7 (1990) 6-20.

22. H. F. Busch, "Integrated Materials Management," *IJDP & MM,* 18 (1990) 28-39.

23. Stalk and Hout, *Competing Against Time.*

24. A. Sorge and M. Warner, "Manpower Training, Manufacturing Organization, and Work Place Relations in Great Britain and West Germany," *British Journal of Industrial Relations,* 18 (1980), 318-333; and R. Jaikumar, "Postindustrial Manufacturing," *Harvard Business Review* (November-December 1986), 72-83.

25. M. L. Dertouzos, R. K. Lester, and R. M. Solow, *Made in America* (Cambridge, Mass.: MIT Press, 1989).

26. J. Hoerr, "The Payoff from Teamwork," *Business Week,* July 10, 1989, pp. 56-62.

27. Staff reporter, "The Trouble with Teams," *Economist,* January 14, 1995, p. 61.

28. See the articles published in the special issue of the *Academy of Management Review* on total quality management [volume 19(3), 1994]. The following paper provides a good overview of many of the issues involved from an academic perspective: J. W. Dean and D. E. Bowen, "Management Theory and Total Quality," *Academy of Management Review,* 19 (1994), 392–418. Also see T. C. Powell, "Total Quality Management as Competitive Advantage," *Strategic Management Journal,* 16 (1995), 15–38.

29. For general background information, see "How to Build Quality," *Economist,* September 23, 1989, pp. 91–92; A. Gabor, *The Man Who Discovered Quality* (New York: Penguin, 1990); and P. B. Crosby, *Quality Is Free* (New York: Mentor, 1980).

30. W. E. Deming, "Improvement of Quality and Productivity Through Action by Management," *National Productivity Review,* 1 (Winter 1981-1982), 12–22.

31. L. Therrien, "Spreading the Message," *BusinessWeek,* October 25, 1991, p. 60; and Staff reporter, "The Straining of Quality," *Economist,* January 14, 1995, pp. 55–56.

32. N. Gross, "Rails that Run on Software," *BusinessWeek,* October 25, 1991, p. 84.

33. Data came from personal interviews conducted by Charles Hill in Japan during the summer of 1992.

34. D. Kearns, "Leadership Through Quality," *Academy of Management Executive,* 4 (1990), 86–89; and J. Sheridan, "America's Best Plants." *Industry Week,* October 15, 1990, pp. 27–40.

35. J. Bowles, "Is American Management Really Committed to Quality?" *Management Review* (April 1992), 42–46.

36. O. Port and G. Smith, "Quality," *Business Week,* November 30, 1992, pp. 66–75. See also Staff reporter, "The Straining of Quality," *Economist,* January 14, 1995, pp. 55–56.

37. For a similar list, see T. C. Powell, "Total Quality Management as Competitive Advantage." Many of the same imperatives are also discussed by J. W. Dean and D. E. Bowen, "Management Theory and Total Quality."

38. Bowles, "Is American Management Really Committed to Quality?" and Staff reporter, "The Straining of Quality."

39. Gabor, *The Man Who Discovered Quality.*

40. Deming, "Improvement of Quality and Productivity."

41. W. E. Deming, *Out of the Crisis* (Cambridge, Mass.: MIT Center for Advanced Engineering Study, 1986).

42. J. F. Siler and S. Atchison, *"The Rx at Work in Utah," BusinessWeek,* October 25, 1991, p. 113.

43. E. Mansfield, "How Economists See R&D," *Harvard Business Review* (November-December 1981), 98–106.

44. Ibid.

45. Booz, Allen, & Hamilton, "New Products Management for the 1980's," privately published research report, 1982.

46. A. L. Page, "PDMA's New Product Development Practices Survey: Performance and Best Practices." PDMA 15th Annual International Conference, Boston, October 16, 1991.

47. See S. L. Brown and K. M. Eisenhardt, "Product Development: Past Research, Present Findings, and Future Directions," *Academy of Management Review,* 20 (1995), 343–378; M. B. Lieberman and D. B. Montgomery, "First Mover Advantages," *Strategic Management Journal,* 9 (Special Issue, Summer 1988), 41–58; D. J. Teece, "Profiting from Technological Innovation: Implications for Integration, Collaboration, Licensing and Public Policy," *Research Policy,* 15 (1987), 285–305; and G. J. Tellis and P. N. Golder, "First to Market, First to Fail?" *Sloan Management Review,* (Winter 1996), 65–75.

48. Stalk and Hout, *Competing Against Time.*

49. Sources: R. L. Hudson, "Philips Official Calls DCC Launch Flawed, Vows Division Comeback," *Wall Street Journal,* August 19, 1993, p. A7; A. Kupfer, "The Next Wave in Cassette Tapes," *Fortune,* June 3, 1991, pp. 153–158; and P. M. Reilly, "Sony's Digital Audio Format Pulls Ahead of Philips's, but Both Still Have Far to Go," *Wall Street Journal,* August 6, 1993, p. B1.

50. G. Stalk, and T. S. Hout, Competing Against Time (New York: Free Press, 1990); and B. Buell and R. D. Hof, "Hewlett Packard Rethinks Itself," *BusinessWeek,* April 1, 1991, pp. 76–79.

51. K. B. Clark and S. C. Wheelwright, *Managing New Product and Process Development* (New York: Free Press, 1993).

52. Ibid.

53. P. Sellers, "Getting Customers to Love You," *Fortune,* March 13, 1989, pp. 38–42.

54. O. Port, "Moving Past the Assembly Line," *BusinessWeek Special Issue, Reinventing America,* 1992, pp. 177–180.

55. G. P. Pisano and S. C.Wheelwright, "The New Logic of High Tech R&D," *Harvard Business Review* (September-October 1995), 93–105.

56. K. B. Clark and T. Fujimoto, "The Power of Product Integrity," *Harvard Business Review* (November-December, 1990), 107–118. Clark and Wheelwright, *Managing New Product and Process Development*; S. L. Brown and K. M. Eisenhardt, "Product Development: Past Research, Present Findings, and Future Directions"; and Stalk and Hout, *Competing Against Time.*

57. C. Christensen, "Quantum Corporation—Business and Product Teams," *Harvard Business School Case* No. 9-692-023.

58. S. Caminiti, "A Mail Order Romance: Lands' End Courts Unseen Customers," *Fortune,* March 13, 1989, pp. 43–44.

59. P. Sellers, "Getting Customers to Love You," *Fortune,* March 13, 1989, pp. 38–42.

60. S. Caminiti, "A Mail Order Romance: Lands' End Courts Unseen Customers."

61. K. West, "Boeing 2000," *Seattle Times,* October 21, 1992, pp. A7, A10, A11.

62. B. J. Pine, *Mass Customization: The New Frontier in Business Competition* (Boston: Harvard Business School Press, 1993).

63. Sources: J. D. Goldhar and D. Lei, "The Shape of Twenty-first Century Global Manufacturing," *Journal of Business Strategy* (March/April 1991), pp. 37–41; "Factories that Turn Nuts into Bolts," pp. 44–45; and J. Kotkin, "The Great American Revival," *Inc.* (February 1988), pp. 52–63.

64. Stalk and Hout, *Competing Against Time.*

65. P. Bradley, "Global Sourcing Takes Split-Second Timing," *Purchasing,* July 20, 1989, pp. 52–58.

66. Sources: R. Howard, "The CEO as Organizational Architect," *Harvard Business Review* (September-October 1992), 106–123; D. Kearns, "Leadership Through Quality," *Academy of Management Executive,* 4 (1990), 86–89; M. E. McGrath and R. W. Hoole, "Manufacturing's New Economies of Scale," *Harvard Business Review* (May-June 1992), 94–102; T. Rohan, "In Search of Speed," *Industry Week,* September 3, 1990, pp. 78–82; J. Sheridan, "America's Best Plants," *Industry Week,* October 15, 1990, pp. 27–40; and J.

Sheridan, "Suppliers: Partners in Prosperity," *Industry Week,* March 1990.

Chapter 6: Business-Level Strategy

1. D. McGinn, "For Ford, Making Wall Street Happy Is Job One," *Newsweek,* April 8, 1996, p. 48.
2. O. Suris, "Ford's Earnings Plunged 58% in 1st Quarter," *Wall Street Journal,* April 18, 1996, p. A4.
3. Derek F. Abell, *Defining the Business: The Starting Point of Strategic Planning* (Englewood Cliffs, N.J.: Prentice-Hall, 1980), p. 169.
4. R. Kotler, *Marketing Management,* 5th ed. (Englewood Cliffs, N.J.: Prentice-Hall, 1984); and M. R. Darby and E. Karni, "Free Competition and the Optimal Amount of Fraud," *Journal of Law and Economics,* 16 (1973), 67–86.
5. Abell, *Defining the Business,* p. 8.
6. Michael E. Porter, *Competitive Advantage: Creating and Sustaining Superior Performance* (New York: Free Press, 1985).
7. R. D. Buzzell and F. D. Wiersema, "Successful Share Building Strategies," *Harvard Business Review* (January–February 1981), 135–144; and L. W. Phillips, D. R. Chang, and R. D. Buzzell, "Product Quality, Cost Position, and Business Performance: A Test of Some Key Hypotheses," *Journal of Marketing,* 47 (1983), 26–43.
8. Michael E. Porter, *Competitive Strategy: Techniques for Analyzing Industries and Competitors* (New York: Free Press, 1980), p. 45.
9. Abell, *Defining the Business,* p. 15.
10. Although many other authors have discussed cost leadership and differentiation as basic competitive approaches—e.g., F. Scherer, *Industrial Market Structure and Economic Performance,* 2nd ed. (Boston: Houghton Mifflin, 1980)—Porter's model (Porter, *Competitive Strategy*) has become the dominant approach. Consequently, this model is the one developed here, and the discussion draws heavily on his definitions. The basic cost-leadership/differentiation dimension has received substantial empirical support—e.g., D. C. Hambrick, "High Profit Strategies in Mature Capital Goods Industries: A Contingency Approach," *Academy of Management Journal,* 26 (1983), 687–707.
11. Porter, *Competitive Advantage,* p. 37.
12. Ibid., pp. 13–14.
13. D. Miller, "Configurations of Strategy and Structure: Towards a Synthesis," *Strategic Management Journal,* 7 (1986), 217–231.
14. L. Armstrong, "Altima's Secret: The Right Kind of Sticker Shock," *BusinessWeek,* January 18, 1993, p. 37.
15. Neil A. Martin, "On the Wheel," *Barron's,* August 12, 1996, pp. 18–20; Edith Updike, "Japan Turns a Corner," *Business-Week,* February 26, 1996, pp. 108–112.
16. Porter, *Competitive Advantage,* pp. 44–46.
17. Charles W. Hofer and D. Schendel, *Strategy Formulation: Analytical Concepts* (St. Paul, Minn.: West, 1978).
18. W. K. Hall, "Survival Strategies in a Hostile Environment," *Harvard Business Review,* 58 (1980), 75–85. Hambrick, "High Profit Strategies," pp. 687–707.
19. J. Guyon, "Can the Savoy Cut Costs and Be the Savoy," *Wall Street Journal,* October 25, 1994, p. B1.
20. L. Nathans Spiro and M. Landler, "Less-Than-Fantastic Plastic," *BusinessWeek,* November 9, 1992, pp. 100–101.
21. Edward Baig, "Platinum Cards: Move Over, Amex," *Business-Week,* August 19, 1996, p. 84; John N. Frank, "American Express's Attention Getter," *Credit Card Management,* August 1996, pp. 36–37.
22. Porter, *Competitive Strategy,* p. 46.
23. J. W. Verity, "They Make a Killing Minding Other People's Business," *BusinessWeek,* November 30, 1992, p. 96.
24. Mark Willis, "Outsourcing Benefits Administration: A Disciplined Process for Conducting a Thorough Cost-Benefit Analysis," *Compensation & Benefits Management,* Winter 1996, pp. 45–53; and Jane Gebhart, "Beyond the Information Systems Outsourcing Bandwagon: The Insourcing Response," *Sloan Business Review,* Winter 1996, p. 117.
25. Peter F. Drucker, *The Practice of Management* (New York: Harper, 1954).
26. Porter, *Competitive Advantage,* pp. 44–46.
27. "The Holiday Inns Trip; A Breeze for Decades, Bumpy Ride in the 1980s," *Wall Street Journal,* February 11, 1987, p.1.
28. Holiday Inn, Annual Report, 1985.
29. Bureau of Labor Statistics, *U.S. Industrial Output* (Washington, D.C., 1986); Mark Gleason and Alan Salomon, "Fallon's Challenge: Make Holiday Inn More 'In'," *Advertising Age,* September 2, 1996, p. 14; and Julie Miller, "Amenities Range from Snacks to Technology," *Hotel and Motel Management,* July 3, 1996, pp. 38–40.
30. The development of strategic-group theory has been a strong theme in the strategy literature. Important contributions include R. E. Caves and Michael Porter, "From Entry Barriers to Mobility Barriers," *Quarterly Journal of Economics* (May 1977), 241–262; K. R. Harrigan, "An Application of Clustering for Strategic Group Analysis," *Strategic Management Journal,* 6 (1985), 55–73; K. J. Hatten and D. E. Schendel, "Heterogeneity Within an Industry: Firm Conduct in the U.S. Brewing Industry, 1952–1971," *Journal of Industrial Economics,* 26, 97–113; and Michael E. Porter, "The Structure Within Industries and Companies' Performance," *Review of Economics and Statistics,* 61 (1979), 214–227.
31. For details on strategic-group structure in the pharmaceutical industry, see K. Cool and I. Dierickx, "Rivalry, Strategic Groups, and Firm Profitability," *Strategic Management Journal,* 14 (1993), 47–59.
32. Hofer and Schendel, *Strategy Formulation,* pp. 102–104.
33. Our discussion of the investment, or posturing, component of business-level strategy draws heavily on Hofer and Schendel's discussion in *Strategy Formulation,* especially Chapter 6.
34. Hofer and Schendel, *Strategy Formulation,* pp. 75–77.
35. J. Weber, "Campbell Is Bubbling, But for How Long," *BusinessWeek,* June 17, 1991, pp. 56–58.
36. Judann Pollack, "Another Helping for Campbell," *Advertising Age,* September 9, 1996, pp. 4, 62; and Linda Grant, "Stirring It Up at Campbell," *Fortune,* May 13, 1996, pp. 80–86.
37. K. R. Harrigan, "Strategy Formulation in Declining Industries," *Academy of Management Review,* 5 (1980), 599–604.
38. Hofer and Schendel, *Strategy Formulation,* pp. 169–172.
39. L. R. Feldman and A. L. Page, "Harvesting: The Misunderstood Market Exit Strategy," *Journal of Business Strategy,* 4 (1985), 79–85.
40. C. W. Hofer, "Turnaround Strategies," *Journal of Business Strategy,* 1 (1980), 19–31.

41. Hofer and Schendel, *Strategy Formulation,* p. 172.
42. N. Darnton, "The Joy of Polyester," *Newsweek*, August 3, 1992, p. 61.
43. Cyndee Miller, "Liz Claiborne Throws a Curve with New Brand for Gen Xers," *Marketing News*, July 1, 1996, pp. 1, 10; and Elaine Underwood, "Claiborne Back in Media," *Brandweek*, January 15, 1996, p. 2.

Chapter 7: Competitive Strategy and the Industry Environment

1. R. Gibson, "Bigger Burger by McDonald's: A Two Ouncer," *Wall Street Journal,* April 18, 1996, p. B1.
2. M. Porter, *Competitive Strategy: Techniques for Analyzing Industries and Competitors* (New York: Free Press, 1980), pp. 191-200.
3. S. A. Shane, "Hybrid Organizational Arrangements and Their Implications for Firm Growth and Survival: A Study of New Franchisors," *Academy of Management Journal,* 1 (1996), 216-234.
4. Much of this section is based on Charles W. L. Hill, Michael Heeley, and Jane Sakson, "Strategies for Profiting from Innovation," *Advances in Global High Technology Management* (Greenwich, Conn.: JAI Press, 1993), III, 79-95.
5. The importance of complementary assets was first noted by D. J. Teece. See D. J. Teece, "Profiting from Technological Innovation," in *The Competitive Challenge*, ed. D. J. Teece (New York: Harper & Row, 1986), pp. 26-54.
6. M. J. Chen and D. C. Hambrick, "Speed, Stealth, and Selective Attack: How Small Firms Differ from Large Firms in Competitive Behavior," *Academy of Management Journal,* 38 (1995), 453-482.
7. E. Mansfield, M. Schwartz, and S. Wagner, "Imitation Costs and Patents: An Empirical Study," *Economic Journal*, 91 (1981), 907-918.
8. E. Mansfield, "How Rapidly Does New Industrial Technology Leak Out?" *Journal of Industrial Economics*, 34 (1985), 217-223.
9. Charles P. Wallace, "Can the Body Shop Shape Up?" *Fortune,* April 15, 1996, pp. 118-120; and Anat Arkin, "Open Business Is Good for Business," *People Management,* January 11, 1996, pp. 24-27.
10. This argument has been made in the game theory literature. See R. Caves, H. Cookell, and P. J. Killing, "The Imperfect Market for Technology Licenses," *Oxford Bulletin of Economics and Statistics*, 45 (1983), 249-267; N. T. Gallini, "Deterrence by Market Sharing: A Strategic Incentive for Licensing," *American Economic Review*, 74 (1984), 931-941; and C. Shapiro, "Patent Licensing and R&D Rivalry," *American Economic Review*, 75 (1985), 25-30.
11. J. Brander and J. Eaton, "Product Line Rivalry," *American Economic Review*, 74 (1985), 323-334.
12. P. Milgrom and J. Roberts, "Predation, Reputation, and Entry Deterrence," *Journal of Economic Theory*, 27 (1982), 280-312.
13. Sharon M. Oster, *Modern Competitive Analysis* (New York: Oxford University Press, 1990), pp. 262-264.
14. Donald A. Hay and Derek J. Morris, *Industrial Economics: Theory and Evidence* (New York: Oxford University Press, 1979), pp. 192-193.
15. Anthony L. Velocci, Jr., "Fuel Prices Fail to Ground Soaring Airline Profits," *Aviation Week & Space Technology,* September 23, 1996, pp. 33-37; and Tim Smart, "Finally We Have Ignition," *BusinessWeek,* September 16, 1996, p. 45.
16. Porter, *Competitive Strategy*, pp. 76-86.
17. O. Heil and T. S. Robertson, "Towards a Theory of Competitive Market Signaling: A Research Agenda," *Strategic Management Journal*, 12 (1991), 403-418.
18. F. Scherer, *Industrial Market Structure and Economic Performance,* 2nd ed. (Boston: Houghton Mifflin, 1980), ch. 8.
19. The model differs from Ansoff's model for this reason.
20. H. Igor Ansoff, *Corporate Strategy* (London: Penguin Books, 1984), pp. 97-100.
21. Robert D. Buzzell, Bradley T. Gale, and Ralph G. M. Sultan, "Market Share—A Key to Profitability," *Harvard Business Review* (January-February 1975), 97-103. Robert Jacobson and David A. Aaker, "Is Market Share All That It's Cracked Up to Be?" *Journal of Marketing*, 49 (1985), 11-22.
22. Ansoff, *Corporate Strategy*, pp. 98-99.
23. S. L. Brown and K. M. Eisenhardt, "Product Development: Past Research, Present Findings, and Future Directions," *Academy of Management Review,* 20 (1995), 343-378.
24. M. Maremont and G. Bowens, "Brawls in Toyland," *BusinessWeek*, December 21, 1992, pp. 36-37.
25. Dawn Wilensky, "TRU Jumps Ahead to 2000," *Discount Store News,* August 5, 1996, pp. 1, 107; and Richard Halverson, "Kids World to Strengthen Market Position," *Discount Store News,* May 20, 1996, pp. 1, 40.
26. The next section draws heavily on Marvin B. Lieberman, "Strategies for Capacity Expansion," *Sloan Management Review*, 8 (1987), 19-27; and Porter, *Competitive Strategy*, pp. 324-338.
27. K. Pope, "Out for Blood, for Compaq and Dell Accent Is on Personal in the Computer Wars," *Wall Street Journal,* February 13, 1993, pp. A1, A6.
28. Gary McWilliams, "Dial Dell for Servers," *BusinessWeek,* September 16, 1996, p. 102; and John Wyatt, "Three Top Pros Take Stock of the Market," *Fortune,* June 10, 1996, pp. 145-146.
29. Cynthia Scanlon, "Not Just a Meeting; It's an Adventure," *Nations Business,* August 1996, pp. 52-54.
30. Jack Willoughby, "The Last Iceman," *Forbes,* July 13, 1987, pp. 183-202.
31. P. Nulty, "The Bounce Is Back at Goodyear," *Fortune,* September 7, 1992, pp. 70-72.
32. Zachary Schiller, "Goodyear Gets a Grip on Its Future," *BusinessWeek,* March 4, 1996, p. 4; and Anonymous, "A Bumpy Ride," *Economist*, February 17, 1996, pp. 59, 60.

Chapter 8: Strategy in the Global Environment

1. Sources: "Furnishing the World," *Economist*, November 19, 1994, pp. 79-80; and H. Carney, "Struggle to Save the Soul of IKEA," *Financial Times,* March 27, 1995, p. 12.
2. Sources: Kathleen Deveny et al., "McWorld?" *BusinessWeek,* October 13, 1986, pp. 78-86; "Slow Food," *Economist*, February 3, 1990, p. 64; Harlan S. Byrne, "Welcome to McWorld," *Barron's*, August 29, 1994, pp. 25-28; and Andrew E. Serwer, "McDonald's Conquers the World," *Fortune,* October 17, 1994, pp. 103-116.
3. C. S. Tranger, "Enter the Mini-Multinational," *Northeast International Business*, March 1989, pp. 13-14.
4. I. Metthee, "Playing a Large Part," *Seattle-Post Intelligence,* April 9, 1994, p. 13.

5. "Matsushita Electrical Industrial in 1987," in *Transnational Management*, ed. C. A. Bartlett and S. Ghoshal (Homewood, Ill.: Irwin, 1992).

6. C. K. Prahalad and Yves L. Doz, *The Multinational Mission: Balancing Local Demands and Global Vision* (New York: Free Press, 1987). Also see J. Birkinshaw, A. Morrison, and J. Hulland, "Structural and Competitive Determinants of a Global Integration Strategy," *Strategic Management Journal*, 16 (1995), 637-655.

7. Prahalad and Doz, *The Multinational Mission*.

8. "The Tire Industy's Costly Obsession with Size," *Economist*, June 8, 1993, pp. 65-66.

9. T. Levitt, "The Globalization of Markets," *Harvard Business Reveiw* (May-June 1983), 92-102.

10. C. A. Bartlett and S. Ghoshal, *Managing Across Borders: The Transnational Solution* (Boston: Harvard Business School Press, 1989).

11. Ibid.

12. Bartlett and Ghoshal, *Managing Across Borders*.

13. Sources: Guy de Jonquieres and C. Bobinski, "Wash and Get into a Lather in Poland," *Financial Times*, May 28, 1989, p. 2; Anonymous, "Perestroika in Soapland, *Economist*, June 10, 1989, pp. 69-71; Anonymous,"After Early Stumbles P&G Is Making Inroads Overseas," *Wall Street Journal*, February 6, 1989, p.B1; and Bartlett and Ghoshal, *Managing Across Borders*.

14. T. Hout, M. E. Porter, and E. Rudden, "How Global Companies Win Out," *Harvard Business Review* (September-October 1982), 98-108.

15. Guy de Jonquieres, "Unilever Adopts a Clean Sheet Approach," *Financial Times*, October 21, 1991, p. 13.

16. This section draws on the following studies: C. W. L. Hill, P. Hwang, and W. C. Kim, "An Eclectic Theory of the Choice of International Entry Mode," *Strategic Management Journal*, 11 (1990), 117-128; and C. W. L. Hill and W. C. Kim, "Searching for a Dynamic Theory of the Multinational Enterprise: A Transaction Cost Model,"*Strategic Management Journal*, 9 (1988), Special Issue on Strategy Content, 93-104. See also E. Anderson and H. Gatignon, "Modes of Foreign Entry: A Transaction Cost Analysis and Propositions,"*Journal of International Business Studies*, 17 (1986), 1-26; and F. R. Root, *Entry Strategies for International Markets* (Lexington, Mass.: Heath, 1980).

17. F. J. Contractor, "The Role of Licensing in International Strategy," *Columbia Journal of World Business* (Winter 1982), 73-83.

18. O. E. Williamson, *The Economic Institutions of Capitalism* (New York: Free Press, 1985).

19. J. H. Dunning and M. McQueen, "The Eclectic Theory of International Production: A Case Study of the International Hotel Industry," *Managerial and Decision Economics*, 2 (1981), 197-210.

20. B. Kogut, "Joint Ventures: Theoretical and Empirical Perspectives," *Strategic Management Journal*, 9 (1988), 319-332.

21. D. G. Bradley, "Managing Against Expropriation," *Harvard Business Review* (July-August 1977), 78-90.

22. Sources: R. Howard, "The CEO as Organizational Architect," *Harvard Business Review* (September-October 1992), 106-123; D. Kearns, "Leadership Through Quality," *Academy of Management Executive*, 4 (1990), 86-89; K. McQuade and B. Gomes-Casseres, "Xerox and Fuji-Xerox," *Harvard Business School Case* No. 9-391-156; and E.Terazono and C. Lorenz, "An Angry Young Warrior," *Financial Times*, September 19, 1994, p. 11.

23. C. W. L. Hill, "Strategies for Exploiting Technological Innovations," *Organization Science*, 3 (1992), 428-441.

24. See K. Ohmae, "The Global Logic of Strategic Alliances," *Harvard Business Review* (March-April 1989), 143-154; G. Hamel, Y. L. Doz, and C. K. Prahalad, "Collaborate with Your Competitors and Win!" *Harvard Business Review* (January-February 1988), 133-139; and W. Burgers, C. W. L. Hill, and W. C. Kim, "Alliances in the Global Auto Industry," *Strategic Management Journal*, 14 (1993), 419-432.

25. "Asia Beckons," *Economist*, May 30, 1992, pp. 63-64.

26. R. B. Reich and E. D. Mankin, "Joint Ventures with Japan Give Away Our Future," *Harvard Business Review* (March-April 1986), 78-90.

27. Sources: D. Darlin, "Daewoo Will Pay GM $170 Million for Venture Stake," *Wall Street Journal*, November 11, 1992, p. A6; and D. Darlin and J. B. White, "Failed Marriage," *Wall Street Journal*, January 16, 1992, p. A1.

28. W. Roehl and J. F. Truitt, "Stormy Open Marriages Are Better," *Columbia Journal of World Business* (Summer 1987), 87-95.

29. K. McQuade and B. Gomes-Casseres "Xerox and Fuji-Xerox," *Harvard Business School Case* No. 9-391-156.

30. Hamel, Doz, and Prahalad, "Collaborate with Your Competitors and Win!" pp. 133-139.

31. B. Wysocki, "Cross Border Alliances Become Favorite Way to Crack New Markets," *Wall Street Journal*, March 4, 1990, p. A1.

32. Sources: J. B. Treece, K. Miller, and R. A. Melcher, "The Partners," *BusinessWeek*, February 10, 1992, pp. 102-107; C. Rapoport, "Mazda's Bold New Global Strategy," *Fortune*, December 17, 1990, pp. 109-113; "Car Industry Joint Ventures: Spot the Difference," *Economist*, February 24, 1990, p. 74; and J. P. Womack, D. T. Jones, and D. Roos, *The Machine That Changed the World* (New York: Rawson Associates, 1990).

Chapter 9: Corporate Strategy—Vertical Integration, Diversification, and Strategic Alliances

1. Sources: S. Lubove "New Tech, Old-Tech," *Forbes*, July 17, 1995, pp. 58-62; Rockwell International's *1995 Data Book and Annual Report*. Available from Rockwell's World Wide Web site at http://www.rockwell.com.

2. T. J. Peters and R. H. Waterman, *In Search of Excellence* (New York: Harper & Row, 1982).

3. D. P. Hamilton, "Red-Faced Matsushita Gets Back to Basics," *Wall Street Journal*, April 10, 1995, p. A14.

4. K. R. Harrian, "Formulating Vertical Integration Strategies," *Academy of Management Review*, 9 (1984), 638-652.

5. This is the essence of Chandler's argument. See Alfred D. Chandler, *Strategy and Structure* (Cambridge, Mass.: MIT Press, 1962). The same argument is also made by Jeffrey Pfeffer and Gerald R. Salancik, *The External Control of Organizations* (New York: Harper & Row, 1978). See also K. R. Harrigan, *Strategic Flexibility* (Lexington, Mass.: Lexington Books, 1985); K. R. Harrigan, "Vertical Integration and Corporate Strategy," *Academy of Management Journal*, 28 (1985), 397-425; and F. M. Scherer, *Industrial Market*

Structure and Economic Performance (Chicago: Rand McNally, 1981).

6. This section is based on the transaction cost approach popularized by Oliver E. Williamson, *The Economic Institutions of Capitalism* (New York: Free Press, 1985).

7. Williamson, *The Economic Institutions of Capitalism.*

8. Williamson, *The Economic Institutions of Capitalism.*

9. J. F. Hennart, "Upstream Vertical Integration in the Aluminum and Tin Industries," *Journal of Economic Behavior and Organization*, 9 (1988), 281-299.

10. Hennart, "Upstream Vertical Integration."

11. A. D. Chandler, *The Visible Hand* (Cambridge, Mass.: Harvard University Press, 1977).

12. Julia Pitta, "Score One for Vertical Integration," *Forbes,* January 18, 1993, pp. 88-89.

13. Joseph White and Neal Templin, "Harsh Regimen: A Swollen GM Finds It Hard to Stick with Its Crash Diet," *Wall Street Journal,* September 9, 1992, p. A1.

14. Harrigan, *Strategic Flexibility,* pp. 67-87.

15. For a detailed theoretical rationale for this argument, see G. R. Jones and C. W. L. Hill, "A Transaction Cost Analysis of Strategy-Structure Choice," *Strategic Management Journal,* 9 (1988), 159-172.

16. Kevin Kelly, Zachary Schiller, and James Treece, "Cut Costs or Else," *BusinessWeek,* March 22, 1993, pp. 28-29.

17. X. Martin, W. Mitchell, and A. Swaminathan. "Recreating and Extending Japanese Automobile Buyer-Supplier Links in North America," *Strategic Management Journal,* 16 (1995), 589-619; and C. W. L. Hill, "National Institutional Structures, Transaction Cost Economizing, and Competitive Advantage," *Organization Science,* 6 (1995), 119-131.

18. Standard & Poor's, *Industry Surveys,* "Autos—Auto Parts," June 24, 1993.

19. See James Womack, Daniel Jones, and Daniel Roos, *The Machine That Changed the World* (New York: Rawson Associates, 1990); and James Richardson, "Parallel Sourcing and Supplier Performance in the Japanese Automobile Industry," *Strategic Management Journal,* 14 (1993), 339-350.

20. Williamson, *The Economic Institutions of Capitalism.*

21. J. H. Dyer, "How Chrysler Created an American Keiretsu," *Harvard Business Review* (July–August 1996), 42-56.

22. Richardson, "Parallel Sourcing," pp. 339-350.

23. W. H. Davidow and M. S. Malone, *The Virtual Corporation* (New York: Harper & Row, 1992).

24. Davidow and Malone, *The Virtual Corporation.*

25. "The Outing of Outsourcing," *Economist,* November 25, 1995, pp. 57-58.

26. Davidow and Malone, *The Virtual Corporation*; and H. W. Chesbrough and D. J. Teece. "When Is Virtual Virtuous? Organizing for Innovation." *Harvard Business Review* (January–February 1996), 65-74.

27. Source: Interviews by Charles Hill of Bob Dryden, executive vice president for the Boeing Commercial Aerospace Group, and Larry Clarkson, vice president of strategic planning at Boeing.

28. This resource-based view of diversification can be traced to Edith Penrose's seminal book, *The Theory of the Growth of the Firm* (Oxford: Oxford University Press, 1959).

29. See, for example, Jones and Hill, "A Transaction Cost Analysis," pp. 159-172; and Oliver E. Williamson, *Markets and Hierarchies* (New York: Free Press, 1975), pp. 132-175.

30. See C. W. L. Hill, "Profile of a Conglomerate Takeover: BTR and Thomas Tilling," *Journal of General Management,* 10 (1984), 34-50.

31. See C. W. L. Hill, M. A. Hitt, and R. E. Hoskisson, "Declining U.S. Competitiveness: Reflections on a Crisis," *Academy of Management Executive,* 2 (February 1988), 51-59; and R. E. Hoskisson, M. A. Hitt, and C. W. L. Hill," Managerial Incentives and Investment in R&D in Large Multiproduct Firms," *Organization Science,* 4 (1993), 325-341.

32. D. J. Teece, "Economies of Scope and the Scope of the Enterprise," *Journal of Economic Behavior and Organization,* 3 (1980), 223-247.

33. For a detailed discussion, see C. W. L. Hill and R. E. Hoskisson, "Strategy and Structure in the Multiproduct Firm," *Academy of Management Review,* 12 (1987), 331-341.

34. Michael E. Porter, *Competitive Advantage: Creating and Sustaining Superior Performance* (New York: Free Press, 1985), p. 326.

35. M. E. Porter, "From Competitive Advantage to Corporate Strategy," *Harvard Business Review* (May–June 1987), 43-59.

36. For reviews of the evidence, see V. Ramanujam and P. Varadarajan, "Research on Corporate Diversification: A Synthesis," *Strategic Management Journal,* 10 (1989), 523-551; and G. Dess, J. F. Hennart, C. W. L. Hill, and A. Gupta. "Research Issues in Strategic Management," *Journal of Management,* 21 (1995), 357-392.

37. C. R. Christensen et al., *Business Policy Text and Cases* (Homewood, Ill.: Irwin, 1987), p. 778.

38. For evidence, see C. W. L. Hill, "Conglomerate Performance over the Economic Cycle," *Journal of Industrial Economics,* 32 (1983), 197-212; and D. T. C. Mueller, "The Effects of Conglomerate Mergers," *Journal of Banking and Finance,* 1 (1977), 315-347.

39. Sources: Scott McMurray, "ICI Changes Tack and Splits Itself into Two Businesses," *Wall Street Journal,* March 5, 1991, p. B3; and Anonymous, "Hanson Likes the Look of ICI," *Economist,* May 18, 1991, pp. 69-70.

40. For example, see C. W. L. Hill, "Diversified Growth and Competition," *Applied Economics,* 17 (1985), 827-847; and R. P. Rumelt, *Strategy, Structure and Economic Performance* (Boston: Harvard Business School Press, 1974); and G. R. Jones and C. W. L. Hill, "A Transaction Cost Analysis of Strategy Structure Choice," *Strategic Management Journal* (1988), 159-172.

41. See H. K. Christensen and C. A. Montgomery, "Corporate Economic Performance: Diversification Strategy Versus Market Structure," *Strategic Management Journal,* 2 (1981), 327-343; and Jones and Hill, "A Transaction Cost Analysis," pp. 159-172; Dess, Hennart, Hill, and Gupta, "Research Issues in Strategic Management"; and C. W. L. Hill, "The Role of Headquarters in the Multidivisional Firm," in R. Rumelt, D. J. Teece, D. Schendel, *Fundamental Issues in Strategy Research* (Cambridge, Mass.: Harvard Business School Press, 1994), pp. 297-321.

42. Sources: "The Flawed Vision of Edzard Reuter," *Economist,* April 27, 1991, pp. 65-66; Krystal Miller, "BMW Zooms Ahead of Mercedes-Benz in Worldwide Sales for the First Time," *Wall Street Journal,* January 20, 1993, Section B1; and John Templeman, "Daimler's Drive to Become a High-Tech Speedster," *BusinessWeek,* February 12, 1990, pp. 55-58.

Chapter 10: Corporate Development—Building and Restructuring the Corporation

1. Sources: T. Jackson, "Giant Bows to Colossal Pressure," *Financial Times,* September 22, 1995, p. 13; Staff reporter, "AT&T's Three Way Split," *Economist,* September 23, 1995, pp. 51–52; Staff reporter, "Fatal Attraction," *Economist,* March 23, 1996, pp. 73–74; and A. Ramirez, "Opportunity and New Risk for a Spinoff," *New York Times,* September 22, 1995, pp. C1, C4.

2. C. W. Hofer and D. Schendel, *Strategy Formulation: Analytical Concepts* (St. Paul, Minn.: West, 1979); and R. A. Bettis and W. K. Hall, "Strategic Portfolio Management in the Multibusiness Firm," *California Management Review,* 24 (1981), 23–28.

3. G. Hamel and C. K. Prahalad, *Competing for the Future* (Cambridge, Mass.: Harvard Business School Press, 1994).

4. D. J. Collis, "Portfolio Planning at Ciba-Geigy and the Newport Investment Proposal," *Harvard Business School Case* No. 795-040, 1995. Ciba-Geigy's World Wide Web page at http://www.cina.com.

5. Subrata N. Chakravarty, "White Slacks and Carbon Black," *Forbes,* October 26, 1992, pp. 122–124.

6. G. Hamel and C. K. Prahalad, *Competing for the Future* (Cambridge, Mass.: Harvard Business School Press, 1994).

7. D. Leonard Barton and G. Pisano, "Monsanto's March into Biotechnology," *Harvard Business School Case* No. 690-009, 1990. See Monsanto's home page for details of its genetically engineered seed products (http://www.monsanto.com).

8. See Booz, Allen, & Hamilton, *New Products Management for the 1980's,* privately published research report, 1982; A. L. Page, PDMA's *New Product Development Practices Survey: Performance and Best Practices,* PDMA 15th Annual International Conference, Boston, October 16, 1991; and E. Mansfield, "How Economists See R&D," *Harvard Business Review* (November–December 1981), 98–106.

9. See R. Biggadike, "The Risky Business of Diversification," *Harvard Business Review* (May–June 1979), 103–111; R. A. Burgelman, "A Process Model of Internal Corporate Venturing in the Diversified Major Firm," *Administrative Science Quarterly,* 28 (1983), 223–244; and Z. Block and I. C. Macmillan, *Corporate Venturing* (Cambridge, Mass.: Harvard Business School Press, 1993).

10. Biggadike, "The Risky Business of Diversification"; and Block and Macmillan, *Corporate Venturing.*

11. I. C. Macmillan and R. George, "Corporate Venturing: Challenges for Senior Managers," *Journal of Business Strategy,* 5 (1985), 34–43.

12. See R. A. Burgelman, M. M. Maidique, and S. C. Wheelwright. *Strategic Management of Technology and Innovation* (Chicago: Irwin, 1996), pp. 493–507.

13. See Block and Macmillan, *Corporate Venturing;* and Burgelman, Maidique, and Wheelwright, *Strategic Management.*

14. G. Beardsley and E. Mansfield, "A Note on the Accuracy of Industrial Forecasts of the Profitability of New Products and Processes," *Journal of Business,* 23 (1978), 127–130.

15. J. Warner, J. Templeman, and R. Horn, "The Case Against Mergers," *BusinessWeek,* October 30, 1995, pp. 122–134.

16. For evidence on acquisitions and performance, see R. E. Caves, "Mergers, Takeovers, and Economic Efficiency," *International Journal of Industrial Organization,* 7 (1989), 151–174; M. C. Jensen and R. S. Ruback, "The Market for Corporate Control: The Scientific Evidence," *Journal of Financial Economics,* 11 (1983), 5–50; R. Roll, "Empirical Evidence on Takeover Activity and Shareholder Wealth," in *Knights, Raiders and Targets,* ed. J. C. Coffee, L. Lowenstein, and S. Rose (Oxford: Oxford University Press, 1989); A. Schleifer and R. W. Vishny, "Takeovers in the 60s and 80s: Evidence and Implications," *Strategic Management Journal,* 12 (Winter 1991), Special Issue, 51–60; and T. H. Brush, "Predicted Changes in Operational Synergy and Post Acquisition Performance of Acquired Businesses," *Strategic Management Journal,* 17 (1996), 1–24.

17. D. J. Ravenscraft and F. M. Scherer, *Mergers, Selloffs, and Economic Efficiency* (Washington, D.C.: Brookings Institution, 1987).

18. See J. P. Walsh, "Top Management Turnover Following Mergers and Acquisitions," *Strategic Management Journal,* 9 (1988), 173–183.

19. See A. A. Cannella and D. C. Hambrick, "Executive Departure and Acquisition Performance," *Strategic Management Journal,* 14 (1993), 137–152.

20. R. Roll, "The Hubris Hypothesis of Corporate Takeovers," *Journal of Business,* 59 (1986), 197–216.

21. "Coca-Cola: A Sobering Lesson from Its Journey into Wine," *BusinessWeek,* June 3, 1985, pp. 96–98.

22. M. Murray and J. Rebello, "Mellon Bank Corp.: One Big Unhappy Family," *Wall Street Journal,* April 28, 1995, pp. B1, B4; and K. Holland. "A Bank Eat Bank World—With Indigestion," *BusinessWeek,* October 30, 1995, p. 130.

23. P. Haspeslagh and D. Jemison, *Managing Acquisitions* (New York: Free Press, 1991).

24. For views on this issue, see L. L Fray, D. H. Gaylin, and J. W. Down, "Successful Acquisition Planning," *Journal of Business Strategy,* 5 (1984), 46–55; C. W. L. Hill, "Profile of a Conglomerate Takeover: BTR and Thomas Tilling," *Journal of General Management,* 10 (1984), 34–50; D. R. Willensky, "Making It Happen: How to Execute an Acquisition," *Business Horizons* (March–April 1985), 38–45; Haspeslagh and Jemison, *Managing Acquisitions;* and P. L. Anslinger and T. E. Copeland. "Growth Through Acquisition: A Fresh Look," *Harvard Business Review* (January–February 1996), 126–135.

25. P. B. Carroll, "IBM, Motorola Plan Radio Link for Computers," *Wall Street Journal,* January 29, 1990, pp. B1, B5.

26. For a recent review of the evidence and some contrary empirical evidence, see D. E. Hatfield, J. P. Liebskind, and T. C. Opler, "The Effects of Corporate Restructuring on Aggregate Industry Specialization," *Strategic Management Journal,* 17, 1996, 55–72.

27. For example, see A. Schleifer and R. W. Vishny, "Takeovers in the 60s and 80s: Evidence and Implications," *Strategic Management Journal,* 12 (Winter 1991), Special Issue, 51–60.

28. See G. A. Patterson and F. Schwadel, "Back in Time," *Wall Street Journal,* September 30, 1992, p. 1; J. Flynn, "Smaller but Wiser," *BusinessWeek,* October 12, 1992, pp. 28–29; and B. Bremner, "The Big Store's Trauma," *BusinessWeek,* July 10, 1989, pp. 50–55.

29. See J. Argenti, *Corporate Collapse: Causes and Symptoms,* (New York: McGraw-Hill, 1976); R. C. Hoffman, "Strategies for Corporate Turnarounds: What Do We Know About

Them?" *Journal of General Management,* 14 (1984), 46-66; D. Schendel, G. R. Patton, and J. Riggs, "Corporate Turnaround Strategies: A Study of Profit Decline and Recovery," *Journal of General Management,* 2 (1976), 1-22; and S. Siafter, *Corporate Recovery: Successful Turnaround Strategies and Their Implementation* (Hammondsworth, England: Penguin Books, 1984), pp. 25-60.

30. D. B. Bibeault, *Corporate Turnaround* (New York: McGraw-Hill, 1982).

31. Hoffman, "Strategies for Corporate Turnarounds," pp. 46-66.

32. Hoffman, "Strategies for Corporate Turnarounds," pp. 46-66.

33. Lee Iacocca, *Iacocca: An Autobiography* (New York: Bantam Books, 1984), p. 254.

34. Sources: L. Hooper, "Xerox Plans to Withdraw Completely from the Financial Services Industry," *Wall Street Journal,* January 19, 1993, p. A3; T. Smart, "So Much for Diversification," *BusinessWeek,* February 1, 1993, p. 31; and T. Smart, "A Cloud Over Xerox," *BusinessWeek,* November 9, 1992, p. 48.

Chapter 11: Designing Organizational Structure

1. D. Woodruff and E. Lesly, "Surge at Chrysler," *Fortune,* November 9, 1992, pp. 88-96.

2. "Chrysler Reengineers Product Development Process," *Information Week,* September 7, 1992, p. 20.

3. J. R. Galbraith, *Designing Complex Organizations* (Reading, Mass.: Addison-Wesley, 1973).

4. J. Child, *Organization: A Guide for Managers and Administrators* (New York: Harper & Row, 1977), pp. 50-72.

5. R. H. Miles, *Macro Organizational Behavior* (Santa Monica, Calif.: Goodyear, 1980), pp. 19-20.

6. Galbraith, *Designing Complex Organizations.*

7. V. A. Graicunas, "Relationship in Organization," in *Papers on the Science of Administration,* eds. L. Gulick and L. Urwick (New York: Institute of Public Administration, 1937), pp. 181-185; and J. C. Worthy, "Organizational Structure and Company Morale," *American Sociological Review,* 15 (1950), 169-179.

8. Child, *Organization,* pp. 50-52.

9. G. R. Jones, "Organization-Client Transactions and Organizational Governance Structures," *Academy of Management Journal,* 30 (1987), 197-218.

10. H. Mintzberg, *The Structuring of Organizations* (Englewood Cliffs, N.J.: Prentice-Hall, 1979), p. 435.

11. B. Woolridge and S. W. Floyd, "The Strategy Process, Middle Management Involvement, and Organizational Performance," *Strategic Management Journal,* 11 (1990), 231-241.

12. Child, *Organization,* p. 51.

13. R. Carzo, Jr., and J. N. Yanousas, "Effects of Flat and Tall Organization Structure," *Administrative Science Quarterly,* 14 (1969), 178-191.

14. A. Gupta and V. Govindardan, "Business Unit Strategy, Managerial Characteristics, and Business Unit Effectiveness at Strategy Implementation," *Academy of Management Journal,* 27 (1984), 25-41; and R. T. Lenz, "Determinants of Organizational Performance: An Interdisciplinary Review," *Strategic Management Journal,* 2 (1981), 131-154.

15. W. H. Wagel, "Keeping the Organization Lean at Federal Express," *Personnel* (March 1984), 4.

16. J. Koter, "For P&G Rivals, the New Game Is to Beat the Leader, Not Copy It," *Wall Street Journal,* May 6, 1985, p. 35.

17. G. R. Jones, "Task Visibility, Free Riding and Shirking: Explaining the Effect of Organization Structure on Employee Behavior," *Academy of Management Review,* 4 (1984), 684-695.

18. "Operation Turnaround—How Westinghouse's New Chairman Plans to Fire Up an Old Line Company," *BusinessWeek,* December 14, 1983, pp. 124-133.

19. C. Chandler and J. B. White, "Honda's Middle Managers Will Regain Authority in New Overhaul of Company," *Wall Street Journal,* May 16, 1992, p. A2.

20. R. L. Daft, *Organizational Theory and Design,* 3rd ed. (St. Paul, Minn.: West, 1986), p. 215.

21. Alfred D. Chandler, *Strategy and Structure* (Cambridge, Mass.: MIT Press, 1962).

22. The discussion draws heavily on Chandler, *Strategy and Structure;* and B. R. Scott, *Stages of Corporate Development* (Cambridge, Mass.: Intercollegiate Clearing House, Harvard Business School, 1971).

23. J. R. Galbraith and R. K. Kazanjian, *Strategy Implementation: Structure System and Process,* 2nd ed. (St. Paul, Minn.: West, 1986); Child, *Organization;* and R. Duncan, "What Is the Right Organization Structure?" *Organizational Dynamics* (Winter 1979), 59-80.

24. O. E. Williamson, *Markets and Hierarchies: Analysis and Antitrust Implications* (New York: Free Press, 1975).

25. P. R. Lawrence and J. Lorsch, *Organization and Environment* (Boston: Division of Research, Harvard Business School, 1967).

26. K. Pope, "Dell Refocuses on Groundwork to Cope with Rocketing Sales," *Wall Street Journal,* June 18, 1993, p. B5.

27. Chandler, *Strategy and Structure;* Williamson, *Markets and Hierarchies;* and L. Wrigley, "Divisional Autonomy and Diversification" (Ph.D. diss., Harvard Business School, 1970).

28. R. P. Rumelt, *Strategy, Structure, and Economic Performance* (Boston: Division of Research, Harvard Business School, 1974); Scott, "Stages of Corporate Development"; and Williamson, *Markets and Hierarchies.*

29. The discussion draws on each of the sources cited in endnotes 20-27 and on G. R. Jones and C. W. L. Hill, "Transaction Cost Analysis of Strategy-Structure Choice," *Strategic Management Journal,* 9 (1988), 159-172.

30. H. O. Armour and D. J. Teece, "Organizational Structure and Economic Performance: A Test of the Multidivisional Hypothesis," *Bell Journal of Economics,* 9 (1978), 106-122.

31. Alfred Sloan, *My Years at General Motors* (New York: Doubleday, 1983), Ch. 3.

32. C. Soloman, "Amoco to Cut More Jobs and Radically Alter Its Structure." *Wall Street Journal,* July 22, 1995, p. B4.

33. S. M. Davis and R. R. Lawrence, *Matrix* (Reading, Mass.: Addison-Wesley, 1977); and J. R. Galbraith, "Matrix Organization Designs: How to Combine Functional and Project Forms," *Business Horizons,* 14 (1971), 29-40.

34. Duncan, "What Is the Right Organizational Structure?"; and Davis and Lawrence, *Matrix.*

35. P. R. Lawrence and J. Lorsch, *Organization and Environment* (Homewood, Ill.: Irwin, 1967), pp. 50-55.

36. Galbraith, *Designing Complex Organizations,* Ch. 1; and Galbraith and Kazanjian, *Strategy Implementation,* Ch. 7.

37. Henry Mintzberg, *The Nature of Managerial Work* (Englewood Cliffs, N.J.: Prentice-Hall, 1973), Ch. 10.

38. Lawrence and Lorsch, *Organization and Environment,* p. 55.

39. Bro Uttal, "Behind the Fall of Steve Jobs," *Business Week,* January 31, 1983, pp. 20–24.

40. Ibid.

Chapter 12: Designing Strategic Control Systems

1. J. Pettet, "Wal-Mart Yesterday and Today," *Discount Merchandiser,* December 1995, pp. 66–67.

2. M. Reid, "Stores of Value," *Economist,* March 4, 1995, pp. ss5–ss7.

3. www.walmart.com.

4. G. Hamel and C. K. Prahalad, "Strategic Intent," *Harvard Business Review* (May–June 1989), 64

5. R. Simmons, "Strategic Orientation and Top Management Attention to Control Systems," *Strategic Management Journal,* 12 (1991), 49–62.

6. R. Simmons, "How New Top Managers Use Control Systems as Levers of Strategic Renewal," *Strategic Management Journal,* 15 (1994), 169–189.

7. R. S. Kaplan and D. P. Norton, "The Balanced Scorecard—Measures that Drive Performance," *Harvard Business Review* (January–February 1992), 71–79.

8. R. S. Kaplan and D. P. Norton, "Using the Balanced Scorecard as a Strategic Management System," *Harvard Business Review* (January–February 1996), 75–85.

9. R. S. Kaplan and D. P. Norton, "Putting the Balanced Scorecard to Work," *Harvard Business Review* (September–October 1993), 134–147.

10. Kaplan and Norton, "The Balanced Scorecard," p. 72.

11. W. G. Ouchi, "The Transmission of Control Through Organizational Hierarchy," *Academy of Management Journal,* 21 (1978), 173–192; and W. H. Newman, *Constructive Control* (Englewood Cliffs, N.J.: Prentice-Hall, 1975).

12. P. F. Drucker, *The Practice of Management* (New York: Harper & Row, 1954).

13. S. J. Carroll and H. L. Tosi, *Management by Objectives: Applications and Research* (New York: Macmillan, 1973).

14. R. Rodgers and J. E. Hunter, "Impact of Management by Objectives on Organizational Productivity," *Journal of Applied Psychology,* 76 (1991), 322–326.

15. Bureau of Business Practice, *Profiles of Malcolm Baldrige Award Winners* (Boston: Allyn & Bacon, 1992).

16. E. Flamholtz, "Organizational Control Systems as a Managerial Tool," *California Management Review* (Winter 1979), 50–58.

17. O. E. Williamson, *Markets and Hierarchies* (New York: Free Press, 1975); and W. G. Ouchi, "Markets, Bureaucracies, and Clans," *Administrative Science Quarterly,* 25 (1980), 129–141.

18. "In Praise of the Blue Suit," *Economist,* January 13, 1996, p. 59.

19. H. Mintzberg, *The Structuring of Organizations* (Englewood Cliffs, N.J.: Prentice-Hall, 1979), pp. 5–9.

20. L. Smircich, "Concepts of Culture and Organizational Analysis," *Administrative Science Quarterly,* 28 (1983), 339–358.

21. General Electric, *Harvard Business School Case* No. 9-385-315, 1984.

22. Ouchi, "Markets, Bureaucracies, and Clans," p. 130.

23. G. R. Jones, *Organizational Theory* (Reading, Mass.: Addison-Wesley, 1997).

24. J. Van Maanen and E. H. Schein, "Towards a Theory of Organizational Socialization," in *Research in Organizational Behavior,* ed. B. M. Staw (Greenwich, Conn.: JAI Press, 1979), pp. 1, 209–264.

25. G. R. Jones, "Socialization Tactics, Self-Efficacy, and Newcomers' Adjustments to Organizations," *Academy of Management Journal,* 29 (1986), 262–279.

26. For details of the HP Way, see chapter 5 in J. P. Kotter and J. L. Heskett, *Corporate Culture and Performance* (New York: Free Press, 1992).

27. J. P. Kotter and J. L. Heskett, *Corporate Culture and Performance.*

28. T. J. Peters and R. H. Waterman, *In Search of Excellence: Lessons from America's Best-Run Companies* (New York: Harper & Row, 1982).

29. W. G. Ouchi, *Theory Z: How American Business Can Meet the Japanese Challenge* (Reading, Mass.: Addison-Wesley, 1981).

30. E. E. Lawler III, *Motivation in Work Organizations* (Monterey, Calif.: Brooks/Cole, 1973); and Galbraith and Kazanjian, *Strategy Implementation,* Ch. 6 (St. Paul, Minn.: West, 1992).

31. E. E. Lawler III, "The Design of Effective Reward Systems," in *Handbook of Organizational Behavior,* ed. J. W. Lorsch (Englewood Cliffs, N.J.: Prentice-Hall, 1987), 386–422; and R. Mathis and J. Jackson, *Personnel,* 2nd ed. (St. Paul, Minn.: West, 1979), p. 456.

32. H. L. Tosi, Jr., and L. R. Gomez-Mejia, "CEO Compensation and Firm Performance," *Academy of Management Journal,* 37 (1994), 1002–1016.

33. T. Y. Hausman, "Second Behind," *Wall Street Journal,* April 11, 1996, p. A4.

Chapter 13: Matching Structure and Control to Strategy

1. A. Choi, "Digital's New Attitude Towards Old Enemies Puts It Back in the Game," *Wall Street Journal,* April 9, 1996, pp. A1, A10.

2. W. G. Ouchi, "The Relationship Between Organizational Structure and Organizational Control," *Administrative Science Quarterly,* 22 (1977), 95–113.

3. K. M. Eisenhardt, "Control: Organizational and Economic Approaches," *Management Science,* 16 (1985), 134–148.

4. J. R. Galbraith, *Designing Complex Organizations* (Reading, Mass.: Addison-Wesley, 1973); P. R. Lawrence and J. W. Lorsch, *Organization and Environment* (Cambridge, Mass.: Harvard University Press, 1967); and D. Miller, "Strategy Making and Structure: Analysis and Implications for Performance," *Academy of Management Journal,* 30 (1987), 7–32.

5. Michael E. Porter, *Competitive Strategy: Techniques for Analyzing Industries and Competitors* (New York: Free Press, 1980); and D. Miller, "Configurations of Strategy and Structure," *Strategic Management Journal,* 7 (1986), 233–249.

6. D. Miller and P. H. Freisen, *Organizations: A Quantum View* (Englewood Cliffs, N.J.: Prentice-Hall, 1984).

7. J. Woodward, *Industrial Organization: Theory and Practice* (London: Oxford University Press, 1965); and Lawrence and Lorsch, *Organization and Environment.*

8. C. J. Loomis, "The Reed That Citicorp Leans On," *Fortune,* July 12, 1993, pp. 90-93.

9. R. E. White, "Generic Business Strategies, Organizational Context and Performance: An Empirical Investigation," *Strategic Management Journal,* 7 (1986), 217-231.

10. Porter, *Competitive Strategy;* and Miller, "Configurations of Strategy and Structure."

11. E. Deal and A. A. Kennedy, *Corporate Cultures* (Reading, Mass.: Addison-Wesley, 1985); and "Corporate Culture," *BusinessWeek,* October 27, 1980, pp. 148-160.

12. B. Saporito, "How to Revive a Fading Firm," *Fortune,* March 22, 1993, p. 80.

13. D. Miller, "Configurations of Strategy and Structure," in R. E. Miles and C. C. Snow, *Organizational Strategy, Structure, and Process* (New York: McGraw-Hill, 1978).

14. Lawrence and Lorsch, *Organization and Environment.*

15. J. Stopford and L. Wells, *Managing the Multinational Enterprise* (London: Longman, 1972).

16. C. A. Bartlett and S. Ghoshal, *Managing Across Borders: The Transnational Solution* (Cambridge, Mass.: Harvard Business School Press, 1991).

17. G. R. Jones and C. W. L. Hill, "Transaction Cost Analysis of Strategy-Structure Choice," *Strategic Management Journal,* 9 (1988), 159-172.

18. Jones and Hill, "Transaction Cost Analysis."

19. R. A. D'Aveni and D. J. Ravenscraft, "Economies of Integration Versus Bureaucracy Costs: Does Vertical Integration Improve Performance?" *Academy of Management Journal,* 5 (1994), 1167-1206.

20. Lawrence and Lorsch, *Organization and Environment;* Galbraith, *Designing Complex Organizations;* and Michael Porter, *Competitive Advantage: Creating and Sustaining Superior Performance* (New York: Free Press, 1985).

21. P. R. Nayyar, "Performance Effects of Information Asymmetry and Economies of Scope in Diversified Service Firm," *Academy of Management Journal,* 36 (1993), 28-57.

22. L. R. Gomez-Mejia, "Structure and Process of Diversification, Compensation Strategy, and Performance," *Strategic Management Journal,* 13 (1992), 381-397.

23. C. C. Markides and P. J. Williamson, "Related Diversification, Core Competencies, and Corporate Performance," *Strategic Management Journal,* Special Issue, 15 (1994), 149-165.

24. Porter, *Competitive Strategy.*

25. M. S. Salter and W. A. Weinhold, *Diversification Through Acquisition* (New York: Free Press, 1979).

26. F. T. Paine and D. J. Power, "Merger Strategy: An Examination of Drucker's Five Rules for Successful Acquisitions," *Strategic Management Journal,* 5 (1984), 99-110.

27. G. D. Bruton, B. M. Oviatt, and M. A. White, "Performance of Acquisitions of Distressed Firms," *Academy of Management Journal,* 4 (1994), 972-989.

28. C. K. Prahalad and R. A. Bettis, "The Dominant Logic: A New Linkage Between Diversity and Performance," *Strategic Management Journal,* 7 (1986), 485-501; and Porter, *Competitive Strategy.*

29. Porter, *Competitive Strategy.*

30. H. Singh and C. A. Montgomery, "Corporate Acquisitions and Economic Performance," Unpublished manuscript, 1984.

31. N. D. Fast, "The Future of Industrial New Venture Departments," *Industrial Marketing Management,* 8 (1979), 264-279.

32. R. A. Burgelman, "Managing the New Venture Division: Research Findings and the Implications for Strategic Management," *Strategic Management Journal,* 6 (1985), 39-54.

33. Fast, "The Future of Industrial New Venture Departments."

34. Burgelman, "Managing the New Venture Division."

35. R. A. Burgelman, "Corporate Entrepreneurship and Strategic Management: Insights from a Process Study," *Management Science,* 29 (1983), 1349-1364.

36. B. Kogut, "Joint Ventures: Theoretical and Empirical Perspectives," *Strategic Management Journal,* 9 (1988), 319-332.

37. "The Outing of Outsourcing," *Economist,* November 25, 1995, p. 36.

38. G. S. Capowski, "Designing a Corporate Identity," *Management Review* (June 1993), 37-38.

39. J. Marcia, "Just Doing It." *Distribution,* January 1995, pp. 36-40.

40. "Andersen's Androids," *Economist,* May 4, 1996, p. 72.

41. J. Cole, "New CEO at Hughes Studied Its Managers, Got Them on His Side," *Wall Street Journal,* March 30, 1993, pp. A1, A8.

Chapter 14: Implementing Strategic Change

1. E. A. Deavenport, Jr., "Winning the Baldridge Award," *Management,* June 1994, pp. 36-38.

2. M. T. Hannan and J. Freeman, "Structural Inertia and Organizational Change," *American Sociological Review,* 49 (1984), 149-164.

3. D. Miller, *The Icarus Paradox* (New York: Harper Business, 1990).

4. J. Thackray, "Restructuring in the Name of the Hurricane," *Euromoney* (February 1987), 106-108.

5. M. Hammer and J. Champy, *Reengineering the Corporation.* (New York: HarperCollins, 1993).

6. Hammer and Champy, *Reengineering the Corporation,* p. 39.

7. G. D. Bruton, J. K. Keels, and C. L. Shook, "Downsizing the Firm: Answering the Strategic Questions," *Academy of Management Executive,* May 1996, pp. 38-45.

8. G. R. Jones, *Organizational Theory* (Reading Mass.: Addison-Wesley, 1997); and R. A. Burgelman and M. A. Maidique, *Strategic Management of Technology and Innovation* (Homewood, Ill.: Irwin, 1988).

9. G. R. Jones and J. E. Butler, "Managing Internal Corporate Entrepreneurship: An Agency Theory Perspective," *Journal of Management,* 18 (1992), 733-749.

10. "Synergen Inc.," *Wall Street Journal,* August 2, 1994, p. B6.

11. R. A. Burgelman, "Designs for Corporate Entrepreneurship in Established Firms," *California Management Review,* 26 (1984), 154-166.

12. D. Frey, "Learning the Ropes: My Life as a Product Champion," *Harvard Business Review* (September-October, 1991), 46-56.

13. R. Beckhard, *Organizational Development* (Reading, Mass.: Addison-Wesley, 1969); and W. L. French and C. H. Bell, Jr., *Organizational Development,* 2nd ed. (Englewood Cliffs, N.J.: Prentice-Hall, 1978).

14. Beckhard, *Organizational Development.*

15. L. C. Coch and R. P. French, Jr., "Overcoming Resistance to Change," *Human Relations* (August 1948), 512-532; and P. R. Lawrence, "How to Deal With Resistance to Change," *Harvard Business Review* (January-February 1969), 4-12.

16. J. O. Huff, A. S. Huff, and H. Thomas, "Strategic Renewal and the Interaction of Cumulative Stress and Inertia," *Strategic Management Journal,* Special Issue, 13 (1992), 55-75.

17. P. Kotter and L. A. Schlesinger, "Choosing Strategies for Change," *Harvard Business Review* (March-April 1979), 106-114.

18. J. R. Galbraith, "Designing the Innovative Organization," *Organizational Dynamics* (Winter 1982), 5-25.

19. J. A. Litterer, "Conflict in Organizations: A Reexamination," *Academy of Management Journal,* 9 (1966), 178-186; and S. M. Schmidt and T. A. Kochan, "Conflict: Towards Conceptual Clarity," *Administrative Science Quarterly,* 13 (1972), 359-370.

20. L. R. Pondy, "Organizational Conflict: Concepts and Models," *Administrative Science Quarterly,* 2 (1967), 296-320.

21. A. C. Amason, "Distinguishing the Effects of Functional and Dysfunctional Conflict on Strategic Decision Making: Resolving a Paradox for Top Management Teams," *Academy of Management Journal,* 1 (1996), 123-148.

22. R. H. Miles, *Macro Organizational Behavior* (Santa Monica, Calif.: Goodyear, 1980).

23. A. M. Pettigrew, *The Politics of Organizational Decision Making* (London: Tavistock, 1973).

24. J. G. March, "The Business Firm as a Coalition," *Journal of Politics,* 24 (1962), 662-678; D. J. Vredenburgh and J. G. Maurer, "A Process Framework of Organizational Politics," *Human Relations,* 37 (1984), 47-66.

25. T. Burns, "Micropolitics: Mechanisms of Institutional Change," *Administrative Science Quarterly,* 6 (1961), 257-281.

26. R. A. Dahl, "The Concept of Power," *Behavioral Science,* 2 (1957), 201-215; and G. A. Astley and P. S. Sachdeva, "Structural Sources of Intraorganizational Power," *Academy of Management Review,* 9 (1984), 104-113.

27. This section draws heavily on D. J. Hickson, C.R. Hinings, C. A. Lee, R. E. Schneck, and D. J. Pennings, "A Strategic Contingencies Theory of Intraorganizational Power," *Administrative Science Quarterly* 16 (1971), 216-227; and C. R. Hinings, D. J. Hickson, J. M. Pennings, and R.E. Schneck, "Structural Conditions of Intraorganizational Power," *Administrative Science Quarterly,* 19 (1974), 22-44.

28. Hickson et al., "A Strategic Contingencies Theory."

29. H. Ibarra, "Network Centrality, Power, and Innovation Involvement: Determinants of Technical and Administrative Roles." *Academy of Management Journal,* 36 (1993), 471-501.

30. Pettigrew, *The Politics of Organizational Decision Making.*

31. Hickson et al., "A Strategic Contingencies Theory."

32. H. A. Landsberger, "The Horizontal Dimension in Bureaucracy," *Administrative Science Quarterly,* 6 (1961), 299-322.

33. G. R. Salancik and J. Pfeffer, "The Bases and Use of Power in Organizational Decision Making: The Case of a University," *Administrative Science Quarterly,* 19 (1974), 453-473.

34. Hickson et al., "A Strategic Contingencies Theory of Intraorganizational Power."

35. J. Pfeffer, *Managing with Power* (Boston: Harvard Business School Press, 1992).

36. J. F. McDonnell, "Learning to Think in Different Terms: TQM & Restructuring at McDonnell Douglas." *Executive Speeches,* June/July 1994, pp. 25-28.

37. P. Annin and A. Underwood, "A Week of Woes Raises More Questions About Saint Merck," *Newsweek,* August 2, 1993, p. 35.

38. E. Tanouye, M. Waldholz, and G. Anders, "Stunning Departure of Merck Chief Signals Turmoil Inside and Out," *Wall Street Journal,* July 16, 1993, pp. A1, A4.

INDEX

° °

Abell, Derek F., 43–46, 186
Abernathy, William J., 51
Absolute cost advantage, 74
A.C. Nielsen, 341
Acquisitions
    as entry strategy, 326–331
    management of, 433–434
Active matrix liquid crystal displays
        (AMLCDs), 52
Activity ratios, C11
Adolph Coors Co., 78
Advanced Micro Devices (AMD), 3, 107–108
AEG, 310
Agee, Bill, 35–37, 52, 54, 55
Airbus Industrie, 296, 310
Airline industry, 225
Airline Pilots Association (ALPA), 40
Akers, John, 339
Alcan, 284–285
Alcatel, 312
Alcoa International, 284–285, 354
Alco Standard, 430–431
Allaire, Paul, 343
Allegis Corporation, 40
Alliances
    as corporate strategy, 306–307
    global, 268–274
    long-term contracts as, 291–292
AlliedSignal, 12–13, 14
Allstate Insurance, 281, 333–334
American Business Products (ABP), 434
American Express
    strategy, 195
    mentioned, 56, 132, 194, 389
American Quality Foundation, 162
American Stauffer Chemical, 304
American Telephone & Telegraph (AT&T)
    case study, 312–313
    strategy, 375
    mentioned, 73, 74, 220, 232, 269, 314,
        327, 333, 355, 356, 451
America Online (AOL), 19, 281
Amgen, 262
AMLCDs (active matrix liquid crystal
        displays), 52
Amoco, 365, 426
AMPEX, 51, 167
Amstrad, 252
Andersen Consulting, 437
Anderson, Robert, 279
Andreessen, Mark, 1
Anheuser-Busch, 78, 216
Anne Klein, 212
Apollo Computer, 170
Apple Computer
    case study, 378–379

mentioned, 3, 90, 93, 105, 110–111, 131,
        167, 168, 196, 217, 219, 293, 358,
        389, 398, 447, 462
Applied Materials, 182
Armstrong, C. Michael, 440–441
Arthur Andersen, 394
Arthur D. Little, 162
Asahi, 76
Asset reduction strategy, 208
Assets
    complementary, 218–219, 220
    specialized, 285–287
AST Research, 110–112, 379
AT&T. See American Telephone and
        Telegraph
AT&T Wireless, 295, 297
Au Bon Pain, 420
Automobile industry, 114–115
Average collection period, C11
Average unit costs, 154
Avery, Seawell, 27

Balanced scorecard model, 384–385
Bang & Olufsen, 192
BankAmerica, 460
Barad, Jill, 2–4, 9, 14
Bargaining power
    of buyers, 81–82
    of suppliers, 82–83
Barrett, Tom, 242
Barriers to entry, 74–75, 76, 191, 194,
        223–226, 284–285
Barriers to exit, 80–81
Barriers to imitation, 128–130, 219, 220
Bartlett, Christopher, 252, 255–256, 258
Bath and Body Works, 221
Bausch & Lomb, 117, 167
Beall, Donald, 279–280
Beatrice Company, 304
Behavior controls, 392–394
Bell Atlantic, 74
Ben & Jerry's, 187
Benchmarking, 135
Bendix, 35
Bertelsmann, 377
Best industrial practice, 135
Bethlehem Steel, 80, 90
Biases, cognitive, 26–28
Bidding strategy, 291
Bisys Group, 198
Bizmart, 283
Blockbuster Entertainment, 215, 216
Bloomingdale's, 212
BMW, 192, 199, 211, 310–311, 317
Boards of directors, 54–56

Bodman, Sam, 320
Body Shop International
    case study, 66–67
    strategy, 221
Boeing
    strategy, 296
    mentioned, 49–50, 75, 177, 248,
        292–294
Boise Cascade, 35
Bonus systems, 403–405
Bookcrafters, 434
Booz, Allen, & Hamilton, 167
Bose Corporation, 178–179
Boss, project vs. functional, 366
Bossidy, Larry, 12–13
Boston Consulting Group (BCG), 315–320,
        322
Bottom-up change, 466
Bowman, Edward H., 63, 217
Brand loyalty, 74, 193
Brand names, 128–129
Brennan, Edward, 334
Bridgestone, 242
British Petroleum, 365
Broad differentiator, 193
BTR Inc., 298
Budgets, operating, 392–394
Bureaucratic costs
    defined, 290, 350
    and differentiation, 350
    and diversification, 300–303
    in divisional structures, 365–366
    and integration, 290
    sources of, 353
Burgelman, Robert, 17
Burger King
    case study, 213–214
    mentioned, 215, 217, 395
Business definition, 42–46
Business ethics. See Ethics, business
Business-level strategy, 185–212
    choice of generic, 188–201
    defined, 186
    global expansion and, 249
    investment strategy and, 203–209
    strategic groups and, 202–203
    structure and control in, 414–421
Business process, 445
Buyers
    bargaining power of, 81–82
    powerful, 193
Buyouts, leveraged, 57–59

Cabot Corporation, 320
Cadillac, 211

Cahouet, Frank, 329
Campbell Soup, 208, 403–404
Canon, 25, 126, 183, 217, 264–265,
    321–322, 342
Canon of Japan, 268
Capabilities, 123–125
Capable competitors, 219–220, 221
Capacity control, 230–233
Capacity and demand, 94–95, 231
Capital structure, C11
Carnation, 428
Carter Wallace, 87–88
Case studies
    American Telephone & Telegraph
        (AT&T), 312–313
    Apple Computer, 378–379
    Body Shop International, 66–67
    Burger King, 213–214
    Chrysler, 346–347
    Daimler-Benz, 310–311
    Digital Equipment Corporation (DEC),
        410–411
    Eastman Chemicals, 442–443
    Ford Motor Co., 185–186, 277–278
    Goodyear Tire & Rubber, 242
    Hughes Aircraft, 440–441
    IKEA, 243–244
    Intel, 107–108
    Liz Claiborne, 212
    Lloyds Bank, 142–143
    Marks & Spencer, 138–139
    Mattel, 2–3
    Mazda, 277–278
    McDonald's, 213–214, 408–409
    Merck, 470–471
    Micron Technology, 71
    Morrison Knudsen (MK), 35–36
    Rockwell International, 279–280
    Southwest Airlines, 33–34
    Wal-Mart, 380–381
    Wang Laboratories, 105–106
    Xerox, 183–184, 342–343
Case study analysis, C2–C14
    case analysis, C3–C7
    financial analysis, C9–C13
    writing of, C7–C9
Cash cows, 316–317
Cash flow, C13
Cash flow, free, 58
Casio, 149
Casual Corner, 212
Caterpillar, 25, 121, 128, 179, 257–258
Centrality, and power, 461–462
Centralization, vs. decentralization,
    356–357, 364
Century 21 Real Estate, 216
CEOs
    compensation of, 52–53, 56–57
    as corporate managers, 11–12
    domination of boards by, 55
    empire building by, 53
    power of, 465

Chaining, 215–216
Chain of command, minimum, 352–353
Champion International, 339
Chandler, Alfred D., 358
Change. *See* Strategic change
Chaparral Steel, 90
Chase Manhattan Bank, 145–146
Chemical Bank, 145–146
Chief executive officers. *See* CEOs
Child World, Inc., 229
Chips & Technologies, 288
Chrysler
    case study, 346–347
    strategy, 293
    mentioned, 14, 27, 81, 114–115, 129,
        130, 133, 196, 209, 227, 288,
        291–292, 337, 348, 350, 354,
        356, 382–384, 419, 423
Ciba-Geigy
    strategy, 318
    mentioned, 204, 315, 319
Cincinnati Bell, 295, 297
Citibank, 116
Citicorp
    strategy, 118
    mentioned, 416
Clausewitz, Carl von, 16–17
Clayton Dubilier & Rice, 343
Club Med, 427
Coca-Cola, 6, 53, 96, 129, 217, 219, 229,
    235, 245, 251, 281–282, 328, 401,
    418
Cognitive biases, 26–28
Cognizant Corporation, 341
Coldwell Banker Real Estate, 281, 333–334
Coleco Industries, 3
Columbia Pictures, 281–282
Commercialization, poor, 167–168
Commission systems, 403
Compaq Computer
    strategy, 234
    mentioned, 3, 86, 110–112, 129, 131,
        152, 174, 219, 283, 326, 355, 379,
        389
Compensation
    of CEOs, 52–53, 56–57
    for performance, 158
    stock-based, 56–57
    see also Reward systems
Competencies. *See* Distinctive
    competencies
Competition
    bargaining power of buyers and
        suppliers, 81–83
    capability of competitors, 219–220, 221
    entry and, 73–75
    five forces model, 72–87, 89–92
    industry evolution and, 92–96
    national state and, 97–102
    potential competitors, 73–74
    rivalry, 75–81
    substitute products and, 83–84

Competitive advantage
    building blocks of, 113–119
    durability of, 127–131
    functional-level strategy and, 142–184
    loss of, 131–133
    strategy and, 125–126
    sustainability of, 134–135
    value creation and, 110–113, 119–123
Competitive bidding strategy, 291
Competitive structure, 76–78
Complementary assets, 218–219, 220
Computer World, 283
Concentration on single business, 281–282
Conflict, organizational, 453–456
Conflict process, stages in, 453–455
Coniston Partners, 40
Consolidated Foods, 299
Consolidated industries, 75–78
Consumer-oriented business, 43–46
Consumer tastes, global differences,
    251–253
Contadina, 428
Continental Airlines, 200
Contracting, long-term vs. short-term,
    291–292
Control, 380–409
    at business level, 414–421
    at corporate level, 427–433
    at functional level, 412–414
    matching to structure and strategy,
        410–441
    organizational culture and, 396–402
    reward systems, 402–405
    strategic, 380–409
    strategic defined, 382–384
    strategic levels of, 387–395
    and structure, 410–441
    systems, 380–409
    types of systems, 385–395
Control span, 351
Cooperative relationships, 290–295; *see
    also* Alliances
Coordination among businesses, 301–302
Core competencies, portfolio of, 320–322
Corporate development, 312–343
    acquisitions, 326–331
    defined, 313
    entry strategies, 326–333
    internal new venturing, 323–326
    joint ventures, 331–333
    portfolio review, 314–322
    restructuring, 333–336
    turnaround strategies, 336–339
Corporate governance, 51–59
Corporate-level managers, 11–12
Corporate-level structure and control,
    427–433; *see also* Control
Corporate raiders, 57
Corporate strategy, 279–311
    concentration on single business,
        281–282
    cooperative relationships, 290–295

diversification, 297–306
outsourcing, 290–295
strategic alliances, 306–307
vertical integration, 282–290
Corporate takeovers, 57
Costco, 334
Cost leadership, 188–191, 194–196,
    415–419
Cost reductions
and entry mode, 268
global, 249–253
Costs
absolute advantages, 74
production, 147
unit, 147, 150–151, 154
see also Bureaucratic costs
Cross-functional integration, 172
Cross-functional teams, 419
Cross-licensing, 262
Crown Books, 456
Crowne Plazas, 201
Crum and Forster, 330, 342–343
Culture
leadership and, 398–399
organizational, 396–402
Cunningham, Mary, 35, 36
Currency exchange, 85
Customer defection rates, 154–156
Customer loyalty, 154–156
Customer needs, 186–187
Customer orientation, 42–46
Customer responsiveness
as competitive advantage, 117–119
functional-level strategy, 175–186
strategic control system for,
    383–384
Customization, 152, 177, 251–253
Cyrix, 107–108

Daewoo Motor Company, 270–271
Daimler-Benz, case study, 310–311
Dart Group, 456
D'Avani, Richard, 91
Days sales outstanding (DSO), C11
DCC (digital compact cassette), 169
Dean Witter Reynolds, 281, 333–334
Debt-to-assets ratio, C12
Debt-to-equity ratio, C12
Decision making
ethics and, 60–62
improvement of, 26–30
and politics, 457
Decline strategies, 207–208
Declining industries, 95–96, 235–239
Deere & Co., 135
Definition of business, 42–46
Dell Computer
strategy, 234
mentioned, 3, 86, 90, 110–112, 129, 131,
    192, 360, 379, 389, 452
Delta Airlines, 355

Demand
and capacity growth, 94–95
industry conditions and, 78–80
national conditions and, 98–99
uncertainty in, 289
Deming, W. Edwards, 160–161, 164
Demographic environment, 86
Den Fujita, 247
DeSimone, L.D., 44
Deutsche Aerospace, 310–311
Development funnel, 171
Development. *See* Corporate development
Devil's advocacy, 29–30
Dialectic inquiry, 29–30
Differentiation, 349–371
definitions, 349–350
horizontal, 358–371
of products, 187
vertical, 350–357
Differentiation strategy, 191–196
advantages and disadvantages of,
    193–194
cost leadership and, 194–196
objective of, 191–192
and structure, 417–419
Digital compact cassette (DCC), 169
Digital Equipment Corporation (DEC)
case study, 410–411
strategy, 134
mentioned, 3, 56, 85, 132, 133, 283, 285,
    389, 414, 452, 464
Dillard Department Stores, 212, 216, 370
Directors. *See* Boards of directors
Disney, Walt, 398
Distinctive competencies
and capabilities, 123–125
defined, 123
and entry modes, 266–268
global transfer of, 245–246
portfolio of core, 320–322
and resources, 123–125
Diversification
bureaucratic costs and, 300–303
as corporate strategy, 297–306
related vs. unrelated, 305–306, 429–433
unrelated, 298, 305–306, 429–433
Divestiture, 209
Divestment, 239, 335–336
Dividend yield, C13
Divisional goals, 390
Divisions, defined, 12
Domino's Pizza, 176
Donna Karan, 212
Dornier Aircraft, 310–311
Dover, 430
Dow Chemical, 306, 307
Doz, Yves, 274
DRAMs (dynamic random access
    memories), 70–72, 78, 80
Drew, Richard, 17, 18
Dreyfus Corporation, 329
DSO (days sales outstanding), C11

Dubinsky, F.C., 40
Dun & Bradstreet, 341
Du Pont. *See* E.I. du Pont de Nemours
Dyment, Roy, 176
Dynamic environment, 130–131
Dynamic random access memories
    (DRAMs), 70–72, 78, 80

E.I. du Pont de Nemours, 86–87, 145, 166,
    306, 323, 358, 361, 374, 426
Eastman Chemicals
case study, 442–443
mentioned, 447, 450
Eastman Kodak, 46, 97, 207, 233, 265, 268,
    287–288, 402, 403, 436
Eckerd, 456
Economies of integration, 429
Economies of scale, 74, 145–147, 148
Economies of scope, 299–300, 429
Edmark, Tomina, 436
EDS, 436
Efficiency
defined, 144
human resource strategy and,
    157–158
superior, 144–160
Eisner, Michael, 56, 125, 399
Electronic Data Systems (EDS), 198, 294
Eli Lilly, 83, 87–88, 122, 202, 203
Ellen Tracy, 212
Embassy Suites, 201
Embryonic industries, 93, 217–222
Emergent strategies, 18–21, 205
EMI, 217, 220
Employee attitudes, 176
Employee input, 164
Employee stock ownership plan (ESOP),
    405, 412
Employee training, 157–158
Entine, Jon, 66
Entry barriers. *See* Barriers to entry
Entry into foreign market, 260–268
choice of entry mode, 266–268
exporting, 260–261
franchising, 262–263
joint ventures, 263–264
licensing, 261–262
wholly owned subsidiaries, 264–266
Entry strategies
acquisitions, 326–331
internal new ventures, 323–326,
    434–436
joint ventures, 321–333
Epson, 369
Equilibrium, punctuated, 90–91
Erickson, 99, 101
Escalating commitment, 26
Esmark corporation, 301
ESOP (employee stock ownership plan),
    405, 412
Estée Lauder, 221

Ethics, business
  decision making and, 60-62
  purpose of, 59-60
  social responsibility, 62-63
  strategy and, 59-63
Ethyl, 55
Excess capacity, 226, 231-232
Exit barriers, 80-81
Experience curve, 248-249
Exporting, 260-261, 267
Express Mail, 118, 17
External analysis, 76-106
  five forces model, 72-87
  global vs. national factors, 96-102
  industry life cycle model, 92-96
  overviews, 7, 72
  strategic group model, 87-92
Exxon, 22, 126, 365

Factor conditions, 98
Factor endowments, 98
Failure of companies, 131-133
Fast-food industry, 213-214
Federal Express, 192, 194, 353, 370, 371
Feedback loop, 10
Feigenbaum, A.V., 160
Ferguson, Jim, 52
Ferris, Dick, 40
Fife, William J., 393
"Fill in the blanks," 321-322
Financial controls, 387-389
Fisher, George, 46
Fit model, 24-25
Five forces model, 72-87, 89-92
Flat structures, 351-352, 413-414
Flexible machine cells, 152
Flexible manufacturing technology,
  151-152
Florida Power & Light, 135, 164
Focus strategy, 196-200, 420
Folley, Clyde, 393
Foodmaker, 217
Ford Motor Co.
  case studies, 185-186, 277-278
  mentioned, 81, 97, 114-115, 128, 129,
    130, 145, 153, 156, 168, 191, 227,
    253, 270, 274, 285-286, 288, 291,
    292, 389, 399-400, 423
Ford, Henry, 399
Ford, Henry II, 399
Foreign market entry. *See* Entry into
  foreign market
Foreign operations department, 424
Four Seasons Hotels, 176
Fragmented industries, 215-216
Fragmented structures, 76-78
Franchising
  advantages and disadvantages of, 262, 267
  in fragmented industries, 216
  international, 262-263
Free cash flow, 58

Friedman, Milton, 63
Fuji Photo Film, 97, 272, 273
Fuji-Xerox
  strategy, 264-265
  mentioned, 183, 262, 263, 270, 274
Fuller, H. Laurance, 365
Full integration, 284, 289
Functional boss, 366
Functional-level managers, 13-14
Functional-level strategy, 142-184
  customer responsiveness, 175-186
  efficiency, 144-160
  innovation, 166-178
  overviews, 8, 143-144
  quality, 160-166
  structure and control in, 412-414
Functional structures, 358-360
Furman Selz, 342-343

GAF, 63
Gallo, 235
Gartner Group, 341
Gates, Bill, 19, 127, 399, 411
Gateway 2000, 131
Gault, Stanley, 242
Geneen, Harold, 134, 304-305
General Electric, 12, 14, 24, 41, 46-47, 86,
    158, 217, 220, 238, 272, 294,
    298-301, 306, 333, 341, 354, 390,
    393
General Foods, 234, 286
General Motors
  strategy, 271
  mentioned, 25, 56, 63, 81, 97, 109,
    114-115, 116, 121, 128, 130, 132,
    156, 168, 187, 196, 197, 199, 202,
    207, 227, 238, 270, 274, 288-292,
    299, 318, 355, 358, 362-364, 383,
    389, 402, 403, 423, 433, 445-446,
    449, 450
Generic groups, 87
Generic strategies, 188-201, 415
Geographic structure, 370-371, 417-418
Gerstner, Lou, 339, 369
Ghemawat, Pankaj, 130
Ghoshal, Sumantra, 252, 255-256, 258
Giddings and Lewis, 393
Glaxo, 87
Glidden, 304, 335
Global expansion, 245-249
Global Information Systems, 312
Global learning, 256
Global-matrix structures, 426
Global production, 96
Global strategy, 243-278
  choice of strategies, 253-259
  cost reduction pressures, 249-253
  entry modes, 260-268
  industry structure and, 96-97
  local responsiveness, 249-253
  strategic alliances, 268-274

Global structures, 421-427
  international, 421-425
  multidomestic, 421-423
  transnational, 425-427
Goals of organization, 6
Goizueta, Roberto, 53
Goodyear Tire & Rubber, case study, 242
Governance mechanisms, 54-59
  board of directors, 54-56
  corporate takeovers, 57
  leveraged buyouts, 57-59
  stock-based compensation, 56-57
Governmental regulation, 74-75
Governments, host global, 252-253
Greenmail, 57
Greenwald, Jerry, 337
Gross profit margin, C10
Group-based bonus systems, 404-405
Groupthink, 28
Grove, Andy, 17
Growth industry, 93
Growth vs. profitability, 53-54
Growth-share matrix, 315
Growth strategies, 205-206
GTE, 313
Guglielmi, Joe, 398
Gulf & Western, 133, 299, 458
Gulfstream, 27

H.E. Ahmanson, 118
H.J. Heinz, 53, 190, 245, 404, 416, 421,
    432
Haft, Herbert, 456
Haft, Robert, 456
Hallmark Cards, 419, 445, 447
Hamel, Gary, 24-25, 274, 314, 320-322
Hampton Inns, 201
Hanley, John, 375
Hanson PLC, 298, 304, 331, 335
Harbor, James, 114-115
Harbor Associates, 114-115
Harvest, 336
Harvest strategy, 206, 208, 238-239
Haspeslagh, Philippe, 330
Hay Associates, 199
Hayes, Robert H., 51
Heathwood, Desmond, 329
Hertz, 40
Heskett, James, 400
Hesterberg, Earl J., 190
Hewlett, Bill, 60, 399
Hewlett-Packard, 48, 60, 85, 117, 149, 170,
    219, 224, 356, 369, 399, 401, 418,
    427, 432, 435
Hilton Hotels, 40, 262-263, 268
Hitachi, 162
Hoffman, Richard, 337
Hold-and-maintain strategy, 207
Holiday Inns, 200-201
Holly Farms, 55
Honda, Shoichiro, 357

Honda Motor
  strategy, 357
  mentioned, 18-20, 25, 168, 177, 178, 190, 192, 202, 230, 253, 347, 383, 394, 447
Hoover, 93
Horizontal differentiation, 349, 358-371
Horizontal merger, 216
Hostage taking, 292-294
Howard Johnson, 29
Hubris hypothesis, 28
Hughes Aircraft
  case study, 440-441
  mentioned, 299, 366
Human resource function, 122-123
Human resource strategy, 157-158, 159
Hypercompetitive industries, 91

Iaccocca, Lee, 14, 129, 209, 337, 354, 356
IBM, 46, 52, 56, 63, 85, 127, 131, 132, 174, 194, 198, 217, 219, 230, 232, 253, 265, 272, 276, 283, 285, 294, 323, 332, 337, 338, 355, 362, 369, 379, 398, 400, 401, 433, 435, 449, 450, 452
IBM Credit, 446
Icahn, Carl, 53
Icarus paradox, 133, 134
ICN Pharmaceuticals, 87-88
IKEA
  case study, 243-244
  mentioned, 249, 251, 255
Illusion of control, 28
Imitation, 128-130
Imitation barriers. *See* Barriers to imitation
Imperial Chemical Industries (ICI), 304, 335
Imperial Group, 29-30
Implementation, poor, 325
Incumbent companies, 73-74
Industry
  declining, 235-239
  definition of, 72
  embryonic, 217-222
  fragmented, 215-216
  growth, 217-222
  mature, 222-235
Industry life cycle, 92-96, 204
Inert cultures, 400
Inertia, 132-133, 135
Inflation, 85
Information control, 452
Informix, 391
Infrastructure
  of company, 123
  and efficiency, 159
Ingersoll Milling Machine Company, 177
Innovation
  competencies in, 169-175
  embryonic industries and, 217-222
  failure rate, 166-169

incremental, 167
quantum, 167
strategic change and, 447-449
and structure, 89-92
superior, 166-178
Innovative Software, 391
Intangible resources, 123
Integrating departments, 372, 374
Integrating mechanisms, 371-374
Integrating roles, 372, 374
Integration, 371-375
  and control, 374-375
  defined, 349
  full, 284
  mechanisms of, 371-374
  taper, 284
  vertical, 9, 282-290, 430-432
Intel
  case study, 107-108
  strategy, 414
  mentioned, 17, 46, 82, 86, 109, 149, 174, 196, 283, 288, 323, 396, 413
Intended strategies, 17-21
Interest rates, 85
Intermountain Health Care, 165
Internal analysis, 107-139
  avoiding failure, 131-136
  business functions, 119-123
  competitive advantage, 110-119
  distinctive competencies, 123-127
  durability, 127-131
  overview, 7, 109-110
Internal new ventures, 323-326, 434-436
International Harvester, 303
International Business Machines. *See* IBM
International strategy, 253-254, 256-258, 421-425; *see also* Global strategy
Internet, 338
Inventory turnover, C11
Investment strategy, at business level, 203-209
Irimajiri, Shoichiro, 357
ITT, 133, 134, 299, 301, 304-305
Iverson, Ken, 15
Ivory tower planning, 24

Jack-in-the-Box, 61, 217
Jaguar, 424
Janis, Irvin, 28
J.C. Penney, 192, 212, 215
Jemison, David, 330
Jen-Coat, 434
Jensen, Michael, 58
JIT (just-in-time) inventory, 156, 165
Jobs, Steven, 167, 168, 324, 358, 378-379
John Fluke Manufacturing, 419
Johnson, David W., 208, 404
Johnson, Lyndon B., 27

Johnson & Johnson, 47-48, 234
Joint ventures
  advantages and disadvantages of, 267
  as entry strategy, 331-333
  international, 263-264
Jones, Reg, 300
Joseph E. Seagram & Sons, 328
Joseph Schlitz Brewing, 191
Juran, Joseph, 160
Just-in-time (JIT) inventory, 156, 165
JVC, 97

Kamprad, Ingvar, 243
Kao, 256
Kaplan, 384
Kawamoto, Nobuhiko, 357
Kazarian, Paul, 448
Kearns, David, 343
Keiretsu system, 292
Kelleher, Herb, 14, 15, 34
Kellogg, 245, 253, 421
Kennedy, John F., 14, 28
Kentucky Fried Chicken, 263
Kim Woo Choong, 271
King, Martin Luther Jr., 14
Kirin, 76, 262, 394
Kmart, 3, 156, 195, 212, 229, 232
Knight, Philip, 437
Kobe Steel Inc., 268
Kodak. *See* Eastman Kodak
Kohlberg, Kravis & Roberts, 333, 336
Komatsu, 25, 179, 257
Kotter, John, 400
Kroc, Ray, 408
Krull, Timm, 428
Kyocera, 283, 394

Land's End, 176-177
LBOs (leveraged buyouts), 57-59
Leadership strategy, 14-16, 236-237
Lean production, 151-152
Learjet, 192
Learning effects, 145-147, 148
Lee, Tim Bernes, 18
Legal environment, 86
Lego, Paul, 56
Leveraged buyouts (LBOs), 57-59
Leverage ratios, C11-C12
Levi Strauss, 96, 251, 402
Levitt, Theodore, 45, 252
Lexmark, 369
Lexus, 199, 211
Liaison roles, 373
Licensing, 221, 261-262, 267
Life cycle effects, 204
Life cycle of industry, 92-96
Lincoln Electric, 47, 405, 416
Lincoln Savings & Loan, 55
Lionel, 229
Liquidation, 206, 209, 336

Liquidity ratios, C10–C11
Liz Claiborne
    case study, 212
    mentioned, 351
L.L. Bean, 135, 164
Lloyds Bank, case study, 142–143
Local responsiveness, global, 249–253
Location economies, 246–248
Lockheed, 448
Long-term contracts, 291–292; *see also*
        Strategic alliances
Lopez de Arriortua, Ignacio, 130
Lotus Development, 55
LTV Steel, 80, 90, 306
Lucent Technologies, 312
Luck, 126–127

Macroeconomic environment, 84–85
Macroenvironment, role of, 84–87
Macy's, 212
Magna International, 293
Management buyout (MBO), 335–336
Management by objectives (MBO),
        390–392
Management team, top, 401
Managers, 10–14
    business-level, 12–13
    corporate-level, 11–12
    functional, 11
    functional-level, 13–14
    general, 11
    middle, 355
Mankin, Eric, 270, 272
Mann, Marvin, 369
Manufacturers Hanover Bank, 146
Manville Corporation, 59–60
Marion Labs, 87–88, 89
Market concentration strategy, 206, 208
Market development, 230
Market globalization, 96
Marketing
    and efficiency, 159
    and sales, 121
    strategy, 15
Market penetration, 228
Market segmentation, 187
Market share, 204, 315–316
Market-to-book value, C13
Markham, Richard J., 470–471
Marks & Spencer
    case study, 138–139
    mentioned, 128, 155
Mary Kay, 447
Mason, R.O., 29
Mass customization, 152
MasterCard, 195
Materials management, 121, 156, 159
Matrix in the mind, 427
Matrix structure, 366–368, 372, 374, 417,
        426

Matsushita Kotobuki Electronics (MKE),
        51, 97, 149, 248–249, 252, 255,
        260, 267, 269, 282, 309
Mattel
    case study, 2–3
    mentioned, 4, 9
Mature industry strategies, 222–235
    entry deterrence, 223–261
    overview, 222
    rivalry management, 226–233
    supply and distribution, 233–235
Maucher, Helmut, 428
Maytag, 192
Mazda
    case study, 277–278
    mentioned, 168, 191, 192, 270, 274
MBO (management buyout), 335–336
MBO (management by objectives), 390–392
MCA, 282
McDonald's
    case studies, 213–214, 408–409
    strategy, 246–247
    mentioned, 96, 196, 207, 215, 216, 217,
        223–224, 233, 245, 251, 262–263,
        268, 281, 287, 395
McDonnell Douglas, 261, 466
MCI Long Distance, 74, 295, 297
McKinsey and Company, 319, 328
McKnight, William, 17
McNealy, Scott, 19
Medco, 470
Mellon Bank, 328–329
Mercedes-Benz, 187, 192, 193, 200,
        310–311, 424
Mercer Management Consulting, 327
Merck
    case study, 470–471
    mentioned, 65, 87–88, 129, 166, 202,
        203, 413, 450
Mergers, 433–434
Merrill Lynch, 356
MES (minimum efficient scale), 145, 150
Messerschmitt-Boelkow-Blohm (MBB),
        310–311
Michelin, 242
Micron Technology, case study, 71
Microsoft
    strategy, 127
    mentioned, 17, 18–19, 70, 86, 107, 131,
        229, 338, 396, 399, 411, 413, 427
Midas International, 215
Middle managers, 355
Miller, Danny, 133, 134
Miller Brewing, 78, 86, 297, 299, 433
Minimum chain of command, 352–353
Minimum efficient scale (MES), 145, 150
Mintzberg, Henry, 17–18, 20, 22
Mission of organization, 6
Mission statement, 39–51
    goals and, 49–51
    values and, 46–49

Mobil, 365
Mobility barriers, 89, 203
Monaghan, Tom, 176
Monsanto, 322, 323
Montgomery Ward, 27
Moody's Investors Service, 334, 343
Morrison Knudsen (MK)
    case study, 35–36
    mentioned, 37, 54, 55
Motorola, 99, 101, 135, 149, 162, 196,
        233, 268–270, 273, 283,
        312–313, 332, 413, 418, 414
Multidivisional structure, 361–366
Multidomestic strategy, 254–255, 259,
        421–423

National state, and competition,
        97–102
Naval Inc., 237–238
NCR Corp., 312–313, 327
NEC Corp., 52, 269, 414
Neiman Marcus, 192, 370–371, 402
Nestlé Enterprises, 421, 428
Net profit margin, C10
Netscape, 17–19
Network structure, 436
New United Motor Manufacturing Inc.,
        274
New venturing, 323–326, 434–436
NeXT, 168, 324
NextGen, 107
Niche strategy, 237–238
Nielsen Media Research, 341
NIKE, 295, 436–437
Nissan
    strategy, 190
    mentioned, 114–115, 121, 189, 194
Nokia
    strategy, 101
    mentioned, 99
Nonprice competition, 227–228
Nonsuitability, 462–463
Nordstrum, 192
Northrop Grumman, 55, 292–294
Norton, 384
Nucor, 15, 90, 109, 124–125, 129, 158

Offsetting, 296
Olsen, Pat, 410
Olson, Ken, 134
O'Neill, Paul, 354
On-the-job consumption, 52
Opel, 271
Operating budgets, 392–394
Operating responsibility, 362
Opportunities, environmental, 72
Oracle, 411
O'Reilly, Anthony J.F., 53, 404

Organizational conflict, 453–456
Organizational culture, 396–402
Organizational design
    defined, 347
    and profitability, 351
    see also Organizational structure
Organizational politics, 456–465
Organizational socialization, 397
Organizational structure, 346–379
    definitions, 349–350
    horizontal differentiation, 358–371
    integration, 371–375
    leadership and, 399–400
    role of structure, 348–350
    vertical differentiation, 350–357
    see also Structure
Ouchi, William, 401–402
Outsourcing, 198, 290–296

Packard, David, 60, 399
Palmer, Robert, 410–411
Panasonic, 375
Panasonic Bicycle Company, 177
Parallel sourcing, 294
Partly parallel development processes, 173–174
Partner selection, in alliances, 270–272
Pascale, Richard, 18
Patents, 129
Pay for performance, 158; *see also* Compensation
People Express, 200, 225
PepsiCo, 48, 129, 217, 229, 235, 416
Perelman, Ronald O., 334
Permanent teams, 372–374
Perot, Ross, 198
Perrier, 121, 428
Peters, Thomas J., 22, 401
Pfeffer, Jeffery, 16
Pfizer, 83, 87–88, 121, 122, 202, 203
Philip Morris, 78, 86, 237, 297, 299, 331, 427, 433
Philips NV, 97, 169, 248–249, 255, 269
Piecework plans, 403
Planning, 4–10
    basic model for, 4–6
    goals of, 6
    ivory tower, 24
    mission of, 6
    in practice, 22–26
    for the present, 24–26
    under uncertainty, 22–24
Polaroid, 125
Political environment, 86–87
Politics, organizational, 456–465
Pondy, Lou R., 453
Porsche, 197
Porter, Michael E.
    on acquisitions, 433
    on competitive advantage, 113

on diversification, 300
five forces model, 72–87, 89–92, C8
on innovation, 90
on nation state and global competition, 97–102
Portfolio planning matrices, 314–319
Portfolio review, 314–322
Positioning strategy, 168
Power, and politics, 454–465
Power balance, 464
Prahalad, C.K., 24–25, 274, 314, 320–322
Pressures for cost reduction vs. local responsiveness, 249–253
Price cutting, 224–225
Price-earnings ratio, C12
Price leadership, 227
Price signaling, 226–227
Principle of the minimum chain of command, 352–353
Prior hypothesis bias, 26
Procter & Gamble
    strategy, 79, 256–257
    mentioned, 75, 135, 192, 228, 234, 245, 253–254, 258, 300, 353, 355, 402, 421
Product development, 228–230
Product development teams, 172–173
Product differentiation, 187
Product-group structure, 425
Production efficiency, 148–151, 159
Production globalization, 96
Product-oriented business, 43–44
Product proliferation, 223–224, 230
Product quality, 286–287
Product-team structures, 368–369, 417–418
Product variety, 151–152
Profitability vs. growth, 53–54
Profit per customer, 155
Profit rate, 110
Profit ratios, C10
Profit sharing, 405
Profit strategy, 207
Project boss, 366
Project management, 170–171
Promotion, 403–404
Proprietary groups, 87
Prudential Insurance, 192
Punctuated equilibrium, 90–91

Quality
    measurement of, 164–165
    superior, 160–166
    TQM, 160–166
Quantum Corporation, 173, 309

R & D. *See* Research and development
Raiders, corporate, 57
Ravenscraft, David, 328

Raw material to consumer chain, 283
RBOCs (Regional Bell Operating Companies), 74–75, 313
RCA, 51, 52, 238, 261
Realized strategy, 17
Reasoning by analogy, 27
Reduction strategy, 208
Reed, John, 416
Reengineering, 444–445
Regional Bell Operating Companies (RBOCs), 74–75, 313
Regulation, governmental, 74–75
Reich, Robert, 58, 270, 272
Related diversification, 297, 305–306, 432–433
Relative market share, 315–316
Representativeness, 27
Research, basic and applied, 170
Research and development
    and efficiency, 157, 159
    functional strategy, 413
    and new venturing, 325–326
    overview, 120
Resource flows, 430
Resources
    control over, 463–464
    distinctive competencies and, 123–125
Responsibility, operating and strategic, 362
Restructuring, 333–336, 445–447
Return on capital employed (ROK), 110
Return on investment (ROI), 50–51, 388, 389
Return on stockholder equity, C10
Return on total assets, C10
Reuben H. Donnelley, 341
Reuter, Edzard, 310
Reward systems
    group, 404–405
    individual, 403–404
    organizational, 405
    strategic, 402–405
    see also Compensation
Richardson Electronics, 237–238
Ricoh, 25, 126, 183, 217, 264–265, 342
Risk of holdup, 286
Rivalry
    among companies, 75–81
    in mature industries, 226–233
RJR Nabisco, 55, 330, 333
Rockwell International
    case study, 279–280
    mentioned, 281–282, 299
Roddick, Anita, 66, 221
Roddick, Gordon, 66
ROI (return on investment), 50–51, 388, 389
ROK (return on capital employed), 110
Rolex, 192, 194
Roll, Richard, 328
Rolls-Royce, 196, 202
Rowntree Mackintosh, 428

Royal Crown Cola, 217, 229
Royal Dutch/Shell, 22-24
Rumelt, Richard, 91
Russ Togs, 212

Saatchi & Saatchi DFS Compton Inc., 199
Safeway, 456
Sales strategy, 413-414
Sandoz, 204
Sapporo, 76
SBUs (strategic business units), 315-319,
     425-426, 428
Scale economies. *See* Economies of scale
Scale of entry, 324-325
Scenario planning, 22-23
Scheduling, improved, 288
Schendel, Dan, 209
Scherer, Mike, 328
Schoemaker, Paul, 23-24
SCM Corporation, 333, 335
Scott-Levin and Associates, 122
Sculley, John, 105, 378-379
Seagate Technologies, 309, 416
Sears, Roebuck
    strategy, 334
    mentioned, 24, 156, 192, 215, 232, 281,
       333, 338, 403
Seattle City Light, 41-43, 49
Seattle Computer, 127
Security Pacific, 460
Seiko, 191
Self-managing teams, 158
Sequential resource flows, 430
Service function, 121
Shaheen, George, 437
Shakeout industry, 93-94
Shakeout strategies, 206
Share-building strategy, 205
Shareholder-return ratios, C12-C13ts
Sharp, 52
Single business concentration, 281-282
Skunk works, 448
Sloan, Alfred, 363
Smale, John, 56
Smith, Jack, 445-446
Smith, Robert, 460
Smith, Roger, 271
SmithKline Beecham, 83
Snecma, 272
Social environment, 86
Social responsibility, 62-63
Socialization, organizational, 397
Sony, 51, 96, 97, 117, 166, 167, 169, 196,
     248-249, 251, 252, 260, 272, 375,
     412
Southwest Airlines
    case study, 33-34
    mentioned, 14, 15, 200, 225
Span of control, 351
Specialized assets, 285-287

Spinoff, 335
Sprint, 74
Stakeholders, 37-39
    defined, 37
    external, 38-39
    internal, 38-39
Standardization, 394-395
Stempel, Robert, 56
Stockholder returns, 50-51
Stock options, 405
Stock price, 388-389
Stouffer Foods, 428
Strategic alliances
    as diversification alternative, 306-307
    global, 268-274
    long-term contracts as, 291-292
    partner selection in, 270-272
Strategic business units. *See* SBUs
Strategic change, 442-471
    defined, 444
    evaluation of, 465-467
    implementation of, 456-465
    kinds of, 444-449
    management of, 465-467
    need for, 449-450
    obstacles to, 450-456
Strategic choice, 8
Strategic commitment, 130
Strategic control systems
    defined, 382-384
    design of, 380-409
    see also Control
Strategic groups, 87-92
    and business-level strategy, 202-203
    defined, 87
    limitations of, 89-92
Strategic intent, 25, 41
Strategic responsibility, 362
Strategies
    asset reduction, 208
    bidding, 291
    business-level, 185-212
    corporate, 279-311
    decline, 207-208
    differentiation, 191-194, 417-419
    embryonic, 18-21, 205
    emergent, 18-21, 205
    entry, 321-331
    focus, 420
    functional-level, 142-184
    generic, 188-201, 415
    global, 243-278
    growth, 205-206
    harvest, 206, 208, 238-239
    hold-and-maintain, 207
    human resource, 157-159
    innovation, 220-222
    international, 253-254, 256-258,
       421-425
    investment, 203-209
    leadership, 14-16, 236-237

    market concentration, 206, 208
    marketing, 15
    mature industry, 222-235
    multidomestic, 254-255, 259, 421-423
    niche, 237-238
    shakeout, 206
    share building, 205
    transnational, 255-259, 421-422,
       425-427
    turnaround, 209, 336-339
Strategy
    and change, 442-471
    competitive advantage and, 142-184
    and control, 380-441
    corporate development and, 312-343
    corporate governance and, 51-59
    defined, 3-4
    as emergent process, 16-21
    ethics and, 59-63
    in global environment, 243-278
    implementation of, 6, 9-10
    industry environment and, 213-242
    management of, 2-34
    matching structure and control to,
       410-441
    planning of, 4-10
Structure
    business-level, 414-421
    competitive, 76-78
    and control, 410-441
    corporate-level, 427-432
    functional-level, 412-414
    global, 421-427
    organizational, 346-379, 399-400
    special issues in, 433-437
    see also Organizational structure
Stuck in the middle companies, 200
Subsidiaries, wholly owned, 264-265, 267
Substitute products, 83-84, 194
Sunbeam-Oster company, 448
Sun Microsystems, 17, 19, 86, 170, 396, 452
Suntory, 76
Suppliers
    bargaining power of, 82-83
    powerful, 193
    relationship with, 165-166
Supply-and-distribution strategy, 233-235
Support activities, 121-123
Swan Optical, 247-249
SWOT analysis, 7-8, C4-C6
Sybase Corp., 469
Synergen, 447
Systematics Company, 198
Systems & Computer Technology Corp.,
     198

Taco Bell, 213
Taiichi, Ohno, 153
Takeover constraint, 57
Takeovers, corporate, 57

Taligent, 398
Tall structure, 351–353
Tangible resources, 123
Taper integration, 284, 289
Target Stores, 229
Task forces, 372
TCI Communications, 75
Teams
    permanent, 372–374
    product, 368–369, 417–418
    product development, 172–173
    self-managing, 158
    top management, 401
Technological environment, 85–86
Technological myopia, 168
Techsonic, 177
Tenneco, 301, 452–453
Texas Air, 200
Texas Instruments (TI)
    strategy, 149
    mentioned, 133, 157, 217, 263–264, 268,
        288, 417, 435
Textron, 301, 430
Thatcher, Margaret, 14
The Boston Company, 328–329
The Gap, 116, 334
The Limited, 221
Threats, environmental, 72
3M
    strategy, 419
    mentioned, 17, 18, 42, 44, 126, 129, 166,
        170, 224, 314, 323, 435, 459
Thurow, Lester, 51
Tiffany, 192
Times-covered ratio, C12
Timex, 191
Tit-for-tat strategy, 226
Top-down change, 466
Topsy Tail, 436
Toshiba, 52, 177, 268, 269, 270, 272–273
Total quality control (TQC), 264
Total quality management. *See* TQM
Total shareholder returns, C12
Toyota
    strategy, 153
    mentioned, 25, 109, 114–115, 116, 121,
        135, 157, 168, 190, 196, 202, 230,
        253, 274, 288, 292, 294, 383, 394,
        412, 427
Toys 'R' Us, 90, 116, 229, 253
TQC (total quality control), 264
TQM (total quality management), 160–166,
    412–413, 416, 445

Trak Auto, 456
Training programs, 157–158
Transfer pricing, 364
Transnational strategy, 255–259, 421–422,
    425–427
Trans Union Corporation, 55
Trotman, Alex, 185, 389
TRW Systems, 272–273, 366, 417
Turnaround strategies, 209, 336–339
Two-boss employees, 366
Tylenol, 47

Unilever
    strategy, 79
    mentioned, 257–258
Union Carbide, 63
Union Pacific, 452
Unit-cost curve, 147
Unit production costs, 150–151, 154
United Airlines, 4–5, 40
United Technologies, 301, 307
Unrelated diversification, 298, 305–306,
    429–431
Upjohn, 203
U.S. Industries, Inc., 333
US Steel, 80, 90, 109
US West, 74
USX, 80–81, 306

Vagelos, P. Roy, 470–471
Value chain, 119–120
Value creation
    by company functions, 119–123
    and competitive advantage, 110–113
    and customer responsiveness, 180
    and efficiency, 159
    and superior innovation, 175
Value dissipation, 303–305
Values of a company, 46–49
Van Kampen Merritt, 342–343
Ventures
    internal new, 323–326
    joint, 331–333
Vertical differentiation, 349, 350–357
Vertical integration, 9, 282–290, 430–432
Viacom, 75
Virtual corporation, 295
"Virtual organization," 437
Visa, 195
Vision. *See* Mission
Volkswagen, 130

Walesa, Lech, 257
Wal-Mart
    case study, 380–381
    mentioned, 3, 48, 90, 121, 122, 156, 212,
        215, 216, 229, 232, 233, 241, 370,
        396, 397, 462
Walsh, Michael H., 452–453
Walt Disney, 56, 125, 398–399
Walton, Sam, 380–381, 396, 397
Wang, An, 105–106
Wang Laboratories
    case study, 105–106
    mentioned, 133
Watermen, Robert H., 22, 401
Weissman, Robert E., 341
Welch, Jack, 6, 12, 14, 41, 46–47, 301, 333,
    354, 396, 390
Wendy's, 213, 217
Western Electric, 238
Westin Hotel, 40
Westinghouse, 52, 56, 238, 351, 356, 389,
    403, 450
Wexner, Leslie, 221
Weyerhaeuser, 41, 335
Whirlpool, 86
White, Philip, 391
Wholly owned subsidiaries, 264–265, 267
Wilson, Kemmons, 201
W.L. Gore, 152
W.N. Procter, 179
World Wide Web, 338
Wozniak, Steven, 358, 378
Wrapp, Edward, 15–16

Xerox
    case study, 183–184, 342–343
    strategy, 264–265
    mentioned, 25, 93, 117, 126, 135, 162,
        164, 167, 217, 219, 233, 272–273,
        295, 330, 389, 419, 436

Yamaha, 178
Yechsonic Industries, 172
Yokogawa Hewlett-Packard (YHP), 162

Zeneca, 304
Zenith, 196
Zytec, 392